THE DIVINE CURRICULUM

THE BÁB

VOLUME 5 (PART 1)

Minneapolis, Minnesota

FIRST EDITION October 2019

THE DIVINE CURRICULUM: The Bab–Part 1

Printed in the United States of America.

10 9 8 7 6 5 4 3 2 1

Cover and interior design: Gary Lindberg

ISBN: 978-1-950743-14-8

Photo images from *The Gate: Dawn of the Bahá'í Faith*, with permission of Spring Green Films.

To the Lord and to all of the Divine Educators.

To Glenford Mitchell, who told me to do this.

To my wife, my daughter, and my mother.

O true companions! All humankind are as children in a school, and the Dawning-Points of Light, the Sources of divine revelation, are the teachers, wondrous and without peer...

—'Abdu'l-Bahá

O thou true friend! Read, in the school of God, the lessons of the spirit, and learn from love's Teacher the innermost truths. Seek out the secrets of Heaven, and tell of the overflowing grace and favour of God...

—'Abdu'l-Bahá

THE DIVINE CURRICULUM

THE BÁB

VOLUME 5 (PART 1)

EDWARD PRICE

with special assistance by Behrad Majidi

Minneapolis, Minnesota

Contents

List of Figures

The Divine Curriculum Series

1. The Divine Curriculum: Divine Design
2. The Divine Curriculum: Abraham and Moses
3. The Divine Curriculum: Jesus
4. The Divine Curriculum: Muhammad
5. The Divine Curriculum: The Báb (Parts 1 & 2)
6. The Divine Curriculum: Bahá'u'lláh

Would you like to be informed when future editions of the Divine Curriculum series are released? Send an email to info@calumeteditions.com.

ACKNOWLEDGMENTS

Once again, with a sense of relief and satisfaction after a long journey, I lift my head up and ponder the names of those precious souls who have given me the most of their heart, offered encouragement, sustained me during difficult days, suggested improvements, created opportunity, and labored with me on this thrilling project. One thing is abundantly clear to me. This book would be impossible without the assistance of many people.

First, and above all others, my wife, Ellen, is the best there is. She is solid as a rock, my sustainer, and constant encourager. As we journey through life together, I cannot think of adequate words to express my gratitude for her love and partnership. Absolutely, in so many ways, without her, this book would not be. Second, our daughter, Alyssa, is a constant supporter as well. The three of us have taken this journey together as a family.

Second, as you will learn inside these pages, my friend, Behrad Majidi, has been an astonishing colleague. Behrad opened the door for me to the vast body of Persian-language scholarship which I had hardly known anything about. He labored literally hundreds of hours, perhaps a thousand, assisting me. He meticulously reviewed the Persian sources, discovered the precious historical gems hidden inside them, related them to me with the enthusiasm of a little-kid, and, upon my repeated request, translated them into English for me. We spent hours on the phone going over all sorts of details in perfect harmony and consultation. For instance, one day we spent thirty minutes on figuring out the best way to translate one word. (I think we got it right at the end!) From the beginning, we both agreed upon the exacting standards of scholarly rigour, striving always to get it right. There were days when I imagined that Behrad might possibly care more about this project than I did myself, his enthusiasm for the work was so great. And, I must add, whenever I mentioned the possibility of compensating him for his work, Behrad always adamantly refused. I can honestly say, in my entire career, I've never worked with so giving and joyful a collaborator.

Next I must mention Gary Lindberg, CEO of Calumet Editions, my publisher. Gary, too, has his heart in what he does. He is brilliant, successful, dedicated, deepened in the Faith, and, more important, a very caring friend. If you like this book, he deserves much of the credit. I want to thank Sue Benjamin for her tireless efforts as my editor. The writing is much better thanks to Sue. I also want to thank Martha Schweitz who made suggestions leading to significant improvements of the text.

Like any Bahá'í, I've always had a strong interest in the Báb. Then, one day in 2016, after a talk I had given, Steve Sarowitz, owner of Spring Green Films, offered me the extraordinary opportunity to be the co-writer and producer of *The Gate: Dawn of the Bahá'í Faith* (which was released in 2018), the first documentary film on the life and teachings of the Báb. The Gate was an award-winning film, with an award-winning director, Bob Hercules. It was shot in the United States, England, Spain and Israel. It was shown on ABC television, screened more than 500 times, and seen in about twenty countries. Working on that film afforded me an extraordinary opportunity to go very, very deep into the Báb's story. The project lasted three years, and I can honestly say that having the opportunity to spend so much time "with" the Báb was life changing. That experience, in turn, has helped me to fashion a better book on the Báb, which is now in your hands.

With a happy heart, I express my profound thanks to all these people who have meant so much to me in my life and in this journey.

Finally, there would be no Divine curriculum without the Divine Educators. I feel quite strongly that I would know nothing and be nothing without Them. And in this book, I can only hope and pray that the Báb will be happy with this work, and bless it, and that it will bring joy to all those who pick it up and read it.

After all this help, let me say what should be obvious to everyone. If there are any flaws remaining in this work, they must remain my responsibility.

ABOUT THE AUTHOR

EDWARD PRICE is a former atheist from a Jewish background who became a Bahá'í more than forty years ago. He holds a B.A. in Psychology and Religious Studies and an M.S. Ed. in Curriculum and Instruction. As an instructional designer, he has developed training programs for numerous government and corporate clients. For many years, Edward has been investigating what God has taught humanity for the last 4,000 years, and the goals toward which God's curriculum is striving. Edward lives in Illinois with his family and his Yorkie-poo, Spy.

OTHER WORKS BY THE AUTHOR

The Divine Curriculum: Divine Design (Volume 1)

The Gate: Dawn of the Bahá'í Faith (award-winning documentary film on the life of the Báb)

Chapter 1

WELCOME TO THE DIVINE CURRICULUM

INTRODUCING THE BÁB

The Báb is the first of the two Founders of the Bahá'í Faith, a world religion with more than five million followers in over 200 countries today. The story began in Persia (Iran) in the middle of the 19th century. His ministry spanned the years of 1844 to 1850 AD. At the center of the great drama which unfolded was the Figure of the Báb Himself, Who is described as "gentle", "youthful", "irresistible in His charm", "matchless in His meekness", "imperturbable in His serenity", "magnetic in His utterance", "infinite in His tenderness", "unsurpassed in His heroism" and "unrivaled in the dramatic episodes of His swift and tragic ministry".[1]

The Báb was born, Siyyid 'Alí Muhammad, in October 1819, to a prosperous merchant family in the city of Shíráz, Persia. Declaring His mission to His first disciple in May 1844, He appeared at a time of great millennial expectation. He stated that His Revelation fulfilled ancient prophecies of Islám and all the religions of the world. He claimed that, in addition to revealing the Word of God, His mission also encompassed preparing the way for the imminent appearance of a Divine Educator even greater than Himself. He referred to this Figure yet to come as Him Whom God shall make manifest. Today, we know this was Bahá'u'lláh. The Báb was arrested, exiled, tortured and imprisoned by the government and religious authorities of His day. Thousands of His followers were killed during violent waves of persecution which took place throughout the country.

As an individual, the Báb was known for His spirituality and devotion to God, His integrity, His exceptional wisdom, His uncanny endurance in the face of opposition, and His astonishing and spell-binding ability to reveal Divine verses of extraordinary power, beauty and eloquence. From the beginning of His ministry, He longed to promote the Cause of God, and even lay down His life as a sacrifice for humanity. Then, six years after His ministry began, in mysterious and surprising circumstances, in July 1850, He did heroically lay down His life.

Bahá'u'lláh, the second Founder of the Bahá'í Faith, and the One for Whom the Báb sacrificed everything, stated this about the Báb:

[Note: In the next quote, "the year sixty" refers to the year 1260 AH, the Islámic calendar. This year was 1844 AD on the Gregorian calendar.]

> No sooner had mankind attained the stage of maturity, than the Word revealed to men's eyes the latent energies with which it had been endowed – energies which manifested themselves in the plenitude of their glory when the Ancient Beauty appeared, in the year sixty, in the person of 'Alí-Muhammad, the Báb. – Bahá'u'lláh[2]

'Abdu'l-Bahá, the Son of Bahá'u'lláh, and His Successor, eloquently described the life and mission of the Báb:

> As for the Báb—may my soul be His sacrifice!—it was at a young age, that is, in the twenty-fifth year of His blessed life, that He arose to proclaim His Cause. Among the Shí'ihs it is universally acknowledged that He never studied in any school, nor acquired learning from any teacher. To this the people of Shíráz, each and all, bear witness. Nevertheless, He suddenly appeared before the people, endowed with consummate knowledge, and though but a merchant, confounded all the divines of Persia... This illustrious Being arose with such power as to shake the foundations of the religious laws, customs, manners, morals, and habits of Persia, and instituted a new law, faith, and religion. Though the eminent men of the State, the majority of the people, and the leaders of religion arose one and all to destroy and annihilate Him, He single-handedly withstood them and set all of Persia in motion. How numerous the divines, the leaders, and the inhabitants of that land who with perfect joy and gladness offered up their lives in His path and hastened to the field of martyrdom!
>
> The government, the nation, the clergy, and prominent leaders sought to extinguish His light, but to no avail. At last His moon rose, His star shone forth, His foundation was secured, and His horizon was flooded with light. He trained a large multitude through divine education and exerted a marvelous influence upon the thoughts, customs, morals, and

manners of the Persians. He proclaimed the glad-tidings of the manifestation of the Sun of Bahá to all His followers and readied them for faith and certitude.

The manifestation of such marvelous signs and mighty undertakings, the influence exerted upon the thoughts and minds of the people, the laying of the foundations of progress, and the establishment of the prerequisites of success and prosperity by a young merchant constitute the greatest proof that He was a universal Educator—a fact that no fair-minded person would ever hesitate to acknowledge. – 'Abdu'l-Bahá[3]

In addition to telling the stirring drama of the life and ministry of the Báb, this book will also share with the reader an extensive discussion of the teachings of the Báb. Through His story and His teachings, it will be possible to appreciate why the Báb had such an electrifying effect on the people of His time, how He fully and faithfully consummated His mission, the way in which He prepared the people for the coming of Bahá'u'lláh, the next Divine Educator soon to appear, and the manner in which He contributed brilliantly to the advancement of the age-long process of the Divine curriculum.

We will get back to the Báb very shortly, but first we must discuss the basic ideas of the Divine curriculum and the general organization of the Divine Curriculum series, of which this is the 5th volume.

ALL OF CREATION IS A CLASSROOM

Imagine the existence of a single, all-encompassing, ancient process that is leading all of creation toward an ultimate, meaningful purpose. If it existed, what would that process and that purpose be?

Imagine the existence of a vast, all-embracing, Divinely conceived plan that is binding together the major religions of the world, advancing civilization, unfolding over time according to rational principles and guiding the human race. If it existed, towards what goal would that plan be striving?

Imagine trying to prove the existence of such a plan. What evidence would you seek? And if you found evidence, how would you go about exploring it?

The premise of this book series is that:

- *All of creation is a classroom.*
- The classroom is part of the universal school of God, which encompasses both the observable universe and the spiritual realms beyond.
- The Creator/Owner/Director of the school is Almighty God Himself.

- The Teachers in the school are the Divine Educators.

A complete telling of the story of humanity's Divine education would go back to the beginning—to the Big Bang, to the formation of our world, to the emergence of life on this planet and to the evolution of our species.

The starting point for this series

But we're not going back to the Big Bang.

The Divine Curriculum book series picks up the story of Divine education at the "moment" in history when monotheism – the belief in only one God – was permanently established in a viable living population, when it was decisively established on the stage of recorded human history.

That significant turning point occurred with the mission of Abraham about 4,000 years ago. That historic realization marked a crucial turning point in the history of the human race and provided the impetus for humanity's subsequent rapid spiritual and social development in the millennia which followed. It was further developed by later Divine Educators.

The Divine Educators in the lineage of Abraham—Moses, Jesus, Muhammad, the Báb and Bahá'u'lláh and Abraham Himself—are the focus of this series. Other Divine Educators, such as Krishna, Zoroaster and Buddha, are truly worthy of inclusion in the story of the Divine curriculum, but my expertise as a writer is mainly focused on the Abrahamic lineage, so I have concentrated my efforts on that which I think I have a reasonable chance of doing well. Hopefully, in the future, more expert writers will come along to fill out the story of the Divine curriculum. I sincerely hope this approach will be sufficient to provide a satisfying journey for the reader.

The book series so far

The volumes of the Divine Curriculum series are as follows.

- Volume 1, Divine Design
- Volume 2, Abraham and Moses
- Volume 3, Jesus
- Volume 4, Muhammad
- Volume 5, The Báb (Parts 1 & 2)
- Volume 6, Bahá'u'lláh

This book is Volume 5, Part 1 in the series on the Báb.

Note to readers of the first edition of Volume 5:

Vol. 1 – Divine Design was published in 2015. After this, I was working on the other volumes and they were mostly written several years ago. Then, in 2016, an exceptional opportunity came along. I was invited to serve as Co-Writer and Producer for the first film documentary on the Báb, entitled *The Gate: Dawn of the Bahá'í Faith*, which was released in 2018. From my perspective, I could not pass up this opportunity of a lifetime. What a privilege it was to play a key role in bringing to the world the story and teachings of the Báb! It was an incredible learning experience. It was so rewarding to write the business plan, to co-author the script, to collaborate with an award-winning director, to solve in the Bahá'í context the problem of not portraying on screen the Báb or any other Divine Messenger, to work with some of the best cameramen in the business, to work with special effects experts, cast members, music and set designers, to see the finest production crew in action, to help select shooting locations, to consult with the finest world-class scholars and experts, to travel the world, to spend time at the Bahá'í World Center Archives, to interact with the Bahá'í administrative institutions, to speak with audiences repeatedly about the Báb and more.

An unfortunate side effect, however, was that the work on my book series was delayed for about three years. When I resumed work on it, it was already late 2018. 2019 happens to be the 200th anniversary of the Birth of the Báb. So, in honor of this great occasion, *I've decided to publish Volume 5 out of sequence.* I've worked hard to get this volume to you, the reader, in time.

I hope you enjoy reading this volume. And as soon as I can, I plan to go back and complete the entire series.

The unfolding educational program taught by these Divine Educators is a Divine curriculum authorized by God Himself. The textbooks of the Divine curriculum are the Holy Scriptures of the Faiths of the world.

Each Divine Educator is authorized to teach a portion of the Divine curriculum during His Ministry; and that portion is given through Divine revelation. Each successive revelation may be considered as a grade in the school of God. The Divine Educator adapts the revelation, the curriculum, to the needs of mankind for the age in which He appears.

Although each Divine Educator appears as a unique Individual at a unique time and place in human history, spiritually They are all Revealers of the same Light of God. Although each One delivers a specific and unique Revelation, They are one. 'Abdu'l-Bahá described Their inherent state of unity:

> In the Word of God there is still another unity—the oneness of the Manifestations of God, Abraham, Moses, Jesus Christ, Muhammad, the Báb and Bahá'u'lláh. This is a unity divine, heavenly, radiant, merciful—the one reality appearing in its successive Manifestations. For instance, the sun is one and the same, but its points of dawning are various... Although these dawning points are different, the sun is the same sun which has appeared from them all. The significance is the reality of Prophethood which is symbolized by the sun, and the holy Manifestations are the dawning places... – 'Abdu'l-Bahá[4]

The Divine curriculum itself is never-ending because the knowledge of God and His gracious giving to humanity cannot be exhausted. Progress towards the goals of the Divine curriculum is grade-by-grade, as progressively revealed by one Divine Educator after another. The Divine curriculum benefits both individuals and society, in this world and the next.

The purpose of each Grade in the school of God is to prepare humanity to advance to the next level. Success occurs when students choose to advance; failure occurs when they don't. There is continuity in the Divine curriculum. The combined effect of advancing through these Divine grades, which have been progressively revealed over thousands of years, is cumulative and purpose driven.

The organization of this book

Volume 5 is published in two parts. Volume 5, Part 1 includes material on the following:

- The condition of Persia prior to the Báb's declaration as the Promised Divine Messenger
- The milieu of the time, and specifically the widespread expectation regarding the coming of the Promised One, in Persia and the United States
- The Báb's childhood
- The Báb's time as a merchant in Búshihr
- The Báb's time in Karbilá as a spiritual pilgrim
- His marriage to Khadíjih
- The declaration of His mission to Mullá Husayn in May of 1844
- His pilgrimage to Mecca

- His return home to Shíráz
- The initial spread of His Cause
- His encounter with Vahíd, the king's scholar
- The initial expansion phase of the Faith
- The rise of opposition and the persecution of His followers
- His expulsion from Shíráz by the religious and political authorities in 1846
- A detailed presentation of the teachings of the Bab.

Volume 5, Part 2 concentrates on the remainder of the Báb's ministry. The following material is included:

- The Báb's arrival in Isfahán and His close relationship with the illustrious and powerful Governor
- After the Governor's death, the Báb is sent to Tihrán, with the expectation that He will meet the Sháh of Persia, but this is thwarted by the Prime Minister
- Instead of meeting the king, the Báb is sent into exile and imprisonment in northwest Persia, first at Máh-kú and then at Chihríq
- The mock trial in Tabríz was intended to humiliate the Báb in front of the leading clergy, but instead the Báb transformed the event into a proclamation of His Mission as the Promised One awaited by all
- At Badasht, the Báb's followers execute a controversial break with the traditions of Islám, disavow violent holy war and proclaim the full station and claims of the Báb
- Soon after, three violent upheavals occur – at Fort Tabarsí, Nayríz and Zanján – when the the Báb's followers come under vicious attack by the government's forces
- The Báb's return to prison and the completion of His Revelation
- In 1850, the Báb was publicly executed
- After 1850, under the pressure of violent waves of persecution, the Báb's Cause appeared to be teetering on the brink of extinction
- And then, the Báb's Faith is rescued by the only leader of the Faith remaining alive, Who turns out to be Him Whom God shall make manifest, Baha'u'llah

Part 1 also provides an appendix which includes the same the overview chapters of all six of the Abrahamic Divine Educators that were presented in Volume 1. These overview chapters are included in each volume of the Divine Curriculum series. The intention is to enable the reader to see, at a high level *the entire Divine curriculum*—as delivered through the Abrahamic lineage—in the proper sequence and in the context of history. Likewise, when the reader is examining one of these Divine Personages closeup, he or she can always remain mindful of how He always fits into a larger school of God as well. He shines as an individual Teacher and He also shines as a collaborating member of a Divine Faculty of Teachers.

One advantage in using this approach is that it recognizes there is no way to know which book in the series someone will pick up first. Perhaps someone will find the Divine curriculum series while looking for a book on Jesus and someone else will be looking for one on Moses, and still another one will be looking for a book on Muhammad. By providing the overview chapters, the reader has the opportunity to see the entire curriculum God taught in the Abrahamic lineage that has spanned about 4,000 years, and hopefully become interested in all of the other Divine Educators in the sequence of the Abrahamic lineage, regardless of which volume in the series they happen to start with. By using this innovative approach, I hope that every reader will be enabled to see the longer historical context of *the entire school of God* covered in this series while also learning about a specific Divine Educators close up. This also helps the reader to begin making connections between all of these great Divine Messengers.

Full disclosure—My stance

My own religious affiliation is the Bahá'í Faith, which was founded in the 19th century by the Báb and Bahá'u'lláh. That said, I personally believe in each and every One of the Divine Educators covered in this series. I benefit from Their teachings in my own personal life and I look upon Them with the utmost reverence and respect. Once the reader understands the true extent of the transcendent monotheism presented in this series, he or she will not find it surprising to know that I look upon each of Them, individually and together, as the pathway to salvation, in this world and in the next.

As the reader, you can benefit from this perspective in very specific ways. As you will discover, *my approach is not sectarian in nature*. Taking an uncommon stance, each of the Divine Educators in this series – Abraham, Moses, Jesus, Muhammad, the Báb and Bahá'u'lláh, each of these towering historical Figures is studied with equal enthusiasm, respect, admiration and even devotion. To the utmost of my ability, no favoritism is shown, no partisanship of any kind is on display. I have made every effort to find unbiased, reliable sources of information and have tried my best to document everything. I've tried to cut through the prejudices and misunderstandings which have occurred all too often in humanity's discourse about religion. The teachings of the Divine Educators, that is, Their curriculum, will be viewed in their accurate historical context, within the events of Their own lifetimes, in Their continuity with one another and in light of Their overall contribution to the advancement of human civilization. My aim is to give you an unbiased, appreciative and connected inquiry into each Divine Educator and into the entire centuries-long process of the Divine curriculum.

THE GOAL OF THE DIVINE CURRICULUM

Creation—indeed, reality itself—is spiritual, unified, intentional, instructional and always surprising. God's revealed Words, scientific knowledge, and indeed the records of human history all testify to different but connected aspects of the Divine education offered by God. All creation serves as a classroom. With all of its magnificent scale and complexity, the entirety of heaven and earth is designed to be educational for complex conscious beings such as ourselves.

Throughout the Divine Curriculum Series, we have made repeated reference to the purpose underlying all of creation. The logic has been as follows: Assuming that God has purposes in mind for calling into existence all of creation in the first place, it stands to reason that whatever He ultimately creates will, according to His wisdom, be designed to be capable of achieving those very purposes. Moreover, assuming that God decided to offer an educational curriculum in the first place, the goals of that curriculum will also be aimed at achieving the purposes underlying all of creation.

Given that logic, let's revisit this quote from Bahá'u'lláh:

> Having created the world and all that liveth and moveth therein, He, through the direct operation of His unconstrained and sovereign Will, chose to confer upon man the unique distinction and capacity to know Him and to love Him—a capacity that must needs be regarded as the generating impulse and the primary purpose underlying the whole of creation.... – Bahá'u'lláh[5]

If the purpose underlying all of creation is knowing and loving God, what kind of creature does God create in order to achieve this? This is discussed in depth in Volume 1 of the series. Suffice to say here that the creature must have the conscious ability to know and learn things, and it must be able to consciously give and receive love. Of necessity, such a creature must be able to choose, and not merely behave as if programmed like a computer. The knowing and the loving this creature offers must be chosen freely; otherwise, such a creature would be merely a mind-controlled automaton. To avoid such a fate, this means the creature, in addition to knowing and loving, must have the capacity for choosing. It must be equally able to say no to God as to say yes. In addition, if the creature has a physical body, there must be a complex central nervous system which would make all that knowing, loving and choosing doable in everyday behavior. Also, to have a truly knowing and loving relationship with God, the relationship must be as eternal as God is eternal, thus the creature must have an immortal soul which survives the death of the body. Finally, that soulful creature must live in a social environment in which the art of knowing, loving and choosing God can be passed on from one generation to the next and through which civilization can continuously improve both materially and spiritually over time. Obviously, we, the human beings who inhabit this planet, are the very creatures which satisfy these exacting "design specifications". Put differently, all of the human race are the students who are "enrolled" in the universal school of God.

The argument of this book series is simply this: In the universal school of God, which is all of creation, the curriculum taught by the Divine Educators across the millennia has been developing this ability of knowing, loving and choosing God and of carrying forward an ever-advancing civilization. Every Divine Messenger has been on this mission, but at different times in history, and at different stages of the curriculum. The lessons brought by the Manifestations of God have been in sequence, given the timeline of history, and they have been cumulative, each one preparing the students, all of humanity, for the next stage to come. Despite many setbacks, humanity has been advancing towards its predestined goal.

In this series so far, we have focused on the Divine curriculum taught by Abraham, Moses, Jesus and Muhammad. This volume (#5) is dedicated to the next Educator in the sequence, the Báb. The next volume (#6), and the last of this series, will focus on the curriculum brought by Bahá'u'lláh. Through these six volumes we are hopefully gaining a good understanding of the overall Divine curriculum as presented by the Founding Figures within the Abrahamic lineage. Since the Divine curriculum is never-ending, we'll all have to wait and see what learning God has in store for us all after Bahá'u'lláh. We have centuries to go before that Great Teacher is destined to appear.

THE DIVINE CURRICULUM SO FAR

All of creation is a classroom. The Divine Educators are spiritually one. As explained by Bahá'u'lláh, They are "all sent down from the heaven of the Will of God"; They all "all arise to proclaim His irresistible Faith"; and They all are therefore "regarded as one soul and the same person".[6] During Their individual ministries on earth, at different times and places, They pursue Their work in mutual respect as Teachers of a single Divine faculty. They acknowledge one another, praise each other, build on the previous lessons that have been taught, honor the suffering of Their Predecessors, glory in Their sacrifices and labor as a team to achieve the mission set for Them by God, the school's Creator. Spiritually, each of these Manifestations of God is well able to claim, "I am all the Prophets" and "Our Cause is but one". They are "all abiding in the same tabernacle, soaring in the same heaven, seated upon the same throne, uttering the same speech, and proclaiming the same Faith".[7] The Divine curriculum They reveal is given to humanity progressively, in a step-by-step fashion, each stage being different from the others in some ways, while the overall process accumulates its benefits age to age.

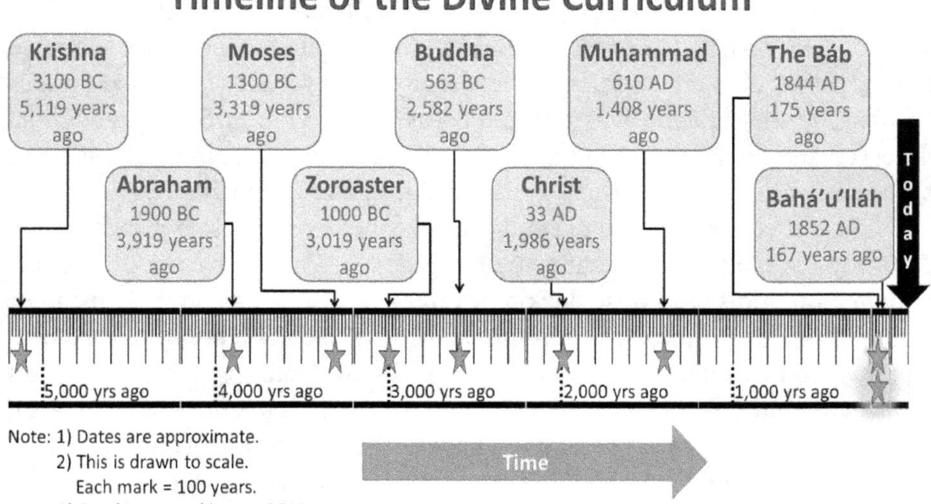

Figure 1 The Divine Educators on the timeline of history

Abraham

Abraham is not the only historical figure that talked about the oneness of God. But His "moment" in history, 4000 years ago, is unique because He is the Divine Educator Who first established what is known as ethical monotheism amidst a viable, living population bound together in a Covenant with God. Abraham's people, the Hebrews, established themselves as the only monotheistic culture amidst a sea of other cultures that were practicing human sacrifice, polytheism and idolatry.

Abraham was an iconoclast, devoting much of His ministry to defeating and destroying idol worship. Abraham's monotheism is known as ethical monotheism because His teaching didn't merely reduce the number of gods to one, but established this God as the one Creator and source of all moral and ethical goodness, who is capable of entering into a Covenant which provides blessings to the people, and also affirms the sacredness of human life. Initially, the unit of social integration was at the scale of the family. A small family in the beginning, Abraham's family grew in the centuries which followed into a population of hundreds of thousands.

Although Abraham's focus was only on one God, His descendants didn't embrace all of the implications of monotheism in one leap. In the ancient near east, the common understanding was that different cultures and different tribes all had their own God. So, monotheism was first understood as a claim of loyalty rather than an assertion of how many gods were in existence. Initially, the God of Abraham was understood as the one God of many gods that deserved and demanded the total loyalty of the Hebrew people and this bond between God and people was expressed through a Covenant with God. The monotheism concept would expand in subsequent centuries to a recognition that only the God of Abraham actually existed. All others were mere human imagination, idols, and false, lacking even existence. This comprehension of God evolved over time, but overall Abraham's Revelation conveyed the idea that this God was the actual Creator, the source of goodness, far more powerful than any other imagined god, and Who was willing to enter into Covenant with His followers. In other words, this was the time in history when ethical monotheism began to take root in human consciousness.

Moses

Moses lived about 3,300 years ago. He was a descendent of Abraham. He acknowledged and honored Abraham and Abraham's God fully. He built on the ethical monotheism of Abraham, strengthening it greatly, and took it a step further with His introduction of the Law of God from this one God. Again, through Moses, this God, now known as Yahweh, entered into Covenant with His chosen people. Moses is known for having accomplished the arduous task of freeing the Hebrew people from cruel bondage in Egypt, revealing to them the Law of God, and especially the Ten Commandments, and guiding their forty-year journey to the land of Canaan, which God had promised them. They named this land Israel, and themselves became known as Israelites and later on as Jews. Moses commanded loyalty to the one God, forbade all idol worship, taught a strong ethical code, and established certain ceremonials such as worshipping at the Temple and observing the Sabbath day.

Initially, the unit of social integration was at the scale of the tribe, based on the twelve tribes which had descended from Abraham, Isaac and Jacob, the patriarchs of Israel. Just tribes in the beginning, the followers of Moses, a population of people which had recently been slaves suffering under cruel bondage, became the exponents of a thriving and brilliant monotheistic civilization in their Promised Land.

Jesus

Jesus lived about 2,000 years ago. He was a descendent of Abraham. He acknowledged and honored Noah, Abraham and Moses fully. He came to the Jewish people when they were once again suffering in their own land under the cruel oppression of the Roman Empire. When Jesus appeared, the Mosaic religion and civilization had already seen better days. The Jews had lost their civilization when they were conquered repeatedly by the Assyrians, the Babylonians, the Greeks, and then the Romans. They had been taken off into exile and then later a remnant had been allowed to return home and reestablish their residence in the Promised Land.

Their religion, at the time of Jesus, had become formulaic and rigid, a stifling remnant of the original Faith which Moses had imparted to the people. In this milieu, Jesus advocated a religion which was a brilliant step forward from the Law. He still offered the one God of Abraham and Moses, but He strengthened their ethical monotheism further by referring to God as "the Father", thus indicating the possibility and even the necessity of forming a close personal relationship with God through Jesus, His Son. Going beyond the Law, without negating it, He emphasized the love of God, forgiveness, the Kingdom of God, and salvation in another world above and beyond earthly existence, which He called Heaven. His intention was not to reject the Law of God, rather His aim was to revitalize and breathe new life into man's Covenant with God. God, the Father, under Jesus' teaching, is truly loving, forgiving, and full of grace. Initially, the unit of social integration was the Jewish people, based on the remnant which had been allowed to return to the Holy Land after years of exile. In the end, however, the scope of the new Covenant with God was expanded to a scale which invited Jews and Gentiles alike into a deeply spiritual loving Covenant relationship with God. After Jesus, His religion flourished in many directions, bringing salvation to millions of souls, ultimately winning over the vast Roman civilization and empire.

Note to readers regarding Muhammad and Islam

Let me offer a clarifying word about Muhammad. At the time of this writing, in 2019, in the Western world, the public's understanding of Muhammad has been demonstrably distorted by the activities and rhetoric of the militant jihadi extremists. Their resort to militancy and terrorism in the name of Islám, the religion Muhammad founded, has tarnished the name of Islám in the West and (understandably) led to gross distortions of how most westerners perceive Muhammad.

To generate a clear and accurate image of Muhammad, a brief effort is made in the overview chapter devoted to Muhammad (in the Appendix of this book) to separate the Faith of Muhammad from the ideology of the terrorists. This effort is based on relying upon authentic sources of information and sound logical reasoning. I invite you to explore that material, especially if up to now your exposure to Muhammad or Islám has been through either the mass media or churches and synagogues.

Muhammad

Muhammad lived about 1,400 years ago. He was a descendent of Abraham. Muhammad was sent to the Arabs living in Arabia who were mainly polytheistic idolaters. Their central shrine, in the center of Mecca, known as the Ka'bih, was the center of their economy and the focus of their idol worship. In the year 610 AD Muhammad claimed to receive Divine Revelation from the same God that had previously spoken to Adam, Noah, Abraham, Moses and Jesus. The Arabic word for God is "Allah", which means literally "the God". Muhammad taught an emphatic monotheism, asserting that there is no God but God and that Muhammad is His Messenger. His Holy Book, the Qur'án, identified Him as the latest in a long line of Divine Messengers sent by God, such as Adam, Noah, Abraham, Moses and Jesus, all of Whom He acknowledged and honored fully.

Like His predecessors, Muhammad was an iconoclast, bent on destroying the idols and establishing the truth of God's Prophets. Though Himself illiterate, He revealed a sacred Scripture, the Qur'án, in His native tongue of Arabic. The beauty and eloquence of the Qur'án, in its original Arabic, being uttered by an illiterate Man, was at such an exalted level that it was considered a miracle. (Thirteen centuries would pass before anyone else would come along and reveal verses on a par with the Qur'án, equally perfect and uplifting.)

Muhammad's central teaching was Islám, which means submission to the will of God. Submission to the will of God is the logical next thing to do with the love of God. It is common for people to cling to their own will, even in one's relationship to God, but when the lover loves the Will of the Divine Beloved, and joyfully submits to His greater wisdom and Divine will, then the love of God attains to transcendent levels. Muhammad taught His followers to pray to God multiple times each day, to give to charity, to go on pilgrimage to Mecca, and to struggle towards self-improvement.

Muhammad faced severe persecution by the Meccans who clung to their idolatrous ways, and was compelled to seek refuge in the city of Medina in the year 622 AD. The Medinans, a community of Jews, Christians, and pagans, were plagued by internal disputes and they asked Muhammad resolve their disputes, offering Him refuge from His enemies in Mecca in return. In a short time, He became, in practical terms, their Leader. As Leader, He established a pact, known as the Constitution of Medina, which established the umma, a pluralistic multi-faith society, bound together in a covenant. Citizens were not asked to change religion, although conversions were welcome. Social harmony, cohesion and prosperity were established, the Muslims were now safe, and Muhammad was the chief arbiter of all issues in Medina. He was at this point both a Prophet of God and a Statesman.

The Meccans, unfortunately, mounted several military attacks on the Muslims, so it became necessary to take up the sword in self-defense of His new nation, the umma. Eventually Muhammad's forces were victorious, Mecca was conquered without bloodshed, the idols were purged from the Ka'bih, and Islám as a religion was fully launched. Initially, the unit of social integration was at the scale of a small nation, or a city-state, but after Muhammad, the Arab military forces exploded out of Arabia and a vast civilization and a vast empire was established. That civilization grew. It was brilliant in science, literature, philosophy, astronomy, architecture, medicine and art.

THE DIVINE CURRICULUM GOING FORWARD

The Báb

The Báb was born on October 20, 1819 AD, in Shíráz, Persia, which is Iran today. This year is the 200th anniversary of His birth (I'm writing this in 2019 AD). The Báb was a descendent of Muhammad, which automatically makes Him a descendent of Abraham as well. The Báb acknowledged and honored all of the Divine Educators which preceded Him, including Adam, Noah, Abraham, Moses, Jesus and Muhammad. Initially the unit of social integration was at the scale of nations, but from the beginning the Báb anticipated an all-inclusive global perspective. The Revelation in this era was intended for all the peoples of the world, in the East and in the West.

The Báb came from a respected family of cloth merchants, and was a merchant in His early years. From His earliest Youth, He demonstrated an unusual attraction to prayer and meditation. His family attempted to send Him to school, but the teacher brought Him back saying He seemed already to possess innate knowledge.

The Báb lived at a time of great millennial expectation in Persia. Large numbers of people were looking for their Promised One. On the evening of May 22, 1844 AD, Mullá Husayn, a brilliant religious student on a quest to find the Promised One, encountered the Báb on the outskirts of the city of Shíráz, Persia. The Báb greeted Mullá Husayn affectionately and invited him to His home for dinner, refreshments, prayers and conversation. It was that night, after prayers, that the young Merchant declared to Mullá Husayn that He was the Báb, the Promised One of Islám and, in fact, all of the world's major religions. He said God had given Him a great Revelation for all of humanity, and also that He had come to prepare the way for another Divine Messenger even greater than Himself. In a short time, a small group of spiritual seekers discovered the Báb on their own and they became His first disciples, whom He called the Letters of the Living. The Báb sent them out throughout the country to teach His message to the people.

The Báb's message was attractive to the people of Persia. In addition to announcing that an even greater Messenger of God was coming, He also taught numerous extremely beautiful ethical and spiritual teachings. Continuing the strong monotheism of earlier revelations, the Báb taught what could be called an enhanced and intensified monotheism. That is, with the Báb, monotheism was not just the oneness of God, He also stressed the utter infinity of God. The Báb placed an emphasis on God as an utterly transcendent Being. God is the only God, God is absolutely infinite and yet He is also caring, loving and responsive to the prayers of His human children.

By His actions and His words, the Báb made clear that each person is invited to have a pure, selfless, loving and personal relationship with God. Moreover, this relationship does not need to be mediated through the services of a priest or a mullá. Each individual should investigate the truth, and humbly decide for Himself his relationship with God. He taught the purity of worship. He explained that that there is an underlying unity between all of the religions of the world, that there is a continuity and progression to all of religion. His ethical principle was as simple as it was graceful; bring no sorrow or grief upon any soul, rather do all in your power to bring joy to others. He taught the responsibility to elevate. In all one's encounters, always strive to elevate the well-being, faith, virtue and understanding of others. Women were to be empowered. His movement was non-aggressive, making strides towards eliminating the use of the sword, especially in the name of religion. The core of His worldview was that all people, of whatever race, religion, class or nationality, are spiritual beings, and the radiant light of God is reflected in every soul. This He taught was the basis of peace an unity, a recognition and perception from the heart.

Both the Báb Himself and His teachings were inspiring and wildly popular with the masses, but were met with vehement hostility by the Shí'ih Islámic religious orthodoxy. The government violently suppressed the movement, forcing the Bábís to defend themselves a number of times. The Báb Himself was exiled, imprisoned, tortured, put through a mock trial, and finally on July 9, 1850 AD He was executed by a firing squad of 750 soldiers. Approximately 20,000 Bábí followers were massacred in the early years of the Faith.

During all these trials, the Báb was extraordinarily prolific as a Revealer of the Word of God. His ability to rapidly and spontaneously reveal God's word became a source of amazement repeatedly throughout His short career. He was the first Person, since Muhammad Himself, to demonstrate the ability to reveal Divine verses, in Arabic, and also in Persian, on the same level of eloquence and perfection as Muhammad had done for the Qur'án. The Báb's original Writings are carefully preserved in archives at the Bahá'í World Center in Haifa, Israel.

One of the most consistent themes repeated throughout the Báb's Writings is the near Advent of the next Divine Educator, Whom He called "Him Whom God shall make manifest".

> ...were I to be assured that in the day of His Manifestation thou wilt deny Him, I would unhesitatingly disown thee and repudiate thy faith.... If, on the other hand, I be told that a Christian, who beareth no allegiance to My Faith, will believe in Him, the same will I regard as the apple of Mine eye. – The Báb[8]

This theme permeates His Writings. At the time these words were revealed (1844-1850) the identity of Him Whom God shall make manifest was not publicly known. Bahá'u'lláh, one of the foremost Bábí followers at the time, eventually announced in 1863 that He was the One foretold by the Báb.

In retrospect, it can now be seen that the Báb's mission was extremely successful as the Forerunner of Bahá'u'lláh because, after 1863, about 99% of the Bábís embraced Bahá'u'lláh and became Bahá'ís, thus rescuing the Faith from impending oblivion under government persecution and bringing to fruition the Báb's dearest hopes and intentions.

Bahá'u'lláh

Bahá'u'lláh was born on November 12, 1817 AD, in Tihrán, Persia, which is Iran today. His given name was Mírzá Husayn 'Alí. He was a descendent of Abraham. Initially a follower of the Báb, Bahá'u'lláh declared that He was the One promised by the Báb and, indeed, by all previous religions. He made this announcement to a small group of followers in a garden outside of Baghdád, Iraq, in 1863. He fully acknowledged and honored all of the Divine Educators which preceded Him, including Adam, Noah, Abraham, Moses, Jesus, Muhammad and the Báb.

Bahá'u'lláh came from a respected and wealthy family based in northern Persia. 'Abdu'l-Bahá says that,

> ...it is well known throughout Persia that He never studied in a school or associated with the learned and the divines. – Abdu'l-Baha[9]

Although not formally educated, He was known since early childhood for His unusual wisdom and seemingly innate knowledge. As a young adult, He refused a prestigious government position and instead used His vast wealth to care of the poor and needy in His region. The people of the region called Him "the Father of the poor" and His wife, Navváb, who was His partner in these activities, was known as "the mother of consolation".

In 1844, when the message of the Báb first reached Bahá'u'lláh in Tihrán, Bahá'u'lláh embraced the Cause instantly, and very quickly became one of the Báb's foremost followers. Bahá'u'lláh embarked upon teaching efforts in northern Persia, in the region near the Caspian Sea, and was highly successful, enrolling thousands in the Cause.

Bahá'u'lláh's career as a follower of the Báb was illustrious. He was a key Player at many events which carried the Faith forward. Like many of the Bábís who sacrificed everything for the Faith, Bahá'u'lláh was caught up in a country-wide wave of persecution against the Bábís. Though He had done nothing wrong, He was thrown into a loathsome dungeon pit, called the Siyáh Chál (Black Pit), three stories underground. In this icy-cold, dark, and vermin infested dungeon, with His body burdened by infamous hundred-pound chains, He received Divine revelation which told Him to arise and proclaim that He was Him Whom God shall make manifest, the One promised by the Báb, and indeed all the world's religions. Describing those moments of Divine Revelation, He stated:

> ...I felt as if something flowed from the crown of My head over My breast, even as a mighty torrent that precipitateth itself upon the earth from the summit of a lofty mountain. Every limb of My body would, as a result, be set afire. At such moments My tongue recited what no man could bear to hear. – Bahá'u'lláh[10]

Bahá'u'lláh did not die in prison. After several months the government had to release Him in early 1853. He was stripped of all His wealth and banished from Persia. Forced to make the journey during the worst winter in memory, He and His family were sent to Baghdád, in Iraq. He was there for about ten years, concentrating His efforts on revitalizing the spirits of the Bábís who, under the weight of the persecution, had fallen into despair in the years following the execution of the Báb.

Baha'u'llah's efforts were highly successful. The Bábí community experienced a profound rebith. Bahá'u'lláh's influence grew and the people held a deep affection for Him. Noticing these trends, the government, in 1863, ordered another exile, this time to Constantinople (which is Istanbul today). But before He left the region on this next exile, He met with some of His followers in a garden outside the city, and He publicly announced that, in fact, He is He Whom God Shall Make Manifest.

Bahá'u'lláh's exiles continued. From Baghdád to Constantinople. From Constantinople to Adrianople (Erdine today). From Adrianople to the city of 'Akká, in what was then known as Ottoman Palestine, which is Israel today. In Israel, He imprisoned again in what is now known as the Most Great Prison. He remained in the Holy Land under various degrees of house arrest until His passing in 1892 and is buried in 'Akka. Like the Shrine of the

Báb in Haifa, the resting place of Bahá'u'lláh, in 'Akká, is a site for sacred pilgrimage for Bahá'ís from all over the world.

Like the Báb, Bahá'u'lláh was also an extremely prolific Revealer of the Word of God, eventually revealing the equivalent of 100 volumes. His act of spontaneous, flowing revelation was as miraculous as the Báb's. Historical accounts all say the same thing; the very room seemed to throb with power and majesty as the Divine verses flowed from Him so fast that the secretaries charged with writing down His words and teachings could hardly keep up.

Bahá'u'lláh's verses, also in Arabic and Persian, soared with the same miraculous eloquence and beauty as the Qur'án and the Báb had achieved. His Writings contained a vast body of teachings that affirmed the transcendent oneness of God, the unity of all the Divine Educators sent by God, and that the purpose of all the Divine Educators of the past, and of God in this Day, is to establish on earth the oneness of humanity. All the teachings of the past, relating to the oneness of God, the sacredness of human life, the law of God, the love of God, the Kingdom of God, the submission unto God, and seeing in all things the reflection of God, have been for the purpose of enabling humanity to, at long-last, establish in this age God's Kingdom on earth, the age of universal peace. While offering a bright pathway to spiritual awakening and universal peace, Bahá'u'lláh also warned that, if humanity ignored God's teachings, that much suffering would result. The suffering would not in the long run defeat the mission, rather humanity would eventually emerge from it chastened and with lessons learned. Whatever the path taken, humanity, according to Bahá'u'lláh, is destined to achieve the Most Great Peace eventually.

> Yet so it shall be; these fruitless strifes, these ruinous wars shall pass away, and the 'Most great Peace' shall come. – Bahá'u'lláh[11]

Bahá'u'lláh brought numerous supplemental teachings to serve as a blueprint for actually attaining to world peace, such as the equality of women and men, the independent investigation of truth, the need for universal education for all girls and boys in the world, the importance of overcoming division through the process of consultation, eliminating prejudices, harmonizing the world's economy through spiritual principles, and forbidding strife and contention, which includes abolishing the use of the sword, especially in the name of religion. Bahá'u'lláh's teachings advocate for the nations to establish by universal consent some sort of world federation of nations, demilitarizing the planet, adopting a universal auxiliary language, and promoting love and fellowship among the peoples of every religion, race and nationality. The moral teachings of Bahá'u'lláh, consistent with the Voices of all the Divine Educators of the past, call humanity to the highest standards of personal behavior, of integrity, love, truthfulness, justice, fellowship, hospitality, kindness and service to humanity in all one's endeavors. The family is strongly emphasized. Prayer is a vital obligation for every soul. Members of the Bahá'í Faith are admonished to avoid *partisan* politics. Bahá'u'lláh appointed, in Writing, His own Successor, His Son, 'Abdu'l-Bahá, who took over leadership of the Faith after Bahá'u'lláh's passing in 1892. As a result, the Bahá'í Faith successfully avoided schism; it is one Faith all over the world. Bahá'u'lláh eliminated the role of the clergy and placed the everyday governance of His Faith in the hands of elected institutions. The Bahá'í Faith has encircled the globe and become a world religion. All over the planet, the Bahá'ís, through numerous lines of activity, are promoting interfaith understanding, interracial harmony, moral and spiritual education, awakening and empowerment, an atmosphere of devotion to God, meaningful conversations, and spiritual community building, all of which are fundamental building blocks for the eventual emergence of world peace and Divine civilization. Membership in the Faith of Bahá'u'lláh now exceeds five million, in over two hundred countries.

***

Although the Divine curriculum is never-ending, the Writings do say that this age has been the goal towards which humanity has ever been striving – the age when all of humanity would unite in the knowledge and the love of God, and freely choose Him, thus establishing on earth the world-embracing, peaceful, ever-advancing Divine civilization which has been the goal of the Divine curriculum from the start.

What follows the achievements of the Divine curriculum?

What comes after the Most Great Peace?

Honestly, no one knows.

I have my ideas and perhaps you have yours. I sense personally that the peaceful unification of the planet is but the launching pad for unimaginably great things in humanity's future. In my view, what God has in store for humanity is so brilliant that it cannot as yet be even dimply visualized. Surely it entails the flowering of civilization to levels as yet beyond our view. But attaining to the Most Great Peace, as wonderful as that will be, should not be imagined as some sort of static ending of history; on the contrary, I see it as the true beginning point of human history, all else that has led up to that is but prologue and preparation.

People love to speculate about what is to come. So long as no one takes too seriously their speculations about what God will do many centuries from now, such conversations can be fun. What we do know is this: with the transition from childhood to adulthood, the potentialities of the human race are unimaginably wonderful. Having put away, for good, the endless strife and wars, having ended the prejudices and the corruptions, having shed the dark ideologies of rampant materialism, unbridled nationalism, brutal totalitarianism and cruel racialism, having achieved the unity of the entire human race, having established a world-embracing Divine civilization, the future for humanity is very, very bright.

As everyone can imagine, attaining to world peace and global Divine civilization is a tall order. The Writings say that humanity's success is inevitable, fast approaching, and necessarily to be achieved over the course of the centuries to come. Obviously, looking at world events today, through the headlines of the mass media, one would think humanity is moving in the opposite direction. This contrary movement is not denied, but fully acknowledged in the Writings. Nevertheless, although mounting difficult times still lie ahead, the outcome of establishing world peace, Divine civilization and God's Kingdom on earth is a matter that is predestined according to the Scriptures. God, the Scriptures say, is with us. His Will be done, on earth as it is in heaven. Divine justice, and mercy, will in the long run prevail.

***

We will turn to the Báb in just a moment, but first I have one more important thing to tell you.

MY PARTNER IN THIS ENDEAVOR

Dear reader, please do not skip over this section.

When I met my good friend, Behrad Majidi, for the first time in September 2018, I was thinking at the time that this book was almost ready for publication because I believed I had made good use of the available English language sources about the life and teachings of the Báb. But I was in for a big surprise.

Behrad and I met at a conference and hit it off very quickly. He too is an author of Bahá'í history, as well as a physician and a highly respected Bahá'í. Our interests converged very quickly, and we began discussing our projects with one another. Behrad also happens to be from Persian background and, having grown up in Iran, he is fluent in Persian. His writing project involved documenting the history of the Bahá'í Faith in the province of south Khurásán, which is where he is from. Mine, as you know, was this book about the Báb. In the course of our conversations it came up that I was trying to puzzle out whether or not Mullá Husayn and the Báb knew each other before the night of His declaration in Shíráz (the answer is in Chapter 1 of this book). Behrad told me that he had scholarly books at home, written in Persian, that might contain the answer and he generously offered to go and look for the answer for me that night. When we saw each other at the conference the next day, sure enough, he had found the answer to my question. And the information was from a solid source, and properly cited, thus it was totally legitimate in my eyes. For me the only catch was that the info was in Persian, so I could not read it for myself. Behrad had foreseen this and prepared for me a first draft translation of the material. So, I was able to accept and use his information. I was thrilled.

Well, our collaboration blossomed from there. Behrad generously offered to scan his books for me to find me content about the Faith that *isn't found* in the English language sources available at this time.

How many books do you have, Behrad? I asked at one point.

He said, Oh, at least seventy.

I was shocked.

I questioned him about these books. I learned that there is a lively body of scholarly work on the Faith written in the Persian language. These are highly proficient, world-class scholars, known in the Persian community, but not known to us in the English-speaking world. In one case, a certain scholar, Mázindaráni, had written nine volumes on the Faith!! This took place in the 1930s at the request and encouragement of Shoghi Effendi. For various reasons, only one volume has ever been published. The others are readily available online, but of course you have to know Persian to read it. The other Persian scholars have equally sterling reputations among those who are familiar with their work. Their books have gone through the rigors of review, editing and the publication process with reputable publishing companies. Many of them are 500 or more pages long, and with copious footnotes. This was an amazing body of knowledge. The only thing wrong with it? I couldn't read it because it is all in Persian!

Figure 2 Behrad and his books (at least some of them)

To make a long story short, Behrad and I developed a joyful collaboration so that some of this content could be brought into my book, and of course to the English-speaking world. Behrad has translated for me nearly 200 pages of content. We spent countless hours on the phone. One phone conversation was six hours long and through it all Behrad was laser focused on getting the job done! We discussed everything.

During the process of translating and paraphrasing from the Persian sources, expertise in Arabic was required. For this, Ziyaollah Seddigh Sarvestani, a friend of Behrad's, provided expert assistance. Ziya was raised in Iran, he received his education through the Baha'i Institute for Higher Education, and his knowledge of Arabic, as well as of the Writings of the Faith, is highly advanced. He provided invaluable expertise in clarifying Arabic phrases and terms found in the Persian sources. On another note, Ziya's ancestry goes to one of the early believers and companions of Vahid in the episode of Nayriz. I wish to extend my deep thanks to Ziya as well.

There are many surprises waiting for you, the reader. First of all, we will answer the question about whether Mullá Husayn and the Báb knew each other beforehand. You will read about the movements of the Letters of the Living in the Faith's first expansion phase. You will learn much more about what happened when the Báb went on pilgrimage to Mecca – for example, about the man who literally chased after the boat the Báb was on – and even how the Báb may have had a plan to create what we might call the 19th century equivalent of social media buzz. You will read about the letter the king's scholar, Vahíd, wrote explaining to his why he was so won over by the Báb. Vahíd's father was, himself, a great scholar who had met the Báb in Mecca. You'll read about the deadly intentions of certain leaders in the government, and even witness the exact moment when the Prime Minister – the man whom Shoghi Effendi christened as "the Antichrist of the Bábí Revelation" – decided to become an archenemy of the Faith, and about the various ways the religious leaders embarrassed themselves again and again. You'll read the heartwarming story of the Báb's childhood teacher and you'll find out what happens to the chief constable of Shíráz after he pleaded with the Báb to save his son's life on the night of the cholera epidemic, and you'll read about the ironic twist of history that takes place with his descendants. You'll read about the surprising relationship the number one Shí'ih leader in the world had with the Báb and His Faith and you'll ponder how history might have turned out differently if this one man had chosen a different path. You'll read in depth about the behind the scenes happenings at the historic conference of Badasht and gain an insight into the high stakes issues the leaders and the faithful were trying to decide. You'll read about the heartfelt actions of an elderly man, the venerable figure Mullá Sadiq, on the morning after He converted to the Cause of the Báb. Heroes you thought you knew, such as Táhirih, Vahíd and Manúchihr Khán, will appear more fully to your eyes. You'll explore the motivations of Sam Khán, the Christian officer who desperately sought to avoid the duty to kill the Báb. You'll read about the dedicated young man who, though he had been left for dead for three days, manages to survive the massacre at Fort Tabarsí, sees a vision of the Báb, is almost disowned by his mother, and then lives to be 100 years old. You'll read some very touching stories about the people who early on arose to find the truth and then to serve it with everything they had.

And much more.

I can hardly wait to share all of this with you.

Behrad and I developed a very systematic method that we hope produces an optimal result. First, we selected twelve books we thought would give us the best chance for really useful content. (It's just not possible to try to read all 70 books.) Then, Behrad reads for me the Persian sources and tells me of things he finds. We discuss it and, about 90% of the time, the content is so interesting that I ask Behrad to give me a translation of that content. Usually in each case it is a few paragraphs or a couple of pages long. He then sends it to me, and I weave it into the manuscript very carefully, combining it with the material from English sources as well, and always with precise footnotes documenting the source. When I actually quote Behrad's translation directly, I modify it slightly so that it will read well in the English. So technically it is a paraphrasal, not a translation. Therefore, each time I do this, without exception, it is footnoted and there is a clear statement like this:

> The following passage is paraphrased from the Persian by Husaini.

Or Faizi, or Rouhani, or Mázindarání, etc. Every one of these sources is listed in the bibliography.

You will never be in doubt as to where the information is coming from. Moreover, other Persian-capable scholars can, if they wish, go back and check my work. The final step is that after I have done the paraphrasal, I ask Behrad to carefully scrutinize it. Did I make any mistakes? Do any of the words need to be changed? Does the paraphrasal convey the mood as well as the facts? Sometimes this has led to thirty-minute conversations about the best way to convey one idea in the passage. Only then, after the work has been double-checked, did we consider that section good to go.

So, to be clear, the material from Behrad is not a translation. It is a paraphrasal which is carefully scrutinized to make sure the presentation in English is faithful to the original Persian, but it is in my words. Therefore, I, and not the scholars I am quoting, must bear full responsibility for any errors or shortcomings that may remain. Put simply, if you think well of this process, much of the credit should go to Behrad. If you don't, then the shortcoming are mine.

Anyway, my collaboration with Behrad has lasted about eight months now. My book was clearly NOT finished last September, but it is ready for you now! With all my heart, I must humbly thank Behrad for the nearly unlimited generosity of his time, his purely altruistic and selfless dedication to this project even as he was finishing his own book and carrying forward his own family and career, his formidable intellectual and professional abilities, for the opportunity to learn so many things from him, and for what has become the most rewarding friendship *and* collaboration I have ever experienced.

Throughout this experience, I can honestly say that my heartfelt affection for the Báb, and all of the heroes of that era, has increased immeasurably. The texture of those times, the lived complexity of that moment in time and the lives that were touched, are now richer and more present in my awareness. I can only hope that this collaboration which Behrad and I now offer to you, will have a similar effect for you.

Both of us have engaged in this labor of love so that you, the reader, might have this book this year, 2019, during the year of the 200th anniversary of the Birth of the Báb.

Let's begin!

Chapter 2
THE HISTORY BEGINS

INTERMENT OF THE BÁB'S SACRED REMAINS

It was 1909. 'Abdu'l-Bahá, Son of the Founder of the Bahá'í Faith, removed His shoes, cast aside His turban, and threw off His cloak. Shoghi Effendi described this moment.

> [The] earthly remains of the Martyr-Prophet of Shíráz were, at long last, safely deposited for their everlasting rest in the bosom of God's holy mountain… ['Abdu'l-Bahá] bent low over the still open sarcophagus, His silver hair waving about His head and His face transfigured and luminous, rested His forehead on the border of the wooden casket, and, sobbing aloud, wept with such a weeping that all those who were present wept with Him. That night He could not sleep, so overwhelmed was He with emotion. – Shoghi Effendi[12]

There was no need to speculate on the reason for 'Abdu'l-Bahá's tears.

From His first breath, 'Abdu'l-Bahá's life had been linked with the life and death of the Báb. He was born on the same night in 1844 when the Báb first declared His Mission to the first disciple, Mullá Husayn.[13]

From 1844 to 1850, the Báb had wielded

> …to a degree unrivaled by the Messengers gone before Him the scepter of independent Prophethood… – Shoghi Effendi[14]

In just six years, the Báb had miraculously revealed hundreds of thousands of verses, the equivalent of many volumes of inspired Sacred Scripture. Beginning with one follower, His young Faith had spread throughout Persia and neighboring Iraq, attracting to its fold high ranking clerics and ordinary folk. The Báb had faced a mock trial. He was identified as a heretic. Fulfilling both Biblical and Islámic prophecy, He had claimed Divine status as the long-awaited Promised One of Islám and other world Faiths. He had announced the imminent appearance of Bahá'u'lláh, a second Divine Messenger Who would be even greater than Himself.

The Báb had given birth to a movement that in time would become a world religion.

The Báb had achieved all this while enduring severe torture, exile and imprisonment. After a meteoric ministry, the Báb was brought to Tabríz in 1850 to be executed by firing squad. At the event, which was witnessed by thousands of people and confirmed by historians, all 750 bullets of the first volley mysteriously missed their target. The stunned regiment Captain and his soldiers refused to continue, so a second regiment had to be found to finish the grim task. The Báb's remains were discarded in the moat outside the city, with the expectation that the remains would be eaten by wild animals, but in a daring mission by His devoted followers they were rescued and kept hidden for decades.

In 1890, while visiting Mount Carmel, Bahá'u'lláh pointed out a cluster of cypress trees, indicating to 'Abdu'l-Bahá the exact spot where the Bab's eternal Shrine would be constructed. In 1892, after the passing of His Father and becoming the Head of the Faith, 'Abdu'l-Bahá carried forward His Father's wishes. For decades, first Bahá'u'lláh and then 'Abdu'l-Bahá had guarded the secret of the locations and movements of the remains of the Báb. For years, machinations of fanatical Muslim leaders and government officials had delayed the journey of the Báb's remains to Mount Carmel. And 'Abdu'l-Bahá, a prisoner of the Ottoman Empire until his release in 1909 after the Young Turk Revolution, had been unable to openly inter the remains of the Báb as directed by His Father.

Now, fifty-nine years after the Báb's execution by firing squad, His sacred remains were finally being laid to rest "in the presence of believers from the East and from the West".[15] After decades of being hidden, of being moved again and again when danger drew near and of being secretly carried vast distances, the interment ceremony was finally taking place within the innermost chamber of the sacred Shrine that 'Abdu'l-Bahá had lovingly erected halfway up the steep slope of Mount Carmel, in the Holy Land, at the exact spot pointed out by His own Father, Bahá'u'lláh. This location would become the focal center of the world Faith Bahá'u'lláh and the Báb had founded. It was destined to be the scene of holy pilgrimage for millions of devoted followers in the centuries to come.[16]

After overcoming countless obstacles and fulfilling His mission, after all that, 'Abdu'l-Bahá finally released a flood of tears. He later wrote:

[Note: In the following quote, "Abhá Beauty" refers to Bahá'u'lláh and "Naw-Rúz" refers to the Persian and Bahá'í new year.]

> The most joyful tidings is this, that the holy, the luminous body of the Báb ... after having for sixty years been transferred from place to place, by reason of the ascendancy of the enemy ... has, through the mercy of the Abhá Beauty, been ceremoniously deposited, on the day of Naw-Rúz, within the sacred casket, in the exalted Shrine on Mt. Carmel..."
> – 'Abdu'l-Bahá[17]

One of the signal acts of His Ministry was at last accomplished.

PRE-BÁBÍ PERSIA

The condition of Persia

In the 7th century AD, armies of the expanding Islámic empire conquered Persia. In little more than a century, Islamic armies overtook territories as far west as Spain and as far east as western China. During the Golden Age of Islám, the Islámic world established far-reaching networks of commercial trade and sophisticated centers of culture. Theologians, philosophers, scientists, astronomers, mathematicians, and doctors practiced their arts. They built houses of worship with dazzling architecture, and steeped populations in the daily rhythms of piety and faith.

After nearly 1,300 years of Islámic domination, Persia followed an Islámic way of life, characterized by the Shí'ih branch of Islam. But by the 19th century, Persian civilization was far past its peak. Instead,

> ...all observers agree in representing Persia as a feeble and backward nation divided against itself by corrupt practices and ferocious bigotries. Inefficiency and wretchedness, the fruit of moral decay, filled the land. From the highest to the lowest there appeared neither the capacity to carry out methods of reform nor even the will seriously to institute them. National conceit preached a grandiose self-content. A pall of immobility lay over all things, and a general paralysis of mind made any development impossible. – Shoghi Effendi[18]

This pall and paralysis of mind showed in the spiritual realm. 'Abdu'l-Bahá observed:

[Note: In the following passage, "the Shí'ihs of Persia" are the followers of Shi'ih Islam. The "blessed Imáms" refer to the twelve spiritual leaders in the early years of Shí'ih Islám.]

Know that in the latter days the Shí'ihs of Persia had forgotten the truth of the religion of God and had become entirely devoid and deprived of the morals of the spiritually minded. They were cleaving to empty husks and remained entirely heedless of the pith and substance. They had nothing to show but outward observances, such as prayer, fasting, pilgrimage, almsgiving, and the commemoration of the blessed Imáms. The people of true knowledge would therefore call them "Qishrí" (superficial), for amongst them the inner truths and meanings were absent, spiritual perceptions were non-existent, and heavenly morals had become but an idle matter. – 'Abdu'l-Bahá[19]

The government, led by the Qájár dynasty, was a church-state.

Venal, cruel, and immoral as it was, [the government] was formally religious. Muslim orthodoxy was its basis and permeated to the core both it and the social lives of the people. But otherwise there were no laws, statutes, or charters to guide the direction of public affairs. – Shoghi Effendi[20]

There was no parliament or civil judiciary "to check or modify the power of the monarch."[21] The law was the Shah's command, arbitrary and capricious.

The right to take life was vested in him alone; and so were all the functions of government, legislative, executive, and judicial. His royal prerogative was limited by no written restraint whatever. – Shoghi Effendi[22]

Punishments included being crucified, blown from guns, buried alive, impaled, or shod like a horse. The Sháh was praised with superlatives such as King of Kings, Shadow of God and Pivot of the Universe. He surrounded himself with self-serving courtiers. A commentator observed:

Half the money voted with his consent never reaches its destination, but sticks to every intervening pocket... – Lord Curzon[23]

And also:

From the Sháh downward, there is scarcely an official who is not open to gifts, scarcely a post which is not conferred in return for gifts, scarcely an income which has not been amassed by the receipt of gifts. – Lord Curzon[24]

The Hidden Imám

The Shí'ih Muslims say all political and spiritual legitimacy comes from Muhammad's appointment of 'Alí, as His successor as the first Imám. The Shí'ih claim that 'Alí was followed by eleven Imáms, all of his lineage. Muhammad appointed 'Alí and then each of the Imáms assumed office by the dual criteria of family lineage and being selected by his predecessor. The Shí'ih claim these Imáms were endowed by God with exceptional spiritual powers and entitled to whole-hearted obedience.

The Twelfth Imám, Muhammad ibn al-Hassan, was a child when he became the Imám in the year 874 AD (260 AH) after His father, the Eleventh Imám, died. All eleven previous Imáms had been assassinated. When his father was killed, the young Twelfth Imám went into hiding, and according to their beliefs remains in that state to this day.

When referring to the Imams, this state of hiding is referred to as "occultation", meaning concealment or disappearing from sight. The Shí'ih describe two kinds of occultation for the Twelfth Imam, a lesser and then a greater occultation. During the lesser occultation, he

> ...disappeared from view and communicated with his followers only through a certain chosen intermediary known as a Gate. Four of these Gates followed one another in order, each appointed by his predecessor with the approval of the Imam. – Shoghi Effendi[25]

This process continued from the year 874 to 941 AD (260 to 329 AH). But, in 941 AD the fourth Gate did not appoint a fifth, successor Gate. Shoghi Effendi states:

> But when the fourth [Gate] was asked by the faithful, before he died, to name his successor, he declined to do so. He said that God had another plan. On his death all communication between the Imam and his church therefore ceased. – Shoghi Effendi[26]

Sachedina, author of *Islamic Messianism*, adds further detail about the beliefs of the Shi'ih:

> ...the Shi'ites came and asked him about his successor, and he said, "The matter is in the hands of God, and He will bring it to accomplishment" ... A few days before his death a note came from the Imám which read as follows: "...your death ... is going to take place in six days' time. So, take care of your affairs and do not appoint anyone in your place, since the complete occultation has taken place.

> I will not appear until God permits me to do so … and that will be after a long time and after the hearts become hard and the earth is filled with wickedness…" – Sachedina[27]

The lesser occultation of communicating through the Gates ended after 67 years and the period of the greater occultation began. Communication with the Imám was cut off. Today, many centuries later, the Shí'ihs believe this Twelfth Imám is still alive, residing in the mysterious and far distant cities known as Jábulqá and Jábulsá. Though he is over a thousand years old, they claim he is being supernaturally preserved from aging. They prophesy that he will return as the Qá'im ("He who arises") and also be followed by another greater Figure, known as the Imám Husayn. (This second Promised One is to be the return of the Third Imám, Husayn. Yes, it can get a little confusing.) When the Twelfth Imám returns, this youthful thousand-year-old man will conquer the world with his sword, punish the enemies of Islam, and establish justice and peace on earth.[28]

The Shí'ih ideas about the Imám led to a critical question. Only the Imám may rule. And since the Twelfth Imám stopped communicating with the world in 941 AD, who today has authority to rule? The answer: In the Imám's absence, the Shí'ih clergy bestowed upon themselves *collective deputyship* from the hidden Imám.

This theological answer became their political theory and their justification to rule. Self-interested religious leaders then allied with corrupt power of State. The clergy affirmed the monarch's legitimacy and the Shah granted the clergy extraordinary affluence, privilege and position. The clergy accommodated to whoever wielded power and the ruler paid homage to the clergy. Each symbiotically supported the status of the other.

> The shahs successfully presented themselves as patrons of the faith and defenders of the Shi'ite kingdom, whereas [the Muslim clerics] consolidated their social base under the aegis of the state. – Abbas Amanat[29]

The clergy intensified their power over the people through certain doctrines.[30] For example, the doctrine of finality affirmed that after Muhammad there would be no future Prophets from God. Muhammad as the final Prophet assured that the religious leaders' privileged position could never be challenged. By weaving a web of fantastic, physically impossible images of the signs of the Last Day, no one could fulfill the prophecies. Even if the Promised One might somehow appear, the clergy's doctrines would triumph.

[Note: In the following passage, the term "Qá'im" refers to the Promised One of Islám, "He who arises".]

> There are many authentic traditions showing that the Qá'im on His appearance would bring new laws with Him and would thus abrogate Islám. But this was not the understanding of the established hierarchy. They confidently expected that the promised Advent would not substitute a new and richer revelation for the old, but would endorse and fortify the system of which they were the functionaries. It would enhance incalculably their personal prestige, would extend their authority far and wide among the nations, and would win for them the reluctant but abject homage of mankind. – Shoghi Effendi[31]

Over centuries, the masses were indoctrinated through lectures in religious schools and repetitious weekly sermons at mosques. Religious leaders extended their positions of power, affluence and influence.[32] Thus, by the 19th century, Persia had become a dark scene.

[Note: In the following passage, the term "Qájár" refers to the ruling dynasty in 19th century Persia.]

> The Qájárs, members of the alien Turkoman tribe, had, indeed, usurped the Persian throne... [The reigns of the Qájár kings] are marked by the stagnation of the nation, the illiteracy of the people, the corruption and incompetence of the government, the scandalous intrigues of the court, the decadence of the princes, the irresponsibility and extravagance of the sovereign, and his abject subservience to a notoriously degraded clerical order. – Shoghi Effendi[33]

These conditions bear a striking resemblance to those dark times when earlier Divine Educators—such as Abraham, Moses, Jesus, and Muhammad—appeared. Higher spiritual aspirations of entire nations were smothered by corrupt clergy of a debased religion, subservient and unquestioning followers, rampant immorality, and tyranny in politics.

In 19th century Persia, afflicted "with its attendant corruption, confusion, intolerance, and oppression, in both the civil and religious life of Persia,"[34] who would arise? Who would champion reform? Who could overcome the vehement resistance of an entrenched system? Who would achieve a breakthrough for the people?

Mosque and State

As the 19th century opened, Persia was controlled by mutually reinforcing institutions. The Qájár dynasty wielded secular power. The Shí'ih religious leadership controlled religious and social matters.

> The Qájárs consolidated their position in the urban centers by means of a military and administrative presence, while the [religious leaders] strengthened their stand by exerting a religious authority that embraced a variety of judicial, educational, and executive functions… Their relation with the Qájár state can be defined as one of guarded coexistence… – Abbas Amanat[35]

The religious leaders were not unified. Within 19th century Persian Shí'ih Islám, two schools of religious and legal practice were active, influential and in conflict. The Akhbárís interpreted the Qur'án and the hadiths about Muhammad literally, while the Usúlís, claimed freedom to interpret the Qur'án symbolically. As noted by Abbas Amanat:

- The Akhbárís "preached sole, largely uncritical, reliance on the Traditions of the Prophet and the Imáms, rejecting the use of rational criteria."[36]
- The Usúlís relied primarily on "deductive reasoning to draw conclusions applicable to practical needs, based on premises inherent in the Qur'án and the Shi'ite Traditions."[37]

The Usúlís identified themselves as uniquely qualified to make legal decisions. According to the Usúlí doctrine of collective deputyship, they ruled on behalf of the Hidden Imám. They eventually won the power struggle with the Akhbárís as the legal decision-makers in Persia. Usúlí legal decisions were arbitrary; decided through their own "deduction", thus giving themselves great flexibility to decide legal matters in their favor. This suited the symbiotic relationship with the State. It made Usúlís a useful tool of the government.[38]

Emergence of the Shaykhí movement

19th century Persia also witnessed the emergence of another, smaller, highly influential school of theological and legal scholarship. Known as the Shaykhís, this school was founded by a saintly man, Shaykh Ahmad Ahsá'í (1756 – 1825 AD). Shaykh Ahmad felt a strong mystical attraction to the

Imáms. He claimed they mentored him in his dreams. Famous for his erudition, he had little regard for material wealth and attracted numerous followers.[39] Shaykh Ahmad was versed in Súfí mysticism and Akhbárí jurisprudence.[40] The author of 96 books, he traveled from town to town to teach theological and legal insights.[41]

Nabíl, a Bahá'í historian, described the character and mission of Shaykh Ahmad:

> At a time when the shining reality of the Faith of Muhammad had been obscured by the ignorance, the fanaticism, and perversity of the contending sects into which it had fallen, there appeared above the horizon of the East that luminous Star of Divine guidance, Shaykh Ahmad-i-Ahsá'í. He observed how those who professed the Faith of Islám had shattered its unity, sapped its force, perverted its purpose, and degraded its holy name... He knew, and was destined by the Will of God to demonstrate, that nothing short of a new and independent Revelation, as attested and foreshadowed by the sacred Scriptures of Islám, could revive the fortunes and restore the purity of that decadent Faith... [He] became increasingly conscious that the Day which was to witness the birth of the promised One could not be far distant.
> – Nabíl[42]

Bahá'u'lláh seems to indicate Shaykh Ahmad intuitively knew the name of the Báb years in advance. Mázandarání notes that in Bahá'u'lláh's book, the Kitáb-i-Badí', Bahá'u'lláh recounts that Shaykh Ahmad had a mysterious conversation with a friend during their time in Mecca together. Shaykh Ahmad told this friend, Hájí Muhammad Ismá'íl from Isfahán (as paraphrased from the Persian by Mázandarání), "Give my greetings to His Holiness the Báb". Initially, the friend had no idea what Shaykh Ahmad was talking about. Years later, when He arrived in Isfahán, the Báb's name became widespread. Only then did the friend realize that what Shaykh Ahmad had been talking about was intended for his guidance.[43]

Shaykh Ahmad was not satisfied with either of the orthodox Akhbárí or Usúlí approaches to Islámic law. In addition to being an expression of the strength of his personal mystical connection to the Imáms, Shaykh Ahmad's extreme veneration was also an implied criticism of the religious leaders' claim of collective deputyship.[44] Shaykh Ahmad supported the age-old doctrine of the Perfect Shí'ih, a man of extraordinary virtue who could derive spiritual authority from the Imáms directly through spiritual illumination and have exceptional intuitive insight. In every generation, only the perfect Shí'ih is able to speak for the Hidden Imám. Belief in the perfect Shí'ih eventually led the Shaykhís to rethink the possibility of Prophets after Muhammad.[45]

Shaykhís understood the Qur'án symbolically rather than literally. For example, Shaykh Ahmad understood "the Resurrection at the advent of the [Qá'im] not as bodies physically rising from the graves, but as a renaissance of the soul of humanity."[46]

Figure 3 Shaykh Ahmad, artist sketch based on historical sources, from *The Gate: Dawn of the Bahá'í Faith*

Shaykh Ahmad said Muhammad's night journey to Jerusalem and heaven was a spiritual rather than a physical journey. He objected to the Súfí idea that a soul could merge with God, because according to the Qur'án God is far beyond all human perception:

> No vision taketh in Him, but He taketh in all vision; He is the Subtile, the All-Perceiving. (Qur'án 6:103)[47]

The Shaykhís accepted that a person, though not equal with God, could receive mystical knowledge from God.

Shí'ih orthodoxy anticipated the future twin appearances of the the Hidden Imám (the Twelfth Imám), and the Imám Husayn (the third Imám, who was martyred). The Islámic traditions relating to these expectations were a contradictory jumble. The "end-times" predictions simultaneously foretold the destruction of the natural universe and the establishment of justice and peace throughout the earth. Passages pertaining to Resurrection Day spoke of reanimation of dead bodies, parts of the human body testifying before God against their owners, shattering of the earth, oceans bubbling, the moon flying into the sun, mountains being crushed to powder, and angels whose wingspan extend thousands of years.[48]

If these cataclysmic images are taken literally, there is no way the prophecies of the return of the Qá'im and the Imám Husayn can possibly be realized by a human being in historical time on planet Earth. It would not be possible for the Qá'im to establish justice on earth *after* the earth itself has been pulverized by a cosmic cataclysm.

Although the Qur'án never commanded it, orthodox religious leaders prohibited setting a date for the Advent. They punished those who attempted to set the time, and forbade their followers from speculating about the name of the Imám when he returned.

Figure 4 Siyyid Kázim, artist sketch based on historical sources, from *The Gate: Dawn of the Bahá'í Faith*

> [Their doctrines] had served to undermine the possibility of any tangible existence of the Imám, relegating him to the timeless oblivion of a never-coming future. The mainstream [Shí'ih] theology … replaced his authority with the general deputyship of the religious leaders. [The Shaykhís] paved the way not only for contact with the

> Imám, but for his eventual reappearance in the 'real' world... – Abbas Amanat[49]

Contrary to orthodox teaching, the Shaykhís said the universe would not be destroyed in a universal cataclysm. Instead, the Shaykhís spoke of a near Advent of the Promised One. They used the word "Manifestation",[50] the Presence among men of a Divine human Personage, a Divine Educator, a Messenger of God, just as Muhammad had been. Shaykhís said two Manifestations were expected, the Hidden Twelfth Imám and then the Imám Husayn. Momen explains the designations of the first of these Promised Ones:

> The Hidden Imám has a large number of titles including the following: Sáhib az-Zamán (Lord of the Age), Sáhib al-Amr (Lord of Command), al-Mahdí (the Rightly-Guided One), al-Qá'im (He who will arise), al-Imám al-Muntazar (the Awaited Imám) and the Baqiyyat Alláh (Remnant of God). – Momen[51]

The Qá'im would be known as the Lord of the Age. He would redress injustices, begin a new age of fulfillment, abrogate the laws of the previous age, exalt the accomplishments of the previous age, establish justice in society, and, far from terminating human history, would propel it forward.[52]

Hundreds of students flocked to Shaykh Ahmad. One student—a young Siyyid, a lineal descendent of Muhammad—stood out brilliantly. Shaykh Ahmad recognized the future greatness of this disciple, According to Nabíl:

> ...Siyyid Kázim had already, from his early boyhood, shown signs of remarkable intellectual power and spiritual insight. He was unique among those of his own rank and age. At the age of eleven, he had committed to memory the whole of the Qur'án. At the age of fourteen, he had learned by heart a prodigious number of prayers and recognized traditions of Muhammad. At the age of eighteen, he had composed a commentary on a verse of the Qur'án ... which had excited the wonder and the admiration of the most learned of his day. His piety, the gentleness of his character, and his humility were such that all who knew him, whether young or old, were profoundly impressed. – Nabíl[53]

Shaykh Ahmad selected Siyyid Kázim to be his successor before passing away in 1825 AD while on pilgrimage to Mecca and Medina. Nabíl describes their final time together:

> Ere he departed from Karbilá, he confided to Siyyid Kázim, his chosen successor, the secret of his mission, and instructed him to strive to kindle in every receptive heart the fire that had burned so brightly within him…
>
> 'You have no time to lose,' were the last words which he addressed to him. 'Every fleeting hour should be fully and wisely utilized. You should gird up the loin of endeavour and strive day and night to rend asunder, by the grace of God and by the hand of wisdom and loving-kindness, those veils of heedlessness that have blinded the eyes of men. For verily I say, the Hour is drawing nigh…' – Nabíl[54]

Siyyid Kázim continually emphasized the nearness of the promised Qá'im. He often quoted a famous tradition from the sixth Imám, Ja'far (702-765 AD):

> Verily, in the year sixty His Cause shall be revealed, and His name shall be noised abroad. – Imám Ja'far[55]

(The "year sixty" was the year 1260 AH in the Islámic calendar and exactly 1,000 years after the passing of the 11th Imám. The year 1260 AH corresponds to 1844 AD in the Gregorian calendar.)

Siyyid Kázim's career as Shaykhí leader was lengthy and highly successful. Under his leadership the movement expanded and spread throughout Persia. As the end of Siyyid Kázim's life drew near, he was asked who his successor would be. He replied there was no need for a successor because "soon the cause of God would reach maturity."[56] The great millennial Event was very near. Siyyid Kázim spoke with glowing anticipation of the Promised One. According to TK Cheyne, Siyyid Kázim was fond of saying,

> I see him as the rising sun. – Siyyid Kázim[57]

1844 and other millennial movements

The Shaykhí movement was not the only significant instance of millennial expectation in the 19th Century. During the same time, there was a phenomenal expectation of prophetic fulfillment in the United States.

The Hebrew Bible foretold a time when God's Covenant with Israel would be fulfilled by the coming of the Son of Man (see for example, Daniel 7:13 and 8:17). The New Testament refers to the Son of Man 84 times and

Jesus explicitly spoke about Daniel's prophecies concerning the messianic Son of Man figure.

Daniel 9:24-25 presented specific prophecies foretelling the coming of Jesus:

> Seventy weeks are determined upon thy people and upon thy holy city, to finish the transgression, and to make an end of sins, and to make reconciliation for iniquity, and to bring in everlasting righteousness, and to seal up the vision and prophecy, and to anoint the most Holy. Know therefore and understand, that from the going forth of the commandment to restore and to build Jerusalem unto the Messiah the Prince shall be seven weeks, and threescore and two weeks: the street shall be built again, and the wall, even in troublous times. (Daniel 9:24-25. See also verse 26.)

'Abdu'l-Bahá explained how this prophecy applied to Jesus:

> The Book of Daniel fixes the period between the rebuilding of Jerusalem and the martyrdom of Christ at seventy weeks, for it is through the martyrdom of Christ that the sacrifice is ended and the altar destroyed. This prophecy thus refers to the advent of Christ.
>
> These seventy weeks begin with the restoration and rebuilding of Jerusalem, concerning which four edicts were issued by three kings... The third was issued by Artaxerxes in the seventh year of his reign, that is, in 457 B.C., and this is recorded in the seventh chapter of Ezra...
>
> What Daniel intended is the third edict, which was issued in 457 B.C. Seventy weeks makes 490 days. Each day, according to the text of the Bible, is one year, for in the Torah it is said: "The day of the Lord is one year." [Num. 14:34] Therefore, 490 days is 490 years. The third edict of Artaxerxes was issued 457 years before the birth of Christ, and Christ was thirty-three years old at the time of His martyrdom and ascension. Thirty-three added to 457 is 490, which is the time announced by Daniel for the advent of Christ. – 'Abdu'l-Bahá[58]

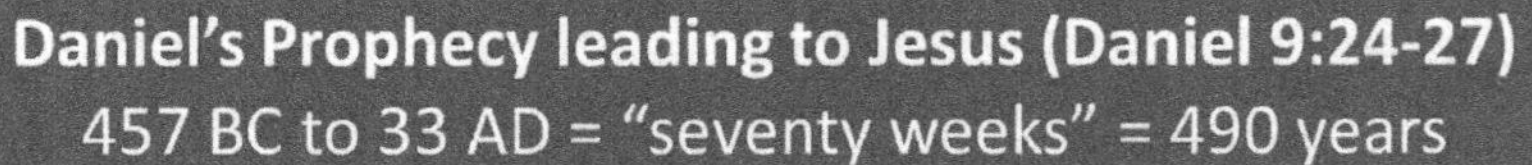

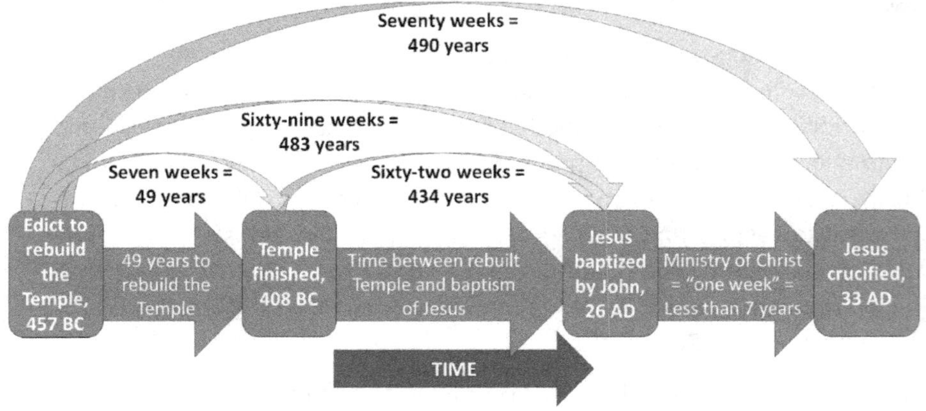

Figure 5 Seventy weeks prophecy

According to Daniel, the prophetic clock began ticking in the year 457 BC when Artaxerxes issued the order allowing the Jewish people to begin rebuilding their sacred Temple in Jerusalem. Michael Sours summarized the calculations as follows:[59]

- 70 weeks = 70 x 7 days/week = 490 days
- In prophecy, each day equals one year, thus, 490 days = 490 years[60]
- 490 years, the total duration of the prophecy - 457 BC (the year of the 3rd decree for the restoration of the Temple) = 33 years

Therefore, Daniel clearly foresaw 33 AD, when Jesus was crucified.

This passage mentions two methods of counting: 70 weeks (in verse 9:24) and 69 weeks (in verse 9:26 where it says "seven weeks, and threescore and two weeks"). 'Abdu'l-Bahá explains there is no real discrepancy:

> But in Daniel 9:25 this is expressed in another manner, that is, as seven weeks and sixty-two weeks, which outwardly differs from the first statement. Many have been at a loss to reconcile these two statements. How can reference be made to seventy weeks in one place and to sixty-two weeks and seven weeks in another? These two statements do not accord.

> In reality Daniel is referring to two different dates. One begins with the edict Artaxerxes issued to Ezra to rebuild Jerusalem, and corresponds to the seventy weeks which came to an end with the ascension of Christ, when sacrifice and oblation were ended through His martyrdom. The second begins after the completion of the rebuilding of Jerusalem, which is sixty-two weeks until the ascension of Christ. The rebuilding of Jerusalem took seven weeks, which is equivalent to forty-nine years. Seven weeks added to sixty-two weeks makes sixty-nine weeks, and in the last week the ascension of Christ took place. This completes the seventy weeks, and no contradiction remains... [The] advent of Christ has been proven through the prophecies of Daniel... – 'Abdu'l-Bahá[61]

Biblical scholars were impressed that the Advent of Jesus and the time of the Crucifixion were so accurately predicted by Daniel. But what of the other mysterious prophecy which Daniel made? Daniel also wrote:

> Then I heard one saint speaking, and another saint said unto that certain saint which spake, How long shall be the vision concerning the daily sacrifice, and the transgression of desolation, to give both the sanctuary and the host to be trodden under foot? And he said unto me, Unto two thousand and three hundred days; then shall the sanctuary be cleansed. (Daniel 8:13-14)

These scholars reasoned that the prophetic clock which had been so accurate in predicting the first coming of Jesus would be *equally accurate* in predicting the second coming of Jesus. They were sure the 2,300 days mentioned in Daniel chapter eight referred to His return because Jesus directed them to heed Daniel's prophecy (Matthew 24:3,15). Jesus also gave a warning:

> Watch therefore: for ye know not what hour your Lord doth come. (Matthew 24:42)

Based on this counsel, they knew it might not be possible to predict exactly *the hour* of Jesus' return, but this command to watch and be ready told them it might be possible to have some reasonably approximate idea of when to expect Him.

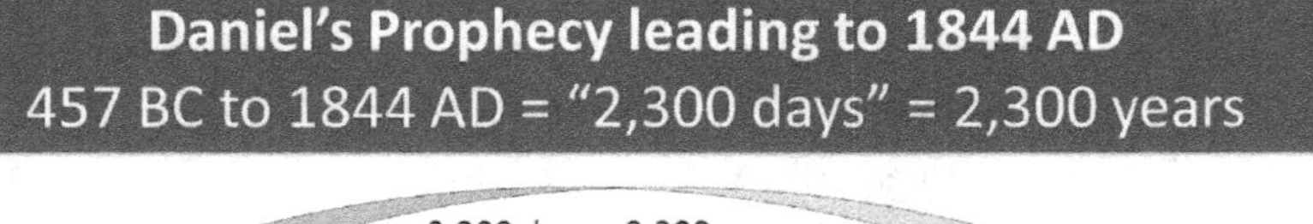

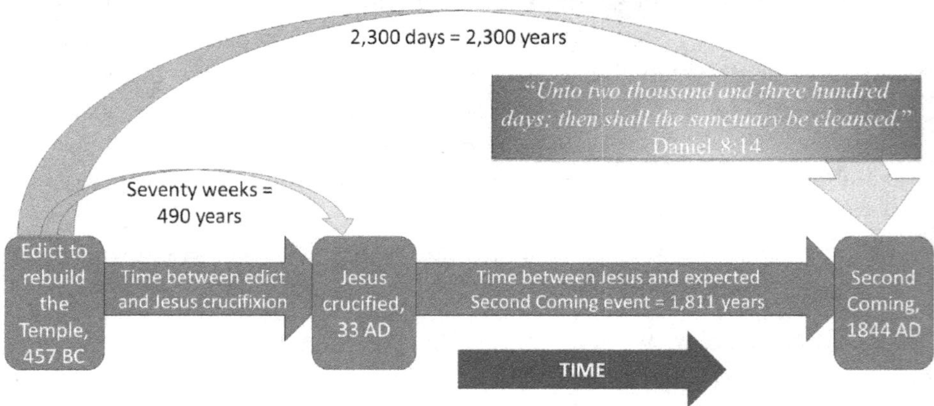

Figure 6 Daniel's 2,300 days prophecy leading to 1844 AD

The core insight was that both prophecies – the one for the first coming of Jesus, which was already known to be correct, and the one for the Second Coming – had the same starting point, the year 457 BC. Using the same prophetic timetable, they calculated the time of the Second Coming of Jesus. The calculation itself was simple:

- 2,300 days ➔ 2,300 years
- 2,300 years - 457 BC ➔ 1843 AD

Due to partial overlap between the Hebrew and Gregorian calendars, some scholars noted the 2,300 years might end in the year 1844 AD. They predicted the Second Advent would occur sometime in either 1843 or 1844 AD.

In the United States in the early 19th Century, one person, above all others, promoted this idea of the imminent return of Jesus. That man, William Miller, was born February 15, 1782. Miller's father had been a soldier in the American Revolutionary War. Miller was educated at home, in Low Hampton, New York, and enjoyed reading widely. Similar to many around him, he had deistic religious views, thinking of God as distant and unconcerned with human affairs. Miller was a farmer and engaged in public service until 1812, when he became a soldier and fought against the British. During one battle, when "bombs, rockets, and shrapnel fell as thick as hailstones", one bomb exploded two feet in front of him.[62] Three other men were wounded. When

Miller survived without injury, he felt it was a miracle. He experienced a full religious conversion. Miller's religious views became more God-centered. However, he was unprepared for debate with his deistic friends, who challenged his newly found faith. Challenged, he spent two years examining the Bible methodically, beginning with the Book of Genesis.

Figure 7 William Miller

Miller stated, in 1818, that his study led him to an astonishing conclusion. Based on Daniel 8:14, Miller thought that the cleansing of the sanctuary represented the Earth's purification by fire at Christ's Second Coming. Using the same prophetic clock that had predicted the First Advent so accurately, he concluded the 2,300 days represented 2,300 years and the counting of the years began in the year 457 BCE with the decree to rebuild Jerusalem by Artaxerxes. Calculations revealed this period would end in 1844. In 1822 Miller wrote,

> I believe that the second coming of Jesus Christ is near, even at the door, even within twenty-one years—on or before 1844. – William Miller[63]

In 1832 Miller wrote an article with these views for a Baptist publication. Miller said he was "flooded with letters of inquiry", that "visitors flocked to converse with me on the subject", and he received many invitations to travel and teach. To meet the demand, he published a lengthy explanation titled, *Evidence from Scripture and History of the Second Coming of Christ, about the Year 1843: Exhibited in a Course of Lectures.*[64] Miller's views gained so much publicity that his presentations took on the character of a national movement; "he gave over 3,200 lectures, wrote a number of books and pamphlets on the subject, and led out in a religious revival in the United States that came to be known as the Millerite movement".[65]

Miller, in accord with the counsel of Jesus, never set an exact date for the long awaited Second Coming. He narrowed the time frame:

> My principles in brief, are, that Jesus Christ will come again to this earth, cleanse, purify, and take possession of the same, with all the saints, sometime between March 21, 1843, and March 21, 1844. – William Miller[66]

These dates passed uneventfully, so far as anyone in the United States knew, so Miller felt compelled to apologize for his "error" and "disappointment."

Further dates, such as October 22, 1844, were offered by other Millerites. When October 23 dawned uneventfully, the thousands who had followed the teachings of William Miller concluded they had suffered what later came to be known as The Great Disappointment. One participant later wrote:

> The day had then passed and our disappointment became a certainty. Our fondest hopes and expectations were blasted, and such a spirit of weeping came over us as I have never experienced before... We wept, and wept, till the day dawn. – A Millerite believer[67]

Many of the Millerites gave up on their beliefs, but Miller expressed his undying faith:

> I have set another day, today, Today, TODAY until He comes. – William Miller[68]

Miller believed in the timely Second Coming until his death on December 20th, 1849. Miller was laid to rest near his home, where he had discovered the secret of Daniel 8:14. His home is a National Historical Landmark. The Millerite movement evolved into the Seventh-Day Adventist Church, with over 16 million followers today. They honor him, preserve his home and keep his archives for posterity.

The disappointment experienced by the Millerites in 1844 was piercing, tragic, and instructive. The Bible had never said Jesus would descend from the heavens *in upstate New York*, a part of the world unknown to Daniel the prophet. But the Millerites were not entirely wrong. According to 'Abdu'l-Bahá, they had the timing right for God's prophetic clock.[69]

Thus, the millennial expectation of the Shaykhís in the East had its counterpart in the West. Two groups, one from an Islámic background and the other from within the Christian Faith, each following guidance from their separate belief systems, mysteriously converged on the same time period of 1843-1844 as the predestined time for their ancient prophecies to be fulfilled.

Signs of the Promised One

Both groups were correct on the timing. Only the Shaykhís were destined to also be in the right place at the right time. The Shaykhís understood the Promised One would be a new Personage, not the literal reincarnation of Jesus or the physical return of the Hidden Imam. They had insight into what to look for, where to look, and when to be looking.

As 1843 wore on, Siyyid Kázim urged his followers to purify and prepare themselves to attain unto true recognition of the Promised One. He continuously said His appearance was near. He listed the signs:

- He is of noble lineage, that is, a descendent of the Prophet Muhammad.
- He is between 20 and 30 years old.
- He is free of any bodily deficiency.
- He is of medium height.
- He abstains from smoking.
- He exemplifies extreme devoutness and piety towards God.
- He is endowed with innate knowledge.[70]

Some Shaykhís thought Siyyid Kázim might be the Promised One, an assertion he vehemently rejected. Although Siyyid Kázim was the author of 135 books, and the most eminent Shaykhí in all Persia, he said,

> My knowledge is but a drop compared with the immensity of His knowledge; my attainments a speck of dust in the face of the wonders of His grace and power. Nay, immeasurable is the difference.
> – Siyyid Kázim[71]

As the 19th Century dawned, the struggle between the two main schools of Islamic legal practice had narrowed orthodoxy and bound it to literalism. For instance, according to the religious leaders, the twelfth Iman had gone into hiding, presumably to escape being assassinated like his eleven predecessors, and he never died during his occultation. So "logically" he must now be more than a thousand years old. Meanwhile, in his absence, the religious leaders took the authority of the Hidden Imám upon themselves, and they liked it that way. Submerged in the self-serving and symbiotic corruption of church and state, religious thought was suffocating and ethically barren.

Amidst this despair, the Shaykhís offered a vitalizing path for the conceptual world. They preached the necessity of returning to the spiritual and ethical core of religion, the importance of being holy, the usefulness of spiritually understanding sacred Scripture, and the real possibility that the Qá'im would come into the world as a youthful living person to restore justice to humanity, but not as a thousand year old man. Making the prophecies actually realizable in human terms shifted thinking and gave a hopeful new view to human destiny.

The twin leaders, Shaykh Ahmad and Siyyid Kázim, emphasized that this Person was about to appear and that he would bring a new, independent Revelation from God. The year prophesied was 1260 AH on the Islámic calendar, the 1,000th year after the death of the 11th Imám.

1844 AD corresponds with that year.

Prior to his passing, Siyyid Kázim urged his followers to search for the Promised One. The Shaykhí movement caused thousands of souls to become receptive to the Promised One. These thousands, mainly from the clerical and merchant classes of society, actively awaited His appearance throughout the country of Persia. When the Promised One appeared, earnest and open-minded seekers were already eager to embrace His Cause and place themselves at his service.

THE BÁB'S EARLY YEARS

Beginnings in Shíráz

Siyyid 'Alí Muhammad, the Báb, was born in the city of Shíráz, in southern Persia, now Iran.[72] He was born before dawn on the 1st of Muharram in the year 1235 AH, which is October 20, 1819 AD.[73]

The Báb's mother was Fátimih Bagum. His father was Siyyid Muhammad Rizá, a respected cloth[74] merchant. He was their only Son. The Báb's father was known throughout the province "for his piety and virtue, and was held in high esteem and honor".[75] His mother, Fátimih, had three brothers; so the Báb had three maternal uncles.

His birth took place in the upper room of the house of His paternal granduncle, Mírzá Siyyid 'Alí, because an infant of another relative had died in His parents' house. Following a custom of the time, they did not want the next baby to be born in the same house. The Báb's delivery was moved to the granduncle's house.[76]

The following is paraphrased from the Persian by Faizi:

> Shíráz had been around for centuries. Its official founding (as an Islámic city) was soon after the region's invasion and conquest by the Arabs in the 7th Century during the time of the Caliph Marván (ruled 685 – 705 AD). Marvan's Prime Minister appointed his brother, Muhammad Ibn-i-Yúsuf Saqafí, as governor of the region. And Saqafí founded the city of Shíráz because one night in a dream he saw a group of heavenly angels descending to the earth. When they came to the land where Shíráz would be located, they prostrated themselves and told him,
>
> "This is a land from which those who are imbued with virtues will arise; it will become the footsteps of holy personages. This is a place from which the wayfarers of the invisible divine worlds will benefit. It will be the focal point of guardianship; a leaven for those who are poor in God; the source of knowledge and wisdom; the inheritor of holiness and purity".
>
> While in his dream, Saqafí drew a line around that land which had been illumined by the heavenly lights.
>
> The next day, he travelled to that land, and saw it and recognized it [from his dream]. And that land appeared to him as full of light and dazzling brightness, just as he had seen in his dream, and he became confident and assured.
>
> He commanded architects and master builders to begin building the city. Later, mosques and temples were added during the reign of the best of the Umayyad Caliphs, 'Umar ibn-i-'Abdu'l-'Azíz (known as 'Umar II, ruled 717 – 720 AD), who was known for his righteousness and piety. More mosques were added later. – Faizi[77]

The Báb was a descendant of Husayn, the Third Imám. (Refer to the graphic.)[78] The Imám Husayn was the grandson of Muhammad, and Muhammad was descended from Abraham. Therefore, the Báb was descended from Abraham. This makes the Faith of the Báb an Abrahamic religion, alongside Judaism, Christianity, Islám, and the Bahá'í Faith.

As the graphic shows,[79] the Báb was a descendent of the Imám Husayn on both sides of His family. The term "siyyid" and the green turban which He wore symbolized His distinguished lineage from Muhammad. His wife, Khadíjih, was also descended from the Imám Husayn, and thus from Muhammad.

The Báb was from a family of merchants, highly regarded for their integrity. Similar to His beloved ancestor, Muhammad, the Báb's father, Siyyid Muhammad Rizá, died when He was very young.[80] In accordance with tradition, His father's earthly remains were buried in Karbilá. In a decision that would later prove consequential,[81] Rizá had chosen the Báb's uncle, Hájí Mírzá Siyyid 'Alí, to be His trustee. As a result, the Báb, His mother, and their property were all placed under his care.[82]

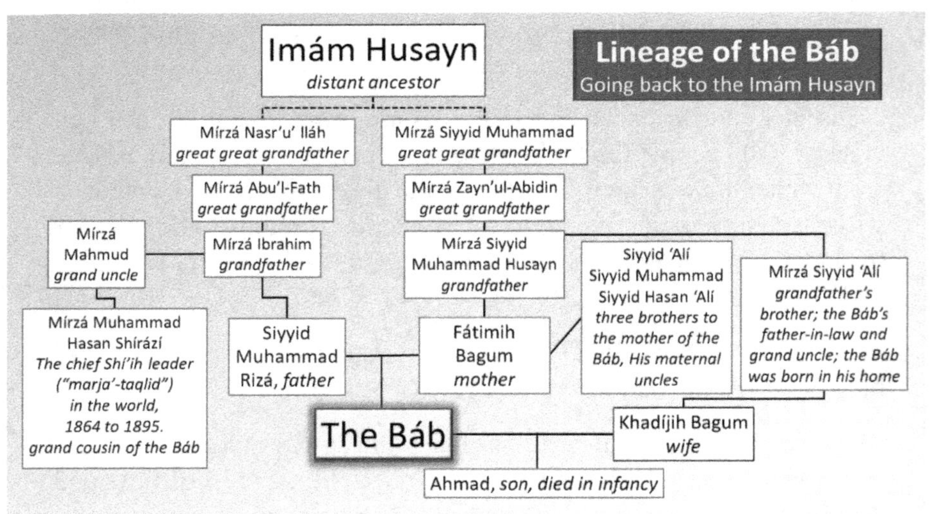

Figure 8 The Lineage of the Báb

From the beginning, the Báb was different from other children. For example, the Báb had a remarkable dream when He was five years old. The following passage is paraphrased from the Persian by Mázindarání.

[Note: In the following passage, the Báb mentions the Imám Sádiq. Ja'far Sádiq was the sixth Imám, a very illustrious and holy figure in Shí'ih Islám.]

The Báb told his father that he had had a dream. He said he saw His ancestor, Imám Ja'far Sádiq, sitting on one side of a balance. The other side of the balance was empty, He said. A dignified person whom the Báb did not recognize picked Him up and placed Him on the empty side of the balance. As this happened, the Báb said, the empty side became heavy and the other side of the Imám became light and went up.

As His father, Siyyid Muhammad Rizá, heard and observed things like this, he began to wonder. He told the family and his relatives,

"I do not know what will come of this Child, as hearing this from a five-year-old is unusual. He is not like His peers." – Mázindarání[83]

When the Báb was about six or seven, His uncle, Siyyid 'Alí, decided that He should receive the education customary for a boy of the merchant class. Education was in religious schools and only for boys. He took the Báb to a nearby religious school, a *maktab*. The students were introduced to the Qur'án, theology, reading, writing, and penmanship. It was run by the schoolmaster, Shaykh 'Ábid, a mullá who had been a disciple of both Shaykh Ahmad and Siyyid Kázim. The uncle enrolled Him in the school.[84]

The Shaykh one day asked the Báb to recite the opening words of the Qur'án.

In the name of God, the Compassionate, the Merciful. – The Qur'án[85]

The Báb said that He would not recite the words unless He was told what they mean. At this, Shaykh 'Ábid pretended not to know their meaning. The Báb said He knew the meaning and would explain if asked to do so. The Shaykh told what happened next:

He spoke with such knowledge and fluency that I was struck with amazement. He expounded the meaning of 'Alláh' [God], of 'Rahmán' [Compassionate], and 'Rahím' [Merciful], in terms such as I had neither read nor heard. The sweetness of His utterance still lingers in my memory. I felt impelled to take Him back to His uncle and to deliver into his hands the Trust he had committed to my care. I determined to tell him how unworthy I felt to teach so remarkable a child.

I found His uncle [Hájí Mírzá Siyyid 'Alí] alone in his office.

[I said:]

> "I have brought Him back to you and commit Him to your vigilant protection. He is not to be treated as a mere child, for in Him I can already discern evidences of that mysterious power which the Revelation of [The Lord of the Age] alone can reveal. It is incumbent upon you to surround Him with your most loving care. Keep Him in your house, for He, verily, stands in no need of teachers such as I." – Shaykh 'Ábid[86]

The uncle rebuked the Báb and reminded Him of his prior instructions to be like the other students, to be silent and listen to every word spoken by the teacher. The young Boy promised to obey and returned to school. Shaykh 'Ábid further comments:

> The soul of that child could not, however, be restrained by the stern admonitions of His uncle. No discipline could repress the flow of His intuitive knowledge. Day after day He continued to manifest such remarkable evidences of superhuman wisdom as I am powerless to recount. – Shaykh 'Ábid[87]

Occasionally, the Báb would not arrive in the morning for school, so the Shaykh sent other pupils to His home and ask Him to come to school. They invariably found him occupied with prayers. One day, when the Báb was ten, He again came late to school. The Shaykh questioned Him about this and the Báb replied gently that He had been in the house of His "Grandfather." The Báb had no living grandfather. This is the term the Siyyids use to describe their esteemed great ancestor, Muhammad. The Shaykh told Him that he was just ten and, therefore, such complete attention to devotions was not required of Him. To this the Báb again gently replied:

> I wish to be like My Grandfather. – The Báb[88]

According to a report from Shaykh 'Ábid, the Báb enjoyed extremely cordial relations with the other students at school. The following is paraphrased from the Persian by Mázindarání.

> ...His manners and conduct were the cause of wonder. He demonstrated qualities and manners, and deeds and actions that were not like other children. He was often wrapped in thoughts ... [and yet] He showed kindness to his fellow classmates and shared whatever food or drink He had, and they would eat and drink with joy and happiness. Whenever they needed help for their homework, He would help them with utmost gentleness, without expecting any return for a favor. There was never any sign of hurt feelings between Him and

His classmates, and no one ever heard any complaints from Him. He never needed His teacher to repeat anything. Whatever His teacher would tell Him, He would learn it the first-time… – Mázindaráni[89]

One distinguished mullá, Hájí Siyyid Javád Karbilá'í, had met the Báb when He was eight or nine years old. Previously, Siyyid Javád had met Shaykh Ahmad, and later had become one of Siyyid Kázim's students.[90] The following is paraphrased from the Persian by Husaini:

In Shíráz, I was in the presence of His Holiness, the Primal Point, Glorified be His Name… This was the first thing that caused me to become attracted to Him. The Báb's uncle and I were sitting on the porch and having a conversation. At this time from the prayer room, I heard the voice of a child who was chanting a prayer … in such a way that the effect of His voice created an attraction and excitement in the hearer. After a little while, I saw a child of about eight or nine years old come out of the prayer room. – Hájí Siyyid Javád Karbilá'í[91]

Later, Hájí Siyyid Javád Karbilá'í would become a follower of the Báb and of Bahá'u'lláh.

One day some older students in Shaykh 'Ábid's school were discussing a difficult topic. After considerable debate it remained unresolved. The Shaykh promised to study some authoritative books that evening and discuss the matter again the next day. The Báb, too young to have been included in the discussion, had been listening. At this moment, He spoke up, and with sound reasoning gave the answer they sought. Full of amazement, the Shaykh asked how He had gained this knowledge. The Báb smiled and offered this couplet from Háfiz:[92]

Should the grace of the Holy Spirit once again deign to assist,

Others will do what Christ could perform. – A verse from Háfiz, recited by the Báb[93]

The Báb spent five years at Shaykh 'Ábid's school. Given His apparent innate knowledge, He wasn't inclined to study. He tried to follow His uncle's instructions. While there, He was taught the basics of the Persian language.

Later, the Báb's uncle made one more attempt to give Him an education. Another teacher in Shíráz, the son of Mullá 'Abdu'l-Kháliq, was assigned to teach a few lessons in Arabic to the Báb. The son was teaching a higher level of Arabic. The son protested to his father, why was he being asked to teach

Him, since He didn't know the basic fundamentals? He refused to teach the Báb, so the Báb did not receive training in the Arabic language.[94]

Years later, this teacher was in the city of Mashhad in a gathering discussing the Writings of the Báb. One of the believers read aloud a Tablet of the Báb which had been revealed in Arabic. As reported by Husaini, he was amazed that a person untrained in the Arabic language was able to create such Writings. At this point, the teacher told his experience from years before. (Husaini states that this account was given by the teacher to Mullá 'Abdu'l-Rahím Qazvíní, when they met each other in Mashhad and the name of the Báb entered the conversation.)[95]

Merchant in Búshihr

His uncle decided to bring the Báb into his business as a textile merchant in Shíráz and Búshihr. Nabíl reports:

> There, too, He revealed signs of a power and greatness that few could approach and none could rival. – Nabíl[96]

The Báb engaged in commerce for six years, beginning at about age sixteen, He came into contact with diverse levels of society. Many of the Báb's trading documents have been preserved. From 1835 to 1840 these documents show the family's large-scale trading activities throughout Persia and to far distant cities, such as Bombay, India and Ishqábád, Turkmenistán. They exported agricultural products and imported fabrics, tea, sugar, and spices. Abbas Amanat observes:

> These documents confirm that the Báb had acquired the necessary skill for keeping accounts and handling commercial orders, and illustrate his acquaintance with the merchant network... – Abbas Amanat[97]

In all His business activities, people noted the Báb's praiseworthy qualities and fair dealing. Hájí Siyyid Javád Karbilá'í was a friend of the family who saw the Báb a number of times in Búshihr. He told about a merchant who asked the Báb to sell some merchandise on his behalf while he was away on pilgrimage to Mecca. The Báb accepted this custodial responsibility. By the time the sale was accomplished, the merchandise had suffered a significant decline in price. When the man returned from Mecca, the Báb gave him the proceeds from the sale plus a significant amount extra, to make up for the drop in price. The Báb was not legally responsible to pay for losses due to changing market conditions. Nevertheless, without being asked to do so, the Báb volunteered the generous extra payment to His client.[98]

The Báb had a stern side to His character. Disapproving of some usual business practices, He resisted attempts to get Him to do something He thought was wrong. As this report indicates, He could be as unmovable as a mountain. Abbas Amanat writes:

> On another occasion, the sale of a cargo of indigo was agreed between [the Báb] and some merchants in Búshihr. After the delivery of the goods, at the time of the payment, the purchasers came back to [Him] and asked for a discount; a general method of after sale bargaining practiced in all Iranian markets and known as *dabbih*. When the Báb declined to consider the customary reduction, he found himself with the purchasers' objection who argued that such reduction is a 'national custom' … and should be observed by everyone. But it is reported that the Báb insisted that 'soon many unlawful customs will be abolished', and further in response to their refusal to pay the full sum, took back the merchandise and made the contract void. The merchants who regarded the cancellation of the deal and the return of the merchandise as a blow to their commercial credit, wrote complaints to his uncle Hájí Sayyid Muhammad, who in turn blamed [the Báb] for not 'acting in accordance with people's wishes and neglecting accepted customs and practices'. – Abbas Amanat[99]

The Báb refused to yield.

> The Báb replied that there are many customs that are wrong and soon they will come to an end. The more they insisted, the more the Báb did not comply. He then asked for the goods to be returned as He did not agree to this custom. – Husaini[100]

Hájí Siyyid Javád Karbilá'í had extensive opportunities to observe the Báb in Búshihr, in the days prior to His declaration and after, in business and in His personal life. Although he eventually became a dedicated Bábí and a devout follower of Bahá'u'lláh, and despite being impressed with the Báb personally, He had no inkling of the Báb's future stature. As Adib Taherzadeh explained,

> Hájí Siyyid Javád [Karbilá'í] was one of the early believers of the Bábí Dispensation. He had known the Báb from the days of His childhood, years before His Declaration, and was fascinated by

> the remarkable qualities which were so strikingly apparent in Him. Some years later, he went to Búshihr and *for almost six months lived in the building where the Báb and His uncle had their business premises*. There he became attracted to the Báb and attained His presence many times, but never did it cross his mind that the Promised One of Islám could be any other than one of the divines or men of learning. – Adib Taherzadeh (Note: Italics not in original.)[101]

Siyyid Javád Karbilá'í made the following observation:

> Every time I met Him, I found Him in such a state of humility and lowliness as words fail me to describe. His downcast eyes, His extreme courtesy, and the serene expression of His face made an indelible impression upon my soul. I often heard those who were closely associated with Him testify to the purity of His character, to the charm of His manners, to His self-effacement, to His high integrity, and to His extreme devotion to God. – Siyyid Javád Karbilá'í[102]

The Báb was very good in business, but He did not find business to be His life calling. He was more inclined to spend His time in prayer. The following is paraphrased from the Persian by Faizi:

> ...He would often leave the business and occupy Himself with prayers. Every time He prayed on the roof of His shop, He would face toward Tihrán, a city that in His Writing was known as a Holy Land, as the Place of Manifestation and the appearance of a Hidden Divine Treasure. – Faizi[103]

It was widely known that the Báb spent hours on the roof of the business intensely absorbed in prayer. Later, when enemies tried to find fault with the Báb, they accused Him of going crazy due to His extreme exposure to the sun. Ironically, there was an engraved inscription above the door of the Báb's business. It was from the Qur'án (68:51) and it said that the people often look at a Prophet of God and call Him crazy.

[Note: The Arabic term (al-dhik'ra) translated in this quote as "the Reminder" is also translatable as "the Message"; indeed, some translators have done exactly that. It is also translatable as "the Remembrance". Either way, in Muhammad's time it would have referred to the Qur'án, the Book revealed by Muhammad. Later on, the Báb will use this Arabic term to refer to Himself as the Remembrance of God.]

> The unbelievers well-nigh strike thee down with their glances, when they hear the Reminder, and they say, 'Surely he is a man possessed!' (Qur'án 68:51)[104]

Faizi saw this door in 1958 during a trip to Búshihr. He reports that everyone could read the inscription clearly. The door had been imported from India.[105]

Sojourn in Karbilá

After about six years in trade, the Báb felt inspired to go to Karbilá in Iraq, to pray at the shrine of the Imám Husayn, one of the holiest spots in Shí'ih Islám. This revered ancestor, the Third Imám, was martyred in the 7th Century, and extolled as a focus of Shí'ih piety ever since.

The Báb appealed to his uncles to come to Búshihr to take over the family businesses. The uncles were slow in coming, so the Báb, eager to move on, settled every transaction, paid all the bills, and updated the accounting records. Nothing was going to stop Him. He locked the door and entrusted the business records and the key to a trustworthy individual, He departed for Karbilá. When the uncles arrived months later, they found everything in perfect order.

The Báb was 21 years old when He arrived in Karbilá. He stayed there about eleven months, but Abbas Amanat states that "even this short stay was enough to draw the attention of observers" amongst the Shaykhís, who noticed "the unusual character" of the young Merchant from Shíráz. "The state of presence in which he was seen, astonished a great number of people." Another merchant, from the town of Qazvín, commented that "he never saw any other person", from the religious leaders, the mystics, the nobles, and the merchants, who could match "the humility, devotion, or magnificence" in his visits to the shrine of Imám Husayn.[106]

In Karbilá, one student, Shaykh Hasan, reported that he often felt an urge to approach the Báb to "fathom His mystery".

> I watched Him several times as He stood in an attitude of prayer at the doorway of the shrine of the Imám Husayn. So wrapt was He in His devotions that He seemed utterly oblivious of those around Him. Tears rained from His eyes, and from His lips fell words of glorification and praise of such power and beauty as even the noblest passages of our Sacred Scriptures could not hope to surpass. The words

"O God, my God, my Beloved, my heart's Desire"

> were uttered with a frequency and ardour that those of the visiting pilgrims who were near enough to hear Him instinctively interrupted the course of their devotions, and marvelled at the evidences of piety and veneration which that youthful countenance evinced. Like Him they were moved to tears, and from Him they learned the lesson of true adoration.
>
> Having completed His prayers, that Youth, without crossing the threshold of the shrine and without attempting to address any words to those around Him, would quietly return to His home. I felt the impulse to address Him, but every time I ventured an approach, a force that I could neither explain nor resist, detained me.
>
> My enquiries about Him elicited the information that He was a resident of Shíráz, that He was a merchant by profession, and did not belong to any of the ecclesiastical orders. I was, moreover, informed that He, and also His uncles and relatives, were among the lovers and admirers of Shaykh Ahmad and Siyyid Kázim...
>
> That Youth had set my heart aflame. The memory of that vision haunted me. My soul was wedded to His till the day when the call of a Youth from Shíráz, proclaiming Himself to be the Báb, reached my ears. The thought instantly flashed through my mind that such a person could be none other than that selfsame Youth whom I had seen in Karbilá, the Youth of my heart's desire. – Shaykh Hasan[107]

The Báb encountered many of the Shaykhí students during His time in Karbilá. This included Mullá Husayn, Quddús, Mullá Sádiq and others. They knew each other in Karbilá at least as acquaintances.

This fact is of significant interest to the Bahá'ís of the West. Their most widely known and beloved chronicle of early Bábí and Bahá'í history, *The Dawn-Breakers*, written by Nabíl, was written in a style that has given readers the impression that the Báb and Mullá Husayn were strangers when they later met in Shíráz. To this day, this is the understanding of many Bahá'í followers in the West. It is astonishing, therefore, to discover a significant aspect about the origin story of their Faith is different. Based on credible sources we can say that *the two men did know each other from their days in Karbilá*. How well they knew each other is a separate question.

'Abdu'l-Bahá, in a talk that was *recently translated*, confirmed they knew each other:

> As Mullá Ḥusayn had met the Báb before in Karbilá and knew Him, he became His guest... – 'Abdu'l-Bahá[108]

Other accounts provide greater detail concerning the encounter between the Báb, Mullá Husayn and the other Shaykhí students. The following account was given by Ibn-i-Asdaq, the son of Mullá Sadiq.

Mullá Sadiq, as we will soon see, is a towering figure in early Bábí and Bahá'í history. Ibn-i-Asdaq, his son, also became a luminary of the Faith in a later period. Bahá'u'lláh appointed Ibn-i-Asdaq to the high-ranking position of Hand of the Cause of God, which means he was a highly trusted, distinguished servant and teacher of the Faith. Ibn-i-Asdaq was as distinguished as his father. Bahá'u'lláh had singled out Ibn-i-Asdaq for distinction when he was still a child. Like his father before him, he endured violent persecution. As a child, he was whipped with lashes against his body. Like Bahá'u'lláh and other Bábís, he spent time in the prison dungeon known as the Síyáh-Chál (the Black Pit) in Tihrán. He attained the presence of Bahá'u'lláh several times and received several Tablets addressed to him. He performed numerous services for the Cause, including travelling and teaching the Faith, helping to initiate the construction of the House of Worship in Ishqábád, Turkmenistán, establishing the first Spiritual Assembly in Tihrán, and defending the Faith against its enemies. Bahá'u'lláh designated him Shahíd Ibn-i-Shahíd, which is translated as Martyr, Son of the Martyr.[109]

Figure 9 Ibn-i-Asdaq, son of Mullá Sádiq, appointed Hand of the Cause of God by Bahá'u'lláh

I am talking about Ibn-i-Asdaq because this account comes to Ibn-i-Asdaq from his father, Mullá Sádiq, an eyewitness present with the Báb in Karbilá. This account of their encounter took place at Mullá Sadiq's home in Karbilá, and Mullá Sadiq was present in the room. Think of this as an intimate meeting in someone's living room.

Mullá Sádiq was one of the Báb's earliest followers, and, with Quddus, the first to be persecuted on Persian soil for the sake of their Faith. Mullá Sádiq, through his son's writing published in a book by Fuádi, tells of an occasion when he met the Báb in Karbilá.

Fuádi states that he read this story from Ibn-i-Asdaq's writings, in a manuscript he saw at the home of Ibn-i-Asdaq's eldest daughter. The following passage is paraphrased from Persian by Fuádi.

[Note: In the passage below the Báb is invited to a meeting to be held in the utmost reverence in honor of the Third Imám, the Imám Husayn. Reverently reciting the story of the Third Imám's tragic martyrdom is a central feature of Shí'ih Muslim devotional life.]

> [Mullá Sádiq] was often a close companion of Quddús and associated with Mullá Husayn. He finally moved to Karbilá and there he met the Báb *before His declaration*. That meeting was in this manner:
>
> One day in the front of the sacred shrine of Imám Husayn, he saw a dignified Siyyid [the Báb] of about age of twenty who with utmost lowliness and humility was standing there. Tears were descending from His eyes. Upon observing this, Mullá Sádiq became attracted to that Youth. The next day, he saw the Báb in the same state and approached Him and said:
>
> "Since at my house there is a meeting for *the remembrance of Imám Husayn* and Siyyid Kázim with his disciples will be present there, my request is that You honor our meeting with Your presence."
>
> The Báb replied that it would be an honor and a privilege to attend such a gathering for the remembrance of the Imám Husayn, whom He described as the Light of God.
>
> That night, the Báb went to the house of Mullá Sádiq while Siyyid Kázim and his disciples were sitting. Mullá Husayn was on the pulpit giving a sermon. When the Báb arrived, Siyyid Kázim, contrary to his customary ways, stood and pointed to the elevated spot of the meeting and said: "Please be seated here." However, the Báb

situated Himself close to the entrance door. All were puzzled and wondered who is this Siyyid that has been welcomed in this manner. Mullá Husayn became silent for a while and was unable to continue, until Siyyid Kázim said: "It is good to recite a few poems of the late Shaykh Ahmad in regard to the martyrdom of Imám Husayn". Mullá Husayn obeyed and began to recite.

During this recitation the Báb began to weep in such a way that all those present began to weep as well. After the recitation ended, sharbat (a fruit drink) was brought, although the Báb did not partake of that. Siyyid Kázim excused himself because he and his disciples were expected at a similar gathering to be held at his home. After they left, the Báb arose and sat where Siyyid Kázim had been sitting. He still did not partake of sharbat and then he left for his house. – Mullá Sádiq, through the report of Ibn-i-Asdaq[110]

As we picture this scenario in our minds, it is clear that everyone in the room had to be aware of these two people. Mullá Husayn was the featured speaker and initially the center of attention. However, when the Báb enters the room he momentarily becomes speechless. Obviously, he was affected by the Báb's Presence in the room. The Báb, however, also became the center of attention. He caused quite a scene. Under these emotional circumstances – with everyone in the room weeping because of the Bab! –these two people, in the same intimate space at the same time, *must* have been aware of one another. This report doesn't prove they were close friends, but it does prove that the Báb, Mullá Husayn, Siyyid Kázim, and Mullá Sadiq were clearly all acquainted with one another.

Ibn-i-Asdaq's account continues:

A few days later, the Báb met Mullá Sádiq in the courtyard of the shrine of Imám Husayn and mentioned to him that His uncle had arrived from Shíráz. He asked if he would be interested in meeting Him.

The same afternoon, Mullá Sádiq went to the house where the Báb was staying and noticed that the uncle was sitting at the high point of the gathering and a group of dignitaries, ulama and merchants from Iran were present and the Báb was offering tea and sharbat to them. During conversations, Mullá Sádiq began to extol the Báb's qualities. In response, the uncle said:

"Yes, all of our descendants are known for their distinction and praiseworthy character in Shíráz, and this Youth is distinguished above them all; however, despite my insistence, He shows no inclination for study and it is considered to be a great deficiency in our family for a person not to be educated."

Mullá Sádiq responded:

"If you do not take Him with you back to Shíráz, I will guarantee that He study."

The uncle said:

"Despite the difficulty that the family feels about His absence (in Shíráz), since you are making such a commitment, I consent to His staying here longer."

After a few days, the uncle returned to Shíráz; however, after that the Báb and Mullá Sádiq did not discuss this matter. – Mullá Sádiq, through the report of Ibn-i-Asdaq[111]

Faizi has provided a nearly identical version of this incident, except its source is Nicolas' history of the period rather than from Ibn-i-Asdaq. Given the great similarity of the account, Nicolas may have received his information from Ibn-i-Asdaq. It is impossible to know. The differences in detail are excerpted below (paraphrased from the Persian by Faizi):

...One day, at the Shrine of the Imám Husayn, his eyes fell upon the Báb Whose face was in the utmost attraction, humility and attention. He was standing a distance from the tomb of the Imám and tears were pouring from His eyes. Mullá Sádiq was amazed at this scene. The next day, he observed Him in the same state. He approached the Youth and greeted Him; however, the Báb was so much immersed in a spiritual state and attraction that He did not answer back. Mullá Sádiq then waited till the Báb completed His pilgrimage and then with utmost courtesy as He was leaving, he approached the Báb again and greeted Him. This time the Báb answered...

...Mullá Husayn, who was on the pulpit, abruptly stopped reciting his sermon, and was puzzled and bewildered of the situation...

...Then, those who were present were served with sharbat (a fruit drink) and the Báb and all those who were present drank...

> …Despite this promise, Mullá Sádiq was unable to speak with the Báb on this matter, as he was so much affected by His manner and moral qualities. Although the opportunity came on multiple occasions, he found himself helpless to bring the matter to the Báb's attention. – Mullá Sádiq[112]

This is also reported by Husaini.[113] Among these accounts, the only difference in factual detail is whether or not the Báb drank the sharbat. Other than that, while they differ on some points of nuance, they agree on the substantive facts.

Abbas Amanat also mentioned Mullá Sádiq's encounter with the Báb at the shrine of the Imám Husayn. He mentions the Báb's exceptional display of reverence and the difficulty of approaching Him at first. In this account, the Báb explains to Mullá Sádiq this mosque was a holy place where one's attention should not be placed on anything besides God. He said that one must be forgetful of self and set aside all worldly matters.[114] According to Amanat, the Báb "was said to have been affected when Mullá Husayn Bushrú'í, his future "First Believer", recited some of the poetry of Shaykh Ahmad…"[115]

In what might be a different encounter, the Báb inspired a strong reaction in Siyyid Kázim when He entered a meeting.

> [The Báb] sat close to the threshold, and with the same modesty and dignity of bearing listened to the discourse of the Siyyid. As soon as [Siyyid Kázim's] eyes fell upon that Youth [the Báb], the Siyyid discontinued his address and held his peace. Whereupon one of his disciples begged him to resume the argument which he had left unfinished.
>
> 'What more shall I say?' replied Siyyid Kázim, as he turned his face toward the Báb. 'Lo, the Truth is more manifest than the ray of light that has fallen upon that lap!'
>
> I immediately observed that the ray to which the Siyyid referred had fallen upon the lap of that same Youth… This added still further to my perplexity. I had already heard my teacher observe that so great is the perversity of this generation, that were he to point with his finger to the promised One and say: 'He indeed is the Beloved, the Desire of your hearts and mine,' they would still fail to recognize and acknowledge Him. I saw the Siyyid actually point out with his finger the ray of light that had fallen on that lap, and yet none among those who were present seemed to apprehend its meaning... – Shaykh Hasan[116]

Hájí Muhammad Rizá was a respected merchant of Isfahán and Baghdád who thought often about the appearance of the Promised One. This story is paraphrased from the Persian by Mázindarání.

> One night in a dream, while living in Baghdád, he actually saw the Promised One at the Shrine of the Imám Husayn occupied with prayers. He appeared in the utmost perfection, beauty, and reverence as tears of devotion poured from His eyes. In the dream, the Promised One expressed the utmost affection towards Rizá and promised him that he would be with Him during their pilgrimage to Mecca. After this dream, a year had passed, and he found himself in Karbilá. Then one day in Karbilá He saw the Báb appearing exactly as he had seen in his dream and the Báb repeated His statement. Even before He declared His Mission, he became enchanted with the Báb and was devoted to Him. ...[Subsequently,] He was in the Báb's presence on several occasions in Mecca. This added to his attraction and faith in the Báb. After the pilgrimage, he returned to Persia and wherever he went he talked about the perfections and spiritual station of the Báb.
> – Mázindarání[117]

Muhammad 'Alí, Hádí and Ibráhím were three wealthy brothers known to Bábí and Bahá'í history as the Nahrí brothers. The word 'nahr" means 'large conduit of water'. They were called Nahrí because their father financed construction of a large water conduit for the city of Baghdád, earning appreciation and respect. The Nahrí brothers repeatedly intersect with the life of the Báb beginning in Karbilá.

One day in Karbilá, two of the brothers, Muhammad 'Alí and Hádí, saw the Báb in the area just outside the Shrine of the Imám Husayn. The following story is paraphrased from the Persian by Mázindarání:[118]

> And in the days that the Báb was living in Karbilá, several times Muhammad 'Alí and Hádí saw the Báb during His pilgrimage to the shrine of Imám-Husayn, and in Siyyid Kázim's classes. The manner of the Báb's worship, His state of humility, the tenderness of His heart, the grandeur of his station, and the respect paid to Him by Siyyid Kázim attracted their attention. Several times the thought passed through Hádí's mind: Might it be possible that this dignified Siyyid could be the Promised One? – Mázindarání

Later on, when the call of the Báb arose from Shíráz, Muhammad 'Alí and Hádí heard of it. Right then, Hádí told his brother,

> Indeed, the Owner of this Call is the same young Siyyid from Shíráz.
> – Hádí

Both men soon departed for Shíráz. On their way, they learned the Báb had already departed to Mecca. Hádí decided to return to Karbilá and Muhammad 'Alí continued on to Isfahán. Both men and their brother, Ibráhím, would meet the Báb in the future.

The Báb visited the meetings of Siyyid Kázim. Balyuzi states that the Báb's "occasional visits" to Siyyid Kázim's sessions "did not ... make him a pupil or disciple of Siyyid Kázim."[119] Abbas Amanat cites pro-Bábí sources which also claim that the Báb's attendance in Siyyid Kazem's classes was "short and infrequent". While these visits were "sufficient to acquaint" Him with the Shaykhí movement, they were not enough to give a "sense of affiliation" with the Shaykhís.[120] The Báb sympathized with the Shaykhí cause. He referred to Siyyid Kázim, in His Writings, as "the revered scholar and friend, my teacher". One of the Báb's famous works, the Commentary on the Súrih of the Cow, was written in honor of Siyyid Kázim.[121] (The Súrih of the Cow is the second chapter of the Qur'án, and the longest.) On his part, Siyyid Kázim had sufficient spiritual vision to sense the as yet undisclosed high station of the Báb.[122]

AUTHOR'S REFLECTION: Why the Shrine of the Imám Husayn evoked so much reverence and tears for the Báb

> With what assiduous care He [the Báb] attended those gatherings at which the virtues of [the Prince of Martyrs], the Imám Husayn, were being extolled! With what attention He listened to the chanting of the eulogies! What tenderness and devotion He showed at those scenes of lamentation and prayer! Tears rained from His eyes as His trembling lips murmured words of prayer and praise. How compelling was His dignity, how tender the sentiments which His countenance inspired! – Hájí Siyyid Javád-i-Karbilá'í[123]

During the Báb's time in Karbilá, we notice the powerful and overwhelming emotions evoked in His heart at the Shrine of the Imám Husayn or hearing his story. Why is the Báb so extremely reverent towards him? Why does remembrance of the Third Imám bring the Báb to tears whenever He hears it?

An important part of Islámic history continues its impact to this day, over 1,400 years later. The Báb had a profound, personal relationship to the story of the Imám Husayn.

A brief telling of the Third Imám's story follows:

The Prophet Muhammad saw the days of His Ministry were coming to an end. During one of His excursions through the territory of Arabia, at a place called Qadír-i-Khumm, Muhammad called a meeting of all the believers with him. He called 'Alí, who was married to His daughter, Fátimih, and the father of His two grandchildren, Hasan and Husayn, to the front of the gathering. 'Alí was also His cousin. Most importantly, at the very beginning of His Mission, 'Alí had been the second person, after His wife, Khadíjih, to believe in His Mission as a Messenger of God. Before all those assembled, Muhammad announced that 'Alí was His chosen successor, and after him his descendants would continue in honor. All those present – including Abu Bakr, the Prophet's elderly closest friend, and 'Umar and 'Uthman, pledged their obedience to 'Alí.

Several months later, on His deathbed, Muhammad called for paper and ink to write His final instructions. It is related that Muhammad wished to confirm 'Alí and his descendants as His successor, leaving both His Book and His family as His legacy. But 'Umar intervened to prevent it. He complained out loud that the Prophet was ill and delirious on His deathbed. The members of the family and 'Umar quarreling, which greatly displeased the dying Prophet, so He banished them all from His presence that day. He died soon after. 'Umar prevented Muhammad's last chance to put His final wishes in writing. Adib Taherzadeh wrote:

> Through his misguided opposition to 'Alí, 'Umar frustrated Muhammad's intentions regarding His successorship and the direction of the affairs of Islám… 'Umar's response was the fateful remark: 'The Book of God is sufficient unto us.' This short statement has echoed through the centuries. 'Abdu'l-Bahá … describes its woeful consequences, saying that this statement caused the foundation of the religion of God in the Islámic Dispensation to be shattered… 'Abdu'l-Bahá explains that as a result of this statement Imám Husayn, the most illustrious of the Imáms, was decapitated on the plain of Karbilá, the other holy Imáms were inflicted with great suffering, imprisonment and death, and the blood of countless innocent souls was shed for almost twelve hundred years…
>
> 'Abdu'l-Bahá attributes all these and many more atrocities committed during the Islámic Dispensation to the influence of the simple statement 'The Book of God is sufficient unto us'. It deprived the greater part of the Islámic nation not only of divine guidance and

> the wealth of spiritual knowledge imparted by the holy Imáms to their followers through their interpretation and elucidation of the many abstruse passages in the Qur'án, but also of their illuminating prophecies concerning the advent of the Qá'im, the Promised One of Islám. – Adib Taherzadeh[124]

Muhammad's supposed friends, Abu Bakr and 'Umar and others, schemed to give the successorship to themselves instead of 'Alí. Following a debate, Abu Bakr, not 'Alí, became the first Caliph of Islám ("caliph" means successor). The elderly Abu Bakr ruled Islám for two years. Then Umar became Caliph. He ruled for ten years before being assassinated. The next Caliph was 'Uthman, who ruled about twelve years before he too was assassinated. At last, after about sixteen years, the community turned to 'Alí, and he was chosen as the fourth Caliph. 'Alí ruled about five years. Then he too was assassinated.

The tragic years after Muhammad were simultaneously turbulent and triumphant. Internal rebellions within the dominions of Islám led to bloodshed and strife, to multiple civil wars. Externally, the Islámic government rapidly expanded into a vast empire, reaching as far west as Spain and the Atlantic Ocean, and as far east as Persia and the Indus Valley, and to the border of China. At its peak, the Islámic empire was the largest empire in history.

The reign of 'Alí was particularly challenging. After waiting so long to become Caliph, he faced a military rebellion from the appointed Governor of Syria, Muáwiyah. In a complex struggle, although 'Alí nearly had Muáwiyah defeated, the struggle ended in a draw. Muáwiyah was left in place, and 'Alí remained Caliph. 'Alí was assassinated in 661 AD and Muáwiyah, the Founder of the Umayyad dynasty, became the new Caliph. He converted the role of Caliph from a spiritual ruler, the head of Islám, into a ruling royal dynasty and worldly empire. This hereditary dynasty, which held power until it was overthrown in 750 AD, became known among Muslim historians, as the most worldly, corrupt, cruel and barbaric in Islámic history.

After Muáwiyah, the Caliphate was passed to his son, Yazid, who vehemently hated the family of the Prophet Muhammad. After 'Alí, the second Imám was his son, Hasan. Yazid pressured Hasan into retiring from his position as Imám. In time Hasan was assassinated. The Third Imám was Husayn, the next son of 'Alí and Fátimih.

Abdullah Yúsuf 'Alí, the famed Sunní Qur'án translator, wrote this about Yazid:

> Yazid assumed the power at Damascus. He cared nothing for the

> most sacred ideals of the people. He was not even interested in the ordinary business affairs of administration. His passion was hunting, and he sought power for self-gratification.
>
> The discipline and self-abnegation, the strong faith and earnest endeavour, the freedom and sense of social equality which had been the motive forces of Islám, were divorced from power. The throne at Damascus had become a worldly throne based on the most selfish ideas of personal and family aggrandisement, instead of a spiritual office, with a sense of God-given responsibility. The decay of morals spread among the people.
>
> There was one man who could stem the tide. That was Imám Husayn. He, the grandson of the Prophet, could speak without fear, for fear was foreign to his nature. But his blameless and irreproachable life was in itself a reproach to those who had other standards. They sought to silence him, but he could not be silenced. – Abdullah Yúsuf 'Alí[125]

'Abdu'l-Bahá gave a theological perspective concerning the Umayyads, stating that they are in fact "the beast" spoken of in Chapter 11 of the Book of Revelation:

> "The beast that ascendeth out of the bottomless pit shall war against them, and shall overcome them, and kill them." (Revelation 11:7)
>
> [This] beast means the Umayyads who attacked them from the pit of error, and who rose against the religion of Muhammad and against the reality of 'Alí—in other words, the love of God. – 'Abdu'l-Bahá[126]

The two protagonists took their places on the stage of history – Yazid as the sworn enemy of the family of the Prophet, and the usurper of the Caliphate, and Husayn, the Third Imám, the noble, prayerful and devoted second son of 'Alí, grandson of Muhammad. These descriptions are not caricatures. History records that Yazid was dark-hearted, and Husayn was noticeably holy and noble of character.

Yazid was envious and fearful of the admiration a multitude of Muslims expressed for Husayn. Yazid felt his position on the throne was not secure unless he could get Husayn to pledge loyalty to him. Yazid had made a number of attempts to force Husayn into pledging loyalty to his Caliphate. Simultaneously, Yazid's rule was brutal and harsh. Noting his worldliness, cruelty and corruption, Husayn repeatedly refused. Abdullah Yúsuf 'Alí continued:

> Medina was the centre of Husayn's teaching. They made Medina impossible for him. He left Medina and went to Mecca, hoping that he would be left alone. But he was not left alone. The Syrian forces invaded Mecca. The invasion was repelled, not by Husayn but by other people. For Husayn, though the bravest of the brave, had no army and no worldly weapons.
>
> His existence itself was an offence in the eyes of his enemies. His life was in danger, and the lives of all those nearest and dearest to him. He had friends everywhere, but they were afraid to speak out. They were not as brave as he was. But in distant Kúfih, a party grew up which said: "We are disgusted with these events, and we must have Imám Husayn to take asylum with us." – Abdullah Yúsuf 'Alí

The people of the city of Kúfih wrote thousands of letters to Husayn asking him to come from Mecca to their city. Many friends warned Husayn that going to Kúfih was a trap, that the people of Kúfih would not resolutely stand by him while he stood by them. Warned that it was dangerous, Husayn decided to go anyway, out of his love for the people. He gathered up his family and loved ones, including wives and children, and rode out from Mecca. Yazid told his army generals to block Husayn and his group of seventy from reaching their destination. Yazid's army was four thousand.[127]

Yazid's soldiers confronted Husayn on the desert plains of Karbilá. In addition to blocking them from passing, they also blocked access to water from a nearby oasis. Husayn asked for permission to pass. He spoke peacefully with the soldiers. His words were beginning to have some effect, when suddenly an arrow struck deep into his body. That arrow was shot by the commander who cried out, "I was the first to shoot an arrow!" A blizzard of arrows soon covered the plain of Karbilá.

Though severely injured, Husayn continued alive for a while. At Noon, he asked for a break in the fighting so that he and his family could perform their prayers. Permission was granted.

Abu'l-Qasim Faizi, author of The Prince of Martyrs, described the carnage:

> After prayers, he again counselled his opponents in gem-like words, but they surrounded him like beasts of prey, striking so many blows with iron bars, spears and swords that he could no longer support

> himself on his charger and fell to the ground. His horse galloped towards the tents where the Imám's family had taken shelter, paused there a little, then disappeared into the endless desert.
>
> The full brunt of the wrath of that frantic mob fell heavily on the Imám. His face was streaming with blood. He lifted up his garment to wipe it away. In that moment [another] arrow sank deep in his chest, causing him to fall to his knees. The wounds were all on his chest and arms, for he never turned his back to his foes. Then a soldier gave the Imám such a severe blow on the head that he fell on his face.
>
> In the confusion, a group of soldiers ... started to invade the Imám's tents for the purpose of looting and putting all to death. Husayn shouted at them, "If you do not follow the religion of God, behave, at least, as true Arabs, and spare the women and children!" – Abu'l-Qasim Faizi[128]

Surprisingly, Husayn's order was obeyed and the soldiers temporarily withdrew from the tents.

> The hand of death was not yet on Husayn, and although fallen he inspired such awe in the hearts of the soldiers that no one dared to commit the heinous deed of decapitating him. Some approached but shuddered in fear and rejoined their ranks... Then this envoy of the Governor of Kúfih fell like a thunderbolt on Husayn's body and severed his head with nearly ten strokes. This sealed the contemptible victory of four thousand over barely seventy... – Abu'l-Qasim Faizi[129]

That day, the 10th of Muharram 61 AH (10 October 680 AD) the army brutally slaughtered the men in the group. The men, including the Imám Husayn, were beheaded. Their heads were mounted on spears for display. Then other members of the family were attacked. The women and some children were marched to Kúfih in captivity. Husayn's only son, also called 'Alí, who was sick and bedridden, was barely spared, but marched back as well. (All future descendants of the Prophet's lineage were descended from this one sick son. If that one life had been killed, all future Siyyids, that is, all future descendants of the Prophet, including all the future Imáms, and the future Promised One of Islám, the Báb, would never have been born.)

During his last painful moment, the only concerns of Husayn were the protection and upliftment of the religion of God, the sanctity of the Prophet's Holy Book, the preservation of the teachings of His Faith, the welfare of his family, and the comfort of his people. Husayn is recognized as the most noble, sincere, and self-sacrificing martyr for the Cause of God. Most of the Imáms suffered, but Husayn's martyrdom became the symbol of holy sacrifice within Shí'ih Islám.

A few brief paragraphs cannot adequately recount the horror and misery inflicted upon the family of the Prophet that day. Among the Shí'ih Muslims throughout history, a prominent part of their religious culture is to rehearse and recount in detail the atrocities of Yazid's men on the plain of Karbilá. Artworks portray the massacre. Books are written about it. A special day of observance is on the Islamic calendar.

A Christian or a Jew can recognize the depths of feeling evoked by the story of Husayn in the hearts of the Shí'ih Muslims by recalling emotions felt about the Crucifixion of Jesus or the binding of Isaac in the Bible. In the psyche of the devout Shí'ih Muslim, the martyrdom of the Imám Husayn ranks as supremely sacred and important, stirs the emotions to their depths, and is commemorated in his culture with devotion and intensity.

With a thoughtful understanding of the story of the Imám Husayn, we can answer the original questions: Why is the Báb so extremely reverent towards him? Why does remembrance of the Third Imám bring the Báb to tears whenever He hears his story? I would like to offer three potential answers. Let the reader decide if these are good answers.

First, having been brought up on the tragic story of the Imám Husayn since childhood, and given the importance of the story, the Báb cared deeply about the Imám Husayn and his loved ones. Meir Litvak states:

> Visitation to the shrines of the Imáms in Iraq became a major feature of popular Iranian Shi'ism. It was intended to acknowledge the Imáms' authority as leaders of the community, and to maintain the contract between the Shi'i believer and the Imám, who would intercede with God on his behalf on the Day of Resurrection. Equally important, the visitation, particularly at Karbilá', aimed at preserving Shi'i collective memory and identity… [The] visitation became a most popular pilgrimage destination. – Meir Litvak[130]

As a devout Shí'ih, the Báb had the tragedy of the Imám Husayn ingrained in His mind from childhood. This explains a normal level of culturally appropriate attachment to the Imám Husayn. It doesn't fully explain the Báb's remarkable devotion and sensitivity to the story of Imám Husayn.

The second reason was personal to the Báb. Moses saw the Burning Bush and heard the Voice of God calling out to Him. Jesus saw the Dove descending upon Him and heard the Voice of Heaven proclaim Him to be the Son of God. Muhammad saw the all-encompassing Vision of the Angel Gabriel on the vast horizon and heard Gabriel's insistent demand to recite the Qur'án. Buddha received enlightenment under the Bodhi tree. Bahá'u'lláh, in the future, would see the glorious Maiden of Heaven addressing Him with God's revelation. The Báb felt an intense kinship and connection to the Imám Husayn. Yet to come, after His days in Karbilá and His return to Shíráz, would be His moment of Revelation. The Báb's vision at in that moment of Revelation yet to come would be of the severed head of the Imám Husayn. Of that vision of Revelation, the Báb later wrote this:

> ...When I awoke, I felt that the Spirit of God had permeated and taken possession of My soul. My heart was thrilled with the joy of His Divine presence, and the mysteries of His Revelation were unfolded before My eyes in all their glory. – The Báb[131]

The third reason is equally profound. We see the Báb at the Shrine of the Imám Husayn in Karbilá, standing humbly near its entrance, lost for long periods in silent reverie, oblivious to His surroundings, with tears flowing down His face. We've noticed how many observers found this display of devotion far beyond the norm, and how they paid attention to His intensely prayerful activities. A few even see in His heartfelt devotions a glimpse that He might be that long-awaited Promised One. We see Him sitting quietly in meetings of the Shaykhís listening to recitations of the sorrowful story of the sacrifice of the Imám Husayn. Overcome with such tenderness of heart that He begins to weep, others in the room weep with Him. We saw this occur in the very meeting which establishes that Mullá Husayn and the Báb knew each other in Karbilá.

Nabíl recorded the internal reflections of the Báb during one of those times when the Imám Husayn's story was read aloud. That reading praised the virtues, mourned the death and described the martyrdom of the Imám Husayn. The Báb explained His thoughts to His followers. As Nabíl continues, the narrative shifts from outward signs to inward thoughts:

> The recital of those sufferings would provoke intense emotion in the heart of the Báb. His tears would keep flowing as He listened to the tale of the unutterable indignities heaped upon him, and of the agonising

> pain which he was made to suffer at the hands of a perfidious enemy.
>
> As the circumstances of that tragic life were unfolded before Him, the Báb was continually reminded of that still greater tragedy which was destined to signalise the advent of the promised Husayn. To Him those past atrocities were but a symbol which foreshadowed the bitter afflictions which His own beloved Husayn was soon to suffer at the hands of His countrymen. He wept as He pictured in His mind those calamities which He who was to be made manifest was predestined to suffer, calamities such as the Imám Husayn, even in the midst of his agonies, was never made to endure. – Nabíl[132]

The Báb claimed to be the Promised One, recipient of Divine revelation. He called Himself the Báb, the Gate, to show He was the forerunner of a Divine Messenger yet to come, He yearned to lay down His life for this Divine Educator, Who was greater than Himself. He called this Divine Educator, Him Whom God shall make manifest.

Islámic prophecy had predicted two Divine trumpet blasts (please see Qur'án 39:68), the coming of two Divine Messengers. According to Shí'ih Muslims, the first One to appear would be known as the Qá'im ("He who arises"), and as the return of the Twelfth Imám. He would probably announce Himself in the year 1260 AH (1844 AD). After this, the Shí'ih believe the Third Imám, Husayn, would return as the second Divine trumpet blast, the second Divine Messenger. We know today that this second sacred Personage was Bahá'u'lláh, but at the time this was a well-guarded Secret. Bahá'u'lláh's birth name was Husayn 'Alí. Husayn was in His name. The Báb wrote this about Him:

[Note: In this passage, the reference to "the Most Great Remembrance" refers to Bahá'u'lláh, Who had not yet declared His mission to the world. The Umayyads are the Umayyad dynasty, of whom Yazid, the killer of Husayn, was the second king.]

> O peoples of the earth! Inflict not upon the Most Great Remembrance what the Umayyads cruelly inflicted upon Husayn in the Holy Land. By the righteousness of God, the True One, He is indeed the Eternal Truth, and unto Him God, verily, is a witness. – The Báb[133]

When listening to the story of the Imám Husayn, or when praying devoutly at his Shrine, in addition to looking to the tragic past of the Imám Husayn, the Báb aspired to suffer in the present in the path of God like the

Third Imám. He was also envisioning the future, when the Promised Husayn, His Successor, Him Whom God shall make manifest, would appear and face even greater sorrows than faced by the Imám Husayn, His namesake.

None of this was revealed to the world when the Báb was in Karbilá, but how much did He know? Perhaps He knew all of it, and it stirred Him to His depths. He later wrote this about the coming of Bahá'u'lláh:

> Bear Thou witness that, through this Book, I have covenanted with all created things concerning the mission of Him Whom Thou shalt make manifest, ere the covenant concerning My own mission had been established. – The Báb[134]

For all these reasons, the Báb was powerfully stirred by the remembrance of the Imám Husayn, the noblest example of self-sacrifice in all of Shí'ih Islám. He was awed by the Shrine of the Imám Husayn, the greatest scene of spiritual pilgrimage in the Shí'ih world. He was inspired by the coming of the Promised Husayn, Him Whom God shall make manifest, Bahá'u'lláh. He was moved to tears at the thought of the excruciating suffering Bahá'u'lláh was destined to endure. The Báb revered the past, was inspired in the present, and knew the future secrets, hidden at the time. Whenever He heard the story of the Imám Husayn, He held the entire past, present and future dear to His heart. Those around Him could not help but notice, and themselves become deeply moved.

Marriage in Shíráz

After the Báb had been in Karbilá for less than a year, His mother wanted Him to return home to Shíráz. He wanted to stay longer in Karbilá. According to Abbas Amanat, the Báb's uncle, Hájí Mírzá Siyyid 'Alí, journeyed to Karbilá. Faced with his Nephew's reluctance to leave, the uncle begged Siyyid Kázim to intervene. At first, the distinguished teacher was reluctant to interfere. The uncle insisted, so Siyyid Kázim told the Báb He could go. At this, the Báb agreed to go. A different source says that the Báb's uncle sought assistance from a different person, not Siyyid Kázim. Regardless of the discrepancy, there is no doubt the uncle was seeking assistance to bring the Báb back home at His mother's request.[135]

The Báb returned home to Shíráz in early 1842 and resumed His trading activities. He was twenty-two. He was restless and wanted to go back to Karbilá. His mother wanted to keep Him in Shíráz, so she and the Báb's uncle decided that He should be married soon. Khadíjih Bagum was chosen (born in 1822).[136] They were close in age and were playmates in childhood.[137]

Interestingly, Khadíjih stated that she had a premonition in a dream that she would be married to the Báb. She said this brought her much joy.

The wedding was on 25 August 1842 AD, in the Báb's home.[138] One of the leading religious leaders of Shíráz presided over the ceremony. Marriage feasts were held in the next-door homes of the Báb's uncle and of Khadíjih's father. Khadíjih recalled those days:

> His kindness towards me and His care for me were indescribable. He and His mother alike showered me with kindness and consideration.
> – Khadíjih Bagum[139]

Soon Khadíjih was pregnant. When the time came to give birth, the delivery was difficult and dangerous. Their son, named Ahmad, lived only a short time. The Báb later penned a letter to His wife in which He offered assurances about the well-being of their son in the worlds beyond:

> Thou art unique amongst women... Verily Thy son Ahmad is, in very truth, with the exalted Fátimih,[140] nurtured by knowledge in the heaven of holiness. – The Báb[141]

Echoing the probable sentiments of Abraham, this is a portion of a heartfelt prayer He revealed concerning their son:

> O my God, my only Desire! Grant that the sacrifice of My son, My only son, may be acceptable unto Thee. Grant that it be a prelude to the sacrifice of My own, My entire self, in the path of Thy good pleasure. Endue with Thy grace My life-blood which I yearn to shed in Thy path. Cause it to water and nourish the seed of Thy Faith. Endow it with Thy celestial potency, that this infant seed of God may soon germinate in the hearts of men, that it may thrive and prosper, that it may grow to become a mighty tree, beneath the shadow of which all the peoples and kindreds of the earth may gather. Answer Thou My prayer, O God, and fulfil My most cherished desire. Thou art, verily, the Almighty, the All-Bountiful.
> – The Báb[142]

After they were married, Khadíjih, one night dreamt that a frightening male lion came into the courtyard of their home. In the dream, the lion grabbed hold of her and dragged her around the courtyard in a circle. One time. Another time. Half a time around the courtyard. She awoke, alarmed and disturbed by this dream. When she told the Báb about it, He answered that she awoke too soon from the dream. He said the meaning of the dream was that the two of them were destined to have only two and a half years together. This brought her much distress, but the Báb consoled and comforted her.

Khadíjih reported that in Shíráz her Husband had no definite occupation. Evidently, His prior successful business activities provided the family enough money. His time in Shíráz was spent mainly in the upper chamber of the house, engaged in devotions. He would sometimes go to His uncle's trading office in the morning and take walks in the fields outside the city, returning home by sunset. He would write in the evenings.[143]

EARLIEST INTIMATIONS OF DIVINE REVELATION

The Báb continued His daily activities, living with His wife, focusing His attention on prayers and writings through the early portion of the year 1260 AH (1844 AD). One night, during this period, He had a dream. He wrote:

> The spirit of prayer which animates My soul is the direct consequence of a dream which I had in the year before the declaration of My Mission. In My vision I saw the head of the Imám Husayn, [the Prince of Martyrs], which was hanging upon a tree. Drops of blood dripped profusely from His lacerated throat. With feelings of unsurpassed delight, I approached that tree and, stretching forth My hands, gathered a few drops of that sacred blood, and drank them devoutly. When I awoke, I felt that the Spirit of God had permeated and taken possession of My soul. My heart was thrilled with the joy of His Divine presence, and the mysteries of His Revelation were unfolded before My eyes in all their glory. – The Báb[144]

This is the moment He identified as the birth of His Revelation.

Another night, probably in March or April of 1844 AD, Khadíjih witnessed something extraordinary. He left their bed, but after a while, when He did not return, she became worried. In her memoirs she later wrote,

> Then I went out to look for Him, but He was nowhere to be found. Perhaps, for some reason, He had left the house, I thought; but, trying the street door I found it locked from within, as usual. Then I walked to the western side of the house, looked up at the roof-top, and saw that the upper chamber was well lighted. This added to my surprise, because I had never known Him to go to that part of the house at that hour of the night, unless He had guests. And He always told me when a visitor was expected. He had not said that He was to have a guest that night. So, with both astonishment and trepidation, I went up the steps at the northern side of the courtyard. There I saw Him standing

> in that chamber, His hands raised heavenwards, intoning a prayer in a most melodious voice, with tears streaming down His face. And His face was luminous; rays of light radiated from it. He looked so majestic and resplendent that fear seized me, and I stood transfixed where I was, trembling uncontrollably. I could neither enter the room nor retrace my steps. My will-power was gone, and I was on the point of screaming, when He made a gesture with His blessed hands, telling me to go back. This movement of His hands gave me back my courage, and I returned to my room and my bed. But all that night long I remained deeply disturbed… Sleep was impossible that night, and then came the dawn, so foreboding, and I heard the muezzin's call to prayer. – Kadíjih Bagum[145]

That morning, when she saw Him again, He seemed to have been transformed. Her narrative continues:

> …as usual, He went to His mother's room to take tea. I followed Him there, and as soon as my eyes alighted on Him, that attitude and that majesty which I had witnessed the night before took shape before me. I paled and shuddered involuntarily. His mother had, at that moment, gone out of the room, and He was quietly drinking His tea. He raised His face to me, and received me with great kindness and affection, bidding me be seated. Then He passed to me what was left of the tea in His own cup, which I drank.
>
> His kindness restored my courage, and when He asked me what it was that troubled me, I boldly replied that it was the change in Him which weighed heavily on my mind.
>
> [I told Him:]
>
> "You are no longer the same person I knew in our childhood. We grew up together, we have been married for two years, living in this house, and now I see a different person before me. You have been transformed."
>
> I further remarked that this had made me anxious and uneasy. He smiled and said that although He had not wished to be seen by me in the condition of the previous night, God had ordained otherwise.
>
> [He said:]
>
> "It was the will of God … that you should have seen Me in the way you

did last night, so that no shadow of doubt should ever cross your mind, and you should come to know with absolute certitude that I am that Manifestation of God Whose advent has been expected for a thousand years. This light radiates from My heart and from My Being."

As soon as I heard Him speak these words I believed in Him. I prostrated myself before Him and my heart became calm and assured. From that moment I lived only to serve Him, evanescent and self-effacing before Him, no thought of self ever intruding. – Kadíjih Bagum[146]

This profound experience shows that Khadíjih Bagum was the very first person to believe in the Báb's Revelation, and also the first woman. Soon after this time, Mullá Husayn would appear, and thus become the first man, the first disciple and the first member of the clergy to embrace His Cause.

THE DECLARATION OF THE BÁB

Mullá Husayn, one of the leading Shaykhí students, was away, in Isfahán and Mashhad, on a mission for Siyyid Kázim when the Siyyid passed away. When he returned to Karbilá, three weeks after his teacher's passing, he found the Shaykhís in a state of confusion. They were still mourning the loss of their great teacher. But something else was going on – claims of leadership. These claimants sought to reintegrate the Shaykhís with the mainstream Shí'ih orthodoxy. Hájí Muhammad Karím Khán Kirmání claimed leadership of the Shaykhí movement and, betraying a central tenent of the Shaykhí movement, tried to remove millennial expectations from the group's teachings.[147]

Mullá Husayn's outlook was the opposite of Kirmání's. More than anything, he wanted to find the Promised One and fulfill the millennial vision of the Shaykhí movement.

No figure embodies the prevailing spirit of Shaykhí yearnings better than Mullá Husayn… He is a key figure in the shaping of the Bábí movement, and the chief architect of its expansion. The background and character of "the Gate of the Gate (Báb al-Báb), as the Báb later named Mullá Husayn, exemplifies the making of a millenarian. – Abbas Amanat[148]

Born in 1814, Mullá Husayn was the son of a small landowner from a town near Bushrúyih, who was moderately affluent and owned a number of shops. He was probably a cloth dyer and part-time religious leader in his community. In 1835, Mullá Husayn moved to Karbilá to study with Siyyid Kázim, where he was distinguished as a superior student. While in Karbilá, Mullá Husayn lived a humble life. He studied extensively with Siyyid Kázim and mastered the Shaykhí writings. At Siyyid Kázim's request, he supervised the junior students.[149] Historical sources report that Mullá Husayn was a physically frail individual suffering from poor health, including trembling hands, heart trouble, restlessness and even anxiety. It is possible he had some sort of heart ailment.[150]

Mullá Husayn asked his fellow Shaykhí disciples what their departed leader said in his last wishes. They reported that repeatedly and emphatically, Siyyid Kázim had urged them to purify their hearts, to leave their homes, to scatter in every direction, and to commit themselves to the search for the Promised One. Siyyid Kázim stated:

> The veils that intervened between you and Him are such as only you can remove by your devoted search. Nothing short of prayerful endeavour, of purity of motive, of singleness of mind, will enable you to tear them asunder. Has not God revealed in His Book: 'Whoso maketh efforts for Us, in Our ways will We guide them?' – Siyyid Kázim[151]

Mullá Husayn then asked:

> Why, then have you chosen to tarry in Karbilá? Why is it that you have not dispersed, and arisen to carry out his earnest plea? – Mullá Husayn[152]

When he received only excuses, a disappointed Mullá Husayn walked away, leaving them to their own pursuits.[153] After failing to arouse his fellow Shaykhís, Mullá Husayn left his mother, sister and all his belongings behind. He departed Karbilá for Iran in the company of his brother and his cousin.[154]

Their first stop was the city of Kúfih. He took shelter in a mosque in Kúfih. Centuries before, 'Alí, the first Imám, had been murdered in this mosque. About a dozen other Shaykhís arrived later. Mullá Husayn planned to pray, meditate and fast for forty days. Joining him was fellow Shaykhí and close friend Mullá 'Alí Bastámí.[155] (Faizi observes an Islámic prophecy, quoted in a famous book, which says the disciples of the Promised One will first pray in the mosque in Kúfih and then go forth in search of Him and His Cause.)[156]

While in Kúfih, Mullá Husayn received a mysterious letter, possibly from his departed teacher. Once he read it, Mullá Husayn decided to leave

Kúfih.[157] According to Amanat, as Mullá Husayn prepared to leave, some of his companions asked him the reason for his departure. He said:

> I am ordered to undertake a journey and go to the service of a great personage.

And they said to him:

> We presumed that this is your turn to be leader.

Mullá Husayn burst into tears, saying,

> How far from me!... – An eyewitness account, reported by Abbas Amanat[158]

Mullá Husayn departed from Kúfih with his brother and his cousin and headed for Basrih. The following passage is paraphrased from the Persian by Baraqi.

> In this trip, contrary to Mullá Husayn's previous travels, he chose the sea route from Basrih to Búshihr. In the type of ship of those days, since it was carrying much merchandise in addition to the passengers, the weight of the ship, the wind, and the waves of the sea greatly affected the trip. Through all those hours, Mullá Husayn sat in the corner of the ship and with concentration of mind wrote in his notebook the difficult questions he would ask from the inner teachings of the Shaykhí school and from the abstruse questions from the Islámic tradition. He wanted to be ready for the recognition and testing of whoever would claim to be the Hidden Imám, or the Guardian, or the Qá'im. He envisioned that if that Person would write a commentary on the Súrih of Joseph, it would need to be unique and new in terms of its style and interpretation… – Baraqi[159]

Balyuzi mentions that Mullá Husayn journeyed by sea.[160] Baraqi states that after the dangerous sea journey ended, in Búshihr Mullá Husayn began to feel a special joy and comfort in the atmosphere of Búshihr. He began to feel a sense of calm assurance he had never felt before. After a few days, according to Baraqi "an attractive and mysterious force and a wonderous inspiring feeling was attracting him toward Shíráz" (Paraphrased from the Persian by Baraqi.).[161] Nabíl reports a similar stirring, saying that he was "drawn as if by a magnet" to Shíráz.[162]

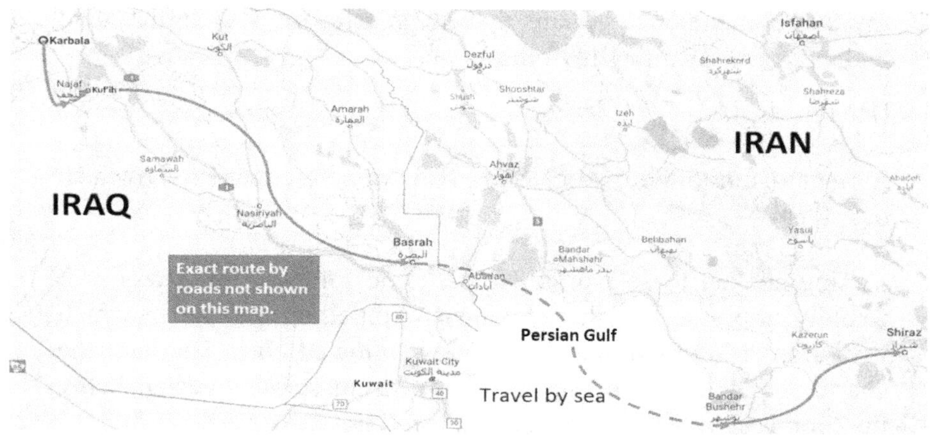

Figure 10 Mulla Husayn's journey from Karbilá to Shíráz via Najaf, Kúfih, Basrih and Búshihr

The journey from Búshihr to Shíráz is about 184 miles. When he arrived in the early afternoon on May 22nd, 1844, he told his brother and cousin to go directly to the mosque and wait there for his arrival. Meanwhile, he intended to walk for a while outside the city. Baraqi reports that "the air was soft and the valleys were green and luscious".[163]

He approached the city from the south. It was from that direction, at the Kázarún Gate, that Mullá Husayn encountered the Báb. (There is no trace of that gate today.) According to Faizi, the first auspicious words of the Báb to Mullá Husayn were in praise of God that he had arrived safely.[164] Mullá Husayn's lengthy account of the dramatic events of that evening is reported by Nabíl:[165]

> On that very day, a few hours before sunset, whilst walking outside the gate of the city, his eyes fell suddenly upon a Youth of radiant countenance, who wore a green turban and who, advancing towards him, greeted him with a smile of loving welcome. He embraced Mullá Husayn with tender affection as though he had been his intimate and lifelong friend…
>
> [Mullá Husayn later wrote:]
>
> 'The Youth who met me outside the gate of Shíráz overwhelmed me with expressions of affection and loving-kindness. He extended to me a warm invitation to visit His home, and there refresh myself after the fatigues of my journey. I prayed to be excused, pleading that

my two companions had already arranged for my stay in that city, and were now awaiting my return.

[He replied:]

"Commit them to the care of God… He will surely protect and watch over them."

Having spoken these words, He bade me follow Him. I was profoundly impressed by the gentle yet compelling manner in which that strange Youth spoke to me. As I followed Him, His gait, the charm of His voice, the dignity of His bearing, served to enhance my first impressions of this unexpected meeting.

We soon found ourselves standing at the gate of a house of modest appearance. He knocked at the door, which was soon opened by an Ethiopian servant.

"Enter therein in peace, secure." (Qur'án 15:46)

were His words as He crossed the threshold and motioned me to follow Him. His invitation, uttered with power and majesty, penetrated my soul. I thought it a good augury to be addressed in such words, standing as I did on the threshold of the first house I was entering in Shíráz, a city the very atmosphere of which had produced already an indescribable impression upon me. Might not my visit to this house, I thought to myself, enable me to draw nearer to the Object of my quest?…

Figure 11 Entrance to the House of the Báb, from *The Gate: Dawn of the Bahá'í Faith*

As I entered the house and followed my Host to His chamber, a feeling of unutterable joy invaded my being. Immediately we were seated, He ordered a ewer of water to be brought, and bade me wash away from my hands and feet the stains of travel. I pleaded permission to retire from His presence and perform my ablutions in an adjoining room. He refused to grant my request, and proceeded to pour the water over my hands. He then gave me to drink of a refreshing beverage, after which He asked for the samovar and Himself prepared the tea which He offered me. ...I renewed my ablutions and prepared for prayer. He, too, stood beside me and prayed. Whilst praying, I unburdened my soul, which was much oppressed, both by the mystery of this interview and the strain and stress of my search. I breathed this prayer:

"I have striven with all my soul, O my God, and until now have failed to find Thy promised Messenger. I testify that Thy word faileth not, and that Thy promise is sure."

That night, that memorable night [Wednesday, May 22, 1844 AD], in the year 1260 AH. It was about an hour after sunset when my youthful Host began to converse with me.

[He asked me:]

"Whom, after Siyyid Kázim do you regard as his successor and your leader?"

[I replied:]

"At the hour of his death our departed teacher insistently exhorted us to forsake our homes, to scatter far and wide, in quest of the promised Beloved. I have, accordingly, journeyed to Persia, have arisen to accomplish his will, and am still engaged in my quest."

[He further enquired:]

"Has your teacher given you any detailed indications as to the distinguishing features of the promised One?"

[I replied:]

"Yes, He is of a pure lineage, is of illustrious descent, and of the seed of Fátimih [the daughter of Muhammad]. As to His age, He is more than twenty and less than thirty. He is endowed with innate knowledge. He is of medium height, abstains from smoking, and is free from bodily deficiency."

He paused for a while and then with vibrant voice declared:

"Behold, all these signs are manifest in Me!"

He then considered each of the above-mentioned signs separately, and conclusively demonstrated that each and all were applicable to His person.

I was greatly surprised, and politely observed:

"He whose advent we await is a Man of unsurpassed holiness, and the Cause He is to reveal, a Cause of tremendous power. Many and diverse are the requirements which He who claims to be its visible embodiment must needs fulfil…"

No sooner had those words dropped from my lips than I found myself seized with fear and remorse, such as I could neither conceal nor explain. I bitterly reproved myself, and resolved at that very moment to alter my attitude and to soften my tone. I vowed to God that should my Host again refer to the subject, I would, with the utmost humility, answer and say: 'If you be willing to substantiate your claim, you will most assuredly deliver me from the anxiety and suspense which so heavily oppress my soul. I shall truly be indebted to you for such deliverance.'…

I had previously requested Siyyid Kázim, in private, to write a commentary on [the Súrih of Joseph, a chapter of the Qur'án which relates the Biblical story of Joseph], which he refused, saying:

"This is, verily, beyond me. He, that great One, who comes after me will, unasked, reveal it for you. That commentary will constitute one of the weightiest testimonies of His truth, and one of the clearest evidences of the loftiness of His position."

I was revolving these things in my mind, when my distinguished Host again remarked:

"Observe attentively. Might not the Person intended by Siyyid Kázim be none other than I?"

I thereupon felt impelled to present to Him a copy of the treatise which I had with me.

[I asked him:]

"Will you read this book of mine and look at its pages with indulgent eyes? I pray you to overlook my weaknesses and failings."

He graciously complied with my wish. He opened the book, glanced at certain passages, closed it, and began to address me. Within a few minutes He had, with characteristic vigour and charm, unraveled all its mysteries and resolved all its problems. Having to my entire satisfaction accomplished, within so short a time, the task I had expected Him to perform, He further expounded to me certain truths which could be found neither in the reported sayings of the Imáms of the Faith nor in the writings of Shaykh Ahmad and Siyyid Kázim. These truths, which I had never heard before, seemed to be endowed with refreshing vividness and power.

[He afterwards observed:]

"Had you not been My guest your position would indeed have been a grievous one. The all-encompassing grace of God has saved you. It is for God to test His servants, and not for His servants to judge Him in accordance with their deficient standards.

"Were I to fail to resolve your perplexities, could the Reality that shines within Me be regarded as powerless, or My knowledge be accused as faulty? Nay, by the righteousness of God! it behoves, in this day, the peoples and nations of both the East and the West to hasten to this threshold, and here seek to obtain the reviving grace of the Merciful. Whoso hesitates will indeed be in grievous loss. Do not the peoples of the earth testify that the fundamental purpose of their creation is the knowledge and adoration of God? It behooves them to arise, as earnestly and spontaneously as you have arisen, and to seek with determination and constancy their promised Beloved."

He then proceeded to say:

"Now is the time to reveal the commentary on the Súrih of Joseph."

> He took up His pen and with incredible rapidity revealed … the first chapter of His commentary on the Súrih of Joseph. The overpowering effect of the manner in which He wrote was heightened by the gentle intonation of His voice which accompanied His writing. Not for one moment did He interrupt the flow of the verses which streamed from His pen. Not once did He pause till [He] was finished. I sat enraptured by the magic of His voice and the sweeping force of His revelation. At last I reluctantly arose from my seat and begged leave to depart.
>
> He smilingly bade me be seated, and said:
>
> "If you leave in such a state, whoever sees you will assuredly say: This poor youth has lost his mind."
>
> At that moment the clock registered two hours and eleven minutes after sunset...
>
> [He declared:]
>
> "This night … this very hour will, in the days to come, be celebrated as one of the greatest and most significant of all festivals. Render thanks to God for having graciously assisted you to attain your heart's desire, and for having quaffed from the sealed wine of His utterance. "Well is it with them that attain thereunto."' – Nabíl[166]

Let us interrupt Nabíl's narrative briefly to include some additional detail reported by Faizi about this moment of when the Commentary on the Súrih of Joseph was being revealed. The following is paraphrased from the Persian by Faizi:

> The pen of the Blessed was engaged in writing with an unbelievable speed. And during their revelation, He was reciting those same verses with a sweet voice and attractive melody. And after each sentence He would repeat this verse from the Qur'án:
>
> "Glory be to thy Lord, the Lord of Glory, above that [which] they describe! And peace be upon the Messengers. And praise be to God, Lord of the Worlds!" (Qur'an 37:180-182)
>
> Mullá Husayn was so enchanted and attracted that he imagined himself to be in the promised paradise. Then the Báb told him that this

> exact hour and minute is the dawn of the Sun of Truth. He praised God that Mullá Husayn had attained such a great bounty. – Fazi[167]

While the Báb fluidly and rapidly revealed the Commentary on the Súrih of Joseph, He melodiously incorporated this verse from the Qur'án into the process of revelation. Mullá Husayn found himself mesmerized.

Mázindaráni shared some additional details of this moment. Paraphrased from the Persian, Mázindaráni adds:

> ...He picked up the pen and held the paper and began to write with a rapidity that was incomprehensible and revealed within minutes its first súrih [of the Commentary on the Súrih of Joseph]... The Supreme Pen was moving over the page while [Mullá Husayn listened to] the heavenly voice of His Holiness. Mullá Husayn lost control of his will and found a new state to the point that he could not bear it... – Mázindaráni[168]

Let us now resume Mullá Husayn's narrative from Nabíl:

> At the third hour after sunset, my Host ordered the dinner to be served. That same Ethiopian servant appeared again and spread before us the choicest food. That holy repast refreshed alike my body and soul. In the presence of my Host, at that hour, I felt as though I were feeding upon the fruits of Paradise. I could not but marvel at the manners and the devoted attentions of that Ethiopian servant whose very life seemed to have been transformed by the regenerating influence of his Master...
>
> I sat spellbound by His utterance, oblivious of time and of those who awaited me. Suddenly the call [to prayer], summoning the faithful to their morning prayer, awakened me from the state of ecstasy into which I seemed to have fallen. All the delights, all the ineffable glories, which the Almighty has recounted in His Book as the priceless possessions of the people of Paradise—these I seemed to be experiencing that night. Methinks I was in a place of which it could be truly said: "Therein no toil shall reach us, and therein no weariness shall touch us..."
>
> Sleep had departed from me that night. I was enthralled by the music of that voice which rose and fell as He chanted; now swelling forth as He revealed verses ... again acquiring ethereal, subtle harmonies as He uttered the prayers He was revealing. At the end of each invo-

cation, He would repeat this verse:

"Far from the glory of thy Lord, the All-Glorious, be that which His creatures affirm of Him! And peace be upon His Messengers! And praise be to God, the Lord of all beings!" (Qur'án, 37:180)

He then addressed me in these words:

"O thou who art the first to believe in Me! Verily I say, I am the Báb, the Gate of God, and thou art the Bábu'l-Báb, the gate of that Gate.

"Eighteen souls must, in the beginning, spontaneously and of their own accord, accept Me and recognize the truth of My Revelation. Unwarned and uninvited, each of these must seek independently to find Me.

"And when their number is complete, one of them must needs be chosen to accompany Me on My pilgrimage to Mecca and Medina. There I shall deliver the Message of God to the Sharif of Mecca. I then shall return to Kufih, where again, in the Masjid of that holy city, I shall manifest His Cause.

"It is incumbent upon you not to divulge, either to your companions or to any other soul, that which you have seen and heard. Be engaged in [the mosque] in prayer and in teaching. I, too, will there join you in congregational prayer. Beware lest your attitude towards Me betray the secret of your faith. You should continue in this occupation and maintain this attitude until our departure for [Mecca and Medina].

"Ere we depart, we shall appoint unto each of the eighteen souls his special mission, and shall send them forth to accomplish their task. We shall instruct them to teach the Word of God and to quicken the souls of men."

Having spoken these words to me, He dismissed me from His presence. Accompanying me to the door of the house, He committed me to the care of God.

This Revelation, so suddenly and impetuously thrust upon me, came as a thunderbolt which, for a time, seemed to have benumbed my faculties. I was blinded by its dazzling splendour and overwhelmed by its crushing force. Excitement, joy, awe, and wonder stirred the depths of my soul. Predominant among these emotions was a sense of gladness and strength which seemed to have transfigured me. How feeble and impotent, how dejected and timid, I had felt previously! Then I could neither write nor walk, so tremulous were my hands and feet. Now, however, the knowledge of His Revelation had galvanized my being. I felt possessed of such courage and power that were the world, all its peoples and its potentates, to rise against me, I would, alone and undaunted, withstand their onslaught. The universe seemed but a handful of dust in my grasp. I seemed to be the Voice of Gabriel personified, calling unto all mankind:

"Awake, for lo! the morning Light has broken. Arise, for His Cause is made manifest. The portal of His grace is open wide; enter therein, O peoples of the world! For He who is your promised One is come!"
– Mullá Husayn, cited by Nabíl[169]

Thus, through this unparalleled night of Revelation, the first dawning hours of the new Dispensation were unfolded. As to the Revelation itself, Mullá Husayn was the first disciple to hear the Báb's momentous claims. In His Revelation that night, the Báb claimed to be the Mouthpiece of God, the One promised by the Prophets of earlier times.

All praise be to God Who hath, through the power of Truth, sent down this Book unto His servant, that it may serve as a shining light for all mankind... This is the Mystery which hath been hidden from all that are in heaven and on earth… – The Báb[170]

He wrote that the kings and princes of the earth should heed His summons and spread His message to the far lands of the earth.

O concourse of kings! Deliver with truth and in all haste the verses sent down by Us to the peoples of Turkey and of India, and beyond them, with power and with truth, to lands in both the East and the West.... – The Báb[171]

He asserted that He was the Herald of One Whose revelation was immensely greater than His own. He warned leaders not to place their faith in the things of this world:

O concourse of kings and of the sons of kings! Lay aside, one and all, your dominion which belongeth unto God...

Let not thy sovereignty deceive thee, O Sháh, for 'every soul shall taste of death,' [Qur'án 3:182] and this, in very truth, hath been written down

> as a decree of God. – The Báb[172]

And the Báb asserted the self-sufficiency of His revelation. If the leaders would listen to it, it would be for their own spiritual and practical benefit.

> By God! If ye do well, to your own behoof will ye do well; and if ye deny God and His signs, We, in very truth, having God, can well dispense with all creatures and all earthly dominion. – The Báb[173]

The Báb and Siyyid Kázim had met in private and public settings. The Báb's unique devotional attitude had attracted the attention of many observers. Siyyid Kázim had a strong inkling of the undisclosed station of the Báb. Mullá Husayn had met the Báb at the home of Mullá Sadiq. And the Báb had cause quite an emotional scene at that meeting. We know that, while praying for guidance at the mosque in Kúfih, Mullá Husayn received a letter which was possibly from his departed teacher which instructed him to go looking for the Promised One, at which point he headed to Shíráz.

We might wonder. Did Siyyid Kázim and Mullá Husayn privately discuss their insights concerning this unusual Merchant from Shíráz? Did prior encounters with Him provide a partial reason for why Mullá Husayn felt drawn to the home city of that young Merchant during his quest for the Promised One? Did Mullá Husayn plan to visit at some point his merchant acquaintance in Shíráz before seeking the Promised One in earnest? On the other hand, in his narrative, Mullá Husayn refers to this encounter as an "unexpected meeting".

Whatever Mullá Husayn might have been thinking as he approached the city of Shíráz, some things are clear: When he sets eyes on the Báb, he recognized Him. The Báb too, welcoming him with such tender affection, of course must have recognized Mullá Husayn. And finally, Mullá Husayn did not anticipate that the Báb that night would claim to be the Promised One for Whom he was searching.

Prior to the evening of May 22, 1844, Mullá Husayn had not seen anyone, including the young Merchant, show the key signs of the Promised One. He had not witnessed the act of revealing Divine verses as impressive as those found in the Qur'án. He had not seen the revelation of the Commentary on the Súrih of Joseph. Mullá Husayn had not seen anyone exhibit that innate knowledge and power by which the Promised One would be recognized.

Mullá Husayn mentions that he did not respond with instant receptivity when presented with these tell-tale signs. Instead, he put the young Merchant to the test, an act he later deeply deplored. In later years Mullá Husayn lamented that his extensive prior education nearly caused him to miss his destiny of being the first person to find the Promised One. Writing in 1987, Mehrabkhani offered the following comments:

> The Báb chose the most learned of men to demonstrate to the world His overwhelming power. A century and a half now separates us from that event. Looking back, one might now wonder if so much learning was of any use to Mullá Husayn as he came face to face with the Promised One of all ages. Did his achievements make the way any easier for him? All his studies, all his erudition, in fact, led him to the verge of denial. He was the only one of the first disciples, the Letters of the Living, who questioned the Báb and sought to test Him. How much, for the rest of his life, did he regret his behavior before the Beloved of all hearts!
>
> One of Mullá Husayn's fellow countrymen ... has left a fascinating story. He had attended school with Mullá Husayn and in later years came to believe in the Báb through his former classmate. He relates:
>
> > Once I was walking with Mullá Husayn in the street and we passed a religious school for mullás. Mullá Husayn looked at it and recited this poetry:
> >
> > > 'Never from this school has come learning,
> > > 'This house of ignorance is fit for burning.'
> >
> > I asked him: 'Why should we complain about these schools, when they have produced a man like you?
> >
> > 'No, my friend,' interrupted Mullá Husayn, 'if it were not for the education I received in these schools, I would not have argued with my Lord.' – R. Mehrabkhani[174]

Mullá Husayn regretted that he did not recognize the station of the Báb until the events in the upper room had run their course.

As to those events in the upper room, Shoghi Effendi emphasizes the almost hidden nature of the dramatic scene which unfolded.

> The opening scene of the initial act of this great drama was laid in the upper chamber of the modest residence of the son of a mercer of Shíráz, in an obscure corner of that city. The time was the hour before sunset, on the 22nd day of May 1844. The participants were the Báb, a twenty-five-year-old siyyid, of pure and holy lineage, and the young Mullá Husayn, the first to believe in Him. Their meeting immediately

before that interview seemed to be purely fortuitous. The interview itself was protracted till the hour of dawn. The Host remained closeted alone with His guest, nor was the sleeping city remotely aware of the import of the conversation they held with each other. – Shoghi Effendi[175]

Only three others could have been privy to the events as they were happening – two women and one man. The first woman was the Báb's wife, Khadíjih. The second woman was Fiddih, the servant of the Báb's wife. And the man was Mubárak, the Báb's faithful servant. Fiddih and Mubárak were Ethiopian, of African descent.

Khadíjih's participation began earlier in the day. The Báb had appears to have had foresight that Mullá Husayn was coming. Before going out to meet him, the Báb told her of his expected guest. Later that evening, and wide awake throughout the night, she listened to the great drama unfolding in the upper chamber of the house. She could hear the Báb trying to convince Mullá Husayn of the truth of His claims. In her memoirs, she later wrote:

What an extraordinary night that was!

The Báb said to me:

"Tonight we will entertain a dear guest."

His whole being was ablaze. I was most eager to hear what He had to say, but He turned to me and told me:

"It is better if you go and sleep."

I did not wish to disobey Him, but I remained awake all night and could hear His blessed voice until the morning, conversing with [Mullá Husayn], chanting verses, and presenting proofs and arguments. – Khadíjih Bagum[176]

Fiddih was a female servant of Khadíjih and wholly devoted to her. Little is known about Fiddih during this period. She was brought into the Báb's household at about seven years of age in 1842. At the time of the Báb's Declaration in 1844 she was about nine years old. Historical records do not mention her whereabouts on that night, but given her age it is highly likely that she was in the house that night.[177] We cannot assume that she was a believer or aware of the significance of the events transpiring that night. We know she was loved by the family and that she spent her life devoted to serving the family. (She passed away, in 1882, on the very same night Khadíjih passed away.)[178]

Mubárak played a significant role in the events of that evening. It was he who welcomed the Báb and Mullá Husayn at the door. He provided them with refreshments and served them dinner. Mubárak would have most likely stood just outside the door of the upper chamber as the Báb and Mullá Husayn conversed, or waited in the adjoining room where he resided, ready to be of service when called upon.[179] Probably, he was awake all night and able to hear the words spoken between the Báb and Mullá Husayn. Mubárak was an educated, literate man. He had been a member of the household for a long time, so it is likely that he heard and understood the religious claims his Master was making.

Since Mubárak was living in the house when months before Khadíjih had suddenly observed the Báb's revelation, we wonder if he was *already* aware of the Báb's claim to be the Promised One. Like Khadíjih, he became a staunch believer in the Báb.

The Báb extolled Mubárak's significance. Though a servant in the household, the Báb praises him spiritually as "he who raised me." Saiedi observes, "The Báb mentions Mubárak numerous times in His writings, where the person known as the Ethiopian servant is transformed into the Ethiopian king… [The] Báb explains that upon rejecting him, the king of Iran, Muhammad Sháh (d. 1848), and his prime minister, Hájí Mírzá Áqásí (d. 1849), descended to the lowest abyss, while Mubárak, who to outward appearance, was bereft of any power or earthly rank, ascended to the heaven of glory for 'having done good in the realm of faith'"[180] This signified, what He called the Great Reversal, mentioned in His Writings:

> …the abased shall be exalted and the exalted shall be abased. – The Báb[181]

Mullá Husayn was impressed with the dignity and the gentleness of Mubárak. As noted, he wrote,

> I could not but marvel at the manners and the devoted attentions of that Ethiopian servant whose very life seemed to have been transformed by the regenerating influence of his Master. – Mullá Husayn[182]

Thus, that night, two other distinguished souls, Khadíjih and Mubárak, and possibly a third, Fiddih, were in the house. They were awake and aware of the magnificent events that were unfolding. As astounding as it may seem, that night only four (or at most five) people were aware that the dawning of the Day of Resurrection had taken place.

The Báb explained in His Writings the meaning of the Day of Resurrection. He wrote:

[Note: In the quote below, the "Tree of divine Reality" = The Divine Messenger, the Manifestation of God, the Divine Educator; Shí'ih Islám is the branch of Islám which predominates in Persia; "Him Who is the Tree of divine Reality" is another reference to the Manifestation of God.]

In the estimation of God .... what is meant by the Day of Resurrection is this, that from the time of the appearance of Him Who is the Tree of divine Reality, at whatever period and under whatever name, until the moment of His disappearance, is the Day of Resurrection. – The Báb[183]

From the Báb's perspective, most people, including the Shí'ih Muslims who lived in Persia, have misunderstood the meaning of the Day of Resurrection.

...what is intended by the Day of Resurrection is the Day of the appearance of the Tree of divine Reality, but it is not seen that any one of the followers of Shí'ih Islám hath understood the meaning of the Day of Resurrection; rather have they fancifully imagined a thing which with God hath no reality. – The Báb[184]

The Day of Resurrection is not the end of the universe, a one-time cataclysmic event. It is not the end of history. The earth is not pulverized to dust. The moon is not cleft in two. The sun does not fall from the sky.

Instead, the Day of Resurrection represents spiritual rebirth and renewal. It is repeated many times throughout history. The Day of Resurrection is the period of time on earth when the Manifestation of God appears. There is a sequence. The Day of resurrection comes when the Divine Messenger promised by the previous Messenger appears in fulfillment of prophecies. The Báb's passage continues:

For example, from the inception of the mission of Jesus – may peace be upon Him – till the day of His ascension was the Resurrection of Moses. For during that period the Revelation of God shone forth through the appearance of that divine Reality, Who rewarded by His Word everyone who believed in Moses, and punished by His Word everyone who did not believe; inasmuch as God's Testimony for that Day was that which He had solemnly affirmed in the Gospel. – The Báb[185]

The Day of Resurrection for Moses was when Jesus appeared. The Báb explains that the process continued throughout history. Therefore, the Day of Resurrection for Jesus was when Muhammad appeared; the Day of Resurrection for Muhammad was when the Báb appeared. It was happening that very night when the Báb was proclaiming His mission in the upper room of a modest house in an obscure corner of the city of Shíráz.

The Báb had fixed, in His Writings, the exact time of the great event:

[Note: In this quote, "the Apostle of God" refers to Muhammad. The "Resurrection of the Apostle of God" refers to the appearance of the Báb. The date given, 4 Jamádíyu'l-Avval, 1260 AH in the Islámic calendar, is 22 May 1844 in the Gregorian calendar. For further information regarding the date, see the footnote.][186]

> ...the Resurrection of the Apostle of God, as is divinely foretold in the Qur'án; the beginning of which was when two hours and eleven minutes had passed on the eve of the fifth of Jamádíyu'l-Avval, 1260 AH. – The Báb[187]

The Báb continued this passage:

> The stage of perfection of everything is reached when its resurrection occurreth. The perfection of the religion of Islám was consummated at the beginning of this Revelation; and from the rise of this Revelation until its setting, the fruits of the Tree of Islám, whatever they are, will become apparent. – The Báb[188]

Following this logic, the Báb says the Day of Resurrection for His own Revelation will occur with the appearance of Him Whom God shall make manifest, the Promised One Whose coming the Báb foretold.

The Báb explained that the glorious Day of Resurrection has happened in the past; it was happening with the declaration of the Báb, and it will happen again in the future. It is a time of renewal, a time for the birth of a new Truth in the world, the coming of a Divine Educator. And it typically occurs outside the view of most of humanity. He wrote:

> The Day of Resurrection is a day on which the sun riseth and setteth like unto any other day. How oft hath the Day of Resurrection dawned, and the people of the land where it occurred did not learn of the event.
> – The Báb[189]

Shoghi Effendi said that the "opening scene" of this momentous Day of Resurrection, the conversation between the Báb and Mullá Husayn, began an hour before sunset. The Báb noted that the exact moment of Mullá Husayn's recognition occurred two hours and eleven minutes after sunset. In just three hours and eleven minutes, the entire process of *initiating* the Day of Resurrection was completed. In just a few short hours, everything had changed.

The ancient prophecies of the Bible in the Book of Daniel, mentioned by Jesus, which converged in the year 1844, were fulfilled. The prophecies of the Book of Revelation in the New Testament, focused on 1844, were fulfilled. The prophecies for the coming of the Promised One of Islám, which converged in the year 1844 (1260 in the Islámic calendar), were fulfilled. The Declaration of the Báb took place on a Wednesday evening. During that same night, in Tihrán, 'Abdu'l-Bahá[190] was born. The ancient God-given prophecies were fulfilled with the beginning of a new Day of Resurrection. The Day of Resurrection prophesied by all the Prophets of old had dawned on the horizon of human history. It had occurred "like a thief in the night." (2 Peter 3:10, 1 Thessalonians 5:2)[191] Yet, it was a day in which the sun rose and set normally. The earth did not stop spinning on its axis. The rest of humanity continued to slumber.

Chapter 3
GROWTH OF THE MOVEMENT

THE BEGINNING OF THE MOVEMENT

The Báb called His first disciples the Letters of the Living. Mullá Husayn was the first. Seventeen more were expected.

This Age was destined to be different.

Previous Manifestations of God went out to find Their disciples. For example, the Bible says Jesus searched for His first disciples (see Mark 1:16-17, Matthew 4:18-19). In this Day, however, the Báb explained that the followers, beginning with Mullá Husayn, by listening to an inner inspiration driving them forward, must seek out and find the True Beloved, the Promised One themselves. Free-will and the ability to independently search for truth are signs of maturity for any individual. As first demonstrated by the Letters of the Living, free will and the ability to search for truth are indispensable features of the Divine design and destined to become key attributes of humanity. As foretold by the Báb, the seventeen souls would independently soon seek Him out and embrace His Revelation.

These eighteen souls were named the Letters of the Living. The term "living" is derived from the Persian word, *hayy*, which refers to God's attribute, the ever living. This means that God's transcendent Being is, from all eternity to all eternity, fully alive in Himself and of Himself. The Báb, by calling these first disciples the Letters of the Living, indicated they were the vanguard of a new era. They were the individuals through whom humanity will eventually attain unto true spiritual awakening and abundant well-being.

The first forty days

Mullá Husayn met frequently with the Báb after His Declaration. Among the followers of Siyyid Kázim, Mullá Husayn was famous, due to Siyyid Kázim showering conspicuous favor and trust upon him previously. Mullá Husayn began teaching classes at the local mosque. It wasn't long before he developed a large following of people attending his lectures at the mosque as he taught from one of the books of Siyyid Kázim. The Báb sometimes attended his lectures, but, following the Báb's instructions, Mullá Husayn did not reveal that the Promised One was sitting right there among them. Mullá Husayn said:

> As I began to organise my classes and perform my devotions, a vast concourse of people gathered gradually about me. Ecclesiastical dignitaries and officials of the city also came to visit me. They marvelled at the spirit which my lectures revealed, unaware that the Source whence my knowledge flowed was none other than He whose advent they, for the most part, were eagerly awaiting. – Mullá Husayn[192]

For forty days no one else knew about the Báb's declaration. During this time the Báb continued to meet with and educate Mullá Husayn. Often the Báb sent Mubárak to summon Mullá Husayn to His home at night and the two of them would spend hours together until dawn. Mullá Husayn wrote:

> Wakeful until the dawn, I sat at His feet fascinated by the charm of His utterance and oblivious of the world and its cares and pursuits. How rapidly those precious hours flew by! At daybreak I reluctantly withdrew from His presence. How eagerly in those days I looked forward to the approach of the evening hour! With what feelings of sadness and regret I beheld the dawning of day! – Mullá Husayn[193]

The Báb completed the entire Commentary on the Súrih of Joseph and some other Writings during this forty-day period.[194]

The arrival of the Letters of the Living

One night, the Báb told Mullá Husayn to expect the arrival of several of his fellow Shaykhís and to greet them warmly. One of these friends, Mullá 'Alí Bastámí, met Mullá Husayn at the mosque. He noticed that Mullá Husayn seemed to have attracted a large following at the mosque and had settled down into a new life in Shíráz, seemingly having abandoned his quest. Thinking he might have been tempted by his worldly success as a teacher in Shíráz, Mullá 'Alí Bastámí and his companions wanted an explanation. Mullá Husayn replied:

> Your companions may naturally attribute my peace and composure to the ascendancy which I seem to have acquired in this city. The truth is far from that... I yearn not for the things of this world. I crave only the good pleasure of my Beloved. Not until I shed my blood for His name will the fire that glows within me be quenched. Please God you may live to witness that day. Might not your companions have thought that ... God has, in His infinite mercy, graciously deigned to unlock before the face of Mullá Husayn the Gate of His grace, and, wishing, according to His inscrutable wisdom, to conceal this fact, has bidden him engage in such pursuits? – Mullá Husayn[195]

Nabíl says these words "stirred the soul of Mullá 'Alí" and he instantly "perceived their meaning".[196] (We can only wonder if Mullá 'Alí noticed the hidden clue in Mullá Husayn's statement, referring directly to "the Gate" in his answer.) In any case, Mullá 'Alí now knew Mullá Husayn had found what he had been seeking.

Mullá 'Alí Bastámí pleaded with Mullá Husayn to tell him the name of the One they were seeking. Recalling that the Báb had forbidden him from divulging to anyone "that which you have seen and heard", Mullá Husayn said that he could not reveal it.[197] So Mullá 'Alí went to the other Shaykhís and they went to their private rooms to fast and to pray for,

> ...the early removal of the veil that intervened between them and the recognition of their Beloved. They prayed while keeping their vigils. – Nabíl[198]

Nabíl recorded their prayer:

> 'O God, our God! Thee only do we worship, and to Thee do we cry for help. Guide us, we beseech Thee, on the straight Path, O Lord our God! Fulfil what Thou hast promised unto us by Thine Apostles, and put us not to shame on the Day of Resurrection. Verily, Thou wilt not break Thy promise.' – Mullá 'Alí and other Shaykhís[199]

After three days of continuous effort, Mullá 'Alí had a vision.

> There appeared before his eyes a light, and, lo! that light moved off before him. Allured by its splendour, he followed it, till at last it led him to his promised Beloved. At that very hour, in the mid-watches of the night, he arose and, exultant with joy and radiant with glad-

> ness, opened the door of his chamber and hastened to Mullá Husayn. He threw himself into the arms of his revered companion. Mullá Husayn most lovingly embraced him and said: 'Praise be to God who hath guided us hither! We had not been guided had not God guided us!' – Nabíl[200]

Mullá Husayn was now confident that Mullá 'Alí had, on his own effort, discovered the identity of the Promised One. According to Faizi, Mullá Husayn took him to the house of the Báb the next morning at dawn. Mubárak was already waiting for them at the door.[201]

This meeting was similar to the Declaration with Mullá Husayn, but it differed in a significant way.

> ...whereas at the previous meeting the proofs and testimonies of the Báb's mission had been critically scrutinised and expounded, at this one all argument had been set aside and nothing but the spirit of intense adoration and of close and ardent fellowship prevailed. The entire chamber seemed to have been vitalised by that celestial potency which emanated from His inspired utterance. – Nabíl[202]

Mullá 'Alí Bastámí became the second Letter of the Living. Faizi mentions that the Báb later wrote that among the servants of God there was one – Mullá 'Alí Bastámí – who was able to attain unto the truth by hearing one verse and without seeking proof.[203]

In the days following, one by one, and through their own unaided efforts, others came to the Báb and recognized Him. Some recognized Him through their dreams, others through visions, others while in prayer.

One exceptional individual who became a Letter of the Living was Táhirih, the only woman and the only one never to meet the Báb face-to-face. She recognized Him at a distance through a vision.

Táhirih was from the town of Qazvín. In a radical departure for the time, her father allowed her to be educated. Táhirih heard about the Shaykhís and their unorthodox teachings, and desired to become a student of Siyyid Kázim. Initially she corresponded with him, and he was quite impressed with her, giving her the honorable title of Qurratu'l-'Ayn (Solace of the Eyes). She travelled to Karbilá to meet him, but Siyyid Kázim passed away ten days before she arrived.[204] Undaunted, she joined the Shaykhí community and spent her time in prayer and meditation. She became renowned for her poetry and extraordinary ability to overcome in debate the most learned scholars and religious leaders of her time. She spent much of her time educating the women of the Shaykhí community.

Her brother-in-law, Muhammad 'Alí Qazvíní, was also interested in the search for the Promised One, and, because he was a man, was free to travel wherever he wished. She gave him a letter from herself to be given to the Promised One when he found Him. She said,

> Say to Him, from me, "The effulgence of Thy face flashed forth, and the rays of Thy visage arose on high. Then speak the word, 'Am I not your Lord?' and 'Thou art, Thou art!' we will all reply." – Táhirih, cited by Nabíl[205]

At this point she did not know the identity of the Promised One. But she had great confidence her brother-in-law would find Him very soon. And he did. He found the Báb and was accepted as one of the Letters of the Living. After this, the brother-in-law handed the letter from Táhirih to the Báb.

Upon receiving Táhirih's letter, the Báb instantly accepted Táhirih as a believer and immediately admitted her as one of the Letters of the Living, even though Táhirih had not yet consciously recognized Him and had not yet explicitly heard His name.

According to Nader Saiedi, the phrase which is translated above as "Say to Him, from me" really means "Make mention of me in His presence." The Báb later wrote in a Tablet to Táhirih that this act of faith, of asking to be mentioned in the presence of the Promised One, was more important than anything she had ever done in her life. It was so mysteriously profound in His view, He said, that He immediately elevated her to the status of a Letter of the Living.[206]

At this point in the story, Táhirih is already a Letter of the Living, but she does not know it yet. Months passed and then one night, Táhirih had an extraordinary dream. 'Abdu'l-Bahá wrote:

> One night when it was getting along toward dawn she laid her head on her pillow, lost all awareness of this earthly life, and dreamed a dream; in her vision a youth, a Siyyid, wearing a black cloak and a green turban, appeared to her in the heavens; he was standing in the air, reciting verses and praying with his hands upraised. At once, she memorized one of those verses, and wrote it down in her notebook when she awoke. After the Báb had declared His mission, and His first book [The Commentary on the Súrih of Joseph] was circulated, Táhirih was reading a section of the text one day, and she came upon that same verse, which she had noted down from the dream. Instantly offering thanks, she fell to her knees and bowed her forehead to the ground, convinced that the Báb's message was truth. – 'Abdu'l-Bahá[207]

Mullá 'Alí Bastámí is the disciple whom the Báb eventually sent to Karbilá to proclaim the advent of the Báb. In Karbilá, he eventually met with Táhirih and shared with her the verses revealed by the Báb in the Commentary on the Súrih of Joseph. When shown these words of the Báb, she recognized the same words she had seen in her dream. This confirmed her faith in the revelation of the Báb. Although she never got to meet the Báb face-to-face, she became one of His most energetic and effective disciples.

Figure 12 Táhirih encounters Mullá 'Alí Bastámí. She is shown the Báb's Writings and is confirmed in her Faith. Image used with permission from *The Gate: Dawn of the Bahá'í Faith*

Sixteen men and one woman were now enrolled as Letters of the Living. The Báb told Mullá Husayn that the final disciple was soon to arrive. Nabíl tells how this last disciple came to the Báb:

> The next day, in the evening hour, as the Báb, followed by Mullá Husayn, was returning to His home, there appeared a youth dishevelled and travel-stained. He approached Mullá Husayn, embraced him, and asked him whether he had attained his goal. Mullá Husayn tried at first to calm his agitation and advised him to rest for the moment, promising that he would subsequently enlighten him. That youth, however, refused to heed his advice. Fixing his gaze upon the Báb, he said to Mullá Husayn:

'Why seek you to hide Him from me? I can recognize Him by His gait. I confidently testify that none besides Him, whether in the East or in the West, can claim to be the Truth. None other can manifest the power and majesty that radiate from His holy person.'

Mullá Husayn marvelled at his words. He pleaded to be excused, however, and induced him to restrain his feelings until such time as he would be able to acquaint him with the truth. Leaving him, he hastened to join the Báb, and informed Him of his conversation with that youth.

[The Báb observed:]

'Marvel not … at his strange behaviour. We have in the world of the spirit been communing with that youth. We know him already. We indeed awaited his coming. Go to him and summon him forthwith to Our presence.' – Nabíl[208]

This youth, Quddús, a young man from the town of Bárfurúsh (the city of Babol today), was just twenty-two years old. Quddús had been a member of Siyyid Kázim's circle of students and was known to Mullá Husayn and the other Letters of the Living from their days together in Karbilá. The Báb and Quddús were not strangers to one another; Faizi, paraphrased from the Persian, states,

Quddús had met the Báb during His time in Karbilá. – Faizi[209]

Quddús, the youngest of the Letters of the Living, was destined to become the highest ranking amongst them all.

These are the names of the Letters of the Living, as recorded by Nabíl:[210]

- Mullá Husayn-i-Bushrú'í
- Mullá 'Alíy-i-Bastámí
- Muhammad-Báqir, cousin of Mullá Husayn
- Muhammad-Hasan, brother of Mullá Husayn
- Mullá Khudá-Bakhsh-i-Qúchání, later named Mullá 'Alí
- Mullá Hasan-i-Bajistání
- Siyyid Husayn-i-Yazdí
- Mírzá Muhammad Rawdih-Khán-i-Yazdí

- Sa'íd-i-Hindí ("Hindí")
- Mullá Mahmúd-i-Khu'í ("Khu'í")
- Mullá Jalíl-i-Urúmí ("Urúmí")
- Mullá Ahmad-i-Ibdál-i-Marághi'í ("Ibdál")
- Mullá Báqir-i-Tabrízí ("Báqir")
- Mullá Yúsif-i-Ardibílí ("Ardibílí")
- Mírzá Hádí, son of Mullá Abdu'l-Vahháb-i-Qazvíní ("Hádí")
- Mírzá Muhammad-'Alíy-i-Qazvíní
- Táhirih
- Quddús

We pause to reflect on the different types of conversion stories exemplified by the earliest believers. The Writings of the Bahá'í Faith mention several pathways to the discovery of truth: sense perception, logic and reason, traditions, inspiration and the Revelation of the Holy Spirit.[211] The first four pathways to understanding truth each have their strengths and their shortcomings. The fifth one – the Revelation of the Holy Spirit through the Divine Educator, the Manifestation of God – is flawless. The four approaches do not necessarily operate in isolation; they are complementary and may act as inputs to one another. For example, ideas or practices from a tradition might cause one to engage in reason and logic concerning the Scriptures. One's reasoning might lead to an inspiration or the use of one's senses to observe happenings in the world. We see in the stories of the earliest believers that all four modes are utilized.

- Mullá Husayn engaged with the Báb both on the level of tradition and logic and reason. He did not instantly accept the Báb's claims. Rather, he painstakingly scrutinized them.
- Táhirih and Mullá 'Alí Bastámí both experienced dreams and visions which led them to the Báb, which is one type of inspiration.
- Quddús simply saw the Báb walking in the street and, perhaps assisted by inspiration, was able to recognize the Báb's station. For Quddús, his senses were enough. He saw Him and he knew Him.
- Vahíd and Mullá Husayn were both extensively guided by tradition to know what the signs of the Promised One would be. They used tradition to guide them to acceptance.

What these stories all have in common is, regardless of the method of approach, each individual was an active seeker of truth. Each relied upon the Revelation from the Divine Educator, the Báb in this case. Each had striven hard to independently discover the truth. So compelling was their drive to find the truth for themselves that they walked on foot, in some cases covering great distances in short periods of time. They sacrificed their time and comforts to reach their goal, which was nothing less than the discovery of the truth of God's Cause. All these heroes exemplify this quality, but in the story of Mullá Sádiq (which we'll read about in the next section), as his friend found him departing the city early in the morning, we heard him say the essential truth of the matter: 'This is not a matter that I can leave to others. This is a matter of the verities of the Faith that I must pursue myself.' Yet, each is an individual using their own unique combination of the pathways to truth to reach their goal. Looking back on this period of history, we can see a new pattern of spiritual discovery emerging for humanity's age of maturity. We see earnest striving combined with unity in diversity in their independent search for the truth.

EXPANSION OF THE MOVEMENT

Mullá 'Alí Bastámí is sent forth

The Báb soon began assigning missions to each one of the Letters of the Living.

Mullá 'Alí Bastámí was called to the Báb's presence. He was given the mission of going to the towns of Karbilá and Najaf to proclaim the advent of the new Day. The Báb said he was destined to be the first one to suffer persecution for the Cause. He then told him,

> You are called to partake of the celestial banquet prepared for you in the immortal realm. You are the first to leave the House of God, and to suffer for His sake... [G]reat will be your reward... – The Báb[212]

The Báb told him to proclaim the appearance of the Promised One, but during *this initial stage* of the new Faith, His name was not yet to be disclosed. Mullá 'Alí instantly accepted the Báb's instructions and arose to fulfill His mission.

Outside of Shíráz, on the way to his destination, Mullá 'Alí was overtaken by a young-man, 'Abdu'l-Vahháb, who had abandoned his shop to follow after Mullá 'Alí. Mullá 'Alí urged him to go back, lest trouble fall upon both of them, but 'Abdu'l-Vahháb would not listen. Soon, trouble came. 'Abdu'l-Vahháb's father chased after them, outraged that Mullá 'Alí had "taken" his son away from his duties at the store. Explanations were not heeded, and 'Abdu'l-Vahháb's father relentlessly beat Mullá 'Alí with a club. The father took his son back with him and, in later years, through the direct teaching effort of Bahá'u'lláh, realized he had done wrong.

Though beaten, Mullá 'Alí continued on to the towns of Búshihr, Kúfih, Karbilá and Najaf. In Búshihr, Mullá 'Alí presented the news of the Báb's revelation to His uncle, Hájí Siyyid Muhammad.

In Najaf, Mullá 'Alí Bastámí went to the Shrine of the Imám 'Alí, the first Imám, and recited a lengthy prayer of visitation revealed by the Báb, given to him to be read in that holy spot. After fulfilling the prayer of visitation, Mullá 'Alí met with one of the highest-ranking clerics in Najaf, Shaykh Muhammad-Hasan Najafi, to give him a letter from the Báb. Mullá 'Alí told this cleric that already the Báb had revealed in a forty-eight-hour period a quantity of Divine verses equivalent to the entire Qur'án (about 6,600 verses, which Muhammad had revealed over a twenty-two-year period).

The meeting didn't go well. Nabíl writes:

> In the presence of Shaykh Muhammad-Hasan, one of the most celebrated ecclesiastics of Shi'ah Islám, and in the face of a distinguished company of his disciples, Mullá 'Alí announced fearlessly the manifestation of the Báb, the Gate whose advent they were eagerly awaiting… 'His proof,' he declared, 'is His Word; His testimony, none other than the testimony with which Islám seeks to vindicate its truth…' That proud and fanatic leader … forthwith pronounced Mullá 'Alí a heretic and expelled him from the assembly. His disciples and followers, even the Shaykhís, who already testified to Mullá 'Alí's piety, sincerity, and learning, endorsed, unhesitatingly, the judgment against him... – Nabíl[213]

Mullá 'Alí Bastámí went on to Karbilá, in Iraq, where he proclaimed the Faith.[214] It was in Karbilá that Mullá 'Alí met with Táhirih. Although not yet permitted to reveal His name, he informed her of the advent of the Báb and shared with her some of the verses of the Commentary on the Súrih of Joseph. When shown these words, she recognized they were the same as the words she had seen in her dream. This confirmed her faith. Although she never got to meet with the Báb face-to-face, she became one of His most energetic and effective disciples.

While in Iraq, Sunní and Shí'ih religious leaders arose in opposition to Mullá 'Alí's teaching activities. He was arrested and beaten "on charges of blasphemy, dissemination of heretical literature, and disturbing the public peace".[215] The Ottoman Governor ordered him brought to Baghdád, where he was put in prison for about six months. He simply taught the Faith while in prison. He was put through a mock trial which generated an enormous amount of public excitement. It was reported widely in the news media of the day. The news reached all the way to Europe. The news included testimony of Major Henry Rawlinson, the British political agent in Baghdád, who filed reports, beginning in January 1845, to his superiors in Constantinople.[216] Amanat states, "the official gathering of twenty prominent Sunní 'ulema [i.e. religious leaders] and twelve of their Shi'ite counterparts was in itself an unprecedented event."[217] With no final verdict from the trial, the Ottoman government ordered Mullá 'Alí's transfer to Constantinople, where he was very probably martyred for the Faith.[218]

The ending of Mullá 'Alí Bastámí's brief mission was tragic – eventually the Persian government, possibly concerned about the treatment of its citizens – even heretics – by the Ottoman Empire, sent a request to help his circumstances. As Abbas Amanat writes, "When they sent orders to lift his chains and release him from forced labor, he had already passed away a few days earlier..."[219] No one knows how he died.[220] Shoghi Effendi wrote of his ending:

> ...the energetic and audacious Mullá 'Alíy-i-Bastámí, one of the Letters of the Living, "the first to leave the House of God (Shíráz) and the first to suffer for His sake," ... had been excommunicated, chained, disgraced, imprisoned, and, in all probability, done to death. – Shoghi Effendi[221]

Mullá 'Alí was able to attract a large number of souls to the Faith. Husaini offers this assessment of Mullá 'Alí's accomplishments (paraphrased from the Persian by Husaini):

> The mission of Mullá 'Alí had great results in Iraq's holy places and it was due to his efforts, and later the effort of Táhirih, that many numbers enlisted under the Faith of God, and it found a special place amongst the Iranians and the Arabs residing in Baghdád, Karbilá, Najaf, and other regions of Iraq, and from this nucleus a number of pure souls travelled to other regions in Iran and in the field of service exceeded others. – Husaini[222]

In addition to Mullá 'Alí's historic encounter with Táhirih, Mullá 'Alí also met Hájí Siyyid Javád [Karbilá'í.] This is how he became a Bábí:

In a spoken chronicle[223] recorded by Mírzá Abu'l-Fadl [one of the most eminent scholars of the Faith], [Javád] recalls with excitement the circumstances which led him to embrace the Faith of the Báb in Karbilá:

...It was in 1844 that Mullá 'Alíy-i-Bastámí returned to Karbilá from Shíráz, bringing the news of the appearance of the Báb and announcing that he himself together with other disciples had already attained His presence. This news, which spread rapidly, created a great excitement among the divines who trusted Mullá 'Alí and had regard for his dignity and pious life...

Mullá 'Alí only mentioned the title of the Báb, however, and refused to disclose His identity. He used to say: 'The Báb has appeared and some of us have attained His presence, but He has forbidden us to mention His name or disclose His identity or that of His family at the present time. Soon however His Message will be noised abroad and His name will be disclosed to all.'

This news brought about an amazing sensation in Iraq. In all the gatherings the appearance of the Báb was the topic of discussion. Many people speculated as to His identity, but no one ever suspected that Siyyid 'Alí-Muhammad could be the Báb, owing to the fact that He was only a youth and a merchant by profession. The people without exception thought that the Báb, the Gate of the knowledge of God, would appear from among the learned and not from the trading and professional classes. The Shaykhís, in particular, thought that He would be one of the leading disciples of Siyyid Kázim.

One day I [Hájí Siyyid Javád [Karbilá'í]] invited Mullá 'Alí to my home... We talked about this wonderful event, but in spite of the strong bonds of love and friendship which existed between us, I could not extract from him any clues by which I could recognize the person of the Báb. In the end I became desperate. *Jokingly I gripped his arms and pushed him hard against the wall... There I held him, demanding that he disclose the name of that wondrous Being*. But Mullá 'Alí calmly reminded me that he was forbidden to do so... In the midst of all this, Mullá 'Alí quite inadvertently mentioned that the Báb had requested him to collect any letters He had written to people in Karbilá and send them back to Shíráz. – Hájí Siyyid Javád [Karbilá'í], as told to Mírzá Abu'l-Fadl. (Note: Italics added.)[224]

Let us pause and read a slightly different version of this climactic moment in Siyyid Javád's life. Husaini gives a more colorful version in his scholarly account. This is from the account recorded by Mírzá Abu'l-Fadl. This portion is paraphrased from the Persian by Husaini:

> By the virtue of his deep friendship with Bastámí, Siyyid Javád tried to discover from Bastámí's conversation a clue as to the identity of the Gate but he was unable to do so. The pressure on Siyyid Javád became such that *with a humorous gesture and tone, and with some seriousness, he grabbed Bastámí by both arms and held him against the wall and pressured him, saying, while keeping a humorous tone and yet with a begging voice, "O, Mullá 'Alí, I must kill you! Why don't you tell me who is His Holiness and What is our duties?"*
>
> [Bastámí] said: "[Javád], the mention of His Name is forbidden to share by His Holiness, Himself."
>
> And in between, Bastámí said without realizing it that His Holiness told him, 'Ask any with whom I have corresponded to send back to Shíráz any of their letters from Me.' – Hájí Siyyid Javád [Karbilá'í], as told to Mírzá Abu'l-Fadl, and cited by Husaini (Note: Italics added.)[225]

Let us now continue with the previous account.

> On hearing this, the thought of Siyyid 'Alí-Muhammad [the Báb] suddenly flashed through my mind. Although it seemed very unlikely, I wondered whether it could be Him. So, I rushed to my room and fetched some of His letters which were addressed to me. As soon as Mullá 'Alí's eyes fell upon the seal of the Báb, he burst into tears. I was so filled with emotion that I too wept. Between his sobs Mullá 'Alí's constant plea to me was: 'I did not mention His name. Please do not disclose it to anyone'…
>
> Soon after this interview, Hájí Siyyid Javád [[Karbilá'í]] travelled to Shíráz and attained the presence of the Báb, this time as an ardent believer. He dedicated his life to the service of the Cause in Karbilá. It was in this city in the year 1851 that he met Bahá'u'lláh for the first time. He immediately recognized the greatness of Bahá'u'lláh, but did not appreciate His glorious station until sometime later. – Hájí Siyyid Javád [Karbilá'í], as told to Mírzá Abu'l-Fadl[226]

Javád personally knew both Divine Messengers – the Báb and Bahá'u'lláh – before either of Them made public any of Their spiritual claims.

In both cases, Javád at first had no inkling of Their stature as Manifestations of God. Fortunately for Javád, however, he realized and ultimately served the Faith with distinction. Readers may be comforted by Javád's example. He is not aware in the beginning, but his passion to discover the truth carries him through and twice he reaches his goal. Javád was in somewhat frequent correspondence with the Báb, whom he knew as simply a merchant and family friend. Javád had a store of letters from the Báb to show to Mullá 'Alí! Although he knew Him personally, and was in possession of a stack of letters from Him, he didn't realize what he had. Thankfully, eventually, he makes sense of it. Javád's passion is amusing and touching as he lovingly thrusts his friend against the wall, begging him to reveal the Name he is longing to discover. Meanwhile, rather than rejoice over his friend's life-changing realization, Mullá 'Alí is worrying about himself, sobbing because he doesn't want the Báb to think he has disobeyed His orders. The humanity of it all.

The great commission to teach the Cause

After Mullá 'Alí was sent forth on his mission, in Shíráz the Báb gathered the other Letters of the Living and delivered His final instructions before sending each one away on his assigned mission. (See the following graphic for the destinations of the Letters of the Living. See the Appendix for further detail.)

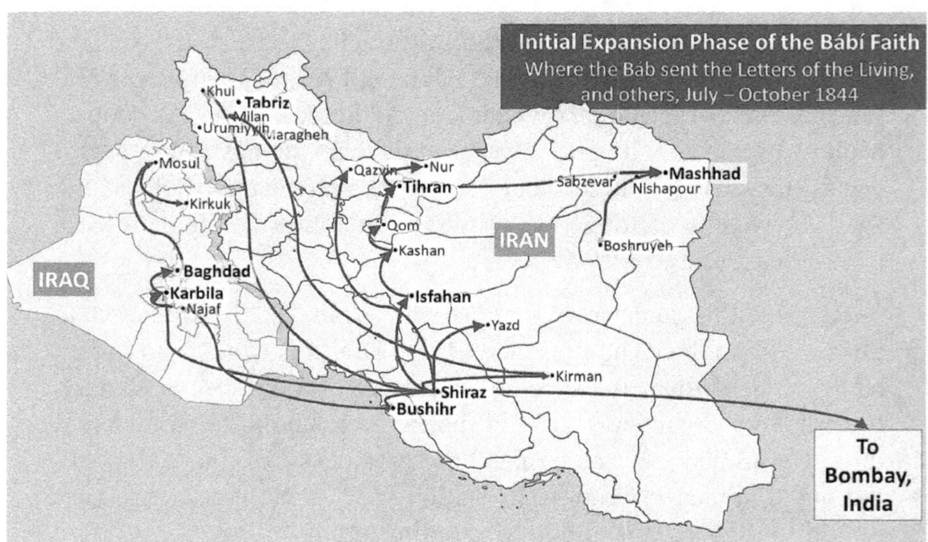

Figure 13 Initial Expansion Phase of the Bábí Faith, 1844. Letters of the Living and others are sent in all directions.

In a lengthy speech, the Báb set forth a highly demanding standard of moral conduct, He urged them to adhere to His teachings and to raise the Call of the new Faith throughout the land. Again, for the time being, He told them His name was not to be disclosed.

> O My beloved friends! You are the bearers of the name of God in this Day. You have been chosen as the repositories of His mystery. It behoves each one of you to manifest the attributes of God, and to exemplify by your deeds and words the signs of His righteousness, His power and glory. The very members of your body must bear witness to the loftiness of your purpose, the integrity of your life, the reality of your faith, and the exalted character of your devotion… Ponder the words of Jesus addressed to His disciples, as He sent them forth to propagate the Cause of God. In words such as these, He bade them arise and fulfil their mission:
>
> 'Ye are even as the fire which in the darkness of the night has been kindled upon the mountain-top. Let your light shine before the eyes of men. Such must be the purity of your character and the degree of your renunciation, that the people of the earth may through you recognize and be drawn closer to the heavenly Father who is the Source of purity and grace. For none has seen the Father who is in heaven. You who are His spiritual children must by your deeds exemplify His virtues, and witness to His glory. You are the salt of the earth, but if the salt have lost its savour, wherewith shall it be salted? Such must be the degree of your detachment, that into whatever city you enter to proclaim and teach the Cause of God, you should in no wise expect either meat or reward from its people. Nay, when you depart out of that city, you should shake the dust from off your feet. As you have entered it pure and undefiled, so must you depart from that city. For verily I say, the heavenly Father is ever with you and keeps watch over you. If you be faithful to Him, He will assuredly deliver into your hands all the treasures of the earth, and will exalt you above all the rulers and kings of the world.'
>
> O My Letters! Verily I say, immensely exalted is this Day above the days of the Apostles of old. Nay, immeasurable is the difference! You are the witnesses of the Dawn of the promised Day of God. You are the partakers of the mystic chalice of His Revelation… Purge your hearts of worldly desires, and let angelic virtues be your adorning… The days when idle worship was deemed sufficient are ended. The time is come

> when naught but the purest motive, supported by deeds of stainless purity, can ascend to the throne of the Most High and be acceptable unto Him… You are the first Letters that have been generated from the Primal Point,[227] the first Springs that have welled out from the Source of this Revelation. Beseech the Lord your God to grant that no earthly entanglements, no worldly affections, no ephemeral pursuits, may tarnish the purity, or embitter the sweetness, of that grace which flows through you. I am preparing you for the advent of a mighty Day. Exert your utmost endeavour that, in the world to come, I, who am now instructing you, may, before the mercy-seat of God, rejoice in your deeds and glory in your achievements. The secret of the Day that is to come is now concealed. It can neither be divulged nor estimated. The newly born babe of that Day excels the wisest and most venerable men of this time, and the lowliest and most unlearned of that period shall surpass in understanding the most erudite and accomplished divines of this age. Scatter throughout the length and breadth of this land, and, with steadfast feet and sanctified hearts, prepare the way for His coming. Heed not your weaknesses and frailty; fix your gaze upon the invincible power of the Lord, your God, the Almighty… Arise in His name, put your trust wholly in Him, and be assured of ultimate victory.' – The Báb[228]

The term "the Báb" means the Gate or Door.

He is the Gate through Whom humanity attained the Revelation of Bahá'u'lláh, just as John the Baptist prepared the way for Jesus. However, as Shoghi Effendi later clarified, the Báb's station is also an independent Manifestation of God:

> …no matter how short the duration of His Dispensation, and however brief the period of the operation of His laws, the Báb had been endowed with a potency such as no founder of any of the past religions was, in the providence of the Almighty, allowed to possess. That He was not merely the precursor of the Revelation of Bahá'u'lláh, that He was more than a divinely-inspired personage, that His was the station of an independent, self-sufficient Manifestation of God, is abundantly demonstrated by Himself, is affirmed in unmistakable terms by Bahá'u'lláh, and is finally attested by ['Abdu'l-Bahá]. – Shoghi Effendi[229]

And also:

> Indeed the greatness of the Báb consists primarily, not in His being the divinely-appointed Forerunner of so transcendent a Revelation, but

> rather in His having been invested with the powers inherent in the inaugurator of a separate religious Dispensation, and in His wielding, to a degree unrivaled by the Messengers gone before Him, the scepter of independent Prophethood. – Shoghi Effendi[230]

The Báb told the Letters of the Living that the people of this generation were steeped in the attitude of resistance. The religious leaders would undoubtedly arise to oppose His Message and strive to turn the people against Him. As a mercy to the people, He therefore followed a practice of gradual disclosure of His station. At first, only His title, not His name should be disclosed.

The people would think that by the title Báb He meant the "modest" claim of being the Gate to the long-hidden twelfth Imám. The full truth of the Báb's station was present from the beginning of His Revelation and is evident in His Writings. Nevertheless, although some religious and political leaders, such as Husayn Khán and Hájí Mírzá Áqásí grasped rather quickly the challenging nature of His claims, many among the mullas and the masses and even some of the Bábís only understood the His claim to Gatehood as indicative of a lesser station—the Gate to the Hidden Imám, who was at last reopening communication with his people after one thousand years of silence. The Báb would gradually make increasingly explicit over time the full scope of His claims. The people would come to recognize that His Gatehood meant that He was the Hidden Imám, the Qá'im. After this, with a little more time, the Báb's full double claim would be made fully explicit. All in all, the Báb would take about four years to patiently train the people and gradually 'peel away the layers', disclosing the inner truth of His station.

- He was, first of all, the Revealer of an Independent Revelation from God, equal in rank to the revelations brought by Moses, Jesus and Muhammad, and authorized by God to reveal new divine verses, abrogate Islám, change its laws and institute new ones.
- He was the Gate to a still greater Manifestation of God destined to come soon after Him, one known as "Him Whom God shall make manifest."

The Báb understood the overwhelming sway the religious leaders held over the minds of their followers. He knew they had distorted Islám and crafted a theology which perpetuated their power and prestige. He would have understood that the Mission of Shaykh Ahmad and Siyyid Kázim created a crack in that worldview. Shaykh Ahmad and Siyyid Kázim carefully prepared a community of devout seekers to be willing and ready to embrace the promised Qá'im when He appeared. Already Shaykh Ahmad and Siyyid Kázim had achieved victory, because about half of the Letters of the Living had been Shaykhís and were trained by them to seek and find Him.[231] This was now accomplished. However, as numerous as the Shaykhís were throughout the country, they were a minority, vastly outnumbered by the Usúlí-led orthodoxy. The announcement of the Báb could not cause anything less than a great tumult throughout the country. In this situation, the Báb chose to gradually make explicit His claims to the public. Even this gradual method of disclosure did not enable the Bábís to escape the clergy and the State's fierce opposition and the persecution.[232]

Mullá Husayn is given a special mission

Mullá Husayn wanted to go with the Báb on pilgrimage to Mecca, but the Báb said, no, He had something extraordinary in mind for him. The Báb told Mullá Husayn to teach the Faith throughout the country and, more importantly, to seek out a Secret in the city of Tihrán:

> Gird up the loins of endeavour, and arise to diffuse My Cause. Be not dismayed at the sight of the degeneracy and perversity of this generation, for the Lord of the Covenant shall assuredly assist you. Verily, He shall surround you with His loving protection, and shall lead you from victory to victory... Raise the cry: 'Awake, awake, for, lo! the Gate of God is open, and the morning Light is shedding its radiance upon all mankind! The promised One is made manifest; prepare the way for Him, O people of the earth! Deprive not yourselves of its redeeming grace, nor close your eyes to its effulgent glory.' ... Follow the course of your journey towards the north, and visit on your way Isfahán, Káshán, Qum, and Tihrán. ... A secret lies hidden in that city. When made manifest, it shall turn the earth into paradise... Be assured that the high mission for which you have been created will, in its entirety, be accomplished by you. Until you have consummated your work, if all the darts of an unbelieving world be directed against you, they will be powerless to hurt a single hair of your head... – The Báb[233]

Mullá Husayn, as the first Letter of the Living, wanted to be the disciple chosen to go on pilgrimage with the Báb to Mecca. Instead, the Báb had an infinitely precious, historic mission in store for him. Nabíl writes:

> [In the following quote, the Báb makes an allusion to Hijáz and Shíráz. Hijáz is the region in Arabia from which Muhammad had come, and Shíráz, was the Báb's own hometown. Therefore, in

this poetic way, the Báb was making an allusion to both Muhammad and Himself. It is the region where Mecca and Medina, the key places of Islámic pilgrimage, are located. What was waiting for Mullá Husayn in Tihrán was something greater than Muhammad and Himself combined.]

As the hour of his departure approached, the Báb spoke these words to Mullá Husayn:

[Note: In the passage which follows the word "'ulamás" refers to the Islámic scholars and learned ones. The word 'ulamá is plural.]

The days of our companionship are approaching their end. My Covenant with you is now accomplished. Gird up the loins of endeavour, and arise to diffuse My Cause. Be not dismayed at the sight of the degeneracy and perversity of this generation, for the Lord of the Covenant shall assuredly assist you. Verily, He shall surround you with His loving protection, and shall lead you from victory to victory. Even as the cloud that rains its bounty upon the earth, traverse the land from end to end, and shower upon its people the blessings which the Almighty, in His mercy, has deigned to confer upon you. Forbear with the 'ulamás, and resign yourself to the will of God. Raise the cry:

> 'Awake, awake, for, lo! the Gate of God is open, and the morning Light is shedding its radiance upon all mankind! The promised One is made manifest; prepare the way for Him, O people of the earth! Deprive not yourselves of its redeeming grace, nor close your eyes to its effulgent glory.'

Those whom you find receptive to your call, share with them the epistles and tablets We have revealed for you, that, perchance, these wondrous words may cause them to turn away from the slough of heedlessness, and soar into the realm of the Divine presence. In this pilgrimage upon which We are soon to embark, We have chosen Quddús as Our companion. We have left you behind to face the onslaught of a fierce and relentless enemy. Rest assured, however, that a bounty unspeakably glorious shall be conferred upon you. Follow the course of your journey towards the north, and visit on your way Isfahán, Káshán, Qum, and Tihrán... A secret lies hidden in that city. When made manifest, it shall turn the earth into paradise. My hope is that you may partake of its

> grace and recognize its splendour. From Tihrán proceed to Khurásán, and there proclaim anew the Call... Be assured that the high mission for which you have been created will, in its entirety, be accomplished by you. Until you have consummated your work, if all the darts of an unbelieving world be directed against you, they will be powerless to hurt a single hair of your head. All things are imprisoned within His mighty grasp. He, verily, is the Almighty, the All-Subduing. – The Báb[234]

And this:

> Grieve not that you have not been chosen to accompany Me on My pilgrimage to Hijáz. I shall, instead, direct your steps to that city [Tihrán] which enshrines a Mystery of such transcendent holiness as neither Hijáz nor Shíráz can hope to rival... The hosts of the invisible Kingdom, be assured, will sustain and reinforce your efforts. The essence of power is now dwelling in you, and the company of His chosen angels revolves around you. His almighty arms will surround you, and His unfailing Spirit will ever continue to guide your steps..." – The Báb[235]

The Báb told Mullá Husayn that He would wait for a report of his success before embarking with Quddús and Mubárak upon His journey to Mecca and Medina. Soon, Mullá Husayn traveled north to the places the Báb told him to approach—Isfahán, Káshán, Qum, Tihrán, and Khurásán.

Figure 14 Mulla Husayn's journey from Shíráz to Isfahán, Káshán, Qum, Tihrán and Khurásán, 1844

Mullá Husayn was well known in Isfahán due to his previous mission there at the request of Siyyid Kázim. Upon his arrival, he went to a religious school and found lodgings. It was not long before a group of students who knew him from his previous visit gathered about him. Fearlessly he taught the new message of the Báb. The distinguished teacher of this school, with whom Mullá Husayn had had dealings, had died, and the son now held the reigns of the school. Several of the students attending the school opposed Mullá Husayn's activities and went to the teacher's son to denounce him. They said:

> Mullá Husayn ... was able, in the course of his last visit, to win the support of your illustrious father to the cause of Shaykh Ahmad. No one among [our teacher's] disciples dared to oppose him. He now comes as the upholder of a still more formidable opponent and is pleading His Cause with still greater vehemence and vigour. He is persistently claiming that He whose Cause he now champions is the Revealer of a Book which is divinely inspired, and which bears a striking resemblance to the tone and language of the Qur'án. In the face of the people of this city, he has flung these challenging words: 'Produce one like it, if you are men of truth.' The day is fast approaching when the whole of Isfahán will have embraced his Cause! – The students of the religious school in Isfahán[236]

The son of the distinguished teacher replied calmly:

> What am I to say? ... Let each man dispassionately examine these claims... – The son of the distinguished teacher, head of the school[237]

The students went to another eminent teacher who replied,

> Hold your peace... Mullá Husayn is not the person to be duped by anyone, nor can he fall a victim to dangerous heresies. If your contention be true, if Mullá Husayn has indeed espoused a new Faith, it is unquestionably your first obligation to enquire dispassionately into the character of his teachings, and to refrain from denouncing him without previous and careful scrutiny... If my health and strength be restored, it is my intention, God willing, to investigate the matter myself, and to ascertain the truth... – Another distinguished teacher[238]

Finally, the students approached Manúchihr Khán, the Governor of the city, who refused to interfere in the matter. He warned them to cease disturbing the peace. Defeated, the students were not able to stop Mullá Husayn from bringing the Message of the Báb to many souls.

Mullá Husayn's mission to Isfahán was a success; some people opposed the Message, but, unexpectedly, several of the religious leaders encouraged the Message and showed him respect. Rather than condemn without justification, the notables of this city urged individual investigation, careful consideration, and fair-minded conclusions.

Often, throughout history, the high-ranking religious leaders and the most prestigious individuals in a city are not the ones who first embrace the bearer of a new message from God. Instead, often it is the lowly members of society who first receive the spark of the new Faith. This was the case in Isfahán.

The first person to embrace the new revelation was a humble sifter of wheat, known as Mullá Ja'far Ghandum-Pák-Kun. This individual is praised by both the Báb and Bahá'u'lláh in Their Writings because, although he was an illiterate wheat sifter, he possessed elevated spiritual perception.[239] Nabíl says of him:

> The first to embrace the Cause of the Báb in that city was a man, a sifter of wheat, who, as soon as the Call reached his ears, unreservedly accepted the Message. With marvellous devotion he served Mullá Husayn, and through his close association with him became a zealous advocate of the new Revelation… Such was the devotion of this youth, that the Báb, in the Persian Bayán, refers to him in such terms:
>
> "Isfahán, that outstanding city, is distinguished by the religious fervour of its Shi'ah inhabitants, by the learning of its divines, and by the keen expectation, shared by high and low alike, of the imminent coming of the [Lord of the Age]. In every quarter of that city, religious institutions have been established. And yet, when the Messenger of God had been made manifest, they who claimed to be the repositories of learning and the expounders of the mysteries of the Faith of God rejected His Message. Of all the inhabitants of that seat of learning, only one person, a sifter of wheat, was found to recognize the Truth, and was invested with the robe of Divine virtue!" – Nabíl, citing the Báb[240]

The Báb mentioned that men like the Wheat Sifter personify an important spiritual principle, the principle of the great reversal. He states in the Persian Bayán:

The lowliest of the creatures shall become the most exalted, and the most exalted shall become the most debased. – The Báb[241]

While in Isfahán, Mullá Husayn was able to bring into the Faith another distinguished soul, Mullá Sádiq. Mullá Sádiq was destined to become the first to suffer for the Cause on Persian soil.

Mullá Sádiq had been a follower of Siyyid Kázim. As a student, he had done so well that Siyyid Kázim had bestowed upon him the rank of "mujtahid". This means he was authorized to render legally binding decisions of Islámic law, a position reserved only for the most learned clerics.

Siyyid Kázim had asked Mullá Sádiq to go to Isfahán and prepare the way for the appearance of the expected Promised One. Mullá Sádiq went to Isfahán and became one of the leading clerics of the city. His congregation at the Mosque grew to be very large, at least four thousand souls.[242]

Here is Mullá Sádiq's account of how he discovered the identity of the Báb, as reported by Nabíl:

> Mullá Sádiq-i-Khurásáni … was also among the first believers who identified themselves with the Message proclaimed by the Báb. As Soon as he learned of the arrival of Mullá Husayn in Isfahán, he hastened to meet him. He gives the following account of his first interview [which took place at the home of one of the Nahrí brothers]…
>
> I asked Mullá Husayn to divulge the name of Him who claimed to be the promised Manifestation.
>
> [He replied:]
>
> 'To enquire about that name and to divulge it are alike forbidden.'
>
> [I asked:]
>
> 'Would it, then, be possible for me, even as the Letters of the Living, to seek independently the grace of the All-Merciful and, through prayer, to discover His identity?'
>
> [He replied:]
>
> 'The door of His grace is never closed before the face of him who seeks to find Him.'
>
> I immediately retired from his presence and requested his host to allow me the privacy of a room in his house where, alone and undisturbed, I could commune with God. In the midst of my contemplation, I sud-

denly remembered the face of a Youth whom I had often observed while in Karbilá, standing in an attitude of prayer, with His face bathed in tears at the entrance of the shrine of the Imám Husayn. That same countenance now reappeared before my eyes. In my vision I seemed to behold that same face, those same features, expressive of such joy as I could never describe. He smiled as He gazed at me. I went towards Him, ready to throw myself at His feet. I was bending towards the ground, when, lo! that radiant figure vanished from before me.

Overpowered with joy and gladness, I ran out to meet Mullá Husayn, who with transport received me and assured me that I had, at last, attained the object of my desire. He bade me, however, repress my feelings.

[He said:]

'Declare not your vision to anyone, the time for it has not yet arrived. You have reaped the fruit of your patient waiting in Isfahán. You should now proceed to Kirmán, and there acquaint Hájí Mírzá Karím Khán with this Message. From that place you should travel to Shíráz and endeavour to rouse the people of that city from their heedlessness. I hope to join you in Shíráz and share with you the blessings of a joyous reunion with our Beloved.' – Mullá Sádiq[243]

After Siyyid Kázim's death, Karím Khán, a fellow Shaykhí, had been making claims of leadership among the Shaykhís. He wasn't claiming to be the Promised One. He was claiming leadership of the Shaykhís, and de-emphasizing the millennialist aspirations which gave birth to the Shaykhí movement in the first place. Mullá Sádiq was entrusted with the important mission of going to Hájí Mírzá Karím Khán and presenting the message and the claims of the Báb. History records that Karím Khán did not respond favorably. He became an opponent of the new Faith.

Mullá Sádiq's realization that the Báb was the Promised One was not surprising. Mullá Sádiq and the Báb had known each other from their days in Karbilá. We recall that Sádiq was impressed by the Báb's extreme devotion and spirituality outside the Shrine of the Imám Husayn. Sádiq had received Him as a guest in his home at least once, and had spoken with the Báb's uncle about helping Him study the Shaykhí beliefs with Siyyid Kázim in Karbilá. In the tight circle of Shaykhí followers in Karbilá, he and Quddús and Mullá Husayn and the Báb had all known each other. It is through Sádiq's account, written and handed down through his son, Ibn-i-Asdaq, that we learned the details of the encounter of the Báb and Mullá Husayn at Sádiq's home in Karbilá in the days prior to the Báb's declaration. When seeking the Promised One through the inspiration of prayer, the Báb was already a known presence in Mullá Sádiq's mind and memories. While in such a seeking state, it would have been easy for him to draw on memories to acquire spiritual insights which drew him to the recognition of the Báb.[244]

Mullá Sádiq's response to discovering the identity of the Báb was dramatic. The very next morning, he changed his clothing from that of a high-ranking religious leader to that of a simple villager, Sádiq abandoned his four thousand followers[245] and set out on his journey to Shíráz. His life had been completely changed in less than twenty-four hours.[246]

We have a fascinating glimpse into the intensity of that transformation, as he began his journey to Shíráz on foot. The following is paraphrased from the Persian by Mázindarání:

[Note: In the following passage the term "Cháhár-Bágh" refers to a large square-shaped public square outside of the Islámic mosque in Isfahán. The impression being conveyed is that the crowds were so large that not only was the space inside the mosque filled up, but also the large public square outside of the mosque.]

> Faraj Tabrízí, a believer of the Báb … has related that in those days he had gone to Isfahán for business. [Mullá Sádiq] had quite a reputation in that city. The local inhabitants were attracted to him for his righteousness and holiness and had been sincerely drawn to him… The crowd of people during his prayers was so large, about 4,000 people, that they could not fit in the court of the mosque and in the Cháhár-Bágh square.

Figure 15 The Cháhár-Bágh. The large mosque in Isfahán where Mullá Sádiq preached and led prayers (Painting by Chardin. Built in the 16th century.)

> I [Faraj] attended his prayers. One day, while walking down the street in Isfahán, I saw a man in the distance who looked like Mullá Sádiq, however, he was not dressed in his usual clothes. Instead of his turban, I saw a small hat, and instead of his Abá (cloak), he was wearing a simple short overcoat, had sandals on his feet and [was carrying] a wooden staff in his hand. I was surprised and wondered, if this is Mullá Sádiq, why he is dressed like this? I stared at him from a distance and then went towards him. As I got near him, to ascertain his identity, I greeted him. As soon as he answered, I knew it was him, and we began a conversation.
>
> I kissed his hand and asked: "Why are you wearing these clothes?"
>
> He answered: "I am going to Shíráz."
>
> I asked: "For what reason?"
>
> He replied: "A Voice and a Call has arisen there, and a Personage has appeared Who is claiming a high station. I am going there to investigate."
>
> I said: "Why are you bothering yourself? Send a few of your trusted believers who can bring the news to you."
>
> He said: "This is a matter of the verities of the Faith and not for blind imitation that I can leave to others.
>
> I have to discover the matter myself."
>
> I said: "Then wait until I can arrange for you a horse, a servant and some provisions."
>
> He said: "This is doable, however, I want to walk this path of search by foot."
>
> Then, he said his goodbye to me and began to walk. – Faraj Tabrízí, paraphrased from the Persian by Mázindaráni[247]

Shíráz is approximately 300 miles south of Isfahán, a journey that Mullá Sádiq, an elderly man, was determined to undertake on foot.

With Mullá Sádiq on his way to Shíráz, and with so many other new believers, including the Sifter of Wheat, entering the fold, Mullá Husayn's visit to Isfahán had been a triumph for the Báb. This success provoked the hostility of Isfahán's religious leaders. Given that Mullá Husayn still had a long way to go, he yielded and left the city.

Mullá Husayn continued his journey north, first to Káshán and then to Qum. In these places, the reaction was mixed. While others turned away, at least three people embraced the Cause in Káshán. One of these, Mírzá Jání, would go on to meet the Báb in Mecca, to host the Báb in Káshán for two nights, to bring many family members and friends in Káshán to the Faith, to write the first history of the Faith, and to become a martyr in 1852.

Mullá Husayn made his way further north to Tihrán, the capital city of Persia. Again, he found lodgings at a religious school. The leader of this school was a Shaykhí, so Mullá Husayn expected a positive response. Instead, that teacher rudely rebuked Mullá Husayn, accusing him of betraying the cause of Siyyid Kázim. Mullá Husayn assured him that he had not betrayed Siyyid Kázim. One of the students of the school, Mullá Muhammad Mu'allim Núrí, overheard the entire conversation. Impressed with Mullá Husayn and ashamed of the rude speech of his teacher, he discretely approached Mullá Husayn at midnight. Mullá Muhammad recalled their conversation, as reported by Nabíl:

[Note: In the following passage a certain Individual by the name of Husayn 'Alí is identified. This is the given name of Bahá'u'lláh.]

> He received me affectionately, and spoke to me with extreme courtesy and tenderness. I unburdened my heart to him, and as I was addressing him, tears, which I could not repress, flowed from my eyes.
>
> [Mullá Husayn asked:]
>
> '...is there to-day among the family of the late Mírzá Buzurg-i-Núrí,[248] who was so renowned for his character, his charm, and artistic and intellectual attainments, anyone who has proved himself capable of maintaining the high traditions of that illustrious house?'
>
> [Mullá Muhammad replied:]
>
> 'Yea, among his sons now living, one has distinguished Himself by the very traits which characterised His father. By His virtuous life, His high attainments, His loving-kindness and liberality, He has proved Himself a noble descendant of a noble father.'
>
> 'What is His occupation?'
>
> 'He cheers the disconsolate and feeds the hungry.'
>
> 'What of His rank and position?'

> 'He has none, apart from befriending the poor and the stranger.'
>
> 'What is His name?'
>
> 'Husayn-'Alí.'…
>
> 'How does He spend His time?'
>
> 'He roams the woods and delights in the beauties of the countryside.'
>
> 'What is His age?'
>
> 'Eight and twenty.'
>
> The eagerness with which Mullá Husayn questioned me, and the sense of delight with which he welcomed every particular I gave him, greatly surprised me. Turning to me, with his face beaming with satisfaction and joy, he once more enquired:
>
> 'I presume you often meet Him?'
>
> 'I frequently visit His home.'
>
> 'Will you deliver into His hands a trust from me?'
>
> 'Most assuredly.'
>
> He then gave me a scroll wrapped in a piece of cloth, and requested me to hand it to Him the next day at the hour of dawn.
>
> 'Should He deign to answer me, will you be kind enough to acquaint me with His reply?'
>
> I received the scroll from him and, at break of day, arose to carry out his desire. – Mullá Muhammad Mu'allim Núrí, a student at the school[249]

Husayn 'Alí, the given name of Bahá'u'lláh, was the name by which He was known at that time. Mírzá Buzurg-i-Núrí, Bahá'u'lláh's father, was a high-ranking nobleman. For some reason, not reported by Nabíl, Mullá Husayn thought to ask about this particular prestigious family.

At dawn the next day, Mullá Muhammad went to the home of Bahá'u'lláh and was greeted by Bahá'u'lláh's brother, Mírzá Músá, who invited him inside. Mullá Muhammad said,

> I was ushered into [Bahá'u'lláh's] presence, and presented the scroll to Mírzá Músá [the brother of Bahá'u'lláh], who laid it before

Bahá'u'lláh. He bade us both be seated. Unfolding the scroll, He glanced at its contents and began to read aloud to us certain of its passages. I sat enraptured as I listened to the sound of His voice and the sweetness of its melody. He had read a page of the scroll when, turning to His brother, He said:

'Músá, what have you to say? Verily I say, whoso believes in the Qur'án and recognizes its Divine origin, and yet hesitates, though it be for a moment, to admit that these soul-stirring words are endowed with the same regenerating power, has most assuredly erred in his judgment and has strayed far from the path of justice.'

He spoke no more. Dismissing me from His presence, He charged me to take to Mullá Husayn, as a gift from Him, a loaf of Russian sugar and a package of tea, and to convey to him the expression of His appreciation and love. – Mullá Muhammad[250]

Mullá Muhammad quickly returned to Mullá Husayn and joyfully gave him the gift and the message from Bahá'u'lláh. Mullá Husayn was overcome with joy.

Words fail me to describe the intensity of his emotion. He started to his feet, received with bowed head the gift from my hand, and fervently kissed it. He then took me in his arms, kissed my eyes, and said:

"My dearly beloved friend! I pray that even as you have rejoiced my heart, God may grant you eternal felicity and fill your heart with imperishable gladness."

I was amazed at the behaviour of Mullá Husayn. What could be, I thought to myself, the nature of the bond that unites these two souls? What could have kindled so fervid a fellowship in their hearts? Why should Mullá Husayn, in whose sight the pomp and circumstance of royalty were the merest trifle, have evinced such gladness at the sight of so inconsiderable a gift from the hands of Bahá'u'lláh? I was puzzled by this thought and could not unravel its mystery. – Mullá Muhammad[251]

Soon after these events, Mullá Husayn departed for Khurásán. As he said farewell to Mullá Muhammad, He said:

> Breathe not to anyone what you have heard and witnessed. Let this be a secret hidden within your breast. Divulge not His name, for they who envy His position will arise to harm Him. In your moments of meditation, pray that the Almighty may protect Him, that, through Him, He may exalt the downtrodden, enrich the poor, and redeem the fallen. The secret of things is concealed from our eyes. Ours is the duty to raise the call of the New Day and to proclaim this Divine Message unto all people. Many a soul will, in this city, shed his blood in this path. That blood will water the Tree of God, will cause it to flourish, and to overshadow all mankind. – Mullá Husayn to Mullá Muhammad[252]

Bahá'u'lláh begins His teaching efforts, quickly distinguishes Himself

Soon after accepting the Báb's Revelation, Bahá'u'lláh set out for the province of Mázindarán, north of Tihrán. His home region of Núr, which means 'Light', was in Mázindarán. In that place, in a short time, Bahá'u'lláh was highly successful in bringing many, many souls into the Faith of the Báb. Here are two of His encounters.

One day, Bahá'u'lláh and some traveling companions came upon a disheveled man, wearing the attire of a dervish. By a brook he had lit a fire and was cooking his food. Bahá'u'lláh lovingly approached him and asked what he was doing. He bluntly replied,

> I am engaged in eating God. I am cooking God and am burning Him.

Bahá'u'lláh was touched by the unpretentious sincerity of this man, so He sat with Him by the side of the road. They talked for a long time. With extreme patience, loving-kindness and eloquence, Bahá'u'lláh opened this man's mind to the true nature of God. In a short time, Bahá'u'lláh had changed him completely. The man, in his part, was so filled with joy and happiness that he left behind his cooking equipment and followed Bahá'u'lláh to Mázindarán singing His praises and composing poems in His honor as they walked. One of his poems became popular in later years:

> Thou art the Day-Star of guidance, Thou art the Light of Truth.
>
> Unveil Thyself to men, O Revealer of the Truth.

Few understood that the object of the poem had been Bahá'u'lláh, and that this lonely dervish had "recognized His station and discovered His glory".[253]

Another time, Bahá'u'lláh was walking by a religious school. The teacher was speaking to a gathering of over two hundred students and asked the students to answer a complex theological question. When none of the students could answer, Bahá'u'lláh asked if He might answer. He then gave a clear, concise and lucid explanation. The teacher was very annoyed.

> For years I have been instructing you … and yet you allow, after all these years of persistent study, this youth … who has no share in scholarly training, and who is entirely unfamiliar with your academic learning, to demonstrate his superiority over you! – Mírzá Muhammad Taqíy-i-Núrí, the teacher of the religious school[254]

After Bahá'u'lláh had gone on His way, the teacher told his disciples that he had experienced some significant dreams concerning Bahá'u'lláh before that day. In one of these dreams, he saw boxes filled with books belonging to Bahá'u'lláh. He stated,

> Every word and letter recorded in these books was set with the most exquisite jewels. Their radiance dazzled me. I was so overpowered by their brilliance that I awoke suddenly from my dream. – Mírzá Muhammad Taqíy-i-Núrí, the teacher of the religious school[255]

Through encounters such as these Bahá'u'lláh attracted much attention. "Ecclesiastical dignitaries, State officials, traders, and peasants all flocked to the residence of Bahá'u'lláh. A considerable number among them willingly espoused the Báb's Cause."[256]

One who did not approve was 'Azíz, one of Bahá'u'lláh's uncles. He went to the leading religious authority of Núr and complained:

> A youth, a layman, attired in the garb of nobility[257] has come to Núr,[258] has invaded the strongholds of orthodoxy, and disrupted the holy Faith of Islám. Arise and resist his onslaught. Whoever attains his presence falls immediately under his spell, and is enthralled by the power of his utterance. I know not whether he is a sorcerer, or whether he mixes with his tea some mysterious substance that makes every man who drinks the tea fall a victim to its charm. – 'Azíz, Bahá'u'lláh's uncle[259]

The leader jokingly asked, "Have you not partaken of his tea?" Replying with all seriousness, the uncle said yes, but he had remained immune. This religious leader was not willing to confront so beloved a Citizen, so he offered 'Azíz no assistance. Bahá'u'lláh was free to continue His activities.[260] Nabíl writes:

> Bahá'u'lláh's visit to Núr had produced the most far-reaching results and had lent a remarkable impetus to the spread of the new-born Revelation. By His magnetic eloquence, by the purity of His life, by the dignity of His bearing, by the unanswerable logic of His argument, and by the many evidences of His loving-kindness, Bahá'u'lláh had won the hearts of the people of Núr, had stirred their souls, and had enrolled them under the standard of the Faith. Such was the effect of words and deeds, as He went about preaching the Cause and revealing its glory to His countrymen in Núr, that the very stones and trees of that district seemed to have been quickened by the waves of spiritual power which emanated from His person. – Nabíl[261]

Figure 16 Muhammad Sháh Qájár and Hájí Mírzá Áqásí

Mullá Husayn meets the Prime Minister and other tasks

With the discovery of Bahá'u'lláh, Mullá Husayn was satisfied that he had found the great Secret which the Báb promised he would find in Tihrán. However, Mullá Husayn's work in Tihrán was not completed. The Báb had given him another important task – to deliver the Báb's messages to Muhammad Sháh, the King of Persia, and to his Prime Minister, Hájí Mírzá Áqásí.

According to Mázindarání, Mullá Husayn was able to gain an audience with the Prime Minister. The following is paraphrased from the Persian by Mázindarání.

> Then Mullá Husayn and his companions met with Hájí Mírzá Áqásí, the well-known minister who was the teacher and the spiritual guide of Muhammad Sháh. He presented an invitation and some Tablets from the Báb. Áqásí, who considered himself a person on the path of truth, had full control over the affairs [of the country]. He was opposed to the Akhbárí and Shaykhí religious leaders. When he became aware of the Báb's address to him and the king, especially in the Báb's Commentary on the Surih of Joseph, he began to oppose the Báb and he did not give the Tablets of the Báb to the king.—Mázindarání[262]

Upon reading the Báb's Words, Áqásí began to perceive the claims and greatness of the Cause of the Báb, and to feel afraid. From his actions, it is clear that he believed that the Báb, if ever given the chance, would replace Him as spiritual guide to the Sháh. What then would happen to him? Given that Áqásí was mainly motivated to serve himself, one can at least fathom the reasons for his fearful reaction. Consider these two passages from that commentary:

> All praise be to God Who hath, through the power of Truth, sent down this Book unto His servant, that it may serve as a shining light for all mankind... Verily this is none other than the sovereign Truth; it is the Path which God hath laid out for all that are in heaven and on earth. Let him then who will, take for himself the right path unto his Lord... This is the Mystery which hath been hidden from all that are in heaven and on earth, and in this wondrous Revelation it hath, in very truth, been set forth in the Mother Book by the hand of God, the Exalted... O concourse of kings and of the sons of kings! Lay aside, one and all, your dominion

which belongeth unto God... Let not thy sovereignty deceive thee, O Sháh, for 'every soul shall taste of death,' and this, in very truth, hath been written down as a decree of God. – The Báb[263]

O Minister of the Sháh! Fear thou God, besides Whom there is none other God but Him, the Sovereign Truth, the Just, and lay aside thy dominion, for We, by the leave of God, the All-Wise, inherit the earth and all who are upon it, and He shall rightfully be a witness unto thee and unto the Sháh. Were ye to obey the Remembrance of God with absolute sincerity, We guarantee, by the leave of God, that on the Day of Resurrection, a vast dominion shall be yours in His eternal Paradise. Vain indeed is your dominion, for God hath set aside earthly possessions for such as have denied Him; for unto Him Who is your Lord shall be the most excellent abode, He Who is, in truth, the Ancient of Days... – The Báb[264]

From this moment, Áqásí was a vehement opponent of the Báb and His followers. Áqásí decided not to share with the Sháh the information given to him by Mullá Husayn. Intimidated by Mullá Husayn's fearless presentation of the Message, he blocked Mullá Husayn from meeting the Sháh. His agitation was so great that other servants of the court privately informed Mullá Husayn that his safety was in jeopardy if he remained long in Tihrán. They advised him to leave the city soon. As he had further to go on his assigned journey, Mullá Husayn was willing to go. But before he did, Mullá Husayn was able to invite eighteen key people of the King's court to the Faith and give them copies of the Báb's Writings. One can only wonder if the Writings of the Báb quietly reached the Sháh at this time through the agency of one of these other key people at court.

Rizá Khán, the son of the Sháh's Stable Master, is one individual who was influenced by Mullá Husayn. The following is paraphrased from the Persian by Mázindarání.

[Rizá Khán] was one of the known Bábís of Tihrán. He was a handsome youth with good character and a unique courage. He lived in Tihrán with grandure, fame, power and wealth. His father[265] was in the court of Muhammad Sháh, working as his Stable Master, and he owned several palaces and lived in opulence. He became a believer through Mullá Husayn and others when they raised the Call of the Báb in Tihrán. He arose with love to assist and support the believers. His house was the gathering place of the friends. By virtue of his power, courage and position, and due to the respect given to his father, he did not have fear. [Later on,] he was courageous in

> the village of Kulayn, at the city of Bárfurúsh, during the Mashhad upheaval, at [the conference of] Badasht, and then upon his ultimate martyrdom at Shaykh Tabarsí. – Mázindaráni[266]

Despite the Prime Minister's obstruction, Mullá Husayn achieved great results during his trip to Tihrán. Mullá Husayn and his traveling companions left Tihrán and continued their efforts to propagate the Faith.[267]

Mullá Husayn set his feet toward Khurásán, a province in the north-east of Persia. Heading east, he came first to the town of Sabzivár and then Níshápúr before arriving at Mashhad, the largest city of Khurásán province, near the eastern border of Iran. His visit to Sabzivár was brief. He would not stay for the night, but only stayed long enough to have dinner and tea before moving on.

Mullá Husayn went to Níshápúr next, where he had a significant impact. According to the French scholar Gobineau, Mullá Husayn achieved two significant conversions in Níshápúr. One man, Mullá 'Abdu'l-Kháliq, a student of Shaykh Ahmad, was noted for his knowledge of science, his eloquence, and the respect he received from the people. The other man, Mullá 'Alí, was known for his ethics and deep understanding, and served as the city's chief religious leader, a lofty position. Both men became ardent Bábís. They took to the pulpits in the mosques and spoke forcefully against the old religion. Over several weeks, the old religion seemed to be defeated. The other religious leaders, observing the defection of their chief and frightened by the public addresses which criticized them, either refused to face them or fled the area.[268]

Mullá 'Abdu'l-Kháliq had been the teacher in Shíráz to whom the Báb's uncles had turned to make a second attempt at furthering the Báb's education. The teacher assigned his son to teach the Báb; the son came back to his father whining that he did not want to teach Him. Now, in Níshápúr, this man had become a devoted Bábí. 'Abdu'l-Kaliq's son also became a Bábí and later a martyr at the upheaval of Shaykh Tabarsí. 'Abdu'l-Kháliq's faith was tested later in Tihrán. He received a Tablet from the Báb which expressed the Báb's claim to a greater station than the Gate to the 12th Imám, and he found himself unable to accept it. He emphatically protested and turned away from his faith in the Báb.[269]

As a result of such controversies, Mullá Husayn's next destination, Mashhad, was already in turmoil when he arrived. On the one hand, the clergy were anxious about his arrival. On the other hand, they were determined to resist Mullá Husayn's efforts. Despite the unstable conditions, several of the eminent scholars of that city, mostly from among the ranks of the Shaykhís, embraced the Cause of the Báb.

Mullá Husayn reports back to the Báb

After these victories, and after arriving in Mashhad, it was time to send a report to the Báb in Búshihr.

> In his communication he referred at length to his sojourn in Isfahán and Káshán, described the account of his experience with Bahá'u'lláh, referred to the departure of the latter for Mázindarán, related the events of Núr, and informed Him of the success which had attended his efforts in Khurásán. In it he enclosed a list of the names of those who had responded to his call, and of whose steadfastness and sincerity he was assured. – Nabíl[270]

Before sending Mullá Husayn out on his mission, He told him:

> Not until I receive your letter from Khurásán shall I be ready to set out from this city on My pilgrimage... – The Báb[271]

According to Nabíl, the letter was sent "by way of Yazd, through the trustworthy partners of the Báb's maternal uncle who were at that time residing in Tabas."[272] Thus, the route of the letter was Mashhad – Tabas – Yazd – Shíráz – Búshihr, which is 1096 miles.

When the Báb received the report, it contained all the vital information He needed. It told of the many people who had joyfully embraced the Cause, including the wonderful news of Bahá'u'lláh's enrollment as a new believer and the beginning of His service as an excellent teacher of the Bábí Faith. Quddús was with the Báb when the report was received, and they both expressed the greatest joy and happiness. Nabíl reports:

> The only companion of the Báb, when that letter reached Him that night, was Quddús, with whom He shared a number of its passages... The Báb's maternal uncle himself described ... the circumstances attending the receipt of Mullá Husayn's letter by the Báb:
>
> 'That night I saw such evidences of joy and gladness on the faces of the Báb and of Quddús as I am unable to describe... As He was reading the communication addressed to Him by Mullá Husayn, He turned to Quddús and, showing him certain passages of that letter, explained the reason for His joyous expressions of surprise...'

> [Mírzá Ahmad, who related this to Nabíl, commented that this story convinced him] "...that in the city of Tihrán there lay hidden a Mystery which, when revealed to the world, would bring unspeakable joy to the hearts of both the Báb and Quddús. – Nabíl[273]

The astonishing speed of Mullá Husayn's travels

Let's pause to make one more observation concerning the initial expansion phase of the young Bábí Faith. The astonishing speed with which it occurred was based on the exceptional dedication of the Letters of the Living as they carried out their assigned missions.

We have some hard data to work with. We know, from various historical sources, the exact dates when certain actions took place. For example, we know the following timeline facts:

- The timeline of the Faith begins on the evening of May 22, 1844, at two hours and eleven minutes after sunset, when the Báb declared His mission to Mullá Husayn.
- The month in the Islámic calendar when Bahá'u'lláh received the message from Mullá Husayn.
- The date Mullá Husayn left Tihrán for Mashhad.
- The date the Báb left Shíráz for Búshihr.
- The date the Báb arrived in Búshihr.
- The date the Báb in Búshihr received the letter from Mullá Husayn.
- The date the Báb departed Búshihr for Mecca.

In addition to the above timeline facts, the historical sources also say that Mullá Husayn was in relatively poor health, possibly with a heart condition.

Using these facts, we can make reasonable estimates regarding other dates and thereby construct a *plausible* timeline for this entire period. With this construct, we can mathematically calculate a reasonable estimate of the speed of Mullá Husayn's travel and the movement of his letter to the Báb.[274]

It is important to stress that these calculations are a hypothesis derived from partial historical information and should not be taken as firmly established. Rather, they offer an estimate of what possibly or probably happened. Future research will determine the accuracy of this estimate.

Hopefully, the aim of this constructed timeline will be achieved even if the calculations are ultimately proven by future scholars to be off a day or two. That aim is to demonstrate the extreme speed of Mullá Husayn's travel, the rapidity of his accomplishments, his extraordinary dedication and his seemingly superhuman endurance.

<table>
<tr><th>Event/ Explanation</th><th>Gregorian Date</th><th>Islámic date[275]</th><th>Sources of information</th></tr>
<tr><td colspan="4">The timeline of the Faith begins May 22, 1844 AD.</td></tr>
<tr><td>The Báb declares His mission to Mullá Husayn in Shíráz</td><td>The night of May 22, 1844.</td><td>Jamádíyu'l-Av-val 4, 1260.</td><td>All histories of the Faith report this information. See Shoghi Effendi, GPB & Nabíl.</td></tr>
<tr><td colspan="4">The Báb states that for 40 days Mullá Husayn was the only believer in the Cause. So, we must add 40 days.</td></tr>
<tr><td>Period of no new believers</td><td>July 1, 1844, calcu-lated as +40 days)</td><td>Jamádíy'th-Thání 14, 1260 (calculated as +40 days)</td><td>Nabíl, p. 66; Perigord, p. 8; A. Amanat, p. 175.</td></tr>
<tr><td colspan="4">Given that the Báb says there are no new believers for 40 days, we assume the next believer was on the 41st day. So, we must add 1 day.</td></tr>
<tr><td>The 2nd believer, Mullá 'Alí Bastámí, is enrolled in the Faith.</td><td>July 2, 1844, (calcu-lated as +1 day)</td><td>Jamádíy'th-Thání 15, 1260 (calculated as +1 day)</td><td>This is a calculated date.</td></tr>
<tr><td colspan="4">How long does it take for the remaining Letters of the Living, including Quddús and Táhirih, to be enrolled? Quddús, the youngest, was the 18th and last Letter. I assume all the Letters must have been enrolled no later than 14 days after Bastámí was enrolled because (in the next row) the Báb was going to need to spend some time with them as a group so they would be able to teach the Faith. It must have been quite a crash course!
We will add 14 days as an estimate.</td></tr>
<tr><td>The remaining 16 Letters of the Liv-ing are enrolled.</td><td>July 16, 1844, (calculated as +14 days)</td><td>Jamádíy'th-Thání 29, 1260 (calculated as +14 days)</td><td>This is an estimated calcu-lation.</td></tr>
</table>

<table>
<tr><th>Event/ Explanation</th><th>Gregorian Date</th><th>Islámic date[275]</th><th>Sources of information</th></tr>
<tr><td colspan="4">How long were the 17 Letters all together in Shíráz? (Táhirih was not present in Shíráz.)
The Báb needed to have some time with the Letters to prepare them for their missions to go out and teach the Faith, but the time available to be together could not have been too much because Mullá Husayn had to get on the road. We know he arrives in Tihrán by a certain point in time, about 8 August. He will be traveling on foot. If he doesn't leave soon, he won't get there by the date recorded in the history books!
We will add 8 days as our best guess.</td></tr>
<tr><td>Mullá Husayn leaves Shíráz.</td><td>July 24, 1844 (calculated as +8 days)</td><td>Rajab 8, 1260 (calculated as +8 days)</td><td>This is an estimated calculation.</td></tr>
<tr><td colspan="4">Baraqi says Mullá Husayn arrived in Tihrán towards the latter part of the month of Rajab. He also mentions that that the Báb stated that Bahá'u'lláh received Mullá Husayn's message in Tihrán during the latter part of the month of Rajab. Therefore, to have time in Tihrán to get the message to Bahá'u'lláh also in Rajab, he cannot have arrived on the last day of Rajab. It is reasonable therefore to estimate that he arrived near the end of the month, as Baraqi indicates, but not at the end of the month. For this reason, I estimate his arrival to occur around the 23rd of Rajab, which is the 8th of August.

On foot, the journey is 544 miles.[276] From July 24 to August 8 is 15 days.

Therefore, to estimate the date of his arrival in Tihrán, we will add 15 days.

We also know that momentous teaching activities took place en route to Tihrán – especially in Isfahán, Káshán and Qum. For example, Mullá Husayn taught Mullá Sadiq in Isfahán. It is obviously necessary to assume that Mullá Husayn is not walking between cities when he is in one of the cities teaching. So how many days did he spend teaching in those cities?

If we assume 5 days in those cities teaching the Faith, then only 10 days are available for walking the distance between Shíráz and Tihrán.

Now we can calculate Mullá Husayn's estimated walking speed. 544 miles in 10 days equals 54.4 miles per day.</td></tr>
<tr><td>Mullá Husayn arrives in Tihrán</td><td>August 8, 1844 (calculated as +15 days)</td><td>Rajab 23, 1260 (calculated as +15 days)</td><td>Baraqi, p. 73, 76.

Although based on information from Baraqi, this is an estimated calculation.</td></tr>
</table>

<table>
<tr><th>Event/ Explanation</th><th>Gregorian Date</th><th>Islámic date[275]</th><th>Sources of information</th></tr>
<tr><td>Bahá'u'lláh receives message from Mullá Husayn</td><td>August 11, 1844 (estimated)</td><td>Rajab 26, 1260 (estimated)</td><td>Baraqi, p. 76; Nabíl, p. 127-128
According to Baraqi, the Báb mentions that Bahá'u'lláh received the message from Mullá Husayn near the end of the month of Rajab.</td></tr>
<tr><td colspan="4">How long did Mullá Husayn stay in Tihrán? It must have been a while because he had enough time to reach out to Bahá'u'lláh, gain an audience with the Prime Minister and teach many souls in the court of the Sháh. He was very busy during this time!
As far as this writer knows, the historical sources do not give a specific date for Mullá Husayn's departure from Tihrán, but we do know Mullá Husayn's arrival date in Mashhad – September 7th! Therefore, we will attempt to estimate his departure date based on the previously calculated rate of speed.
The trip from Tihrán to Mashhad is 612 miles.[277] At an estimated pace of 54.4 miles per day, Mullá Husayn would need a minimum of 11 days for walking between the two cities. If we subtract 11 days from the 7th of September we get the 27th of August. This gives an estimate that he should have left Tihrán no later than the August 27, 1844.
If this calculation is correct – and we must remind the reader that this is only a calculated estimate – then he would have spent about 19 days total in Tihrán.</td></tr>
<tr><td>Mullá Husayn leaves Tihrán</td><td>August 27, 1844 (calculated as -11 days from September 7th)</td><td>Sha'bán 12, 1260 (calculated as -11 days from Sha'bán 23)</td><td>This is an estimated calculation.</td></tr>
<tr><td>Mullá Husayn arrives in Mashhad</td><td>September 7, 1844</td><td>Sha'bán 23, 1260</td><td>Baraqi, p. 75
Baraqi says Mullá Husayn arrived in Mashhad at the latter part of the month of Sha'ban. Baraqi also says Mulla Husayn's total journey from Shiraz to his arrival to Mashhad was 45 days. This gives an estimated arrival date of September 7, 1844.</td></tr>
</table>

<table>
<tr><th>Event/ Explanation</th><th>Gregorian Date</th><th>Islámic date[275]</th><th>Sources of information</th></tr>
<tr><td>The Báb leaves Shíráz for Búshihr</td><td>September 10, 1844</td><td>Sha'bán 26, 1260</td><td>Husaini #1, p. 232; Faizi, p. 132

Nabíl, p. 129 says that the Báb departed Shíráz in October 1844. Since the Báb receives the letter in Búshihr on September 30th, this is impossible.</td></tr>
<tr><td>The Báb arrives in Búshihr</td><td>September 19, 1844</td><td>Ramadán 6, 1260</td><td>Husaini #1, p. 232; Faizi, p. 132</td></tr>
<tr><td colspan="4">How much time does Mullá Husayn spend teaching the Faith in Mashhad before sending his report to the Báb in Búshihr? And how long did the letter take to get to the Báb in Búshihr. This is not reported in the historical sources, but we do know when the Báb received the letter in Bushihr.

When he arrived in Mashhad in early September, he immediately began propagating the new Faith, and this led a group of people to embrace the Cause.[278]

According to Nabíl, Mullá Husayn sent his report "by way of Yazd, through the trustworthy partners of the Báb's maternal uncle who were at that time residing in Tabas." Thus, the route of the letter was Mashhad – Tabas – Yazd – Shíráz – Bushihr, which is 1096 miles.[279] They probably used the local postal service which, by changing horses periodically, were able to cover greater distances.

The letter arrived in Bushihr on 30 September.

So, when did he send it?

If he spends 10 days teaching in Mashhad (an estimate), then he would have had to send the letter on September 17. This would give the letter 13 days to go 1,096 miles and arrive on the 30th of September.

The letter would have to travel a stunning 84.3 miles per day. So perhaps it was sent even sooner.</td></tr>
<tr><td>Mullá Husayn sends his written report to the Báb in Búshihr.</td><td>September 17, 1844 (calculated as +10 days from September 7th)</td><td>Ramadán 4, 1260 (calculated as +10 days from Sha'bán 23)</td><td>This is an estimated calculation.</td></tr>
</table>

Event/ Explanation	Gregorian Date	Islámic date[275]	Sources of information
Mullá Husayn's letter reaches the Báb in Búshihr	September 30, 1844	Ramadán 17, 1260	Baraqi, p. 75 Baraqi mentions that the letter arrived early at night. He says that Quddús, and the Báb's uncle, Siyyid 'Alí, were present. Baraqi, p. 173, in a footnote, indicates that Nabíl says the letter arrived October 9th. See Nabíl, p. 126, 129 for this discrepancy. Nabíl cannot be correct in this instance because he has the letter arriving in Búshihr after the Báb has already departed Búshihr. Nabíl also errs when he states the Báb received the letter in Shíráz.
The Báb leaves Búshihr for His pilgrimage to Mecca	October 2, 1844	Ramadán 19, 1260	Shoghi Effendi, *GPB*, p. 9; Baraqi, p. 75; Husaini #1, p. 232; Faizi, p. 132 Baraqi says the Báb left two days later, after receiving the report from Mullá Husayn. Husaini #1 quotes a tablet of the Báb stating the departure occurred on the 19th of Ramadán.

Mullá Husayn's speed of travel suggests that he must have pushed himself very, very hard on his travel days. Mehrabkhani states that "he abandoned rest and sleep, travelling day and night". Mehrabkhani adds: "If he maintained such a pace, he must have crossed extraordinary distances in far fewer days than normally required."[280]

This discussion is not limited to a mere computation of multiplying speed times time. If Mullá Husayn actually walked at the calculated pace of 54.4 miles per day, how many hours per day would he have been actually walking? If he walked at an *above average* human walking speed of

4.5 miles per hour, he would have to walk for no less than 12 hours each day when he is walking between cities. This calculation does not include time for stopping for rest, prayers, water, eating or relieving himself. And even if he could do it for one day, the idea that this frail man did not succumb to exhaustion and that he was able to maintain this pace day after day seems quite astounding. And then to think that when he arrived in a city after such a long trek that he was fresh and ready to teach the Faith with the vigour he obviously demonstrated appears to border on the miraculous.

The loving dedication and the physical endurance required to achieve all this activity is most impressive. Candidly, it is hard to believe that it really happened because Mullá Husayn, in particular, was known to be physically frail, tremulous, and possibly suffering with heart problems. Nevertheless, the facts speak for themselves. The mere fact that Mullá Husayn accomplished so many teaching victories, overcame so much opposition, and covered such vast distances in such a short period of time, exhibiting an apparent superhuman endurance, is surely a notable achievement in the annals of religious history and a testament to his indefatigable faith.

THE BÁB'S PILGRIMAGE TO MECCA

The Báb decides to go

The journey to Arabia held many dangers, both physical and social. In the Báb's time and in His part of the world, there were no fast transportation vehicles, such as cars, buses, trains, or airplanes. The only options for a long journey were to walk on foot, ride on the back of an animal, or travel by sea. The Báb used all three modes of transport during His nearly year-long journey. Each had its risks. While traveling on foot one was vulnerable to attack by robbers, and waves and storms at sea could be treacherous. Socially, the Báb was fully aware that by making a bold spiritual claim to be the Promised One, awaited by all Islám, He was putting His life in danger. He knew he was setting in motion events which could only result in vehement and violent opposition to Him and His followers.

The Báb was waiting to confirm that the Cause He had launched would be in good Hands and able to survive His death, should some disaster occur while en route. The report from Mullá Husayn gave the Báb precisely the confirmation He wanted. Now that Bahá'u'lláh had enthusiastically entered the fold, the Báb knew that no matter what happened, Bahá'u'lláh's masterful Hand would guide the infant Bábí community, and that the Cause would flourish despite the obstacles it would inevitably encounter. Nabíl reports:

> [In the following quotes, Núr, which is north of Tihrán, was the hometown of Bahá'u'lláh. Nabíl speaks of "pilgrimage to Hijáz". Hijáz is the region in western Arabia from which Muhammad had come and it is the region where Mecca and Medina, the key cities of Islámic pilgrimage, are located. The Ethiopian servant mentioned is Mubárak.]

> The letter of Mullá Husayn decided the Báb to undertake His contemplated pilgrimage to Hijáz... Quddús was His only companion, and the Ethiopian servant His personal attendant. – Nabíl[281]

> The references in Mullá Husayn's letter to Bahá'u'lláh's immediate response to the Divine Message, to the vigorous campaign which He had boldly initiated in Núr, and to the marvellous success which had attended His efforts, cheered and gladdened the Báb, and reinforced His confidence in the ultimate victory of His Cause. He felt assured that if now He were to fall suddenly a victim to the tyranny of His foes and depart from this world, the Cause which He had revealed would live; would, under the direction of Bahá'u'lláh, continue to develop and flourish, and would yield eventually its choicest fruit. The master-hand of Bahá'u'lláh would steer its course, and the pervading influence of His love would establish it in the hearts of men. Such a conviction fortified His spirit and filled Him with hope. From that moment His fears of the imminence of peril or danger entirely forsook Him. Phoenix-like He welcomed with joy the fire of adversity, and gloried in the glow and heat of its flame. – Nabíl[282]

In Persian society at the time, women of the family needed to be under the protection of a man. The Báb found it necessary to place both His mother and His wife in the care of His maternal uncle, Hájí Mírzá Siyyid 'Alí. This is like giving the uncle benevolent legal guardianship. The historical record demonstrates that Siyyid 'Alí took his responsibilities seriously.

The journey itself

The Báb departed from Shíráz on September 9, 1844.[283] His route to Mecca was:

Portion of route	Mode of travel
• Shíráz to Búshihr	Over land
• Búshihr to Musqat ○ With a brief stop in Kangen	By sea
• Musqat to Jaddih	By sea
• Jaddih to Mecca	Over land
• Mecca to Medina	Over land
• And the journey home was the same in reverse.	

Figure 17 The Bab's route on foot and by sea to Mecca

The travelers began by heading southwest from Shíráz to the port city of Búshihr. Mullá Husayn's letter reached them in Búshihr. They waited for a ship and departed Búshihr on a sailing vessel on October 2, 1844.[284] Traveling south through the Persian Gulf, they stopped briefly in Kangen and then exited the Gulf into the Indian Ocean and soon arrived at their next destination, the city of Musqat, at the southeastern corner of Arabia. They tarried in Musqat for several days, and then continued on their journey by sea, sailing in dangerous open waters around the coast of Arabia. Their ship, turning north, entered the Red Sea and arrived at Jaddih, their entry point into the western region of Arabia, the Hijáz. From there, they treked over land to Mecca, where their pilgrimage would begin.[285] Shoghi Effendi states:

> Landing at Jaddih after a stormy voyage of over a month's duration, He donned the pilgrim's garb, mounted a camel, and set out for Mecca, arriving on [December 12th, 1844]. Quddús, holding the bridle in his hands, accompanied his Master on foot to that holy Shrine. – Shoghi Effendi[286]

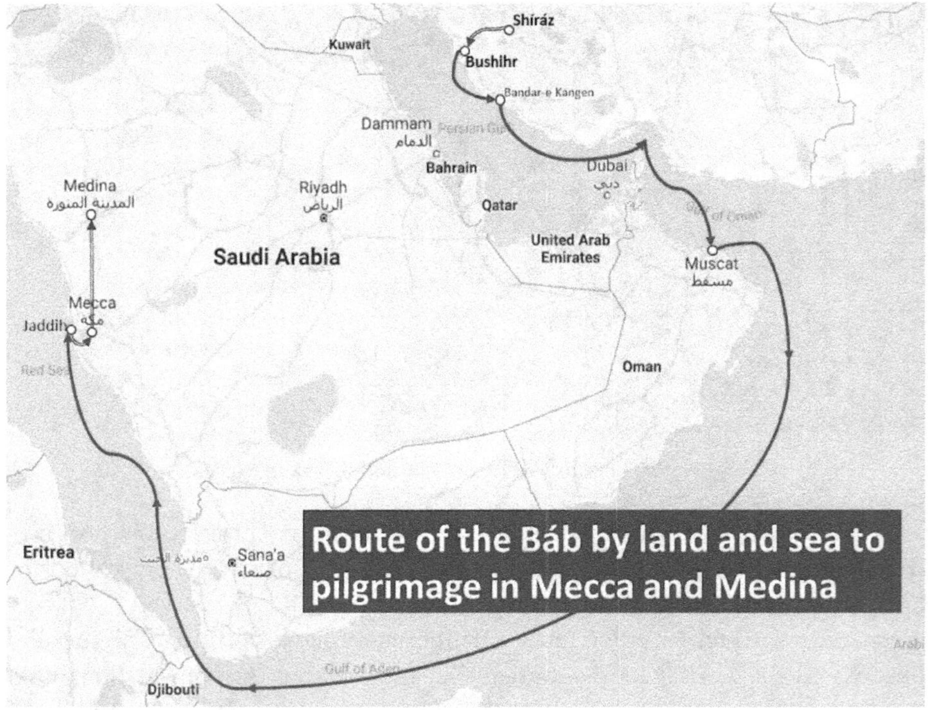

Figure 18 The Báb's pilgrimage journey from Shíráz to Búshihr to Musqat to Jaddih to Mecca

Nabíl only mentions that the Báb was accompanied by Quddús and Mubárak. There is more information to report, however. Given the many months of the journey it is not surprising that other sources indicate that a number of individuals intersected with or shared parts of the Báb's pilgrimage journey, and events along the way. A large crowd went to Mecca that year. More than 70,000 pilgrims were in attendance, including Arabs, Turks, Iranians, Kurds and Indians.[287] Faizi describes the reason for such a large number of pilgrims. The following is paraphrased from the Persian by Faizi.

> In that year, in the sight of the Muslims visiting the Ka'bih it was considered especially important. There was also the hope that the expected Promised One might make His appearance there as well. Therefore, the number of pilgrims that year was more than in previous years. – Faizi[288]

Meir Litvak made a similar observation:

In fact, 1260 AH/1844-45 AD, the millennium of the Twelfth Imám's Occultation, witnessed a record number of pilgrims, due to the heightened messianic expectations in the Shí'i world. – Meir Litvak[289]

Many encounters along the way

We will briefly mention some of the individuals with whom the Báb interacted:

- Siyyid Javád Muharrí Isfahání
- Muhammad Rizá of Isfahán
- Muhammad Rizá of Káshán, also known as Makhmal-Báf
- Abu'l-Hasan-i-Shírází, also called Abu'l-Hasan-i-Bazzáz (the mercer)
- Mírzá Jání
- Siyyid Ja'far Kashfí
- Sulaymán Khán
- The ulema (i.e. religious leaders) of Musqat

Siyyid Javád Muharrí Isfahání

Siyyid Javád Muharrí Isfahání was a scribe, about 38 years old, and a Shaykhí, who learned of the Faith from Mullá Sádiq in Isfahán. He may have had an earlier encounter with Mullá Husayn when the latter came to Isfahán. Javád had been very interested in the rising expectations concerning the prophesied appearance of the Promised One in the year 1260 AH (1844 AD). He had even consulted an expert astronomer for guidance on how to find the Promised One.

When he heard of the Faith, he rushed to Shíráz to meet with the Báb personally. Unfortunately, when he arrived, he discovered that the Báb had already departed for Búshihr on His pilgrimage. He then went to Búshihr, only to discover he had arrived too late. The Báb was already on the boat to Musqat. Determined to chase after the Báb, Javád got on the next available boat and followed the Báb to Musqat. As we know, the Báb tarried there for a few days. This enabled Javád to catch up with Him.

Upon arrival, Javád changed his clothes, performed ablutions, and washed in preparation for meeting the Báb. When he entered the room at the home of the Vali, the local governor, he saw that the Vali, the Báb and Mubárak were present. Mubárak was fanning the room, due to the heat. The Báb courteously gave him permission to sit down and join the gathering. As Javád was sitting, the Báb moved His turban slightly, making visible a small mole on His forehead, which Javád observed. Islámic tradition had in fact predicted this small mark on the forehead of the Promised One.[290] Javád took this as a small first sign that he had found the Promised One.

During one of their encounters, Javád asked the Báb what is the proper path to gain recognition of Him, the Promised One? The Báb asked, how did you recognize Shaykh Ahmad and Siyyid Kázim? Javád answered by saying through being with each other, companionship. The Báb replied that it would be the same way with Him as well. Javád continued to be with the Báb during the journey to Jaddih and Mecca, and then on the return trip as far as Búshihr. During the trip, he met with the Báb several times. All these encounters increased his faith, attraction, commitment and understanding of the Báb. After separating from the Báb in Búshihr, he went to Basrih, Karbilá and then back to Isfahán. In these locations, he constantly described and praised the Báb. This persistent action led the opponents of the Faith to make him a target of persecution.[291]

Muhammad Rizá of Isfahán

When the Báb was in Karbilá, Muhammad Rizá was a merchant in Baghdád and Isfahán. The year before, Rizá, then living in Baghdád, had a dream about the Báb. In the dream, the Báb offered him His tender affection, and promised that Rizá would be with him during His pilgrimage to Mecca. Now, after encountering Him in Karbilá, and with the pilgrimage journey underway, Rizá found himself joining the Báb for part of His pilgrimage to Mecca. After the pilgrimage, Rizá returned to Persia. Wherever he went throughout Persia, he taught the Faith, talking about the perfections and spiritual station of the Báb. In 1850, he was cast into the horrible, infamous Black Pit dungeon prison in Tihrán. Eventually surviving the ordeal, he was released, but in 1852, he was arrested again and ultimately killed.[292]

Muhammad Rizá of Káshán, also known as Makhmal-Báf

Makhmal-Báf met the Báb during the pilgrimage to Mecca and Medina. His attraction to the Faith began with one glance from the Báb. He was responsible for bringing the first Zoroastrian convert into the Faith. The following is paraphrased from the Persian by Mázindarání.

> Muhammad Rizá, known as Makhmal-Báf, a reputable and dignified merchant of Káshán, attained the presence of the Blessed Báb in that year during the pilgrimage. With one glance from Him he became attracted to His beauty and he said to companions: "I swear by God, this illumined Youth is either the Imám or His deputy". And everywhere that he saw Him, it only added to his attraction and love. When he came to His presence in Medina, he attained to the station of faith. With that state of mind, he subsequently returned to Káshán, and became a target of the religious leaders, the rulers and the people. – Mázindarání[293]

The story of Makhmal-Báf helps to demonstrate the way the Faith was spread. Numerous people encountered the Báb during His pilgrimage journey. Many of them were profoundly affected by His holiness and spirituality, impressed by His manner, and inspired by His Revelation. After such encounters they went home and began to talk about their experiences with family and friends. Some, like Makhmal Báf, became targets of oppression, and this attracted more conversions to the Faith. The following is paraphrased from the Persian by Mázindarání.

> Makhmal-Báf of Káshán was attacked by the people of Káshán at the instigation of the religious leaders and the governmental [agents]. They attacked his house and took him to the seat of the government. They tied his feet and beat them, they took off his clothes and covered his face and body with mud. They hung him upside down and tied his hands to the tail of a donkey and dragged him through the streets and the bazaar of Káshán. A large crowd of people watched. A few spat on him and cursed him. At this time, one man, Bahman Púr-Kávús, a Zoroastrian, who was in his shop, came out and recognized him. Since he was aware of Makhmal-Báf's religiosity, affluence, wisdom and perception, he began to search [for the truth] about the Faith and became a believer. He was the first person among Zoroastrians who became a Bábí and now his descendants are known [as members of the Faith as well]…" – Mázindarání[294]

'Abdu'l-Bahá discusses the story of Makhmal-Báf. He explains that at one point the Prime Minister, without authorization from the Sháh, issued orders for a widespread persecution of the believers. Further elaborating on the example of Makhmal-Báf, He states:

> …he [the Prime Minister] issued orders to persecute the Bábís, imagining that by overweening force he could eradicate and suppress matters

of this nature ... whereas (in fact) to interfere with matters of conscience is simply to give them greater currency and strength; the more you strive to extinguish the more will the flame be kindled, more especially in matters of faith and religion, which spread and acquire influence so soon as blood is shed, and strongly affect men's hearts... Thus they relate that the possessions of a certain Bábí in Káshán were plundered, and his household scattered and dispersed. They stripped him naked and scourged him, defiled his beard, mounted him face backwards on an ass, and paraded him through the streets and bazaars with the utmost cruelty, to the sound of drums, trumpets, guitars, and tambourines. A certain [Zoroastrian][295] ... chanced to be seated apart in a corner of a caravansary. When the clamor of the people rose high he hastened into the street, and, becoming cognizant of the offence and the offender, and the cause of his public disgrace and punishment in full detail, he fell to making search, and that very day entered the society of the Bábís, saying, "This very ill-usage and public humiliation is a proof of truth and the very best of arguments. Had it not been thus it might have been that a thousand years would have passed ere one like me became informed."
– 'Abdu'l-Bahá[296]

Abu'l-Hasan-i-Shírází

Abu'l-Hasan-i-Shírází travelled on the same sailing vessel as the Báb from Búshihr. Like the Báb, Abu'l-Hasan was a cloth merchant. Much of what is known about the Báb's sailing journey comes from Hasan's eyewitness reports. Although he was on the same boat as the Báb, Abu'l-Hasan remained neutral concerning the Báb's religious claims. It was only later, when he observed the Báb's masterful handling of the confrontation at the Vakíl mosque back in Shíráz, that he finally decided to identify himself as a follower of the Báb. Back in Shíráz, Abu'l-Hasan's wife was a close friend and could be considered an ally of the Báb and His family.

Mírzá Jání

Mírzá Jání and his brother became believers in Káshán. Jání then went to Mecca to meet with the Báb. Through his encounter with the Báb, his faith was confirmed. Eventually, when he was in Tihrán, Jání would write the first history of the Faith in 1852. He was martyred in Tihrán in that same year.

Siyyid Ja'far Kashfí

Siyyid Ja'far Kashfí met the Báb in Mecca, but he did not recognize Him as the Promised One. Born in 1180 A.H (1766-1767 AD), Kashfí was about 77 years old when he met the Báb in Mecca.[297] Kashfí was one of the most distinguished and celebrated religious leaders of his time. About him Nicholas stated, "His high moral character, his righteous ways had attracted to him universal esteem and consideration. His science had won for him the glorious name of Kashfi, that is to say, one who discovers and explains the divine secrets."[298]

Kashfí was well informed about the importance of the year 1260 AH (1844 AD). Despite meeting the Báb in Mecca, and despite his high attainments, Kashfi did not recognize the Báb as the Promised One. Abu'l-Hasan-i-Shírází reported that he met Kashfí in Mecca. As paraphrased from the Persian by Faizi, Shírází stated, "I, myself, saw him in Mecca, and he saw [what happened] with his own eyes, and he heard with his own ears, and yet he did not become a believer".[299] The Báb, nevertheless, held him in high esteem. It is interesting that Kashfí was the father of Vahíd, whom we will read about in a little while.

Sulaymán Khán

Another co-traveler to Mecca was Sulaymán Khán, a notable from Tabríz, who had been in the court of the Crown Prince of Persia and then in the Court of Muhammad Sháh. The following is paraphrased from the Persian by Mázindarání.

> As a youth he was attracted to prayers and he loved to be in the company of people of knowledge and virtue. He moved to Karbilá and became an admirer of Siyyid Kázim and he lived his life there in prayers. After the declaration of the Báb, he became informed of the new Faith through two Letters of the Living (Ardibílí and Khu'í). – Mázindarání[300]

Later on, Sulaymán Khán was destined to play a significant role in the history of the Faith, in the period after the Martyrdom of the Báb.[301] He suffered a heroic martyrdom later on Tihrán.

Musqat religious leaders

It is important to note that the Báb was actively declaring His mission prior to arriving in Mecca. In Musqat, the Báb met with the religious leaders at the home of the Imám Jum'ih, the chief religious leader. Only one convert resulted. For the most part, His appeal for recognition fell on deaf ears. Siyyid Javád Isfahání, according to his memoirs, was present in those meetings.[302] Nicholas provides some additional information.

> In time he arrived at Masqat where he rested for several days during which he sought to convert the people of that country but without success… That he attempted a conversion and did not succeed is an indisputable fact because he affirms it:
>
> "The mention of God, in truth, descended upon the earth of Mascate… Say: We have not seen in Mascate men of the Book willing to help him, because they are lost in ignorance…" – Nicolas[303]

After this visit, the Báb again attempted to communicate with one of the religious leaders of Musqat, named Sulaymán. From the context, it is clear this was written sometime after the pilgrimage journey. The Báb spoke to him in a stern tone with the authority of a Messenger of God even as He offered him forgiveness. Here is a small excerpt:

[Note: The following passage mentions "the sacred House." This is a reference to the Ka'bih in Mecca, the holiest shrine in of all Islám, the spot where all Muslims go to worship on their pilgrimage.]

> This is an Epistle from God, the Help in Peril, the Self-Subsisting, unto Sulaymán in the land of Masqat, to the right of the Sea. In truth there is none other God but Him, the Help in Peril, the Self-Subsisting... From this land We then proceeded to the sacred House, and on Our return journey We landed once again at this spot, when We perceived that thou hadst heeded not that which We sent thee, nor art thou of them that truly believe. Although We had created thee to behold Our countenance, and We did actually alight in thy locality, yet thou didst fail to attain the object of thy creation, and this despite thy worshipping God all thy life… In truth We tested thee and found that thou wert not of them that are endowed with understanding… However, shouldst thou return unto Us, We would convert thy negation into affirmation. Verily We are the One Who is of immense bounteousness. But should the Primal Point cease to be with you, then the judgement given in the Words of God shall be final and unalterable and every one will assuredly uphold it… Our grace assuredly pervadeth all that dwell in the kingdoms of earth and heaven and in whatever lieth between them, and beyond them all mankind.

> However, souls that have shut themselves out as by a veil can never partake of the outpourings of the grace of God. – The Báb[304]

In the time of the Báb, the journey by boat was a lengthy one, and the seas were stormy and turbulent. While other passengers were afflicted with seasickness, the Báb and Quddús worked without pause – the Báb dictating Divine verses and Quddús taking down all the words He revealed. Mubárak looked after their needs.

Unprovoked, some of the pilgrims on the ship were hostile to the Báb. According to Abu'l-Hasan-i-Shírází, one man in particular harassed the Báb continuously, both verbally and physically. The captain of the ship admonished this man to stop bothering the passengers, but he would not stop. In fact, he even began to argue with the captain to such an extent that the captain ordered his sailors to seize him and throw him into the sea. As the sailors moved to comply with his orders, the Báb realized what the captain was about to do and, although He had been the primary victim of this man's assault, threw Himself on top of this man and would not let him go. The Báb pleaded with the captain to forgive him one more time and not throw him into the sea. The captain asked: He wronged you more than anyone else on this ship, why are you stopping us? The Báb replied that such people only harm themselves and that we should look upon them with tolerance and forgiveness. The Báb's vigorous defense of this man changed the hearts of many, resulting in a friendlier atmosphere on board.[305]

The Báb later wrote about the behavior of the pilgrims which He witnessed during His pilgrimage journey:

> The saddest thing that I saw on my pilgrimage to Mecca was the constant disputes of the pilgrims between themselves, disputes which took away the moral benefit of the pilgrimage. – The Báb[306]

And :

> I have seen (on the way to Mecca) acts of the vilest kind, in the eyes of God, which were sufficient to undo the good resulting from the pilgrimage. These were the quarrels among the pilgrims! Verily, the House of God has no need of such people! – The Báb[307]

Proclamation in Mecca

After arriving at Jaddih, the Báb made His way to Mecca. There He observed all the traditional rites of pilgrimage. Other Shaykhís were pilgrims that year.

Although Siyyid Kázim had explicitly appointed no successor, several individuals were jockeying for the leadership position among the Shaykhís. One of these claimants, a man named Muhít, was in Mecca at the same time the Báb was there. The Báb confronted Muhít directly, presenting His claims and demanding an answer. Muhít gave an evasive response.
The Báb sent a letter to the Sherif of Mecca, the leading religious authority in that city, but received no response.

Near the end of the pilgrimage a vast multitude was present in the vicinity of the Ka'bih and the Báb made His intentions known to all. He approached the Ka'bih. He placed His back against the wall and took hold of the ring on its door. He then made His announcement.

Faizi states that Quddús, Hájí Abu'l-Hasan-i-Shírází and some other believers were present at this scene.[308] From the account of Shírází, we know that an extraordinary silence fell over the more than 70,000 pilgrims. The following is paraphrased from the Persian by Faizi:

> Hájí Abu'l-Hasan-i-Shírází said that the miracle was this, that despite all the crowd that was present and the noise they normally were making that, suddenly, all became silent, to the degree that even if a sparrow moved its wings, all would hear it. After the silence of all who were present, again, He repeated:
>
> "Indeed, I am that Qá'im for whom you have all been waiting".[309]
>
> Three times, with utmost clarity, He said this phrase so that all the pilgrims received it and then the pilgrims began to translate and interpret this blessed phrase for each other. – Faizi[310]

Though His claims were not embraced by the multitude of pilgrims, many of them began to tell stories of this event. News began to spread to all regions that a young merchant of Shíráz, a Siyyid twenty-five years of age, had taken hold of the Ka'bih's door and claimed to be the Promised One.[311] Interestingly, these stories told by pilgrims returning home created what in modern terms would be called 'a local buzz'. That is, since it was news, pilgrims would naturally tell their friends and families about what they had seen and heard in Mecca. It didn't matter if they believed the Báb's claims or not. It was interesting to talk about. It was fresh. It was uplifting, and it had an air of mystery. It was the talk of the town. The curiosity of many was piqued. In due course, actual teachers of the Faith would arrive in the towns and start to teach. It was then that many people, already primed to be curious, would ask and receive answers to their questions. As a result, conversions to the young Cause exploded.

Onward to Medina

With His pilgrimage to Mecca completed, the Báb went north to the city of Medina, recognized as the city of the Prophet Muhammad. 1,260 years before on the Islámic calendar, Muhammad had been forced to flee Mecca, the city of His birth, to save His life and the lives of many of His followers. The citizens of Medina, about 280 miles north, invited Him to relocate and, ultimately, He became their Leader. In a historic journey, known as the Hijra, He and His followers emigrated there in 622 AD, and established a multi-faith, pluralistic society, which embraced Jewish, Christian, pagan and Muslim elements, which prospered and ultimately expanded throughout Arabia and into the entire Islámic Empire. The Islámic calendar, named the Hijri calendar, had its beginning at this time, the most crucial turning point in Islámic history. Muhammad died in the year 632 AD, and His remains are buried in a sacred mosque in Medina. Although the sacred Ka'bih in Mecca is the primary site ordained for Islámic pilgrimage, Medina is a secondary site for pilgrimage. When finished with His duties in Mecca, the Báb, accompanied by Quddús and Mubárak, naturally went on to Medina.

The Báb's journey to Medina began on Friday, January 10, 1845.[312] Nabíl's chronicle reports the interior reflective thoughts of the Báb as He walked towards the city of Medina. The Báb recalled the immortal scenes which had been enacted in that city by the Prophet Muhammad, His Genius, and His creative power. In this meditation, the dust of the ground upon which He was walking called out to Him, fervently asking Him to stay here and remain safe from His growing number of enemies. The Báb's Spirit confidently replies that He longs to sacrifice Himself for the Glory of God, that His life is the seed which will enable the Tree of God to grow, and that this is His destiny. Nabíl writes:

> As He approached [that holy city] … He prayed as He drew nigh unto that holy sepulchre which enshrined the mortal remains of the Prophet of God. He also remembered, as He trod that holy ground, that shining Herald of His own Dispensation [Shaykh Ahmad who] had decided to spend the evening of his days within the precincts of that hallowed shrine [the Ka'bih, and who was laid to rest nearby].
>
> There came to Him also the vision of those holy men, those pioneers and martyrs of the Faith, who had fallen gloriously on the field of battle, and who, with their life-blood, had sealed the triumph of the Cause of God.

> Their sacred dust seemed as if reanimated by the gentle tread of His feet. Their shades seemed to have been stirred by the reviving breath of His presence. They looked to Him as if they had arisen at His approach, were hastening towards Him, and were voicing their welcome. They seemed to be addressing to Him this fervent plea:
>
> "Repair not unto Thy native land, we beseech Thee, O Thou Beloved of our hearts! Abide Thou in our midst, for here, far from the tumult of Thine enemies who are lying in wait for Thee, Thou shalt be safe and secure. We are fearful for Thee. We dread the plottings and machinations of Thy foes. We tremble at the thought that their deeds might bring eternal damnation to their souls."
>
> [The Báb's indomitable Spirit replied:]
>
> "Fear not, I am come into this world to bear witness to the glory of sacrifice. You are aware of the intensity of My longing; you realise the degree of My renunciation. Nay, beseech the Lord your God to hasten the hour of My martyrdom and to accept My sacrifice. Rejoice, for both I and Quddús will be slain on the altar of our devotion to the King of Glory. The blood which we are destined to shed in His path will water and revive the garden of our immortal felicity. The drops of this consecrated blood will be the seed out of which will arise the mighty Tree of God, the Tree that will gather beneath its all-embracing shadow the peoples and kindreds of the earth. Grieve not, therefore, if I depart from this land, for I am hastening to fulfil My destiny." – Nabíl[313]

The return trip home

After the pilgrimage to Medina, the Báb, Quddús and Mubarak returned to Jaddih, and from there returned by sea again to Musqat. The Báb stayed about three months in Musqat.[314]

Nader Saiedi states that previously,

> …He had called on His followers to gather in Karbilá… [This] summons would have been understood as signaling preparation for the beginning of the apocalyptic holy war foretold in the Islámic Traditions. Yet, in issuing this call, what the Bab was actually doing was something very different. The most important function of that call was to implicitly announce His identity as not merely the Gate to the Hidden Imam, as the Qá'im Himself. – Nader Saiedi[315]

At that time in Persia, the orthodox and widespread understanding of the Shí'ih Muslims was that the Promised One would gather His followers in Karbilá to launch a violent holy war against the forces of evil and unbelief, ushering in the cataclysmic Day of Judgment and Resurrection. Although the Báb claimed to be the Promised One, His vision of what that entailed did not include moving towards violent holy war. Saiedi continues:

[Note: In this next passage, the word "jihad" refers to violent holy war. Islám speaks of different types of jihad, and not all of them are violent. In this quote, however, the intended meaning is violent jihad. The "Báb's messenger" is Mullá 'Alí Bastámí.]

> Although the Bábís had gathered in Karbilá for the expected jihad, the Báb unexpectedly cancelled that decree, and instead of going to Karbilá, He returned to Iran. He explained that the reason He did so was the persecution of His followers by the Muslin clergy, who had imprisoned the Bab's messenger and rejected His message. As the Bab explains, it was His desire to see no harm or sadness befall anyone that led Him to alter His previous command… – Nader Saiedi[316]

Baráqí, as paraphrased from the Persian, states:

> Mullá 'Alí Bastámí was sent in chains to Istanbul. Bastámí began his fateful journey on April 14, 1845 AD. The totality of these sorrowful events caused the Bab to alter His decision for the sake of protecting the Bábís.[317]

Therefore, the Báb directed His steps to Shíráz instead, where His family was waiting for Him. This decision, likely in early 1845, might have been made during His three months in Musqat.

The Báb sent messages to His followers advising them of the change of plan. He told the followers to go to Isfahán and wait there for further instructions. There was to be no violent Holy War at this time.

After Musqat, the Báb continued by sea to Búshihr. He arrived at Búshihr nine months after leaving home. Friends and relatives came to meet Him at the same Búshihr inn where He had stayed previously. By this time, the Faith was spreading to Iraq, to Isfahán, Káshán, Tihrán, Mazandaran and Mashhad. While in Búshihr, the Báb addressed Tablets (letters) to Muhammad Sháh, the King of Persia, and the Prime Minister, Hájí Mírzá Áqásí, seeking an audience to present His claims.

The Báb summoned Quddús to His presence and urged him to depart ahead of Him for Shíráz, while the Báb intended to stay a little longer at His uncle's place in Búshihr. He told him,

> The days of your companionship with Me are drawing to a close. The hour of separation has struck, a separation which no reunion will follow except in the Kingdom of God, in the presence of the King of Glory. In this world of dust, no more than nine fleeting months of association with Me have been allotted to you. On the shores of the Great Beyond, however, in the realm of immortality, joy of eternal reunion awaits us. The hand of destiny will ere long plunge you into an ocean of tribulation for His sake. I, too, will follow you; I, too, will be immersed beneath its depths. Rejoice with exceeding gladness, for you have been chosen as the standard-bearer of the host of affliction, and are standing in the vanguard of the noble army that will suffer martyrdom in His name. In the streets of Shíráz, indignities will be heaped upon you, and the severest injuries will afflict your body. You will survive the ignominious behaviour of your foes, and will attain the presence of Him who is the one object of our adoration and love. In His presence you will forget all the harm and disgrace that shall have befallen you. The hosts of the Unseen will hasten forth to assist you, and will proclaim to all the world your heroism and glory. Yours will be the ineffable joy of quaffing the cup of martyrdom for His sake. I, too, shall tread the path of sacrifice, and will join you in the realm of eternity. – The Báb[318]

The Báb gave Quddús a letter for His maternal uncle, Hájí Mírzá Siyyid 'Alí, and a copy of a recently revealed treatise, named "The Seven Qualifications".[319] In this treatise He explained some essential practices for those who had joined in His Cause. He also asked Quddús to convey His greetings to His loved ones in Shíráz. While in Búshihr, the Báb sent letters to both the Sháh and to the Prime Minister.

THE BÁB RETURNS TO SHÍRÁZ

Quddús, Mullá Sádiq, and Ardistání face torture

Fortified by his months of close fellowship with the Báb, Quddús departed Búshihr in a state of eagerness and determination. On the one hand, he understood that severe persecution and tribulation were ahead for him.

On the other hand, the Báb had promised him he would survive its cruel rigours and eventually enter the Presence of Him Whom God shall make manifest, the One for Whom both he and the Báb longed to lay down their lives. The bliss of that meeting, He told him, would be such that all the suffering which Quddús was destined to endure would become a thing forgotten. Although destined to never again meet during this earthly existence, the Báb had promised him that they would be reunited in the realm of eternity.

Upon arriving in in Shíráz, he was warmly received in the home of the Báb's maternal uncle, Hájí Mírzá Siyyid 'Alí. This uncle was open-minded and receptive, so Quddús taught him the Faith. Prior to this time, the magnitude of the newly born Faith had been kept secret, but with Quddús' assistance 'the veil' was removed and this uncle fully embraced the Cause.

After the Letters of the Living, Siyyid 'Alí was the first person in Shíráz to embrace the new Divine revelation. His love for the Báb grew so intense that he steadfastly devoted his whole life to the Báb. Disregarding any discomfort or danger to his life, and though "recognized as an outstanding figure among the businessmen" of Shíráz, "he never allowed material considerations to interfere with his spiritual responsibility of safeguarding the person, and advancing the Cause, of his beloved Kinsman". At a later time, he would lay down his life as one of the Seven Martyrs of Tihrán, "in circumstances of exceptional heroism".[320]

Mullá Sádiq had already accepted the Faith from Mullá Husayn in Isfahán and had left behind four thousand followers in Isfahán. He had travelled on foot three hundred miles to meet the Báb in Shíráz. He arrived in Shíráz before either Quddús or the Báb. Recalling that the two men were well acquainted with one another, when Mullá Sadiq met up with Quddús he was further enkindled by Quddús. His faith became intensified and confirmed. Quddús shared with him a copy of "The Seven Qualifications" which the Báb had recently revealed.

One of its teachings was that when a Bábí stands up in a mosque to give the call to prayer, he should add the Báb's name to the list of holy Persons mentioned at the start of the prayer. (This is like a Christian saying "In Jesus' name...") Mullá Sádiq arose to accomplish this task. The four statements which Mullá Sádiq made were as follows (paraphrased from the Persian by Faizi):

> I testify that there is no God but God.

> I testify that Muhammad is the Messenger of God.
>
> I testify that 'Alí is the Guardian of the Faith.
>
> I bear witness that He whose name is 'Alí-Qabl-i-Muhammad is the servant of the Baqíyyattu'lláh. – Words recited by Mullá Sádiq[321]

The first three lines were familiar Shí'ih doctrine. The fourth one was new. The phrase "'Alí-Qabl-i-Muhammad" is one way of stating the name of the Báb. And the phrase "Baqíyyattu'lláh" means Remnant of God. According to Nabíl, in this instance it is a reference to Bahá'u'lláh.[322]

Prior to this time, the Báb had asked His followers not to divulge His name to anyone. Now, with this act, His name was dramatically and openly proclaimed. Siyyid 'Alí Muhammad, the merchant of Shíráz, was now to be known as the Báb (the Gate), a bold claim of being the Promised One. Moreover, the mention of the Remnant of God was a reference to Him Whom God shall make manifest. This is a reference to Bahá'u'lláh, although the people of the time did not yet know the identity of Him Whom God shall make manifest. Thus, from the very beginning the claim of the Báb to be the Forerunner to Him Whom God shall make manifest, was present is His declarations and Writings. According to Nabíl, the populace was astounded.

> Dismay and consternation seized the entire congregation. The distinguished divines, who occupied the front seats and who were greatly revered for their pious orthodoxy, raised a clamour, loudly protesting: 'Woe betide us, the guardians and protectors of the Faith of God! Behold, this man has hoisted the standard of heresy. Down with this infamous traitor! He has spoken blasphemy. Arrest him, for he is a disgrace to our Faith.' … The whole city had been aroused, and public order was, as a result, seriously threatened. – Nabíl[323]

Husayn Khán, the Governor of the province, ordered the arrest of Quddús, Mullá Sádiq and Mullá 'Alí Akbar Ardistání, another believer.[324] The police authorities seized a copy of the Báb's Commentary on the Súrih of Joseph from them, handcuffed them, and brought them to the Governor. At first, Husayn Khán focused his attention on the elderly Mullá Sádiq.[325] After looking at the manuscript, he asked Mullá Sádiq about its opening passage, which called upon the rulers to give up their sovereignty now that the Promise One had appeared. Husayn Khán attempted to quote the passage, with these words:

> Divest yourselves of the robe of sovereignty, for He who is the King in truth, hath been made manifest! The Kingdom is God's, the Most Exalted. Thus hath the Pen of the Most High decreed! – Husayn Khán attempting to quote the Báb[326]

Husayn Khán asked: Does this apply to our sovereign the Sháh? And since I represent the Sháh in this province, must I too abdicate my position?

Mullá Sádiq answered that the truth of the Báb's words would be established and that, if these are the Words of God, the abdication of the Sháh and others like him "can matter but little", nor can the sovereignty of God be diminished, or His Divine purpose be turned aside.[327]

Husayn Khán was outraged at this response. He ordered his aides to strip Mullá Sádiq of his clothes and whip him with a thousand lashes. According to Nabíl,

> He then commanded that the beards of both Quddús and Mullá Sádiq[328] should be burned, their noses be pierced, that through this incision a cord should be passed, and with this halter they should be led through the streets of the city.
>
> [Husayn Khán declared:]
>
> "It will be an object lesson to the people of Shíráz, who will know what the penalty of heresy will be." – Nabíl[329]

Mullá Sádiq remained calm and assured. He raised his eyes to heaven and was heard reciting a prayer:

> O Lord, our God! We have indeed heard the voice of One that called. He called us to the Faith – 'Believe ye on the Lord your God!' – and we have believed. O God, our God! Forgive us, then, our sins, and hide away from us our evil deeds, and cause us to die with the righteous. – Mullá Sádiq[330]

A nonbeliever eyewitness of the torture scene found it strange that Mullá Sádiq seemed to be smiling while the violent lashes were being inflicted upon his body. He reported:

> I was present when Mullá Sádiq was being scourged… No one believed that Mullá Sádiq, so advanced in age and so frail in body, could possibly survive fifty such savage strokes. We marvelled at his fortitude when we found that, although the number of the strokes of the scourge he had received had already exceeded nine

hundred, his face still retained its original serenity and calm. A smile was upon his face, as he held his hand before his mouth. He seemed utterly indifferent to the blows that were being showered upon him. When he was being expelled from the city, I succeeded in approaching him, and asked him why he held his hand before his mouth. I expressed surprise at the smile upon his countenance. He emphatically replied:

'The first seven strokes were severely painful; to the rest I seemed to have grown indifferent. I was wondering whether the strokes that followed were being actually applied to my own body. A feeling of joyous exultation had invaded my soul. I was trying to repress my feelings and to restrain my laughter. I can now realise how the almighty Deliverer is able, in the twinkling of an eye, to turn pain into ease, and sorrow into gladness. Immensely exalted is His power above and beyond the idle fancy of His mortal creatures.'

Mullá Sádiq, whom I met years after, confirmed every detail of this moving episode. – An eyewitness to the scourging of Mullá Sádiq[331]

The three men serenely accepted their tortures. After this, they were expelled from the city. Nabíl says they "earned the immortal distinction of having been the first to be persecuted on Persian soil for the sake of their Faith."[332] (Mullá 'Alí Bastámí had suffered first for *the Cause*, but outside of Persia.) Quddús went to Kirmán, Mullá Sádiq to Yazd, and Ardistání to his hometown of Ardistán, near Isfahán.[333] In 1845, news of the violent persecution in Shíráz was sent to the west and published in the *Times of London*[334] and even in a small town in Missouri.[335]

BOON'S LICK TIMES.

"ERROR CEASES TO BE DANGEROUS, WHEN REASON IS LEFT FREE TO COMBAT IT."—Jefferson.

Vol. 7. FAYETTE, MISSOURI, SATURDAY, APRIL 4, 1846. No. 4.

A MODERN MAHOMET—We see by late London papers that a schism has lately taken place among the followers of Mahomet, and a new sect set itself up in Persia, at the head of which is a 'merchant who had returned from a pilgrimage' to Mecca, and proclaimed himself a successor of the prophet. The following account is given of the treatment of those followers of a 'new light.'

Four persons being heard repeating their profession of faith, according to the form prescribed by the imposter, were apprehended, tried and found guilty of unpardonable blasphemy. They were sentenced to lose their beards by fire being set to them.—The sentence was put into execution with all the zeal and fanaticism becoming a true believer in Mahomet. Not deeming the loss of beards a sufficient punishment, they were further sentenced the next day to have their faces blacked and exposed thro'-out the city. Each of them was led by a mirgazah, (executioner,) who had made a hole in his nose and passed through it a string, which he sometimes pulled with such violence that the unfortunate fellows cried out alternately for mercy from the executioner and vengeance from Heaven.—It is the custom in Persia, on such occasions, for the executioners to collect money from the spectators, and particularly from the shopkeepers in the bazaar. In the evening, when the pockets of the executioners were well-filled with money, they led the unfortunate fellows to the city gate, and there turned them adrift. After which the Moll[ah]s at Shiraz sent men to Bushire with power to seize the imposter, and take him to Shiraz, where, on being tried, he very wisely denied the charge of apostacy laid against him, and thus escaped from punishment.—*N. Y. Mirror.*

The Boon's Lick Times article, in Fayette, Missouri, dated April 4, 1846, was sourced from the **N.Y. Mirror**.

Another article, with very similar wording, was published in the **Times of London** on Wednesday, November 19, 1845.

Figure 19 Boon's Lick Times article about the persecutions in Shíráz.

The Báb enters Shíráz, "truly majestic"

As these events unfolded, the Báb was on His way home from pilgrimage. Shoghi Effendi states that His return home to Shíráz in February - probably in July (or August) of 1845 "was the signal that rocked the entire country".[336]

The fire which the declaration of His mission had lit was being fanned into flame through the dispersal and activities of His appointed disciples. Already within the space of less than two years it had kindled the passions of friend and foe alike... With the Báb's return to Shíráz the initial collision of irreconcilable forces [had begun]... The people of Shíráz were by that time wild with excitement. A violent controversy was raging in the masjids, the madrisihs, the bazaars, and other public places. Peace and security were gravely imperiled. Fearful, envious, thoroughly angered, the mullás were beginning to perceive the seriousness of their position... Meanwhile the fever that had seized His followers was communicating itself to the members of the clergy and to the merchant classes, and was invading the higher circles of society. Indeed, a wave of passionate inquiry had swept the whole country, and unnumbered congregations were listening with wonder to the testimonies eloquently and fearlessly related by the Báb's itinerant messengers. – Shoghi Effendi[337]

The Governor, Husayn Khán, had dispatched troops to Búshihr with orders to arrest the Báb and bring Him back to Shíráz bound in chains. On the way to Shíráz, the Báb spotted them from a distance. He asked Mubarak to approach the soldiers and ask who they were looking for. The commander told what happened:

Having completed the third stage of our journey to Búshihr, we encountered, in the midst of the wilderness a youth who wore a green sash and a small turban after the manner of the siyyids[338] who are in the trading profession... As we approached him, he saluted us and enquired as to our destination... He smilingly observed:

"The Governor has sent you to arrest Me. Here am I; do with Me as you please. By coming out to meet you, I have curtailed the length of your march, and have made it easier for you to find Me."

I was startled by his remarks and marvelled at his candour and straightforwardness. I could not explain, however, his readiness to subject himself, of his own accord, to the severe discipline of government officials, and to risk thereby his own life and safety. I tried to ignore him, and was preparing to leave, when he approached me and said:

"I swear by the righteousness of Him who created man, distinguished him from among the rest of His creatures, and caused his heart to be made the seat of His sovereignty and knowledge, that all My life I have uttered no word but the truth, and had no other desire except the welfare and advancement of My fellow-men. I have disdained My own ease and have avoided being the cause of pain or sorrow to anyone. I know that you are seeking Me. I prefer to deliver Myself into your hands, rather than subject you and your companions to unnecessary annoyance for My sake."

These words moved me profoundly. I instinctively dismounted from my horse, and, kissing his stirrups, addressed him in these words:

"O light of the eyes of the Prophet of God! I adjure you, by Him who has created you and endowed you with such loftiness and power, to grant my request and to answer my prayer. I beseech you to escape from this place and to flee from before the face of Husayn Khán, the ruthless and despicable Governor of this province. I dread his machinations against you; I rebel at the idea of being made the instrument of his malignant designs against so innocent and noble a descendant of the Prophet of God. My companions are all honourable men. Their word is their bond. They will pledge themselves not to betray your flight. I pray you, betake yourself to the city of Mashhad in Khurásán, and avoid falling a victim to the brutality of this remorseless wolf."

To my earnest entreaty he gave this answer:

"May the Lord your God requite you for your magnanimity and noble intention. No one knows the mystery of My Cause; no one can fathom its secrets. Never will I turn My face away from the decree of God. He alone is My sure Stronghold, My Stay and My Refuge. Until My last hour is at hand, none dare assail Me, none can frustrate the plan of the Almighty. And when My hour is come, how great will be My joy to quaff the cup of martyrdom in His name! Here am I; deliver Me into the hands of your master. Be not afraid, for no one will blame you."

I bowed my consent and carried out his desire. – The leader of the escort[339]

Instead of running away from the soldiers, as many people would have done, the Báb boldly surrendered to them. His motive, He explained, was to avoid causing the soldiers any sorrow or inconvenience. The soldiers were moved by the attitude and actions of the Báb. As ordered, they brought the Báb back to Shíráz. Balyuzi observes that His entry to the city "was truly majestic. His arrival bore no resemblance to the condition envisaged by the Governor. He had wanted the Báb to be brought before him in chains. Instead, here was the Báb riding, calm and serene, at the head of the horsemen."[340] And Nabíl adds,

> Free and unfettered, He went before His escort, which followed Him in an attitude of respectful devotion. By the magic of His words, He had disarmed the hostility of His guards and transmuted their proud arrogance into humility and love. – Nabíl[341]

The Báb was taken directly to the Governor. Nabíl says,

> He received Him with the utmost insolence… He publicly rebuked Him, and in abusive language denounced His conduct.
>
> "Do you realise," he angrily protested, "what a great mischief you have kindled? Are you aware what a disgrace you have become to the holy Faith of Islám and to the august person of our sovereign? Are you not the man who claims to be the author of a new revelation which annuls the sacred precepts of the Qur'án?" – Husayn Khán, cited by Nabíl[342]

Figure 20 Husayn Khán, Governor of Fárs and of the city of Shíráz

Figure 21 The Báb's turban goes flying after He has been struck in the face. (Photo from reenactment in *The Gate: Dawn of the Bahá'í Faith*)

The Báb responded calmly to his questions with a verse from the Qur'án which instructs Muslims to "clear up the matter at once, lest through ignorance ye harm others", that is, to investigate and ascertain the facts of any situation. (Qur'án, 49:6)[343]

The Governor misunderstood the quote. He ordered one of his aides to strike the Báb in the face. So violent was the blow that the Báb's turban was thrown to the ground. The leading cleric of the city, Shaykh Abú-Turáb, who was present, and he had a more kindly disposition. He gently placed the turban back on the Báb's head. This cleric understood the Qur'ánic reference which the Báb had made and urged Husayn Khán that the better course would be a calm investigation.

According to Nabíl, "The Báb denied the claim of being either the representative of the Promised Qá'im or the intermediary between Him and the faithful."[344] This was accepted in that meeting as a recantation, but it was nothing of the sort. He was neither of the things which He had denied; in fact, He claimed to be no less than the Qá'im Himself, the Promised One, and the Gate to a still greater Manifestation of God yet to come.

The Governor demanded He pay a fine. His uncle paid it and then the Báb was allowed to return home, where His family was waiting for Him. For a time, the Báb lived quietly, engaged in prayer and writing, and only His wife, mother, uncles and servants had access to Him.

The Báb's non-recantation at the Vakíl mosque

The Báb was ordered to make a public "recantation" at the Vakíl mosque. The Báb came to the mosque on a Friday, accompanied by His uncle, Hájí Mírzá Siyyid 'Alí. An eyewitness tells of the events of that day. The following passage is paraphrased from the Persian by Faizi.

[Note: In the following passage, the Báb is referred to as "this Siyyid". The term Siyyid refers to a person who is a descendent of Muhammad. As noted earlier, the Báb was a Siyyid.]

> I [Sádiq-i-Mu'allim] was about twenty years old… The government announced, at the request of the religious leaders, that all the inhabitants of Shíráz, from all classes of society, should gather in the Vakíl mosque to hear the Báb deny His claims. I went and tried to get as close as possible [to the pulpit] so I could hear what He said. The people began to come to the mosque in groups from morning until three hours before sunset. The crowd was so large that they filled up the area near the pulpit, the courtyard, the gardens, the rooftops, and even the minarets of the mosque. Then the Governor, Husayn Khán, the religious leaders, the merchants, and other dignitaries entered the mosque and sat close to the pulpit. The pulpit was one large piece of marble with fourteen steps.

Figure 22 Mosque Vakíl in Shíráz where the Báb spoke.

I sat close and suddenly heard noises and the whispering of the people, saying: "He is coming". The Blessed One had a turban on His head and had a cloak on His shoulders, entering with such majesty, greatness and power, that I cannot describe it. He paid no attention to the presence of the multitude. He asked the religious leaders and the Governor to explain their purpose in summoning Him there.

They answered: "The purpose is this that You go over to the pulpit and recant from Your false claim, so this disturbance will be extinguished."

Without answering, the Báb went and stood on the first step. A certain Shaykh[345] said forcefully: "Go to the top of the pulpit so that all can see You and hear Your voice."

His Holiness ascended higher and sat at the top; suddenly the whole crowd became as silent as if there was no one in the mosque at all. All became attentive.

With utmost eloquence and in a clear voice, He began to deliver a sermon in Arabic on the Unity of God. Upon hearing this, all present from high and low, learned and illiterate, became attracted. This lasted about half an hour.

The silence of the crowd agitated the Shaykh and he told the Governor:

"Have you invited this Siyyid here to prove His claim or to recant it? Tell Him what He needs to say."

Husayn Khán said: "Siyyid, say what they told you to say."

His Holiness paused for a moment and then He cried out to the people. He affirmed that He says what His ancestor, Muhammad, the Messenger of God, said 1,260 years ago. He asserted that what Muhammad has approved is true until the Day of Resurrection, and that what He has forbidden is forbidden until the Day of Resurrection. He cited a tradition that has come down from the Imams, 'Whenever the Qá'im arises, that will be the Day of Resurrection.' 346

And then He stepped down from the pulpit. After that, the Shaykh raised his walking-stick to strike the Báb. The late Mírzá Abu'l-

> Hasan Khán,[347] who was a young man at that time, moved his shoulder forward and his shoulder took the blow." – An account from an eyewitness[348]

Nabíl gives a slightly different version of these events.[349] The chief religious leader in Shíráz, Shaykh Abú-Turáb, is given a more prominent role in the narrative. Nabíl indicates that he was on the pulpit while the Báb spoke. He asked the Báb to ascend the pulpit a little higher. When another Shaykh in the crowd spoke insolently to the Báb, Shaykh Abú-Turáb, rebuked him. Nabíl reports that the amount of time the Báb spoke was much less and that the words He spoke were different. He said:

> The condemnation of God be upon him who regards me either as a representative of the Imám or the gate thereof. The condemnation of God be also upon whosoever imputes to me the charge of having denied the unity of God, of having repudiated the prophethood of Muhammad, the Seal of the Prophets, of having rejected the truth of any of the messengers of old, or of having refused to recognize the guardianship of 'Alí, the Commander of the Faithful, or of any of the Imáms who have succeeded him. – The Báb[350]

Nabíl indicates that Shaykh Abú-Turáb was a wise and moderate man and he was concerned for the Báb's safety after His speech. According to Nabíl, he intervened and advised the Báb to return home, rather than to complete His prayers at the mosque.

> "Your family," he said, "is anxiously awaiting your return. All are apprehensive lest any harm befall you. Repair to your house and there offer your prayer; of greater merit shall this deed be in the sight of God."
>
> Hájí Mírzá Siyyid 'Alí also was, at the request of the [chief religious leader], asked to accompany his nephew to his home.
>
> This precautionary measure which Shaykh Abú-Turáb thought it wise to observe was actuated by the fear lest, after the dispersion of the congregation, a few of the evil-minded among the crowd might still attempt to injure the person of the Báb or endanger His life. But for the sagacity, the sympathy, and the careful attention which the [chief religious leader] so strikingly displayed on a number of such occasions, the infuriated mob would doubtless have been led to gratify its savage desire, and would have committed the most abom-

> inable of excesses. He seemed to have been the instrument of the invisible Hand appointed to protect both the person and the Mission of that Youth. – Nabíl[351]

Though some people took the Báb's words as a recantation, in reality He repudiated none of His claims. At the Vakíl mosque, the Báb affirmed truths that all Muslims and Bábís could agree upon and rejected claims that He was *not* actually making. Since the multitude had not yet fathomed the Báb's higher stature as the Promised One Himself, this careful statement sufficed to restore calm in the city.

'Abdu'l-Bahá explained the more precise meaning of the Báb's claim to be the Gate.

> One day they summoned Him to the mosque urging and constraining Him to recant, but He discoursed from the pulpit in such wise as to silence and subdue those present and to stablish and strengthen His followers. It was then supposed that He claimed to be the medium of grace from His Highness the Lord of the Age (upon Him be peace); but afterwards it became known and evident that His meaning was the Gatehood of another city and the mediumship of the graces of another Person Whose qualities and attributes were contained in His books and treatises. – 'Abdu'l-Bahá[352]

Some people who had been hostile towards the Báb were no longer hostile after listening to Him. Some who had known the Báb before this day became more ardent admirers. Nabíl reported,

---

[Note: In the following passage the term "Masjid-i-Vakíl" refers to the Vakíl mosque. The word "masjid" refers to a mosque.]

> A few among those who were present on that memorable occasion in the Masjid-i-Vakíl, and had listened to the statements of the Báb, were greatly impressed by the masterly manner in which that Youth had, by His unaided efforts, succeeded in silencing His formidable opponents. Soon after this event, they were each led to apprehend the reality of His Mission and to recognize its glory. – Nabíl[353]

This event led to the birth of a small community of believers in Shíráz, including a nephew of Shaykh Abu-Turab.[354] One name stands out. Hájí Abu'l-Hasan Shírází had been attracted to the Báb while a passenger on the ship travelling to Mecca. Despite his prior close companionship with the Báb on that journey, it was only in witnessing the events at the Vakil mosque that he became certain of the Faith. Later on, he demonstrated his devotion by suffering for the Faith.

After the events at the Vakíl mosque, the Báb returned to His home. Effectively under a form of house arrest, by order of the government, He was not allowed to see most of His followers. He could only have interaction with a few close friends and with His family. For a time, He lived a relatively quiet existence.

Meanwhile, the news of the Báb's claims had caused a commotion throughout the nation. As Nabíl explains:

> His disciples, who had spread throughout the length and breadth of the country, fearlessly proclaimed to the multitude of their countrymen the regenerating power of the new-born Revelation. The fame of the Báb had been noised abroad and had reached the ears of those who held the highest seats of authority, both in the capital and throughout the provinces. A wave of passionate enquiry swayed the minds and hearts of both the leaders and the masses of the people... The dignitaries of State and Church either attended in person or delegated their ablest representatives to enquire into the truth and character of this remarkable Movement. – Nabíl[355]

Mullá Husayn returns to Shíráz

When the Báb had earlier cancelled the expected meeting with His followers in Karbilá, he had told them to go to Isfahán and await further instructions. The expected "holy war" many of the followers anticipated, based at that point on their understanding of their prophecies, was cancelled. Most of the followers received the news joyously and immediately arose to go to Isfahán. A small number of the followers[356] were discontented because, in their eyes, the Báb had broken His promise. Clearly, the Báb's decision not to conform to their expectations or the "the script" they held in their minds was a test for them. Despite their inner state of agitation, outwardly they went along with the Báb's instructions.

The Báb's instructions had not reached Mullá Husayn, so, after His triumphant journey to Isfahán, Tihrán and Mashhad, he was now heading back to Karbilá as he thought he was supposed to do. Then a fortunate coincidence occurred. Some of those believers who were en route to Isfahán encountered Mullá Husayn in the city of Kangávar as he was en route to Karbilá. Nabíl explains:

> They were greatly delighted by this unexpected encounter, and requested Mullá Husayn to prolong his stay in Kangávar, with which request he readily complied... Mullá Husayn decided to join the company of his friends and to proceed with them to Isfahán. – Nabíl[357]

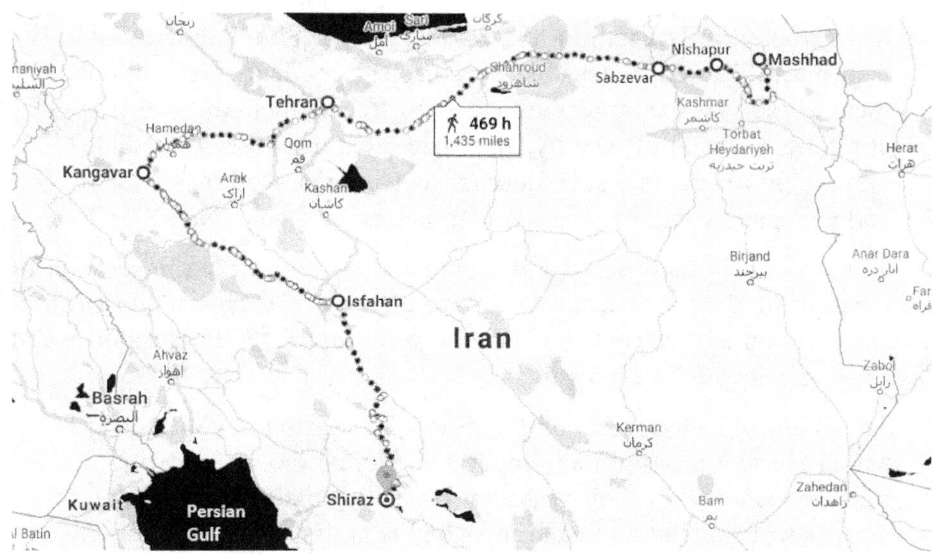

Figure 23 Mullá Husayn's return journey from Mashhad to Shíráz, via Kangávar

Mullá Husayn walked about four to six miles ahead of the group. He stopped periodically during the day to offer his prayers, and this gave his traveling companions an opportunity to catch up with him. When prayers were completed, they would resume their march together. When they came near Isfahán, Mullá Husayn said they should enter the city in small groups, to avoid causing a stir.

After arriving in Isfahán, they received news of the agitation going on in Shíráz and that it was forbidden for anyone, except His family, to meet with the Báb. Going to Shíráz, they concluded, would be quite dangerous. Nabíl says that Mullá Husayn was undaunted by this news and decided to go to Shíráz anyway. He changed his clothes to that of a horseman and, with his brother and cousin, set out for Shíráz:

> As he approached its gate, he instructed his brother to proceed in the dead of night to the house of the Báb's maternal uncle and to request him to inform the Báb of his arrival. Mullá Husayn received, the next day, the welcome news that Hájí Mírzá Siyyid 'Alí was expecting

> him an hour after sunset outside the gate of the city. Mullá Husayn met him at the appointed hour and was conducted to his home. Several times at night did the Báb honour that house with His presence, and continue in close association with Mullá Husayn until the break of day. Soon after this, He gave permission to his companions who had gathered in Isfahán, to leave gradually for Shíráz, and there to wait until it should be feasible for Him to meet them. He cautioned them to exercise the utmost vigilance, instructed them to enter, a few at a time, the gate of the city, and bade them disperse, immediately upon their arrival, into such quarters as were reserved for travellers, and to accept whatever employment they could find. – Nabíl[358]

The men who had become discontented by the Báb's cancellation of the meeting in Karbilá, became even more so when they saw the extraordinary affection and esteem the Báb showered upon Mullá Husayn. Nabíl describes the envy of the three men:

> The manifold evidences of the Báb's increasing favour towards Mullá Husayn aroused their anger and excited the smouldering fire of their jealousy. In their impotent rage, they resorted to the abject weapons of fraud and of calumny. Unable at first to manifest openly their hostility to Mullá Husayn, they sought by every crafty device to beguile the minds and damp the affections of his devoted admirers. Their unseemly behaviour alienated the sympathy of the believers and precipitated their separation from the company of the faithful. – Nabíl[359]

At Mullá Husayn's bidding, the Báb's followers tried to show forbearance towards these three men, but they caused such a commotion in the city that it was the civil authorities – the government of Husayn Khán – that "despised and feared their plottings" so much that they expelled them from the city.[360] The Báb, in a Tablet, later commented on these three men and described them as false believers. Later on, all three in fact joined forces with the enemies of the Faith.

By showing so much favor to Mullá Husayn, the Báb was striving to educate the believers both concerning His own station and the station of Mullá Husayn. Though He never deviated, most of the Bábís early on understood Him to be making a claim of being the Gate to the Hidden Imám. The Báb's station was vastly higher than that, and, by extension, so was the rank of Mullá Husayn as the first believer. As Faizi explains (paraphrased from the Persian):

> It was on this occasion that the Báb gave the title of 'the Báb' to Mullá Husayn and He Himself became known as the "The Remembrance of God"; and thereby He was the path of true faith and recognition. His Reality was shedding Its light according to the capacities of the believers, and was bringing the believers closer to the truth and the essence of their goal. – Faizi[361]

We must not be confused by this new terminology. The Báb was still known throughout all Persia as the Báb, the Gate, and Mullá Husayn, the first believer, was still known as "Bábu'l-Báb", the Gate of the Gate. Instead of changing the common usage, the Báb was assigning additional meanings and esoteric insights to the terms. In so doing, He was striving to help them to understand profound concepts.

Another factor was at work. The Báb knew that the period in which He could freely interact with the followers was coming to an end. In the future, He would be isolated from the believers for lengthy periods of time. Hence, the believers would need to rely on Mullá Husayn, the Letters of the Living and the other heroes of the Faith for their guidance. Increasing the stature of His first disciple, while simultaneously providing further enlightenment as to His own station, fit perfectly the needs of the Faith at this moment.

Consequently, this period in Shíráz saw the first emergence of the the Bábí community. This community was not an organized congregation, at least not yet. Such a thing was not remotely possible in the young Faith's perilous environment of persecution. Rather, a rapidly expanding network of active followers who understood the station, claims and mission of the Báb was coming into existence. These followers were now working together, assuming significant responsibilities, and winning converts. They spread the message throughout the nation and to neighboring Iraq. The millennial spirt of the age was being harnessed and stimulated, and the masses were becoming interested in the new Faith. This may well be what the earliest phase of the birth of a world religion looks like.

Despite the disturbance caused by the handful of discontents, and notwithstanding the opposition of the government and clergy, the community of the believers was developing nicely. A number of conversions took place. One of these conversions is especially interesting – Shaykh 'Ábid-i-Mu'allim, the Báb's childhood teacher.

We recall earlier, that Hájí Siyyid Javád Karbilá'i, who had known the Báb since childhood, excitedly discovered the name of the Báb while talking with Mullá 'Alí Bastámí during the latter's visit to Karbilá. Javád came back to Shíráz. One day in Shíráz, Javád asked the Báb for permission to teach the Faith to Shaykh 'Ábid. Javád delivered the following report to the distinguished scholar Mírzá Abu'l-Fadl, who wrote it down. The report was later published by both Faizi and Husaini. The following passage is paraphrased from the Persian by Husaini.

> Shaykh 'Ábid had interactions with the family of the Báb, especially His uncles. Sometimes he visited them to perform recitations of the Scriptures, other times to perform certain religious duties and ceremonies. According to Siyyid Javád-i-Karbalá'í, 'Ábid was a very educated man and was informed of the sciences of his time... The story of the conversion of Shaykh 'Ábid is as follows:
>
> 'Ábid had been traveling in the period after the Báb returned from Mecca. After his return, he heard about the events related to the Appearance, so he began to inquire about it. I (Javád) asked His Holiness (the Báb) for permission to have a conversation with him at a gathering.
>
> After obtaining His permission, a time and place was determined to form a gathering where a number of individuals could attend. As all the invitees were assembled, we began to talk about different matters and then it was determined that a Tablet of the Báb's, written in Arabic, would provide an answer to a question [that had been asked].
>
> I said: "Gentlemen, our habit is that no one should speak and no one should occupy himself with anything else during the reading of the Tablet. If anyone wants to smoke or drink tea, he should do so before the reading and if anyone has an objection, he must wait until the reading is finished [before he can speak]".
>
> All promised and made a firm covenant that no one would speak [or interrupt] during the reading of the Tablet. One of the individuals present began to recite the Tablet. I (Javád) was watching the face of Shaykh 'Ábid and at the beginning I saw his face was becoming disturbed and was changing colors. I could see he was angry. After a few pages of the Tablet were read, I noticed his facial expression returned to normal. I knew that his protestation had vanished. But the Tablet was not yet finished. As the reading continued, I watched the tears pouring from his face. His denial had changed to acceptance and his protest had been converted to confession. – Hájí Siyyid Javád Karbilá'i, reported by Husaini[362]

Siyyid Javád had seen the full range of emotions transparently displayed, in a short time, on the face of the Báb's former teacher. One can only wonder as to the thoughts rapidly flooding through his mind. By the end of the reading, the beloved Shaykh had fully accepted his former pupil as his master. Husaini offers this closing comment about Shaykh 'Ábid, paraphrased from the Persian by Husaini.

> Shaykh 'Ábid ascended to the Eternal Kingdom in the month of Rajab 1263 AH (June-July, 1847) with utmost certitude and his resting place is in the Musallá cemetery in Shíráz. On a white headstone, in Arabic, are written beautiful descriptions of his spiritual and learned station… It has been reported that Shaykh 'Ábid wrote a manuscript of his memories of the Báb's childhood, but unfortunately this writing is not available. – Husaini[363]

Alongside these positive events, the disturbances continued among the people of Shíráz. This led the Báb to make a decision. Nabíl says:

> Soon after the arrival of Mullá Husayn at Shíráz, the voice of the people rose again in protest against him. The fear and indignation of the multitude were excited by the knowledge of his continued and intimate intercourse with the Báb.
>
> [They clamoured:]
>
> "He again has come to our city; he again has raised the standard of revolt…"
>
> So grave and menacing became the situation that the Báb instructed Mullá Husayn to regain, by way of Yazd, his native province of Khurásán. He likewise dismissed the rest of His companions who had gathered in Shíráz, and bade them return to Isfahán…
>
> These precautionary measures which the Báb deemed wise to undertake, relieved Him from the immediate danger of violence from the infuriated people of Shíráz, and served to lend a fresh impetus to the propagation of His Faith beyond the limits of that city. His disciples, who had spread throughout the length and breadth of the country, fearlessly proclaimed to the multitude of their countrymen the regenerating power of the new-born Revelation.
>
> The fame of the Báb had been noised abroad and had reached the ears of those who held the highest seats of authority, both in the

> capital and throughout the provinces. A wave of passionate enquiry swayed the minds and hearts of both the leaders and the masses of the people… – Nabíl[364]

Mullá Husayn set forth for Mashhad in the province of Khurásán, his second journey to that city, this time by way of Yazd.[365] Other believers travelled in other directions.

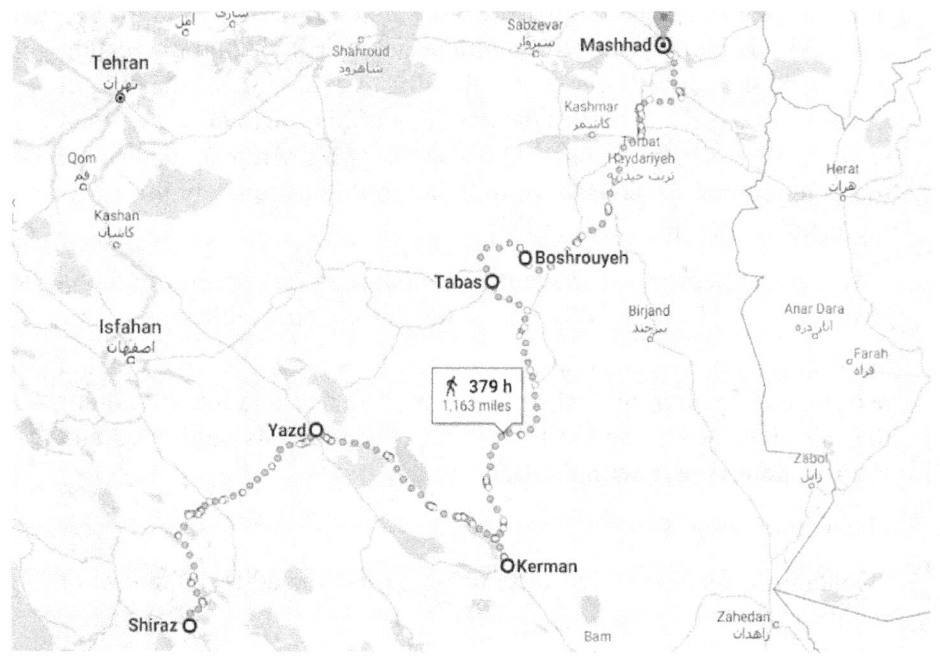

Figure 24 Mullá Husayn's second journey from Shíráz to Mashhad, via Yazd and Bushrúyih

Vahíd arrives. The Sháh wants to know what is going on

Meanwhile, contradictory reports about the new Movement were reaching the ears of the king, Muhammad Sháh. His chamberlain, the Master of Ceremonies at his court, Mírzá Lutf-'Alí, was aware of the Faith, possibly through the visit of Mullá Husayn. Presumably he was telling the Sháh good things about the Báb and His teachings. At the same time, the Sháh was receiving disturbing reports from Governor Husayn Khán in Shíráz.[366] According to Nicolas, the news of the gathering at the Vakíl mosque had reached the Sháh.[367]

The Sháh wanted to find the meaning of these events. Was this a spiritual movement? Was it compatible with Islám? Or was it subversive and intent upon overthrowing His regime? He decided to investigate.

> The commotion had assumed such proportions that the Sháh, unable any longer to ignore the situation, delegated the trusted Siyyid Yahyáy-i-Dárábí, surnamed Vahíd, one of the most erudite, eloquent and influential of his subjects – a man who had committed to memory no less than thirty thousand traditions – to investigate and report to him the true situation. – Shoghi Effendi[368]

> He delegated [Vahíd], the most learned, the most eloquent, and the most influential of his subjects, to interview the Báb and to report to him the results of his investigations. The Sháh had implicit confidence in his impartiality, in his competence and profound spiritual insight. He occupied a position of such pre-eminence among the leading figures in Persia that at whatever meeting he happened to be present … [none] would dare to assert his views in his presence. They all reverently observed silence before him; all testified to his sagacity, his unsurpassed knowledge and mature wisdom…
>
> In those days [Vahíd] was residing in Tihrán in the house of Mírzá Lutf-'Alí, the Master of Ceremonies to the Sháh, as the honoured guest of his Imperial Majesty. The Sháh confidentially signified through Mírzá Lutf-'Alí his desire and pleasure that [Vahíd] should proceed to Shíráz and investigate the matter in person.
>
> [The Sháh said;]
>
> "Tell him from us that inasmuch as we repose the utmost confidence in his integrity, and admire his moral and intellectual standards, and regard him as the most suitable among the divines of our realm, we expect him to proceed to Shíráz, to enquire thoroughly … and to inform us of the results of his investigations; We shall then know what measures it behoves us to take." – Nabíl[369]

Vahíd was interested in obtaining first-hand knowledge of the Báb's claims. According to Taherzadeh, "It is reported that the Sháh gave him a horse, a sword and the sum of one hundred túmáns for the journey."[370] Málmírí also states that the Sháh gave him a horse, a sword and expense money.[371] He set out for Shíráz, but since he had a home in Yazd, he stopped there on the way, to visit with his wife and sons. In that city, he spoke to thousands of people who came to hear him speak about his mission. He was mounted on his horse and carrying his sword as he addressed the populace. He said:

> O inhabitants of Yazd, a certain distinguished Siyyid in Shíráz has claimed to be the Promised Qá'im. I am intending to go to Shíráz to have an interview with Him. If I find him to be an impostor, I shall deal with him with this sword but if I find His claim to be true I shall be willing to give my life in His path. – Vahíd[372]

Concluding his speech, he invited anyone in the crowd to join him on his journey. The crowd declined his offer and instead unanimously said they would follow whatever decision he made. After this, he departed.

Upon arriving in Shíráz, he stayed at the home of Governor Husayn Khán. After a few days, he moved to the home of a friend who was a Bábí. This friend advised him to exercise caution so that he would not act towards the Báb in ways he might later regret.

Vahíd's first meeting with the Báb was held at the home of His uncle, Hájí Mírzá Siyyid 'Alí. For two hours Vahíd asked the Báb to respond to questions about the most difficult to comprehend and deeply philosophical aspects of Islámic teachings, with the most obscure passages of the Qur'án, and with the numerous sayings and prophecies of the Imáms of the Faith. Nabíl says,

> The Báb at first listened to his learned references to the law and prophecies of Islám, noted all his questions, and began to give to each a brief but persuasive reply. The conciseness and lucidity of His answers excited the wonder and admiration of Siyyid Yahyá. He was overpowered by a sense of humiliation at his own presumptuousness and pride. His sense of superiority completely vanished. – Nabíl[373]

Vahíd arose to depart and promised that he would submit all his remaining questions at their next interview. Vahíd returned to his friend and said,

> I have in His presence [expounded] unduly upon my own learning. He was able in a few words to answer my questions and to resolve my perplexities. I felt so abased before Him that I hurriedly begged leave to retire. – Vahíd[374]

Before the next interview, his friend urged him to remember his counsel to act with all humility towards the Báb. As the second interview began, Vahíd discovered that all the questions he had planned for the Báb had vanished from his mind. He was soon amazed to hear the Báb answering, one by one, all the questions he had forgotten to ask. Vahíd still doubted. He thought the Báb's surprising performance might be a coincidence.

For the third and final interview, Vahíd decided on one single proof. He would in his mind ask for a commentary on a certain chapter of the Qur'án, Súrih 108, known as the Súrih of Kawthar, but not state the request verbally. Vahíd was thinking that if the Báb revealed such a commentary, and if it was obviously of equal or greater quality to the verses of the Qur'án, that he would believe in the Báb's Mission. But upon arrival, Vahíd felt an overwhelming sense of fear as soon as He was brought into the presence of the Báb.

[Note: In the following passage, the Báb offers to reveal a commentary on the Súrih of Kawthar, the 108th chapter of the Qur'án. According to Islámic traditions, the term Kawthar refers to a river in Paradise from which great abundance and goodness flows. This river is poetically mentioned in the first verse of that Súrih.]

The Báb, beholding my plight, arose from His seat, advanced towards me, and, taking hold of my hand, seated me beside Him.

[He said:]

'Seek from Me whatever is your heart's desire. I will readily reveal it to you.'

I was speechless with wonder. Like a babe that can neither understand nor speak, I felt powerless to respond. He smiled as He gazed at me and said:

'Were I to reveal for you the commentary on the Súrih of Kawthar, would you acknowledge that My words are born of the Spirit of God? Would you recognize that My utterance can in no wise be associated with sorcery or magic?'

Tears flowed from my eyes as I heard Him speak these words…

It was still early in the afternoon when the Báb requested Hájí Mírzá Siyyid 'Alí to bring His pen-case and some paper. He then started to reveal His commentary on the Súrih of Kawthar.

How am I to describe this scene of inexpressible majesty? Verses streamed from His pen with a rapidity that was truly astounding. The

> incredible swiftness of His writing, the soft and gentle murmur of His voice, and the stupendous force of His style, amazed and bewildered me. He continued in this manner until the approach of sunset. He did not pause until the entire commentary of the Súrih was completed.
>
> He then laid down His pen and asked for tea. Soon after, He began to read it aloud in my presence. My heart leaped madly as I heard Him pour out, in accents of unutterable sweetness, those treasures enshrined in that sublime commentary. I was so entranced by its beauty that three times over I was on the verge of fainting. He sought to revive my failing strength with a few drops of rose-water which He ... sprinkled on my face. This restored my vigour and enabled me to follow His reading to the end. – Vahíd[375]

Vahíd was captured utterly by the astonishing speed of the Báb's Revelation, about 2,000 verses in less about five hours![376] He was deeply moved by His exquisite and rapid handwriting and by the incomparable beauty of His words. He found himself edified by the profound insights the verses contained.

In the days which followed, Vahíd and another Bábí worked carefully to transcribe and copy the Text of the Báb's Revelation.

> [We] devoted three days and three nights to this work. We would in turn read aloud to each other a portion of the commentary until the whole of it had been transcribed. We verified all the traditions in the text and found them to be entirely accurate. Such was the state of certitude to which I had attained that if all the powers of the earth were to be leagued against me they would be powerless to shake my confidence in the greatness of His Cause. – Vahíd[377]

Málmírí summarized the progression which Vahíd had experienced:

> At the first meeting, which took about an hour, he saw himself superior to the Báb. In the second session, which lasted an hour, he saw himself equal to Him. And by the third time, again about an hour, he saw himself as a lowly servant and observed in Him the Exalted Lord. The truth of the Cause became apparent to him. – Malmírí[378]

Rouhani gives another insight into the spiritual journey of Vahíd. He explains that Vahíd visited Qazvín at least five times during his journeys. Three of those times were before He met the Báb. Vahíd had always been continuously learning. His insights about religion were constantly evolving, even before he met the Báb. The following is paraphrased from the Persian by Rouhani.

- On his first visit to Qazvín, Vahíd was an eminent but orthodox scholar. He condemned the Shaykhí teachings from the pulpit.
- On his second visit, his tone was changed, and he approved the teachings of both the Shaykhís and the orthodox religious leaders.
- On his third visit, he approved of the Shaykhí teachings and rejected the teachings of the orthodox religious leaders.

After his third visit he was in Tihrán, and this is when the Sháh told him to go and investigate the Call of the Báb.

- On his fourth visit to Qazvin, in the home of one of the local religious leaders, he taught the proofs of the Báb's mission, explained the signs of the Dawn of His revelation, and removed the doubts of the people.
- On his fifth visit to Qazvín, Vahíd gave more sermons and spoke at many other venues in town. He gave more proofs of the Báb's mission. His audience was generally receptive.[379]

On this fifth trip, he answered questions from the people. Mullá Ja'far-i-Qazvíní recorded one of these answers which he heard from Vahíd. We can surmise from his answer that the question was, 'How do you know the claims of the Báb are true?' This was his answer. The following is paraphrased from the Persian by Rouhani.

> After I heard of this call, I went to Shíráz and sat next to the Báb and asked for proof and writings. He consented. I requested a commentary of the Súrih-i-Kawthar, the shortest Súrih in Qur'án. He asked if I wanted it verbally or in writing. I requested in writing.
>
> Then He held the pen and the paper by His hand, and He poured words like as jewels and pearls upon those pages. The pen was moving with a speed and His writing was so rapid that the movement of His blessed fingers was incomprehensible. Without thinking, reflection, or pause, He wrote more than two thousand verses and He then offered it to me. I realized that this is beyond the power of a human being writing these words without thinking and pause. Therefore, I became certain and assured of His Truth, and of the falsehood of anything but Him. Then He said I was now His defender and supporter. – Vahíd, as recorded by Mullá Ja'far-e-Qazvíní[380]

Mázindarání shares another report of Vahíd's interactions with the Báb, this one taking place outside the context of the three interviews. The report is from Siyyid Javád Karbilá'i, an eyewitness and the writer of this account, and later recorded in the history books by the great scholar Mírzá Abu'l-Fadl. The event unfolds at the home of the Báb's uncle. We have it from Mázindarání. The following is paraphrased from the Persian by Mázindarání.

> …During the times when he was meeting with the Báb, Vahid brought me a notebook of difficult questions and abstruse problems that he himself had written. He said to please give them to the Báb and ask Him to give the answers.
>
> The Báb came to the uncle's home early in the evening. The hour was getting late as we talked and ate food. After the food, the Báb returned to His house to rest. I gave Mubarak the notebook of Vahíd's questions and asked him to give it to the Báb and to explain that these are questions from Vahíd.
>
> When we rose up at dawn and were getting ready for the dawn prayers, suddenly the Báb arrived and brought a notebook of a stack of papers in His own handwriting in answer to the questions asked by Vahíd.
>
> This delighted Vahíd as he read some of it under the light of a candle and [I observed] strange behavior from him. Although he had been calm and dignified, he began to demonstrate silly movements as if he was going to dance.
>
> [Karbilá'i said to Vahíd:] "What is wrong?"
>
> [Vahíd said:] "Javád, it took me a whole week to write these questions. Tonight, from sunset to late in the evening, the Báb was here with us for four or five hours, and then He returned home to rest for four to five hours. [And now it is early morning.] I swear by God! How He revealed these Writings in such a short time is a clear Book by itself…" – Comments of Siyyid Javád Karbilá'i[381]

These stories of Vahíd give a glimpse of a man already on a spiritual journey even before he arrived in Shíráz to meet with the Báb. Vahíd was a mixture of qualities. He was overly confident in his learning and initially thought himself superior to the Báb. He was a dynamic personality that, despite his attitude, was already on the move, thoroughly engaged with the process of learning and evolving his views. He was sufficiently engaged in that process that, when presented with astonishing demonstrations of Divine power, he was willing to be convinced. The fact that he was the king's scholar, an impediment at first, did not prevent him from finding the Faith. He allowed his skepticism to be conquered by the profound evidence he saw with his own eyes. In the end, by evolving, he became assured and, before long, a heroic champion of the Cause.

'Abdu'l-Bahá states that, after Shíráz, Vahíd…

> …wrote without fear or care a detailed account of his observations to Mírzá Lutf-'Alí the chamberlain in order that the latter might submit it to the notice of the late king, while he himself journeyed to all parts of Persia… – 'Abdu'l-Bahá[382]

While in the court of the Sháh, Mírzá Lutf-'Alí later became a Bábí through Vahíd.[383] Málmírí states that Vahíd wrote to the people of Yazd. At the top of his letter he composed the following poem. The poem is paraphrased from the Persian by Málmírí.

[Note: In the second line of the poem, "Túr" refers to the Revelation to Moses through the Burning Bush (i.e. Túr-i-Síná, Mount Sinai). The fire refers to the Voice of God within the Burning Bush. Vahíd is equating the voice of the Báb to the Voice of God in the Burning Bush. Vahíd's vision is not limited to the Báb's claim to be the Gate. He sees in Him the Manifestation of the Light of God's Revelation, God's "Divine-Self".]

I see a fire, O friends, from far
warmth felt upon my eye from the palm tree of Túr
flame-like, it is showing itself
Unveils, the claim of its Divine-self.[384]

Vahíd left Shíráz and went to all parts of Persia.

As requested by the Báb, his first destination was the town of Burújird, the home of Vahíd's father. His first mission was to inform his illustrious father, Siyyid Ja'far Kashfí, about the Cause of the Báb. Recall that Kashfí had met the Báb in Mecca but did not recognize His station. Rouhani mentions that Kashfí had written many books, had established himself in numerous cities, and formed an extensive family. He spent his time "on spiritual practices such as seclusion and fasting and had become known for his spiritual intuition and virtues."[385] Rouhani notes that the Báb had not approved of most of the renowned Islámic philosophers of His day, but had looked upon Kashfí with respect and approval.[386]

Vahíd presented eight reasons for how he knew the truth of the Báb to his father. The following is paraphrased from the Persian by Rouhani.

[Note: In the 8th item below, Vahíd makes reference to the Imám 'Alí. 'Alí was the son-in-law and cousin of the Prophet Muhammad and, according to the Shi'his, the chosen successor to Muhmmad, the very first Imám and one of the holiest figures in Islám.]

---

1. The Báb is unlettered, devoid of formal education.
2. He expresses and solves difficult and abstruse questions with brevity.
3. His words are not like those of the religious leaders. They are unique and coming from His own innate knowledge.
4. During answering a question, if there is a very small piece of paper in His hand that He can only write one sentence on, He is able to give a sufficient answer on that paper, and it is so complete and perfect that the questioner is satisfied, whereas the religious leaders need to answer with lengthy arguments.
5. With all the beauty of His penmanship that is special to Him, He writes with utmost rapidity, while the norm [for most people] is that beautiful handwriting [can only be produced] with slowness of pen.
6. More important is His character, which in every way is distinct from others. Even his sitting and his standing is unique and not like anyone else.
7. The drinking and eating of His Holiness is not similar to others. I have attentively observed this myself. All the food that He has for the day is less than two bites of a man… And when He sits and eats with others it is as an equal (that is, even if that person is from a lower social class).
8. No one has the power and perseverance of His worship, which is similar to the manner of His Holiness, Imám 'Alí... – Vahíd[387]

These were the signs of the Báb's greatness which Vahíd chose to share with his father. Vahíd explains what happened when he approached his father:

> [The Báb] urged me to exercise towards him the utmost forbearance and consideration. From my confidential conversations with him I gathered that he was unwilling to repudiate the truth of the Message

I had brought him. He preferred, however, to be left alone and to be allowed to pursue his own way. – Vahíd[388]

Rouhani stated that Vahíd's father was sufficiently impressed with the eight points that he forwarded them on to a friend of his, Mu'ín'ul-Saltanih of Tabríz. This friend later became a Bábí and subsequently wrote an extensive history of the Faith, which has been used by many scholars. We have Vahíd's eight points because Saltanih recorded them in his history. In any case, Kashfí told his son, "I am too old to actively serve."[389]

Vahíd continued his journeys throughout Persia. In the course of the next four years, he crisscrossed the entire country of Persia. I was unable to clearly draw his route on a map because he went back and forth across Persia – east to west, north to south, covering great distances. The best I could do was to place his many destinations on a map without lines for his itinerary. The list on the right of the graphic is in chronological order.[390] (See the graphic.)

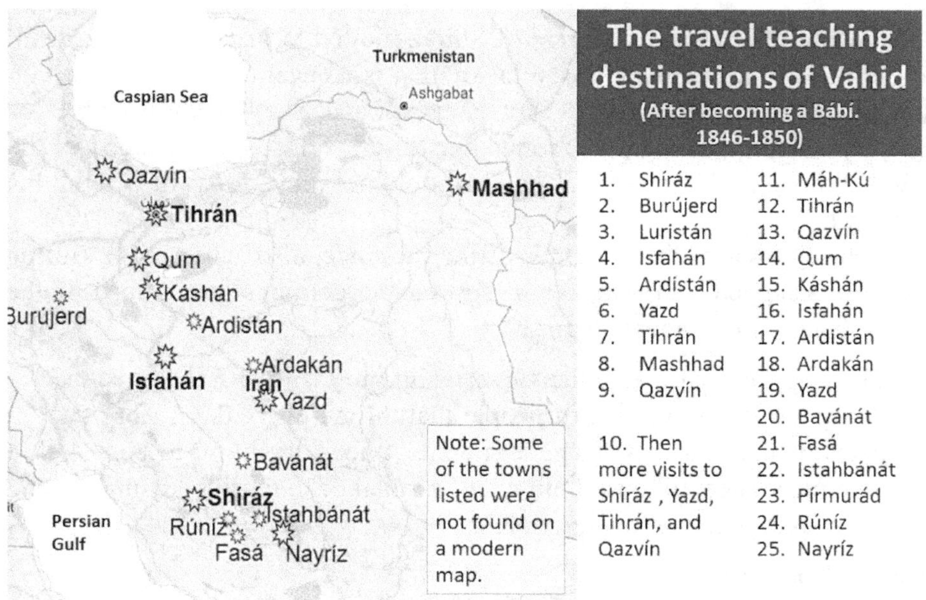

Figure 25 The travel teaching destinations of Vahíd, 1844-1850

It seems logical to assume that Vahíd still had the horse that the king had given him for his journey to Shíráz. On a horse, he would have been more able to cover greater distances. As "the king's scholar", everywhere he went his reputation attracted vast audiences. He ascended the pulpit at the mosques and addressed the crowds wherever he went. On some occasions, he spoke to thousands of people, proclaiming the message of the Báb and bringing many people to the Faith. This disconcerted the other religious leaders to such an extent that, as 'Abdu'l-Bahá put it, they "decided that he must be mad, accounting it a sure case of bewitchment."[391] Muhammad Sháh, however, continued to trust Vahíd's wisdom. He reportedly told his Prime Minister, Hájí Mírzá Áqásí,

> We have been lately informed that [Vahíd] has become a Bábí. If this be true, it behooves us to cease belittling the cause of that siyyid [the Báb]. – Muhammad Sháh, King of Persia[392]

In fact, Vahíd was not the only dignitary who was won to the Cause of the Báb. Many were attracted and converted. So many, in fact, that it can be stated this period witnessed the birth of the Bábí community in Shíráz.

Midnight raid and a cholera epidemic

Meanwhile, the religious leaders of Shíráz plotted to bring about the death of the Báb. To accomplish this, a fatwá, that is, a legal order, was drawn up and signed by all the clerics of Shíráz, except one, Shaykh Abú-Turáb. This Shaykh, who ranked highest among all in Shíráz, refused to sign because the Báb had done nothing wrong. The plot could not move forward without his signature.

Husayn Khán, the governor of the province, also schemed to kill the Báb. He assigned secret agents to spy on the comings and goings of the Bábís. One of these agents reported:

> The eager crowd that gathers every night to visit the Báb surpasses in number the multitude of people that throng every day before the gates of the seat of your government. Among them are to be seen men celebrated alike for their exalted rank and extensive learning. – An agent reporting to Husayn Khán[393]

Husayn Khán asserted:

> I swear by the imperial diadem of Muhammad Sháh that this very night I shall have the Siyyid-i-Báb executed... – Husayn Khán[394]

Husayn Khán was not acting alone. Secretly, and contrary to the wishes of the Sháh, Prime Minister Áqásí had been telling him to bring about the Báb's death. The following is paraphrased from the Persian by Husaini.

> The Prime Minister had secretly ordered Husayn Khán to prepare a

> way to execute the Báb… Therefore, Husayn Khán consulted with 'Abdu'l-Hamíd Khán, the chief constable of Shíráz, and they agreed to have a local group of vigilantes do the deed because a public government-led execution was contrary to the order of the Prime Minister, and also because it would cause a tumult due to the Báb being a Siyyid, and if they caused unrest they would then be answerable to the central government… [Despite this], Husayn Khán ordered the chief constable to invade the house of the Báb's uncle with his agents, not the vigilantes, and arrest the Báb and his followers to bring them to the seat of the government. So, during the night of September 23, 1846, 'Abdu'l-Hamíd and his agents climbed up the wall of the house of the Báb's uncle and from the roof they invaded the house. Despite the reports of a large number of people at the house, they found no one but the Báb, [the uncle] and [a friend] Siyyid Kázim Zanjání." – Husaini[395]

The uncle was ordered to stay in his home. The other two were arrested and the Sacred Writings in their possession were confiscated.[396] The plan was to bring the Báb and Siyyid Kázim Zanjání to Governor Husayn Khán. But while the soldiers were en route, they discovered the city was in a panic. Suddenly, people were screaming in anguish. Citizens were fleeing in every direction from the city. The chief constable "was struck with horror" when he saw a long procession of coffins being carried through the city streets.[397]

The city was suddenly in the grip of a severe cholera epidemic.

Bewildered and dismayed by what he saw, the constable asked a citizen about these events. He was told,

> This very night, a plague of exceptional virulence has broken out. We are smitten by its devastating power. Already since the hour of midnight it has extinguished the lives of over a hundred people. Alarm and despair reign in every house. The people are abandoning their homes, and in their plight are invoking the aid of the Almighty. – A citizen during the epidemic in Shíráz.[398]

When the constable heard this, he hurried with his captives to the home of Husayn Khán, only to discover that the governor's home had been ravaged by the disease and that Husayn Khán himself had fled the city, leaving the dead unburied in his home. The constable then decided to bring his three captives to his own home, pending further instructions.[399] Nabíl says,

> As he was approaching his house, he was struck by the sound of weeping and wailing of the members of his household. His son had been attacked by the plague and was hovering on the brink of death. In his despair, he threw himself at the feet of the Báb and tearfully implored Him to save the life of his son. He begged Him to forgive his past transgressions and misdeeds.
>
> "I adjure you," he entreated the Báb as he clung to the hem of His garment, "by Him who has elevated you to this exalted position, to intercede in my behalf and to offer a prayer for the recovery of my son. Suffer not that he, in the prime of youth, be taken away from me. Punish him not for the guilt which his father has committed. I repent of what I have done, and at this moment resign my post..."
>
> The Báb ... directed him to take some of the water with which He was washing His face to his son and request him to drink it. This He said would save his life.
>
> No sooner had [the constable] witnessed the signs of the recovery of his son than he wrote a letter to the Governor in which he acquainted him with the whole situation and begged him to cease his attacks on the Báb.
>
> "Have pity on yourself," he wrote him, "as well as on those whom Providence has committed to your care. Should the fury of this plague continue its fatal course, no one in this city, I fear, will by the end of this day have survived the horror of its attack." – Nabíl[400]

According to 'Abdu'l-Bahá, Husayn Khán replied with instructions to release the Báb on condition of His leaving the city.[401] Earlier that night Husayn Khán had declared his intention to murder the Báb. He found instead that he was the one fleeing for his life.

Nevertheless, when he later reentered the city, Governor Husayn Khán resumed the harsh treatment of the Bábís. After the Báb had left the city, Husayn Khán rounded up the believers and beat many of them with sticks. The following is paraphrased from the Persian by Husaini.

> ...After the Báb left for Isfahán, the epidemic of cholera in Shíráz lessened and the Governor of Shíráz returned to the seat of the government and resumed his oppression. He realized he could not reach the Báb who had left for Isfahán, so he began to harass the Báb's relatives... He ordered his agents to go to the house of the Báb's brother-in-law,

Jinab-i-Mírzá Abul-Qásim Afnán, and bring him to the seat of the government. Mírzá Abul-Qásim was in bed, still sick from cholera.

Disregarding his promise to the Báb, Abdul-Hamid Khán, [the chief constable], followed the Governor's order and with a group of his agents and a few troublemakers invaded the brother-in-law's home. As the servant of the house opened the door, they barged in and began to search for the Báb. The more Mírzá Abul-Qásim and his family said that they had no knowledge of the Báb's whereabouts, the more the agents harassed them. Finally, they carried Mírzá Abul-Qásim on their shoulders to the Governor who angrily demanded that he produce the Báb for him. Mírzá Abul-Qásim said, "I have been sick, and I don't know where the Báb is." The Governor gave him fifteen days to bring him the Báb, otherwise he would have to pay 15,000 túmáns to the Governor.

After the fifteen days, the Governor brought Mírzá Abul-Qásim back and demanded payment of the 15,000 túmáns. Again, the brother-in-law said that he had no knowledge of the Báb's whereabouts, but the Governor would not accept it and increased his verbal abuse.

At this moment a special messenger arrived from Manúchihr Khán, the Governor of Isfahán, with an order that he should stop harassing the Báb's relatives. Out of fear, the Governor calmed down and agreed to accept only 1,500 túmáns, [1/10th of what he was demanding], from Mírzá Abul-Qásim.

Husayn Khán's oppression continued. He ordered that if the Writings of the Báb were found in anyone's home, the owner of that house would be executed, and his properties taken away. – Husaini[402]

Husayn Khán's order led many in the city to relinquish their holdings of the Báb's Writings. Stacks of Writings, many of them written on exquisite cashmere paper, were delivered to the home of the Báb's brother-in-law. Balyuzi states that the Báb's uncle, Hájí Mírzá Siyyid 'Alí, out of respect for the Sacred Writings revealed by the Báb, "advised the members of that household to wash away the ink and bury the sodden paper".[403]

Nabíl states that the Sháh was displeased when he heard of the severe treatment Husayn Khán was inflicting upon the Báb and His loved ones, so he sent an imperial edict to Shíráz ordering Husayn Khán's dismissal from office. Nabíl further states:

> From the day of his dismissal, that shameless tyrant fell a victim to countless misfortunes, and was in the end unable to earn even his daily bread. No one seemed willing or able to save him from his evil plight. When, at a later time, Bahá'u'lláh had been banished to Baghdád, Husayn Khán sent Him a letter in which he expressed repentance and promised to atone for his past misdeeds on condition that he should regain his former position. Bahá'u'lláh refused to answer him. – Nabíl[404]

Husaini gives a slightly different version of the ending of Husayn Khán. He states that Husayn Khán was not dismissed by Muhammad Sháh, and that he remained in office until after the death of Muhammad Sháh, some two years later. The following is paraphrased from the Persian by Husaini:

[Note: In the next passage, reference is made to "the people of Fars". Fars is the name of the province of Persia in which the city of Shíráz is located.]

> After the death of Muhammad Sháh and the dismissal of Hájí Mírzá Áqásí, the people of Fars revolted against Husayn Khán and he was dismissed by the new Prime Minister] from his post. He then became a wanderer and he sought protection from the ambassadors of foreign countries, but this did not help. Formerly the Governor of Fars, he and his family became poor and homeless. He lived by begging for food and died in poverty." – Husaini[405]

Regardless of the date of his dismissal, both Nabíl and Husaini agree that Husayn Khán never recovered his career or personal well-being. Nabíl says, "Sunk in misery and shame, he languished until his death."[406] Husaini reports that he was seen as a beggar outside the house of a government official in Tihrán. So great was his abasement, that when he died none who knew him attended his funeral.[407]

'Abdu'l-Hamíd Khán, the chief constable of Shíráz, whose son's life was saved, was not faithful to his promise to the Báb. He did not resign his post. He continued to work for Husayn Khán. Being so tied to the governor, his fortunes deteriorated when Husayn Khán lost his position and was disgraced. The following is paraphrased from the Persian by Faizi.

> The fate of 'Abdu'l-Hamíd, the chief constable of Shíráz, was that after a few years he became disfavored in the court of the Sháh. He was killed, his stomach was torn open, and his body was thrown to the wild animals. – Faizi[408]

Two generations later, fate took an interesting turn. The following is paraphrased from the Persian by Faizi.

> 'Abdu'l-Hamíd's son – the one who was saved from the cholera epidemic by the Báb – was named Mihdí. After Mihdí reached maturity, he chose two wives, and from his second wife, Fátimih, was born a son whose name was Rahmat'u'lláh [i.e. mercy of God], who lived in the city of Hamadán. Attaining to a good ending, Rahmat'u'lláh, recognized and accepted the Cause of the Báb and Bahá'u'lláh. He worked for the railroad in the southern part of Iran.
>
> I [Mr. Faizi] met him in the town of Ahvaz when he was more than sixty and benefited from his spiritual state. Now, his children are all serving the Cause of God with devotion and steadfastness. – Faizi[409]

There were many cholera epidemics in Persia during the 19th Century in Persia, infant mortality rising to over 50% from this disease.[410] The occurrence of a cholera epidemic in Shíráz is not, by itself, noteworthy. However, it was an extremely unlikely coincidence that the massive outbreak occurred *exactly* in Shíráz, *on the very same night, in the same hours, while the police were on the way* to fulfill the Governor's plot to murder the Promised One Who just happened to be residing in *that* city. The Báb later suggested that the cholera epidemic had been an instance of Divine intervention:

> Call thou to remembrance the early days of the Revelation. How great the number of those who died of cholera! That was indeed one of the prodigies of the Revelation, and yet none recognized it! During four years the scourge raged among Shí'ah Muslims without any one grasping its significance!" – The Báb[411]

THE BÁB LEAVES FOR ISFAHÁN

No good-bye

While staying at the home of the constable, the Báb had foreseen His impending expulsion from Shíráz. He used the time available to set His worldly affairs in order.[412] As His father had previously done, the Báb placed His wife and mother in the loving care of His uncle, Hájí Mírzá Siyyid 'Alí, already an ardent believer. According to the rules of society, this made Siyyid 'Alí the legal guardian of the two most beloved women in the Báb's personal life. That night,

He informed His uncle of His intended departure from Shíráz, entrusted both His mother and His wife to his care, and charged him to convey to each the expression of His affection and the assurance of God's unfailing assistance.

[He told His uncle:]

"Wherever they may be, God's all-encompassing love and protection will surround them. I will again meet you amid the mountains of Ádhirbáyján, from whence I will send you forth to obtain the crown of martyrdom. I Myself will follow you, together with one of My loyal disciples, and will join you in the realm of eternity." – Nabíl, reporting on the Báb[413]

The Báb left the constable's home the next day and traveled to Isfahán never to return. The Báb was not given an opportunity to say good-bye to His family.

The Báb never saw His mother again.

The Báb and Khadíjih never saw one another again.

ONWARD TO THE REST OF THE STORY IN PART TWO

The Báb's expulsion from Shíráz marked a major turning point in His Ministry. During the years to come, He would pour forth His revelation at a speed and productivity never before seen in the annals of humanity's religious history. He would fully reveal His teachings, His laws and the magnitude of His spiritual claims. He would increasingly focus the attention and the hopes of His followers on the near Advent of Him Whom God shall make manifest, the eagerly awaited Promised One of His Faith. His followers would engineer a dramatic break with Islám and then face unspeakable brutality and repression in three notable locations. They would defend themselves valiantly, and in each location only eventually be crushed by the deception and betrayal of the government. The forces of persecution would, in stages, mow down nearly the entire leadership of His fledgling Cause. After Shíráz, the Báb Himself would experience a brief period of tranquility in Isfahán, followed by harsh exile and imprisonment in Máh-Kú and Chihríq, a mock trial in Tabríz and then, as repeatedly predicted by Him, martyrdom, also in Tabríz. The martyrdom itself would be remembered by future generations as one of the most mysterious, possibly miraculous and thoroughly documented events ever recorded in religious history. And then, two years after the crushing blow of His death, when His Cause was finally teetering on the brink of ultimate extinction, it would be miraculously saved by the one Leader providentially left alive.

All this, and more, will be explored in Part Two of this book.

Chapter 4

THE STATION AND TEACHINGS OF THE BÁB

REVEALING HIS TEACHINGS

Upon being banished from Shíráz, the Báb's next destination was Isfahán. He would spend less than a year in Isfahán and then be banished from that city as well. Sent to Tihrán, He hoped to attain the long sought-after meeting with the Sháh. But the Prime Minister engaged in machinations and prevented the meeting from ever taking place. Instead, the Báb was sent to the Máh-Kú prison, to the Chihríq prison, and then finally to His martyrdom in Tabríz. Despite the extreme deprivation of His imprisonment, the Báb was phenomenally productive during His time at Máh-Kú and Chihríq, using His time there to more fully reveal His teachings.

Nader Saiedi discusses the significance of this stage in His ministry:

> The Báb's imprisonment in Mákú marks the most important turning point in His mission… It is during the Mákú period that He begins to declare His true station openly, announcing that not only is He the promised Qá'im but also a new Manifestation of God… [This] stage sees the explicit proclamation of a new religious Dispensation and the abrogation of the laws of Islám. It is also in [this stage] that the Báb begins to employ a completely new set of terms and concepts as vehicles of that Revelation… [One] major term characteristic of this stage is *"Man Yuzhiruhu'lláh"*, He Whom God shall make manifest, referring to the Promised One Who would come after the Báb. In fact, the most visible sign of [this stage] of writing is the presence of this term, which is absent from the Báb's earlier writings. – Nader Saiedi[414]

Although the claim to be "the Gate" (the Báb) to Him Whom God shall make manifest had been present in His Writings from the very earliest days of His revelation, this claim was only now taking on absolutely explicit expression with this new terminology. Most people today, if they know about the Báb, describe Him first as the Forerunner of Bahá'u'lláh (Who in 1863 would claim to be Him Whom God shall make manifest). But, in the years prior to Máh-Kú and Chihriq, if the concept of Him Whom God shall make manifest was not yet being talked about explicitly, what other things was the Báb talking about? Why were the believers willing to endure so much hardship to spread the Faith? Why did they risk bringing down upon themselves the condemnation and hatred of their government and religious leaders?

To answer, we must explore the station and the teachings of the Báb.

THE STATION OF THE BÁB

The Báb and Bahá'u'lláh are the Twin Founders of the Bahá'í Faith.

There is an interesting reversal in the birthdays and ministries of these two great Personages. The Báb, born in 1819, was two years younger than Bahá'u'lláh, but His ministry came first, in 1844. Bahá'u'lláh was born two years earlier, in 1817, but His Ministry came after the Báb, beginning in 1852. Thus, the Báb's ministry was from 1844 to 1850 and Bahá'u'lláh's ministry was from 1852 to 1892. The Báb and Bahá'u'lláh were both descendants of Abraham.

The Báb has a twofold spiritual station:

- He is a Manifestation of the Primal Will of God and the Revealer of His own independent Revelation from God
- He is the Forerunner of Bahá'u'lláh

As a Herald, He prepared His followers for the imminent appearance of Bahá'u'lláh. As a Manifestation, He imparted to the world a vast Revelation body of teachings, some of which are discussed in this chapter, which are well suited for the age in which we live.

Although the Báb devoted an enormous amount of energy to His role as Herald, being the Forerunner of Bahá'u'lláh is *not* the Báb's *primary* claim to greatness:

> Indeed the greatness of the Báb consists primarily, not in His being the divinely-appointed Forerunner of so transcendent a Revelation… – Shoghi Effendi[415]

Instead, His greatness was *primarily* based on the fact that He was a Manifestation of the Primal Will of God, the Author of a distinctive revelation from God. Shoghi Effendi continues…

> …but rather in His having been invested with the powers inherent in the inaugurator of a separate religious Dispensation, and in His wielding, to a degree unrivaled by the Messengers gone before Him, the scepter of independent Prophethood. – Shoghi Effendi[416]

Though He was the Forerunner of Bahá'u'lláh, He wielded "the scepter of independent Prophethood" to an unprecedented degree. This is the primary foundation of His greatness and the reason it is so important to learn how His teachings are a vital chapter in the never-ending, ever-advancing process of the Divine Curriculum.

We note that Shoghi Effendi makes this comparative claim in relation to the Messengers "gone before Him", thus not including Bahá'u'lláh, Who came after Him. Shoghi Effendi is not claiming that the Báb wielded "the scepter of independent Prophethood" in a manner that was greater than Bahá'u'lláh. In this statement, Shoghi Effendi doesn't mention that point. The comparison is with the Messengers "gone before" the Báb.

Unlike the Dispensations which preceded the Báb's, His Dispensation was very short, barely nine years. Bahá'u'lláh explained:

> That so brief a span should have separated this most mighty and wondrous Revelation from Mine own previous Manifestation, is a secret that no man can unravel and a mystery such as no mind can fathom. Its duration had been foreordained, and no man shall ever discover its reason unless and until he be informed of the contents of My Hidden Book. – Bahá'u'lláh[417]

Shoghi Effendi asserts:

> The short duration of His Dispensation, the restricted range within which His laws and ordinances have been made to operate, supply no criterion whatever wherewith to judge its Divine origin and to evaluate the potency of its message. – Bahá'u'lláh[418]

Instead, he says…

> The marvelous happenings that have heralded the [coming of the Báb], the dramatic circumstances of His own eventful life, the miraculous tragedy of His martyrdom, the magic of His influence exerted on the most eminent and powerful among His countrymen … should in themselves

> be regarded as sufficient evidence of the validity of His claim to so exalted a station among the Prophets. – Shoghi Effendi[419]

As already cited, one of the signs of the Báb's greatness was the dramatic circumstances of His life. The most dramatic feature of His life was the nature of His Revelation. Unique in its mastery of language, breathtaking in the scope of its themes, groundbreaking in the exalted spirit of its Message, stunning in the quality and speed with which it was revealed, and impressive for the harsh conditions under which it was produced, the Báb's Revelation was a literal downpour of Divine verses. Bahá'u'lláh affirmed:

> No eye hath beheld so great an outpouring of bounty... [The] verses which have rained from this Cloud of divine mercy have been so abundant that none hath yet been able to estimate their number... Hath any age witnessed such momentous happenings? – Baha'u'llah[420]

In Máh-Kú, by the end of the fourth year of His ministry, the Báb states that He had revealed "no less than five hundred thousand verses."[421] To put this in perspective, the entire Qur'án was 6,236 verses, revealed by one Person. The Bible, the Old and New Testaments, has 31,175 verses, written by different authors spanning centuries. Mathematically, the 500,000 verses of the Báb are equivalent to 80.2 Qur'áns. In sheer quantity, the Qur'án had been the greatest outpouring of Revelation by a single Author that humanity had ever seen. Muhammad had twenty-two years to reveal one Qur'án, but the Báb had only six years total, and only four years to Máh-Kú. To accomplish His feat, the Báb's rate of production exceeded anything ever seen before. Muhammad revealed, on average, 283 verses per year;[422] Up to Máh-Kú, the Báb, on average, revealed 125,000 verses per year. To achieve this incredible pace during the amount of time He had, the Báb had to reveal verses 441 times faster, on average, than Muhammad.

The Báb's output of Divine verses Compared with the Qur'án				
	Total verses revealed	Years to make	Verses per year	Verses per day
By the end of the Báb's time at Máh-Kú (with two more years of His ministry remaining)	500,000	4	125,000	342.5
The Qur'án (with Muhammad's full twenty-two-year ministry)	6,236	22	283	0.8
The Báb's output of verses compared to Muhammad	80.2 times more verses			
The Báb's speed compared to Muhammad	441.0 times faster			

Figure 26 The Báb's revelatory output

One should note that in the 19th Century in Persia, technological innovations such as the computer, the typewriter, a tape recorder or automated voice dictation, were not available. Not even the ball point pen or the lead pencil were available. Any of these innovations would have made the act of Revelation much faster and easier. In the Báb's era writing was done with a quill and an ink bottle, a much slower method of writing. One had to dip the quill into the ink and then write a few words until the ink ran out. Then one had to dip the quill again. One had to be careful not to pick up too much ink, because then the writing would look splotchy. And then repeat this process, again and again and again, through the entire process of writing. The Báb's sheer physical act of writing so rapidly under such physically limiting conditions, with such exquisite penmanship, and such eloquent and insightful utterance, was in itself a stunning achievement.

In addition, the process of making a copy of a manuscript in the 19th Century could not be done with a photocopy machine or a computer printer. A copy was made by hand, slowly, again through the use of a quill and a bottle of ink.

Figure 27 Persian writing with quill and ink bottle, from *The Gate: Dawn of the Bahá'í Faith*

The Báb explained that His revelation experience was different from that of the earlier Prophets. For example, Muhammad said that revelation only came upon Him under certain conditions, when He periodically entered into a trance-like state for short periods of time. This state was obvious to all onlookers. Then, after these episodes, He would announce that new verses had been received from God. We can imagine that the obvious appearance of these episodes made it easier for the people of His time to accept the Words He revealed as the Words of God.

The Báb's experience was something new in history. For the first time in history, God offered the revelation experience continuously. The Báb stated:

> Many a time, so often that none except God can know, [the Primal Reality] is crying out ceaselessly and without interruption… – The Báb[423]

Nader Saiedi commented:

> …the Báb claims to live ceaselessly in that sublime station of intimate converse with the Divine… [The revelation of divine verses] is continuous and ceaseless, unlike the assumed discontinuous way the Qur'án was revealed to Muhammad. The reason it should be noted, is the differing receptivity of the audience… – Nader Saiedi[424]

As Saiedi noted, this difference in the process of revelation does not indicate any difference among the Manifestations of God Themselves. God is able to reveal verses to any of the Manifestations of God at whatever speed or manner God wishes. The key variable is the gradually evolving capacity of the followers. Just as a wise parent carefully guides a child through gradually advancing stages of development, God does not reveal His teachings according to the capacity of the Messengers to deliver them, but according to the capacity of the followers to receive them. In the earlier stages of development, the parent gives knowledge to the child in smaller, more digestible morsels. Later on, as the child makes progress, the parent delivers larger servings and more advanced teachings. This is due to the ever-growing capacity of the child.

The Báb's experience of continuous revelation and His prodigious output of Divine verses are signs of His having wielded, "to a degree unrivaled by the Messengers gone before Him, the scepter of independent Prophethood". These are a demonstration of humanity's growing capacity to receive a vastly intensified Revelation. To reveal the Word of God at this rapid pace, one can assume that the Báb was in the state of Divine revelation nearly constantly.

It is important to examine the content of the Báb's teachings for their intrinsic merit, and to discover what attracted so many fervent followers. What did He teach that so many people, upon simply reading His Words, or hearing someone quote Him, almost immediately believed in Him, transformed their lives, and ultimately gave their lives for His Cause?

We will explore these questions very shortly, but first we'll give equal attention to His role as Forerunner.

THE COMING OF HIM WHOM GOD SHALL MAKE MANIFEST

The Báb, in addition to having His own independent religious Dispensation, was the Forerunner of a Manifestation of God soon to come after Him. He referred to this great Personage in His Writings as Him Whom God shall make manifest. At the time, His identity was undisclosed, but today we know He was referring to Bahá'u'lláh.

The Báb anticipated that abrogation/exaltation (irtifá') would apply equally to His own Dispensation:

> ...the Bayán hath no goal but Him Whom God shall make manifest, inasmuch as none save Him hath ever elevated/abrogated, or will ever elevate/abrogate this Book. – The Báb[425]

The Báb praised Him Whom God shall make manifest repeatedly and in glowing terms. Here is one example:

> I swear by the most sacred Essence of God that but one line of the Words uttered by Him [i.e. Him Whom God shall make manifest] is more sublime than the words uttered by all that dwell on earth. Nay, I beg forgiveness for making this comparison. How could the reflections of the sun in the mirror compare with the wondrous rays of the sun in the visible heaven? The station of one is that of nothingness, while the station of the other, by the righteousness of God—hallowed and magnified be His Name—is that of the Reality of things.... – The Báb[426]

The Báb promised the followers that Him Whom God shall make manifest was already in the world. He was already present among the followers, His true station as yet unrevealed:

> Say, He Whom God shall make manifest is but one of you; He will make Himself known unto you on the Day of Resurrection. – The Báb[427]

Shoghi Effendi summarized the Báb's sense of anticipation for the Revelation yet to come:

> Again and again the Báb admits, in glowing and unequivocal language, the preeminent character of a Faith destined to be made manifest after Him and to supersede His Cause. "The germ," He asserts in the Persian Bayán, the chief and best-preserved repository of His laws, "that holds within itself the potentialities of the Revelation that is to come is endowed with a potency superior to the combined forces of all those who follow me." "Of all the tributes," the Báb repeatedly proclaims in His writings, "I have paid to Him Who is to come after Me, the greatest is this, My written confession, that no words of Mine can adequately describe Him, nor can any reference to Him in my Book, the Bayán, do justice to His Cause." Addressing [Vahíd] … He says: "By the righteousness of Him Whose power causeth the seed to germinate and Who breatheth the spirit of life into all things, were I to be assured that in the day of His Manifestation thou wilt deny Him, I would unhesitatingly disown thee and repudiate thy faith.... If, on the other hand, I be told that a Christian, who beareth no allegiance to My Faith, will believe in Him, the same will I regard as the apple of Mine eye. – Shoghi Effendi[428]

> All that hath been revealed in the Bayán is but a ring upon My hand, and I Myself am, verily, but a ring upon the hand of Him Whom God

shall make manifest... He turneth it as He pleaseth, for whatsoever He pleaseth, and through whatsoever He pleaseth. He, verily, is the Help in Peril, the Most High. – The Báb[429]

A thousand perusals of the Bayán cannot equal the perusal of a single verse to be revealed by 'Him Whom God shall make manifest.'... Today the Bayán is in the stage of seed; at the beginning of the manifestation of 'Him Whom God shall make manifest' its ultimate perfection will become apparent.... The Bayán and such as are believers therein yearn more ardently after Him than the yearning of any lover after his beloved.... The Bayán deriveth all its glory from 'Him Whom God shall make manifest.' All blessing be upon him who believeth in Him and woe betide him that rejecteth His truth. – The Báb[430]

Just as the Báb had come to gather the fruit of the Tree of Islámic Revelation, so too Him Whom God shall make manifest will gather the fruit of the Tree of the Bábí Revelation when He appears:

Praise be to God that He hath enabled us to become cognizant of Him Whom God shall make manifest in the Day of Resurrection, so that we may derive benefit from the fruit of our existence and be not deprived of attaining the presence of God. For indeed this is the object of our creation and the sole purpose underlying every virtuous deed we may perform. Such is the bounty which God hath conferred upon us; verily He is the All-Bountiful, the Gracious. – The Báb[431]

The Báb was entirely focused on preparing the way for Him Whom God shall make manifest:

He—glorified be His mention—resembleth the sun. Were unnumbered mirrors to be placed before it, each would, according to its capacity, reflect the splendour of that sun, and were none to be placed before it, it would still continue to rise and set, and the mirrors alone would be veiled from its light. I, verily, have not fallen short of My duty to admonish that people, and to devise means whereby they may turn towards God, their Lord, and believe in God, their Creator. If, on the day of His Revelation, all that are on earth bear Him allegiance, Mine inmost being will rejoice, inasmuch as all will have attained the summit of their existence, and will have been brought face to face with their Beloved, and will have recognized, to the fullest extent attainable in the world of being, the splendour of Him Who is the Desire of their hearts. If not, My soul will indeed be saddened. I truly have nurtured all things for this purpose. – The Báb[432]

THE TRANSCENDENT INFINITY AND ONENESS OF GOD'S ESSENCE

More than anything else, one must begin a study of the Báb's teachings with His guidance concerning the ultimate Reality of God. In full alignment with the previous Messengers of God, the Báb stressed the oneness of God and a very strong ethical monotheism. His teachings are centered on a conception of God as one, infinite, personally relatable, ultimate goodness, full of grace, and utterly transcendent beyond the reach or the comprehension of any of His creatures.

According to the Báb, there can be no *direct* connection between the exalted Being of God and any created thing, nor can there be any adequate descriptions of God's Nature because, unlike the grasping human minds striving to comprehend God's Essence, God is not in any way limited by the constraints of space, time, energy, matter or physical laws. In the Báb's Writings, God is self-subsisting, that is, His existence is self-sustaining, eternal, and not dependent upon the consent, decree, support, or sustenance from any other being. He stated:

> God indeed is the Sovereign Truth, Who is manifestly Supreme over His servants; He is the Help in Peril, the Self-Subsisting. God testifieth that there is none other God but Him... He is exalted above the comprehension of all things, and is inscrutable to the mind of every created being; none shall be able to fathom the oneness of His Being or to unravel the nature of His Existence. – The Báb[433]

> ...from everlasting God hath been invested with the independent sovereignty of His exalted Being, and unto everlasting He will remain inaccessible in the transcendent majesty of His holy Essence. – The Báb[434]

> God is sanctified from His servants and no direct relationship ever existeth between Him and any created thing, while ye have all arisen at His bidding. Verily He is your Lord and your God, your Master and your King. – The Báb[435]

> He is God, no God is there but Him, the Almighty, the Best Beloved. All that are in the heavens and on the earth and whatever lieth between them are His. Verily He is the Help in Peril, the Self-Subsisting. – The Báb[436]

The Báb explained that,

> ...any reality to which the term 'being' is applicable hath been created by the sovereign Will of the Almighty... – The Báb[437]

The word "being" refers here to existence. Speaking of the Being of God refers to His existence. But in this passage the Báb states that the term "being", can only refer to a *created* thing, not to the Creator. Whatever God is, whatever His existence consists of, even the word "being" cannot do justice to the Reality of God. Rather, it can only refer to things which have been created by Him. So what word can we use to refer to "the being" of God? No such word exists. Language itself is incapable of adequately alluding to the Reality of God. There is nothing we humans can say, with our limited human minds and feeble human language, that would adequately refer to the Existence and "Being" of God.

Even the statement that "God exists" fails to adequately acknowledge the exalted Essence and Existence that is God. This is certainly *not* to suggest that God doesn't exist. Far from it. Rather, we simply must realize that even terms like "being" and "existence", which seem so straight-forward and obvious to us, are nothing more than limited human conceptions that can, in the end, do no justice to His actual infinite Reality. Similarly, the Báb's Writings refer to God as "He", but this too is a result of there being no adequate way to refer to God in human language.

Despite these realizations, we ironically still find ourselves referring in our day-to-day conversations to "the existence of God". This is as it should be because, in our human condition, and with the constraints of our human languages, we have no choice. There is nothing else we can do. It is wisdom, however, to consciously recognize that we are not adequately referring to God with our words, but rather merely doing the best we can within our limited human condition. We simply trust that God knows this as we strive to be of service and rely on His mercy, and leave it at that. And we remember not to claim we're smarter or more certain of truth than we really are, but to humbly walk in recognition of our true status in the cosmos – mere creatures made by God.

The Báb repeatedly extolled the sublimity of God's station:

> In the Name of God, the Most Exalted, the Most Holy... He Himself hath at all times been immeasurably exalted above any association with His creatures. ... He hath been and will ever be one and incomparable in the transcendent glory of His divine being and He hath ever been indescribably mighty in the sublimity of His sovereign Lordship. No one hath ever been able befittingly to recognize Him nor will any man succeed at any

> time in comprehending Him as is truly meet and seemly, for any reality to which the term 'being' is applicable hath been created by the sovereign Will of the Almighty, Who hath shed upon it the radiance of His Own Self, shining forth from His most august station. ... He hath everlastingly existed and will everlastingly continue to exist. He hath been and will ever remain inscrutable unto all men, inasmuch as all else besides Him have been and shall ever be created through the potency of His command. He is exalted above every mention or praise and is sanctified beyond every word of commendation or every comparison. No created thing comprehendeth Him, while He in truth comprehendeth all things. – The Báb[438]

With words like these, we realize that the Báb wanted His followers to appreciate, to the extent possible for human beings, that the full Reality of the Essence of God is totally, utterly, and absolutely far, far above anything humans can conceive or approach. The sanctity and sublimity of God's Essence is so cosmically beyond human understanding or expression that any human references to God's qualities are not adequate.

For example, consider the term "the Creator". In the Báb's view of the Divine Essence even *this* term must be taken as beneath God! *Of course*, so far as human beings can describe reality, God is the Creator. The Báb's assertion is not a denial. But from the Divine perspective, according to the Báb, even that magnificent term is beneath Him. Consider these statements from the quotations we looked at a moment ago:

> ...[He hath been] He Himself hath at all times been immeasurably exalted above any association with His creatures... – The Báb

> God is sanctified from His servants and no direct relationship ever existeth between Him and any created thing, while ye have all arisen at His bidding. – The Báb[439]

Of course, there is a relationship between God and His creation, but, according to the Báb, there is no *direct* relationship between them. As the Báb explained, the exalted, infinite, sanctity of the Essence of God, means that *all* the human words used to describe God, even terms like Creator, Eternal, Loving, Powerful, Just, Merciful and Wise, are beneath Him and insufficient to describe His Reality. Again, as far as humans can say, God *is* all these things, but our understanding of these concepts and our words fall utterly short of His true Reality.

This is certainly very difficult to wrap one's mind around. For example, everyone reading this, if a believer in God, and even non-believers, probably associates the name 'the Creator' with God. While for practical purposes, we treat this as correct, in ultimate terms no human language can adequately refer to God.

It would be easy to react emotionally to the Báb's explanations, especially if one is a believer, and since such thinking probably goes far beyond what any of us were taught growing up. It would be easy to reject what the Bab is saying, simply because it runs counter to all that we think we know and it makes our heads want to explode to even suggest that so obvious a description of God as the Creator might be beneath God.

But we should be patient instead. There is a truth to be understood.

The *newness* of the Báb's teaching is the degree and intensity to which He explicitly and emphatically emphasized the utterly infinite nature of God's Being. God is not body-bound. God does not have a gender, God is not *physically* near or far, inside or outside, above or below. God is not arriving or departing, coming down or going up, not moving or standing still in any physical sense. God is not subservient to any of the laws of nature. God is not limited by time. God isn't limited by space, or distance, or physical closeness. All the energies of the universe, combined, are submissive to God's command. God is not mortal, nor is God remotely human-like in ways of being, knowing, thinking, feeling or acting. God doesn't procreate physically, suffer from diseases, experience injury, sleep, forget things, or have needs. God has no *need* of any creatures at all. In His divine Essence,

> God hath, at all times and under all conditions, been wholly independent of His creatures. – The Báb[440]

Therefore, any conceiving of God *in the image of man* is a deep fallacy from the point of view of the Báb. Moreover, it is implicitly contrary to the Bible's teaching that it is man that is created in the image of God. This culturally accustomed way of viewing God with human-like attributes is anthropomorphism. One of the primary impacts of the deep theological thinking embedded in the Báb's Revelation is to remove any traces of anthropomorphism. Later, Bahá'u'lláh continued to emphasize this. We can understand that removing anthropomorphism is the logical result of ethical monotheism and in keeping with the progression of Revelation, the never-ending Divine Curriculum, and the work of all the Prophets. Logically, it is where the oneness of God inevitably had to go.

Removing anthropomorphism from our conception of God has huge benefits for human society.

If we are like ants trying to understand God as the Báb suggests, then any concept of God we formulate will fall short of true Reality. Spending decades and centuries trying to win debates and fighting with the followers of other religions about the interior Essence of God, ultimately unknowable anyway, is simply not needed. Why kill somebody over an idea, when neither can possibly be correct? All the fighting about dogma within and between mosques, churches and synagogues can be set aside. People can adopt a more friendly, listening style of discourse with each other. We can be put aside anthropomorphic priest-prompted superstitions, fanciful beliefs, and complex man-made dogmas, all promoted energetically through the ages by seemingly learned theologians and philosophers, and sometimes pressed upon others at the point of a sword.

If we feel we must talk about such things, at least we can hold tentative ideas and questions to explore through humble conversations with other souls, rather than argue and forcefully thrust theological beliefs upon one another. Consider this fascinating passage of the Báb:

> Thus these two would dispute: This one sayeth, "Thou art an extremist," and the other one sayeth, "Thou art intolerant," This one adduceth evidence from a word of God, and that one reasoneth by another word of God. But I affirm unto them: Ye both are true and right, on the condition that thou not say unto him, "He is an extremist," and he not say unto thee, "Thou art intolerant." ... Thus, wert thou to acquire wisdom, thou wouldst not reject anyone because of his limitation, but must foster the growth of all in the palm of thy mercy. Shouldst thou succeed in elevating him to the realm of glory, great would be his blessings from thee; and should he fail to ascend to thy height thou shouldst train him within his own rank of existence. For verily he too is a creation of thy Lord; God loveth him and he loveth God... – The Báb[441]

History is littered with accounts of men fighting over realities which are ultimately beyond their ability to know. The Christian Church, for example, in the early centuries of the Faith, spent years fighting about the interior subjective world of God, debating whether or not, or in what way, God was really three persons in one. Tomes were written about the Trinity concept; mobs were violent, fighting in the streets; Church Councils were held and Roman Emperors intervened in theological questions to achieve political goals.

The history of such disputation is long and tragic and it has by no means been limited to one Church or Faith. To mention one example of this extremism, when the Church Council were held, the creeds were negotiated, argued and written to instruct and direct the members of the Faith in the beliefs that were deemed proper. In the course of such writing, doctrines were specified, individuals were condemned and heretics were cursed. The word used to pronounce a curse on someone was "anathema". To illustrate, the creed from the second church council in Constantinople (in the year 553 AD) included eleven statements of anathema. For brevity sake, we'll cite only the first one and the last one:

> Anathema 1: If anyone does not confess that the Father and the Son and the Holy Spirit are one nature or essence, one power or authority, worshipped as a trinity of the same essence, one deity in three hypostases or persons, let him be anathema. For there is one God and Father, of whom are all things, and one Lord Jesus Christ, through whom are all things, and one Holy Spirit, in whom are all things.
>
> Anathema 11: If anyone does not anathematize Arius, Eunomius, Macedonius, Apollinaris, Nestorius, Eutyches and Origen, together with their impious, godless writings, and all the other heretics already condemned and anathematized by the holy catholic and apostolic Church, and by the aforementioned four Holy Synods and all those who have held and hold or who in their godlessness persist in holding to the end the same opinion as those heretics just mentioned; let him be anathema. – Second Council of Constantinople[442]

We note that in the eleventh anathema, if you are not cursing certain other famous people, such as Arius, Nestorius, and Origen, then you too are to be cursed! You can only be in the good graces of the Faith if you are cursing somebody! Honestly, it is of no interest to us to get involved with the centuries old dispute that these declarations represent. (Whoever was right or wrong is for another book to examine.) The point being made here is simply this: The Báb taught a concept of God that makes all of these accusations and counteraccusations vain and pointless. All human beings are but humble creatures when standing before the Almighty God. The last thing God wants us to do with *His religion* is to act like extremists and intolerants, cursing one another on our sayso.

Setting aside the legitimate and sincere endeavor of believers striving to understand God to the best of their ability, and giving credit to all who engage in a loving and heartfelt search for truth, why should anyone engage in strife over something that, in the final analysis, remains unknowable to humans? You can't know the interior thoughts of the person sitting right next to you unless they choose to tell you, so what makes any of us think we can understand definitively the exalted interior Mind of Almighty God? Rather than fight about such unknowable matters, humans can let go of their anthropomorphic concepts of God. We can engage in loving conversation, seek to learn from one another, and stop fighting over things we cannot ever truly know.

We note that in the above quote the Báb seems to imply that between two people in conversation one might be just slightly more advanced in his understanding than the other. He seems to be saying "So what?" to this. It is no excuse for bad behavior. Both people are so far from really understanding God that their differences are not worth fighting over.

Isn't it sometimes the case that we think we're the smarter one, when in fact the other person is really smarter? Don't we often imagine ourselves as " in the know" and the other person isn't? But doesn't the other person think the same thing too? Who is really smarter? Since both of us, according to the Báb, are little more than "ants" trying to fathom the unfathomable existence of God, what difference does it make if two "ants" are not quite equally far away from truly understanding God? Who cares if one is 900 miles away from the truth and the other in 899 miles away? God is beyond us both. Should the one who is 899 miles away tout his superiority over the one who is 900 miles away? Or should one realize that one is still impossibly far from his goal, and reach out with a hand of fellowship to one who is, relatively speaking, very close in position and take the journey together, arm in arm along the way? The Báb advises both parties to drop the extremist/intolerant dynamic between them, to listen and learn from one another, to not bring grief upon one another, to bring joy to other souls, to strive to lovingly elevate one another, and to remember instead that God loves us both, and we love God.

The driving force for this change of heart comes from the Báb's humbling teaching that we're all just mortal creatures trying our best to understand reality.

> Thou hast asked concerning the fundamentals of religion and its ordinances: Know thou that first and foremost in religion is the knowledge of God. This attaineth its consummation in the recognition of His divine unity, which in turn reacheth its fulfilment in acclaiming that His hallowed and exalted Sanctuary, the Seat of His transcendent majesty, is sanctified from all attributes. And know thou that in this world of being the knowledge of God can never be attained save through the knowledge of Him Who is the Dayspring of divine Reality. – The Báb[443]

> Verily I am Thy servant, O my God … I am conscious that all created things are debarred from Thy sublime Essence and the entire creation is denied access to Thine inmost Being… How can one who is but Thy creature seek reunion with Thee and attain unto Thy presence, whereas no created thing can ever be associated with Thee, nor can aught comprehend Thee?... Thus every created thing beareth witness that it is debarred from the sanctuary of Thy presence by reason of the limitations imposed upon its inner reality. It is undisputed, however, that the influence of Thine attraction hath everlastingly been inherent in the realities of Thy handiwork, although that which beseemeth the hallowed court of Thy providence is exalted beyond the attainment of the entire creation. This indicateth, O my God, my utter powerlessness to praise Thee and revealeth my utmost impotence in yielding thanks unto Thee; and how much more to attain the recognition of Thy divine unity or to succeed in reaching the clear tokens of Thy praise, Thy sanctity and Thy glory. Nay, by Thy might, I yearn for naught but Thine Own Self and seek no one other than Thee. – The Báb[444]

Later, Bahá'u'lláh would confirm the Báb's approach:

> …thou wilt readily admit the futility of such efforts as may be attempted by thee, or by any of the created things, to fathom the mystery of the Living God, the Day Star of unfading glory, the Ancient of everlasting days. This confession of helplessness which mature contemplation must eventually impel every mind to make is in itself the acme of human understanding, and marketh the culmination of man's development. – Bahá'u'lláh[445]

Thus, a human reaches the peak of his understanding and attains the height of development, not when he asserts superiority over others, or when he claims to have fully understood God, but when he makes an earnest "confession of helplessness" based on "mature contemplation" before the awe-inspiring Reality that is God.

What would the Báb do if He encountered a person who wanted to argue about God? He would probably offer a better explanation, to elevate the other person. But if He encountered resistance, wouldn't He try to find a way to express the love of God to avoid an unnecessary and futile fight? Wouldn't He let go of the debate, avoid becoming the cause of any grief or sorrow, and focus instead on building a loving relationship. The Báb would surely engage in impressive discourse, but if the other person was not convinced, after a certain point, He would live and let live. As the Báb stated:

> It is better to guide one soul than to possess all that is on earth, for as long as that guided soul is under the shadow of the Tree of Divine Unity, he and the one who hath guided him will both be recipients of God's tender mercy, whereas possession of earthly things will cease at the time of death. The path to guidance is one of love and compassion, not of force and coercion. This hath been God's method in the past, and shall continue to be in the future! – The Báb[446]

The Báb's approach to the infinity and oneness of God, and the humility of all creatures which it induces, takes away conflicting confrontations about religion. It cleanses theological discussions of toxic attitudes. It releases followers from time-wasting discussions about things that are not knowable. It loosens the grip of dogma on the minds of men. It induces an attitude of generosity and good-will towards other seekers. It has a liberating and expanding effect on human hearts.

THE BÁB'S TEACHING ABOUT THE PRIMAL WILL

Given the majestic and soaring transcendence of God just discussed, our limited human minds may still wonder in what sense God is the Creator, and in what sense God is knowable.

Saying earlier that the term "Creator" is beneath God, does not imply that God is not the Creator. Far from it. God is the Creator. The question is how to understand it. Fortunately, the Báb and later Bahá'u'lláh addressed this point.

In past religions, among many philosophers, theologians and mystics, and the people, all reality has been imagined as having two aspects.

- God
- Creation

First, there is the Essence of God , and then there is everything else, that is, all creation. God is self-sufficient, not caused by anything else. Creation is contingent upon God, caused by Him. So naturally it was thought that the Essence of God is the Creator of all creation. At one level of analysis, this is true.

However, the Báb treats the structure of reality differently. He says there are three aspects to reality:

- God (in His Essence)
- The Primal Will of God
- Creation

The first aspect, God in His Essence, is infinite, unapproachable, beyond any direct connection to anything. This aspect is eternally hidden from view and even the term "Creator" is unworthy of God at this sanctified level.

The second aspect of reality is the Primal Will of God. The Báb says the Primal Will of God is, the first thing to *emanate* from God. It has been known throughout history by other names, such as the Holy Spirit, the Most Great Spirit, the Word of God, the Logos, the First Remembrance, and the First Mind. The Báb says that the Primal Will is created by Itself, which is surely a mysterious statement. The Primal Will is co-eternal with God, and outside of time and space, but since It is an emanation from God, It is said to be contingent upon the Essence of God.

The term "to emanate" is defined by the dictionary as a verb, meaning to flow out, issue, or proceed, as from a source or origin; come forth; originate. Some synonyms in the thesaurus are: come forth; emerge; emit; originate; radiate; birth; flow; issue; proceed; spring and send forth.[447]

Here are analogies to help us think about the idea of emanation.

Think of a book. We can say that a book is an emanation from the mind of the author. It proceeds from the writer, having no existence of its own unless the words flow out of the mind of the writer onto the page. No one can know the thoughts of the writer until after the writer gives life to them in his writing.

Think of a painting. We can say that a painting emanates from the mind of the painter. It proceeds from the artist, who is the fashioner of the painting. No one can see the image of the painting in the mind of the painter. It must issue forth through the skillful hand of the painter filling the empty canvas with the artist's imaginative creation.

But emanation is not limited to physical objects. Consider a mathematician's ideas. The theory of relativity, $e = mc^2$, is a brilliant formula, but no one was aware of it until it emanated from the mind of Albert Einstein.

These examples refer to human creations; each has a beginning point in time. No man-made entity can capture the eternity of God. Since God is not limited by time, but is in fact the Creator of it, the Primal Will is understood to be co-eternal with God. It has "existed" as long as God has existed. Even so, It is contingent upon the "prior" existence of God, from Whom It emanates.

Perhaps the closest example is the sun. In itself, its existence is unapproachable, too intensely bright. The rays of the sun are an emanation from its core. From the rays, spreading out in all directions through the entire solar system, all life on earth is generated. The rays have emanated from the sun for as long as the sun itself has existed. This suggests to us the co-eternity of God and the Primal Will. It also conveys the contingency of the rays on the orb of the sun. Without the sun, there would be no rays shining forth. This seems to work, but it is only a limited analogy.

Just as the powerful rays of the sun emanate from the intense internal activity of the sun, so the Primal Will of God is the first emanation from the sanctified Essence of God.

Candidly, even the concept of emanation fails to do ultimate justice to the infinite Reality of the Primal Will. The Báb writes:

> ...verily God, glorified be He, hath ever been, and will ever exist without anything to exist with Him. He verily hath created all things by virtue of His Will, and hath created the Will by Itself, out of nothing else.... All things are created and affected by It.
>
> ...Then behold naught in the heavens, the earth, and that which lieth between them, save as the effects thereof. They all, verily, are fashioned by the Will and have proceeded from It, while It is verily created by Itself and abideth beneath Its Own Essence. It hath proceeded from God... – The Báb[448]

There is no way to fully comprehend the truth that is being alluded to in this statement. Speaking for myself, all I feel able to achieve is strive to perceive with a spiritual sensibility that a truly profound, cosmic Reality is being suggested.

One observation should not escape our attention. Note how the Báb refers to the Primal Will, which is the Holy Spirit, as an "It", not a "He". Thus, the Primal Will is not presented as a Person, rather as a some-thing. This departs from traditional Christian theology which describes the Holy Spirit/Primal Will as one of three "Persons" of God. On the other hand, this is in alignment with both Jewish and Islámic thinking, both of which never attempted to personify the Holy Spirit.

The Báb's purpose was to draw men away from any limited human ideas about God, to acknowledge the absolutely transcendent character of God, and to leave minds unclouded by preconceptions, misconceptions, prejudices, superstitions, dogmas or anthropomorphic ideas.

The Báb says that the Primal Will of God is the cause of all creation, therefore, it is the Creator of all things. Everything that is not God exists because of the creative activity of His Primal Will. The Primal Will is God expressed at the realm of Divine Action.

According to the Báb, the act of creation, the calling into being of the entirety of the universe, including all the realms of heaven and earth, is the action of the Primal Will, which we now understand as the Creator. The Báb stated:

> He verily hath created the Will by virtue of His Will, and hath created the Will by Itself, out of nothing else... All things are created and affected by It. – The Báb[449]

> Everything thou beholdest hath been called into being through the operation of His Will. – The Báb[450]

> ...any reality to which the term 'being' is applicable hath been created by the sovereign Will of the Almighty... He hath been and will ever remain inscrutable unto all men, inasmuch as all else besides Him have been and shall ever be created through the potency of His command. – The Báb[451]

Therefore, in the Báb's teaching, while God is the First Cause of all existence, the actual *agent* of Creative action is the Primal Will of God, which is the first thing which emanated from God. His Primal Will, the Will of God, the Holy Spirit, the Divine Logos, the Universal Mind, is 'the supreme sacred Reality' for mankind.[452] Saying that the Primal Will is the active creative Agent, is like saying that the rays of the sun, rather than the sun itself, are the creator of all life on earth.

- Without the sun there would be no rays at all, but factually speaking it is the rays, which travel through space, that illuminate the earth and supply the energy which enables life to occur.

In this analogy, it is the same with the Primal Will, which is the first emanation from God.

- Without God as the First Cause, there would be no Primal Will at all, and yet it is the Primal Will which actively enables all creation and life to occur.

THE BÁB'S TEACHING ABOUT THE MANIFESTATIONS OF THE PRIMAL WILL OF GOD

The Báb also identified the Primal Will with the Manifestations of God, God's Representatives in this world. The following quote is somewhat lengthy, but due to its importance it will be quoted in full. The reader is invited to pay special attention to the last paragraph.

> [In the following quote, "the Apostle of God" = Muhammad; "the Bayán" = "the Bayán" = the Mother-Book of His Dispensation, His most weighty book and the repository of His laws[453]; "Point of the Bayán" = the Báb; and "Him Whom God shall make manifest" = Bahá'u'lláh (However, at the time the Báb wrote these words, Bahá'u'lláh had not yet made public His claims to be Him Whom God shall make manifest.) Likewise, today, no one on earth has any idea of Who the "One Who will appear after" will be.]

> [There] can be no doubt that from everlasting God hath been invested with the independent sovereignty of His exalted Being, and unto everlasting He will remain inaccessible in the transcendent majesty of His holy Essence. No creature hath ever recognized Him as befitteth His recognition, nor hath any created being ever praised Him as is worthy of His praise. He is exalted above every name, and is sanctified from every comparison. Through Him all things are made known, while too lofty is His reality to be known through anyone but Him. The process of His creation hath had no beginning and can have no end, otherwise it would necessitate the cessation of His celestial grace. God hath raised up Prophets and revealed Books as numerous as the creatures of the world, and will continue to do so to everlasting.

> If thou art sailing upon the sea of God's Names, which are reflected in all things, know thou that He is exalted and sanctified from being known through His creatures, or being described by His servants. Everything thou beholdest hath been called into being through the operation of His Will. How can such a created thing, therefore, be indicative of His essential oneness? God's existence in itself testifieth to His Own oneness, while every created thing, by its very nature, beareth evidence that it hath been fashioned by God. Such is the proof of consummate wisdom in the estimation of those who sail the ocean of divine Truth.

> If, however, thou art sailing upon the sea of creation, know thou that the First Remembrance, which is the Primal Will of God, may be likened

> unto the sun. God hath created Him through the potency of His might, and He hath, from the beginning that hath no beginning, caused Him to be manifested in every Dispensation through the compelling power of His behest, and God will, to the end that knoweth no end, continue to manifest Him according to the good-pleasure of His invincible Purpose.
>
> And know thou that He indeed resembleth the sun. Were the risings of the sun to continue till the end that hath no end, yet there hath not been nor ever will be more than one sun; and were its settings to endure for evermore, still there hath not been nor ever will be more than one sun. It is this Primal Will which appeareth resplendent in every Prophet and speaketh forth in every revealed Book. It knoweth no beginning, inasmuch as the First deriveth its firstness from It; and knoweth no end, for the Last oweth its lastness unto It.
>
> In the time of the First Manifestation the Primal Will appeared in Adam; in the day of Noah It became known in Noah; in the day of Abraham in Him; and so in the day of Moses; the day of Jesus; the day of Muhammad, the Apostle of God; the day of the 'Point of the Bayan'; the day of Him Whom God shall make manifest; and the day of the One Who will appear after Him Whom God shall make manifest. Hence the inner meaning of the words uttered by the Apostle of God, 'I am all the Prophets', inasmuch as what shineth resplendent in each one of Them hath been and will ever remain the one and the same sun. – The Báb[454]

This quote has so much in it. It is fascinating, for example, that the Báb says,

> God hath raised up Prophets and revealed Books as numerous as the creatures of the world, and will continue to do so to everlasting. – The Báb

Although the Báb, in this passage, gives a list of specific Prophets of God Who have been the Manifestations of His Will on earth, in fact, the list is not limited to just these names. Many times, throughout history, innumerable times, the Almighty has sent forth His Messengers. As Bahá'u'lláh and 'Abdu'l-Bahá would later elucidate, this means that other Manifestations, not on the specific list offered here by the Báb, have also been sent forth. In many cases, Their names are lost to the mists of history, but in some instances additional names are known. Thus, Krishna, Zoroaster, and Buddha, Who are not part of the Abrahamic lineage, are explicitly recognized as Divine Educators in the Bahá'í Writings. There are other fascinating possibilities which are discussed by scholars. For example, perhaps the Native American peoples have, in the past received a Divine Messenger.[455] Also, the Báb indicates that this process of sending Divine Educators into creation has no ending point. It will continue everlasting because, as the Báb indicates,

> The process of His creation hath had no beginning and can have no end, otherwise it would necessitate the cessation of His celestial grace. – The Báb

This never-ending quality of Divine Revelation will be discussed further in a section below, "*The final word on finality.*"

When a specific Manifestation of God is mentioned, as the above quotation implies, He is "the Point", or "the Primal Point". Thus, the Báb referred to Himself as the Primal Point and as the Point of the Bayán, the Bayán being the Book which was the centerpiece of His revelation. Similarly, He designates Muhammad as the Point of the Qur'án.

Although the Báb wrote of Himself as the Primal Point, in another sense every Divine Educator is the Primal Point. Moreover, since the Primal Will of God is identified as the Creator, the Manifestation of God, as the resplendent appearance of the Primal Will, is, as indicated in the analogy, in some sense similarly the Creator.

This idea of the Logos/Word of God/Primal Will as Creator was implied in a famous passage in the Gospel of John:

> In the beginning was the Word, and the Word was with God, and the Word was God. He was with God in the beginning. Through him all things were made; without him nothing was made that has been made. (John 1:1-3)

Saying that "through Him all things were made" is other language which refers to the Word of God as the Creator. We recall that the Word of God is another term for the Primal Will of God.

So, we have an interesting implication emerging about the Manifestation of God, as the appearance of the Primal Will of God, and as the Creator. This is not to suggest that the physical person Moses, or Jesus, or Muhammad was the Creator. Rather, it is the spiritual radiance, bounty and perfection of God, the Light of the Holy Spirit, the Primal Will "which appeareth resplendent in every Prophet and speaketh forth in every revealed Book" which is involved with the act of creation. The Báb pulls these fascinating threads together:

> I am the Primal Point from which have been generated all created things. – The Báb[456]

> ...God called you into being through the Primal Point... – The Báb[457]

We see that in some mysterious and fascinating way, due to the splendor of the Primal Will shining radiantly within Them, the Manifestations of God are in some sense involved with the act of creation. Noted scholar Adib Taherzadeh offered these comments about the Primal Will of God:

> The Holy Spirit is usually associated with the Manifestations of God. It is the Holy Spirit which has animated them all, and the Holy Spirit itself has been generated through the instrumentality of the 'Most Great Spirit', referred to as the 'Primal Will'. Through it all creation has come into being and all Revelations have been sent down. – Adib Taherzadeh[458]

These ideas are confirmed by Bahá'u'lláh. He equates God's "command" and "wish" to the Primal Will and He uses the phrase "stepped out of nothingness" to indicate the Divine act of creation:

> ...by a word of His command all that are in heaven and on earth have come to exist, and by His wish, which is the Primal Will itself, all have stepped out of utter nothingness into the realm of being, the world of the visible. – Bahá'u'lláh[459]

The Báb's teachings mesmerized His followers. They were familiar with Islámic conceptions of God's oneness, power, compassion, and mercy. The Báb's portrayal of the majestic Essence of God, the power of His Primal Will to bring into being all things, and the connection of that same Primal Will with the Manifestations of God, while consistent with the Qur'án and its doctrine of God's oneness, was a stirring vision they had never before encountered. The Báb's attack on anthropomorphism enabled the followers to shake themselves loose from the conceptual restraints and clouded dogmas imposed upon them by their religious leaders.

THE SEVEN STAGES OF CREATIVE ACTION

The Báb and Bahá'u'lláh explain that all things come into existence through a seven-stage process. While this is described in linear terms, it seems plausible to also envision this as a coexisting list of specifications for existence. For something to exist, all elements/stages must be present.

The seven stages of creation apply to individual creatures and objects as well as to the entire cosmos. The idea of applying the seven stages of creation principle to individual objects comes from Bahá'u'lláh.[460] (See the footnote for the source citation.) To facilitate understanding, I've created the table below and chosen a simple example of creating a musical instrument, a flute. The reader is free to think of other examples of created things as a way of crystalizing his or her understanding.

The seven stages are:

Name	Arabic name	Description, using the flute as an example
1. Will	Mashíyyat	The desire to have the musical instrument, the flute, to create melodies and happiness
2. Determination	Irádih	Imagining an instrument like a flute
3. Destiny	Qadar	Envisioning the shape, size and material of the flute
4. Decree	Qadhá'	Drawing the specifications on a piece of paper. (This is the final stage of subjective thinking.)
5. Permission	Izn	Taking action to gather the material to build the flute based on the written design specification. Actually making the flute.
6. Duration	Ajal	This is the period of time for the flute. How long it will be used and endure.
7. Book	Kitáb	The fruition of creation. This is the actual usage of the flute while its duration lasts.

Figure 28 Brief overview of the Seven Stages of Creative Action

Several points are worth noticing.

First, although the example is creating a flute, the seven stages also apply to God's Primal Will acting to create all of the realms of heaven and earth—that is, all things.

Second, let me offer an opinion. In addition to objects, the seven stages may apply to individual actions and acts of service. For example, let's say a person is thinking of making a donation to charity. When we think of the steps to perform the act of donating, we see that it begins first with the will, then it progresses to specifics such as deciding how much to give, which charity to give it to, when to make the donation, and so on. After this subjective thinking, the money is collected from a source, such as one's bank account, and the donation is made. The fruit of the donation is the use of the money for the stated duration and purpose of the charity. All human actions can be seen through the seven stages. In my opinion, the act of creating refers to both tangible and intangible objects.[461]

Third, notice that the Creator/creator of the universe or of the flute, is not one of the seven stages. The Being/being that is doing the actions, in relation to the object being created, is pre-existent, existing effectively outside the time and space of the creative process. The Creator/creator could have been busy with other things before one day deciding to make a flute. His pre-existence, *from the perspective of the flute*, is in fact eternal, because he could have been around for any length of time before making the flute. Nothing happens at all without this prior Existence/existence. In a sense, this is why the Essence of God is hidden; He exists before anything else comes into existence. All things other than Himself have a dependent existence.

Fourth, and this is of crucial relevance, notice that the first stage of creation is the Will. Thus, whether the universe is being created, or a flute is being created, there must first be the Will, *emanating* from the Essence of the Creator, to create. The Will (or the will) is the first agency of creating anything.

The seven stages of creation is a deep, mystical subject. Nader Saiedi's book, *The Gate of the Heart,*[462] delves into this subject at length. Hopefully, this brief discussion and the example of the flute is a helpful introduction to the topic.

THE PERSONAL GOD

An equally appealing feature of the Báb's message was His image of an infinite AND intimately personal God. Typical human thinking about an infinite God often led to the attitude that such a God must be impersonal and remote from our everyday lives. The thinking typically went like this:

> If God is so big that He's running the universe, then He's obviously too busy or tired to pay attention to tiny and insignificant individual people like you and me.

The least helpful word in that statement is "obviously". In fact, it isn't obvious because this line of thinking erroneously makes the assumption that God is powerful, but not powerful enough, aware but not infinitely so. This led to the idea that an infinite God is an impersonal God. Upon closer examination, however, if God is truly *infinite* this limited view is logically false and commits the error of anthropomorphizing God.

If God is infinite enough to create the universe in the first place, and infinite enough to run the entire cosmos on a second by second basis, the idea that God would be too busy to hear your prayers, or too tired 'after all that work', is an idea of a limited God. Yes, it is a very, Very, VERY big God, but not an infinite one. The God that can create the universe is already extremely different from an ordinary human being, so why assume He has human traits like limited attention or getting tired after a big workout? Those are human qualities. With an infinite God, there is no reason to assume that God would get tired like humans do. That is the error of anthropomorphism.

A concept of real infinity would, I think, go like this. God has the capacity to create the entire expanding universe. Doesn't get tired. Plenty of Him left over. (Even the concept of "left over" implies the human condition!) God can run the entire universe, minute by minute, day by day, year after year, for uncounted billions of years, non-stop. God is Ruler of every person and living creature, of the earth, all the other billions of planets in the galaxy, all the other trillions of galaxies, throughout the observable universe, and beyond. God doesn't get tired. Plenty of Him left over. Why doesn't God get tired? Because He's infinite! God doesn't even "break a sweat" with all this activity. (Even the concept of "break a sweat" implies a human attribute!) Why? Because God is infinite! What does an infinite God do with all the untapped capacity "left over"? Whatever He pleases to do! He is free to create even more worlds, both physical and in the realms of heaven. And God gives some of His attention to the beloved creatures He has created! No creature is too small for His loving attention. God knows everything about them. He especially attends to His human children and listens to their prayers because He gave them some god-like qualities, such as intellect, wisdom, love, compassion, truthfulness, and much more. God can hear every prayer, in all languages, spoken out loud, whispered, and even the ones that are silent thoughts in the mind of every prayerful soul. And guess what? Since God is infinite, He doesn't get tired or run out of abilities. God's Essence is eternal. He doesn't need to sleep, or take a break, and God never asks anyone to repeat what they prayed because He hears everything correctly the first time, in every language, from every soul, on this world and on every other world in the vast expanding universe. Even with all this activity, God still has infinite capacities left over. God is never too busy running the universe to pay attention to the most humble or needy of His children. Why? Because God is infinite! Infinite never runs out, never encounters any limits. Infinite means infinite.

Everything about the Báb's teachings declare the truth of the one infinite God. To the Báb, the infinity of God does not imply an impersonal distance from people, but rather close intimacy. The infinite God is also loving, attentive, just, gracious, forgiving, and the answerer of prayers.

Among religious Figures in history, the Báb displayed His own exemplary and profound relationship with God. From earliest childhood, He showed extreme dedication to prayer and devotion to God. Those who encountered Him, in business, in His family, during His days in Karbilá, and during the active phases of His ministry, were moved by observing His devotional practices. He was one of the greatest mystics of all time.

The Báb's Writings contain endless references to the intimate and personal nature of not only His relationship with God, but of what is available to ordinary followers. The following are some examples.

The Báb explained that God's grace is universal:

> Our grace assuredly pervadeth all that dwell in the kingdoms of earth and heaven and in whatever lieth between them, and beyond them all mankind. However, souls that have shut themselves out as by a veil can never partake of the outpourings of the grace of God. – The Báb[463]

The Báb testified to the intimacy and intensity of His feelings for God:

> Verily I am Thy servant, O my God, and Thy poor one and Thy suppliant and Thy wretched creature. I have arrived at Thy gate, seeking Thy shelter. I have found no contentment save in Thy love, no exultation except in Thy remembrance, no eagerness but in obedience to Thee, no joy save in Thy nearness, and no tranquility except in reunion with Thee... Whenever I attempt to approach Thee, I perceive nothing in myself but the tokens of Thy grace and behold naught in my being but the revelations of Thy loving-kindness. How can one who is but Thy creature seek reunion with Thee and attain unto Thy presence, whereas no created thing can ever be associated with Thee, nor can aught comprehend Thee? How is it possible for a lowly servant to recognize Thee and to extol Thy praise, notwithstanding that Thou hast destined for him the revelations of Thy dominion and the wondrous testimonies of Thy sovereignty?... It is undisputed, however, that the influence of Thine attraction hath everlastingly been inherent in the realities of Thy handiwork, although that which beseemeth the hallowed court of Thy providence is exalted beyond the attainment of the entire creation... Nay, by Thy might, I yearn for naught but Thine Own Self and seek no one other than Thee. – The Báb[464]

The Báb extolled the fullness of God's forgiveness:

> Glorified art Thou, O Lord, Thou forgivest at all times the sins of such among Thy servants as implore Thy pardon. Wash away my sins and the sins of those who seek Thy forgiveness at dawn, who pray to Thee in the day-time and in the night season, who yearn after naught save God, who offer up whatsoever God hath graciously bestowed upon

them, who celebrate Thy praise at morn and eventide, and who are not remiss in their duties. – The Báb[465]

Thy loving providence hath encompassed all created things in the heavens and on the earth, and Thy forgiveness hath surpassed the whole creation. Thine is sovereignty; in Thy hand are the Kingdoms of Creation and Revelation; in Thy right hand Thou holdest all created things and within Thy grasp are the assigned measures of forgiveness. Thou forgivest whomsoever among Thy servants Thou pleasest. Verily Thou art the Ever-Forgiving, the All-Loving. Nothing whatsoever escapeth Thy knowledge, and naught is there which is hidden from Thee. – The Báb[466]

The Báb appealed to God for justice for the way He was being mistreated. This quotation refers to the period of His exile in the mountain of Máh-Kú.

Thou seest, O my Lord, my dwelling-place in the heart of this mountain and Thou dost witness my forbearance. Verily I have desired naught else but Thy love and the love of those who love Thee. How can I extol the effulgent beauty of Thy Lordship, conscious as I am of my nothingness before the habitation of Thy glory? Yet the sorrow of solitude and loneliness prompteth me to invoke Thee through this prayer… – The Báb[467]

The Báb spoke of turning to God for help and assistance in times of every peril and tribulation.

Verily Thou art the highest aspiration of every earnest seeker and the Goal of the desire of them that yearn after Thee. Thou art He Who is ready to answer the call of such as recognize Thy divine unity, and He before Whom the faint-hearted stand in awe. Thou art the Helper of the needy, the Deliverer of the captives, the Abaser of the oppressors, the Destroyer of the wrong-doers, the God of all men, the Lord of all created things. Thine are the kingdoms of Creation and Revelation, O Thou Who art the Lord of all the worlds.

O All-Sufficient One! Thou dost suffice Me in every hardship that may descend upon Me and in every affliction that may wax great before Me. Thou art My sole Companion in My loneliness, the Delight of My heart in My solitude and My Best Beloved in My prison and in My Abode. No God is there but Thee! – The Báb[468]

The passages indicate the Báb's loving, personal relationship with the infinite God. Equally numerous are the passages inviting every loyal believer to seek a loving, personal relationship with God, the infinite One. This brief sampling gives a comforting look at this aspect of the Báb's teaching. Yes, God is utterly infinite. In fact, God is so infinite that He cannot do less than rule the entire universe AND still have abundant ability left over to hear and answer the prayers of each and every one of His human children. And He is graciously willing to do just that.

THE PROCESS OF CREATION IS ETERNAL

We must observe caution when we speak of the Primal Will, the Holy Spirit, emanating from God. In human terms, the term emanation implies that the source of the emanation existed, in historical time, prior to the emanation and that the emanation itself must have had a specific beginning in time. The sun existed before the rays emanating from it existed. The writer existed before the words emanating from his pen were first written.

With spiritual reality, this time-line may not be valid. Indeed, to hold to such time-bound thinking could be considered an example of anthropomorphic thinking. The Writings of the Báb avoid this error. He says:

> The process of His creation hath had no beginning and can have no end... – The Báb[469]

The Primal Will and all creation which flows from it are eternal, just as God is eternal. The great difference is that God is self-subsisting and that both the Primal Will and creation are dependent upon God for their existence.

Here is an analogy of how something can be both eternal and at the same time dependent upon something else. Consider the existence of numbers. All numbers (1, 2, 3, 4, 5, etc.) exist simultaneously in current time in the human mind as intangible mental realities, as concepts. The number five has existed as a conceptual reality for as long as the number one has existed. In this sense, *as concepts*, all numbers are eternal. On the other hand, *in logic*, the number one arithmetically precedes all the other numbers and all the other numbers (2, 3, 4, 5, etc.) arithmetically proceed from the number one (1 + 1 = 2, 1 + 1 + 1 = 3, etc.). Thus, while all numbers are 'eternal', only one number is sufficient unto itself and only that number is capable of being the source of all the other numbers. In this analogy, what would the number one symbolize? In this writer's view, it would symbolize the Primal Will while God in His transcendent station is too exalted to be symbolized by any number, including the first number. Somehow, from the hidden sanctity of His own transcendent unity, God has generated the number 'one', the Primal Will, and from It have all other numbers, all created things, been generated.

This is a crucial principle of the Báb's teaching—the process of creation is everlasting and the actual agent bringing it into being is the Primal Will. Again, the Báb stated:

> Everything thou beholdest hath been called into being through the operation of His Will. – The Báb[470]

The Primal Will is active as Creator as a result of the boundless, ceaseless grace of God. The most formidable sign of God's grace is Him revealing Himself to humanity through His Prophets and Messengers, the Manifestations of God through the ages. The Báb explained:

> The process of His creation hath had no beginning and can have no end, otherwise it would necessitate the cessation of His celestial grace. God hath raised up Prophets and revealed Books as numerous as the creatures of the world, and will continue to do so to everlasting. – The Báb[471]

If God is never-ending, His grace is never-ending. If God's grace is never-ending, the process of His creation is never-ending. And if grace and creation are never-ending, then the Manifestations of His Will, His Prophets and Messengers, must be never-ending. God will always be sending Divine Educators into the world. This occurs at times and places of His choosing.

MANIFESTATIONS OF THE PRIMAL WILL OF GOD AND PROGRESSIVE REVELATION

If the Primal Will is the eternal Will of God emanating from God, then the Manifestations of God – Abraham, Moses, Jesus, Muhammad, the Báb, Bahá'u'lláh, and others – are the Manifestations of the Primal Will of God. They are, one and all, the Primal Mirrors of the Will of God in the created world. They are not incarnations of the Essence of God, which remains one and "wholly independent of His creation",[472] rather they are perfect Manifestations of the Will of God on earth, the infallible Mirrors of His attributes. To know Them is to know God; to love Them is to love God; to serve Them is to serve God. To attain Their Presence is to attain the Presence of God; as much as any of these things are remotely possible for any human being to attain.

Each of the Manifestations of God, while sharing the same spiritual Reality, appear at different times in history as unique Individuals, for the purpose of advancing humanity in the Divine Curriculum:

> [In the following quote, although *not* in the original quote, bullet points are added to assist the reader. Also, in the following quote, "the Apostle of God" = Muhammad; "the Bayán" = the leading book revealed by the Báb; "Point of the Bayán" = the Báb; and "Him Whom God shall make manifest" = Bahá'u'lláh (However, at the time the Báb wrote these words, Bahá'u'lláh had not yet made public His claims to be Him Whom God shall make manifest.) Likewise, today, no one on earth has any idea of Who the "One Who will appear after" will be.]

If, however, thou art sailing upon the sea of creation, know thou that the First Remembrance, which is the Primal Will of God, may be likened unto the sun...

- In the time of the First Manifestation the Primal Will appeared in Adam;
- in the day of Noah It became known in Noah;
- in the day of Abraham in Him;
- and so in the day of Moses;
- the day of Jesus;
- the day of Muhammad, the Apostle of God;
- the day of the 'Point of the Bayán';473
- the day of Him Whom God shall make manifest;474 and
- the day of the One Who will appear after Him Whom God shall make manifest.

Hence the inner meaning of the words uttered by the Apostle of God, 'I am all the Prophets',[475] inasmuch as what shineth resplendent in each one of Them hath been and will ever remain the one and the same sun.
– The Báb[476]

Let's recap some of the Báb's key concepts.

- In His absolute station, God is utterly independent of His creation. He is, in Himself, Self-Subsisting, utterly infinite.
- The Primal Will, emanating from God as an expression of His grace, from everlasting to everlasting, is ceaselessly creating all things.

- The Manifestations of God, therefore, have a dual reality.
- In Their station of pure unity, periodically, the Primal Will of God is sent forth into the world as a Person, the Manifestation of God. The inner reality of every Manifestation is the same. Spiritually, they are all one, they are "Focal Points of the Primal Will", and the Creator of "everything thou beholdest".[477] As Bahá'u'lláh would later explain,

> …if thou callest them all by one name, and dost ascribe to them the same attribute, thou hast not erred from the truth. Even as He hath revealed: "No distinction do We make between any of His Messengers!" (Qur'án 2:285) For they one and all summon the people of the earth to acknowledge the Unity of God… They are all invested with the robe of Prophethood, and honoured with the mantle of glory… These Countenances are the recipients of the Divine Command, and the day-springs of His Revelation... Thus He saith: "Our Cause is but one." (Qur'án 54:50) Inasmuch as the Cause is one and the same, the Exponents thereof also must needs be one and the same. – Bahá'u'lláh[478]

- In their other station, the station of distinction, each Manifestation appears on the earth, at different times and places. They appear as unique individuals Who are seemingly very different from one another. Bahá'u'lláh elucidated this theme:

> The other is the station of distinction, and pertaineth to the world of creation and to the limitations thereof. In this respect, each Manifestation of God hath a distinct individuality, a definitely prescribed mission, a predestined Revelation, and specially designated limitations. Each one of them is known by a different name, is characterized by a special attribute, fulfills a definite Mission, and is entrusted with a particular Revelation. – Bahá'u'lláh[479]

The Manifestations of God have an infinitely greater spiritual Reality than understood by the followers of Their Faiths. The Manifestations of God are *not God*, because the Essence of God exists alone, far above all other existence. But the Manifestations of God *are God* in the sense that all that can be known of God is revealed to creation through Them, just as the Mirror reflects the Light of the Sun.

We humans perceive only the tiniest fraction of their infinite spiritual glory.

Consider this analogy. Human beings share with the animals the same basic reality of physical life. We share much of our DNA. We all are required to consume food, to breathe oxygen, to eat, sleep and wake. We all use sensory organs, such as eyes and ears, to be aware of our surroundings. Our internal organs are highly similar. We are born, reproduce and die. With all this similarity, how vast is the difference between human beings and our most beloved pets or the beasts of the field! The animals and humans walk on the earth together, share enormous similarities, and yet they inhabit two entirely different kingdoms of creation. Here is a very helpful quote from 'Abdu'l-Bahá:

> Although the mineral, vegetable, animal and man all have actual being, yet the mineral has no knowledge of the vegetable. It cannot apprehend it. It cannot imagine nor understand it.
>
> It is the same with the vegetable. Any progress it may make, however highly it may become developed, it will never apprehend the animal, nor understand it...
>
> It is the same with the animal. However much it may progress in its own kingdom, however refined its feelings may become, it will have no real notion of the world of man or of his special intellectual faculties...
>
> Although the mineral, vegetable, animal and man himself are actual beings, the difference between their kingdoms prevents members of the lower degree from comprehending the essence and nature of those of the superior degree...
>
> Lastly the perfect man, the Prophet, is one who is transfigured, one who has the purity and clearness of a perfect mirror—one who reflects the Sun of Truth. Of such a one – of such a Prophet and Messenger – we can say that the Light of Divinity with the heavenly Perfections dwells in him. – 'Abdu'l-Bahá[480]

So it is that the Manifestations of God walk the earth with human beings, while also occupying a station in the hierarchy of existence that is infinitely exalted by comparison. Their human condition is only a temporary tool, a veil which conceals Their truly infinite spiritual state. Only a tiny portion of Their glory is revealed to human eyes. They are as different from human beings as human beings are from the animals of the earth. Even that comparison is too feeble. The difference between a human being and a bird is vast, but nevertheless finite. Both are *created* beings. The Manifestation of

God, in His Spiritual Essence, is not part of creation, rather He is a Mirror of God in the realm of creation. Therefore, in a way unfathomable to humans, His Reality is utterly infinite, completely transcendent relative to human existence. No true comparison is possible.

Yes, as the Scriptures all say, They are human while on earth. This is only so that They can serve as our Divine Educators. But if, as the Báb says, They are in fact the Focal Points of the Primal Will of God, then They are really far more than human. Being that They are Manifestations of the Primal Will of God, They are a distinct order of Life immeasurably above our own.

To grasp this, I sometimes think of a fish I once had in an aquarium in my home. My daughter was too young to have the dog she really wanted, so my wife and I started with a small fish which my daughter named "Spikey". We hung a little bubble tank on the wall in the bathroom and I looked at it when I brushed my teeth. As I daydreamed about life from the viewpoint of Spikey, I imagined trying to communicate with him, like God strives to communicate with us humans. How would I do it? Obviously, Spikey could not come out and talk to me in my environment since my air-breathing world was impossible for him. And I, a full-sized human being, could never fit into his tiny water tank. This led me to think I would need to insert some representation of myself in the likeness of a fish into his "world", the tiny tank, so I could swim with him and talk to him in his fish language in his bounded fish world. I would need to act enough like Spikey so that he would be able to understand what I was saying at his level of existence. With all that effort, no matter how much I wanted to tell him, Spikey would only be able to manage the tiniest understanding of my world, not just the bathroom area, but the other rooms of my whole house, and the seemingly infinite worlds beyond the walls of my house. He could not conceive of the cars driving by the front of my house, or the houses across the street, or think about the downtown village area a half mile away. From his fishbowl vantage point, he could never conceive of the planet earth, or the solar system, of other worlds, or the Milky Way galaxy, or other galaxies far beyond. He would never be able to grasp any of that. But in his world, I could teach him a few useful things, such as how to be nice to other fish, how to swim better, and so forth. I thought the analogy worked well.

Figure 29 Bubble fish tank

The Divine Educators are the Representatives of God's Primal Will to our world. They are heavenly Beings who *temporarily* take on a human form to reveal the Word of God to us. We should not be confused about Their true Reality, however. Though They look outwardly ordinary, inwardly They are very different from us. They are the pathway for salvation God has provided for His human creatures. They are the Intermediaries to God.

So profound is this relationship of representation that the Báb says attaining to Their presence is *equivalent* to attaining the presence of God. .

[In this quote, the Báb uses two symbolic terms – "Him Who is the Tree of divine Reality" and "the Primal Tree" – to refer to "that which is feasible" with the Manifestations of God.]

> ...all men will be brought before God and will attain His Presence; which meaneth appearance before Him Who is the Tree of divine Reality[481] and attainment unto His presence; inasmuch as it is not possible to appear before the Most Holy Essence of God, nor is it conceivable to seek reunion with Him. That which is feasible in the matter of appearance before Him and of meeting Him is attainment unto the Primal Tree. – The Báb[482]

Attaining to Their presence is treated *as if* it is the same as meeting God, for nothing else is "feasible":

> There is no paradise more wondrous for any soul than to be exposed to God's Manifestation in His Day, to hear His verses and believe in them, to attain His presence, which is naught but the presence of God, to sail upon the sea of the heavenly kingdom of His good-pleasure, and to partake of the choice fruits of the paradise of His divine Oneness. – The Báb[483]

I take this passage literally. There is "no paradise" higher than attainment to recognition of "God's Manifestation in His Day" and following Him. No matter what men may think, this is as high as anyone can go. It is the peak and purpose of existence, the pathway to being able to partake of paradise, which is perfection itself.

The Báb's reference to "in His Day" introduces the element of time to our thinking. Given that He teaches that God sends Divine Educators at many times throughout history, it is clear that each Manifestation "in His Day" is the One who should be the focus of human aspirations and devotion. And given Their oneness, to be loyal and obedient to each One "in His Day" is to, spiritually speaking, be loyal and obedient to them all.

And the reverse also holds true.

The Divine Educators are each sent to humanity at the times prescribed by God. On earth human history must unfold through the process of time. Just as lessons to a child are gradually unfolded over time as the capacities of the child develop, so it is that over the centuries humanity has received Divine Education from the Manifestations of God. Originating from the same Source – the Primal Will of God – His Prophets and Messengers have appeared throughout history in diverse places and times in order to foster the development of humanity in an orderly and progressive fashion.

The Báb articulated this process in terrific detail, with such power, beauty and clarity, that His hearers were swept away. He explained that God's Will for humanity is subject to alteration as humanity evolves socially and spiritually. Just as a parent will give an older child a different set of rules than he or she gives a younger child, so God's teachings for humanity have evolved from age to age. This is no reflection on God or His Prophets. Each Revelation is an expression of God's Primal Will. Divine Revelation is uniquely effective in propelling humanity forward. Progress requires evolution of the teachings, giving gradually increasing knowledge and understanding to humanity. Every stage is an expression of God's will for that stage, following earlier stages, and preparing for stages yet to come. The Báb explained:

> Man's highest station, however, is attained through faith in God in every Dispensation and by acceptance of what hath been revealed by Him, and not through learning; inasmuch as in every nation there are learned men who are versed in divers sciences. Nor is it attainable through wealth; for it is similarly evident that among the various classes in every nation there are those possessed of riches. Likewise are other transitory things.

> True knowledge, therefore, is the knowledge of God, and this is none other than the recognition of His Manifestation in each Dispensation. Nor is there any wealth save in poverty in all save God and sanctity from aught else but Him—a state that can be realized only when demonstrated towards Him Who is the Dayspring of His Revelation. This doth not mean, however, that one ought not to yield praise unto former Revelations. On no account is this acceptable, inasmuch as it behooveth man, upon reaching the age of nineteen, to render thanksgiving for the day of his conception as an embryo. For had the embryo not existed, how could he have reached his present state? Likewise had the religion taught by Adam not existed, this Faith would not have attained its present stage. Thus consider thou the development of God's Faith until the end that hath no end. – The Báb[484]

Thus, in every age, Divine Revelation is adapted to the needs of humanity. The teaching humanity has received, progressing from age to age, is *one unified program* of education bestowed upon humanity by the Primal Will of God as a token of His boundless and unending grace.

From this perspective, Professor Saiedi notes,

> The Báb defines the various religions as products of the interaction between the divine effulgence and the receptivities of human beings… The progressive receptive capacities of human beings in the march of history are accompanied by progressive revelations of the Primal Will. As this process of human spiritual evolution can have no end, there can be no end for divine revelation, and there can be neither a final religion nor any one total revelation of spiritual truth. – Nader Saiedi[485]

The Báb candidly admonished a Muslim cleric who adhered to the belief in finality:

> Thy vision is obscured by the belief that divine revelation ended with the coming of Muhammad, and unto this We have borne witness… – The Báb[486]

The Báb understood that the Revelations which Manifestations of God, like Himself, bring into the world soon become religions. These religions, imbued with Divine spirit, gradually overcome obstacles in their path and attract massive followings. The religions erect social, political and cultural institutions—such as houses of worship, creeds and doctrines, legal codes, charitable endeavors, institutes for the study of sacred scripture, daily practices for followers, and development of a clergy. These provide pattern and structure for collective religious experiences and individual spiritual expressions.

Generated by the initial impulse of Divine revelation, the religion unfolds over the centuries and millennia which follow. Often disputes and schisms occur among the followers. Often, the followers gradually depart from the inner spiritual meaning of the Revelation which gave birth to their Faith, and new expressions of religiosity develop which diverge from the core Teachings of the Faith. Gradually, the organized, orthodox religion becomes a form and structure without life. Like a dead fossil, the outward form of the institutional religion remains in the world, but its spiritual life has vanished. Only traces of the Spirit remain for those dedicated souls who continue to pursue their spiritual journey with intention and vigor. Sincere souls, if they are not mentally imprisoned by dogma and indoctrination, manage to find the Spirit and receive spiritual sustenance, despite the encrusted orthodoxy, but as a body and as a social movement, the Spirit has moved on.

The Báb understood this as a natural process. For Him, religion was neither an absolute, unchanging Truth, as religious fundamentalists maintain, nor was it a purely culturally determined phenomenon, as cultural relativists assert.

> Each religion, with its particular practices and laws, is explained as the product of the *interaction* between the divine Will and a specific set of historical, social, and cultural conditions. The Will of God is not static, but ever-creative, renewing the form in which It manifests itself in accordance with humanity's stage of development; the various religions are all viewed as diverse, sequential expressions of the same divine truth. The writings of the Báb direct attention away from the token or secondary manifestations of religion—those laws and practices that are diverse—and they focus attention instead on the one common source of all those varying expressions: the divine Will. In other words, the Báb's writings combine historical consciousness with mystical consciousness, encompassing both dimensions of religion and emphasizing that the core reality of all the religions is one and the same. – Nader Saiedi[487]

> Because each religion is a product of the interaction between the supreme Source of religion--which is the common reality of all the Prophets--and the specific conditions of culture and society in each age, one should fix one's eyes on the divine revelation itself in order

> to recognize the truth of the new Manifestation beyond the diversity of religious forms. – Nader Saiedi[488]

The Báb understood each and every one of the Manifestations of God to be the representatives of the Primal Will of God. He spoke of the process of Revelation as a process of never-ending Divine creation:

> The process of His creation hath had no beginning and can have no end, otherwise it would necessitate the cessation of His celestial grace. God hath raised up Prophets and revealed Books as numerous as the creatures of the world, and will continue to do so to everlasting. – The Báb[489]

Revelation can have no end because that would indicate that God's grace had been withdrawn from creation, which the Báb says is impossible. Given that the Manifestations all emanate from the same Source, they act as members of a single team. The Báb says,

> The Lord of the universe hath never raised up a prophet nor hath He sent down a Book unless He hath established His covenant with all men, calling for their acceptance of the next Revelation and of the next Book; inasmuch as the outpourings of His bounty are ceaseless and without limit. – The Báb[490]

THE FINAL WORD ON FINALITY

Nearly all the people in the Islámic society held to the view that Muhammad was the last of the Prophets God would ever send to humanity. This idea was based on a certain interpretation of a single verse of the Qur'án – Súrih 33:40 – which announced that Muhammad was the Seal of the Prophets.

> Muhammad is not the father of any one of your men, but the Messenger of God, and the Seal of the Prophets; God has knowledge of everything. (Qur'án 33:40)[491]

The Báb believed in the Qur'án and He accepted this title for Muhammad. What He did not accept was the theologians' interpretation of it, which alleged that God was done sending Divine Educators to humanity. The word "seal" (khátama in Arabic) has multiple meanings. In the Arabic dictionary, one meaning is finality, or last, but that isn't the only possible meaning.

Another meaning is that a seal is like an ornament, or a certification of something. Think of ancient times when a king or queen would attach a molded wax seal to a letter to indicate its authenticity. This meant: "Yes, this letter is really from me, see, here is my seal on it."

The theologians said the "seal" referred to finality of prophethood, but the text itself doesn't necessarily show that. Moreover, neither Muhammad Himself, not His immediate generation of followers subscribed to the doctrine of finality. As Yohann Freidman documented in his book, *Prophecy Continuous*, the finality doctrine became accepted by the theologians about two centuries after Muhammad.[492] (Attributing the doctrine of finality to Muhammad, after the fact, is like anachronistically attributing a modern attitude towards a feature of the Constitution to the Founding Fathers of the United States a couple of centuries after they are gone.)

Even if khátama (seal) is taken to mean finality, look again at the quote. Notice the wording in the Qur'án. Seal is a descriptive applied to the word "prophets"; it is not applied to the other word which was "messenger". If it had been, Muhammad would have written "seal of the messengers and of the prophets". But He didn't write that. He applied the seal description only to prophets, not to messengers. Regardless of orthodox clergy claiming finality about the prophets, God has not declared the ending of sending Messengers to humanity.

Contrary to the static, terminated concept of Divine Messengership espoused by the theologians, the Báb taught that Divine Revelation is a dynamic, ever-evolving, never-ending phenomenon. As a sign of God's grace, God interacts with humanity periodically through His Manifestations and is not limited by the desires or interpretations of men.

Therefore, each time a Manifestation of God appeared in the world He established a covenant with His followers concerning the acceptance of the next Manifestation of God, destined by God's Will to appear in the future.

> The Lord of the universe hath never raised up a prophet nor hath He sent down a Book unless He hath established His covenant with all men, calling for their acceptance of the next Revelation and of the next Book; inasmuch as the outpourings of His bounty are ceaseless and without limit. – The Báb[493]

The Báb described the nature of this covenant in different ways.

For example, both the Báb and Muhammad had been merchants. The Báb compared Divine Revelation to a loan God gives to humanity. Every loan has terms and stipulations. The borrower gets to use "the funds" for a specified period of time but has to pay back the loan when it is due. The Báb said,

> …the divine words … and all other parts of religion are tokens that are bestowed as a bounty from the Supreme Truth unto His created beings. Therefore, upon His revelation, it is incumbent upon all to return this bounteous loan unto Him… – The Báb[494]

Each Revelation is a loan to all human beings. The Báb says that when the Dispensation of a Manifestation of God has run its course and a new Manifestation of God appears, the loan comes due and human beings, borrowers from God, must repay the loan. This repayment is achieved by recognizing the new Manifestation of God as the spiritual return of the previous Manifestation of God, as the next One sent by God, and as the Primal Point of a new religious Dispensation. Saiedi notes:

> At this time the former religion, along with its symbols, is no longer intended to be kept by the believers, but is to be returned to God… – Nader Saiedi[495]

Returning the religion to God requires giving up attachment to the outward forms – not the inner spiritual truth – of the prior religious system. It means investigating the claims of the new Divine Educator. If your investigation leads to recognition, then repayment means embracing and following the Faith revealed by the most recent Messenger. This is the only way to repay the loan and remain faithful to the Divine Covenant. The Báb then adds,

> Were one to repay at once, upon the revelation of his debt, nothing would be reduced from his possessions; rather, he would be acknowledged in both the world and within himself. – The Báb[496]

Unlike an ordinary loan on earth, repayment of the Divine loan, consistent with God's grace, leads to an *increase* in spiritual riches.

> Yet, paradoxically, repaying this loan will not render anyone poorer for doing so. The abrogation of the previous religion is simultaneously its exaltation and fulfillment, as it actually appears renewed in the form of a fresh Revelation. Repayment is thus a means of gaining true riches: the new wealth is attaining the good pleasure of God and recognition of His new Manifestation. – Nader Saiedi[497]

The relationship between a former and succeeding Revelation presents a profound, beautiful continuity. The Báb uses the Arabic word, *irtifá'*, to emphasize this continuity. It has no equivalent in English; it has two simultaneous meanings, both equally important. Irtifá' means *both* abrogation and elevation, removal *and* lifting up.[498]

The Báb used this word to say that when a new Manifestation of God appears in the world, He applies irtifá' to the previous religion. As the inaugurator of a new religious Dispensation, a Divine Educator abrogates (changes) the laws of the previous religion and at the same time elevates the previous religion, bringing about its fulfillment.

All the Messengers of God engage in abrogation. For example, Jesus exercised His authority to abrogate certain of the laws of Moses. Notice the logical structure He used to explain abrogation to the people: "In the past you were told 'x', but now I tell you 'y'." Here are two illustrations of Him using this authority:

> It has been said, 'Anyone who divorces his wife must give her a certificate of divorce.' But I tell you that anyone who divorces his wife … commits adultery. – Jesus (Matthew 5:31-32)[499]

> You have heard that it was said, 'Eye for eye, and tooth for tooth.' But I tell you, do not resist an evil person. If anyone slaps you on the right cheek, turn to them the other cheek also. – Jesus (Matthew 5:38-39)[500]

It was through statements like this that Jesus changed the laws of divorce and retaliation. Jesus made several such statements.

Muhammad also changed laws from the past. One famous example was when He told the followers to stop turning to Jerusalem when offering their prayers and to turn towards the Ka'bih in Mecca instead. Muhammad had already emigrated to Medina and established "the umma", the federation of His followers with the Jews and Christians of the city. One day, following a revelation from God, Muhammad changed the direction of prayer. With a simple command, He told His followers to turn towards the Ka'bih, which He called the Holy Mosque:

> …now We will surely turn thee to a direction that shall satisfy thee. Turn thy face towards the Holy Mosque; and wherever you are, turn your faces towards it. Those who have been given the Book know it is the truth from their Lord… (Qur'án 2:144)[501]

The Báb, as the initiator of His own religious Dispensation, exercised His authority as a Divine Educator to abrogate the laws of the prior Dispensations, including those of Muhammad. There are many examples. The Báb…

- Altered the call to prayer
- Changed the calendar
- Encouraged secular as well as religious education

- Supported the advancement of women
- Negated the doctrine of finality asserted by the Muslim religious leaders
- Announced the imminent appearance of yet another Divine Messenger after Himself
- And much more.

In the Báb's case, He exercised His authority to make a nearly complete break with the prior Dispensation, which was Islám. This is the abrogating half of irtifá' in action.

The other—equally important—half of irtifá' is that the newer Manifestation of God elevates, exalts and fulfills the previous Dispensation. The newest Manifestation of God is the "fruit" of the Tree of the previous Divine Revelation, the culmination of all its striving. Thus, the Dispensation of Abraham found its fulfillment in the Dispensation of Moses, of Moses in Jesus, of Jesus in Muhammad and of Muhammad in the Báb. Without exception, the Scriptures which appeared later honored the ones that came before. For instance, Jesus praised Noah, Abraham, and Moses and, in addition, as the Gospels spread, distributed Their Names to populations who had never heard of them before. The Qur'án repeatedly honored and praised the deeds and rank of Abraham, Noah, Moses, and Jesus and elevated their Names among even more distant populations which had never before embraced either Moses or Jesus.[502]

Later, 'Abdu'l-Bahá took up this theme of elevation. He offered the following explanation of how later Divine Educators support and promote earlier Ones. In this example, the relationship between Moses and Jesus is discussed:

> This Personage, Jesus Christ, declared Moses to have been the Prophet of God... He proclaimed the Torah the very Book of God, summoned all to conform to its precepts and follow its teachings. It is an historical fact that during a period of fifteen hundred years the kings of Israel were unable to promulgate [or] broadcast the religion of Judaism. In fact, during that period the name and history of Moses were confined to the boundaries of Palestine and the Torah was a book well known only in that country. But through Christ, through the blessing of the New Testament of Jesus Christ, the Old Testament, the Torah, was translated into six hundred different tongues and spread throughout the world. It was through Christianity that the Torah reached Persia. Before that

> time there was no knowledge in that country of such a book, but Christ caused its spread and acceptance. Through Him the name of Moses was elevated and revered. He was instrumental in publishing the name and greatness of the Israelitish prophets, and He proved to the world that the Israelites constituted the people of God. Which of the kings of Israel could have accomplished this? Were it not for Jesus Christ, would the Bible, the Torah have reached this land of America? Would the name of Moses be spread throughout the world? Refer to history. Everyone knows that when Christianity was spread, there was a simultaneous spread of the knowledge of Judaism and the Torah. Throughout the length and breadth of Persia there was not a single volume of the Old Testament until the religion of Jesus Christ caused it to appear everywhere so that today the Holy Bible is a household book in that country. It is evident, then, that Christ was a friend of Moses, that He loved and believed in Moses; otherwise, He would not have commemorated His name and Prophethood. This is self-evident… – 'Abdu'l-Bahá[503]

The Báb said that all Divine revelations are each like a seed implanted in the hearts of humans. After the Manifestation of God, the followers are given time—centuries or millennia—to help this seed grow. They have time to receive its spiritual inspiration and express it outwardly through advancing civilization. Outward forms give evidence of the inner inspiration provided by the revealed Will of God. People compile sacred Texts and commentaries, they build magnificent Houses of Worship, they found humanitarian and educational institutions, they explore the profound meanings of sacred Scripture, they write creeds and discuss their beliefs and philosophies, they seek mystical experiences with the Divine, they make advances in science and technology, they develop an entire culture which strives to reflect the spirit of the Revelation which started it all.

Depending on the stage of human development and particular circumstances, certain errors of thinking or behaving creep into the Faith. Alterations and additions to the original teachings are adopted and spread. Sometimes the followers fight with one another. All in all, the civilizations, initially generated by Revelation, with all their accomplishments and shortcomings, continue to develop as far as possible within their capacities. The seed has become a tree, that is, a civilization. More than this, the tree has lived a full cycle and grown to its stage of maturity. In God's inscrutable knowledge, a point in historical time is reached when it is most wise to "pluck" the fruit of the Tree of Revelation to yield a new religious Dispensation by sending a new Manifestation of God into the world. Speaking of His own Revelation, the Báb says:

> He is made manifest in order to gather the fruits of the trees He hath planted… He appeareth not, save for the purpose of gathering the fruits of Islám from the Qur'ánic verses which He [Muhammad] hath sown in the hearts of men. The fruits of Islám cannot be gathered except through allegiance unto Him [the Qá'im] and by believing in Him. – The Báb[504]

Sometimes people worry that recognizing the new Manifestation of God might be an *act of betrayal* towards the previous Manifestation of God to Whom they have been loyal their entire lives. The Báb had an illuminating answer to this question. If only people would understand, they would know that the opposite is true. Accepting the next Manifestation of God is not a betrayal, it is an affirmation of the success of the previous Manifestation in preparing humanity for its next developmental stage. For example, the Báb stated:

> The stage of perfection of everything is reached when its resurrection occurreth. The perfection of the religion of Islam was consummated at the beginning of this Revelation; and from the rise of this Revelation until its setting, the fruits of the Tree of Islam, whatever they are, will become apparent. – The Báb[505]

Embracing the newest Divine revelation is the second half of irtifá', it is the *elevation* of the Cause of God to the next level.

For the same reason, rejecting the next Divine Educator is not affirming the previous Divine Educator. In the Báb's teaching, the purpose of Revelation is continuity and step-by-step progress for the human race.

Let us recall the overarching theme of this book, namely, that all creation is a classroom, which could be called the school of God. Each Dispensation is like a grade in this school, the Manifestations of God are the Divine Educators in this school and Their Revelations constitute the Divine Curriculum at each level of the school. In school, a child begins at the beginning. She enters first grade, proceeds through the school year, and then first grade comes to an end. Then what happens? If the student has learned well, she receives a promotion! It is time to move on to second grade. When the next school year begins, should the child cling to the first-grade teacher and refuse to go on to the second grade? If she does cling, isn't that rejecting everything the first-grade teacher strove to achieve on behalf of the student? Wouldn't that teacher feel as if she had failed? Similarly, if the child cheerfully advances to the next grade, isn't that the only way to affirm and honor the efforts of the earlier teacher? The parents and student realize that all the Teachers are members of the same team, working for the same school Director. The Teachers are all supporters of the same school program, which was designed to bring advancement to all the students, the human race. This principle applies to all of the grades in school. It doesn't matter if we're talking about being promoted from first grade, seventh grade, or twelfth grade. The principle is the same.

The covenant each student makes with his or her teacher is that after being taught by a master teacher in one grade, and after following the curriculum to the best of one's ability in that grade, a *promotion* is earned to the classroom of the next master teacher in the same school. Imagine the situation of a student who has failed to learn, for whatever reason, the lessons prescribed by the teacher. Imagine the parent's feelings when they are told their child will be held back for a year. This is not a moment of joy. No matter how much the present teacher is loved, the parents will not say 'yippee, our child will stay with this teacher for another year.' The parents and the teacher feel sadness because the child is not advancing as they hoped.

So it is in the school of God. The school Director, God's Primal Will, has designed this program for the advancement of humanity. God's Representatives are the Teachers in His school, the Manifestations of God. Through Their deeds and Their Revelation of the Word of God, they provide humanity with the Lessons of the Divine Curriculum. What they all hope is that humanity will embrace Their Lessons and advance from Dispensation to Dispensation in an orderly and timely manner. They are all sorrowful when humanity does not advance.

Some people who are members of an earlier Faiths may feel that comparing their religion to an earlier grade in school is something of *a put down*. In the teachings of the Báb this would be misreading the situation. Are first grade teachers any less valuable to the school program than third grade teachers? Do they get paid less? Do they have a lower rank? Are their views in staff meetings any less appreciated because they teach students who are at a younger age? No, of course not. The teachers in the school all have equal rank. In fact, the teachers are somewhat interchangeable. So great is their knowledge that the first-grade teacher can easily be reassigned by the school Director to the fifth grade and the fifth-grade teacher can easily become a first-grade teacher. Such a reassignment does not imply any change in rank for the teacher.

In addition, the lessons they give are equally important. Even if a student loves his teacher, the student is not supposed to repeat a lesson over and over again after it has been mastered. Instead, each set of lessons is designed to advance the student step-by-step to the next level. The lessons of fourth grade are completely unteachable if lessons of first, second and third grades were not mastered. All the grades in the school are stages in one coherent program of learning. The student who studies more advanced reading, writing and math lessons, if he is fair-minded and appropriately grateful, will recognize that his progress would have been impossible without learning from teachers of earlier stages. Every time he advances, he will praise his former teachers and acknowledge their achievements in him. Now in an advanced stage of study, despite his respect and gratitude to his earlier teachers, he would not wish to go back. Faithful to the intent of those earlier teachers, he will eagerly keep advancing to achieve his fullest potential as a student in the school.

Each new Revelation is a continuation of a single, universal, Divine educational process, which the Báb says has operated as long as humanity has existed and will continue without end. Since the Manifestations of God are one in their essence, it is also true that, spiritually they are the same, even though they are unique Individuals at different times in history. Each new Revelation indicates the termination of laws of the previous Dispensation and also its exaltation. The Báb said that to be truly faithful to the Covenant with God and the intent of the earlier Divine Educator, one must investigate and then embrace the new Manifestation of God, if He is found to be true. Far from being a rejection, this is the best way to show one's loyalty, faithfulness and gratitude to the previous Manifestation of God. It is worthwhile to look at this quote once again:

> True knowledge, therefore, is the knowledge of God, and this is none other than the recognition of His Manifestation in each Dispensation. Nor is there any wealth save in poverty in all save God and sanctity from aught else but Him—a state that can be realized only when demonstrated towards Him Who is the Dayspring of His Revelation. This doth not mean, however, that one ought not to yield praise unto former Revelations. On no account is this acceptable, inasmuch as it behooveth man, upon reaching the age of nineteen, to render thanksgiving for the day of his conception as an embryo. For had the embryo not existed, how could he have reached his present state? Likewise had the religion taught by Adam not existed, this Faith would not have attained its present stage. Thus consider thou the development of God's Faith until the end that hath no end. – The Báb[506]

There is one additional aspect of the Báb's treatment of the question of finality. The Báb asserts the essential principle that God does whatsoever He wills to do, regardless of what humans may think. This principle is captured succinctly in this statement from Bahá'u'lláh:

> The spirit that animateth the human heart is the knowledge of God, and its truest adorning is the recognition of the truth that "He doeth whatsoever He willeth, and ordaineth that which He pleaseth." – Bahá'u'lláh[507]

It is so with the appearance of the Divine Messenger. Ultimately, He makes an *empirical* argument. That is, despite the theories of the theologians and the philosophers who say He isn't coming, He comes. The ultimate proof of a Manifestation of God is when He is right in front of you saying, "Here am I."

All the seemingly sound theories about why and how this is not possible turn to ashes when you are confronted with *the empirical evidence* of His Presence. All your expectations and everything you think you know are turned upside-down by the simple fact of His coming with all the essential signs and proofs. In this moment, one is faced with a straight-forward choice, retreat into denial or face reality. Then you must decide what to do about it.

In the end, it was this empirical proof that convinced both Mullá Husayn and the king's scholar, Vahíd. At the beginning of their encounters with the Báb, both men were skeptical of the Báb's claims. But then, something astounding happened. For Mullá Husayn it was the sudden and unprompted revelation of the Commentary of the Surih of Joseph, the final sign which Mullá Husayn had kept secret in his mind. Likewise, when Vahíd planned a similar test, the Báb suddenly revealed a Commentary on the Surih of Kawthar, the chapter of the Qur'án which he had on his mind. In these cases, the empirical evidence before the eyes of both men was stunning and undeniable.

- Unprompted Revelation, as if the Báb had read their minds and answered an unspoken prayer.
- Thousands of verses revealed.
- At astonishing speed.
- With no pause or hesitation.
- In exquisite penmanship (nearly impossible to do given the quill and ink bottle writing tools of the day).
- Brilliant, beautiful, eloquent words.

- Ideas, words and teachings as profound and elevated as the Qur'án itself. A feat no one in nearly 1,300 years had ever been able to accomplish.
- And all this by a young merchant with no formal religious education, by one Who is not a member of the clergy.

Let's put ourselves in the position of these two men. By all logic, this astounding achievement should not be humanly possible. Neither man, nor any other illustrious member of the clergy was able to do it. It *should* be impossible. The doctrine of finality told them it was impossible. They would not have believed it if they had not seen it with their own eyes. And yet, there they are, in the room, with the Báb, seeing it unfold before their very eyes.

This is literally the ultimate scientific, empirical argument. The Manifestation of God is saying (allow me to put this in my words), "Put aside your theology that tells you this will never happen, forget your logical arguments about why this cannot be. The proof is Myself, here, in this room with you, right now, revealing the Word of God. What else do you need to know?" We know from the history, as sincere seekers, both Mullá Husayn and Vahíd accepted the clear evidence presented to their eyes. And accepting the evidence transformed them.

The Báb explains that the Manifestation of God is like the sun, shining upon all things. Humans are no more than mirrors reflecting the sun. From God's perspective, how can a mere mirror dispute with the brilliant illumination of the sun? The proof of the sun is the sun itself.

The Báb's presence on earth as a Divine Educator was His ultimate refutation of the doctrine of finality that was embraced by the orthodox Muslim religious leaders. That doctrine was based primarily upon their reading of the Qur'án which stated in Súrih (Chapter) 33:40 that Muhammad is the "seal of the prophets." These clerics and theologians argued, therefore, that there were no more Prophets after Muhammad until the Day of Resurrection and until that Day they themselves were in charge of the Cause of God. This became their finality doctrine. The Báb upheld the Qur'án as the revealed Word of God. He agreed with what the Qur'án revealed. From the Báb's perspective, the Islámic leaders had misunderstood the meaning of the Resurrection, they had not understood the concept of the seal, and they had not appreciated that God does whatsoever He will. God acts as He deems best.

God doeth what He willeth. (Qur'an 14:27, translated by Yusuf 'Alí)

That passage of the Qur'án – Surih 33:40, which refers to Muhammad as the seal of the prophets – simply doesn't mean what they claimed it meant.

Books could be written about their finality doctrine. In the final analysis, however, none of the theologians' interpretations matter if God one day chooses to send another Divine Messenger. All the arguments become irrelevant when a new reality emerges, when God sends a new Manifestation of God into the world with all the signs and proofs necessary to establish His claim.

The opponents could say what they wished, but here He was among them. Here He was, giving His proofs, in exactly the same manner that Muhammad had done, through the revelation of Divine verses. Given this evidence, it was now up to each individual to investigate and to respond according to his or her conscience, not through blind imitation of others. The Báb wrote:

[In the following quote, Him Whom God shall make manifest = Bahá'u'lláh, the Messenger of God Who came after the Báb. Note: Italics are added for emphasis.]

Thus on the Day of Resurrection God will *ask everyone of his understanding and not of his following in the footsteps of others*. How often a person, having inclined his ears to the holy verses, would bow down in humility and would embrace the Truth, while his leader would not do so. Thus *every individual must bear his own responsibility*, rather than someone else bearing it for him. At the time of the appearance of Him Whom God will make manifest the most distinguished among the learned and the lowliest of men shall both be judged alike. How often the most insignificant of men have acknowledged the truth, while the most learned have remained wrapt in veils. Thus in every Dispensation a number of souls enter the fire by reason of their following in the footsteps of others. – The Báb[508]

Nevertheless, from the beginning of their lives till the end thereof, in conformity with the laws established in the previous religion, they worship God, piously adore Him, bow themselves before His divine Reality and show submissiveness toward His exalted Essence. At the hour of His manifestation, however, they all *turn their gaze toward their own selves* and are thus shut out from Him, inasmuch as they *fancifully regard Him as one like unto themselves*. Far from the glory of God is such a comparison. Indeed that august Being resembleth the physical sun,

> His verses are like its rays, and all believers, should they truly believe in Him, are as mirrors wherein the sun is reflected. Their light is thus a mere reflection. – The Báb[509] **(Note: Italics added.)**

The Báb's teaching opened the door from the stagnant, closed, self-serving ideology of the orthodox religious leaders. He stimulated a new openness of mind and opened shining new horizons for humanity. The followers were inspired to achieve unprecedented levels of devotion and sacrifice. The Báb wrote:

> The process of His creation hath had no beginning and can have no end, otherwise it would necessitate the cessation of His celestial grace. God hath raised up Prophets and revealed Books as numerous as the creatures of the world, and will continue to do so to everlasting. – The Báb[510]

God's celestial requires the continuation of His creative activity and progressive Revelation through the ages. Explicitly, in the Báb's Writings, this is the final word on finality. It shook the nation to its core.

DIVINE PROOF

The Manifestation of God appears in the world. He is literally or metaphorically standing in front of you, saying, "Here am I". If true, the fact of His Presence in the world ends all debate about whether or not the previous Divine Messenger was the final one.
But honestly, a seeker must ask a crucial question, "How do I know if your claim to be a Divine Educator is really true?" Every person *must* confront this question, because (we can assume) God would not want you to embrace someone as a Divine Teacher if his claim were false. Yes, by definition, God wants you to embrace a TRUE Divine Educator, but it is safe to assume He doesn't want you to embrace someone making a false claim either. Right?

To do your duty towards God, to the best of your ability you must decide about the Divine Educator's claim. How do you fulfill this duty faithfully and honorably?

In one way or another this challenge has been mentioned in all the Scriptures – the Hebrew Bible, the Gospels, the Qur'án, and the Writings of the Báb. To evaluate the Báb's claim, we will explore three points which He specifically addressed:

- He did not want His followers to teach His Faith to others by relating miracles about Him.

- The proof of His legitimate claim to be a Divine Educator is His revelation of Divine verses.
- To recognize that His verses were authentically from God one needs purity of heart.

Are miracles proof?

The Báb never claimed He could not do miracles. He wasn't worried about any lack of ability. Miracles are easy to do if one is a Manifestation of the Primal Will of God. History records that the Bab performed miracles from time to time.

But you won't hear much about these miraculous events because the Báb didn't want His followers talking about them. Specifically, He did not want His followers *to teach* the Cause by talking about His miracles. He didn't want people believing in Him because of miracles. From His perspective, turning God's revelation into some sort of magician's trick was beneath the dignity of God's Cause. The Báb states:

> He who recounteth any miracle, other than the verses, is veiled from any truth. – The Báb[511]

Moreover, as Dr. Saiedi explained, asking for and teaching through stories of miracles is a sign of spiritual weakness, not strength.

> In this new age, the Báb explains, physical miracles are no longer the conclusive testimony of the Prophet; those who ask for miracles are merely testifying to the immaturity of their own spiritual level. – Nader Saiedi[512]

When a person is in the Presence of a Manifestation of God, or when exposed to His Writings, sometimes a selfish spiritual blindness and skepticism prompts an individual to demand a miracle. The one seeking the miracle is often a disbeliever, and likely wants to stay a disbeliever. He doesn't want the miracle in order to become convinced, nor does he wish to assume his proper place as a humble believer; he demands the miracle because he thinks the Manifestation of God is bluffing. He wants the Prophet to fail so that he can pridefully vindicate his skepticism and mock the Prophet. He oversteps his bounds in the cosmic scheme seeking to put God to the test, when in fact it is God who tests His servants. This attitude trivializes the purposes of God's Messenger – to bring the hearts of God's human children closer to Him, to rectify their conduct, to reorient their minds, to edify their souls and to reawaken civilization itself.

The Báb clearly indicates that God doesn't wish to play this game. Why ask for a cheap trick, when one could ask for love, wisdom and salvation from the Teacher Whom God has empowered to give it to you? From the Báb's perspective, the request for a miracle is not a sincere request for proof, it is an indication of hardness of heart. The Báb speaks harshly of such individuals:

> Were any man to be adorned with all spiritual virtues in utmost contentment in all the worlds, and yet assert in this Day that his heart is not utterly satisfied with the revelation of verses in the absence of witnessing miracles, then all his acquiescence would be brought to naught in the Book of God, and no other mode of resignation would be of any profit to him. – The Báb[513]

The Báb's point was not that He hadn't performed any miracles. As a Manifestation of the Primal Will of God, a miracle was well within His abilities, if God willed Him to perform one.

One example was the Báb's ability to ride a wild horse when He was in Urúmíyyih, on the way to His trial in Tabríz in the Summer of 1848. It was *the people, not the Báb,* who claimed the Báb had performed a miracle. The reader may wonder, was it really a miracle? Even if every detail of the story is proven true, it doesn't matter. From the Báb's perspective, how can His ability to ride a wild horse have anything to do with whether He was truly a Divine Educator sent from God? How can the crowd's excitement show anything other than the peoples' immaturity? How can all the attention given to this feat be anything other than a distraction from the serious message He was trying to convey?

Here is the report:

[Note: The miraculous account of the Báb calmly riding the wildest horse in the city of Urúmíyyih is presented in Chapter 4: Opposition Builds.]

> When the Báb arrived at Urúmíyyih, [the prince] ceremoniously received Him and accorded Him the warmest hospitality… On a certain Friday when the Báb was going to the public bath, the prince, who was curious to test the courage and power of his Guest, ordered his groom to offer Him one of his wildest horses to ride. Apprehensive lest the Báb might suffer any harm, the attendant secretly approached Him and tried to induce Him to refuse to mount a horse that had already overthrown the bravest and most skillful of horsemen.

[The Báb replied:]

"Fear not, do as you have been bidden, and commit Us to the care of the Almighty."

The inhabitants of Urúmíyyih ... filled the public square, eager to witness what might befall the Báb. As soon as the horse was brought to Him, He quietly approached it and, taking hold of the bridle which the groom had offered Him, gently caressed it and placed His foot in the stirrup. The horse stood still and motionless beside Him as if conscious of the power which was dominating it. The multitude that watched this most unusual spectacle marvelled at the behaviour of the animal. To their simple minds this extraordinary incident appeared little short of a miracle. – Nabíl[514]

The crowd watching this spectacle went crazy.

[Note: The mention below of "the dreadful treatment meted out to Him in Tabríz" refers to the eventual martyrdom of the Báb, which would take place two years later in Tabríz.]

They hastened in their enthusiasm to kiss the stirrups of the Báb... All the way, the prince's footmen were endeavoring to restrain the people who, from every side, were pressing forward to catch a glimpse of the Báb... On His return from the bath, He again mounted the same horse and was acclaimed by the same multitude...

No sooner had the Báb left the bath than the people of Urúmíyyih rushed to take away, to the last drop, the water which had served for His ablutions. Great excitement prevailed on that day... When He was subsequently informed how the overwhelming majority of the people had spontaneously arisen to proclaim their undivided allegiance to His Cause, He calmly observed:

"Think men that when they say, 'We believe,' they shall be let alone and not be put to the proof?" [Qur'án 29:2]

This comment was fully justified by the attitude which that same people assumed towards Him when the news of the dreadful treatment meted out to Him in Tabríz reached them. Hardly a handful among those who had so ostentatiously professed their faith in Him

> persevered, in the hour of trial, in their allegiance to His Cause…
>
> The tales of the signs and wonders which the Báb's unnumbered admirers had witnessed were soon transmitted from mouth to mouth, and gave rise to a wave of unprecedented enthusiasm which spread with bewildering rapidity over the entire country… – Nabíl[515]

Thus, as the Báb predicted, the majority who witnessed what they proclaimed as a miracle did not persevere in the Faith when a couple of years later the times grew difficult. From the Báb's perspective, miracles don't do much to advance the people in deep faith, understanding and commitment to God's Cause.

From the Báb's viewpoint, demands for a miracle from doubters and opponents should not be granted. This is why, in an Islamic society, in 1848, when the mullás in Tabríz demanded a miracle during the trial, He offered instead the same proof that Muhammad had given them:

> 'The mightiest, the most convincing evidence of the truth of the Mission of the Prophet of God … is admittedly His own Word. He Himself [Muhammad] testifies to this truth:
>
> > "Is it not enough for them that We have sent down to Thee the Book?" [Qur'án 29:51]
>
> 'The power to produce such evidence has been given to Me by God. Within the space of two days and two nights, I declare Myself able to reveal verses of such number as will equal the whole of the Qur'án.' – The Báb[516]

The revelation of the Word of God

There are at least two ways to evaluate the revelation of the Word of God. First, the revelation itself, the product produced by the Divine Educator is supremely excellent and inspiring. Surely, like the Qur'án in the previous age, God's Primal Will would only reveal something wonderful. When we read the revealed Word of God, it is beautiful, eloquent and profound.

Second, the process by which these words come into existence is marvelous in some way. For example, as I write this paragraph I am slowly, carefully trying to write words that make sense. I have to go back frequently and correct my errors. Though I am considered well educated, I often change my mind, erase what I wrote and start over. Often, I go research something, such as a quotation, before I can move forward. Sometimes, I experience writer's block, which is surely not wonderful. I modified this paragraph at least six times. With so many errors, detours and do-overs, it can take more than an hour to write a good paragraph. It takes me time, lots of time, to get through this process. Clearly my writing abilities are those of a fallible, ordinary human being.

A Manifestation of God should be different. A Manifestation of God *is* different. The Báb makes this point:

[Note: In the quote below, the phrases "His supreme Testimony" and "appearance of this Tree" are metaphorical and poetic references to the revelation of the Manifestation of God. In this case, the image is that of the Tree of Divine Revelation.]

> The evidence set forth by God can never be compared with the evidences produced by any one of the peoples and kindreds of the earth; and beyond a shadow of doubt no evidence is set forth by God save through the One Who is appointed as His supreme Testimony... And if anyone should reflect on the appearance of this Tree, he will undoubtedly testify to the loftiness of the Cause of God. For if one from whose life only twenty-four years have passed, and who is devoid of those sciences wherein all are learned, now reciteth verses after such fashion without thought or hesitation, writes a thousand verses of prayer in the course of five hours without pause of the pen, and produceth commentaries and learned treatises on such lofty themes as the true understanding of God and of the oneness of His Being, in a manner which doctors and philosophers confess surpasseth their power of understanding, then there is no doubt that all that hath been manifested is divinely inspired. Notwithstanding their life-long diligent study, what pains do these divines take when writing a single line in Arabic! Yet after such efforts the result is but words which are unworthy of mention. All these things are for a proof unto the people; otherwise the religion of God is too mighty and glorious for anyone to comprehend through aught but itself; rather by it all else is understood. – The Báb[517]

This important passage describes the Word of God as incomparable to the words of men. We've alredy mentioned these features earlier in the chapter, but let's take a moment to analyze specifically what the Báb is saying. This quotation is structured in three parts.

- The first part may be labeled ‘contrary to expectations’ or as ‘with these disqualifiers’.
- The second part is explicit, “now reciteth verses”.
- The third part may be labeled ‘nevertheless with these amazing characteristics as proof’.

Despite these reasons for thinking an ordinary person shouldn’t be able to do it, the Báb did it, and He did it with these amazing qualities as proof of the Divine origin of His Words. Let’s now look at what He says:

First, He should not be able to do it because:

- He was “only twenty-four years” old. In His culture, being a youth meant He was too inexperienced to have any amazing abilities or qualifications. It was grounds for not giving Him any respect. This isn’t fair, but it was the prevalent prejudice of the religious leaders of the times.
- He was “devoid of those sciences wherein all are learned”. This meant that He wasn’t considered learned, like the mullás were thought to be learned. They had spent many years in their schools of religious training. They had studied the Qur’án, memorized it, perfected the use of Arabic grammar, learned the obscure rules of Islám, discussed the points of theology, and attained positions of power, dominating over the people. The Báb had done none of that. The mullás would have thought, ‘Are you kidding me? He is an untutored merchant. How could He possibly know more than we do? How could he possibly outrank us and tell us what to do?’

Second, the Báb says that, despite these disqualifiers which say He shouldn’t be able to do it, He did it anyway. He “now reciteth verses”.

Third, the Báb lists six outstanding qualities of these verses.

Summary point	The Báb's words
No preparation	"...without thought or hesitation..."
Large quantity	"...writes a thousand verses..."
Little time	"...in the course of five hours..."
Flowing, no pause in revealing the words	"...without pause of the pen..."
On profound topics	"...produceth commentaries and learned treatises on such lofty themes..."
With exceptionally profound understanding	"...in a manner which doctors and philosophers confess surpasseth their power of understanding..."

Figure 30 The miraculous features of the Bab's revelation, in His own words

He then draws the inevitable conclusion: "then there is no doubt that all that hath been manifested is divinely inspired". He concludes His argument by contrasting this work with that of the pretentious religious leaders:

> Notwithstanding their life-long diligent study, what pains do these divines take when writing a single line in Arabic! Yet after such efforts the result is but words which are unworthy of mention. – The Báb[518]

His summary is that the Cause of God is truly mighty, in all the ways that are important.

> All these things are for a proof unto the people; otherwise the religion of God is too mighty and glorious for anyone to comprehend through aught but itself; rather by it all else is understood. – The Báb[519]

This was a powerful, transformative argument. We see it in action repeatedly; eyewitnesses to the act of Revelation are repeatedly dumbfounded by the display of power.

If someone asked you, with no warning, to write a large book in a short amount of time, without taking a moment to prepare, without pausing your pen, in exquisite penmanship, revealing profound insights and at a level of such literary and intellectual excellence that your final product would compare favorably to, say, Shakespeare, how would you do? Could you do that?

Could ten people, working together, do that? And yet, writing in both Arabic and Persian, this is precisely what this young, unschooled Merchant did. No wonder men like Mullá Husayn and Vahíd felt overwhelmed, overjoyed and convinced. They saw it as a true miracle, and the miracle was no cheap trick like flying around the room. It was spiritually meaningful and directly relevant to the Báb's claim to be a Manifestation of God. This, indeed, was all the miracle that true seekers ever needed.

This takes us deeper into additional insights. Professor Saiedi, offers this observation about Divine verses:

> A point should be noted about the term {áyát} (Singular {áyih}), translated as "divine verses." The Arabic word {áyát} is a most complex term, the nuances of which cannot be captured by any single word in English. It means "verses," "signs," and "miracles." Indeed the Báb's frequent discussion of the inimitable and incontrovertible character of the Word of God contains all these meanings at the same time: *the divine words are God's supreme miracle*, which is the sign of His majesty and glory, revealed in the world in the form of the Word – that is, the divine verses. – Nader Saiedi[520]

Thus, the term Divine verses includes within itself the meaning of a sign or miracle from God! According to the Báb, everything in "existence is a divine text, and the entirety of being is a mirror of divine reality: whatever exists in the world is a sign, a verse, and a miracle that proclaims the unity and sovereignty of God."[521] The greatest miracle and the most sublime reality of all, is the Word of God, an expression of His Primal Will.

The Báb spoke of the rapidity of His revelation as an outer expression of His inner experience, which He referred to as an "inner surge". *Thus, the real miracle of the revelation of the Word of God is that "inner surge" of Divine inspiration and revelation flowing within the heart of the Manifestation of God.* The Báb wrote a significant treatise known as the Súrih of Kawthar in which He poetically describes the legendary Kawthar fountain flowing in paradise. The Báb compares the rapid flow of this fountain to His experience revealing the Word of God. Professor Saiedi explains:

[Note: In the next quote the term "the One Whom God willeth" refers to the Manifestation of God.]

> Another significant feature of the Kawthar fountain is the force with which these divine rivers surge and flow. The Báb frequently attests to the speed with which revelation flowed from His lips and pen, as

evidence of the inimitable nature of that revelation. How much more powerful was the inner experience of being the vehicle of revelation:

> ...Verily, by virtue of the rapidity of the flow ... a complete book of prayer streameth forth from My Pen within the course of six hours. Such rapidity is, verily, a most glorious sign within the realm of miracles. For verily the outward rapidity of flow is evidence of the inner surge. This surge is a daunting and highly perplexing matter, recognized by all as being impossible to attain by anyone save the One Whom God willeth. For the supreme honour is not in the mere composition of the outward appearance of the words, but in traversing the kingdom of Names and Attributes in less than the twinkling of an eye. – Nader Saiedi, citing the Báb[522]

In the Age of the Báb, humanity is offered an improved definition of Divine proof. Although physical miracles happen from time to time, they are no longer offered as proofs of the truth of the Divine Messenger. Instead, the Divine Educator offers the proofs of awe-inspiring acts of revelation and the resulting written Word of God itself. Each seeker must see or hear the Words and decide in his conscience whether such verses have originated from God. As Saiedi stated:

> It is the immaterial mystic wisdom of heavenly truth, expressed in the body of words, that constitutes the supreme testimony of God in the Day of the Báb. – Nader Saiedi[523]

Purity of heart

"Proof" isn't what it used to be. In the 21st Century, large numbers of people believe that the earth is flat. The evidence that the earth is round is overwhelming – even a child can understand it – so how can it be that many people still think the earth is flat?

Let's consider the concept of proof. For example, imagine you are a juror in a murder case. The prosecuting attorney sets forth a mountain of evidence. He explains that, thanks to a tip from an eyewitness, the police caught the defendant at the scene of the crime just minutes after the crime had taken place. The medical examiner reports that the cause of death was a bullet to the heart. The bullet that was removed from the body of the victim was traced back to the very gun found in the defendant's hand moments after the murder took place. The defendant's fingerprints are on the gun and elsewhere at the murder scene. Some of the victim's blood was found splattered on the defendant's clothing. The defendant had a motive to commit the killing.

Has the prosecution proven his case? As a juror, would you convict the defendant of murder?

Then the defense attorney stands up to begin making his case.

Well, he says, there were other people at the scene who were arrested by the police. Their fingerprints were also found at the scene and on the gun. They too have blood from the defendant splattered on their clothes. The defendant claims he was trying to stop one of the other people from committing the murder. Sure, he hated the victim for a good reason (the victim had cheated him) and had gone to the scene to give him a nasty scolding and diatribe, and maybe get his money back, but he didn't think anyone should be killed over it. He was at the scene, just as the police reported, but, when the shouting got out of hand, he struggled with the others at the scene who had brought the gun (it wasn't his gun), trying to get the gun away from them. In the chaos, the gun went off and killed the victim. He doesn't know who pulled the trigger on the gun, but he does know that multiple people had their hands on the gun during the struggle. Despite his admitted anger at the victim, he was really trying *to stop* a killing. He grabbed the gun too late and that is when the police arrived.

Has the defense attorney proven his case? As a juror, would you acquit the defendant of the charges?

"Proof" is having evidence sufficient to establish a premise as true, or producing a strong belief in its truth, eliminating the irrationality of denial or alternate explanations. Proof is understood as a pattern of facts that impel a reasonable, rational, objective observer to come to a specific conclusion. Moreover, "proof" is so compelling it would make no difference if this observer loves or hates the defendant. The evidence is so strong that no fair-minded, logical human being would come to a different conclusion.

This is what proof is supposed to look like; it is decisive, undisputed. Even the hostile opponent, if he has integrity, cannot deny it. But *sometimes*, even when proof is vividly clear, doubters remain. Have you ever been in a conversation with someone over some point of disagreement and, to prove your point, you said something that you thought was so elementary, so basic, so fundamental, so obvious, that in your thinking it should be sufficient to end the argument? To you, your statement was as basic as 2 + 2 = 4. To you, the response should have been, "Oh yes, I see the light!" But that is not the response. You are amazed that someone can hear the point you just made and not automatically agree. You're thinking, "How can you not get this?", after you made such an obviously convincing point.

There are four possible explanations for this peculiar behavior. One, your friend really doesn't understand. Two, your friend understands, but doesn't want to admit it. Three, your friend is tired of you "always" being correct. Four, your point wasn't as brilliant as you thought it was. The point seems to be that we think is "proof" isn't necessarily actual proof in all cases. Even proof seems to be in the eye of the beholder, regardless of its objective validity.

There are still people living in the world today who believe that the earth is flat and not round. Twelve jurors in court do not always agree despite the presentation of overwhelming evidence. Despite the proofs given by a Manifestation of God in support of His rank as a Divine Educator, some people continue to deny or be uncertain.

The question is why?

Other qualities are necessary for people to be open to a new idea. They are two sides of the same coin – prejudice and purity of heart.

Prejudice is an attitude or perspective which distorts reality in the mind of an individual. Invariably learned in a social or cultural context of some sort, it is usually focused on one or more external trait; it could be anything, such as sex, ethnicity, culture, social class, tall people, short people, overweight people, skinny people, old people or young people, etc. Then, grasping on to that one external trait, they may say, "All those people are… <expletive deleted>." This is clearly a distortion. The prejudiced attitude is not receptive to facts or logic. It reflects an ill will in the psychology of the individual.

Prejudice has an ominous quality that goes unnoticed by the one caught in its grip. It induces systematic and consistent error. That is, the prejudiced individual, as a habit, will always misread reality somehow. Indeed, the prejudiced individual is usually more attached to their position than to discovering reality. Therefore, prejudice is very difficult to overcome, because the individual who has fallen victim to it is unlikely to recognize it, acknowledge it or be willing to correct it.

Prejudice can be caused by many factors, such as excessive pride in one's knowledge, indoctrination by others, feeling threatened, clinging to an "us" vs. "them" mentally, wanting to feel superior to others, a perceived conflict, dogmatically adhering to a rigid position, seeking to gain wealth, advantage or power at the expense of others, prior painful experiences or institutional discrimination, as well as other factors.. Whatever the cause, prejudice distorts one's perception of reality. Systematic and consistent error is the result. In its worst forms, this error leads to injustice and tyranny between individuals and in society.

The other side of prejudice is purity of heart. A person with purity of heart will be free from prejudice and an eager learner. This person will seek truth, will not be indifferent to truth claims, will be welcoming, and will be willing to invest time and effort in investigating the truth. A person with a pure heart who finds truth embraces it willingly. There are no barriers holding this person back. For this trait to be maintained, other qualities are essential, such as the yearning for truth, the desire for a close relationship with God, the pattern of treating others with respect and dignity, the humility to be a learner instead of a "know-it-all", not holding oneself or one's ideas as inherently superior, and being receptive to new learning, even in unexpected ways. A person with purity of heart will be eager to serve, will not harbor ulterior motives and will gladly let knowledge of the facts lead him wherever they need to go.

We should not oversimplify the challenge of seeking purity of heart instead of prejudice. Many individuals in history made a false claim of Divine revelation. They were pretenders. We acknowledge the existence of this *type* of individual. The psychology, motivations and signs of such individuals could be the subject of a lengthy book.

Nor is every skeptical person prejudiced, or every accepting person pure of heart. The skeptic asks the tough questions that will, in their view, lead them to the truth. Skepticism may be a tough-minded expression of intellectual rigor, showing a commendable effort to investigate reality. Likewise, an accepting person might be gullible or unwilling to make a strong effort to come to their own conclusions. In this case, acceptance isn't purity of heart, it is excessive reliance on others.

The spiritual and intellectual landscape of the types of people one may encounter could be quite diverse. However, prejudice will be a barrier, even if one is presented with "proof", and purity of heart will be a refreshing breeze, bringing new insights and a willingness to consider "proofs".

Neither the prejudiced individual nor the one who is pure of heart should arrogantly reject a false claim nor blindly embrace a true one:

> ...be thou neither a divine without discernment nor a follower without discernment... – The Báb[524]

We should accept true claims and accept false ones, but only after adequate investigation. The Báb acknowledges this dynamic. Referring to the Qur'án, He reports that both types of individuals receive what they deserve from the same Source, the proof of the Divine verses:

[Note: In the following quote, "the year sixty" refers to 1260 AH, on the Islámic calendar, which was 1844 AD, on the Gregorian calendar. "Him Who is the Testimony of God" = a reference to the station of the Manifestation of God.]

> God beareth Me witness, I was not a man of learning, for I was trained as a merchant. In the year sixty God graciously infused my soul with the conclusive evidences and weighty knowledge which characterize Him Who is the Testimony of God – may peace be upon Him – until finally in that year I proclaimed God's hidden Cause and unveiled its well-guarded Pillar, in such wise that no one could refute it. 'That he who should perish might perish with a clear proof before him and he who should live might live by clear proof.' (Qur'án 8:44) – The Báb[525]

The Báb, because He was dealing with the mullás who vehemently and violently opposed His Cause, dwelt extensively on the subject of "learning". He berated acquired human learning as a potential barrier to recognizing the truth of the claim of an authentic Divine Messenger.

The mullás prided themselves on their years of study. They considered themselves above everyone else. They claimed to know the truth of religion, and considered all others as ignorant. They especially considered the Báb ignorant because He was from the merchant class. They imagined that He couldn't possibly know as much as they did. In their many encounters, they belittled the Báb. In His Writings, the Báb claimed that human learning was no guarantee of wisdom or salvation.

> Man's highest station, however, is attained through faith in God in every Dispensation and by acceptance of what hath been revealed by Him, and not through learning; inasmuch as in every nation there are learned men who are versed in divers sciences. Nor is it attainable through wealth; for it is similarly evident that among the various classes in every nation there are those possessed of riches. Likewise are other transitory things. – The Báb[526]

> Verily on that Day the learning of the learned shall prove of no avail, neither the accomplishments of the exponents of knowledge, nor the pomp of the highly honoured, nor the power of the mighty, nor the remembrance of the devout, nor the deeds of the righteous, nor the genuflexion of the kneeling worshipper … nor the nobility of those of noble descent, nor the discourse of the eloquent, nor the titles of the prominent – none of these shall be of any avail unto them… – The Báb[527]

The Báb urged all people to investigate truth for themselves, and not to rely on the opinions of anyone else, especially the mullás:

> [Note: In the following quote, the Báb refers to the Day of Him Whom God shall make manifest. The reader will recall that the Báb was the Forerunner of this Figure, Who, at that time, had not yet revealed Himself publicly. In our era, we now know this Figure was Bahá'u'lláh, Who did appear in due course.]

> Thus on the Day of Resurrection God will ask everyone of his understanding and not of his following in the footsteps of others. How often a person, having inclined his ears to the holy verses, would bow down in humility and would embrace the Truth, while his leader would not do so. Thus every individual must bear his own responsibility, rather than someone else bearing it for him. At the time of the appearance of Him Whom God will make manifest the most distinguished among the learned and the lowliest of men shall both be judged alike. How often the most insignificant of men have acknowledged the truth, while the most learned have remained wrapt in veils. Thus in every Dispensation a number of souls enter the fire by reason of their following in the footsteps of others. – The Báb[528]

He commented on the barriers some people experience, which block them from recognizing the truth of the Divine verses. In the end, He asserts, although "God desireth that all men should be guided aright", they won't let themselves be guided, by virtue of their own ego and other undesirable quality:

> However, such as are conceited will not suffer themselves to be guided. They will be debarred from the Truth, some by reason of their learning, others on account of their glory and power, and still others due to reasons of their own, none of which shall be of any avail at the hour of death. – The Báb[529]

The Báb warns individuals to seek reality rather than the gratification of their personal preferences. Truth often does not conform to the desires of an individual. If he clings to his desires, he may find himself veiled from reality. For a seeker after truth, the only thing that matters is discovering the path which leads to the good-pleasure of God.

> In every nation thou beholdest unnumbered spiritual leaders who are bereft of true discernment, and among every people thou dost encounter myriads of adherents who are devoid of the same characteristic. Ponder for a while in thy heart, have pity on thyself and turn not aside thine attention from proofs and evidences. However, seek not proofs and evidences after thine idle fancy; but rather base thy proofs upon what God hath appointed. Moreover, know thou that neither being a man of learning nor being a follower is in itself a source of glory. If thou art a man of learning, thy knowledge becometh an honour, and if thou art a follower, thine adherence unto leadership becometh an honour, only when these conform to the good-pleasure of God. – The Báb[530]

In the final analysis, the individual must seek purity of heart as the sure means of being able to recognize the truth of God's proofs when they are presented by God's Messenger:

> Know thou that in the Bayán purification is regarded as the most acceptable means for attaining nearness unto God and as the most meritorious of all deeds. Thus purge thou thine ear that thou mayest hear no mention besides God, and purge thine eye that it behold naught except God, and thy conscience that it perceive naught other than God, and thy tongue that it proclaim nothing but God, and thy hand to write naught but the words of God, and thy knowledge that it comprehend naught except God, and thy heart that it entertain no wish save God, and in like manner purge all thine acts and thy pursuits that thou mayest be nurtured in the paradise of pure love, and perchance mayest attain the presence of Him Whom God shall make manifest, adorned with a purity which He highly cherisheth, and be sanctified from whosoever hath turned away from Him and doth not support Him. Thus shalt thou manifest a purity that shall profit thee. – The Báb[531]

THE SYMBOLISM OF "ALL THINGS"

The Báb made extensive use of symbolism and numerology in His teachings. Many of the symbols are complex and directly intelligible only to Bahá'í scholars and Muslim Shí'ih audiences trained in Arabic and Persian languages. We remember that the Báb's initial audiences were people from the Shí'ih background, many from the clergy or former disciples of Shaykh Ahmad and Siyyid Kázim. They would have understood the symbols and numerical expressions used by the Báb as evidence of His spirituality and insight. The Báb spoke to the culture and time in which He lived.

For most non-scholars, especially in the Western world, much of the symbolism would seem obscure and confusing. Nevertheless, it is worthwhile for readers not familiar with the Báb's 19th Century Persian Shí'ih culture, or Islámic theological background, to gain a modest appreciation of the richness of the Báb's use of symbols. Therefore, some basic symbolic concepts used by the Báb will be discussed.

Let us recall the basic constructs of the Báb's teaching.

- There is only one God, infinitely, transcendently beyond human reach or comprehension. There can be no direct connection between the ultimate Essence of God and His creation or His creatures.
- The Primal Will of God is the First Emanation from the Essence of God and it is responsible for all Divine creative action. The Primal Will, therefore, is simultaneously the Creator, the Holy Spirit, the Logos, and the Word of God, from which the massive plurality of all existing beings are derived.
- Periodically, in history, the Primal Will takes a human form and appears to humanity as the Manifestation of God.
- The Báb referred to the Manifestation of God as "the Point" or "the Primal Point". As the current Manifestation of God, the Báb referred to Himself as "the Primal Point".
- Historically, each of the Manifestations of God is an individual, but at the spiritual level they are like the sun. Although appearing as a unique and separate Individuals, the Sun of the Manifestation of God is spiritually the same no matter how many different times It rises above the horizon of human history and It is the same no matter how many times It sets.
- The Manifestations of God reflect the same cosmic spiritual Reality, the Primal Will of God. Though they share a physical form with other human beings, they are as different, spiritually, from humans as humans are from dogs or cats. Indeed, such a comparison fails to express the extent of the difference. Truly, the human form which They temporarily inhabit may be better understood as but a veil that conceals Their infinite spiritual Reality from the eyes of men.

- As noted, the Báb assumed the title of “the Primal Point”. And this was based on His transcendent conception of the unity of God and the Manifestation of the Primal Will in His own Self.

In Arabic (and Hebrew, Greek and Persian) each letter of the alphabet is assigned a numeric value.[532] The first letter of the Arabic alphabet is alif and it has the numeric value of one. The second letter, ba, has a numeric value of two, and so on. Here are three examples:

- The word “Báb”, which means gate or door, is made up of these first two letters of the alphabet, giving a numerical value of 5
    - ba, alif, ba equals 2 + 1 + 2 = 5
- The word “váhid”, which means unity, has the numerical value of 19
    - vav, alif, ha, dal equals 6 + 1 + 8 + 4 = 19
- The phrase “kullu shay’” means all things, and it has a numerical value of 361

The Báb used the numerical values associated with words and phrases to imply deeper spiritual meanings. We will briefly look at this.

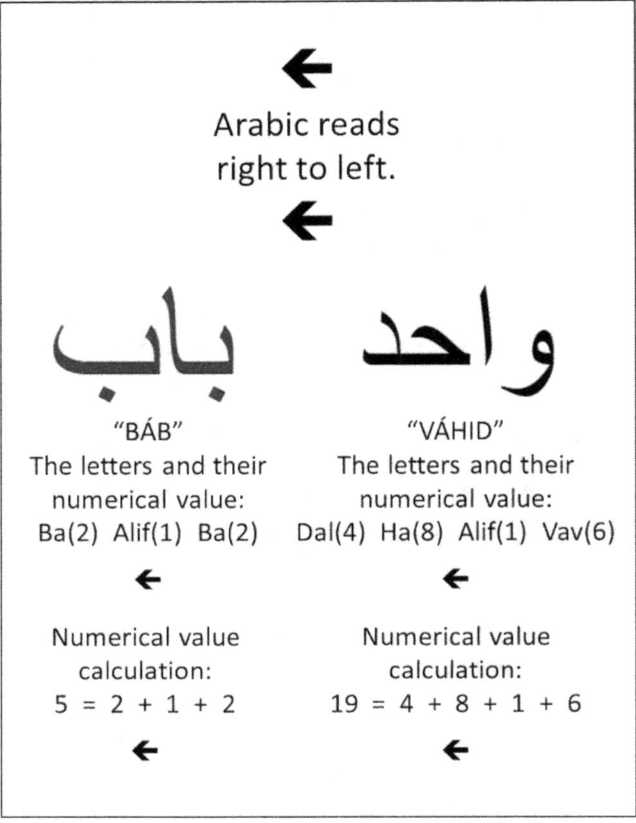

Figure 31 The words "BÁB" and "VÁHID" in Arabic

The Word of God

The word for "one" or "unity" in Arabic is "váhid". Throughout the writings of the Báb, one or unity is represented by its numerical equivalent, 19. The Báb and His eighteen Letters of the Living comprise the Primal Unity [a first váhid] of nineteen figures. This Primal Unity gives rise to "all things" – a term that is particularly important. The numerical value of "all things" (kullu shay') is 361, which is 19 multiplied by 19. In other words, all things literally are manifestations of the Primal Unity, and each unit of the Primal Unity is itself the source of a complete unity. The Báb makes this symbolic structure the organizing scheme of the Bábí community…
– Nader Saidi[533]

The Báb wrote two books which He called "Bayán" (meaning "utterance"). They were the Persian Bayán and the Arabic Bayán, the latter being a shorter and somewhat condensed expression of the former.

The Báb intended to structure His Bayáns to express His teachings about unity.[534] Here is how that worked: The Bayans were divided into sections and the sections were divided into chapters. He intended to have 19 sections, that is, one váhid of sections. He intended to have 19 chapters in each section, that is, one váhid of chapters in each section. Thus, mathematically, there would be 19 sections times 19 chapters – a váhid of váhids, a unity of unities – all together, or 361 chapters: 19 x 19 = 361.

The Arabic word for "all things" is "kullu shay'", and its numerical value is 361.[535] Thus, the Bayans, the central books of the Bábí Dispensation, are intentionally structured to symbolically represent the idea of the unity of unities, that is, all things, which is all *created* reality, also initially symbolically represented by the first 361 believers in the new spiritual community.

He eloquently expressed this idea of all things in one of His letters to "Him Whom God shall make manifest":

> He is God, no God is there but Him, the Almighty, the Best Beloved. All that are in the heavens and on the earth and whatever lieth between them are His. Verily He is the Help in Peril, the Self-Subsisting.
> – The Báb[536]

This statement, and others like it, is interesting and subtle. It states that *every* created thing – the heavens, the earth, and everything in-between – 'is His'; everything is the property of God. As the owner of everything, God stands above it, unique, apart from it, "Self-Subsisting", utterly transcendent. While the idea of "all things" includes all created reality, it does not include God. God is superior above all things. When we speak of all things, we're speaking *only of created* things, not the Uncreated. In other words, God is so great that even the phrase "all things" cannot contain Him. Clearly, no man-made image, description or conception of God can remotely begin to do Him justice.

However, the Bayáns were both unfinished works. The Arabic Bayan contains eleven full váhids (11 váhids x 19 chapters = 209 total chapters). The Persian Bayan contains eight full váhids plus ten chapters of the ninth váhid (8 váhids x 19 chapters + 10 more chapters = 162 total chapters).[537] Nader Saiedi states:

> ...evidently the Báb had no intention at that time to complete either the Persian Bayan or the Arabic Bayan by Himself... The rest of the

> Bayan, therefore, was to be revealed, as the Báb intimates, by Him Whom God shall make manifest. – Nader Saiedi[538]

Thus, the clear implication was that the completion of His work and the success of His Mission was dependent upon the appearance of Him Whom God shall make manifest. Later, during His Ministry, Bahá'u'lláh revealed *The Book of Certitude*. Shoghi Effendi indicated one feature of the importance of The Book of Certitude:

> It was written in fulfillment of the prophecy of the Báb, Who had specifically stated that the Promised One would complete the text of the unfinished Persian Bayán… – Shoghi Effendi[539]

Thus, it can be stated that symbolically and practically, "all things" were only fully realized through the Twin Manifestations of both the Báb and Bahá'u'lláh working together.

The community

The Báb applied this notion of "all things" to His community of followers.

The Báb was the Primal Point.

The Báb had insisted that 18 Letters of the Living must seek Him and find Him of their own accord. The Báb stated that these first followers plus Himself – 19 in all – constituted the first váhid of *the Bábí community*.[540]

He called this group the Primal Unity.[541]

From these first 19 souls, the Primal Unity, came all the future Bábís, and all the future Bahá'ís as well. This first unity, the Primal Unity, had the mission of finding and developing the rapidly growing Bábí community.

As the Báb sent the Letters of the Living out into the world to teach His Message, He instructed them to report the names of the souls who embraced the Cause. They should send reports of these conversions, to His uncle, Hájí Mírzá Siyyid 'Alí, who would give them to the Báb. The Báb grouped them into eighteen additional sets of 19 (váhids). All together, these sets plus the Primal Unity, would constitute 361 souls.[542] This bestowed a great honor upon these souls:

> Of all these believers I shall make mention in the Tablet of God, so that upon each one of them the Beloved of our hearts may, in the Day when He shall have ascended the throne of glory, confer His inestimable blessings, and declare them the dwellers of His Paradise. – The Báb[543]

The Báb laid great emphasis on the spiritual and practical importance of the Primal Unity and the emergence of His spiritual community, represented by these first 361 souls. The first váhid of the Persian Bayán, the first 19 chapters, are an exposition of the Primal Unity and this emerging community. These 361 souls were the nascent community of the Cause of God. They symbolically represented "all things", that is, the hope of all humanity.

All time

The Báb devised a new calendar for the new community. God ordained that,

> ...each year should equal the numerical value of the words "all things" [kullu shay', 19 x 19 = 361], to consist of nineteen months, where each month equaleth nineteen days... – The Báb[544]

There are nineteen months in the calendar introduced by the Báb. Each month is nineteen days. The total number of days is 361. The Báb named the nineteen months after some of the exalted names of God:

Bábí / Bahá'í Calendar 19 Attributes of God			
English name	Arabic name	English name	Arabic name
1. Splendour	Bahá	11. Will	Mashíyyat
2. Glory	Jalál	12. Knowledge	'Ilm
3. Beauty	Jamál	13. Power	Qudrat
4. Grandeur	'Azamat	14. Speech	Qawl
5. Light	Núr	15. Questions	Masá'il
6. Mercy	Raḥmat	16. Honour	Sharaf
7. Words	Kalimát	17. Sovereignty	Sulṭán
8. Perfection	Kamál	18. Dominion	Mulk
9. Names	Asmá'	Intercalary Days (added later by Bahá'u'lláh)	Ayyám-i-Há
10. Might	'Izzat		
		19. Loftiness	'Alá'

Figure 32 The months of the calendar devised by the Báb

The 361 days of the calendar do not equal either a lunar or a solar year, but they do symbolically represent "all things". Later, Bahá'u'lláh modified the Báb's design to create a solar year by adding four or five days to the year. He called these four or five days Ayyám-i-Há. The Bahá'í Writings explain the meaning of this term:

> Known as the Ayyám-i-Há (the Days of Há), the Intercalary Days have the distinction of being associated with "the letter Há". The abjad nu-

> merical value of this Arabic letter is five, which corresponds to the potential number of intercalary days. The letter "Há" has been given several spiritual meanings in the Holy Writings, among which is as a symbol of the Essence of God. – Notes to the Most Holy Book (The Kitab-i-Aqdas)[545]

The symbolism of Ayyám-i-Há is interesting. The letter "Ha" refers symbolically to the Essence of God – Who is one, eternal, and infinite – because "Ha" is the first letter of the phrase "He is God" in Arabic. The Essence of God is one, above, beyond, and outside of time and space. Similarly, the period of Ayyám-i-Há suggests this fundamental truth about God because it too is outside of time, in the sense that it occurs outside of the "normal" flow of the nineteen months of the calendar.

Ayyám-i-Há is a time when Bahá'ís show their dedication to the oneness of God by showing hospitality, giving gifts, serving others, and sharing fellowship with others. Interestingly, the Báb designated that each day of the week should be given a spiritual name.

Bábí / Bahá'í Calendar – Days of the Week 7 Attributes of God		
English name	Arabic name	Gregorian day of week
1. Glory	Jalál	Saturday
2. Beauty	Jamál	Sunday
3. Perfection	Kamál	Monday
4. Grace	Fiḍál	Tuesday
5. Justice	'Idál	Wednesday
6. Majesty	Istijlál	Thursday
7. Independence	Istiqlál	Friday

Figure 33 The days of the Bábí calendar

By naming the days and the months after attributes of God, and by organizing the months to reflect the spiritual meaning of the number 361, the Báb symbolically infused the entire year with the sacred spirit of "all things." As Professor Saiedi explains, His purpose was profound:

> The Báb turns the entire concept of time into a process of spiritualization. Time literally becomes filled with God. – Nader Saiedi[546]

The Báb's symbolism suggests profound meanings. God is one; God stands above, beyond, and transcendent of all things. The Word of God – the

Bayán in the Dispensation of the Báb – teaches all things. The Bábí community, and by implication future humanity, reflects all things. Even the process of time reflects all things. And since all things emanate from God, all things reflect the signs of His Revelation, beginning with the Primal Point Himself, the Báb.

In this brief discussion we have glimpsed a hint of the rich symbolism in the Báb's Writings. For now, we will have to content ourselves with this modest understanding of the symbolism in the Writings of the Báb.

RESURRECTION IS RENEWAL

Contrary to traditional interpretations by theologians of previous religions, the Báb associates the Day of Ressurection with the period of renewal brought by a new Manifestation of God. According to the Báb, the Day of Resurrection is not a one-time-only, end-of-history event. It does not involve the physical destruction of the world, as theologians have claimed. The Báb said:

> The Day of Resurrection is a day on which the sun riseth and setteth like unto any other day. – The Báb[547]

He says:

> [In the following quote, Tree of divine Reality = the Manifestation of God; the Apostle of God = Muhammad; Tree of the Bayán = the Báb; the Qur'án = Muhammad's Holy Book; the Resurrection of the Bayán = the revelation to come after the Báb, i.e. Bahá'u'lláh; Him Whom God shall make manifest = Bahá'u'lláh.]

> ...what is meant by the Day of Resurrection is this, that from the time of the appearance of Him Who is the Tree of divine Reality, at whatever period and under whatever name, until the moment of His disappearance, is the Day of Resurrection.
>
> For example, from the inception of the mission of Jesus – may peace be upon Him – till the day of His ascension was the Resurrection of Moses. For during that period the Revelation of God shone forth through the appearance of that divine Reality, Who rewarded by His Word everyone who believed in Moses, and punished by His Word everyone who did not believe; inasmuch as God's Testimony for that Day was that which He had solemnly affirmed in the Gospel.
>
> And from the inception of the Revelation of the Apostle of God—may the blessings of God be upon Him – till the day of His ascension was

the Resurrection of Jesus – peace be upon Him – wherein the Tree of divine Reality appeared in the person of Muhammad, rewarding by His Word everyone who was a believer in Jesus, and punishing by His Word everyone who was not a believer in Him.

And from the moment when the Tree of the Bayan appeared until it disappeareth is the Resurrection of the Apostle of God, as is divinely foretold in the Qur'án; the beginning of which was when two hours and eleven minutes had passed [after sunset on May 22, 1844]... This was the beginning of the Day of Resurrection of the Qur'án, and until the disappearance of the Tree of divine Reality is the Resurrection of the Qur'án.

The stage of perfection of everything is reached when its resurrection occurreth. The perfection of the religion of Islam was consummated at the beginning of this Revelation; and from the rise of this Revelation until its setting, the fruits of the Tree of Islam, whatever they are, will become apparent.

The Resurrection of the Bayan will occur at the time of the appearance of Him Whom God shall make manifest. For today the Bayan is in the stage of seed; at the beginning of the manifestation of Him Whom God shall make manifest its ultimate perfection will become apparent. He is made manifest in order to gather the fruits of the trees He hath planted...

...For on that Day all men will be brought before God and will attain His Presence; which meaneth appearance before Him Who is the Tree of divine Reality and attainment unto His presence; inasmuch as it is not possible to appear before the Most Holy Essence of God, nor is it conceivable to seek reunion with Him. That which is feasible in the matter of appearance before Him and of meeting Him is attainment unto the Primal Tree. – The Báb[548]

Conventional ideas about Heaven and Hell	
Heaven	**Hell**
Heaven is a place some people go to after death.	Likewise, hell is a place other people go to after death.
If you were in heaven, you would probably know it.	If you were in hell, you would probably know it.
Heaven is a place where life is good. For example, you might sing in the heavenly choir or get to visit with great and holy persons from the past.	Hell is a place where life is bad. For example, real fires might be constantly and painfully burning your flesh.
And, if you were in heaven, you would be in a happy state of mind.	And, if you were in hell, you would be in an unhappy state of mind.

Figure 34 The Báb's explanation of the Day of Resurrection

Saiedi explains:

> Traditionally, in both Christianity and Islám, the doctrines of resurrection and the Day of Judgment have been used to refute historical consciousness and to support a thesis of the 'end of history'—the world and history itself were expected simply to come to an end. This belief was usually accompanied by the doctrine of the finality of one's own religion, which held that revelation itself had come to an end with this 'final' message for humanity... *The Báb reinterprets the doctrine of resurrection not as the end of history but as the substance of history itself.* Resurrection is described not as a single, final event but a recurring, cyclic, and progressive process linking all past, present, and future divine Revelations. Each resurrection is characterised by the abrogation of the former laws and ordinances and the inception of new ones, corresponding to the specific social needs of humanity in the emerging age... Not only is the doctrine of finality replaced by the doctrine of infinite sequential divine Revelations, but the very idea of the Day of Resurrection, traditionally a static notion, itself becomes an affirmation of the dynamic nature of spiritual reality... [The] Báb explains that each spiritual Dispensation has its own life history, with a beginning and an end. The end of each Dispensation is its own Day of Resurrection. This end is a 'resurrection'

because it is also the inception of the next Dispensation, when the religion itself is recreated through the revelation dispensed by a new Manifestation of God. Thus the Day of Resurrection is the period when the new Manifestation of God is present on earth.[549]

One spiritual meaning of the Báb's teaching about the Day of Resurrection is that when the next Manifestation of God appears in the world, believers in the previous Dispensation, especially orthodox clergy, and the unbelievers in the world, are put to the test. So…

> …from the beginning of their lives till the end thereof, in conformity with the laws established in the previous religion, they [i.e. all men] worship God, piously adore Him, bow themselves before His divine Reality and show submissiveness toward His exalted Essence. At the hour of His manifestation, however, they all turn their gaze toward their own selves and are thus shut out from Him, inasmuch as they fancifully regard Him as one like unto themselves. Far from the glory of God is such a comparison. Indeed that august Being resembleth the physical sun, His verses are like its rays, and all believers, should they truly believe in Him, are as mirrors wherein the sun is reflected. Their light is thus a mere reflection. – The Báb[550]

Will humanity recognize the spiritual Light of God when It rises again in a new Dawn in a new place? Will they accept the Primal Will of God when It appears again in the world in the form of a new Human Temple? Or will they turn away through self-satisfaction, indifference and disbelief?

This is the test. The Day of Resurrection brings the Day of Judgment. But contrary to common understanding, the judgment each person experiences is self-imposed. The Heavenly Court, gathering in the Presence of God, the Bridge that leads to heaven or hell, and the process of Divine Judgment are all spiritual symbols. These symbols convey the gravity of each person's spiritual decision. According to the teachings of the Báb, the faithful, honorable, correct thing to do, and the way to remain true to the Eternal Covenant with God, is to investigate the claims of the new Manifestation of God, and if found to be true, to embrace them sincerely.

This time of testing and new beginnings is called the Resurrection because, when the humble follower recognizes the most recent Manifestation of God as the new spiritual Sunrise, he or she finds a new Day of spiritual renewal. This Resurrection is like springtime, bringing a new burst of spiritual energy. The appearance of the Manifestation of God, His rising to undertake His Mission, is the new Spiritual Sunrise, the dawning of a new Day of God, defined as a new era in human history. It brings new spiritual Light into the world, banishing darkness.

[In the following quotes, Mecca = the sacred city of the Muslims; Ka'bah = the sacred Shrine of Islám at Mecca; "forsaken in this mountain" = the Báb is referring to Máh-Kú the prison fortress where He was being held at the time He wrote this passage; the Apostle of God = Muhammad; the Qá'im = meaning 'He Who arises', one of the names of the Promised One of Islám, the Báb Himself; Him Whom God shall make manifest = Bahá'u'lláh]

Thou beholdest how vast is the number of people who go to Mecca each year on pilgrimage and engage in circumambulation, while He, through the potency of Whose Word the Ka'bah hath become the object of adoration, is forsaken in this mountain. He is none other but the Apostle of God Himself, inasmuch as the Revelation of God may be likened to the sun. No matter how innumerable its risings, there is but one sun, and upon it depends the life of all things. It is clear and evident that the object of all preceding Dispensations hath been to pave the way for the advent of Muhammad, the Apostle of God. These, including the Muhammadan Dispensation, have had, in their turn, as their objective the Revelation proclaimed by the Qá'im. The purpose underlying this Revelation, as well as those that preceded it, has, in like manner, been to announce the advent of the Faith of Him Whom God will make manifest. And this Faith—the Faith of Him Whom God will make manifest—in its turn, together with all the Revelations gone before it, have as their object the Manifestation destined to succeed it. And the latter, no less than all the Revelations preceding it, prepare the way for the Revelation which is yet to follow. The process of the rise and setting of the Sun of Truth will thus indefinitely continue—a process that hath had no beginning and will have no end.

Well is it with him who in every Dispensation recognizeth the Purpose of God for that Dispensation, and is not deprived therefrom by turning his gaze towards the things of the past. – The Báb[551]

THE PERSPECTIVE OF UNITY

The Báb offers a deeply spiritualized vision of reality. Professor Saiedi calls it "the perspective of unity".

The Báb perceives all existence as a creation of the Primal Will of God, which emanates, like rays of the sun, from God's own exalted Essence. Like the sun in our physical heaven, the interior Essence of God is too exalted to be approached by any of His creatures. God's Essence is utterly transcendent. God is truly known only to Himself.

> …'No vision taketh in Him but He taketh in all vision. He is the Subtle, the All-Perceiving.' Glory be unto Thee, O my God, indeed no mind or vision, however keen or discriminating, can ever grasp the nature of the most insignificant of Thy signs. Verily Thou art God, no God is there besides Thee. – The Báb[552]

Yet, reality – that is, "All that are in the heavens and on the earth and whatever lieth between them"[553] – is not in darkness according to the Báb. The Báb's approach relies upon pure, mature monotheism. God is one and inaccessible, but He loves His creation.

> Therefore, it is necessary, according to true wisdom, that the Pre-existent God describe Himself to His creatures, that they may recognize their Creator and that, out of the grace of the Pre-existent, the contingent beings may attain their supreme End. – The Báb[554]

God performs this self-description through His Primal Will, which is the Sender of the Manifestations of God into the world. Another part of the self-description of God is the all-pervasive revelation of the signs of God in "all things". The Báb explains:

> And within the inmost reality of all things there hath been, and will forever continue to be, a sign from God through which the unity of the Lord is celebrated. This sign, however, is a reflection of His Will, present within it, through which naught is seen but God. – The Báb[555]

> He hath moreover deposited within the realities of all created things the emblem of His recognition, that everyone may know of a certainty that He is the Beginning and the End, the Manifest and the Hidden, the Maker and the Sustainer, the Omnipotent and the All-Knowing… – The Báb[556]

> God's existence in itself testifieth to His Own oneness, while every created thing, by its very nature, beareth evidence that it hath been fashioned by God. Such is the proof of consummate wisdom in the estimation of those who sail the ocean of divine Truth. – The Báb[557]

Like the rays shining out in every direction from the star at the center of our solar system, God's Primal Will, the Logos, the Holy Spirit of God—all His loving, wise and powerful attributes—is generating all things and radiating throughout all realms of existence. All creation is vitalized by Its effects. Therefore, all things are illuminated spiritually by the Light of His Divine Revelation. This is one of the Báb's core teachings.

Professor Saiedi describes this outlook as "the perspective of unity", as "seeing in all things only the signs and traces of the divine Effulgence that permeates and constitutes all creation."[558] He states:

> ...the perspective of unity ... transforms all of reality into mirrors reflecting the divine names, in every possible form, in all their glory.
> – Nader Saiedi[559]

All created things are imbued with the signs of God's revelation. All things are *reflections* of the attributes of God, which His Primal Will, as Creator, has deposited within every atom and particle of the universe. Reflections of the Creator are within every living creature, including all people, regardless of their race, gender, nationality, social status or outward appearance.

The perspective of unity enables every individual to perceive in all the Manifestations of God, in all created things, in all other people, and even in oneself, the signs of God's handiwork. From the mystical, spiritual perspective of the Báb, there is only one human race. All people are created by God's Will, no matter how noticeable the outward differences seem to be. In fact, the fullness of God's unity is demonstrated on the earthly plane by the near infinite diversity of the human race. Hence, a logical outcome of the perspective of unity is an embrace of the principle of unity *through* diversity.

In their infinitely diverse forms, all things are reflections of *the same* Light of God because, in the Báb's thought universe, there is only one God, so naturally all "the Light" (of the Primal Will) originates from the same Source. All things are united as recipients of His Light. The Creator doesn't descend into the mirrors of each person or created thing. From His exalted heights God's Primal Will shines His Light upon them and they reflect the signs of His revelation. Humankind is one because we are all "mirrors" reflecting the same Light from God.

The Báb wasn't saying that God is "in" all things. Think of the difference between these three statements:

- "All things are God."
- "God is 'in' all things."
- "All things are of God."

The first statement equates God with His creation, a concept called pantheism, which would be abhorrent to the Báb! Given His teaching about the utter transcendence and infinity of God, the idea of equating God with the universe, His creation, of as He would say "joining partners with God", would be flatly rejected. One can even imagine Him calling it a blasphemy.

The second statement is also pantheism, by somehow putting God "inside" all created things, blurring the distinction between Creator and creature. Think of the small fish tank of my daughter's pet fish, Spikey. Could I fit my human-sized body into his tank, or into him? Of course not. Can you fit the entire Pacific Ocean into a small teacup? Again, no; such an idea is absurd. So it is with God; He is so infinite that not even the vast expanding universe can "contain" His Being. Indeed, even these comparisons fall far short of His Reality. Putting God "inside" all created things would be considered outrageous by the Báb.

The third statement would be praised by the Báb. It asserts that God is the Source and that, in some manner, all things are *reflections* of that same Source. The Painter and the painting are not the same. And yet, isn't it wonderful that the painting magnificently reflects the artistry, skill, personality and vision of the painter? The book and the writer of the Book are not the same. The song and the song writer are not the same. And yet, when we hear a song, don't we somehow find expression of the songwriter's mind within the chorus of the song?

Thus indeed, "all things are *of* God".

In all existence, the most important Reality that is *of* God is the Manifestation of God. Sending the Divine Educator, the Manifestation of His Primal Will, into the world is a voluntary act of amazing grace and a never-ending progression. As Dr. Saiedi explains,

> [One] who takes the perspective of unity recognizes the Manifestation of God, the Word of God, in whatever physical body He appears, whatever name He takes, and whatever form of Scripture and laws He brings.[560]

Years later, someone asked Bahá'u'lláh which of the Divine Educators are superior to the others. Responding from the perspective of unity, He said:

> Know thou assuredly that the essence of all the Prophets of God is one and the same. Their unity is absolute... To prefer one in honor to another, to exalt certain ones above the rest, is in no wise to be permitted.
> – Bahá'u'lláh[561]

The perspective of unity is based on:

- The recognition of God's transcendent oneness
- The creative role of His Primal Will
- God's gracious activity as the Sender of the Manifestations of God
- The oneness of the Divine Educators
- The spiritual oneness of each and every person born on the planet
- And the fact that God has deposited within "all things" the signs of His revelation.

The Báb's perspective of unity prompted a social and spiritual attitude, and an exalted moral standard that avoided aggression and violence, mandated bringing no sorrow to any soul, encouraged bringing joy to others, and brought responsibility to elevate "all things" to their highest state of perfection. He exemplified and taught an approach to life that, when followed humbly, faithfully and selflessly, leads to paradise in both this world and the world to come.

This attitude perceives unity in all things and especially the oneness of humanity. Human beings, regardless of race, class, creed, nationality, or other outward feature, are "mirrors" capable of reflecting God's Primal Will, such as His attributes of truthfulness, integrity, love, kindness, wisdom, power, forgiveness, mercy, justice and grace. For example, He writes:

> Become as true brethren in the one and indivisible religion of God, free from distinction, for verily God desireth that your hearts should become mirrors unto your brethren in the Faith, so that ye find yourselves reflected in them, and they in you. This is the true Path of God.... – The Báb[562]

The Báb's mystical perspective of unity has profound implications. A proper study of mysticism would require another book, but essentially the mystic individual seeks a sense of union with God through personal experiences, intuition or insight. This is a common mystic concept, regardless of culture, language, religious tradition, period in history, or location around the world. Commonly, a mystic will claim to have experienced an encounter with God, or something profound that is beyond description. During this encounter, they feel an overwhelming sense of Divine Beauty and Love, a perception of the giving up of "self", and a feeling of "merging" consciousness with a universal Beloved. Practices intended to promote this mystical experience include prayer, meditation, interpreting the hidden meanings in sacred Text, chanting, asceticism, the use of intoxicants, appreciation of nature, and certain prescribed physical movements, such as dancing or drumming.

Mysticism is sometimes monistic in approach, that is, based on the idea of *merging* with the One, often with pantheistic aspects. For example, the Islámic mystic, al-Halláj, of the 10th Century, made an extraordinary claim. Al-Halláj was a monist because he felt that he, a created being, had become virtually the same as Divinity itself. Following one of his experiences, he asserted publicly, "I am Truth." This was cursed by the orthodox Islámic religious leaders because it violated the monotheistic premise behind all of Islam. Truth was considered to be one of the Names of God, so his claim was considered arrogance, blasphemy and heresy. Al-Halláj was put on trial, imprisoned, and then executed in the year 922 AD.

The Báb's mystical perspective of unity leads to oneness, but not to monism or pantheism. One can understand the error. A mystic receives a glimmering of the Light of the infinite God and, overpowered by its Beauty, mistakes it for all the Light produced by the Sun of Truth. This sort of pantheistic mystic errs spiritually and intellectually. Instead of taking his sensation of being overwhelmed by the mystical experience as evidence of his limitation, he imagines that he has encompassed the wholeness of the Divinity and merged with it.

But not all mystics are monists. The Báb and the other Prophets of God were undoubtedly mystics while maintaining a sharp distinction between the individual and God. Any sense of "merging" with God is not taken literally, but regarded as an experience of communion or a highly exalted state of mind. The Báb says the true believer should never err by thinking the creature or the creation can contain the infinite Essence of God. Instead, He says that all things created by God's Primal Will share in the honor of originating from the same one Source and reflect God's Beauty in proportion to their Divinely bestowed potential. This view rejects any monistic idea of literally encountering God directly, of actually merging with the Essence of God, or of equating the Creator with His creation.

> ...from everlasting God hath been invested with the independent sovereignty of His exalted Being, and unto everlasting He will remain inaccessible in the transcendent majesty of His holy Essence. – The Báb[563]

> God is sanctified from His servants and no direct relationship ever existeth between Him and any created thing, while ye have all arisen at His bidding. Verily He is your Lord and your God, your Master and your King. – The Báb[564]

Clearly, the Báb would not condone any approach to oneness which degenerated into pantheism, the sense that "all things *are* God":

> He is not within a thing nor above it nor beside it… He is exalted above every mention or praise and is sanctified beyond every word of commendation or every comparison... Indeed too high and exalted is He for anyone to allude unto Him. – The Báb[565]

However, the Báb honored the mystics' yearning for oneness with the infinite God. As shown in His Writings, His prayers, and His intense dedication to devotional practices, He was Himself a sincere and passionate mystic. He encouraged others to attain a similarly profound mystical and spiritualized orientation to life.

The Báb's perspective of unity might be summed up with the phrase "all things are *of* God." The perspective of unity is a mystical approach to reality which unites all people, all races, and all nations in a vision that discovers in all created things God's blessed handiwork and the signs of His revelation. Everything and everyone are in some fashion a reflection of the glory and revelation of God.. Since all things – all created things – are reflections of the one God, in their innermost essence, and regardless of external differences, they are inherently in unity.

Reflecting upon the profound meaning of the perspective of unity, one finds a fascinating rationale for the oneness of the human race, which is the central teaching of Bahá'u'lláh (referred to by the Báb as Him Whom God shall make manifest). This insight was possibly confirmed decades later, in Bahá'u'lláh's Will and Testament, made public after His passing in 1892:

[Note: Given that this quotation is from Bahá'u'lláh's Will and Testament, it is suggested that it might mean that the phrases "the means of order" and "the instrument of union" are intended to refer to the entire Cause of God and the teachings of His Faith. The phrase "fain would hope" is an archaic expression. The word "fain" means, willing or obliged by circumstances, so the meaning is something like "I would hope and desire", which makes sense in context.]

> Say: O servants! Let not the means of order be made the cause of confusion and the instrument of union an occasion for discord. We fain would hope that the people of Baha may be guided by the blessed words: *'Say: all things are of God.'* This exalted utterance is like unto water for quenching the fire of hate and enmity which smouldereth with-

> in the hearts and breasts of men. *By this single utterance contending peoples and kindreds will attain the light of true unity.* Verily He speaketh the truth and leadeth the way. He is the All-Powerful, the Exalted, the Gracious. – Bahá'u'lláh[566] (Note: Emphasis added.)

THE GIFT OF FREE-WILL VS. PREDESTINATION

Implicit in the Báb's teachings is the vital necessity of exercising your own free-will to discover the Truth and to choose your response to it. For instance, when the Day of Resurrection comes again with the appearance of a new Divine Educator, God does not wish to force anyone to believe. Each person is expected to investigate reality, open his heart, consult his conscience and then make a free choice either to accept or reject:

> The path to guidance is one of love and compassion, not of force and coercion. This hath been God's method in the past, and shall continue to be in the future! – The Báb[567]

The Báb explained that the Revelation is offered to everyone and that each person has the opportunity to express openness of heart and receptivity to the Truth. If they do or do not it is because of their own choice. If they "fail to apprehend the Truth" when it appears it is because of limitations they have imposed upon themselves. If anyone's heart is not open to God it is because he "suffereth himself" to go astray:

> Consider how at the time of the appearance of every Revelation, those who open their hearts to the Author of that Revelation recognize the Truth, while the hearts of those who fail to apprehend the Truth are straitened by reason of their shutting themselves out from Him. However, openness of heart is bestowed by God upon both parties alike. God desireth not to straiten the heart of anyone, be it even an ant, how much less the heart of a superior creature, except when he suffereth himself to be wrapt in veils, for God is the Creator of all things. – The Báb[568]

Certainly, the Bábís were encouraged to engage in discussion and debate, sometimes vigorously, but there was always a line not to be crossed. No one should be forced or pressured into the Faith. No one's free-will should be undermined. Interestingly, the Qur'án had also spoken against using force and coercion to spread the Faith of God.

> Let there be no compulsion in religion. (Qur'án 2:256)[569]

Clearly, the persecutors of the Bábís were not obeying the Qur'án, but the Bábís were respectful of it and the Báb taught the same thing.

The Báb gave the subject of human free-will in-depth treatment. Previous religious traditions have discussed it in detail. It was a topic of intense discussion among Muslim philosophers. One might think there would be by now nothing new which one could say, but that would not be the case. The Báb offered an innovative approach to the topic.[570]

For most of human history, the questions which have been asked always seem to assume an inherent opposition between divine destiny and human free-will. Here are some examples:

- Are human affairs determined by God's will, or do humans have freedom to decide?
- How can humans have free-will if God knows in advance everything we will do?

Taken together these questions seem to assume that predetermination and freedom are mutually exclusive; you can either have one or the other. The Báb discussed the dichotomous approach which typified the Muslim community.

> Indeed, all who have endeavoured to explain the problem of Destiny have advocated either absolute divine determination or human choice, and thus all the philosophers have confessed their powerlessness to explain the truth of this question. – The Báb[571]

Part of the problem lay in the fact that there are numerous passages in the Qur'án (and other Scriptures) which emphasize the absolute power of God, His sovereignty, and His command over all created things while, at the same time, there are numerous passages in the same Books which emphasize human choice and accountability for one's actions. This was troubling to scholars and theologians. Over time, as the Muslims struggled honestly to reason about free-will vs. predestination they seemed divide themselves into opposing camps. The Báb said that all such viewpoints were inadequate because human reason is not adequate to the challenge. The Báb said a spiritual perspective, not just logic, is required to resolve the confusion. The oppositions which men created in reality are all resolved in the unseen realms of infinity, by the insights of the heart. The Báb said:

> [That] which is beyond these two extremes, which is the Middle Path ... can be comprehended by naught save the heart. God hath created the heart to understand His unity and transcendence, and it is through the heart that Divine Unity can be witnessed at the level of action. – The Báb[572]

Unity prevails in the Divine hidden realms. According to Saiedi,

> The basic error in these traditional approaches is that they posit an absolute opposition between divine determination and phenomenal choice… [The] Báb explains that it is the simultaneous truth of both divine determination and human freedom which is the true "Middle Path." … Thus, according to the Báb, God has created not only human beings but all things in such a way that freedom is inherent in their very nature: it is embedded in their reality as a part of the process of creation. God has created human beings with freedom and has enabled them to be shaped in time in accordance with their own decisions and choices – for which they are inevitably accountable. – Nader Saiedi[573]

The Báb wrote:

> Destiny is a mystery among the mysteries of God… Its fathomless depths extend between the heavens and the earth, its width between the East and the West… In its depths there shineth a Sun. – The Báb[574]

The Báb then explains that in the moment of action, man is a free agent because "free choice is bound to the existence of each thing" He continues:

> Verily, at the primordial moment of choice, when God said unto the thing, 'Am I not your Lord?' it would not have replied, 'Yea,' had it been deprived of freedom of choice. – The Báb[575]

This is a lot to take in, but here are some reflections that might be helpful.

The Primal Will of God creates all things with a prescribed amount of free-will. It is inherent in the eternal design of God that every human being is, in the moment of choice, given the freedom to choose. So *free-will IS destiny* in the sense that it is predetermined that each person has some degree of free will to begin with.

The Báb points out that the problem of free-will and destiny is the result of men's exclusive reliance on ordinary human logic. There are false assumptions as well; for instance, assuming that the knowledge of man operates the same as the knowledge of God. For God, the past, present and the future are all known to Him as one and the same thing. For humans, knowledge is limited, it is modified by learning, and it is constrained by things not yet discovered. It is bound by the limits of time and space. With rare exceptions, we cannot know what tomorrow will bring, before tomorrow brings it. When men approach spiritual matters, such as understanding the relation between destiny and free-will, the perspective of unity and insight from the heart is required to make any headway into the realm of understanding.

This writer has struggled to understand the Báb's spiritually unified interpretation of freedom and destiny. Perhaps some everyday examples might help.

I think of a chess game when I ponder the relationship between my knowledge and my will, on the one hand, and the Lord's knowledge and the Lord's Will, on the other. How can human actions be free if God knows in advance everything we will do? Let's assume the game is underway. I make a move on the chessboard. Is there any move I, with my finite knowledge, can make that will not be anticipated and countered perfectly by God, the Possessor of infinite knowledge? The answer is no. I am free to make any move I want on the chess board. And God can do the same. But with His infinite awareness He will always come up with a more brilliant move. God might permit me to put up a good show, so to speak, if He wishes to show mercy, but in the end is there any doubt Who will win? Of course not. Whether He checkmates me in two or six or ten moves does not matter. He will checkmate me. Every step of the way I am a free agent, deciding for myself which way to move on the chess board. *The path may vary, but the outcome is predetermined.*

Another example. I was walking my dog one night when I was pondering this subject of free-will and determination. Our human-dog relationship seemed to me a perfect analog to the God-human relationship. My dog, Spy, is a small black Yorkie-poo, about ten years old at the time of this writing. He is a loving, happy, energetic creature. When he was a younger dog, Spy was so eager to experience the world that, if I did not have him on a leash, he could suddenly bolt into the street if he saw something, such as another dog, on the other side of the street. Spy does not realize that fast onrushing cars could kill him. He does not pause to look and see if it is safe to cross. Through my use of the leash, I set a boundary on his expression of free-will. Within these limits, his free-will remains intact and vigorous. In this analogy, my superior will over Spy is comparable to God's superior will over me. Just as I may sometimes think God's decree in my life is unfair, I imagine, if he were capable of such thoughts, Spy might think I am being unfair to him by not letting him do everything he wants to do. In fact, the opposite is true. Limiting the free-will Spy gets to express, which to him might look like determination, is a gift of freedom because I am keeping him alive so that he can continue to enjoy the range of motion he does have. He has *free-will within his prescribed range of motion* on the leash, and by limiting his range of motion I am *protecting him*, giving him a longer, happier life and more future opportunities to express his free-will in ways that are safe for him to do.

Another example. Let us consider the making of a car at the auto factory. It is designed with four wheels, a motor, gears, a passenger compartment, and, most importantly, a gas pedal, brakes and a steering wheel. Thanks to these last three features, the car has the ability to "choose" between moving, stopping, and turning left or right. These features are predestined for the car by its designers. But the car, even with a full tank of gas, cannot go anywhere just yet. It requires an agent to make the choices of where to drive the car. The human being that sits in the car, who drives it, is symbolic of the feature of free-will. Hence, when the human driver gets in the car, puts the car in gear, presses the gas pedal and steers the car, free-will is expressed. Is this contrary to destiny? No, it affirms destiny because the designer *designed the car to require the driver* to go places. But, the "free will" of the car and driver combo is not absolute. The car was not designed to fly, to float on the water, or to soar into outer space. No matter how much the driver might wish to fly, he cannot do it with this car. The car was not designed for that, so the driver cannot make this choice. If this is a good analogy, then every created thing, including humans, *within its design features*, has the ability to express some degree of free will.

In my understanding, human free-will dynamically *interacts* with the operation of the Will of God. On the one hand,

- God created the physical universe, established the natural laws of physics, chemistry and biology, and launched the entire enterprise of life on the planet.
- God sends the Messengers into human history, He reveals spiritual and social laws, and He provides teachings which provide opportunities, exhortations, explanations, prohibitions, restrictions, punishments and rewards. Through the Divine Educators, human beings gradually advance towards an ever-advancing civilization.

On the other hand, humans use the free will which was designed into our very nature to recognize or reject the Manifestation of God. With that decision we reap the consequences of our thoughts, feelings and actions and *we deliver ourselves* into either the paradise of nearness to God or the hell of remoteness from Him. Clearly, as the Báb indicated, both free-will and determination coexist and dynamically interact with one another.

Another possible meaning of destiny will be mentioned. It can be said that the Will of God has endowed human beings with a certain potential; in fact, a glorious potential. It would be correct to say that every human being has a Divinely ordained destiny, understood as realizing a certain potential that is inherent and waiting to be manifested.

A man who discovers a musical talent might be "destined" to become a world-class pianist. A woman with an extraordinary ability to understand science might be "destined" to discover the cure for cancer. An everyday citizen may have a glorious "destiny" in store due to a particular affinity to serving the poor or helping the community. Whoever a person might be, everyone has talents and faculties, and it would be correct to say that it is God's destiny for every person that they find out how best to use the gifts God has given them. Thus free-will, expressed as earnest efforts to realize one's potential, goes hand-in-hand with predestination, understood as the gift of that potential in the first place.

And above all this, the Báb's teachings, and indeed the teachings of all the Prophets, make it clear that every person has been destined by God to enter into a knowing and loving relationship with Him. This relationship is achieved through the Manifestation of God:

> True knowledge, therefore, is the knowledge of God, and this is none other than the recognition of His Manifestation in each Dispensation. – The Báb[576]

Attaining to spiritual knowledge through the recognition of the most recent Manifestation of God is the destiny of every person; that is, God invites, encourages, and promises to assist every longing soul that strives to attain His Presence and reach this paradise:

> There is no paradise more wondrous for any soul than to be exposed to God's Manifestation in His Day, to hear His verses and believe in them, to attain His presence, which is naught but the presence of God, to sail upon the sea of the heavenly kingdom of His good-pleasure, and to partake of the choice fruits of the paradise of His divine Oneness.
> – The Báb[577]

It is obvious that most souls to some degree fall short of the glorious heights which God has destined for them. Some never attain unto recognition of the Manifestation of God for the Day in which they are living. Some may recognize Him partially but fail to live according to His teachings. I would like to suggest that this is yet another proof of the coexistence of free-will and destiny. Potentialities are destined for every one of us. We choose, during our lives, how much of that potential gets developed and used. Saiedi wrote:

> The true Destiny of all things is the free choice of the good. All human beings are created capable of that choice, and the purpose of creation is the unity of that choice with the attainment of spiritual qualities and the recognition of God. In other words, when freedom is accompanied by the choice of the good, the end and purpose of creation – its true destiny – is realized. For humans to attain this destiny requires turning toward the divine effulgence and annihilating their own will in the Will of God. At that time their essences are as pure mirrors in which divine revelation is manifestly shining. That station is the station of the heart, the very station that makes possible the understanding of the secret of Destiny. – Nader Saiedi[578]

THE REALITY OF PURE WORSHIP

Free-will is especially important in the matter of worshipping God. As mentioned earlier, God could have programmed every human being to automatically testify to His oneness and to declare undying faith in Him. The model of this is the computer, which can be programmed to perform almost any operation the programmer decides. But of what value would the faith of a robot be to God? None. None at all. the Báb said this great power was within His grasp:

> Should it be Our wish, it is in Our power to compel, through the agency of but one letter of Our Revelation, the world and all that is therein to recognize, in less than the twinkling of an eye, the truth of Our Cause.... – The Báb[579]

the Báb did not choose this because

> The path to guidance is one of love and compassion, not of force and coercion. This hath been God's method in the past, and shall continue to be in the future! – The Báb[580]

Evidently, in God's design, it is His wish that every soul approach him in worship freely, lovingly and sincerely.

The Báb explained the true meaning of worship in this context. Worship is not merely the observance of one's daily prayers and prescribed rituals. It is not merely good deeds such as giving to the poor in the name of God, as noble as that is. And worship is not the "price" one pays to get one's ticket into heaven.

Far different from these things, the Báb says the purity of motive and sincerity of the worshipper is the greatest concern:

> Worship thou God in such wise that if thy worship lead thee to the fire, no alteration in thine adoration would be produced, and so likewise if thy recompense should be paradise. Thus and thus alone should be the worship which befitteth the one True God. Shouldst thou worship Him because of fear, this would be unseemly in the sanctified Court of His presence, and could not be regarded as an act by thee dedicated to the Oneness of His Being. Or if thy gaze should be on paradise, and thou shouldst worship Him while cherishing such a hope, thou wouldst make God's creation a partner with Him, notwithstanding the fact that paradise is desired by men.
>
> Fire and paradise both bow down and prostrate themselves before God. That which is worthy of His Essence is to worship Him for His sake, without fear of fire, or hope of paradise.
>
> Although when true worship is offered, the worshipper is delivered from the fire, and entereth the paradise of God's good-pleasure, yet such should not be the motive of his act. However, God's favour and grace ever flow in accordance with the exigencies of His inscrutable wisdom.
>
> The most acceptable prayer is the one offered with the utmost spirituality and radiance; its prolongation hath not been and is not beloved by God. The more detached and the purer the prayer, the more acceptable is it in the presence of God. – The Báb[581]

True worship, according to the Báb, is a selfless affair. One does not worship God because, if you does not, you will not be saved. One does not worship because, if you do, you will be delivered from punishment. Worship instigated by the fire and brimstone sermons of various preachers falls far short of what is truly acceptable and pleasing to God. According to the Báb, the only reason "worthy of His Essence" is to worship God "for His sake, without fear of fire, or hope of paradise."

In theory then, a truly selfless worshipper would worship God for the sake of His spiritual Beauty, even if God, for some reason known only to Himself, decreed eternal punishment for that person. To be clear, this principle does not say that God is either unfair or arbitrary, rather it sets forth the absolute sovereignty of God and it recognizes that God, in His universal wisdom, is not constrained by any morality devised by men. The final goal of worship is not to make a deal with God or to extract from Him certain benefits you desire, but to adore the supreme Reality of His Manifestation, to acknowledge the infinite perfection of the Creator, to conform oneself to His supreme Will, and to seek His Divine good-pleasure. Even the performance of every good deed ultimately depends upon Divine acceptance, good-pleasure, and grace. Worship that is driven by pure motives is the goal of the Báb's teachings. This is a standard of purity that few human beings are able to attain. Nevertheless, in the Báb's teachings, it remains the ideal towards which everyone must strive:

> ...the purer the prayer, the more acceptable is it in the presence of God.
> – The Báb[582]

The Báb expresses a paradox in the above passage. The true worshipper, whose motive for worship is focused on the Supreme Beauty of God, and not on any gain for herself, finds that her acts of worship become the means for attaining paradise and avoiding hell. This is because the Báb defined paradise as attaining a state of perfection, developing one's human and spiritual potentialities fully, recognizing God's Manifestation, and thus attracting to oneself the grace of God's good pleasure. Hell is the opposite. It is not the vindictive wrath of an angry, punitive and cruel God, rather it is the loss of grace and the justice which someone *brings upon himself* through his misdeeds. Hell involves a state of heedlessness, selfishness, absorption in the things of this world, the neglect of one's spiritual potentialities, and, most of all, denying oneself the bounty of recognizing and benefitting from the teachings of the Manifestation of God for the age in which one is living. The Báb stated:

> Paradise is attainment of His good-pleasure and everlasting hell-fire His judgement through justice. – The Báb[583]

Implied in this statement is the realization that paradise and hell-fire exist in both this world and in the world to come. One does not have to wait to experience either the one or the other; both are present right now. One is basking in the joyous grace of God's good pleasure and developing all one's spiritual gifts, the other is the darkness of remoteness. The Báb wrote:

> Verily, the most sublime station of reward ... is naught but the state of the servant's turning towards his Lord with utter devotion... Shouldst thou taste the joy of that ecstatic station, thou wouldst never part with it, even shouldst thou be torn asunder... – The Báb[584]

Addressing of the importance of recognizing the next Manifestation of God, Him Whom God shall make manifest, the Báb imagined the possibility of meeting Him someday. He said He would...

> ...unhesitatingly bow down before Him, solely on account of His intrinsic supreme worth... For recognizing Him by Him, and through the testimony of His own Self, is paradise... – The Báb[585]

Clearly then, truly pure hearted worship and recognition of God's Manifestations, according to the Báb, becomes the means for attaining higher levels of knowledge, perfection, grace and, ultimately, paradise, notwithstanding the fact that one should not worship with the motive that God will pay you back with paradise and reward you by keeping you out of hell-fire.

THE HIGHEST ETHICAL STANDARDS OF CONDUCT

Search for Truth

The Báb emphasized the importance of the search for truth. He recognized the controversies men have engaged in through the centuries. Is Jesus fully God or fully man? How can God, in the form of Jesus, die? Why did 'Alí, the first Imám, claim to be ever living when the tragic circumstances of his death are fully recorded by history? And so on. The Báb instructed His followers that there is a more subtle issue involved in the search for truth. He spoke of two men engaged in a dispute about religion:

> This one sayeth, 'Thou art an extremist,' and the other one sayeth, 'Thou art intolerant.' This one adduceth evidence from a word of God, and that one reasoneth by another word of God. But I affirm unto them: Ye are both true and right, on the condition that thou not say unto him, 'He is an extremist,' and he not say to thee, 'Thou art intolerant.' – The Báb[586]

The Báb was *not* saying all answers to all questions are equally valid; He is not offering relativism. One of these two might have a better understanding than the other concerning the actual point of dispute between them. What concerned the Báb more than the actual debate was the condition of the hearts and the way they served one another. The passage continues:

Thus wert thou to acquire wisdom, thou wouldst not reject anyone because of his limitation, but must foster the growth of all in the palm of thy mercy. Shouldst thou succeed in elevating him to the realm of glory, great would be his blessings from thee; and should he fail to ascend to thy height, thou shouldst train him, within his own rank of existence. For verily he too is a creation of thy Lord; God loveth him and he loveth God… – The Báb[587]

This approach is very interesting. Consider a situation in which both men consider themselves to be in the higher position. Clearly, as these two engage in discourse, *if they follow the Báb's advice*, they will offer the most gentle loving kindness to one another. They will not fall into strife and idle disputation. Neither will view the other as an opponent to be defeated in debate, rather they will conduct themselves as two mutual travelers on the highway of search, in the most loving and humble way constantly striving to be of service to one another. Inevitably, with this approach, friendship and fellowship will blossom and, undoubtedly, both will eventually discover the truth together.

The Báb, beginning with His first disciples, the Letters of the Living, was clear that, in this Day, everyone must fully exercise their free-will and pursue their search for the Truth for themselves. This is what the Báb told Mullá Husayn after he had become the first to believe in Him:

Eighteen souls must, in the beginning, spontaneously and of their own accord, accept Me and recognize the truth of My Revelation. Unwarned and uninvited, each of these must seek independently to find Me. – The Báb[588]

The Báb emphasized that the most essential requirement for an individual's progress in all the worlds of God is the recognition of the Manifestation of God in the age in which they are living.

True knowledge, therefore, is the knowledge of God, and this is none other than the recognition of His Manifestation *in each Dispensation*. – The Báb[589] (Note: Emphasis added.)

Well is it with him who *in every Dispensation* recognizeth the Purpose of God *for that Dispensation*, and is not deprived therefrom by turning his gaze towards the things of the past. – The Báb[590] (Note: Emphasis added.)

O people of the earth! Whoso obeyeth the Remembrance of God and His Book hath in truth obeyed God and His chosen ones and he will, in

> the life to come, be reckoned in the presence of God among the inmates of the Paradise of His good-pleasure. – The Báb[591]

> There is no paradise more wondrous for any soul than to be exposed to God's Manifestation *in His Day*, to hear His verses and believe in them, to attain His presence, which is naught but the presence of God, to sail upon the sea of the heavenly kingdom of His good-pleasure, and to partake of the choice fruits of the paradise of His divine Oneness. – The Báb[592] (Note: Emphasis added.)

Nevertheless, despite the compelling need to recognize the Manifestation of God, difficulties abound. Ordinary reason cannot easily reconcile or transcend the opposing positions of religious debate. He wrote:

> Beseech thou God to open, through His grace, the gate of the heart unto thee, inasmuch as, without the light of that sanctuary, man is unable to conceive of contrary attributes within one and the same thing. – The Báb[593]

He stated:

> Such conclusive truth hath been revealed through the gaze of the heart, and not that of intellect... No one can recognize the truth of the Middle Way between the two extreme poles except after attaining unto the gate of the heart and beholding the realities of the worlds, visible and unseen. – The Báb[594]

As Professor Saiedi observed,

> "...whenever the Báb addresses a complex metaphysical question, He normally begins by explaining it is necessary to attain this higher perspective in order to understand reality: one must traverse the path of unity, submerge oneself in the sea of the heart, journey in the realm of the divine names, and attain the stage of utter servitude in order to be able to discern the truth of things." – Nader Saiedi[595]

"Verily, I do this for God"

At the core of the Báb's view of ethics is that all human action should be "for God" and according to the highest standards of conduct. Finding considerable coherence with the essential Islámic teaching of submitting oneself to the Will of God, and the core Christian teaching of loving God and fellowman with one's entire mind, heart and soul, the Báb used the Arabic phrase "*lilláh*", which means literally "for God" or abiding by the Will of God. Like the previous Manifestations of God, to perform a deed for God means to serve all His creatures with devotion and humility. The Báb wrote:

> ...no behaviour turneth into a real action unless it is performed for the sake of God. It is for this reason that it is enjoined upon all those who perform any act to utter these words at the time of their action:
>
> > 'Verily, I do this for God, the Lord of the heavens and the earth, the Lord of all that is seen and unseen, the Lord of creation.'
>
> Should he recite them in his heart, his action would be rewarded as a result. – The Báb[596]

The Báb sanctified the marriage vow, by having the couple state that they will abide by the Will of God, which was later affirmed by Baha'u'llah.

The Báb urged the followers to attain the highest degree of character, beauty, refinement and perfection possible. It is incumbent on everyone to seek the highest state of excellence for oneself, for others, and for the world, including the natural world. This is best achieved when all one's actions are done "for God", that is, in a spirit of service, worship and pure intent.

Purity and the environment

Indeed, the Báb showed an extraordinary degree of environmental awareness. As Professor Saiedi explains:

> ...the Báb consistently emphasizes the idea of purification. All levels of reality, from the material body to the human heart, must be purified. Natural resources must be preserved in the utmost purity... The Báb turns the idea of the purity of water into protection of the environment ... He writes:
>
> > Nothing is more beloved of God than to keep water in a state of utmost purity, to such an extent that if a believer should become aware that the glass of water he holdeth in his hand hath passed through any impure parts of the earth, he would be grieved. – The Báb
>
> In other words, it is implicitly necessary that all streams, lakes and seas through which the water passes to be clean.[597]

Whether it be one's own character, the education of other souls, the garden where flowers are planted, the structures men build, the societies human beings establish, the natural environment, or the entire family of nations, according to the Báb, every person must do his utmost to promote beauty, refinement, and perfection of "all things", so that all things may attain unto paradise:

> For verily Thou hast desired, by this law, to build the earth anew by virtue of Thy glorious handiwork through the hands of Thy servants. – The Báb[598]

Inflict no sorrow, bring joy to others

The Báb laid down a prohibition against causing others grief and sadness. In fact, His counsel is to enrich others and bring them joy.

> [The] essence of all knowledge is the knowledge of good character and traits. Man must act in conformity with them, that by virtue of such knowledge of ethics he shall neither witness any grief in his soul, nor inflict sorrow upon any other soul. – The Báb[599]

The Báb said that if anyone should receive an inquiry from someone "it is his duty to reply" and to "give a guiding answer."[600] He says that:

> ...he is a man endued with vision who answereth the call of God in all worlds and stations" [and that] "all are enjoined to respond to one another. – The Báb[601]

He continues,

> So much so, that if an infant cry, it is a duty to respond to him through appropriate means. Likewise, should one's condition silently call upon others, it is the duty of men of discernment to answer his call... [It] is binding upon them to reply, that at no time anyone should witness that which would cause him grief. – The Báb[602]

As this passage shows, one must respond to all people through loving action and deeds of service, but especially to the powerless, and even to those who may not be able to express their needs. The Báb "defines the most exalted persons as those who lovingly reply to a call or need even before the request is made, addressing the voice of the inner reality."[603]

To emphasize the importance of not causing anyone grief, the Báb revealed a law which specified a small fine for "he who knowingly causeth grief to any soul..."[604] Saiedi adds:

> ...the Báb declares that God has forbidden anyone to inflict sorrow upon any soul. This rule is also extended to the spiritual community,

> so that causing grief to any member of the community is like causing grief to the Letters of the Living, and inflicting sadness upon the Letters of the Living is like causing grief to the Primal Point. The Báb asks His followers not only to refrain from saddening people but to seek actively to bring them joy and happiness. – Nader Saiedi[605]

Interestingly, and in direct contradiction to the Islámic cultural environment of His day, He indicated this was especially important in relation to the treatment of women:

> ...there is no act of obedience that ensureth greater nearness to God than bringing joy to the hearts of the faithful, even as naught yieldeth more remoteness than causing them grief. This law is doubly binding in dealing with [women], whether in causing them joy or grief. However, man must always be watchful that even if he fail to bring joy to a human being, at least he should refrain from causing him grief. – The Báb[606]

In all that the Báb taught, concern and care of others is paramount. But this is not an absolute command. At any given moment our capacity to reduce or eliminate the sadness, distress and difficulty of another person is subject to limitations according to every situation. Hence, the Báb repeatedly qualifies His command; always act "by any means in your power", "to the extent possible for you" and "to the extent of your ability". He wrote:

> Be lovingly watchful of one another and thus improve your affairs. Should ye find amongst you one who is afflicted with grief, remove his sorrow by any means in your power, and should ye find one stricken with poverty, enrich him to the extent of your ability. If ye find in your midst one who is abased, exalt him to the extent ye can, and if ye find one who is veiled by ignorance, educate him to the degree of your capacity. Should ye find amongst yourselves one who is single, help him to marry, in accordance with the divine law, to the limits of your ability, and should ye find one who is in distress, bring him tranquility by any means in your power... If ye find in your midst one who is hungry, send him, in truth and to the extent of your power, food in such a way that his heart will not be saddened, and if ye find one who has no clothes, provide him with clothes in the most dignified manner, to the extent possible for you. Look then not at your selves and your possessions, but rather look at God, Who hath created you and conferred upon you from His kingdom that which is your lot. – The Báb[607]

The command to inflict no sorrow upon other souls, but rather to enrich them by solving their afflictions and bringing them joy, has profound purposes. It goes beyond the traditional understanding of the Golden Rule – to do unto other AS you would have them do unto you – which emphasizes reciprocity in human interactions. It focuses one's ethical emphasis on the well-being of the other person, on selflessness and pure-hearted altruism.

That said, it is not merely a self-evidently worthy goal in itself (it is). The Báb gives additional justification. Saiedi explains,

> No discussion of the laws and ethics of the Bayán can be complete without reference to [additional] key principles… [The first] is the primacy of Him Whom God shall make manifest… As we have seen, He Whom God shall make manifest is the most fundamental and pervasive theme of the entire Revelation of the Báb… There is virtually no law of the Persian Bayán which is not an affirmation of the Promised One, and indeed, all the principles … exemplify the centrality of Him Whom God shall make manifest. For example, we saw that the Báb prohibits causing grief to any soul. As He has explained, the real purpose of this law is that no one should cause grief to Him Whom God shall make manifest. If the Babis refrain from saddening anyone, they will not unknowingly cause grief to the Promised One.
> – Nader Saiedi[608]

The Báb does indeed have a primary focus on the near advent of Him Whom God shall make manifest, as the very goal of His own revelation. But, in truth, all human souls, in addition to the Person of Him Whom God shall make manifest, are the beneficiaries of the Báb's elevated ethical standards. Decades later, in the period of 1911 to 1913, 'Abdu'l-Bahá, the Son of Bahá'u'lláh, would discuss the significance of bringing joy, not sorrow, to other souls:

> The progress and development of the soul, the joy and sorrow of the soul, are independent of the physical body. If we are caused joy or pain by a friend, if a love prove true or false, it is the soul that is affected…
> – 'Abdu'l-Bahá[609]

> Joy gives us wings! In times of joy our strength is more vital, our intellect keener, and our understanding less clouded. We seem better able to cope with the world and to find our sphere of usefulness. But when sadness visits us we become weak, our strength leaves us, our compre-

> hension is dim and our intelligence veiled. The actualities of life seem to elude our grasp, the eyes of our spirits fail to discover the sacred mysteries, and we become even as dead beings... [The] trials which beset our every step, all our sorrow, pain, shame and grief, are born in the world of matter; whereas the spiritual Kingdom never causes sadness... – 'Abdu'l-Bahá[610]

The responsibility to elevate

The Báb clearly wanted all peoples to attain perfections and the good pleasure of God. He wanted everyone to find their way into paradise and wished for no one to be left out. He emphasized that God's grace and forgiveness were unlimited.

> Thy loving providence hath encompassed all created things in the heavens and on the earth, and Thy forgiveness hath surpassed the whole creation. Thine is sovereignty; in Thy hand are the Kingdoms of Creation and Revelation; in Thy right hand Thou holdest all created things and within Thy grasp are the assigned measures of forgiveness. Thou forgivest whomsoever among Thy servants Thou pleasest. Verily Thou art the Ever-Forgiving, the All-Loving. Nothing whatsoever escapeth Thy knowledge, and naught is there which is hidden from Thee. – The Báb[611]

> O Lord! Enable all the peoples of the earth to gain admittance into the Paradise of Thy Faith, so that no created being may remain beyond the bounds of Thy good-pleasure. – The Báb[612]

These teachings that paradise is perfection and attaining the good pleasure of God suggest an important ethical stance. We recall that the Báb held loving guidance and human free will in the highest regard:

> It is better to guide one soul than to possess all that is on earth, for as long as that guided soul is under the shadow of the Tree of Divine Unity, he and the one who hath guided him will both be recipients of God's tender mercy, whereas possession of earthly things will cease at the time of death. The path to guidance is one of love and compassion, not of force and coercion. This hath been God's method in the past, and shall continue to be in the future! – The Báb[613]

Given this principle of guidance rather than coercion, a key feature of the Báb's teaching is that we all have *the responsibility to elevate* one another. Thus, instead of using force and aggression to convert others to the Cause of

God, or to force them to comply on any issue, one must use loving guidance to influence them, all the while respecting their own free will to choose. Influence (rather than control) becomes a moral responsibility to elevate others to the extent that we are able. And, of course, others must strive to elevate us. In the Báb's moral universe, people are bringing joy to one another, never causing sorrow if they can avoid it, and always striving to elevate one another. This can only be achieved through a specific ethical stance: reliance on God, prayer, moral virtues, listening to one another, consultation, serving one another, exemplary behavior, and lifting others up.

The ethical stance taught by the Báb is that everyone has a *responsibility to elevate* "all things" (kullu shay) to their uttermost state of perfection, so that, to the extent of their God-given potential, all things in creation may magnify, praise and reflect the Beauty of the Lord. Thus, will all things and all people achieve paradise. Saiedi elaborated:

> Paradise is the highest state of perfection and self-actualization that can be attained by a being within its own station. Hell is the state of deprivation of that perfect actualization. Thus, not only human beings but all other created things have their own 'heaven' and 'hell'. This new definition has far-reaching implications for the attitude the believer should take toward all things, including the natural world... *Human beings are invested with the unique responsibility to ensure, to the limits of their power, that all created things achieve their paradise*... [In the Báb's Writings] we find:
>
> [W]hoever possesseth power over anything *must elevate it to its uttermost perfection* that it may not be deprived of its own paradise. For example, the paradise of a sheet of paper on which a few excellent lines are inscribed is that it be refined with patterns of gold illumination, adornment, and excellence that are customary for the most exalted parchment scrolls. Then the possessor of that paper hath elevated it to its utmost degree of glory. Should he know of a higher degree of refinement and fail to manifest it upon that paper, he would deprive it of its paradise, and he would be held accountable, for why hast thou, despite the possession of the means, withheld the effusion of grace and favor?
> – The Báb, cited by Nader Saiedi[614]

If a piece of paper has a right to be elevated to its paradise, then doesn't every member of the human race have an even greater right to the same? The Báb says:

> Man's highest station … is attained through faith in God in every Dispensation and by acceptance of what hath been revealed by Him, and not through learning; inasmuch as in every nation there are learned men who are versed in divers sciences. Nor is it attainable through wealth; for it is similarly evident that among the various classes in every nation there are those possessed of riches. Likewise are other transitory things.
>
> True knowledge, therefore, is the knowledge of God, and this is none other than the recognition of His Manifestation in each Dispensation. – The Báb[615]

Every person must be concerned not only with elevating his reality so that he can recognize the legitimate Manifestation of God for the Day in which he is living but elevate others to achieve the same. Every individual must work ceaselessly to perfect his character and, through love, compassion, wisdom and justice, strive with all endeavor to elevate society and indeed the entire family of nations to its highest level of paradise and perfection. Every soul has a responsibility, in whatever way possible, to elevate his associations – himself, his family, his community and his nation, and extending even to the largest entity of which man is a part, his civilization on this planet.

In time, a world-wide Divine civilization is the logical and inevitable outcome of such teachings when, God willing, they are faithfully and earnestly applied. The perspective of unity, the responsibility to elevate, and its breathtaking possibilities are possible because the Primal Will of God has placed signs of His revelation in every created thing. The Báb wrote:

> And within the inmost reality of all things there hath been, and will forever continue to be, a sign from God through which the unity of the Lord is celebrated. This sign, however, is a reflection of His Will present within it, through which naught is seen but God. – The Báb[616]

PARADISE AND NEARNESS TO GOD, HELL AND REMOTENESS FROM GOD

What happens when every soul and all things are joyfully elevated to their highest possible state?

Every created thing has a potential latent within it, an inherent gift from the Primal Will of God, which enables it to reflect, to some degree, the signs of God's revelation. With Divine and human assistance, every created thing has the capacity to express its full potential, and when that degree of perfection is achieved it has found its paradise:

> No created thing shall ever attain its paradise unless it appeareth in its highest prescribed degree of perfection. For instance, this crystal representeth the paradise of the stone whereof its substance is composed. Likewise there are various stages in the paradise for the crystal itself... So long as it was stone it was worthless, but if it attaineth the excellence of ruby—a potentiality which is latent in it—how much a carat will it be worth? Consider likewise every created thing. – The Báb[617]

Paradise is perfection. And perfection is aligning oneself entirely, according to the capacity of each created thing, with the Will of God. For humans, aligning with the Will of God entails, first of all, recognizing God's latest Divine Educator when He appears. Recognition leads to benefitting from His teachings, serving His Cause, and following His guidance in "all things", and that is attaining His good pleasure.

> There is no paradise more wondrous for any soul than to be exposed to God's Manifestation in His Day, to hear His verses and believe in them, to attain His presence, which is naught but the presence of God, to sail upon the sea of the heavenly kingdom of His good-pleasure, and to partake of the choice fruits of the paradise of His divine Oneness. – The Báb[618]

> Indeed no paradise is more glorious in the sight of God than attainment unto His good-pleasure. – The Báb[619]

> Paradise is attainment of His good-pleasure and everlasting hell-fire His judgement through justice. – The Báb[620]

Hellfire is the opposite of paradise. It is the self-inflicted tragedy of being remote from God by denying oneself opportunities to move closer to God and His Will.

Contrary to the religions of the past, the Báb is not describing paradise and hell as physical places you go to after death. To be sure, the Báb taught that for human beings there is an afterlife that is different from physical reality on earth. But sinners and saints both go to an afterlife environment, so spiritually defining it in terms of "place" is not the true meaning of the concepts of paradise and hellfire. Paradise and hell are not physical places. Instead, paradise and fire are conditions of the mind, the heart and the soul which we bring upon ourselves by our faith or the lack of it, by our selfless good deeds or the lack of them, by our virtues or the absence of them, by our alignment with the Will of God or our failure to achieve alignment, by our attaining of perfections and the good pleasure of God or by letting those opportunities to slip away from us. The Báb makes it clear that the sublimity of true spiritual paradise is far greater than the physical paradise humans have imagined, and the misery and loss of true spiritual hellfire is much worse than the physical versions which have been described in literature. Indeed, the physical descriptions to which we have become accustomed are but symbols of the true reality to which they allude.

> There is no paradise, in the estimation of the believers in the Divine Unity, more exalted than to obey God's commandments, and there is no fire in the eyes of those who have known God and His signs, fiercer than to transgress His laws and to oppress another soul, even to the extent of a mustard seed. On the Day of Resurrection God will, in truth, judge all men, and we all verily plead for His grace. – The Báb[621]

In most peoples' image of the afterlife nowadays, the following statements are probably accepted as true:

Conventional ideas about Heaven and Hell	
Heaven	**Hell**
Heaven is a place some people go to after death.	Likewise, hell is a place other people go to after death.
If you were in heaven, you would probably know it.	If you were in hell, you would probably know it.
Heaven is a place where life is good. For example, you might sing in the heavenly choir or get to visit with great and holy persons from the past.	Hell is a place where life is bad. For example, real fires might be constantly and painfully burning your flesh.
And, if you were in heaven, you would be in a happy state of mind.	And, if you were in hell, you would be in an unhappy state of mind.

Figure 35 Common conceptions about Heaven and Hell (in the culture)

In this common description of heaven and hell, before all else, it is a place. You go there after death. It is a matter of geography. You go to this place or that place. It could be the place where the tormenting fires burn you alive or it could be the place where you hear the heavenly choir singing, but it is a concrete place first and foremost. Second to this fact, the common conception says that the former is unquestionably considered good, and the latter is undeniably considered bad.

Notice that these are objective realities – you're either in the good place or the bad place. At that point it is no longer a matter of opinion or belief.

Notice that two aspects are cognitive in nature. That is, they are in your own mind, internal to yourself. You are assumed to be aware of where you are and you're either happy or sad about it. These two are states of mind which are in reaction to the facts of the surroundings in which you will eventually find yourself.

One factor is external to you, two factors are internal within your own mind. These are the common conceptions of heaven and hell.

It is interesting to observe that the Báb's explanation of paradise and hell turns some of these assumptions upside-down. First, since neither heaven nor hell are "places", there is no objective "geography" available by which to identify whether or not you're in the good or the bad "place". Second, if there is no "geography" to go by, and no objective or predestined things happening to you, you may or may not be consciously aware of where you are.

In theory, a person might not know, for a fact, if they were in heaven or hell. This is further confirmed when we recall the Báb's definition of paradise is that it is a spiritual state of being near to God, of being exposed to God's Manifestation and embracing His truth, of developing perfections, and of attaining God's good pleasure. Is it possible that a person might *think* they have found the truth, be near to God, to have developed perfections, and be the recipient of God's good pleasure, and be mistaken about all that? Have you met people who were surely bad who thought surely that they were good people?! Similarly, is it possible for a person to feel deprived of heavenly blessings and not realize how blessed they really are in God's eyes? The answer to these questions is an unsettling "yes, it is possible". This means one may not know "where" one is headed in the afterlife, despite having a strong feeling of thinking you know. Moreover – here is a real kicker – a person does not have to wait to die to be in either heaven or hell. A person might be in either "place" right now.

Attaining nearness to God, aligning with His Will, being worthy of His good-pleasure, and attaining perfections, is a judgement that the infinite God makes about each one of us individually. You don't decide that, He does. And if we're honest with ourselves we must admit that individually we're not privy to what God thinks of us right now. We just don't know. It is possible that you and I have misjudged and come up with the wrong conclusion. You could be thinking "A" while God is thinking "B".

Consider this remarkable quote, which turns on its head the idea of what punishment from God might really look like.

> All praise be unto Thee, O Thou besides Whom there is none other God. Graciously enable me to ascend unto Thee, to be granted the

> honour of dwelling in Thy nearness and to have communion with Thee alone. No God is there but Thee.
>
> Indeed shouldst Thou desire to confer blessing upon a servant Thou wouldst blot out from the realm of his heart every mention or disposition except Thine Own mention; and shouldst Thou ordain evil for a servant by reason of that which his hands have unjustly wrought before Thy face, Thou wouldst test him with the benefits of this world and of the next that he might become preoccupied therewith and forget Thy remembrance. – The Báb[622]

Like so many of the Báb's prayers, we notice that He pleads humbly for the honour of being close to God, which is the very definition of being in heaven, never taking it for granted. We notice that giving a blessing consists of shielding the individual from becoming too absorbed in all things of the world and to focus entirely on God. And finally – now comes the surprise – punishment ("ordaining evil") is not physical hell-fire and brimstone, rather it comes to the unjust when God allows them to experience the rewards of the material world and to become forgetful of God, the very definition of being in hell.

This does not mean that having material blessings are to be equated with hell. Far from it. But if one has material abundance and that *causes you* to be completely forgetful of God, then, yes, such material abundance and preoccupation with the world could very well be a punishment, "by reason of that which his hands have unjustly wrought". And this is because paradise is closeness to God, and the opposite, worldly *preoccupation*, is by definition a self-imposed state of being distant from God. It is that state which is the defining condition of hell.

This opens up a door of opportunity to every human being, but it takes courage and fearless self-honesty to walk through it. You can examine your own life and ask yourself, Am I someone who is preoccupied the material world? Am I someone who is forgetful of God? If the answer you give yourself is "yes", then regardless of whether you are wealthy or destitute you may already meet the conditions of being in hell. On the other hand, if you can honestly say to yourself, "No, I'm not forgetful of God, nor am I disobedient, nor am I too much preoccupied with the material world", then perhaps, tentatively, you can breath a momentary sigh of relief and view positively the direction of your life. The good fact is that regardless of the answer you give yourself, you can use it as an inspiration to improve whatever you are doing, to either change direction or to strive harder for even greater progress.

And just to be clear, this idea of punishment is radically different from what most people normally think about when the idea of punishment is discussed. Normally, people think of punishment as something that one party does TO another party. And, that act is understood to be something painful or unpleasant. Wrathful images of an angry grey-bearded Deity throwing lightning bolts at people come to mind. The motivation for inflicting such punishment is conceived to be retribution rather than education, to pay someone back for the bad thing they did. In the Báb's description, however, God is not doing anything to you. He is merely withdrawing blessings and leaving you to your own devices, so that you can experience the consequences of your own actions.

Here is an analogy: Think of the merciful blessings as "a shield" given to an individual to protect them *from themselves*, that is, from their own wayward thoughts, feelings and actions. If God removes the shield, "by reason of that which his hands have unjustly wrought", the person is no longer protected. Having "the shield" around you is a mercy and grace from God. You never did anything to deserve it in the first place, at your beginning it was just given to you out of love. But if you don't want God in your life, if you prefer to be selfishly absorbed with worldly comforts and pleasures, then God says, 'OK, I won't force Myself on you. Do things your own way and see how that works out.' Then, inevitably, you become forgetful, and since the shield isn't there protecting you anymore, you then feel the full impact of your own folly. Bad things start happening to you, and, since you're busy ignoring God's guidance, you brought them upon yourself by your own actions. Perhaps that is what Divine justice looks like.

Naturally, the person in this wayward situation will complain when the bad things start happening, blaming God for doing it to them, but God's answer is silence. I imagine, in His exalted Mind, He's simply thinking, 'Why complain? I merely gave you what you asked for.'

God's intention was not retribution, but education. The intention is to let you learn from your own actions how needful of Him you are, and then, to welcome you back, when you make the choice to turn to Him in repentance, seeking forgiveness. And then, the Scriptures provide assurance that God is Ever-Forgiving and Ever-Loving. He graciously welcomes the wayward soul who humbly turns to Him. In my view, I think the Báb is implying that this is what punishment looks like. It is not vindictive, as the world sees it; it is educational, disciplining, and ultimately both merciful and just in its method.

Now let's ask, if a person is thriving materially, and reaping the rewards of the world, will they likely think they are being blessed or punished?

Most people would interpret material abundance as being blessed, not punished. If the Báb's description of spiritual reality is correct, and God lets some individuals acquire wealth and possessions and to forget about Him, then they would be quite unaware of their true situation. They could be in spiritual hell, as the Báb defines it, and not know about it! Or, due to their worldly prosperity, they might think they are happy while simultaneously being entirely oblivious of the much greater joys God has in store for them if only they would redirect their steps. Or, even with their prosperity, their lives could be miserable anyway, and still they might fail to realize they had done it all to themselves. Either way, because they are not cultivating nearness to God, not developing their spiritual virtues and perfections, nor attaining the good-pleasure of God, and because they are placing self above all other concerns, according to the Báb, they are remote from God, and in the real hell, and possibly not even realize it.

One shouldn't conclude from this discussion that the reality of paradise and hell-fire is totally black and white. Everyone knows that people are a healthy mixture of both good and bad qualities. Very few individuals are faithless, selfish, or hateful one hundred percent of the time. Likewise, few souls have fully developed their perfections either. Some people are more spiritually developed than others. Some have strong faith but poor conduct, while others behave well but have no faith commitment whatsoever. But everyone, while still alive and, even if they are not aware of it at the moment, is on the journey in one way or another. It is likely for most people to be aligning with God's perfections in some ways but not in others. The status of people regarding paradise and hell-fire is likely to be more like a continuum and progressive over time. Someone who looks to be remote from God today may repent and make significant strides of faith and behavior towards God later in life. Likewise, over time, someone who appears to be doing well today might backslide and lose sight of God's good pleasure. It is probably unwise to assume that the status of oneself or of other people is fixed and unchangeable. There may be many milestones on the never-ending continuum of progress towards God. The Báb stated:

> Say, this earthly life shall come to an end, and everyone shall expire and return unto my Lord God Who will reward with the choicest gifts the deeds of those who endure with patience. Verily thy God assigneth the measure of all created things as He willeth, by virtue of His behest; and those who conform to the good-pleasure of your Lord, they are indeed among the blissful. – The Báb[623]

In the end, *God decides* how well or poorly each person has done, how to balance mercy with justice in light of each individual's circumstances. God determines what blessings and consequences the soul should receive as it journeys through this life and the life beyond.

In my view, the appropriate reaction to these insights is to show gratitude and humility. One should approach God with a thankful heart and a submissive attitude, with the utmost respect, never complaining about trials, recognizing fully one's position in the cosmos as a creature, never presuming that we know what He is thinking of us in any given moment, never acting with any sense of entitlement, always being willing to reevaluate and get back on track, never loudly asserting to others that we have our salvation already fully worked out. And most of all, we must never transgress the bounds of propriety and assume we know what God thinks about someone else or bring sorrow to any soul by condemning anyone to hell simply because they disagree with the beliefs we hold.

In my opinion, complete humility and gratitude is the only safeguard.

ADVANCING TOWARDS ABOLISHING THE LAW OF THE SWORD

The teachings of the Báb clearly pointed to a peaceful, non-aggressive worldview and way of life. The Báb especially did not want His followers engaging in violence or aggression if it could be avoided. Although the Báb did not forbid His followers from defending themselves when under attack, His preference for non-aggression whenever possible was explicitly stated. For example, He wrote:

> The path to guidance is one of love and compassion, not of force and coercion. This hath been God's method in the past, and shall continue to be in the future! – The Báb[624]

This emphasis on non-aggression and non-coercion, and on guidance through love, comes clearly into focus when considered in light of His teachings about not causing anyone grief or sorrow. We recall, for example, these quotes:

> [The] essence of all knowledge is the knowledge of good character and traits. Man must act in conformity with them, that by virtue of such knowledge of ethics he shall neither witness any grief in his soul, nor inflict sorrow upon any other soul. – The Báb[625]

> ...there is no act of obedience that ensureth greater nearness to God than bringing joy to the hearts of the faithful, even as naught yieldeth more remoteness than causing them grief... However, man must always be watchful that even if he fail to bring joy to a human being, at least he should refrain from causing him grief. – The Báb[626]

The Báb had initially asked His followers to meet with Him in Karbilá when He would be on His way back from pilgrimage. According to the common understanding of Shí'ih prophecies concerning the coming of the Twelfth Imám, many Bábís initially understood this as a call for violent jihad, i.e. holy war.[627] Saiedi explains:

> In the middle of the nineteenth century, the world of Shí'ih Islám was in a state of fervent messianic expectation. Devout believers were awaiting the advent of the holy figure known as the Twelfth Imám, who had been in concealment for a thousand years. According to the prophecies recorded in the Traditions, when the Hidden Imám reappeared he would arise ... to unleash jihad – holy war – on the forces of evil and unbelief, and would usher in the Day of Judgment and the Resurrection. – Nader Saiedi[628]

The religious leaders and the government authorities were aware of the same prophecies and assumed that the Bábí movement intended to become a violent insurrection against the government. Likewise, the religious leaders, who paid pious lip service to the Promised Twelfth Imám, continuously announcing their hope of His coming in their Friday sermons, understood that their power was temporary, and would have to be relinquished to Him if He were ever to re-appear. Despite their public statements of reverence to Him, covertly they didn't really want Him to come, and would vehemently resist anyone making a claim to be the Twelfth Imám.

The eleventh Imám, Hasan al-Askari, had died in the year 874 AD, which had been the year 260 AH on the Islámic calendar. He had been assassinated, as had been many of the Imáms before him. His son, Muhammad al-Mahdi, then only about five years old, immediately became the twelfth Imám. Probably to save the boy from deadly political intrigue, he went into hiding. Theologically, this was referred to as his "occultation", which specifically means hiding or concealment. There had been two types of occultation, called a minor and then a major occultation. During the minor occultation the twelfth Imám was said to have communicated with his followers through deputies (interestingly, called "báb", or gates). After nearly sixty years and a succession of four "gates", the communication is said to have been stopped, in the year 941 AD, thus beginning the major occultation.

The religious leaders – the mullás – claimed that the twelfth Imám had been in hiding for the last thousand years, that he had been supernaturally preserved from aging, that he lived in two far-off cities known as Jábulsá and Jábulqá, and that he would someday return to humanity to bring justice to the earth. The religious leaders claimed that that they were the twelfth Imám's official representatives on earth during the long period of occultation until the day when he would return. It was understood that their hold on power was provisional, that is, it was *only* legitimate in *the absence* of the Twelfth Imám and that they would have to give up their power if he returned.)

So. *How do you fight a violent war without causing someone a great deal of sorrow?* How do you bring joy and elevate other souls when you're killing them with your swords? How do you avoid the sorrows of the families while you're killing their loved ones on the battlefield? Given the horror of war, which is known to all, the absurdity of the question seems overwhelming.

The Báb, on His way back from pilgrimage, became aware of growing opposition to His Cause, and He could foresee that if the meeting were held as planned, violent conflicts would be the result. Many would be hurt due to a perceived provocation by the Bábís. But, as Dr. Saiedi pointed out, the Báb "unexpectedly cancelled that decree, and instead of going to Karbilá, He returned to Iran… *[It] was His desire to see no harm or sadness befall anyone that led Him to alter His previous command…*"[629] (Note: Emphasis added) Both the Bábís, expecting to fight, and their enemies, expecting a rebellion, were spared a great deal of grief and sorrow due to this decision to cancel the meeting.

Let's think about that. The long-prophesied epic "holy war" was cancelled because the fighting it would making people sad. (Especially the people you are slaughtering with your sword!) And, according to the Báb, no one should be put to grief! The great holy war was simply cancelled!! Have you ever heard of such a thing?

Repeatedly, throughout His Ministry, opportunities arose to initiate violent struggle against the religious and political authorities of His day, but in every instance the Báb repeatedly refused to allow the Bábís to take up the sword.

The darkness and ignorance of the times were extreme. The Báb judged that He could not, *in one leap*, abolish the current militant understanding of holy war (jihad). He adopted a gradualist approach. Without abolishing holy war explicitly, according to Professor Nader Saiedi, He "undermines the concept by defining holy war in such a way as to make it contingent on the realization of impossible conditions – thus, in effect, nullifying it."[630] The symbolism and the outward terminology of jihad remained, but the actual practice of fighting religious holy war was virtually abolished. The expectations for what the Promised One would be like were turned upside down.

Holy war in the Báb's Writings was subjected to stringent conditions, which when closely examined show them to be impossible, unfulfillable conditions.

- The Báb states that, while He is alive, only He can declare a holy war. Well, in theory that allows for the possibility of holy war, but, in actual practice the Báb refused all opportunities to call for it.
- The Báb says that, after Him, holy war can only be declared by a king who is a believer in the Bayán, i.e. a Bábí. Well, there were no Bábí kings! All the kings of His day were His enemies.
- Moreover, He knew there never would be any Bábí kings because the revelation of Him Whom God shall make manifest was coming very soon and all the Báb's laws were all going to be superseded by His Laws anyway.

Holy war was permitted only after impossible, unfulfillable conditions were fulfilled, which meant, in practice, that holy war was not permitted. (Let's recall the exception. Not being the aggressor is quite a different thing from defending oneself when under attack. The Bábís were not forbidden from defending themselves when necessary.)

Today's reader might ask, if the Báb's aim was to end the use of violent struggle for promoting religion, why didn't He just say so? The answer is that this circuitous style of rhetoric was designed to make the transition out of the old rigid militaristic mindset more manageable for the people. It is a little like telling an alcoholic he is allowed to drink only if his therapist explicitly gives permission beforehand. Yes, in theory the alcoholic can tell himself that drinking is still possible, but in practice the wise therapist will always say no when asked. Stating the rule this way helps the alcoholic to separate himself from alcohol gradually. Just as the Báb's own increasingly explicit declaration of His Mission was a gradual process, the process of changing some of the most ingrained laws of the society in which He lived required a gradual process as well.

All in all, in practical terms, holy war, as a force within religion, did come to an end with the Báb's teaching. Saiedi states,

> It would remain for Bahá'u'lláh to abolish it formally and indeed the explicit abrogation of the law of the sword … was Bahá'u'lláh's first act in announcing His Mission. – Nader Saiedi[631]

The use of violence was anathema to the Báb. How could it be otherwise when His ethical teachings urged the followers to never be the cause of grief to anyone? Is there any greater cause of grief than war for the purpose of promoting a religion? Is there any act more offensive to human free-will than the coercion of the sword? Therefore, in the Báb's Dispensation, in principle and in practice, offensive holy war was not permitted.

The Báb was taking the people to the future. He was taking them to a time when holy war would be totally abolished. He made great strides toward the abolition of holy war, but at the end of His ministry, the ancient law of the sword was still, officially, "on the books", so to speak. As He intended and fully expected, Bahá'u'lláh changed the law once and for all, and He effected an epochal transformation in the attitudes and practices of the believers. Adib Taherzadeh states that, on the day in April 1863 when Bahá'u'lláh first publicly declared His identity as Him Whom God shall make manifest, "Bahá'u'lláh made three particularly important statements to His followers".

> …The first was to forbid the use of the sword in His Dispensation. During the ministry of the Báb the believers defended themselves against their persecutors; Bahá'u'lláh clearly forbade this. In many Tablets He counselled His followers to teach the Cause with wisdom and prudence and not to arouse the antagonism of a fanatic enemy. He enjoined caution when teaching those who were determined to uproot the foundation of the Faith and harm its adherents. At one stage in His ministry He particularly exhorted His followers to guard against falling into the hands of enemies, but if faced with martyrdom, to lay down their lives in the path of their Faith rather than kill their persecutors. The tongue of the believer who teaches the Cause, He stated in one Tablet, is the mightiest sword he possesses, for his utterances are endowed with a power that can remove veils of ignorance from the hearts of men. Soon, as a result of such counsels and exhortations, the attitude of the believers was radically changed, and swords and other weapons were put away never to be used again. During the ministries of Bahá'u'lláh and 'Abdu'l-Bahá great numbers of Bahá'ís were martyred in Persia, but they did not resort to violence. They gave their lives willingly, and many testified in the

hour of martyrdom that their life-blood proclaimed the truth of the Cause of God for this age. – Adib Taherzadeh[632]

THE BÁB'S DIVINE AUTHORITY

The Báb summoned the kings, the clerics, and the peoples of the world to acknowledge His Revelation and abide by its Teachings. From His point of view, nothing could be more imperative; after all, in addition to His own Revelation of the Word of God, a central focus of His Revelation was to prepare the way for Him Whom God shall make manifest. He well knew that this next Divine Manifestation would bring a Revelation of incomparable importance. It was destined to establish the unity and the spiritual quickening of all mankind.

Nothing could be more important than this, so he called out to the kings of His day to adhere to His guidance:

> O concourse of kings and of the sons of kings! Lay aside, one and all, your dominion which belongeth unto God.... – The Báb[633]

> By God! If ye do well, to your own behoof will ye do well; and if ye deny God and His signs, We, in very truth, having God, can well dispense with all creatures and all earthly dominion. – The Báb[634]

> Vain indeed is your dominion, for God hath set aside earthly possessions for such as have denied Him.... O concourse of kings! Deliver with truth and in all haste the verses sent down by Us to the peoples of Turkey and of India, and beyond them, with power and with truth, to lands in both the East and the West.... – The Báb[635]

To the faithful kings He promised great rewards:

> Fear ye God, O concourse of kings, lest ye remain afar from Him Who is His Remembrance [the Báb], after the Truth hath come unto you with a Book and signs from God, as spoken through the wondrous tongue of Him Who is His Remembrance. Seek ye grace from God, for God hath ordained for you, after ye have believed in Him, a Garden the vastness of which is as the vastness of the whole of Paradise. – The Báb[636]

He addressed the religious leaders:

> O concourse of divines! Fear God from this day onwards in the views ye advance, for He Who is Our Remembrance in your midst, and Who cometh from Us, is, in very truth, the Judge and Witness. Turn away

> from that which ye lay hold of, and which the Book of God, the True One, hath not sanctioned, for on the Day of Resurrection ye shall, upon the Bridge, be, in very truth, held answerable for the position ye occupied.... – The Báb[637]

It was clear to the Báb that if the religious leaders and the rulers of His Day would embrace His Revelation and follow His guidance, they would be able to bring the masses of humanity into the loving embrace of the Cause of God. For instance, He wrote this to one of the Muslim religious leaders:

> Hadst thou faithfully obeyed the Decree of God, all the inhabitants of thy land would have followed thee, and would have themselves entered into the celestial Paradise, content with the good-pleasure of God for evermore. – The Báb[638]

Bahá'u'lláh later asserted that if the cruel and cowardly clerics of that period had not interposed themselves between the Báb and the people, all of Persia would have been won over to the new Revelation within two years.[639] If the religious leaders had led the way, vast numbers would have found their way to the truths enshrined in the Revelation.

Their lives would have been transformed. Their children would have followed them in God's teachings for the new era. As a result of such movement, the human race and countless generations yet unborn would have been spared centuries of strife, violence, corruption, hardship and sorrow. Alas, instead of advancing the Cause of God, instead of joyfully accepting promotion in the school of God, the rulers and the religious leaders stood in the way, thus propelling humanity towards a long road of disunity and suffering which continues to this day. So far, in human history, this tragic pattern of behavior has always been the way humanity, and particularly the established orthodoxy, has "welcomed" the advent of a new Divine Educator.

SOCIAL TEACHINGS ABOUT WOMEN, CHILDREN, HUMAN RIGHTS AND NATURE

The following is a sampling of some of the laws and ordinances of the Báb.

In His society, women were oppressed. The Báb advocated the removal of the hijáb (the veil over a women's face) and He eliminated the confinement of women to the home. The Báb allowed women and men to visit with one another and to speak with one another.[640] This assumes that in one another's company men and women should continue to practice good morality, chastity, and fidelity. The Báb told husbands who are traveling to inform their wives of how long they would be gone.[641] Men and women were to be equal in marriage and the marriage contract itself was to be contingent upon the willing consent of BOTH parties.[642] The practice of temporary marriages is prohibited.[643] The obligation for women to go on pilgrimage was lifted.[644]

In His society, children were not treated much better. The Báb granted children permission to occupy themselves with games and play, and to sit on chairs.[645] Corporal punishment was not totally outlawed, but it was restricted significantly. No physical punishment was permitted prior to the age of five. And after that, punishment was limited to five strokes, and those strokes had to be administered over clothes or covering and not on the bare body. The Báb favored giving children a secular education (such as arts, sciences, mathematics, etc.) in addition to giving them religious education. Education is an obligation so that the people will not have to depend on the religious leaders (the mullás).[646]

The Báb offered guidance on the rights of the individuals. It is important to safeguard the integrity and station of all human beings. Therefore, it is not permissible to confess one's sins to others, as it has been done in the past.[647] (This ruling doesn't stop one person from having a heartfelt conversation with another person concerning one's faults, rather it prohibits the ritualized abasement of someone by requiring them to confess to sins to receive religious blessings.) The hitting, injuring, beating, belittling, imprisonment or exile of someone from one's hometown is no longer permissible, and it is contrary to the divine teachings. One who commits such an act deprives himself from Divine pleasure and is obliged to repent and pay a fine.[648] Rejecting and repulsing one another has been a custom of the clerics. It is now emphatically forbidden.[649] Some people had imagined they were supposed to kill and mutilate the bodies of certain people. The Báb said this is totally banned. Anyone who does this must pay a penalty and will be deprived of Divine forgiveness.[650]

The Báb described certain public rights. He urged the followers to have a will in which they specified their inheritance wishes, and advised giving a portion to one's teacher.[651] The practice of begging (mendicancy) is prohibited.[652] Carrying weapons of war is prohibited.[653] The use of alcohol and addictive substances is prohibited, including the sale and purchase.[654] Congregational prayers are prohibited and ascending the pulpit is forbidden. Sitting on a chair is recommended instead.[655] Attending a feast as a means of promoting love and fellowship is commanded.[656] Considering either objects or animals as being inherently unclean has been removed from the law.[657] It is an obligation to answer letters and questions.[658]

Today, the Báb's ordinances about the environment would be considered enlightened for His time. One might consider Him to be one of the first modern environmentalists. The world is starting to catch up. But the Báb's ideas about refinement and purification were not limited to the physical environment. The Báb's view was more encompassing; all levels of reality, including the sanctuary of the human heart, must be purified. Nader Saiedi writes:

> ...the Báb consistently emphasizes the idea of purification. All levels of reality, from the material body to the human heart, must be purified. Natural resources must be preserved in the utmost purity. The Arabic Bayán prohibits the commodification of the natural elements of fire, air, water, and earth. The Báb turns the idea of the purity of water into the protection of the environment. In the Persian Bayán He writes:
>
> Nothing is more beloved before God than to keep water in a state of the utmost purity, to such an extent that if a believer should become aware that the glass of water he holdeth in his hand hath passed through any impure parts of the earth, he would be grieved. – The Báb
>
> In other words, it is implicitly necessary that all streams, lakes, and seas through which the water passes be clean. – Nader Saiedi[659]

The Báb had interesting comments to make about individuals singing. He revealed an entire treatise on the subject (called the Risálah Fi'l-Ghiná', Treatise on Singing) when He was asked a question about it in Isfahán. In His culture, at that time, singing was forbidden. What did He have to say? The following is paraphrased from the Persian by Husaini.

> The Báb said the true human (insán) is the one who takes assistance from his intelligence, and who with his heart and his action performs the Divine commandments. Such a human is the possessor of inner heart (fu'ád). Inner heart (fu'ád) is the place of the manifestation of intelligence ('aq'l) and the emanation of the heart (qalb).
>
> He said that the reason for the prohibition on singing, as it appears in the traditions from Muhammad, was due to the sinful and misguided way it was used. Otherwise, when music and singing does not result in sinful actions or overstep the bounds of the tree of reality (a reference to human nature and moderation) it should not be prohibited. He said that anytime a human being sings from the Divine aspect of

> human reality (rubúbíyyát-i-muú'dih, the lordship deposited within the human reality), it is praiseworthy in the presence of God and approved by men of knowledge and understanding. Any time man sings from his lower nature, it is forbidden. – Husaini[660]

This ordinance is interesting because it gives a particular insight into the Báb's view of Divine law. In secular society, the thing that is regulated is the outward behavior. Except in a few cases, such as mental incapacity or for crimes of hate, the inner mental state of the perpetrator is not considered the main issue. Look at the actions, either someone has committed a crime, or they haven't. But here, two people singing might in the eyes of God be judged quite differently. If the action is coming from a person's lower nature, God doesn't allow it, but if it is coming from the spiritual aspect of human nature, then it is approved. Thus, in relation to the law of God, a lesson can be learned – one's inner state matters when one acts.

These are just a sampling of the social teachings of the Báb.

THE AGE OF PROPHECY AND THE AGE OF FULFILLMENT

In July of 1950, Shoghi Effendi, then the Guardian of the Bahá'í Faith, its world leader, wrote to the Bahá'ís assembled under the dome of the Bahá'í House of Worship in Wilmette, IL on the occasion of the 100th anniversary of the martyrdom of the Báb. The cornerstone of the temple had been laid by 'Abdu'l-Bahá, Who had been born on the very night the Báb declared His mission to Mullá Husayn. The temple itself was three years away from its public dedication in 1953, which would be about 100 years after the birth of Bahá'u'lláh's revelation in the dark dungeon in Tihrán known as the Black Pit (Siyáh-Chál). The assembled Bahá'ís listened to the opening words of his message.

> Moved to share with assembled representatives of American Bahá'í Community gathered beneath the dome of the Most Holy House of Worship in the Bahá'í world, feelings of profound emotion evoked by this historic occasion of the world-wide commemoration of the First Centenary of the Martyrdom of the Blessed Báb, Prophet and Herald of the Faith of Bahá'u'lláh, Founder of the Dispensation marking the culmination of the six thousand year old Adamic Cycle, Inaugurator of the five thousand century Bahá'í Cycle. – Shoghi Effendi[661]

Shoghi Effendi managed in just thirty-one words to summarize accurately the exalted station and pivotal historic significance of the Báb and His mission.

First, the Báb is a Divine Educator, a Manifestation of God, and independent Prophet of God in His own standing. He came with His own revelation, His own revealed Words. He produced a vast body of Sacred Scripture, inspired His own followers, disclosed His own law, proclaimed His station, fulfilled the prophecies of His coming, unfurled His Banner, abrogated the previous Dispensation, laid down His own life, and launched a movement that shook to its core the very foundations of Persian society. As Shoghi Effendi elsewhere observed, He had wielded the scepter of independent prophethood to a degree unrivaled by any of the Messengers of the past. He was, in every way, an independent Messenger of God, the Promised One of His age.

Second, He was the Herald of a greater Divine Educator yet to come. Referring to this Promised One as Him Whom God shall make manifest, He did everything in His power to prepare His followers for the Advent of this next Manifestation of God, Whose appearance was to be soon, very soon. Although unknown at the time to all but a few, we know this great Figure to be Bahá'u'lláh, who in 1863 told the followers that He was the One Whom the Báb had foretold.

Third, 1844 had been a very significant year for another reason. As the Writings of the Faith have made clear, all recorded history up to that crucial turning point had been one long cycle of history, referred to as the Cycle of Prophecy (or the Adamic Cycle). The earliest Manifestation in that cycle had been Adam, and the final one had been Muhammad. With the appearance of the next Messenger after Muhammad, the Báb, the Dispensation of Muhammad had come to its termination point, and so had this long 6,000-year Cycle of Prophecy. The Báb explained:

> When God sent forth His Prophet Muhammad, on that day the termination of the prophetic cycle was foreordained in the knowledge of God. Yea, that promise hath indeed come true and the decree of God hath been accomplished as He hath ordained. Assuredly we are today living in the Days of God. These are the glorious days on the like of which the sun hath never risen in the past... These are the appointed days which ye have been yearningly awaiting in the past – the days of the advent of divine justice. Render ye thanks unto God, O ye concourse of believers.
> – The Báb[662]

At a later time, Bahá'u'lláh would also affirm the fact:

> The Prophetic Cycle hath verily ended. The Eternal Truth is now come.
> – Bahá'u'lláh[663]

And Shoghi Effendi also stated at a later time:

> The Faith of Bahá'u'lláh should indeed be regarded, if we wish to be faithful to the tremendous implications of its message, as the culmination of a cycle, the final stage in a series of successive, of preliminary and progressive revelations. These, beginning with Adam and ending with the Báb, have paved the way and anticipated with an ever-increasing emphasis the advent of that Day of Days in which He Who is the Promise of All Ages should be made manifest. – Shoghi Effendi[664]

The Dispensations of every Divine Educator known to history, up to and including Muhammad, had taken place within this long cycle of time known as the Prophetic Cycle. As the Báb had stated, when Muhammad's Dispensation ended with the Advent of the Báb's Dispensation, the ending of the 6,000-year Prophetic Cycle was likewise ordained. The Báb's Revelation stood at the crucial point in time when one long cycle of history was ended and a new one was begun.

Fourth, as stated, the Báb's appearance was also the beginning of the much longer Cycle of Fulfillment. The cycle of prophecy had been the childhood of humanity, the Cycle of Fulfillment would be its adulthood. During this new cycle, which would include the Dispensations of many, many Divine Educators yet to come, the undreamt of potentialities of the human race would be fully realized under the care and guidance of a gracious God.

As observed by Shoghi Effendi, this new Cycle of Fulfillment is destined to be much longer, running a minimum of 5,000 centuries or 500,000 years.[665] Bahá'u'lláh is the first of many Divine Educators yet to come within the cycle of fulfillment. The Báb stated:

> Likewise continue thou to ascend through one Revelation after another, knowing that thy progress in the Knowledge of God shall never come to an end, even as it can have no beginning. – The Báb[666]

And in this quote, which we studied earlier, the Báb made specific mention of a Manifestation to come after Bahá'u'lláh:

> In the time of the First Manifestation the Primal Will appeared in Adam; in the day of Noah It became known in Noah; in the day of Abraham in Him; and so in the day of Moses; the day of Jesus; the day of Muhammad, the Apostle of God; the day of the 'Point of the Bayan'; the day of Him Whom God shall make manifest; and the day of the One Who will appear after Him Whom God shall make manifest. – The Báb[667]

The Writings of the Faith state that Bahá'u'lláh's Dispensation will last no less than 1,000 years, and that it will be during this period that the Divine civilization and the Most Great Peace will be realized. After that time, when humanity has finally attained maturity, the real greatness of the human race will begin to become evident. The Writings offer only a hint, a glimpse, a peek at the ineffable destiny which God has in store for humanity.

> Then will the coming of age of the entire human race be proclaimed and celebrated by all the peoples and nations of the earth... Then will the banner of the Most Great Peace be hoisted... Then will the planet ... be made the footstool of His Throne on high, and acclaimed as the earthly heaven, capable of fulfilling that ineffable destiny fixed for it, from time immemorial, by the love and wisdom of its Creator. – Shoghi Effendi[668]

Some useful graphics are provided to help the reader visualize the significance of these changes to come.

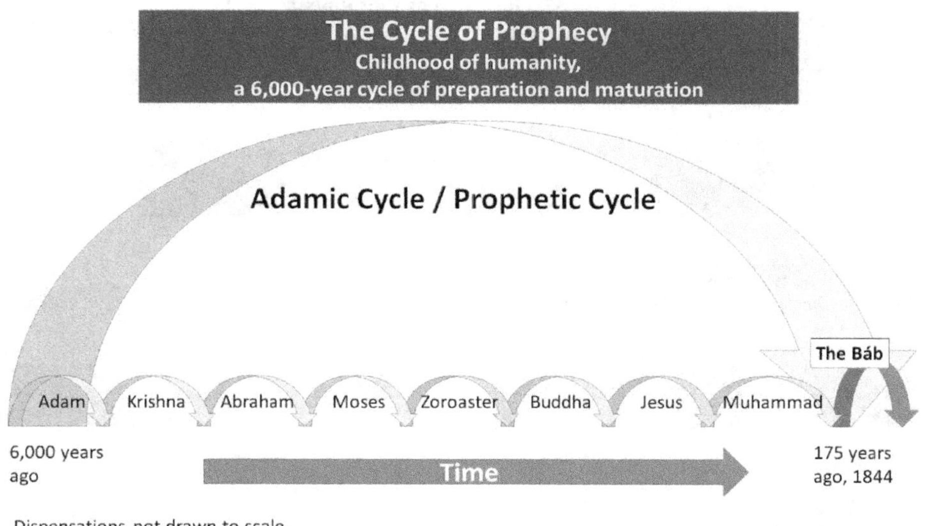

Figure 36 The Cycle of Prophecy

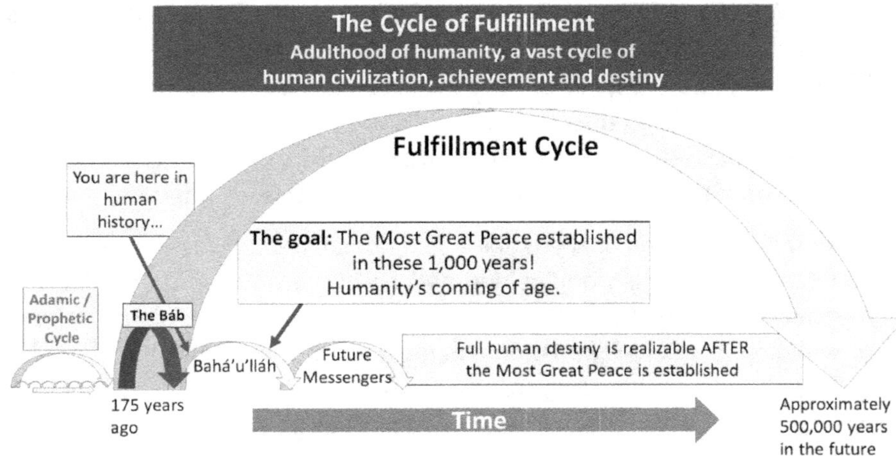

Dispensations not drawn to scale.

Figure 37 The Cycle of Fulfillment

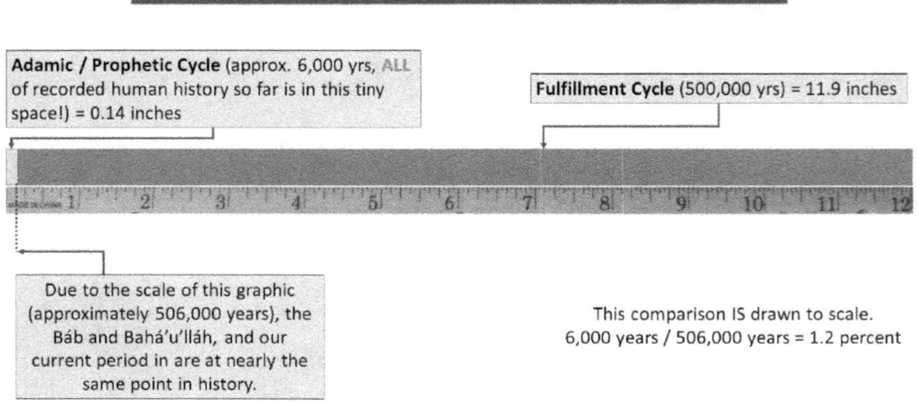

Figure 38 The Cycles of Prophecy and Fulfillment (drawn to scale)

CONCLUSIONS ABOUT THE BÁB'S TEACHINGS

When I pondered the implications of the Báb's teachings a flood of images came to mind. I began to wonder what human society would be like if, when people approached one another, they saw in each other only the workmanship of a great artist and felt only the desire to elevate however humbly the perfections of one another. I pictured everyone as a painting by one of the masters, DaVinci for example. In my mind I saw that everyone was really a walking version of a Mona Lisa. Every person was a demonstration of the beauty of the work of the master artist. And I realized it was my task to bring no sorrow to those works of art, rather joy, and to do whatever I could to help them to be even more beautiful, if possible.

Then I thought, every person is unique, so we would not all be the same painting. Each painting would be unique and different from all the others, as well as have some traits in common (after all, regardless of the subject matter, experts are able to identify a painting as a DaVinci, a Rembrandt, a Picasso, or a Van Gough). I imagined every person as a unique painting and all of us were painted by DaVinci. DaVinci never produced an ugly painting. All his works were beautiful. If everyone were a painting by him everyone would be beautiful as well.

Then I thought this panorama would be even more breathtaking and beautiful if I imagined that the Great Artist was not a mortal human being at all, but the Primal Will of God. I began to understand the Báb's teaching as suggesting that we must see in every person the signs of the handiwork of the Supreme Artist, the Creator of heaven and earth, and do all we can to help others to become even more beautiful and praiseworthy:

> ...every created thing, by its very nature, beareth evidence that it hath been fashioned by God... – The Báb[669]

If the inner reality of everyone and everything is a Divinely crafted work of art and a sign of God's revelation, and if Divine "art" is expressed in all created things through near infinite diversity, and if every person is bringing joy rather than sorrow, and striving to elevate every other person, then, it seems to me that devotion to God and appreciation, compassion, love and unity among individuals, races, and nations must be the eventual result once this truth becomes known, understood and practiced.

I once had a very meaningful conversation with Nader Saiedi. I was newly embarked on writing this book and he graciously arranged to give me a two-hour block of time, during which we had an in-depth discussion about the Báb and His teachings. (Since that time, Dr. Saiedi and I have become friends, and we were close collaborators working on the movie about the Báb, *The Gate: Dawn of the Bahá'í Faith*. Today, we have talked many times.)

On this first occasion we reviewed many aspects of the Báb's teachings, and then I asked a question: "When it is all summed up, whether He was explaining the transcendence of God, teaching the truth about progressive revelation, elucidating the Manifestations of God, encouraging the proper approach to worshipping God, elevating women, setting forth the highest ethical standards, or discussing our roles in society, the Báb was teaching everyone to unite through seeing the Beauty of God in all things and in all people and then to act accordingly. Is that right?"

He said, "Yes, I think so."

I replied, "Well, if that is right, is it correct to say that He laid the mystical and spiritual foundation for the oneness of mankind, which Bahá'u'lláh was soon going to teach?"

He said, "That's correct. The Báb laid the spiritual and logical foundation for the truth of the oneness of mankind, but He made no efforts to establish a civilization operating on that principle. He laid the foundation, but it was Bahá'u'lláh Who was the Architect Who actually taught us how to build it in the world."

After we parted company that day, I reflected deeply on what I had learned. Among other things, understanding what the Báb taught helped me to see more clearly that the Báb and Bahá'u'lláh really were Twin Manifestations of God. It was the Báb, in His role as an independent Manifestation of God and while under strict conditions of confinement and persecution, Who poured forth an abundant and near ceaseless stream of divine verses, Who set forth a number of the most cherished revolutionary social and spiritual principles Who built the community of followers that very soon would help launch Bahá'u'lláh's Revelation into the world. Thus, His dual roles of Divine Messenger and Forerunner are intimately intertwined.

The Báb was preparing mankind for a momentous graduation in the school of God. The Báb's Teachings were a crucial bridge between the Manifestations of God which preceded Him and Bahá'u'lláh, the Manifestation of God that was soon to appear. So vast was the Mission—the establishment of universal Peace among the peoples and nations of the world, that is, establishing the Kingdom of God on earth—that, mysteriously, in the Divine wisdom, two full Manifestations of God were required to bring about the coming of age of the human race. One followed the Other in a mysteriously short span of time and They embraced one another with perfect unity of purpose.

Appendix

OVERVIEW OF THE DIVINE CURRICULUM

The material in this appendix was first published in Volume 1 of the Divine Curriculum series as chapters 2 through 7. They are mostly unchanged in this volume (#5) of the series, with some corrections having been made. The section on Muhammad has undergone a revision and a slight expansion.

There is a very good reason for reprinting these chapters in each volume of the Divine Curriculum series. The entire approach of the Divine Curriculum series is to demonstrate that there is a bigger picture into which the world's major religions fit. Let's recall the initial question asked at the opening of chapter 1.

> Imagine the existence of a single, all-encompassing, ancient process that is leading all of creation toward an ultimate, meaningful purpose. If it existed, what would that process and that purpose be?
>
> Imagine the existence of a vast, all-embracing, Divinely conceived plan that is binding together the major religions of the world, advancing civilization, unfolding over time according to rational principles and guiding the human race. If it existed, towards what goal would that plan be striving?
>
> Imagine trying to prove the existence of such a plan. What evidence would you seek? And if you found evidence, how would you go about exploring it?
>
> The premise of this book series is that: All of creation is a classroom. The classroom is part of the universal school of God, which encompasses both the observable universe and the spiritual realms beyond.

> The Creator/Owner/Director of the school is Almighty God Himself. And the Teachers in the school are the Divine Educators.

The first volume of the series, subtitled Divine Design, gave an overview of the entire Divine Curriculum process based on a contextual view of history, the voices of the Divine Educators as found in Scriptures, the structure, premises and purposes which unify and animate the operations of the curriculum as a whole, and the progression of ideas and teachings through the ages, just like a curriculum. The subsequent volumes, including this one, are designed to give the reader a close-up view of each Divine Educator's heroic story as well as His contribution to the overall curriculum in the context of His own life and times, and in the context of the Divine Educators Who precede and follow Him.

But we do not want that close-up view to become myopic. Therefore, I am providing the overview chapters here so that the reader can maintain the overall view of the curriculum simultaneously. This will also help the reader understand how the specific Divine Educator he is reading about connects to and contributes to the overall curriculum that God has been pursuing for millenia.

Throughout the entire series, the approach taken is non-sectarian, non-partisan. That is, each Divine Educator covered in the series is appreciated as an Individual and in His place in the timeline of human history. No favoritism is shown.

There is another important, somewhat practical reason for including these overview chapters in each volume of the series. When you write a multi-volume series of books and you imagine your future readers encountering your work, you quickly realize they may not encounter the books in the order you have presented them. Most people who go to the library or shop online for a biography of Jesus, for example, may not at the moment of their searching also be interested in material on Muhammad or the Báb. So, my hope is that when the reader encounters this brief content on the other Divine Educators that the stories and the teachings They each brought will be so interesting that he or she will be inspired to go and read about all of the other great, historic Divine Educators! While, of course, I'd be thrilled if the reader goes and reads the other books in my series, in fact I will be satisfied and happy if they go and read any good and unbiased biographies of all of these magnificent Divine Educators. Either way, the mission of the series to promote the knowledge, understanding and appreciation of ALL of the Divine Educators will be served.

With all that said, I hope you enjoy these chapters and the overview of the last 4,000 years of Divine curriculum. As noted in chapter 1, we pick up the story of Divine education at the crucial moment in history when monotheism becomes established in a population bound together in a Covenant with God. We begin our overview of the story of Divine education with Abraham. We will then go on to Moses, Jesus, Muhammad, the Báb and Bahá'u'lláh, all great Divine Educators in the Abrahamic lineage.

ABRAHAM

Introduction

> Among the great Prophets was Abraham, Who, being an iconoclast and a Herald of the oneness of God, was banished from His native land. He founded a family upon which the blessing of God descended, and it was owing to this religious basis and ordination that the Abrahamic house progressed and advanced. Through the divine benediction noteworthy and luminous prophets issued from His lineage.... All this was due to the religion of God which this blessed lineage established and upheld. It is evident that throughout the history of Abraham and His posterity this was the source of their honor, advancement and civilization.—'Abdu'l-Bahá[670]

Abraham lived approximately 4,000 years ago. The Founders of four world religions—Moses (Judaism), Jesus (Christianity), Muhammad (Islám), the Báb and Bahá'u'lláh (the Bahá'í Faith)—were all descended from His lineage. Each one of those subsequent Founders said the God of Abraham was the Source of Their revelations as well.

Abraham was an iconoclast, the greatest man of His age, Who battled against the polytheistic and idolatrous norms of His society. He established the oneness and goodness of God and entered into an everlasting Covenant of faith with God. God promised Him that the land of Canaan would be given to Him and His posterity. God offered even greater promises:

> ...I will bless thee, and in multiplying I will multiply thy seed as the stars of the heaven, and as the sand which is upon the sea shore... And in thy seed shall all the nations of the earth be blessed... (Genesis 22:17-18)

Abraham succeeded in establishing monotheism because He did not impose His teachings by force; rather He embedded His God-given Covenant in a living and growing community of followers. He achieved this by demonstrating enduring faith and loyalty to God and by educating His family in a deeply-held *ethical monotheism*,[671] which is defined as a monotheism which regards the one God as the ultimate Source of all goodness. According to the ethical monotheism established by Abraham, God alone possesses the final authority to define the distinctions between true and false and good and evil. Ethical monotheism was in sharp contrast to the norms of His Day. By turning away from the norms of idolatry, polytheism and the brutal child sacrifice prevalent in His Day, Abraham's view of God also promoted the ethic that human life is sacred.

Not only is Abraham the Father of a multitude, He is also the Founder and Establisher of ethical monotheism. Literally, countless generations and billions of souls have been the beneficiaries of Abraham's life and work.

Information about Abraham is found in both Scripture and tradition. Scriptures that narrate episodes of His life or mention Him are the Old Testament (primarily the Book of Genesis), the New Testament, the Qur'án, and the Baha'i Writings. Considerable supplementary material is found in the records of Jewish and Islámic oral tradition.

Mission and teachings

From the beginning, Abraham was exceptional. According to Jewish legends, He was born in Ur, a province of the Babylonian empire. Under King Nimrod, religion was a state-owned enterprise based on idolatry and polytheism. Abraham's father, Terah, worked for Nimrod as a seller of idols.

When soothsayers told Nimrod that a great leader was about to be born who would oppose his religion and challenge his authority, Nimrod ordered the cruel massacre of many babies in the kingdom. Abraham's mother managed to conceal her pregnancy, however. After Abraham was born, His mother hid Him in a cave to save His life. In the cave, according to legend, the Angel Gabriel cared for Him and, after a long delay, Abraham was eventually reunited with His family.

Jewish tradition tells us that Abraham reasoned His way to the recognition of God. One day he looked at the sun and marveled at its light. Surely this must be God, He thought. Then the sun set below the horizon and He realized that if it could be taken away it couldn't be god. Next, he saw the moon. In a while, it too was taken away, so He knew it could not be God. Then He noticed the stars, but they were taken away by the morning light, so Abraham again reasoned that the stars could not be God. Abraham thought about the idols he saw everywhere around Him. He knew that, since they were fashioned by men, they could not be God either. Abraham thought, Whoever created all these things—the sun, the moon, the stars—though He cannot be seen, must be God.

This recognition inspired Abraham to campaign vehemently to His fellow citizens that idol worship is wrong and that only the one true God is worthy of worship. This became His great mission. Abraham's activities stirred the wrath of Nimrod who, according to legend, had Abraham catapulted into an enormous fire. By a miracle Abraham survived in the midst of the fire. Eventually Nimrod decided to banish Abraham from the kingdom.

Both the Bible and the Qur'án report that God and Abraham spoke to each other on many occasions. Because of these interactions, Abraham came to be known as the Friend of God. This was the first time God spoke to Abraham recorded in the Bible:

> Now the Lord had said unto Abram, Get thee out of thy country, and from thy kindred, and from thy father's house, unto a land that I will shew thee: And I will make of thee a great nation, and I will bless thee, and make thy name great; and thou shalt be a blessing: And I will bless them that bless thee, and curse him that curseth thee: and in thee shall all families of the earth be blessed. (Genesis 12:1-3)

Acting on faith, Abraham followed these instructions. He convinced His father, Terah, to come along on the journey, and also His nephew Lot, and his family. This was the beginning of the migration of the Hebrew people to their land of promise. Abraham and His group went west, stopping first in the town of Harran, in Upper Mesopotamia (southeastern Turkey today), where they stayed for five years. After Terah passed away, God again told Abraham to continue on to the land of Canaan, known today as Israel.

Abraham was a moral leader and well acquainted with the rulers of His Day. On occasion, Abraham showed brilliant capabilities as a military leader, such as when he rescued Lot after his nephew had been captured by hostile forces. Abraham became very prosperous with the years.

In their conversations, God explained more and more about the Covenant between Them and instituted the practice of circumcision for male members of the covenant family. The most important knowledge that Abraham received was absolute certainty that there is only one God, the Creator of all things, and that this one God is the Source of all goodness. This deeply held ethical monotheism, backed by His condemnation of idolatry, became the focus of Abraham's message to the people of His day.

All seemed well for Abraham except for one thing. God's promise that Abraham would be the Father of a multitude seemed increasingly unlikely because Abraham and His wife, Sarah, still had no children. Sarah was elderly and barren. Eventually, Sarah suggested that Abraham take her maidservant, Hagar, as His concubine and conceive a child with her, which He did, naming His first-born son Ishmael. Abraham raised Ishmael to believe in the one Creator God, and Ishmael was circumcised as God had commanded.

At last God told Abraham that the time had come for Sarah to have a child. Sarah laughed at this, but soon Isaac, the long-awaited child of promise, was born. Like his older brother, Isaac was also raised to know and love God.

The Bible records God's promise that His Covenant would continue with Isaac, but years later God made a startling announcement:

> Some time later God tested Abraham. He said to him, "Abraham!" "Here I am," he replied. Then God said, "Take your son, your only son, whom you love—Isaac—and go to the region of Moriah. Sacrifice him there as a burnt offering on a mountain I will show you." Early the next morning Abraham got up and loaded his donkey... (Genesis 22:1-3)[672]

The Bible clearly says the child to be sacrificed was Isaac. By contrast, Muslim scholars have stated that the child to be sacrificed was actually Ishmael who was, after all, the first-born son and also much loved by Abraham. Despite these differences, the Bible and the Qur'án, and also Jewish traditions, depict the son as a willing (even if not entirely knowing) participant in the drama about to unfold. The Qur'án speaks especially well of this son to be sacrificed. In dialogue with his Father, the Qur'án reports that he offered his Father only words of encouragement and strength:

> O my father! do as thou art commanded: thou will find me, if God so wills, one practicing patience and constancy! (Qur'án 37:102-106)

After they arrived at the mountain where the sacrifice was to take place, Abraham and his son prepared the site. Abraham placed His son on an altar, bound him, and then raised a knife. Literally at the last second an angel twice called out to Abraham. Abraham answered, "Here am I!", and then the angel declared:

> Do not lay a hand on the boy… Now I know that you fear God, because you have not withheld from me your son, your only son. (Genesis 22:12)

Abraham stopped. A ram was found tangled in nearby bushes and was sacrificed to God in place of Abraham's son.

To put it mildly, the meaning of this story has been a source of heart-rending discussion and controversy for centuries. A discussion of the various interpretations is presented in Volume 2 of this series.

For the present, let one observation suffice. In the centuries after Abraham, His followers, and the followers of all the monotheistic Faiths in the Abrahamic lineage, abandoned and outlawed the practice of child sacrifice so prevalent in Abraham's time. Hence, it is no exaggeration to say, that at least by example, Abraham's deeply held ethical monotheism began with an affirmation of the sacredness of human life.

After Abraham

Curiously, the Bible doesn't record any promises by Abraham of a future Divine Educator to appear after Him. It does, however, cite the final words of Joseph, the highly distinguished great grandson of Abraham.

> And Joseph said unto his brethren, I die: and God will surely visit you, and bring you out of this land unto the land which he sware to Abraham, to Isaac, and to Jacob. And Joseph took an oath of the children of Israel, saying, God will surely visit you, and ye shall carry up my bones from hence. (Genesis 50:24-25)

Thus, according to Joseph's prophecy, in due time a great Divine Deliverer would come to the Hebrews in Egypt, and He would bring them back to the land promised to them through the Covenant that God had made with their ancestor Abraham. In time, Moses fulfilled this promise.

The stature of Abraham

If ethical monotheism is compared to a tree, Abraham was its planter and first cultivator. He was the first to root it in the soil of human consciousness. He gave His followers the knowledge of one God and identified Him as the Source of all goodness in creation. Abraham succeeded in binding His people to God through an everlasting Covenant, affirmed the sacredness of human life, set forth boundaries of good behavior, and handed down to His ever-expanding lineage a priceless heritage of knowing, loving, and choosing God. He was indeed a wondrous Divine Educator.

MOSES

Introduction

> Among the revelators of the law of God was Moses. ...He promulgated the divine teachings and liberated a nation from the lowest condition of

> degradation and bondage. The people of Israel were ignorant, lowly, debased in morals – a race of slaves under burdensome oppression. Moses led them out of captivity and brought them to the Holy Land. He educated and disciplined them, established among them the foundations of material and divine civilization. Through the education of Moses these ignorant people attained an advanced degree of power and prestige, culminating in the glory of the reign of Solomon... It is evident, therefore, that Moses was an Educator and Teacher...—'Abdu'l-Bahá[673]

Moses lived approximately 3,300 years ago. He was descended from Abraham through His wife Sarah and their son Isaac. The Pharaoh of Egypt tried to kill Moses when He was a baby, just as Nimrod had attempted to kill Abraham hundreds of years earlier. His revelation, Moses said, was from the "the God of Abraham". An iconoclast like Abraham, He vehemently forbade His people from the practice of idolatry or polytheism still prevalent in His Day. He affirmed the oneness and goodness of God—that is, ethical monotheism—as Abraham had done.

Following a historic confrontation with Pharaoh in Egypt, He brought His people, the Israelites, out of cruel bondage from that land. When pursued by Pharaoh's army, and when all seemed lost, God saved the Israelites by miraculously parting the Red Sea and drowning the Egyptian army that was pursuing them. The Israelites celebrated their deliverance after the Egyptians were defeated.

> And Israel saw that great work which the Lord did upon the Egyptians: and the people feared the Lord, and believed the Lord, and his servant Moses. (Exodus 14:30-31)

According to the Bible, the Israelites were a rebellious and disobedient people in desperate need of Divine discipline and education. They wandered in the wilderness for forty years—long enough for a younger and more receptive generation to arise.

Moses brought the Israelites to Mt. Sinai and revealed to them the Ten Commandments and other laws of God. Moses helped the people re-establish their Covenant with God. Although He successfully brought the people to the Promised Land, Moses Himself did not enter. Before dying at age 120, He handed leadership over to Joshua, who led the Israelites into the lands God had given them.

Moses succeeded in embedding the entire construct of Divine law and Covenant into an ever-expanding, living and growing population. The Law infused a new spirit into the Israelites who, with all their shortcomings, became spiritually and socially transformed by its influence. Moses was the Divine Educator Who promoted the oneness and goodness of God, established of the Law of God, and revealed an enduring Covenant between God and His people. Literally, countless generations and billions of souls have been the beneficiaries of Moses' life and work.

Information about Moses is found in both Scripture and tradition. Scriptures that mention Him are the Old Testament, the New Testament, the Qur'án and the Baha'i Writings. Considerable supplementary material is found in the records of Jewish and Islámic oral tradition.

Mission and teachings

Moses revealed God's Covenant to the Israelites at Mt. Sinai. This Covenant was in no sense between equals. God, the Supreme Monarch, gave the Covenant on His own terms and was free to terminate it at any time if the Israelites didn't abide by it. God did not need the adoration of the Israelites; His stated objective was the good of the Israelite people and, eventually, the good of all mankind. God promised that if they would obey Him and keep His covenant, they would become a "holy nation", a unique instrument in His Divine plan (Exodus 19:5).

> Moses asked the people to affirm their loyalty to God: And all the people answered together, and said, All that the Lord hath spoken we will do. (Exodus 19:3-11)

Moses went up to the summit of Mt. Sinai to receive the Ten Commandments, the core of His Law, which God had written on tablets of stone. (Exodus 20:1-17) While He was on the mountaintop, in the famous incident of the Golden Calf, the people below indulged in an orgy of idolatry and debauchery. After coming down from the mountain Moses displayed an intense anger on behalf of God, smashing the precious stone tablets. Many were punished, a few were pardoned, and the people promised again to be good.

Moses ascended the mountain once more to "make atonement for your sin" and to receive from God a second set of stone tablets. (Exodus 32:30) While there, He was allowed to behold the glory of the Lord. This led to an astonishing result:

> When Moses came down from Mount Sinai with the two tablets of the Testimony in his hands, he was not aware that his face was radiant because he had spoken with the Lord. (Exodus 34:27-29)[674]

Moses commanded the Israelites to construct the Ark of the Covenant, an ornate gold-covered box to serve as the permanent repository of the stone tablets and the Torah[675] which the Israelites carried with them on their journeys. In later times, the Ark would be placed within the 'holy of holies' in the Temple in Jerusalem.

Mosaic Law centralized the worship of God around the Ark of the Covenant. The Israelites would come there to worship God, led by the priests whom Moses had appointed. Mosaic Law continued the practice of circumcision, the mark of the Covenant that all male Israelites exhibited, and established the law of the Sabbath, a day of rest after six days of working.

Mosaic Law also taught a special brand of justice. Though harsh sounding today, in fact it softened the way justice was done.

> ...thou shalt give life for life, eye for eye, tooth for tooth, hand for hand, foot for foot, burning for burning, wound for wound, stripe for stripe. (Exodus 21:23-25)

This was a new conception of justice—*proportionality*. Today, we take this concept for granted, but in the context of the times Mosaic Law helped mankind understand that punishment must always fit the crime.

Mosaic Law emphasized love and loyalty. Loyalty to God meant not worshipping idols or giving respect to any other gods.

> Thou shalt not bow down thyself to them, nor serve them: for I the Lord thy God am a jealous God... (Exodus 20:5)

The term "jealous God" may seem off-putting at first, but one should remember what God's jealousy was really about. This was not a petty emotion. Far from it. This was an expression of God's authority as the Creator expressed in language the people could understand. It demanded that the Israelites abandon the wicked and "detestable" practices associated with other gods and idolatry—such as child sacrifice, prostitution and corruption (Deut. 18:9-13)—"lest there be among you a root bearing poisonous and bitter fruit". (Deut. 29)[676] God planned on working His vast redemptive scheme for all of mankind through this tiny "chosen" population.

Within the Covenant, God asked for an exclusive relationship. So, Mosaic Law asked the Israelites to know God, to love God, and to choose God:

> Hear, O Israel: The Lord our God is one Lord: And thou shalt love the Lord thy God with all thine heart, and with all thy soul, and with all thy might. (Deut. 6:4-5)

> Know therefore that the Lord thy God, he is God, the faithful God, which keepeth covenant and mercy with them that love him and keep his commandments to a thousand generations... (Deut. 7:9)[677]

This love of God could also be expressed by loving other people:

> ...thou shalt love thy neighbour as thyself... (Leviticus 19:18)

Extraordinarily, this love was extended to strangers and foreigners:

> ...the stranger that dwelleth with you shall be unto you as one born among you, and thou shalt love him as thyself... (Leviticus 19:33-34)

As mentioned, through Abraham parents learned to value their children and not sacrifice them as burnt offerings in misguided acts of piety. Moses made that teaching explicit and went even further. Now the children were commanded to reciprocate: "Honor thy mother and father". Loving family relationships were thus made sacred in two directions.

The Israelites were held to a high standard of conduct. If they obeyed the Covenant, they would have the Lord's blessings and prosper. If they disobeyed, God's blessings would be withdrawn and, as punishment, God would ultimately scatter them among the nations. (Deut. 4:23-27. See also Deut. 11:26-28; 30:19 - 31:1). Ultimately, it was their choice.

Previously, God had initiated His Covenant with an individual, Abraham, and His family, whose posterity had indeed multiplied with time. Now, with Moses, the descendants of Abraham had grown to about 600,000, so the scope of God's Covenant had also expanded to the size of a small but growing nation.

According to Moses, God's personality is intense and vital, not impersonal, not a mere force of nature. Nature itself was created by Him! He is not an idol made by man, rather the Maker of all things. The God of Moses is powerful and active in history. He cares intensely about the well-being of His chosen people. The God of Moses comes to the rescue and leads His people to the Promised Land. His Law and teachings are the Source of justice, righteousness and virtue in this life. God is both loving and stern. God expected the children of Israel to keep their Covenant with Him and He rewarded, punished, or forgave them as circumstances required. This God, the One God, the God of Abraham and Moses, was truly a Force to be reckoned with.

All of this, and much more, was in the law. God's human children, especially those who were bound to Him in a Sacred Covenant, must, through conscious obedience to the law, come to know and love the God Who directed their destiny.

After Moses

Moses led the Israelites through the desert for forty years and then handed leadership over to Joshua. Moses died at the age of 120, alone with His God.

God had told Abraham's family of the coming of a future Deliverer, a prophecy which Moses fulfilled. In turn, Moses prophesied the coming of another great Revealer of God's Word:

> The Lord thy God will raise up unto thee a Prophet from the midst of thee, of thy brethren, like unto me; unto him ye shall hearken... (Deut. 18:15)

Later, the lesser prophets of Israel would say much more about this Promised One. He would be a Messiah, a Savior, an Anointed One and a Suffering Servant. In due time, Jesus would fulfill these prophecies and claim "he wrote of me". (John 5:46)

The stature of Moses

Israel's spiritual, social, economic, and political development continued in the centuries after Moses. The Israelites achieved a high level of civilization as a result of the powerful spiritual impulse which Moses, their Divine Educator, imparted to them.

> ...in every noble human attribute—learning, stability, determination, courage, honor, generosity—this people came to surpass all the nations of the earth... and even foreign peoples wishing to praise a man would say that he was like an Israelite.—'Abdu'l-Bahá[678]

The Divine Educators Who appeared after Moses all hailed His greatness. Jesus associated Himself with Moses:

> ...had ye believed Moses, ye would have believed me, for he wrote of me... (John 5:46)

Muhammad mentioned Moses 154 times in the Qur'an, calling Him "a man of purity" and an "Apostle" (e.g. Qur'án 19:52). The Báb called Him a Manifestation of the Primal Will of God. And Bahá'u'lláh said that Moses had been armed "with the rod of celestial dominion" and that He "shone forth from the Sinai of light upon the world".[679]

Abraham laid the foundation of the Divine curriculum and Moses built on it. The monotheism established by Abraham provided Moses the authority to bring about the deliverance of the Israelites from their brutal state of bondage, establish the Divine Presence among them, inaugurate the Covenant, promulgate the Law, assert a new social order, establish Divine justice, increase human freedom and dignity, command the unyielding rejection of polytheism and idolatry and give the Promised Land to the Israelites as an inheritance.

Moses schooled the Israelites in Divine discipline. But even with all their shortcomings the Israelites achieved an epic leap forward in human civilization. Thanks to Moses, the Will of God was experienced through the Law of God, and the Law of God was now embedded in a living and growing population bound together in a renewed, expanded and sacred Covenant with God.

Without a doubt, Moses succeeded brilliantly as a Divine Educator. He advanced His people in the great School of God. Despite their shortcomings, the Israelites played their part in history by becoming the first distinct people to invest their entire future in a monogamous relationship with the one God, the God of Abraham, the God Moses had taught them to obey and love.

JESUS

Introduction

> Jesus Christ was an Educator of humanity. His teachings were altruistic; His bestowal, universal. He taught mankind by the power of the Holy Spirit and not through human agency… Galen, the Greek physician and philosopher who lived in the second century… [said:] "There are certain people among us, followers of Jesus, the Nazarene, who was killed in Jerusalem. These people are truly imbued with moral principles which are the envy of philosophers. They believe in God and fear Him. They have hopes in His favors; therefore, they shun all unworthy deeds and actions and incline to praiseworthy ethics and morals. Day and night they strive that their deeds may be commendable and that they may contribute to the welfare of humanity… These people have praiseworthy morals, even though they may be illiterate." The purpose of this is to show that the holy Manifestations of God, the divine Prophets, are the first Teachers of the human race. They are universal Educators, and the fundamental principles they have laid down are the causes and factors of the advancement of nations… If you reflect upon the essential teachings of Jesus, you will realize that they are the light of the world.–'Abdu'l-Bahá[680]

Jesus lived approximately 2,000 years ago in the Galilee region of ancient Palestine, which at that time was a province on the eastern edge of the Roman Empire. He was descended from Abraham, through His wife Sarah, and their son Isaac. Jesus affirmed that He had been sent into the world by the God of Abraham and Moses. As with Abraham and Moses, the life of baby Jesus was threatened, this time by the Roman leader Herod.

According to the New Testament, Jesus gathered a core group of disciples who traveled with Him as He went from town to town preaching His message in the Galilee region of northern Palestine (in Israel today). Along the way, He performed healings and miracles. In His teaching, He emphasized the coming of the Kingdom of God, the spiritual greatness of the afterlife, the opportunity for every true believer to partake of that afterlife, and the necessity of practicing spiritual virtues such as faith, love, mercy, charity, humility, obedience and forgiveness.

At a time when the Jews were expecting their Savior to rescue them from Roman oppression, Jesus acted contrary to these expectations and said:

> My kingdom is not of this world. (John 18:36)

Instead, Jesus cast Himself as the Suffering Servant destined to suffer for the sins of mankind as prophesied in the book of Isaiah.

An iconoclastic and revolutionary tone was present, however, in Jesus' words and deeds. For example: He urged the people to turn away from corrupt and worldly practices, and from sin and temptation; denounced the corruption of the Jerusalem Temple and foretold its destruction; and counseled people to pay more attention to the spirit of the Law than the letter of it. He was offended by the hypocrisy of the Jewish leaders of His day and rejected their rigid interpretation and enforcement of Mosaic Law. Contrary to what some Christians may have heard, Jesus was an observant Jew and had high respect for the Laws of Moses.

While many in the public eagerly embraced Jesus, He did encounter fierce opposition from the religious leaders whom He criticized. During the climactic final week of His life, the religious leaders plotted His demise in collaboration with the Roman authorities aided by a traitor from among His disciples. After what can only be described as a sham of a trial, Jesus was condemned, tortured and crucified. The New Testament records that three days after His execution, His body was missing from the tomb where it had been laid to rest. The New Testament reports that Jesus was seen alive by many people during the following forty days. This event, called the Resurrection of Jesus, was regarded by subsequent generations as the signal event of the Christian Faith. It restored the faith and courage of His followers, convinced them of His ability to conquer death (as they then understood it), and established His legitimacy as the Savior of mankind. This realization led to the founding of the Church.

Jesus succeeded brilliantly as a Divine Educator. He advanced humanity—Jew and gentile alike—in the great school of God. His curriculum unveiled both the love of God and His Kingdom, and further intensified humanity's potential to intimately know and love the Creator. Jesus obviously saw Himself as operating within the same continuity of Divine Revelation as Abraham and Moses, but also brought a fuller revelation. He taught a radical ethical monotheism which emphasized not only the oneness and goodness of God, but also the greatness of His love. Literally, countless generations and billions of souls have been the beneficiaries of Jesus' life and work.

Information about Jesus is found in both Scripture and tradition. Scriptures that narrate episodes of His life or mention Him are the New Testament, the Qur'án and the Baha'i Writings. Supplementary material is found in the records of Islámic oral tradition.

Mission and teachings

The mission of Jesus began when He went to see His famous cousin, John the Baptist, who was baptizing people in the Jordan River. John was telling the people:

> Repent ye: for the kingdom of heaven is at hand. (Matthew 3:2)

The people responded in great numbers, and one day Jesus went to be baptized.

> As soon as Jesus was baptized, he went up out of the water. At that moment heaven was opened, and he saw the Spirit of God descending like a dove and lighting on him. And a voice from heaven said, 'This is my Son, whom I love; with him I am well pleased.' (Matthew 3:16-17)[681]

This moment marked the beginning of Jesus' mission. Immediately after, Jesus went into the wilderness for forty days, where the Bible says He faced numerous temptations from the devil. (Matthew 4:1) After this, Jesus began teaching, continuing the proclamation of the Kingdom:

> Repent: for the kingdom of heaven is at hand. (Matthew 4:17)

For both men, there was an urgent need for individuals to repent of their sins and reform their character or else risk being deprived of the Kingdom. Thus, the first and most vital core of Jesus' message was the proclamation of the Kingdom of God.

The disciples Jesus attracted were simple folk, mainly fishermen. Jesus went into the synagogues in His home town, Nazareth, and announced that He was the Promised One all were waiting for.

> ...The Spirit of the Lord is on me, because he has anointed me to preach good news to the poor... (Luke 4:17-21)[682]

The people in the synagogue could only see the carpenter's son they had known for three decades. They chased Him away.

The Kingdom of God was the central focus of Jesus' mission. It was not a single concept, but rather an interwoven fabric of teachings.

- When Jesus spoke of the Kingdom being *amidst the human world*, and of it being near at hand, He was referring to His own Divine Presence in the world. He understood His own Sonship and Divinity and sought to help people understand their exceptional bounty of being alive in the days when He was present among them. To help people understand, He spoke of Himself as both Son of Man and Son of God.
- When Jesus spoke of the Kingdom being *above the human world*, He radically challenged current conceptions of the afterlife. In His day, there was no knowledge of the sun as a star and no awareness of the earth as a planet revolving around the sun. They thought God lived above the sky. They thought that hell (Sheol in Hebrew, Hades in Greek) was below the ground. People didn't go to be with God above the sky when they died; instead, with the rare exceptions of a few select heroes, it was thought that everyone went down to hell. Heaven was up, beyond the sky, and hell was down, beneath the earth. Life in Sheol was imagined to be exceedingly dismal, eternally devoid of vitality, light, joy or hope. Individuals in Sheol were like ghosts. In stark contrast, Jesus "was preaching something new to his culture."[683] Jesus taught that all true believers could avoid the dark emptiness of Sheol! He offered a bright, joyful, inviting, and inclusive portrayal of the afterlife. He offered good news but that hopeful message collided head-on with what people thought they knew about the life beyond.
- When Jesus spoke of the Kingdom of God being *below the heavenly world*, He made it clear that eventually life on earth should also become heavenly:

> Thy kingdom come, Thy will be done in earth, as it is in heaven. (Matthew 6:10)

- According to Bible scholars Spivey and Smith, while "Jesus claims that the kingdom is inaugurated with his ministry, it is in the process of being realized; but it has not yet fully come, for its completion is still in the future."[684]
- When Jesus said *the Kingdom is within* (Luke 17:20), He revealed that spiritual qualities—such as obeying God's will, faith, righteousness, love, mercy, forgiveness, innocence, purity, and humility—are crucial entrance requirements for the Kingdom! One can perform all the ritual offerings one likes, He explained, but getting into heaven is not possible without these inner Divine virtues. There are many passages stipulating these action-oriented *entrance requirements*.

> Not everyone who says to Me, 'Lord, Lord,' shall enter the kingdom of heaven, but he who does the will of My Father in heaven. (Matthew 7:21)

> For I say to you, that unless your righteousness exceeds the righteousness of the scribes and Pharisees, you will by no means enter the kingdom of heaven. (Matthew 20:5)

> The first of all the commandments is, Hear, O Israel; The Lord our God is one Lord: And thou shalt love the Lord thy God with all thy heart, and with all thy soul, and with all thy mind, and with all thy strength: this is the first commandment. And the second is like, namely this, Thou shalt love thy neighbour as thyself. There is none other commandment greater than these. (Mark 12:29-31)

The Jews mainly thought that the Kingdom of God meant overthrowing the oppressive Roman regime and replacing it with a newly established, politically independent Jewish state. For them, the Kingdom was not within—it was in the world, accomplished by overthrowing oppressive governments and establishing new ones. But Jesus kept explaining:

> My kingdom is not of this world. (John 18:36)

Jesus understood that the Jewish people in the past had been given their own God-sponsored political kingdom and that, despite their achievements, it had crumbled because of corruption, fratricidal power struggles and disloyalty to God's Covenant. He also knew that a violent military struggle against Rome would leave the Jews in a worse condition spiritually and materially. Jesus understood that the real building blocks of the Kingdom of God were the hearts of the people. Put simply, *make better people and you make a better kingdom.* So, Jesus taught virtues, such as inner purity, righteousness, Divine love, mercy and forgiveness. He showed people how to be better from the inside out. Therefore, if you want God's Kingdom "in earth, as it is in heaven" (Luke 11:2), He urged people to learn that "the kingdom of God is within you" (Luke 17:20).

Jesus referred to God as "My Father". He invited His followers to share in closeness with God by asking them to become "sons of God" too. (John 1:12-13) Believing in Him is necessary for salvation, He said, and it was the duty of everyone to obey His teachings, forgive others, love God, love one's neighbor and even love your enemy. Worshipping God "in spirit and in truth" (John 4:24) and altering one's behavior accordingly are essential entrance requirements for attaining to God's Kingdom.

Jesus embraced a variety of titles during His ministry—Son of Man, Son of God, Rabbi and Prophet among them.[685]

After Jesus

Jesus foretold that He would come again at the end of the age to finish the work of establishing God's Kingdom on earth. On the one hand, He spoke of His return using first person language:

> ...I go away, and come again unto you... (John 14:28)

On the other hand, He also spoke of His return using third person language:

> Nevertheless I tell you the truth; It is expedient for you that I go away: for if I go not away, the Comforter will not come unto you; but if I depart, I will send him unto you... I have yet many things to say unto you, but ye cannot bear them now. Howbeit when he, the Spirit of truth, is come, he will guide you into all truth: for he shall not speak of himself; but whatsoever he shall hear, that shall he speak: and he will shew you things to come. (John 16:7-13, see also John 14:16-17; 14:26; 15:26)

Bahá'u'lláh explained that both the first and third person viewpoints are valid, and ultimately indicative of the oneness of the Divine Educators. On one level, The Divine Educators are all Manifestations of the same Spirit; on another level, They are unique Individuals:

...He the Revealer of the unseen Beauty [Jesus], addressing one day His disciples, referred unto His passing, and, kindling in their hearts the fire of bereavement, said unto them: 'I go away and come again unto you.' And in another place He said: 'I go and another will come Who will tell you all that I have not told you, and will fulfil all that I have said.' Both these sayings have but one meaning, were you to ponder upon the Manifestations of the Unity of God with divine insight.—Bahá'u'lláh[686]

Many early Christians believed the return of Christ would occur within their lifetimes. But as the years passed, Christians recognized the return was to be a long-delayed event.

The next Divine Educator, Muhammad, Who would also be a descendant of Abraham, would not appear until almost 580 years later, in the seventh century. Coming from an unexpected place, the Arabian Desert, Muhammad would claim in 610 AD to be the fulfillment of the prophecies of Jesus recorded in the Bible. The Qur'án would say:

And when Jesus son of Mary said: O Children of Israel! Lo! I am the messenger of God unto you, confirming that which was (revealed) before me in the Torah, and bringing good tidings of a messenger who cometh after me... (Qur'án 61:6)[687]

Just as Jesus had been rejected by the religious leaders of His Day, in the seventh century Muhammad would also suffer greatly and face rejection by the religious leaders. Regardless of the differing viewpoints concerning the meaning of certain specific prophecies, the essential point is that Jesus gave numerous indications of the coming of future Divine Educators.

The stature of Jesus

Through Abraham, the oneness of God had been embedded in a rapidly growing family that was bound to God in a sacred Covenant. Through Moses, the law of God had been embedded in a single people, the Israelites, who were bound to God and each other in a sacred Covenant. Now, with Jesus, the love of God and the knowledge of the Kingdom was intensified and embedded in many peoples bound to God in a renewed Covenant:

Is God the God of Jews only? Is he not the God of Gentiles too? Yes, of Gentiles too, since there is only one God... (Romans 3:29; see also Romans 10:12)[688]

Vast numbers embraced the new Covenant with God. When Christ appeared...

> He united varying and divergent creeds and warring people of His time. He brought together Greeks and Romans, reconciled Egyptians and Assyrians, Chaldeans and Phoenicians. Christ established unity and agreement among people of these hostile and warring nations.—'Abdu'l-Bahá[689]

Taken together, the teachings, works, sacrifice and resurrection of Jesus all pointed the way to a complete cleansing of the human being. Those who followed His way would, in this world and in the next, know God, love God, and choose God with far more clarity, intimacy and intensity than they had ever thought possible. Jesus had come as the Suffering Servant. Although He died as a sacrifice for the sins of humanity, even His brutal crucifixion was no impediment to His world-shaping achievements.

Leading no army, though opposed by the determined powers of His age, and working through the agency of his disciples, Jesus performed the greatest miracle of all. His Cause did triumph, and idolatry and polytheism suffered irreversible setbacks. The knowledge of the God of Abraham and Moses burst forth from its regional limitations, the love of the one true God took root in the hearts of millions, the fear of death was overcome, the glories of an abundant afterlife were opened up to the teeming masses, and the seeds of the Kingdom were securely planted. Literally billions of souls were saved, the standards of human virtue were vastly elevated, multitudes were brought closer to the very purpose which underlay their existence, and in due time because of the seeds that He had sown, the Kingdom of God would definitely be realized in earth as it is in heaven. Without a doubt, Jesus is a stunningly powerful Figure in human history, a brilliant Divine Educator.

MUHAMMAD

Separating the Faith of Muhammad from the ideology of the terrorists

This book is being made ready for publication in September of 2019, exactly eighteen years after the September 11, 2001 terrorist attacks in New York, Washington, D.C., and Pennsylvania. Anyone who was aware of the news at that time remembers vividly the horror and shock of those days. Most people in the West prior to that day gave little thought to the Islámic religion, which the terrorists claimed as the inspiration for the attacks. But that changed quickly. Nader Saiedi has commented on the sudden impact of those days on the psyche of most Americans and other Westerners from around the world:

> Before September 11, 2001, few could have imagined that one of the effects of modern Western technological advancement would be the dramatic and violent intrusion, upon the Western world, of the seemingly remote and arcane internal conflicts of Islam. The events of September 11 placed Islám at the center of Western cultural and political discourse as the West struggles to make sense of what seems a bewildering, medieval mindset centering around holy war or jihad as a religious duty. A series of troubling but crucial questions have come to the fore: Is religion, particularly Islam, ultimately only conducive to conflict and hatred? Is the "clash of civilizations" inevitable? What went wrong in the Middle East's encounter with modernity?... Does any possibility exist for genuine reconciliation, mutual respect, and peace among the religions of the world? – Nader Saiedi[690]

At that time, millions of ordinary Muslims were living their everyday lives as either citizens or residents in America. Following the attacks, they found themselves in an uncomfortable position. On the one hand, these violent, cruel and monstrous terrorists claimed they were fighting in the name of Islám. On the other hand, the ordinary peace-loving Muslim citizens saw in the words and deeds of the terrorists an utterly unrecognizable version of the religion they themselves were following. They looked at the terrorists and knew with certainty that Muhammad, if He were alive today, would condemn what they do. Equally distressing, they were put on the defensive in the media, in their houses of worship, at work, at school and perhaps even in their own families. Now, in the heated fervor of public debate – in order to be accepted members of society – they were called upon to defend Islám and/or to denounce the terrorists. In the tribulation of those days, in some instances, they even found that some people they knew now suspected them of secretly being terrorists too, or at least sympathizers. These anguished, decent citizens yearned to disown and distance themselves from the violent and militant terrorists.

At the same time, there was and continues to be a blizzard of media coverage that seems to fan the flames of hatred, confusion and misunderstanding. Many pundits, preachers and politicians do not clarify the distinction between the ideology of the terrorists and the real teachings of Muhammad Himself. They seem eager to treat Islám as if the entire religion is extremist. Or perhaps they are just lazy.

Many people simply absorb the images and the rhetoric swirling about them. Others find it hard to accept that a world religion with 1.6 billion adherents can be as evil, false and violent as "the Islám" that is depicted in mass media and pulpits. Something must be wrong with this picture, they think. But what? Most don't know where to turn for the truth. As a result, they are confused, even oppressed, by the whole issue:

> What 'oppression' is more grievous than that a soul seeking the truth, and wishing to attain unto the knowledge of God, should know not where to go for it and from whom to seek it?—Bahá'u'lláh[691]

Of course, some individuals do search for the truth. They look for unbiased, reputable sources. They are inclined to believe that the terrorists are not real Muslims, but they don't know how to back up that claim if anyone challenges them. They know that merely reciting the slogan that "Islám is a religion of peace" will inevitably fall on deaf ears.

The solution, in my opinion, is to understand the terrorists' movement *in itself*, to pierce its misleading veil of rhetoric, to contrast their beliefs with long-established Islámic teachings and to trace their *militancy* to the true historical sources—which, contrary to their own rhetoric, actually goes back to the origins of the modern jihadi movement in the early 20th Century. Simultaneously, one needs to understand Islám from authentic and reliable resources, unbiased by cross-cultural polemics, and as taught by Muhammad within His own specific historical context. Related to this, one must distinguish between the words of ordinary commentators and those of Muhammad, the Founder. With this knowledge in hand, it becomes simple to contrast historic Islámic practice and jurisprudence with the stated goals and practices of the militant jihadi terrorists. From this, the reader is enabled to judge for himself the distance between them.

Here is a summary of such an investigation—my own. (A more complete presentation will be given in Volume 4 of this series.) My aim in sharing this with you is to obtain a *fair* hearing for Muhammad. I am inspired by this quote from 'Abdu'l-Bahá:

> This is the plain truth—we are not prompted by fanatical attachment, nor do we blindly seek to defend, but we examine and relate matters with fairness. – 'Abdu'l-Bahá[692]

I hope we will be able to discard any prior misconceptions and then, with an openness of mind, go on and learn about Muhammad and His Faith from legitimate sources.

Understanding the militant jihadi terrorists

When the Prophet-Founder of Islám died in the year 632 AD, His followers embarked upon a program of empire expansion. In the last ten years of His life, Muhammad had become the Leader and Protector in the city of Medina on the Arabian Peninsula. He and His followers had been under threat of annihilation from the Arabs in Mecca, His hometown, from which he had been forced to flee in 622 AD. To help them resolve their internal disputes, the Jewish, Christian and Arab tribes invited Muhammad to Medina. He was so successful in this role that He soon became the Head of Medina's multi-cultural community. One of His first acts was to establish a covenant among all these groups, called the Constitution of Medina[693] in which all these parties pledged the mutual protection and support of each other. No one was required to adopt a different religion.

As the Medina community (known as the *ummah*) gradually prospered under Muhammad's leadership, the Meccans continued their efforts to destroy it. Muhammad was obliged to take up the sword in defense of the Jews, Christians and Muslims under His protection. After many battles, betrayals and broken treaties, Muhammad emerged victorious and even succeeded in conquering Mecca, the home-base of the opposition, *without bloodshed.*

Although Muhammad's military activities were mainly defensive, after His death Muhammad's successors aggressively embarked on a campaign of empire building. In less than a century the Arab empire astonishingly extended its reach from Spain in the West to the Indus Valley in the East, including all of Mesopotamia and eventually all of Turkey to the North. In the centuries that followed, as the empire waxed and waned, a brilliant civilization was raised up. Regardless of which dynasty ruled or which sect of Islám dominated the culture, Islám as a whole remained politically victorious. Based on this lived history, Islámic ideology has always been triumphalist in tone.

This all changed in the 19th and 20th centuries when the Islámic empire suffered catastrophic reversals. Islám's history of triumph was transformed into a series of humiliations. Islám's ruling institution, the Caliphate, having been held for centuries by the Ottoman Turks, was permanently abolished in 1924 following the Turkish Revolution. The State of Israel was established in 1948. In 1967 the Israelis virtually wiped out the armies of the neighboring countries that were attacking them, retaking Jerusalem in the process. The Arabs refer to this time, especially the 1948 period, as *al-nakbah*, the Catastrophe. Over time, the memory of repeated defeats has metastasized into a pervasive feeling of victimhood and severe resentment in large parts of the Muslim world.

The Muslim world responded to these defeats in two broad ways. Following the pattern of modern nation-states, a number of autocratic secular states were established including Egypt and Turkey. In addition, a growing fundamentalist movement began to take root. This movement aspired to return Islám to the less-dogmatic and triumphant days of Muhammad and His companions. This latter response, known as *Salafism*, generally has taken two forms. One form is nonviolent and nonpolitical, consisting of the majority of Muslim fundamentalists. For the most part, they are not particularly nationalistic, and mainly focused on achieving a peaceful return to a more pure religious experience. The other form is activist, desiring to pursue their goals through politics, which although they exist in large numbers today, they are not in the majority. A narrower subset of this group are the terrorists. These individuals are obsessed with warfare, and are driven by hatred of the West. Over time, a wide spectrum of opinion developed in which some people remained entirely peaceful, others are sympathetic to the goals of the terrorists but not violent themselves, and still others are dedicated to violent extremist actions against innocent populations.

One should *not* confuse peaceful Islámic fundamentalism with militant jihadi terrorism. The former is about practicing the religion in ways that are deemed to be more suitable by its followers. Many religions, such as Judaism and Christianity, also have peaceful fundamentalist movements. What these fundamentalisms have in common is that they are mainly religious in nature.

Militant jihadi extremism and terrorism, on the other hand, while it may claim to be Islámic in its *motivation*, is highly political in its *aspiration*. It seeks to reconquer, exact revenge, and brutally impose on all nations an extremely intolerant fascism that was *not* the Islám taught by Muhammad. The militant terrorists use Islám to recruit massive numbers of willing extremists into their terrorist army.

The root of militant jihadi extremism, of jihadi terrorism, is not Muhammad of the 7th century, but the defeats and losses in the Muslim world in the 19th and the 20th Centuries and the desire to recover what many believe was wrongly taken from them. While there is a certain rage-induced logic to such motives, the terrorists are certainly not justified in their actions, which the majority of Muslims believe bring shame upon Islám, which cause misery and death to Muslims in great numbers and which inflict untold suffering upon countless innocents from many Faith backgrounds. Let me be clear about this: as will be demonstrated, *their ideology is not that of Muhammad and is widely viewed as a radical militant political ideology under the guise of Islám*.

The modern jihadi extremist movement, as distinguished from modern Islámic fundamentalism, began in Egypt in the first half of the 20th century at about the same time as the founding of the Muslim Brotherhood organization. The Brotherhood initially sought collaboration with the pan-Arab nationalist Egyptian government of Gamal Abdel Nasser, but quickly realized that Nasser was an autocratic secularist rather than an Islámist fundamentalist. Instead, the Brotherhood switched tactics and agitated for the overthrow of the Nasser government. One of the Brotherhood's leaders was an Egyptian named Sayyid Qutb. Born in 1906, Qutb was an educator and prolific fundamentalist Islámic writer[694] who harbored a deep hatred for the West. In particular, he resented the American government's cooperation with Nasser (logically, it could not have been otherwise, since Egypt possessed the Suez Canal).

Qutb and other members of the Brotherhood conspired to kill President Nasser. Qutb was caught, tried, convicted and sent to jail. While in prison, Qutb penned a number of works that incited and swayed many extremists. His manifesto of radical fundamentalist thought, known as *Milestones*,[695] became an enormously influential Arabic-language document in setting the course for the militant extremist fundamentalist movement.

Ten years later, Qutb was released from prison. He soon joined in another plot to assassinate President Nasser. Again, he was caught. Again, he was tried. Again, he was convicted. Sentenced to death this time by the Egyptian court, he was executed in 1966.

The extremists of today consider Qutb as a martyr and the intellectual founder of the modern militant jihadi extremist movement. For example, Ayman al-Zawahiri, Osama Bin Laden's partner in the founding of al-Qaeda, stated that Qutb's ideas were "the beginning of the formation of the modern Islámic jihad movement…"[696] One scholar estimated the significance of Qutb: "The 11 September attacks cannot be understood fully without an understanding of the ideas of Sayyid Qutb, who is widely acknowledged as the intellectual godfather for the various modern radical Islamic movements, including Al-Qaeda. Qutb's writings are important because they define the core elements that have been adopted by all radical Islamic movements. These include: (1) an extreme hostility toward Western culture, especially the role of women and sexual mores in the West; (2) the formation of society under the rule of Sharia, Islamic law; (3) the overthrow of governments not under the rule of Sharia by means of holy war; and (4) an intense hatred of Jews and distrust of Christians."[697]

Qutb and the militant jihadi extremists falsely represent Islámic teaching in several ways.

- Qutb's teaching that Judaism and Christianity are false religions is opposed by the Qur'án.
- Qutb's designation of Jews and Christians as infidels worthy of death is rejected by the Qur'án.
- Qutb's designation of all modern-day societies—even Muslim societies and governments—as *jahiliyya* (barbaric) is not classical Islámic teaching.
- Qutb claimed that the Islámic civilization ("the world of Islám", *dar al-Islám* in Arabic) was in perpetual war with all other civilizations, especially Western civilization ("the world of war", *dar al-harb* in Arabic). The war would end only when "the world of Islám" conquers the entire world. This teaching contradicts Muhammad's example and teaching to always seek peace whenever possible.
- Qutb's interpretation of *jihad*, which means "struggle" in Arabic, is misleading because of his extreme emphasis on offensive war-making and mocking disregard of Islám's teachings on peace-making. Qutb completely dismissed Muhammad's teaching concerning "the greater jihad", the struggle to master one's own egotistical and selfish impulses.
- Qutb's eagerness to practice *takfir*, which means declaring someone an "infidel" and ordering their execution, is contrary to established Islámic law.
- Qutb's attitude of extreme vigilantism is counter to fourteen centuries of Islámic jurisprudence. In traditional Islám, to wage violent jihad one must first gain permission from one's parents, creditors and a qualified Islámic scholar! It is wrong to simply respond to the summons of a self-appointed charismatic leader claiming to act in the name of Islám.
- Qutb's willingness to permit suicide is anti-Islám. For example, to demonstrate His firm teaching concerning suicide, Muhammad once refused to perform burial rites for a follower who, though having fought in His army to defend the ummah, committed suicide.

- Qutb's willingness to order the killing of innocent people while also killing oneself is condemned by Islám. Martyrs, in every religion, have always been heroic victims standing up for their Faith, not perpetrators of crimes. This doctrine is a triple sin in Islám. In Islám you cannot kill other people, kill yourself, and then also expect to receive a reward in Paradise! So-called "martyrdom operations" against innocent non-combatants are an absolute perversion of Islámic teaching.

Finally, the allegedly ideal society that Qutb wanted to establish was not like the pluralistic, multicultural society that Muhammad had painstakingly built. Instead, Qutb's ideal society would look much more like a 20th century totalitarian fascist state in which ultimately everyone, under threat of death, would be forced to submit to Qutb's ideology. In that sense, ironically, Qutb's vision was not based in the 7th century at all. It was a thoroughly modern creation!

Islámic voices against extremism

Although largely ignored by Western media, legitimate Islámic voices have been raised against the extremists.

A good example is Dr. Fadl. The al-Qaeda terrorist organization was originally founded by five men, the most famous of them being Osama Bin Laden. One of these five men was Sayyid Imám al-Sharif, who goes by the name Dr. Fadl.[698] Dr. Fadl wrote influential books justifying terrorist attacks against civilian targets. Consistent with Qutb's teachings, Fadl's doctrine at that time was that jihad—which he defined solely as military struggle—is the natural state of Islám; that Muslims must always be in conflict with nonbelievers; and that one resorts to peacemaking only when one is in a position of abject weakness.

Dr. Fadl was eventually caught and sent to prison for terrorism. Surprisingly, while in prison, he had a change of mind. Although still in prison, he published a new book in which he repudiated the extremely violent jihadi ideology he earlier espoused. In this book Dr. Fadl pleaded:

> Oh, you young people, do not be deceived by the heroes of the Internet, the leaders of the microphones, who are launching statements inciting the youth while living under the protection of intelligence services, or of a tribe, or in a distant cave or under political asylum in an infidel country. They have thrown many others before you into the infernos, graves, and prisons. – Dr. Fadl

Surprisingly, Dr. Fadl has helped the Egyptian government rehabilitate 12,500 militant jihadi extremist prisoners, former terrorists, who were then deemed safe to return to society.

Dr. Fadl himself remains behind bars.

Another remarkable Islámic voice against terrorism is that of Shyakh-ul-Islám Dr. Muhammad Tahrir-ul-Qadri,[699] a courageous and distinguished Pakistani scholar, founder of the world-renowned Minhaj-ul-Quran peace organization, and author of literally hundreds of books. In 2010, Dr. Qadri published and received world-wide attention for his outstanding *Fatwa on Terrorism and Suicide Bombings*.[700] This fatwá, or legal decree, was a 475 page treatise explaining the entire legal basis for the *Islámic* condemnation of terrorism and suicide bombings. It is a thorough presentation of Qur'ánic verses and commentary, and Islámic history, jurisprudence and social policy. To my knowledge, no one else has compiled such a comprehensive and conclusive decree against terrorism and suicide/homicide bombings, nor explained it in terms that would be so convincing to fellow Muslims all over the world.

Dr. Qadri, in his legal decree, makes a striking claim about the terrorists. In several chapters of his fatwa, in exacting detail, he explains why the modern-day terrorists are the "return" of *the Kharijites* from the 7th Century. A little bit of history is required to understand the profound significance of this claim. When Muhammad died in 632 AD, His Faith and the ummah went through several ordeals, called *fitna* (or "tests). Though Muhammad's son-in-law, 'Alí, had been, according to the Shí'ih Muslims, designated by Him to be the chosen successor to the Prophet, 'Alí was not at first allowed to ascend to power. Instead, three men – 'Abu Bakr, 'Umar and 'Uthman – preceded him as Caliph. It was not until the year 656 AD that 'Alí was accepted as the 4th Caliph of Islám. He ruled until the year 661 AD. During those years, 'Alí faced severe challenges, including a rebellion from the Governor of Damascus, by the name of Muawiyah. 'Alí's army was ready to attack and defeat Muawiyah's forces at the Battle of Siffin, but another crisis happening at the same time prevented him from doing so. A sect of extremist Muslims, known today as the Kharijites, were claiming that all other Muslims had deviated from true Islám and they were justified in killing whomever they considered unworthy. Even 'Alí himself, Muhammad's son-in-law and one of the first to believe in Him, and the rightful Caliph, was not a good enough Muslim for the Kharijites. They began killing 'Alí's supporters in the region, including the slaughter of innocent women and children, very much acting like the terrorists of today. Though disadvantageous to him militarily, out of compassion, 'Alí turned his army aside from Muawiyah to deal with this dangerous threat. At first, he tried to reason with the Kharijites and promised forgiveness to those who would put down their weapons and go home. The rest, he said, would be eliminated in battle because in Islám their extremism would not be tolerated. About 4,000 of the Kharijites did in fact listen, and they went home peacefully. The remaining Kharijites would not listen, so 'Alí had to fight them and defeat them. But a few escaped and returned several years later to assassinate 'Alí. But in the immediate aftermath of the struggle with the Kharijites, 'Alí didn't have the military strength to go and defeat Muawiyah. He was forced into an arbitration which left Muawiyah in power, and after 'Alí's death Muawiyah was able to make his claim to be the Caliph stick. Muawiyah became the next Caliph and the first monarch of the Umayyad dynasty, the most corrupt ruling dynasty in all of Islámic history. In any case, these tragic events show that *within Islám, from its first century, its original principle*, established by 'Alí himself, is that *militant extremist terrorists are not to be tolerated.*

With that in mind, the meaning of Dr. Qadri's assertion is clear. If you're a modern-day Kharijite, you may call yourself a Muslim, but the Islámic community will cast you out from its embrace. Dr. Qadri, in his fatwa, went into detail concerning the crimes of the modern-day Kharijites. For example, indiscriminate killing is unlawful in Islám; it is unlawful to indiscriminately kill non-Muslims or to torture them; it is unlawful to kill non-Muslims who are non-combatants; terrorism against non-Muslims – even in wartime – is unlawful; the lives, property and houses of worship of non-Muslims are to be protected; it is unlawful to force one's belief on others; suicide is forbidden and Paradise is denied to them; etc. As mentioned, this fatwa is 475 pages long. Dr. Qadri cites the Qur'án and generations of mainstream Islámic jurists, providing both the Arabic and English texts of what they said. Dr. Qadri's conclusion is inescapable – the modern-day militant jihadi terrorists and what they do are *condemned within and by Islám*.

Dr. Qadri is by no means a lone voice within the Islámic community bringing up the image of the Kharijites. More recently, Shaykh Muhammad Al-Yaqoubi wrote a short book, *Refuting ISIS: Destroying its religious foundation and proving it has strayed from Islám and that fighting it is an obligation*, first published in 2016, which has been distributed worldwide.[701] Yaqoubi was listed in 2012 as one of the 500 most influential Muslims in the world in a joint publication by Georgetown University's Prince Alwaleed Center for Muslim–Christian Understanding and the Royal Islamic Strategic Studies Centre of Jordan (and also honorable mentions in 2015 and 2016).[702]

ISIS was a branch of al-Qaeda which took root in Iraq after the calamitous war in Iraq in the early 2000s. ISIS from the beginning was extremely brutal. As scholar William McCants showed in his book, *ISIS Apocalypse*, even al-Qaeda – the terrorist group behind the September 11 attacks – thought ISIS was too ruthless.[703] In 2014, ISIS managed to declare a new Caliphate, under Abu Bakr al-Baghdadi, and militarily acquire a very large territory in both Syria and Iraq. Their brutality, transmitted through the world's television screens, horrified the world. Their acts of beheading, burning and mutilating people and their genocide against entire innocent populations repulsed peace-loving people across the globe. For a time, it seemed as if a renewed jihad was underway. In 2017 and 2018, western forces were able to defeat ISIS on the battlefield, and ISIS no longer holds any territory, though at this writing al-Baghdadi remains at large.

In this book, Yaqoubi affirms that the ISIS loyalists are modern-day Kharijites. He says that their barbarism and atrocities are condemned within Islám. Their declarations of takfir against the masses who do not follow their line is unauthorized and invalid. In an interesting chapter, Yaqoubi asks, 'But are the Kharijites Muslims?' At first, addressing the Kharijites, he says this: "The general tendency amongst Islámic jurists was to consider them deviators, misguided, and disobedient to Almighty God and His Messenger, but not outside the fold of Islám." And citing a 4th Century AH scholar: "None of the scholars, either in past or recent times, ever disagreed that the *Khawarij* [another word for Kharijites] are an evil group, disobedient to God Almighty and His Messenger. Even if they pray, fast, or strive in worship, it does not benefit them…" Yaqoubi says he was raised in the tradition in Islám that gives the benefit of the doubt to the people, so while the extremists are evil they are not declared non-Muslims. More recently, however, he says the opinion of scholars has changed about their claim to be Muslims, and Yaqoubi reports that now some scholars are openly declaring the Kharijites as outside the fold.

When Yaqoubi directs his focus at ISIS loyalists specifically, he concludes that "their level of extremism" has reached such a level that they can be "declared non-Muslim without hesitation." He states: "The ideology of ISIS is based on a complex system of fallacies that sever the sacred texts from their context… The so-called 'Islámic State is neither Islámic nor a state, but rather a deviant group that is driven by anger, hatred, and a thirst for power, using Islám to reach their goals." And: "Their condemnation, which is based on irrefutable juridical proofs (i.e. authenticated texts from the Islámic tradition), is unequivocally harsh and leaves no room for reservations. It can be summed up in one sentence: ISIS is the modern-day form of *the Khawarij* movement predicted by the Prophet Muhammad and described by him as renegades who will abandon Islám despite their claim to be Muslims." Interestingly, fourteen centuries ago the Prophet Muhammad had made a specific prediction about the appearance of such evil actors within Islám.

Yaqoubi also claims that *the Muslims* are obligated to fight against ISIS and not allow them to win. But first it is necessary to try to reason with them and call upon them to repent, as 'Alí had done, and if they listen to you, very good. Yaqoubi then delivers a fatwa: "I issue here the fatwa that fighting the group known as ISIS is a communal obligation upon Muslims. This group must be fought in order to protect the core of the religion, defend Muslim lands, protect the blood of the innocent, and let the truth prevail. It is not permissible to neglect fighting ISIS... " Yaqoubi then concludes his argument with this statement: "In light of this exposition, it is clear that the Islámic State in Syria and Iraq, known as ISIS or Daesh, is a group of deviators that do not represent Islám in any form. They have in fact left Islám… Its actions are simply a series of crimes perpetrated in the name of Islám… Islám disavows ISIS, the teachings of the Messenger of God disavow ISIS, and the scholars of mainstream Sunni Islám disavow ISIS."

These are just three examples.

The verdict against the militant jihadi terrorists

With these examples clearly in view, it becomes clear that one should not minimize how greatly the jihadi terrorists deviate from Islámic norms. One cannot say the horrific deeds and distorted beliefs of the terrorists merely represent the harsher end of a conservative vs. liberal spectrum of ideas about jihad within the larger Islámic community. One cannot explain away or diminish the horror of what the terrorists do by saying (incorrect) things like "Islám only teaches the greater jihad", or by selectively reinterpreting history to allege that jihad doesn't really include military action or by ignoring that the concept of jihad was the subject of controversy within the Islámic community over time.

For example, one such controversy occurred in the 13th Century when the Mongols invaded the Islámic Empire and overthrew the great Abbasid dynasty. The Mongols were at first recognized as outsiders and the Muslim armies resisted the invaders accordingly. But then, in a surprising move, vast numbers of the Mongols converted to Islám. Now, officially, they were brothers in Islám! So, the controversy became, "Can we still fight jihad against the invaders now that they have become Muslims?" Understandably this was an important controversy to be resolved. To make a long story short, the controversy was ultimately settled when the most eminent jurist of the day, Ibn Taymiyyih, delivered a fatwa which said that, regardless of their outward conversion to Islám, the invaders were still invaders and they were not observing Islám properly anyway, so they should be resisted by the sword. He wrote, "It is obligatory to take the initiative in fighting those people…But if they first attack the Muslims then fighting them is even more urgent…"[704] It took time, but eventually the rule of the Mongols came to an end. Through the ages, jihad has been the subject of various controversies. Nevertheless, in the present era, although not adequately reported by the Western news media, condemnation of the terrorists (the modern-day Kharijites) exists even within the conservative segment of the Islámic community. To mention one example, Abdul-Aziz ibn Abdullah Al ash-Sheikh, the current Grand Mufti of Saudi Arabia, known as a hardliner, declared in 2013 that the suicide bombings were "great crimes" and that the bombers had been "robbed of their minds" and are "criminals who rush themselves to hell by their actions". In 2014, as reported by the Reuters news agency, he condemned ISIS and al-Qaeda saying, "Extremist and militant ideas and terrorism which spread decay on Earth, destroying human civilization, are not in any way part of Islam, but are enemy number one of Islam, and Muslims are their first victims".[705]

There is no shortage of evidence.

Without a doubt, those who follow the militant jihadi terrorist ideology are outside the embrace of Islám. This is not to deny that they, in their own minds, wholeheartedly think they are Muslims and believe they are supporting Islám. In all their rhetoric, the militant jihadi extremists appear to be heartfelt advocates for Islám. So, if one were to just listen to what they say, one *might* call them Muslims. Historically, Islámic scholars and jurists have preferred to give people the benefit of the doubt as much as possible.

The problem arises when one looks at what the terrorists actually do. Their behavior and their teachings can be examined factually and contrasted objectively with the teachings of Muhammad and the example of His life, which are well documented. When these two bodies of information are honestly compared, one quickly perceives that the extremists' behavior and allegedly Islámic teachings violates and contradicts both the Qur'án and centuries of accepted Islámic practice and jurisprudence. In fact, many of the things they do under the umbrella of Islám are actually criminal acts in Islám, that is, among both the Sunni and Shí'ih branches of Islám of the last fourteen centuries. When the words and deeds of the militant jihadi extremists are examined in a dispassionate way, though an observer may acknowledge their claimed Islámic self-identification, as explained by the scholars cited above, it is not possible to overlook their serious deviation, indeed, their divorce, from the well-established Faith of the Prophet Muhammad.

I reject the idea of using the term "Islámic" with regard to the terrorists because it implies that there is something genuinely Islámic about their extremism. I prefer terms like "terrorist", "jihadi terrorist" or "militant jihadi extremist", which all mean the same thing, for three reasons. First, I do not like the idea of tarnishing the word Islám, which refers to submission to the Will of God, with the shameful stain of what the terrorists do. Second, the word jihadi, being of Islámic origin, adequately connotes and acknowledges the claimed Islámic motivations of the terrorists, while at the same time it deprives them of the dignity of explicitly using the word "Islámic". Third, this approach helps us to avoid the confusion, perversion and hatred of Islám induced by calling the terrorists Islámic. It enables us to un-conflate the established Islámic religion founded by Muhammad from the violent and hate-filled ideology of the terrorists. It helps us overcome the prejudice against Islám caused by the terrorists' horrible deeds and the faulty descriptions of Islám in the mass media. And this, hopefully, enables us to recover the dignity and the beauty of the word "Islámic" on behalf of the millions of everyday citizens who follow their religion in a humble, loving, respectful and peaceful way.

Therefore, they may say their Muslim prayers, read the Qur'án and shout "Alláh'u'akbár" even as they release the detonator button during a "martyrdom operation", but they are nothing more than proverbial wolves in sheep's clothing—regarded as an enemy from within by most Muslims and a growing consensus of scholars. In the long run, they fool only themselves, because when they get to the afterlife, in my opinion, Muhammad Himself will turn His back on them and cast them far from His Presence.

This has been a brief explanation of the false and distorted ideology that is unjustly promoted by militant jihadi terrorists as the Islámic religion. Now that we understand how far the extremists have distanced themselves from the established heart of Islám, let's become acquainted with Muhammad, the Founder of Islám.

Introduction

When we review the conditions existing in the East prior to the rise of the Prophet of Arabia, we find that throughout the Arabian Peninsula

> intense mental darkness and the utmost ignorance prevailed among its inhabitants. Those tribal peoples were constantly engaged in war, killing and shedding blood, burning and pillaging... Muhammad appeared as a Prophet among such a people. He educated these barbarous tribes, lifted them out of their ignorance and savagery and put an end to the continuous strife and hatred which had existed among them. He established agreement and reconciliation among them, unified them and taught them to look upon each other as brothers. Through His training they advanced rapidly in prestige and civilization. They were formerly ignorant; they became wise. They were barbarous; they attained refinement and culture. They were debased and brutal; He uplifted and elevated them. They were humiliated and despised; their civilization and renown spread throughout the world. This is perfect proof that Muhammad was an Educator and Teacher.—'Abdu'l-Bahá[706]

Muhammad lived approximately 1,400 years ago. Born in Arabia, in the city of Mecca, He was descended from Abraham through that Patriarch's second wife Hagar and their son Ishmael. Unlike Abraham, Moses and Jesus, no great king tried to kill Muhammad as a baby, but Muhammad was orphaned three times due to the untimely deaths of His father, mother and grandfather.

Muhammad lived, married and prospered in Arabia as a merchant/camel driver. Due to exceptional personal qualities, His nickname was "al-Amin", meaning "the trustworthy one". At the age of 40, in 610 AD, during a period of meditation in the mountains near Mecca, Muhammad experienced Divine revelation for the first time. He saw a vision of the angel Gabriel standing astride the horizon, and Gabriel commanded Him to recite the Word of God.

Muslim tradition looks back at pre-Islámic Arabia as the age of barbarism (*jahiliyya*). Muhammad's hometown, Mecca, was the center of idol worship and polytheism because it was the home of the sacred shrine known as the Ka'bih, the square black shrine that according to legend dated back to the times of Adam and Abraham. The Arabian version of idolatry, in Mecca, was really a commercial enterprise. Tribes from all over Arabia would come to worship at the Ka'bih, around which were assembled as many as 360 idols.

Providing for all these pilgrims was at the foundation of the Meccan social economy, making Mecca the economic powerhouse of the region. As Yahiya Emerick stated, "Idolatry became big business."[707] Arab society, in addition to its crass idolatry, was torn by strife and vendetta among the Arab tribes. The culture was so debased it condoned the practice of burying unwanted infant girls alive in the hot desert sands.

In this climate of idolatry, commerce, strife and barbarism, Muhammad arose to tear down His society's whole system of idolatry and proclaim the oneness of God. Not surprisingly, Muhammad's pagan Arab contemporaries saw His mission as a direct and immediate threat to their way of life.

Muhammad said His revelation was from none other than the God of Abraham, Moses and Jesus. The word for God in Arabic is "Alláh", meaning literally "God". This word is not meant as a proper name, nor does it signify a deity other than the one God. Likewise, the central theme of His revelation was submission to the will of God, so He named His religion "Islám", which means "submission to the will of God" in Arabic. Accordingly, a "Muslim" is one who submits to God.

Like Abraham, Muhammad was a fierce iconoclast Who battled the polytheism and idolatry in His society. Muhammad encouraged friendly relations with Jews and Christians, affirmed the transcendent oneness and mercy of God and promoted an attitude of humility towards God. This particularly irritated His Arab contemporaries because Arab culture cultivated a certain arrogance of bowing to no one. Muhammad was a strong advocate of human rights, of enjoining good and forbidding evil, and for upgrading the status of women. He forbade the barbaric practice of female infanticide.

The Meccans rejected Muhammad's message and persecuted Him. After more than a decade of harsh treatment, Muhammad and His growing community were forced to flee Mecca and take refuge in Medina about 500 miles to the north. Muhammad had been invited to become the Leader in Medina by the strife-ridden Jewish, Christian and Arab tribes residing there at the precise moment when He and His followers were in the most peril. With acute irony, Muhammad fled Mecca as a fugitive and was joyously welcomed by crowds in Medina. As the new virtual head of state, Muhammad brought about peaceful relations among the various groups living in Medina. He caused the Constitution of Medina to be written which, through treaty, established an expanding multi-cultural community (known as *the ummah*), made up of Jews, Christians, pagan Arabs and Muslims.[708] This constitution pledged all its members to mutual respect and protection with no pressure to convert. Muhammad had achieved preeminent status as both a religious leader and a statesman.

Unfortunately, even after His escape, the Meccans continued their aggression toward Him and His ummah. As a result of this hostility, Muhammad was forced to take up arms in self-defense. The Muslims emerged victorious from most battles, but not all. The Meccans were intent on annihilating the ummah. Eventually, however, Muhammad overcame the opposition forces and retook Mecca. The Kaaba was cleansed of all idols and Islám was spread through all of Arabia. Surprisingly, Muhammad's conquest of Mecca was almost bloodless. The entire city was handed over peacefully and without the threat of forced conversion.

According to historical reports, at the end of His life Muhammad planned to appoint a successor but at the last moment was prevented from doing so.[709] This led to much strife and the divisions that continue within Islám to this day. In the centuries after His death, the Muslims embarked upon a seemingly irresistible military expansion, building an empire and a civilization larger than anything the world had ever seen. Today, there are more than 1.6 billion Muslims. The largest concentrations of Muslims actually reside outside the Middle East in places like Bangladesh, Pakistan, India and Indonesia.

For fourteen centuries Muhammad's global influence has been "powerful and pervasive".[710] Literally, as the Divine Educator Who emphasized submission to the will of God, countless generations and billions of souls have been the beneficiaries of Muhammad's life and work.

Information about Muhammad is found in both Scripture and tradition. Scriptures which narrate episodes of His life or mention Him are the Qur'án and the Baha'i Writings. Considerable supplementary material is found in the records of Islámic oral tradition, known as *hadith*. In addition, many biographies have been written about Muhammad beginning in the eighth century with the work of Ibn Ishaq, al-Tabari and others.

Mission and teachings

God, Prophethood, and the Qur'án

Muhammad was one of the few men of Arabia who saw how the idolatry-based economy was causing great harm to His people. As He approached His fortieth year, Muhammad frequently went out into the mountains around Mecca for long periods of reflection. In the year 610 AD, while on one of His spiritual retreats, something entirely new happened. Muhammad felt a Presence and heard a loud, powerful voice. Looking up, He saw the angel Gabriel Who commanded Him to recite what later became known as the first verses of the Qur'án. At first only family members and close friends accepted Muhammad's revelation. After some time Muhammad publicly began proclaiming His message.

The Islámic testimony of faith was straight-forward. The first part of the testimony, "No God is there but God" (Arabic: "*lá iláha illa alláh*"), emphatically asserted the oneness of God. Muhammad was a strict ethical monotheist in the same lineage as Abraham, Moses, and Jesus. Nearly every chapter of the Qur'án begins with the phrase, "In the name of God, the Compassionate, the Merciful". God's love is praised throughout the Qur'án. God is depicted as the supreme Creator, exalted, transcendent, full of majesty, all-knowing.

The testimony begins with the word "no" ("*lá*") precisely because affirming the oneness of God meant refusing the existence of other gods. Muhammad, like the Divine Educators before Him, was determined to establish a pristine faith based on a reborn commitment to the one God. Muhammad was also determined to cleanse the Ka'bih of all traces of idolatry.

The second part of the testimony, "Muhammad is the Apostle of God" (Arabic: "*Muḥammadan rasúl Alláh*"), boldly asserted that God had appointed Muhammad to be His Messenger, an Apostle to the Arab peoples and all of mankind.

Establishing Muhammad as the Prophet of God was vital to establishing the Qur'án as the Word of God and the Holy Book of Islám. Over a period of twenty-two years, He revealed the Qur'án, a volume of 6,236 verses. The word "Qur'án" literally means "recitation" of God's Words.

The eloquence and beauty of the Qur'án in the original Arabic language was astounding to His contemporaries and was regarded as an incomparable literary masterpiece. One biographer stated: "A simple, uneducated Man… suddenly preached a literate, aesthetic, miraculous piece of work... The intoxicating beauty of its verses was ample proof of its divine origin for Muhammad and for all the Arabs."[711] For the Arabic listener, the Qur'án pulsates with spiritual energy. Muhammad said that the Qur'án was His miracle.

> This Qur'án is not such as can be produced by other than God… (Qur'án 17:37-38, 88)

The Qur'án moves in rhythms and rhymes undetectable to a Westerner, but which are completely vivid to one whose native language is Arabic. As Karen Armstrong observed:

> The Arabs found the Qur'án quite astonishing: it was unlike any other literature they had encountered before. Some were converted immediately, believing that divine inspiration alone could account for this extraordinary language... If approached in the right way, believers claim, it yields a sense of the divine presence...[712]

While Arabic listeners are often mesmerized by the verses of the Qur'an, Western readers often find the Qur'án to be unfamiliar in style and structure. Western scholars have frequently been "baffled by the Qur'án."[713] Unlike the Bible, little narrative background is given, instead relying on a largely conversational format. The language is evocative; the listener is expected to already know the stories to which the Text is alluding.

The Qur'án honored the Divine Educators of the past—Adam, Noah, Abraham, Moses, Jesus and others—stating that They had all been sent by the same God. The Qur'án says that God has always been graciously sending great Messengers into the world:

> For We assuredly sent amongst every People a Messenger... (Qur'án 16:36)

Adjusting for differences of time and place, the Divine Educators all proclaimed the ancient and eternal religion of God, which, as Muhammad explained, centered on worshipping one God, submitting to His Will and following His commandments to do good and avoid evil.

The Qur'án stated that no Prophet is distinguished above the others:

> We make no distinction between any of them, and unto Him we have surrendered. (Qur'án 3:84)[714]

The Qur'an did not teach that Jews and Christians were infidels. On the contrary, the Qur'án honored the Jews and the Christians as "People of the Book" because God had previously given them the Torah and the Gospels. They were to be left alone in matters of religion. The Qur'án said:

> Let there be no compulsion in religion. (Qur'án 2:256)

This egalitarian outlook prevailed among the Muslims in their early centuries. Over time, the Muslims deviated from the message and, like the Christians and the Jews before them, began to claim superiority and finality for their Messenger.

The Qur'án says non-Muslims are not excluded from God, nor are they denied spiritual blessing in the Hereafter. What is not acceptable to God is arrogance and pride, or worshipping anything other than God, such as idols or material wealth. Therefore, if an individual surrenders to God, as Abraham, Moses, Jesus and Muhammad all did, then the Qur'án says that individual will be blessed.

Pillars of Islám

Muhammad taught a strong version of ethical monotheism. He was an iconoclast. Only God should be worshipped, and all idol worship should be eliminated. God is the supreme authority, fully sovereign to tell men how to live their lives.

Muhammad revealed certain laws and ordinances for His followers to follow. These are called the five "pillars of Islám."

- The first pillar is the testimony of Faith described above. One converts to Islám by reciting the testimony of faith.
- The second pillar is the law of formal ritual prayer, called *salat* in Arabic, which is performed five times a day. A key phrase, which is used throughout, is "Alláh'u'akbár", which is Arabic for "God is most great".
- The third pillar is the law of almsgiving or charity, called *zakat* in Arabic.
- The fourth pillar is the law of fasting, called *sawm* in Arabic. The Muslims fast during the month of Ramadan, the ninth month of the Islámic lunar calendar, from sunrise to sunset, abstaining from food, drink, smoking and marital relations.
- The fifth pillar is the law of pilgrimage, called *hajj* in Arabic. Muslims, if they have the means, must go on pilgrimage to Mecca and pray at the Ka'bih in person, at least once in their lifetime. Professor Frederick Denny states, "The hajj is a powerful symbol of the worldwide unity of the Muslim community."[715]

Jihad = Struggle

Jihad is not one of the *pillars* of mainstream Islám, but it is a legitimate principle of the Faith. The word jihad literally means struggle in Arabic. Muhammad taught that there are two kinds of jihad.

The "greater jihad" is the struggle to master one's own ego, to overcome the flaws in one's character, to resist temptations that cause one to stray from the straight path of Truth and to draw closer to God. In that sense, the greater jihad is a battle within oneself.

The lesser jihad is to fight with the sword. This is the military meaning and it too had legitimate meaning within the Islámic religion. Though armed struggle (lesser jihad) was always part of Islámic history, it has never been the primary focus of Islám. (By contrast, if one listens to the militant extremists of today, one would get the false idea that Islám is *only* about armed struggle, killing the infidels and conquering the world in the name of Islám.)

Nader Saiedi explained that jihad, as holy war, has always had the dual meaning of both offensive and defensive conflict, that it has been subject to diverse interpretations through time, but that it was always to be practiced with a sense of moderation:

> The concept of holy war -- jihad or {qital} (meaning fighting and slaying) -- waged against unbelievers for the spread and defence of the religion, has been subject to differing interpretations even within Islam… Historically, until the nineteenth century, Islamic jurisprudence defined holy war as offensive (as well as defensive) war. Statements in the Surih of the Cow [Qur'án 2:190-193], which say to fight against those who fight against you but "do not transgress the limits" became the basis of modern arguments that holy war is solely meant to be defensive, but these verses were classically interpreted as meaning that, in the conduct of a holy war, those among the enemy who do not take up the sword (in other words, the elderly, women, and children) should not be slain." – Nader Saiedi[716]

Balyuzi, in his book, *Muhammad and the Course of Islám*, also described the meaning of jihad.

> Jihad (Holy War) is also a subsidiary of the Faith. In the days of the Prophet and in the years immediately following, this Holy War was directed against pagans and idolaters – the polytheists [who were attacking His followers] – and was undertaken in defence of the realm of Islam. With the passage of centuries the sense of jihad was obscured and lost... The Faith of the Arabian Prophet … must never be designated as Muhammadanism. It is Islam: the religion of submission to the Will of God, and it was not imposed by the sword. Surah 2:257 declares:
>
> > No compulsion is there in religion.
> > Rectitude has become clear from error.
> > So whosoever disbelieves in idols
> > and believes in God, has laid hold of
> > the most firm handle, unbreaking; God is
> > All-hearing, All-knowing. (Qur'án 2:257) – Balyuzi[717]

Historically, Muhammad did everything He could to avoid armed struggle. Unfortunately, the Meccans were relentless in their hostility and aggression. While in Mecca during the earlier half of His ministry, He spoke only as a Warner from God. He and His followers suffered persecution patiently. The situation changed when Muhammad went to Medina. Once there, the various groups and tribes had elevated Him to the position of Leader of the community. And He established a treaty of fellowship among the Jews, Christians, Muslims and pagans that were living in Medina. This was called the Constitution of Medina and it was written down and recorded. This Constitution guaranteed mutual protection and safety among the groups, effectively bringing into being a multi-Faith pluralistic society in His lifetime. One feature of this treaty is that no one was required to change their religion. Through the Constitution of Medina, Muhammad was duty-bound to be the protector of the entire ummah, which was the *entire* multicultural community in Medina. Thus, when the Meccans continued their attacks against the ummah, Muhammad received a revelation telling Him that He could fight back and defend His people (Qur'án 22:39-40). It was only when this permission was received from God that Muhammad and His followers fought back against the Meccans.

'Abdu'l-Bahá described the military activities of Muhammad:

> Muḥammad's military expeditions were always defensive in nature. The clear proof is this: For thirteen years both He and His companions endured in Mecca the most intense persecutions and were the constant target of the darts of hatred. Some of His companions were killed and their possessions pillaged; others forsook their native country and fled to foreign lands. Muḥammad Himself was subjected to the severest persecutions and was obliged, when His enemies resolved to kill Him, to flee Mecca in the middle of the night and emigrate to Medina. Yet even then His enemies did not relent, but pursued the Muslims all the way to Medina and to Abyssinia…
>
> It was among such tribes that Muḥammad was sent forth. For thirteen years He suffered at their hands every conceivable tribulation, till at last He fled the city and emigrated to Medina. And yet, far from desisting, these people joined forces, raised an army, and attacked with the aim of exterminating every man, woman, and child among His followers. It was under such circumstances and against such people that Muḥammad was forced to take up arms. This is the plain truth—we are not prompted by fanatical attachment, nor do we blindly seek to defend, but we examine and relate matters with fairness. You should likewise consider in fairness the following: If Christ Himself had been placed in similar circumstances and among such lawless and barbarous tribes; if for thirteen years He and His disciples had patiently endured every manner

of cruelty at their hands; if they were forced through this oppression to forsake their homeland and take to the wilderness; and if these lawless tribes still persisted in pursuing them with the aim of slaughtering the men, pillaging their property, and seizing their women and children—how would Christ have dealt with them? If this oppression had been directed towards Him alone, He would have forgiven them, and such an act of forgiveness would have been most acceptable and praiseworthy; but had He seen that cruel and bloodthirsty murderers were intent upon killing, pillaging, and tormenting a number of defenceless souls and taking captive the women and children, it is certain that He would have defended the oppressed and stayed the hand of the oppressors.

What objection, then, can be directed against Muḥammad?... Moreover, to free these tribes from their bloodthirstiness was the greatest gift, and to curb and restrain them was pure bounty… If Christ had been placed in similar circumstances, He would have undoubtedly delivered, through an all-conquering power, those men, women, and children from the claws of such ravenous wolves. – 'Abdu'l-Bahá[718]

There is a hadith from Muhammad (a reported saying from Him) which was recorded in the hadith collections compiled by Muslim scholars. This hadith demonstrates that, although jihad was permitted when necessary, when it was not necessary Muhammad preferred to focus His followers' attention and efforts on other things:

A man came to the Prophet asking his permission to take part in Jihad. The Prophet asked him, "Are your parents alive?" He replied in the affirmative. The Prophet said to him, "Then exert yourself in their service." – Hadith attributed to Muhammad[719]

Overall, Muslims were directed to seek peace first, accept a truce if offered, and resort to violence only as a last resort. Muhammad praised the martyrdoms of those who had died defending Islám, as any great leader in His position would do, but He always preferred negotiating and peace-making whenever possible. He taught His followers to do the same. That many followers did not listen to their Teacher, of course, is a lamentable fact of history.

After Muhammad

As regards the coming of a future Divine Educator, most Muslims today adhere to the doctrine of finality. Based on their reading of Qur'án 33:40, nearly all Muslims today believe that Muhammad was the last of God's Prophets. That verse says:

> Muhammad is not the father of any man among you, but he is the Apostle of God, and the seal of the prophets: and God knoweth all things. (Qur'an 33:40, transl. by Rodwell)

This verse undeniably describes Muhammad as the Seal of the Prophets. The meaning and interpretation of that title, however, is another matter.

The two Figures most affected by the religious leaders' finality claim were the two Divine Educators which came *after* Muhammad—the Báb and Bahá'u'lláh—Who were in Their time severely persecuted because of resistance from religious leaders. A detailed examination of this issue appears in Volumes 4, 5 and 6 in this series, but here are a few brief points.

- The belief that God would never again send Someone—another Divine Educator—to reveal the Word of God to humankind was not the view of Muhammad or the early Muslims. Instead, by the tenth century, the *finality doctrine* was promoted and established by Islámic religious and political leaders. Similar to the doctrine of the Trinity among Christians, the history of the doctrine of finality *within* the Muslim community has a centuries-long history that must be considered.[720]
- Verse 33:40 uses two terms that refer to Muhammad. The first term is "Apostle" (*rasúl* in Arabic). The second term is "prophet" (*nabí* in Arabic). Looking closely at the verse, we see that the Qur'án did *not* say that Muhammad "is the seal of the apostles and the prophets". It only says that He is "the seal of the prophets", which leaves open the possibility that, *even if* the finality interpretation were correct, God might *still* send Apostles (*rasúl*) to speak for Him—that is, even if He isn't going to send prophets (*nabí*) anymore. The point is, no matter how one chooses to interpret the "Seal of the prophets" statement, God is remains free to speak to humankind however, wherever and whenever He wishes to do so.
- While accepting without question the "Seal of the Prophets" reference in the Qur'an, both the Báb and Bahá'u'lláh offered enlightening spiritual explanations to show what They claimed to be the true meaning of the Seal verse.

Paradoxically, despite their assertions of Muhammad's finality, Muslims do have teachings concerning the coming of future Promised Ones. As noted earlier, the Sunnís say the Mahdí ("the guided one") will appear, followed by the return of Jesus. Shí'ih Muslims expect the Qá'im ("he who arises") and also the return of the Imám Husayn. Detailed signs are given by the theologians for the appearances of these figures. When the time came to deal with these claims, both the Báb and Bahá'u'lláh offered Their proofs to Their respective audiences.

The stature of Muhammad

In today's super-heated, hyper-partisan and geopolitically disturbed society, discovering the true stature of Muhammad is a difficult challenge. It is no wonder that masses of people are confused and suspicious. Nevertheless, throughout this work I have done my best to offer an account of Muhammad that is factual, friendly and fair.

There is no question that Muhammad was one of the most influential Figures in the entire history of humanity. Like Abraham, Moses and Jesus, Muhammad's influence has been world-encompassing and truly enduring. He was the Revealer of Islám's sacred Scripture, the Preacher of its message and the Establisher of a world religion that today claims a membership of over 1.6 billion people. So far, in history there really hasn't been anyone quite like Him. Michael Hart, author of *The 100: A Ranking of the Most Influential Persons in History*, ranked Muhammad as number one because "he was the only man in history who was supremely successful on both the religious and secular levels..."[721]

The rise of Islám was stunning in its speed and scope. Muhammad succeeded in creating a strictly monotheistic, Abrahamic Covenant community, called the ummah, that was multicultural, expanding and welcoming of peoples of other backgrounds. This ummah possessed immense energy and, in the years after Muhammad's passing, and despite internal political stresses, it burst out of the Arabian Peninsula to build the vast Islámic empire. In a couple of centuries, the empire became the foundation for a new civilization with centers in Arabia, Syria, the Holy Land, Egypt, Spain and elsewhere. While the West was immersed in what is known as the dark ages, in Islámic dominions notable advances were being made in architecture, art, astronomy, geography, history, literature, mathematics, medicine, mysticism and philosophy.

'Abdu'l-Bahá summed up the transformative impact of Muhammad as the Divine Educator of His people.

> We entertain no prejudice against Muhammad... The Arabians were in the utmost state of degradation. They were bloodthirsty and barbarous,

so savage and degraded that the Arabian father often buried his own daughter alive. Consider: Could any barbarism be lower than this? The nation consisted of warring, hostile tribal peoples inhabiting the vast Arabian peninsula, and their business consisted in fighting and pillaging each other, making captive women and children, killing each other. Muhammad appeared among such a people. He educated and unified these barbarous tribes, put an end to their shedding of blood. Through His education they reached such a degree of civilization that they subdued and governed continents and nations... Why then should we deny Muhammad?—'Abdu'l-Bahá[722]

THE BÁB

Introduction

As for the Báb... [this] illustrious Soul arose with such power that He shook the supports of the religion, of the morals, the conditions, the habits and the customs of Persia, and instituted new rules, new laws and a new religion. Though the great personages of the State, nearly all the clergy, and the public men arose to destroy and annihilate Him, He alone withstood them and moved the whole of Persia. Many [religious leaders] and public men, as well as other people, joyfully sacrificed their lives in His Cause, and hastened to the plain of martyrdom. The government, the nation, the doctors of divinity and the great personages desired to extinguish His light, but they could not do so... He imparted divine education to an unenlightened multitude and produced marvelous results on the thoughts, morals, customs and conditions of the Persians... The appearance of such wonderful signs and great results; the effects produced upon the minds of the people, and upon the prevailing ideas; the establishment of the foundations of progress; and the organization of the principles of success and prosperity by a young merchant, constitute the greatest proof that He was a perfect Educator. A just person will never hesitate to believe this. – 'Abdu'l-Bahá[(723)]

The Báb was born about 200 years ago, in 1819, in Shíráz, Persia. His given name was Siyyid 'Alí Muhammad. He was a descendant of Muhammad and since Muhammad was descended from Abraham, the Báb was likewise descended from Abraham. The term "siyyid" and the green turban which He wore symbolized his distinguished lineage from Muhammad, through Muhammad's grandson Husayn. Like Muhammad, the Báb's father died when He was very young. Consequently, He was raised by a beloved uncle.

The Báb was brought to a school at a young age, but His innate knowledge was so exceptional that the headmaster soon brought Him back to His uncle and said:

> He is not to be treated as a mere child … He, verily, stands in no need of teachers such as I. – Shaykh 'Ábid(724)

The Báb grew up in the uncle's home in Shíráz and worked as a merchant in His uncle's business. The Báb stood out among the citizens of Shíráz for His luminous moral qualities, especially in business. He was also distinguished by His extraordinary devotion to God and prayer.

Persia in the mid-nineteenth century was a place of the most extreme fanaticism, corruption, degradation, brutality and narrowness of mind, desperately in need of reform and spiritual revival. When the Báb was 24, He experienced a revelation from God revealing that He was in fact the long-awaited Promised One of the Islámic Faith.(725) This Promised One was called the Qá'im (He Who Arises) by the Shí'ih Muslims, the dominant sect of Islám in Persia. He adopted the title of the Báb, however, which means the Gate or Door, to indicate that He was preparing the way for an even greater Divine Educator yet to come.

At the same time that the Báb received His revelation, there was around the world a great millennial fervor. In the West, a group known as the Millerites anticipated the return of Christ sometime in 1843-1844 based on an insightful interpretation of the Book of Daniel in the Old Testament. Meanwhile, in Persia another group known as the Shaykhís anticipated the imminent appearance of the Qá'im during that same period. As the time drew closer, one of the foremost members of the Shaykhís, a young cleric called Mullá Husayn, went searching for the Qá'im throughout much of Persia.

At the hour of dusk on May 22nd, 1844, Mullá Husayn approached the city of Shíráz. The great historian, Nabíl, recounts what happened next. Mullá Husayn saw "a Youth of radiant countenance", wearing "a green turban", Who greeted him lovingly:

> [Mullá Husayn said:]

> The Youth who met me outside the gate of Shíráz overwhelmed me with expressions of affection and loving-kindness. He extended to me a warm invitation to visit His home, and there refresh myself

> after the fatigues of my journey... I was profoundly impressed by the gentle yet compelling manner in which that strange Youth spoke to me. As I followed Him, His gait, the charm of His voice, the dignity of His bearing, served to enhance my first impressions of this unexpected meeting…
>
> [The Youth said:]
>
> 'Enter therein in peace, secure,'
>
> were His words as He crossed the threshold [to His modest home] and motioned me to follow Him. His invitation, uttered with power and majesty, penetrated my soul... – Mullá Husayn[(726)]

The two men shared refreshments and then prepared for evening prayers. Inwardly, he felt "oppressed" by the "mystery of this interview" and the "strain of his search". As they stood together, Mullá Husayn, did not yet realize that he was already in the Presence of the One for Whom he had been searching. While praying, he "unburdened his soul" with these words:

> I have striven with all my soul, O my God, and until now have failed to find Thy promised Messenger. I testify that Thy word faileth not, and that Thy promise is sure. – Mullá Husayn[(727)]

After prayers, the two men enjoyed friendly conversation. Mullá Husayn explained he was a Shaykhí, looking for the Promised Qá'im Who was expected to appear soon. At the request of his youthful Host, Mullá Husayn listed the signs he was looking for in the Promised One. The Promised One would be:

- Between 20 and 30 years old.
- He would be of noble lineage, that is, a descendent of Muhammad.
- He would be free of any bodily deficiency.
- He would be of medium height.
- He would abstain from smoking.
- And, He would be endowed with innate knowledge.[(728)]

When Mullá Husayn finished describing the signs, the Youth confidently asserted that He, Himself, was the One for Whom he was searching. With a vibrant voice, He said:

Behold, all these signs are manifest in Me! – The Báb[(729)]

Perhaps as a result of the fatigue of his journey, Mullá Husayn's first reaction was skeptical, but the Báb kindly answered all his questions. Then, *without being prompted to do so*, the Báb suddenly began to reveal an original commentary on a specific chapter of the Qur'án. This was a key sign of the Qá'im that Mullá Husayn had not mentioned to anyone.[730]

The Báb chanted the verses while writing them down, and Mullá Husayn was captivated by the speed, the wisdom, the eloquence, the beauty, and the rhythmic melody in the Báb's voice. In Mullá Husayn's words:

> I sat spellbound by His utterance, oblivious of time… All the delights, all the ineffable glories, which the Almighty has recounted in His Book as the priceless possessions of the people of Paradise—these I seemed to be experiencing that night… Sleep had departed from me that night. I was enthralled by the music of that voice which rose and fell as He chanted; now swelling forth as He revealed verses… again acquiring ethereal, subtle harmonies as He uttered the prayers He was revealing… – Mullá Husayn[731]

As evening drifted into morning, Mullá Husayn was in a state of ecstasy, his heart overwhelmed with joy. This was indeed the Qá'im!

The Báb told Mullá Husayn that seventeen other souls, seekers like himself, must on their own efforts find Him and declare their belief in Him before His public Mission could begin.

Within forty days, those first disciples, whom the Báb called the Letters of the Living, did indeed find their way to Him. The Báb educated them about the principles of His new revelation and assigned to each of them a task to help spread the Faith.

The first Letter of the Living, Mullá Husayn, was sent to Tihrán, the capital of Persia. The Báb explained the glorious task he was destined to accomplish there:

> Beseech almighty Providence that He may graciously enable you to attain, in that capital, the seat of true sovereignty, and to enter the mansion of the Beloved. A secret lies hidden in that city. When made manifest, it shall turn the earth into paradise. My hope is that you may partake of its grace and recognize its splendour… Be assured that the high mission for which you have been created will, in its entirety, be accomplished by you… – The Báb[732]

With the hindsight of history, we now know that the great "secret" he was seeking was a Person, none other than Bahá'u'lláh, a revered nobleman from one of Persia's wealthiest families. Bahá'u'lláh was in those days renowned in the region because He dedicated His time and vast wealth to caring for the poor and needy. Upon hearing of the Báb's revelation and reading just one page of His Writings, Bahá'u'lláh immediately embraced His Cause. In a short time, Bahá'u'lláh distinguished Himself as one of the foremost leaders within the ranks of the Báb's Faith.

When the Báb received the report from Mullá Husayn that Bahá'u'lláh had entered the fold, He felt immense joy and confidence that, regardless of what might happen to Him, the Cause of God would "continue to develop and flourish". Therefore, with this knowledge and assurance, He decided to embarked upon His anticipated pilgrimage to Mecca, the heart and center of Islám.[(733)] There, in Mecca, He announced Himself as the Promised One.

Although ignored by the religious leaders in Mecca, thanks to the prior influence of the Shaykhí movement in Persia, the masses were highly receptive to the news of the Báb's revelation and it soon spread like wildfire. Tens of thousands joined His new Faith. And, for a time, it appeared as if the entire nation might convert to the new religion.

Most people of that era expected the Promised Qá'im to be a violent revolutionary destined to overthrow of the corrupt Persian government. The Báb, however, had no such intentions. He rejected opportunities to spread the Bábí Faith through aggression and violence. Instead, the Báb set forth nonaggressive guidelines for the promotion of the Faith:

> The path to guidance is one of love and compassion, not of force and coercion. This hath been God's method in the past, and shall continue to be in the future! – The Báb[734]

The Báb was subjected to increasingly severe degrees of imprisonment. After he returned to Shíráz from His pilgrimage to Mecca, He was placed under house arrest. After some time, He was exiled from Shíráz, so He moved to the city of Isfahán. From there, He was moved to the mountain fortress of Máh-Kú, and then to the remote fortress of Chihríq. The Báb spent most of His ministry under confinement.

In July 1848, the Báb was summoned to a meeting in the city of Tabríz with religious leaders for purposes of examination. The significance of the occasion was heightened by the presence of the heir to the throne of Persia. The occasion was part debate, part sham trial. The religious leaders thought to humiliate the Báb through argumentation. Instead, the Báb chose that moment to fully and vividly publicly declare His station. He announced:

> I am, I am, I am the Promised One! I am the One Whose name you have for a thousand years invoked, at Whose mention you have risen, Whose advent you have longed to witness, and the hour of Whose Revelation you have prayed God to hasten... – The Báb[735]

Not surprisingly, the religious leaders refused to investigate His claim in an unbiased manner. The Báb was tortured that day and sent back to Chihríq prison.

The religious and political leaders of Persia found the rapid success of the Bábí movement threatening, so they initiated violent persecution against the Bábís. The Bábís found it necessary to defend themselves in locations throughout Persia, such as the Fort of Shaykh Tabarsí and the cities of Nayríz and Zanján. In each location, although they heroically defended themselves and their families, the Babis were ultimately overwhelmed by government forces and massacred. Over 20,000 Bábís were martyred for their Faith. Twelve of the eighteen Letters of the Living, including Mullá Husayn, laid down their lives.

One of those Letters, known as Táhirih, was a famous poetess, scholar and advocate for women's rights. Giving voice to the heart of the Báb's teachings, before the soldiers strangled her to death she is reported to have said:

> You can kill me as soon as you like, but you cannot stop the emancipation of women. – Táhirih[736]

Then, in 1850, the Prime Minister of the government issued an order to execute the Báb. On July 9, 1850, the Báb was brought to the barracks square in the city of Tabríz. According to historical reports, thousands of citizens gathered on the rooftops surrounding the square to witness the execution. The captain of the Christian Armenian regiment charged with the responsibility to conduct the execution was apprehensive about killing an Individual whom he thought was an innocent Man, so he went to talk with the Báb in His cell. He explained to the Báb that he didn't want God to be angry with him and the Báb comforted him. He replied that he should carry out his orders and if God finds him to be sincere in his heart He will, no doubt, solve his dilemma. So, the captain did as the Báb advised and ordered the execution to go forward. Meanwhile, when the soldiers came for the Báb the Báb was engaged in a conversation with His secretary, giving him some final instructions. The soldiers said to come, and the Báb replied that no power on earth can prevent Him from completing to the last word His mission on earth. The soldiers ignored this warning and took Him away anyway. The Báb and a devoted disciple were suspended from a post in the square. The regiment of 750 soldiers was arranged in three ranks of 250. The order was given, and the soldiers fired their muskets. The square filled with smoke, making it almost as dark as night at midday. When the smoke cleared, the people were astounded by the sight of the Báb's young disciple standing there completely unharmed. The Báb Himself was gone. The had been severed by the bullets.

Upon realizing that the Báb was missing, the crowd went into a frenzy. They shouted that a miracle had occurred. (Witnesses that day, including enemies of the Faith and Western diplomats who were present also confirmed that the first volley of bullets had not killed the Báb.) The soldiers began an anxious and hurried search for the Báb and soon found Him back in the prison cell He had occupied earlier that morning, "unscathed from the shower of bullets which the regiment had directed against Him".[(737)] He was found completing the conversation which had earlier been interrupted by the soldiers. The captain of the regiment, himself a Christian, had seen enough. He ordered his men to leave the scene, promising never again to have anything to do with harming the Báb.

The government authorities quickly found another regiment willing to perform the execution. By the time that the soldiers found Him back in His cell, He had completed His conversation with His aide. The Báb now told the soldiers they could do with Him whatever they wished. The Báb and His young disciple were again brought to the square and suspended again from the same post. At about noon the soldiers fired. When the smoke cleared the second time, the Báb and His disciple were both killed. Their bodies had been fused by the massive onslaught of bullets, but surprisingly their faces were completely unmarred. Nabíl reports:

> The very moment the shots were fired, a gale of exceptional severity arose and swept over the whole city. A whirlwind of dust of incredible density obscured the light of the sun and blinded the eyes of the people. The entire city remained enveloped in that darkness from noon till night. – Nabíl[738]

The authorities tossed the mangled bodies into the moat outside the city where they lay for a few days. Late at night, however, individuals loyal to the Báb secretly rescued the remains. The sacred remains were kept hidden for fifty-nine years before they were brought secretly to Ottoman Palestine (modern day Israel). 'Abdu'l-Bahá lovingly laid the sacred remains to rest in the beautiful Shrine which He had built for the Báb – the Shrine of the Báb on Mt. Carmel, in Haifa, Israel. Today, lovers of the Báb, who are mainly members of the Bahá'í Faith, come on pilgrimage from all over the world to pray at the Báb's Shrine.

Information about the Báb is found in Bábí and Bahá'í Scripture and historical writings. Eyewitness accounts of His life and times are in existence, and His original Writings in Arabic and Persian are carefully preserved in the Bahá'í archives on Mt. Carmel, in Israel. A painting of the Báb exists in the Bahá'í archives. The Báb's Writings are in the process of being translated.

Mission and teachings

Was it merely the claim that the Qá'im had appeared that so excited the population? Surely not. The mission of the Báb had a two-fold aspect.

On the one hand, as an independent Divine Educator in His own right, the Báb summoned the people to a new age of enlightenment. He said that a new age in human history had begun, the age in which humanity would be spiritually reborn and, in due course, finally achieve universal peace. He called for a strict monotheism, education for everyone, equal status for women, non-aggression, protection of the environment, and most importantly a new perspective on God's creation—that all things in creation reflect the qualities of God.

On the other hand, and of equal importance, the Báb proclaimed that He was the Herald of a still greater Manifestation of God that He referred to as "Him Whom God Shall Make Manifest". It would be this next Divine Educator Whose revelation was to come in the very near future, and Who would actually provide the guidance necessary for establishing the Kingdom of God on earth.

The Báb knew all along that Bahá'u'lláh was the next Divine Educator. This is why He was so joyful when He knew that Mullá Husayn had found the great "secret" of Tihrán.(739) From that moment on, the Báb knew that no matter what might happen to Himself, the Cause of God would be in good Hands. The Báb was the Gate, the doorway, between a past age of prophecy and a new age of fulfillment.

Amazingly, despite the horrible conditions of His imprisonment, in just six years the Báb revealed an astounding 500,000 verses of the Divine Word.(740) The Qur'án, by contrast, was just 6,236 verses, revealed over twenty-two years. In objective terms, the Báb's literary output was equivalent to about 80 Qur'áns, which He produced in six years' time. As one can imagine, with such prodigious output, the Báb was able to reveal a considerable body of teachings. A very small sampling of these core teachings will be mentioned here.

At the center of the Báb's teaching lay His soaring, transcendent monotheism, a natural culmination of centuries of Abrahamic ethical monotheism. After centuries of human beings trying to imagine the interior Reality of the Essence of God, the Báb explained that, notwithstanding the noble intention of wanting to know God, no one in creation is capable of knowing God as He is within Himself.

> ...No one hath ever been able befittingly to recognize Him nor will any man succeed at any time in comprehending Him as is truly meet and seemly, for any reality to which the term 'being' is applicable hath been created by the sovereign Will of the Almighty... – The Báb[741]

Even the concept of *being/existence*, which seems so fundamental to the human mind, is ultimately just another part of the creation, not the Creator. Human language, no matter how elevated or precise it may become, even when affirming the existence of God, always falls short of describing God's existence adequately. Whatever the existence of God really is, it is infinitely beyond adequate human comprehension or description. As He says, anything that has "being" is part of the creation, and all of that has been called into existence by the Will of the Almighty God.

The Báb's ethical monotheism was not new. The *newness* of the Báb's teaching was the extent to which He eloquently and repeatedly emphasized the *infinity* of God. This perspective had always been present in the ethical monotheism of the other Abrahamic Faiths, but the theologians, philosophers and scientists of the past had always imagined ways to make God more "human" in their thinking. Now, through continuous emphasis on the oneness and infinity of God, the Báb's teaching sought to put aside any tendency to make God into a human-like creature.[742]

Although interior knowledge of the Essence and Being of God is unattainable for all creatures, the Báb made it equally clear that human beings *can* know a great deal *about* God and are able to experience a deeply personal relationship with Him.

The First Emanation from God, He explained, is the Primal Will of God (also referred to as the Word, the Logos, the Holy Spirit, the First Remembrance, etc.). The Báb said that the Primal Will of God, like an ever-repeating sunrise, is manifested from time to time when God sends a Divine Educator into the world.

> In the time of the First Manifestation the Primal Will appeared in Adam; in the day of Noah It became known in Noah; in the day of Abraham in Him; and so in the day of Moses; the day of Jesus; the day of Muhammad, the Apostle of God; the day of the 'Point of the Bayán'; the day of Him Whom God shall make manifest; and the day of the One Who will appear after Him Whom God shall make manifest. Hence the inner meaning of the words uttered by the Apostle of God, 'I am all the Prophets', inasmuch as what shineth resplendent in each one of Them hath been and will ever remain the one and the same sun. – The Báb[743]

At one time the Primal Will was manifested in Adam, then in Noah, then in Abraham, Moses, Jesus, Muhammad, and the Báb. At the time in history when the Báb wrote those words (1844 to 1850), the Báb said that the Primal Will of God was going to appear again very soon in the Person of Him Whom God Shall Make Manifest, Whom we know today as Bahá'u'lláh. (The term "Point of the Bayán" is a reference to the Báb Himself, as the Author of His main book, the Bayán).

The Báb repeatedly compared these appearances of the Primal Will of God in the world to be like the risings of the sun:

> ...the First Remembrance, which is the Primal Will of God, may be likened unto the sun. – The Báb[(744)]

> ...the Revelation of God may be likened to the sun. No matter how innumerable its risings, there is but one sun, and upon it depends the life of all things... The process of the rise and setting of the Sun of Truth will thus indefinitely continue – a process that hath had no beginning and will have no end. – The Báb[(745)]

> And know thou that He indeed resembleth the sun. Were the risings of the sun to continue till the end that hath no end, yet there hath not been nor ever will be more than one sun; and were its settings to endure for evermore, still there hath not been nor ever will be more than one sun. It is this Primal Will which appeareth resplendent in every Prophet and speaketh forth in every revealed Book. It knoweth no beginning ... and knoweth no end... – The Báb[(746)]

The Báb also said that the Primal Will is the Force which brings into being all created things.[747]

> Everything thou beholdest hath been called into being through the operation of His Will. – The Báb[748]

In the Writings of the Báb, the Primal Will of God is also known as the Primal Point when It is sent into the world in the form of a Manifestation of God. Thus, the Báb referred to Himself as the Primal Point.

> I am the Primal Point from which have been generated all created things. – The Báb[749]

Moreover, it is the power of the Manifestation of God, the intermediary between the Essence of God and all of creation, which is also known as the Primal Will manifested as the Primal Point, which calls creation into being:

> ...God called you into being through the Primal Point... – The Báb[(750)]

Noted scholar Adib Taherzadeh offered these comments about the Primal Will of God:

> The Holy Spirit is usually associated with the Manifestations of God. It is the Holy Spirit which has animated them all, and the Holy Spirit itself has been generated through the instrumentality of the 'Most Great Spirit', also referred to as the 'Primal Will'. Through it all creation has come into being and all Revelations have been sent down. – Adib Taherzadeh[751]

Thus, the Báb taught that the Primal Will was the first emanation from God, that It is the Most Holy Spirit animating all of the Manifestations of God, and that It is the Primal Point which calls into being all of existence.

The Báb taught a fully developed concept of the continuity of Divine revelation. God's grace is unending, so the Divine Educators must continue to be sent into the world, He said. The Divine curriculum has been and always will be never-ending because God's grace cannot ever be stopped:

> The process of His creation hath had no beginning and can have no end, otherwise it would necessitate the cessation of His celestial grace. God hath raised up Prophets and revealed Books as numerous as the creatures of the world, and will continue to do so to everlasting. – The Báb[(752)]

Through His own exemplary piety, through His revealed prayers and through His Writings, the Báb demonstrated that a *truly infinite* God had more than enough capacity to run the universe and to also be concerned with the well-being and prayers of individual human beings, no matter how meek or lowly someone may be. The infinite God is eager to engage in a voluntary, loving and personal relationship with each and every one of His human creatures.

The Báb taught that resurrection is renewal, and not a one-time catastrophic, world-ending, and history-ending event that takes place at a distant future time. According to the Báb, the Day of Resurrection has already happened many times in the past, whenever a new Manifestation of the Primal Will of God, a new Divine Educator, has been sent into the world.

> ...from the inception of the mission of Jesus—may peace be upon Him—till the day of His ascension was the Resurrection of Moses... – The Báb[753]

> The Day of Resurrection is a day on which the sun riseth and setteth like unto any other day. How oft hath the Day of Resurrection dawned, and the people of the land where it occurred did not learn of the event. – The Báb[754]

Thus, Jesus was the Resurrection of Moses, Muhammad the Resurrection of Jesus, the Báb the Resurrection of Muhammad, and so on. Whenever a new Divine Educator appears in the world, His Presence represents the Resurrection of the previous Divine Educator. The spiritually dead are awakened from their graves of sin and unbelief by the newest Divine Educator, people decide whether to embrace or reject the newest Messenger, the Day of the most recent revelation unfolds normally in human history and the Divine curriculum continues to promote the advancement of civilization.

The Báb taught that men should adopt an exceptionally high standard of virtuous conduct. An individual should worship God for His sake alone, and not through fear of hell or hope of heaven. Similarly, an individual should act in his life for the sake of God. One should never bring sadness to anyone. His followers should avoid extremism, protect the environment, encourage education for everyone and elevate the status of women in society. The Báb taught and practiced integrity in His dealings with others.

Noted scholar Nader Saiedi has suggested that one of the most important teachings of the Báb is "the perspective of unity."[755] This is a perspective on life which sees the reflection of God in all things.

> And within the inmost reality of all things there hath been, and will forever continue to be, a sign from God through which the unity of the Lord is celebrated. This sign, however, is a reflection of His Will, present within it, through which naught is seen but God. – The Báb[756]

> ...every created thing, by its very nature, beareth evidence that it hath been fashioned by God... – The Báb[757]

When the perspective of unity is applied to daily living, a person's perspective on life is transformed. Despite whatever shortcomings people may possess—and regardless of superficial differences such as gender, race, creed or nationality—individuals learn to regard others as if they were a DaVinci, a Van Gogh or a Monet masterpiece because within the heart of every individual is an indication that he or she was created by God. The Báb's perspective of unity unites all people through a vision of reality that discovers God's blessed handiwork in all created things. It can be argued that the sanctuary of the heart provides a profound spiritual rationale for the unity of the human race.

After the Báb

A central aspect of the Báb's mission is that He was the Herald of another, greater Divine Educator to come. He referred to this Divine Messenger as Him Whom God Shall Make Manifest, but we now know that He was talking about Bahá'u'lláh, Who was a wealthy nobleman of Tihrán. As mentioned earlier, Bahá'u'lláh joined the Bábí Faith very early in the history of the movement and became one of its leading exponents. But in those early days, Bahá'u'lláh's future role was not known to most of the followers and He was regarded merely as a Bábí.

Beginning around 1847, the Báb began to vigorously emphasize the imminent coming of Him Whom God Shall Make Manifest. The Báb repeatedly spoke of "the year nine" of His revelation as being the key point in time to be on the lookout for Him.

> In the year nine ye shall attain unto all good. – The Báb[758]

To understand this quote, one needs to convert the date from the Islámic calendar:

> The declaration of the Báb took place in the year 1260 AH (1844 AD). The year nine is 1269 AH, which began about the middle of October 1852 when Bahá'u'lláh had already been imprisoned for about two months in the [Black Pit in Tihrán], the scene of the birth of [Bahá'u'lláh's] Revelation. – Adib Taherzadeh[759]

The Báb was emphatic to His followers that loyalty to Him Whom God Shall Make Manifest, Bahá'u'lláh, was the same as loyalty to Him.

> ...If on the day of His Revelation all that are on earth bear Him allegiance, Mine inmost being will rejoice, inasmuch as all will have attained

> the summit of their existence.... If not, My soul will be saddened. I truly have nurtured all things for this purpose. How, then, can anyone be veiled from Him? – The Báb[760]

As a result of teachings such as these, among the Bábís there was no doubt whatsoever that Him Whom God Shall Make Manifest was going to come quickly. The only thing most of the Bábís did not know was that He was already by their side, comforting them and serving the Cause as one of them with exemplary wisdom and devotion.

The stature of the Báb

The Báb infused a dynamic spiritual force into the Bábí community, which brought forth exalted spiritual virtues and heroic fortitude in the face of brutal oppression and persecution. Though the authorities of the day sought to extinguish His Cause, in those early years the Bábí movement continued to expand. The repeated banishments, intended to isolate the Báb, only brought Him into contact with far flung populations, each of whom were attracted to His magnetic personality and eloquent teachings.

One French scholar compared the Báb's life and mission with that of Jesus. He wrote:

> His life is one of the most magnificent examples of courage which it has been the privilege of mankind to behold, and it is also an admirable proof of the love which our hero felt for his fellow countrymen. He sacrificed himself for humanity, for it he gave his body and his soul, for it he endured privations, insults, torture and martyrdom. He sealed, with his very lifeblood, the covenant of universal brotherhood. Like Jesus he paid with his life for the proclamation of a reign of concord, equity and brotherly love… Fear had no hold upon his soul and, perfectly calm, never looking back, in full possession of all his powers, he walked into the furnace. – A. L. M. Nicolas[761]

In addition to bringing about an unprecedented spiritual renewal among His followers, perhaps the signal achievement of the Báb is that He brought into being a large community of committed followers who were prepared, waiting and receptive for the soon-to-be-made-known revelation of Him Whom God Shall Make Manifest.

The Báb succeeded in accomplishing the near total transition of His followers into the Faith of the Divine Educator that came after Him. An estimated ninety-nine percent of His followers accepted Bahá'u'lláh after He made His claims known to them.(762) This is an extraordinary achievement, a first in religious history and no doubt attributable both to the unceasing preparation which the Báb provided to His followers and to the magnificent ability of Bahá'u'lláh to attract those same followers to His Cause. The Báb's followers accepted promotion in the great school of God. They kept current with the ever-advancing Divine curriculum.

By pouring out Divine verses at an unprecedented pace and scope, by bringing four millennia of monotheistic understanding to a culmination, by suffering and laying down His life as a sacrifice for all of humankind, and by brilliantly leading His followers to embrace the next Divine Educator Who appeared soon after Him, literally millions and potentially billions of souls have been the beneficiaries of the Báb's life and mission on earth.

BAHÁ'U'LLÁH

Introduction

In the nineteenth century strife and hostility prevailed among the people of the Orient. Apathy and ignorance characterized the nations. They were indeed gloomy and dark, negligent of God and under the subjection of the baser instincts and passions of mankind... At such a time as this Bahá'u'lláh appeared among them like a luminary in the heavens. He flooded the East with light. He proclaimed new principles and teachings. He laid a basis for new institutions which are the very spirit of modernism, the light of the world, the development of the body politic and eternal honor. The souls who hearkened to these teachings among the various oriental nations immediately renounced the spirit of strife and hostility and began to associate in goodwill and fellowship. From extremes of animosity they attained the acme of love and brotherhood. They had been warring and quarreling; now they became loving and lived together in complete unity and agreement. Among them today you will find no religious, political or patriotic prejudice; they are friendly, loving and associate in the greatest happiness. They have no part in the war and strife which take place in the East; their attitude toward all men is that of goodwill and loving-kindness. A standard of universal peace has been unfurled among them. The light of guidance has flooded their souls. It is light upon light, love upon love. This is the education and training of Bahá'u'lláh...—'Abdu'l-Bahá[763]

Bahá'u'lláh was born about 200 years ago, in 1817, in Tihrán, Persia (modern-day Iran). He was a nobleman born into one of the wealthiest families in Persia. He was descended from Abraham, through that Patriarch's third wife, Keturah.

Bahá'u'lláh was a young man in His twenties when His father, who had been a high-ranking official in the court of the Sháh of Persia, passed away. As was customary in those times, Bahá'u'lláh was offered His father's position in the government. Though the position would have guaranteed prestige and affluence for life, He declined the offer. Instead, Bahá'u'lláh and His wife concentrated on spiritual and humanitarian pursuits, using their vast wealth to take care of the poor. So highly regarded were they that the poor of their region had given them the nicknames of "Father of the Poor" and "Mother of Consolation".

As mentioned previously, in the mid-nineteenth century Persia was a place of extreme fanaticism, corruption, degradation, brutality and narrowness of mind. When news of the Báb's revelation reached Bahá'u'lláh in Tihrán in early 1844, He discerned the truth of the Báb's claims and immediately became a champion of that Cause. Bahá'u'lláh was an exceptionally articulate exponent of the Báb's teachings which helped Him bring large numbers of people into the Movement.

The religious and government leaders in Persia almost immediately began fierce persecutions of the Bábís. Tens of thousands were killed and the Báb Himself was martyred in 1850. By the end of 1852, nearly all of the leaders of the Faith had also been wiped out, with only Bahá'u'lláh remaining as "the sole survivor among the towering figures of the new Dispensation."[(764)] The combined effect of these multiple disasters created a deep sense of despair and decline among the Bábís.

In August of 1852, two emotionally overwrought Bábí youths decided to cast aside all that the Báb had taught them and take revenge on the Sháh. One day, while the Sháh and his entourage were traveling outside the city of Tihrán, these two Bábís attacked and tried to kill the Sháh.

Though injured and thrown from his horse, the Sháh survived the attack. The attackers were punished immediately. Once back in the palace, the government authorities ordered a massive purge against the Bábís. Government officials in every region were ordered to participate personally in the massacres. Thousands were slaughtered.

Bahá'u'lláh deplored the attack on the Sháh. Indeed, Bahá'u'lláh had been counseling wisdom and patience among the Bábís. However, once such a heinous crime had occurred there was no doubt that the authorities would seek to take Him into custody. The Russian Ambassador to Persia offered Him refuge in Russia but Bahá'u'lláh declined the offer. Instead of hiding or running away, Bahá'u'lláh set out on His horse to go towards the closest encampment of the Persian Army to turn Himself in. He was arrested, tortured, and in a march reminiscent of the Passion of Christ the authorities paraded Him through the streets, barefoot and bareheaded in the intense summer heat, while the citizens He had so lovingly served stoned Him.

In Tihrán, Baha'u'llah was thrown into the notorious Black Pit dungeon (known as the *Síyáh-Chál* in Persian) and weighed down with chains so heavy they scarred His body for the rest of His life. Three stories underground, in a space formerly used as a palace cistern, the Black Pit had a loathsome smell, was icy-cold and infested by vermin—a truly unbearable place. Mobs ransacked His homes. Bahá'u'lláh's pregnant wife and children had to flee and were instantly reduced to poverty.

Since Bahá'u'lláh was a renowned nobleman from one of the most prestigious families in Persia, it was not politically expedient for the authorities to simply execute Him. They hoped, instead, that Bahá'u'lláh would die in the prison where He suffered along with about one hundred fifty other Bábís. Bahá'u'lláh later wrote an extraordinary account of how, in that dangerous and dismal place, He experienced His first moments of Divine revelation as "Him Whom God Shall Make Manifest".

> One night, in a dream, these exalted words were heard on every side: "Verily, We shall render Thee victorious by Thyself and by Thy Pen. Grieve Thou not for that which hath befallen Thee, neither be Thou afraid, for Thou art in safety. Erelong will God raise up the treasures of the earth—men who will aid Thee through Thyself and through Thy Name, wherewith God hath revived the hearts of such as have recognized Him."... During the days I lay in the prison of Tihrán, though the galling weight of the chains and the stench-filled air allowed Me but little sleep, still in those infrequent moments of slumber I felt as if something flowed from the crown of My head over My breast, even as a mighty torrent that precipitateth itself upon the earth from the summit of a lofty mountain. Every limb of My body would, as a result, be set afire. At such moments My tongue recited what no man could bear to hear.—Bahá'u'lláh[765]

After about four months in the Black Pit, events moved to bring about the release of Bahá'u'lláh Who was very sick but alive. The mastermind of the crime against the Sháh had been found, Bahá'u'lláh's innocence had been categorically proven and the Russian Minister to Persia was demanding Bahá'u'lláh's release. The government complied but stripped Him of all His wealth. He and His family were banished to Baghdád after allowing just one month to recover from His illness and prepare for the journey. The trek across the perilous mountains took place during the most severe Persian winter in recent memory.

After a journey of great suffering and privation, Bahá'u'lláh and His family managed to get to Baghdád, which at that time was under Ottoman rule. Soon after they arrived, Bahá'u'lláh's wife lost the baby she was carrying. Bahá'u'lláh was allowed to take up residence in a modest home in the city.

Bahá'u'lláh did not immediately reveal His station to the Bábís. At first, only His eldest Son, nine-year-old 'Abdu'l-Bahá possessed the spiritual insight to recognize the great change that had taken place within Him.

As "Him Whom God Shall Make Manifest", Bahá'u'lláh was aware of the degraded state of the Bábí community. His mission was to establish the unity of the human race and to bring about the spiritual rebirth of every human being on the planet. How could such a seemingly impossible mission succeed with such a discouraged band of supporters? The answer was in plain sight.[(766)]

In Baghdád, Bahá'u'lláh worked to revive the spiritual vitality of the Bábís. As a consequence of these efforts, His standing as the true spiritual leader of the community gradually became obvious. During this period, He revealed a number of His most significant works. Among them were: *The Book of Certitude*, His leading theological book; *The Hidden Words*, a marvelously compact guide to spiritual ethics; and *The Seven Valleys*, His most popular mystical treatise.

Bahá'u'lláh's popularity among the general population of Baghdád gradually rose to such a level that he was again banished by the authorities, this time to the ancient city of Constantinople (modern-day Istanbul), the capital of the Ottoman Empire. Upon the eve of His departure, Bahá'u'lláh made the historic announcement to the Bábís that He was in fact "Him Whom God Shall Make Manifest", the Promised One of the Báb. That day, April 21st, 1863, is celebrated world-wide as the greatest Holy Day of Bahá'í history.

Bahá'u'lláh explained that God had chosen Him to reveal a stupendous revelation for our times, one which God had ordained as the pathway to the oneness of humanity and the spiritual awakening of the human race. He stated that the mission of this age is to finally bring about on earth the establishment of God's Kingdom. He said that God had ordained that in this Day the law of the sword was abolished, and like the Báb He ordained that the mighty goal of peace for the planet must be established through love and unity, not force or violence.

After a brief residence in Constantinople, Bahá'u'lláh's growing popularity again caused Him to be banished for five years to the city of Adrianople, and finally, in 1868, to the prison fortress city of 'Akká in the Holy Land. Baha'u'llah and His entire family suffered extreme hardship in the prison fortress, which He called the Most Great Prison.

After a little more than two years Bahá'u'lláh was allowed to move to a house within the city of 'Akká, effectively under house arrest. As the years wore on, the authorities became intensely aware of Bahá'u'lláh's sterling spiritual qualities and gradually softened the restrictions He had been enduring. In 1879, while still under official restrictions, Bahá'u'lláh was allowed to take up residence in an abandoned mansion outside the city of 'Akká. That mansion, known as Bahjí (Delight) to Bahá'ís, is the place where Bahá'u'lláh passed away in 1892. His remains are located in a Shrine next to the mansion surrounded by beautiful gardens added in the years since His passing. It is the primary pilgrimage destination for Bahá'ís around the world.

Bahá'u'lláh's written output during forty-year ministry was on a par with that of the Báb. All told, He revealed the equivalent of about one hundred volumes. His Writings are known for their profound spiritual insight, eloquence and beauty. At times Bahá'u'lláh wrote in the style of a lawgiver, and other times like a philosopher, an interpreter of Scripture, a wise counselor, a mystic or a pragmatic guide and problem-solver. Bahá'u'lláh's Writings provide the necessary guidance for individuals, institutions and the community of mankind to establish salvation, justice and unity.

Bahá'u'lláh was the first Divine Educator to leave behind a written Will & Testament. In this personally handwritten document, He appointed His eldest son 'Abdu'l-Bahá to be His Successor. This single historic act, unique in the annals of human religious history, inaugurated the Covenant of Bahá'u'lláh with His followers and enabled His Faith to avoid the schisms that have afflicted the religious Dispensations of the past.

Bahá'u'lláh ordained in His Writings that there would be no clergy in His Faith. Using a non-partisan election procedure, He placed the administrative affairs of His Faith in the hands of elected governing councils known as Local and National Spiritual Assemblies. He also ordained a world governing body, known as the Universal House of Justice, which has its seat on Mt. Carmel, in Haifa, Israel, and is elected every five years.

In the decades since the passing of Bahá'u'lláh, the Bahá'í Faith has spread throughout the world to over 200 countries. Demographically, the Bahá'í Faith is highly inclusive. More than 2,000 races, tribes and ethnicities comprise its population. Published literature has been translated into about 800 languages. The Bahá'í population world-wide is about five million. Recognized today in most parts of the world, while still being persecuted in some places, the Bahá'í Faith has established itself as a world religion. It is the fourth world Faith in the Abrahamic lineage.

Information about the Bahá'u'lláh is found in Bábí and Bahá'í Scripture and historical writings. Eyewitness accounts of His life and times are in existence and His original Writings in Arabic and Persian are carefully preserved in the Bahá'í archives on Mt. Carmel in Israel. A portrait and a photograph of Baha'u'llah exists in the Bahá'í archives. Bahá'u'lláh's Writings are in the process of being translated.

Mission and teachings

Bahá'u'lláh wrote that God had bestowed upon Him a specific mission for this time in history:

> This Youth hath come to quicken the world and unite all its peoples. The day is approaching when that which God hath purposed will have prevailed and thou shalt behold the earth transformed into the all-glorious paradise.—Bahá'u'lláh[767]

Quickening, originally a medical term indicating the first stirrings of a baby inside the womb of the mother, refers the spiritual and material awakening of the human race. Uniting all the peoples of the earth refers to the oneness of humanity, an emergent state of society in which all the peoples, races and nations of the world are fully reconciled and living in peace with one another. When these things are achieved, inevitably the entire world will become like an all-glorious paradise. Thus, Bahá'u'lláh was sent into the world with the mission of culminating the work of all the Dispensations of the past and fulfilling the ancient goal of the Divine curriculum, the establishment on earth of God's Kingdom.

Bahá'u'lláh knew that God had designated Him to be Him Whom God Shall Make Manifest, the Promised One of the Báb's revelation, and indeed the One to fulfill the prophecies of the Scriptures of the past.

> The time foreordained unto the peoples and kindreds of the earth is now come. The promises of God, as recorded in the holy Scriptures, have all been fulfilled.—Bahá'u'lláh[768]

Bahá'u'lláh recognized that the religious and secular authorities in every age invariably reject the claims made by the Divine Educators because They do not fulfill the expectations and the prophecies as interpreted by the religious leaders. Bahá'u'lláh already knew how the Báb and His followers had been treated, so He expected similar treatment once His claims became known.

Bahá'u'lláh knew that establishing God's Kingdom on earth, a Divine civilization, would signify nothing less than the coming of age of humankind and was a task that would take many generations. But He asserted it was God's will that the time had come to finally achieve it. Bahá'u'lláh realized that an idolatrous, materialistic, chaotic, divided, corrupt and strife-ridden humanity could never achieve this goal without substantial Divine guidance, grace and assistance. Bahá'u'lláh foresaw humanity's long period of tribulation but promised that God had not abandoned humanity. On the contrary, He taught that humanity's trials would in the long run be cleansing and chastening learning experiences that would lead humanity to its ultimate God-ordained destiny.

Bahá'u'lláh and the Báb both shared the same fundamental insight that Jesus had originally taught—the Kingdom of God is within. World peace cannot be achieved merely through the acquisition and exercise of power, nor by merely passing laws, so long as the human heart remained dedicated to sin and selfishness. Evil, He taught, ultimately springs from the ascendency of man's animal nature over his spiritual nature. The truly virtuous society depends on the exercise of free will to choose the path of virtuous conduct.

> All that which ye potentially possess can, however, be manifested only as a result of your own volition. Your own acts testify to this truth.—Bahá'u'lláh(769)

Peace on earth depends upon achieving the intentional conquest of the self, the voluntary subordination of man's animal nature to his angelic side and the education and transformation of the interior soul and character of man.

Bahá'u'lláh also stated a new principle—that universal peace and well-being is not possible unless and until the peoples and nations first learn to unite, and this was possible only with guidance from God. Learned statesmen had imagined that the unity of humanity would come from peace; in fact, Bahá'u'lláh said, the opposite was true. Unity was a necessary prerequisite for lasting peace, and God's help and guidance is necessary to achieve so fundamental a transformation of humankind:

> The well-being of mankind, its peace and security, are unattainable unless and until its unity is firmly established. This unity can never be achieved so long as the counsels which the Pen of the Most High hath revealed are suffered to pass unheeded.—Bahá'u'llá[770]

Bahá'u'lláh's revelation brought an unprecedented dual focus on both the individual and the collective life of humanity. He provided detailed teachings for the spiritual transformation and salvation of the individual person, and also ordained laws and teachings for society as a whole. Combined, His extensive teachings provide a blueprint for humanity to rise to its Divinely ordained destiny.

Some of those teachings will be mentioned below.

Bahá'u'lláh is a Divine Educator firmly in the Abrahamic lineage. Like His Predecessors, Abraham, Moses, Jesus, Muhammad and the Báb, Bahá'u'lláh taught a vigorous ethical monotheism. In His teaching, there is but one God, one Creator.

> There can be no doubt whatever that the peoples of the world, of whatever race or religion, derive their inspiration from one heavenly Source, and are the subjects of one God.—Bahá'u'lláh[771]

Bahá'u'lláh continued the Báb's profound emphasis of the transcendent infinity of God:

> Regard thou the one true God as One Who is apart from, and immeasurably exalted above, all created things. The whole universe reflecteth His glory, while He is Himself independent of, and transcendeth His creatures... All existence is dependent upon Him, and from Him is derived the source of the sustenance of all things. This is what is meant by Divine unity; this is its fundamental principle.—Bahá'u'lláh[772]

Like the Báb, Bahá'u'lláh also emphasized that being utterly infinite in no wise prevented God from entering into a personal relationship with every individual and nation. According to Bahá'u'lláh, God knows us so intimately, and cares for us so deeply, that sometimes He answers our needs before we even ask for His help:

> Unasked, I have showered upon thee My grace. Unpetitioned, I have fulfilled thy wish. In spite of thy undeserving, I have singled thee out for My richest, My incalculable favors....—Bahá'u'lláh[773]

Bahá'u'lláh makes it very clear in His Writings that God wants a loving relationship with His human children:

O SON OF MAN! I loved thy creation, hence I created thee. Wherefore, do thou love Me, that I may name thy name and fill thy soul with the spirit of life.—Bahá'u'lláh[774]

Since God is beyond human comprehension, but still desires to have a relationship with human beings, He chooses to reveal Himself to humanity through Divine Educators, the Manifestations of God, in different times and places throughout history.

[In the next quote, Birds of the celestial Throne = the Divine Educators.]

Inasmuch as these Birds of the celestial Throne are all sent down from the heaven of the Will of God, and as they all arise to proclaim His irresistible Faith, they, therefore, are regarded as one soul and the same person. For they all drink from the one Cup of the love of God, and all partake of the fruit of the same Tree of Oneness… Even as He hath revealed: "No distinction do We make between any of His Messengers."… If thou wilt observe with discriminating eyes, thou wilt behold Them all abiding in the same tabernacle, soaring in the same heaven, seated upon the same throne, uttering the same speech, and proclaiming the same Faith. Such is the unity of those Essences of Being, those Luminaries of infinite and immeasurable splendor!—Bahá'u'lláh[775]

Bahá'u'lláh's teaching concerning the unity of the Prophets provides a new understanding of religious truth, which "by sweeping away the age-long barriers that have so insurmountably separated the great religions of the world, has laid down a broad and unassailable foundation for the complete and permanent reconciliation of their followers."[776]

- Each Divine Educator is recognized for His unique mission from God and for His specific contribution to the advancement of civilization.
- Each Divine Educator is recognized as a Member of the Faculty in the universal school of God, all teaching stages of the Divine curriculum, all serving the same mission.

Bahá'u'lláh stressed the oneness of humankind as His central teaching for the current age. Considered "the pivot round which all the teachings of Bahá'u'lláh revolve",[777] the whole focus of Bahá'u'lláh's social teachings are aimed at promoting the oneness of humanity. The following is a brief and partial listing of teachings that are intended to help bring about the oneness of humankind:

- The independent investigation of truth.
- The abolition of prejudice.
- The elimination of fanaticism and that religion must be the cause of unity.
- The harmony of science and religion.
- The equality of women and men.
- The necessity for universal education. (Including equal treatment for both boys and girls.)
- The voluntary elimination of extremes of wealth and poverty.
- The adoption by the nations of a universal auxiliary language.
- The need for a trustworthy system of world governance.
- The general demilitarization of the planet in conjunction with the principles of collective security and reconciliation among the nations.

Bahá'u'lláh taught that problems should be solved and conflicts resolved through the practice of consultation, which, as He and 'Abdu'l-Bahá taught it, is a unique form of discourse. Not debate, not trying to win an argument, not being emotionally attached to one's own ideas and not trying to seek an advantage at another party's expense, consultation is a type of discourse in which parties search together for the truth of a matter. While differences of viewpoint are freely expressed, belittling the views of another is not permitted. Consultation requires mutual respect, even love, a moderate tone, an attitude of learning and tolerance for the shortcomings of others. Consultation calls for listening for the merits in what each party has to say, with the aim of finding the best answer and outcome for all concerned. Bahá'ís around the world have been practicing this method for over a century with marvelous results overall. Though no one would claim consultation is easy, or that mistakes are not made, in general, consultation is both an attitude and a skill that can be learned. With practice, whether the context is within the Faith, between the world Faiths, among the nations, between the races, in the workplace, in the schoolhouse or between married couples, consultation is an uplifting and effective unity-building method of discourse.

As to the individual, Bahá'u'lláh provided extensive teachings concerning the nature of man, man's relationship with God and the destiny of the soul in the worlds beyond. He prohibited backbiting and enjoined the formation of a noble and virtuous character and conduct here on earth. Bahá'u'lláh ordained daily prayer and study of the Word of God, which, in His perspective, includes the Scriptures of the world's religions. Bahá'ís are expected to practice chastity, to abstain from alcohol and the abuse of drugs, to avoid gambling and to hold themselves apart from any entanglement with partisan politics.

As an extension of the oneness of mankind, Bahá'u'lláh taught the practice of universal fellowship:

> Consort with the followers of all religions in a spirit of friendliness and fellowship." Whatsoever hath led the children of men to shun one another, and hath caused dissensions and divisions amongst them, hath, through the revelation of these words, been nullified and abolished.—Bahá'u'lláh[778]

The ethical standards set by Bahá'u'lláh are very high. It is virtuous conduct on the part of individuals, institutions and the community of nations that provides the key to humanity's spiritual and material advancement.

> Honesty, virtue, wisdom and a saintly character redound to the exaltation of man, while dishonesty, imposture, ignorance and hypocrisy lead to his abasement. By My life! Man's distinction lieth not in ornaments or wealth, but rather in virtuous behaviour and true understanding.—Bahá'u'lláh[779]

> The purpose of the one true God in manifesting Himself is to summon all mankind to truthfulness and sincerity, to piety and trustworthiness, to resignation and submissiveness to the will of God, to forbearance and kindliness, to uprightness and wisdom. His object is to array every man with the mantle of a saintly character, and to adorn him with the ornament of holy and goodly deeds.—Bahá'u'lláh[780]

> By My life! The light of a good character surpasseth the light of the sun and the radiance thereof.—Bahá'u'lláh[781]

> Truthfulness is the foundation of all human virtues. Without truthfulness progress and success, in all the worlds of God, are impossible for any soul. When this holy attribute is established in man, all the divine qualities will also be acquired."—'Abdu'l-Bahá[782]

Bahá'ís around the world are organized along the guidelines set by Bahá'u'lláh. Without a clergy, elected local, national and international administrative bodies run the day to day affairs of the Bahá'í Faith. There is also a non-clergy appointed branch, referred to as "the learned", which serves in a complementary advisory and encouraging capacity at the local, national and international levels. At present there are eight continental Bahá'í Houses of Worship and plans to build several more in the near future. Bahá'ís participate in interfaith activities around the world and undertake various social economic development and humanitarian activities as well. Bahá'ís are non-partisan. Bahá'í communities across the globe celebrate Bahá'í Holy Days and observe an annual period of fasting.

World-wide, Bahá'ís are engaged in a systematic "process that seeks to raise capacity within a population to take charge of its own spiritual, social and intellectual development."[(783)] By focusing on certain core activities, in addition to the ordinary activities of a religious community, increased momentum towards the transformation of civilization is being pursued. These activities include educational activities for children, youth and adults, which emphasize the development of virtuous conduct, insight and spiritual empowerment, especially for youth. Another core activity includes sponsoring devotional meetings where prayers and the Word of God are shared with people of all backgrounds and Faiths.

As the Bahá'í Faith continues to grow around the world, the community and society-building power of all these activities is gradually becoming a visible model of a new and inclusive pattern of life, based on faith, consultation and virtues, which promotes spiritual awakening and the unity of the human race.

After Bahá'u'lláh

Bahá'u'lláh guaranteed the future unity of His Faith by appointing in writing His eldest Son, 'Abdu'l-Bahá, to be His Successor and Head of the Faith after His passing. He also assigned to 'Abdu'l-Bahá the roles of Exemplar and Interpreter of the Teachings. Individuals in the Faith were welcome to have their own personal opinions about the Faith, but no individual other than 'Abdu'l-Bahá was given the right to authoritatively interpret or explain the teachings. No one could form a sect around him or herself, claiming to be either the perfect Bahá'í or in exclusive possession of the truth of the Faith. 'Abdu'l-Bahá traveled widely in His later years and also maintained an extensive correspondence with the Bahá'ís around the world. His letters and books have become an essential body of knowledge assisting the Faith.

When 'Abdu'l-Bahá passed away, He appointed His eldest grandson, Shoghi Effendi, to the role of Guardian of the Bahá'í Faith. As Guardian, Shoghi Effendi continued writing and translating the Writings. He continued 'Abdu'l-Bahá's function as Interpreter of the Writings. He organized world-wide spread of the Faith and he guided the Bahá'ís in raising up thousands of local and national spiritual assemblies. He laid the groundwork for the election and establishment of the Universal House of Justice, the Faith's world governing body. The Bahá'í Faith, with its unity intact, has been under the leadership of the Universal House of Justice since 1963.

As to the next Divine Educator, Bahá'u'lláh was emphatic that God would never stop sending His Messengers to humanity. Very little is known about what to expect, except for one fact. Bahá'u'lláh said the next Divine Educator will not come before one thousand years have passed. We know from the Bahá'í Writings that the one thousand year "clock" began with the inception of Bahá'u'lláh's revelation in the year 1852. Hence, more than eight centuries are remaining, at a minimum, before the next Divine Educator will make His appearance.[784]

The stature of Bahá'u'lláh

How does one estimate the stature of a Divine Educator when the Dispensation He inaugurated is still in progress, when the Faith He founded is still young, and while most of the human race remains unaware of the Revelation that He bestowed upon humankind? What could you say about the achievements of the Israelite, the Christian, or the Muslim civilizations less than two centuries after the founding of their Faiths? Certainly, at this early stage, no adequate assessment of Bahá'u'lláh's stature or His contribution to Divine civilization can be articulated.

Even so, there are useful indicators.

Bahá'u'lláh left over a hundred volumes of the revealed Word of God, much of it already translated. Within these volumes Bahá'u'lláh gave humanity a priceless treasure of exhortations, world-shaping laws and ordinances, stirring warnings and prophecies to mankind, soul-uplifting prayers, meditations, commentaries and explanations, addresses to kings and religious leaders, mystical discourses, ethical teachings, social teachings and organizational guidance.[785]

Contained within these volumes is a blueprint for methodically and patiently establishing the oneness of humanity and God's Kingdom on earth through loving, peaceful, and nonviolent means. When one reads even a small portion of Bahá'u'lláh's guidance, one cannot fail to be impressed by the completeness and wisdom of His road map for humanity. The writings of His Son 'Abdu'l-Bahá, His great-grandson Shoghi Effendi and, of course, the Báb, also are resources vital for achieving the mission of this Day.

Bahá'u'lláh began His mission in the darkness of a dungeon. After His release, He poured out the radiance of a new revelation and spiritually regenerated the hopeless Bábí community. He restored their faith, corrected their morals, and instilled in them heroism, dedication, and the spirit of love, peace and service for all mankind. Throughout His ministry, people who came into contact with Bahá'u'lláh in Person or through His Writings were transformed. Many of them laid down their lives for the Cause of Bahá'u'lláh. Subsequent generations of Bahá'ís voluntarily heeded the call of Bahá'u'lláh; they left their homes and travelled the globe to make sure that the banner of His Faith was planted in every island, town and country. Today, with over five million followers, the Light of the Revelation of Bahá'u'lláh has found its way to almost every part of the planet.

Today, the world-wide Bahá'í community is gaining experience in applying Bahá'u'lláh's teachings in everyday life as it engages in a world-wide process of spiritual community building. Under the influence of Bahá'u'lláh's teachings, barriers of race, religion, ethnicity, class, gender and national origin cease to be divisive influences and a fellowship based on unity in diversity is becoming established. Bahá'ís participate in devotional gatherings, study the Word of God, and invite people of every Faith and background to engage in spiritually meaningful conversations, interfaith activities and humanitarian endeavors. The world governing body of the Bahá'í Faith added the following comments:

> Bahá'u'lláh's Revelation is vast. It calls for profound change not only at the level of the individual but also in the structure of society. "Is not the object of every Revelation", He Himself proclaims, "to effect a transformation in the whole character of mankind, a transformation that shall manifest itself, both outwardly and inwardly, that shall affect both its inner life and external conditions?" The work advancing in every corner of the globe today represents the latest stage of the ongoing Bahá'í endeavour to create the nucleus of the glorious civilization enshrined in His teachings, the building of which is an enterprise of infinite complexity and scale, one that will demand centuries of exertion by humanity to bring to fruition. There are no shortcuts, no formulas. Only as effort is made to draw on insights from His Revelation, to tap into the accumulating knowledge of the human race, to apply His teachings intelligently to the life of humanity, and to consult on the questions that arise will the necessary learning occur and capacity be developed.—The Universal House of Justice[786]

In those places around the world where persecution of Bahá'ís continues, the followers of Bahá'u'lláh have remained steadfast, unbowed by the oppression they face. Where Bahá'ís are free to practice their Faith, one sees a vibrant ascending international religious community contributing its share to the well-being, peace and security of humanity. Most importantly, one sees a world Faith undivided, adhering to its Covenant with God, unbroken by schism. Literally millions and potentially billions of souls have been the beneficiaries of Bahá'u'lláh's life and work.

Building upon the accomplishments of Abraham, Moses, Jesus, Muhammad, the Báb and other Divine Educators, the Dispensation of Bahá'u'lláh still has about eight hundred years to run its course[(787)] and achieve its goal of giving birth to a Divine civilization. Bahá'u'lláh, no less than all the Divine Educators Who preceded Him, has showered upon mankind gracious outpourings of the Holy Spirit sufficient to power humanity's tumultuous journey towards its pre-ordained destiny. Shoghi Effendi, on the 100th anniversary of the birth of the Faith, offered this vision of the future:

> Whatever may befall this infant Faith of God in future decades or in succeeding centuries, whatever the sorrows, dangers and tribulations which the next stage in its world-wide development may engender, from whatever quarter the assaults to be launched by its present or future adversaries may be unleashed against it, however great the reverses and setbacks it may suffer, we, who have been privileged to apprehend, to the degree our finite minds can fathom, the significance of these marvelous phenomena associated with its rise and establishment, can harbor no doubt that what it has already achieved in the first hundred years of its life provides sufficient guarantee that it will continue to forge ahead, capturing loftier heights, tearing down every obstacle, opening up new horizons and winning still mightier victories until its glorious mission, stretching into the dim ranges of time that lie ahead, is totally fulfilled.—Shoghi Effendi[788]

BIBLIOGRAPHY

ENGLISH SOURCES

Sacred Writings

The Bible

The Bible, King James Version: Public: Public Domain

The Bible, English Standard Version: The ESV® Bible (The Holy Bible, English Standard Version®), copyright © 2001, Crossway, Good News Publishers, Wheaton, IL

The Bible, New International Version: The Holy Bible, New International Version®, NIV® Copyright © 1973, 1978, 1984, 2011 by Biblica, Inc.® Used by permission. All rights reserved worldwide.

The Bible, New Revised Standard Version: New Revised Standard Version Bible, copyright © 1989 the Division of Christian Education of the National Council of the Churches of Christ in the United States of America. Used by permission. All rights reserved.

The Bible, Revised Standard Version: Revised Standard Version of the Bible, copyright © 1946, 1952, and 1971 the Division of Christian Education of the National Council of the Churches of Christ in the United States of America. Used by permission. All rights reserved.

The Qur'án

Qur'án, transl. by Arberry: A.J. Arberry, translator, *The Koran Interpreted*, 1996 (1st ed 1955), Touchstone/Simon & Shuster, New York, NY

Qur'án, transl. by Pickthall: Mohammed Marmaduke Pickthall, translator, *The Meaning of the Glorious Koran*, no date given, New American Library, New York, NY

Qur'án, transl. by Rodwell: Public Domain. J.M. Rodwell, translator, *The Koran*, 1876. Url: http://www.sacred-texts.com/isl/qr/qrtp.htm (Last accessed: May 19, 2015)

Qur'án, transl. by Yusuf Ali: Abdullah Yusuf Ali, translator, *The Holy Qur'án: Text, Translation and Commentary*, 1946, McGregor & Werner, USA

Bahá'í Writings

'Abdu'l-Bahá, translated by Edward G. Browne, *A Traveler's Narrative*, publ. 1980, Bahá'í Publishing Trust, Wilmette, IL

‘Abdu’l-Bahá, *‘Abdu’l-Bahá in London*, 1983, Bahá’í Publishing Trust, Wilmette, IL

‘Abdu’l-Bahá, *Foundations of World Unity*, 1945, Bahá’í Publishing Trust, Wilmette, IL

‘Abdu’l-Bahá, *Memorials of the Faithful*, 1971, Bahá’í Publishing Trust, Wilmette, IL

‘Abdu’l-Bahá, *Paris Talks*, 1995, Bahá’í Publishing Trust, London, UK

‘Abdu’l-Bahá, *Selections from the Writings of ‘Abdu’l-Bahá*, 1978, Bahá’í World Centre, Haifa, Israel

‘Abdu’l-Bahá, *Some Answered Questions, Revised Translation*, 2014, Bahá’í World Center, Haifa, Israel

‘Abdu’l-Bahá, *Star of the West, v4*, #6, June 24, 1913, Chicago. Url: http://starofthewest.info/ (Last accessed: May 17, 2015)

‘Abdu’l-Bahá, *Tablet to August Forel*. Original Persian text first published Cairo 1922. This translation taken from *The Bahá’í World, Vol. XV*, pp. 37–43. Url: http://www.bahai.org/library/authoritative-texts/abdul-baha/tablet-august-forel/ (Last accessed: May 17, 2015)

‘Abdu’l-Bahá, *Tablet to the Central Organization for a Durable Peace, The Hague*. Url: http://bahai-library.com/abdulbaha_lawh_hague_bwc (Last accessed: May 15, 2015)

‘Abdu’l-Bahá, *Tablets of ‘Abdu’l-Bahá v1*, 1980, 1st printing 1909, Bahá’í Publishing Committee, New York, NY

‘Abdu’l-Bahá, *Tablets of ‘Abdu’l-Bahá v2*, 1980, 1st printing 1915, Bahá’í Publishing Committee, New York, NY

‘Abdu’l-Bahá, *Tablets of ‘Abdu’l-Bahá v3*, 1980, 1st printing 1916, Bahá’í Publishing Committee, New York, NY

‘Abdu’l-Bahá, *The Compilation of Compilations, v1*, 1991, Bahá’í Publications Australia

‘Abdu’l-Bahá, *The Compilation of Compilations, v2*, 1991, Bahá’í Publications Australia

‘Abdu’l-Bahá, *The Promulgation of Universal Peace, Talks Delivered by ‘Abdu’l-Bahá during His Visit to the United States and Canada in 1912*, 1982 edition, Bahá’í Publishing Trust, Wilmette, IL

‘Abdu’l-Bahá, *The Secret of Divine Civilization*, 1957, 1990 edition, Bahá’í Publishing Trust, Wilmette, IL

‘Abdu’l-Bahá, *Twelve table talks given by ‘Abdu’l-Bahá in ‘Akká*, recently translated. Url: https://www.bahai.org/library/authoritative-texts/abdul-baha/twelve-table-talks-abdul-baha/

Bahá’u’lláh, *Bahá’í Prayers*, 1954, 1991 edition, Bahá’í Publishing Trust, Wilmette, IL

Bahá’u’lláh, *Epistle to the Son of the Wolf*, 1941, 1988 edition, Bahá’í Publishing Trust, Wilmette, IL

Bahá’u’lláh, *Gems of Divine Mysteries*, 2002, Bahá’í World Centre, Haifa

Bahá’u’lláh, *Gleanings from the Writings of Bahá’u’lláh*, 1952, 1983 edition, Bahá’í Publishing Trust, Wilmette, IL

Bahá’u’lláh, *Má’idih-Ásmání*, vol. 8 page 191-192. Url: http://reference.bahai.org/fa/t/b/MAS8/mas8-191.html (Last accessed: 24 June 2019)

Bahá’u’lláh, *Prayers and Meditations by Bahá’u’lláh*, 1938, 1987 edition, Bahá’í Publishing Trust, Wilmette, IL

Bahá’u’lláh, *Tablets of Bahá’u’lláh Revealed after the Kitáb-i-Aqdás*, 1978, Bahá’í World Centre, Haifa

Bahá'u'lláh, *The Book of Certitude (The Kitáb-i-Íqán)*, 1931, 1983 edition, Bahá'í Publishing Trust, Wilmette, IL

Bahá'u'lláh, *The Hidden Words, Arabic and Persian*, 2002 edition, Bahá'í Publishing, Wilmette, IL

Bahá'u'lláh, *The Most Holy Book (The Kitáb-i-Aqdás)*, 1992, Bahá'í World Centre, Haifa

Bahá'u'lláh, translated by Marzieh Gail and Ali-Kuli Khan, *The Seven Valleys and the Four Valleys*, 1945, 1986 edition, Bahá'í Publishing Trust, Wilmette, IL

Bahá'u'lláh, *The Summons of the Lord of Hosts*, 2002, Bahá'í World Centre, Haifa

The Báb, *Selections from the Writings of the Báb*, 1976, Bahá'í World Centre, Haifa

Shoghi Effendi, *Citadel of Faith*, 1965, 1970 edition, Bahá'í Publishing Trust, Wilmette, IL

Shoghi Effendi, *Dawn of a New Day: Messages to India*, 1923-1957, 1970, Bahá'í Publishing Trust

Shoghi Effendi, *Directives from the Guardian*, no date given, Bahá'í Publishing Trust, New Delhi, India

Shoghi Effendi, *God Passes By*, 1944, Bahá'í Publishing Company, Wilmette, Illinois

Shoghi Effendi, *Letters from the Guardian to Australia and New Zealand, 1923-1957*, 1971 edition, National Spiritual Assembly of the Bahá'ís of Australia

Shoghi Effendi, *Messages to America*, 1947 edition, US Bahá'í Publishing Trust, Wilmette, IL

Shoghi Effendi, *Messages to the Bahá'í World—1950 to 1957*, 1971 edition, Bahá'í Publishing Trust, Wilmette, IL

Shoghi Effendi, *The Advent of Divine Justice*, 1939, 1971 edition, Bahá'í Publishing Trust, Wilmette, IL

Shoghi Effendi, translator and editor, *Nabíl's Narrative: The Dawn-Breakers*, 1932, Bahá'í Publishing Trust, Wilmette, IL

Shoghi Effendi, *The Light of Divine Guidance, v2*, 1985 edition, Bahá'í Publishing Trust of Germany (Bahá'í-Verlag) Url: http://reference.bahai.org/en/t/se/LDG2/ (Last accessed: May 17, 2015)

Shoghi Effendi, *The Promised Day is Come*, 1976 edition, Bahá'í Publishing Trust, New Delhi, India

Shoghi Effendi, *The Unfolding Destiny of the British Bahá'í Community*, 1981, Bahá'í Publishing Trust, London, UK

Shoghi Effendi, *The World Order of Bahá'u'lláh*, 1938, 1974 edition, Bahá'í Publishing Trust, Wilmette, IL

The Bahá'í International Community, *Statement on Baha'u'llah*, May 29, 1992. Url: https://www.bahai.org/library/other-literature/official-statements-commentaries/bahaullah/ (Last accessed: September 15, 2019)

The Universal House of Justice, *Messages from the Universal House of Justice, 1963 to 1986, The Third Epoch of the Formative Age*, 1996, Geoffrey W. Marks, ed., Bahá'í Publishing Trust, Wilmette, IL

The Universal House of Justice, letter dated August 22, 1977, *"Clarification on Infallibility"*. Url: http://bahai-library.com/uhj_infallibility_guardianship_uhj (Last accessed: May 15, 2015)

The Universal House of Justice, letter dated March 24, 1998, *"Abrogation of Past Dispensations"*. Url: http://bahairesearch.com/english/Baha'i/Authoritative_Baha'i/The_Universal_

House_of_Justice/Letters/Holy_Texts_and_Publications, elucidation/1998_Mar_24_Abrogation_ of_Past_Dispensations.aspx. (Last accessed: September 23, 2014)

The Universal House of Justice, letter dated 7 April 1999, *"Issues Related to the Study of the Bahá'í Faith".* Url: http://www.bahai.org/library/authoritative-texts/the-universal-house-of-justice/messages/#d=19990407_001&f=f1 (Last accessed: May 14, 2015)

The Universal House of Justice, *Ridván 2010 Message*

Compilations

Helen Hornby, *Lights of Guidance*, 1988, Bahá'í Publishing Trust, Wilmette, IL

Other Sources

(Order based on last name of author)

Sabir Afaqi, editor, *Táhirih in History. Perspectives on Qurratu'l-'Ayn from East to West. Studies in the Bábí and Bahá'í Religions: Volume 16*, 2004, Kalimát Press, Los Angeles

'Abu'l-Qasim Afnan, *Black Pearls*, 1988, Kalimat Press, Los Angeles

Karen Armstrong, *Muhammad, A Biography of the Prophet*, 1991, 2001, Phoenix Press, London, England

Essad Bey, *Mohammed, A Biography*, 1938, Bridges Publishing, Frankfurt, Germany

AHP Bulletin, "Adventism's birthplace purchased", June 1985, Adventist Historical Properties, Battle Creek, Michigan, p. 1. (URL: http://www.adventistheritage.org/site/1/docs/AHPB01-1.pdf, last accessed June 3, 2018)

AHP Bulletin, "William Miller Farm, Low Hampton, New York", Summer 1990, Vol. 3, No. 2, Adventist Historical Properties, Battle Creek, Michigan, p. 1. (URL: http://www.adventistheritage.org/site/1/docs/AHPB03-2.pdf, last accessed June 3rd, 2018)

Abbas Amanat, *Pivot of the Universe: Nasir al-Din Sháh and the Iranian Monarchy, 1831-1896*, 1997, University of California Press, Berkley

Abbas Amanat, *The Early Years of the Babi Movement Background and Development*, Thesis submitted for the degree of Doctor of Philosophy in the University of Oxford St., Catherine's College T Hilary, 1981. (URL: https://bahai-library.com/pdf/a/amanat_early_years_babi.pdf; Last accessed: 10 December 2018)

Abbas Amanat, *Resurrection and Renewal: The making of the Bábí Movement in Iran, 1844-1850*, 1989, Cornell University Press, Ithaca, New York

Kwame Anthony Appiah and Henry Louis Gates, Jr., *Encyclopedia of Africa, Volume 1*, 2010, Oxford University Press, Oxford, p. 197, Section on Hájí Mubarak by Anthony Lee

M.H. Azizi and F. Azizi, *History of Cholera Outbreaks in Iran during the 19th and 20th Centuries*, Middle East Journal of Digestive Diseases, 2010 January, 2(1), p. 51–55. (PMCID: PMC4154910)
(Url: https://www.ncbi.nlm.nih.gov/pmc/articles/PMC4154910/; Last accessed: 22 February 2019)

The Bahá'í World News Service, *Bahá'í shrines chosen as World Heritage sites*, 8 July 2008. Url: http://news.bahai.org/story/642

H.M. Balyuzi, *Bahá'u'lláh: King of Glory*, 1980, George Ronald Publisher, Oxford

H.M. Balyuzi, *Eminent Bahá'ís in the Time of Bahá'u'lláh, With some Historical Background*, 1985, George Ronald Publisher, Oxford

H.M. Balyuzi, *Khadíjih Bagum: The Wife of the Báb*, 1982, George Ronald Publisher, Oxford

H.M. Balyuzi, *The Báb: The Herald of the Day of Days*, 1973, George Ronald Publisher, Oxford

Kazem Big, "Báb et les Bábís", published in *Journal Asiatique*, 1866, p. 379. Found in the University of Michigan collection, uploaded to the Internet archive. URL: https://archive.org/details/journalasiatiqu134frangoog/page/n407. The exact quote is on p. 407 of the internet file. (Last accessed: 30 May 2019)

Sylvester Bliss, *Memoirs of William Miller, Generally known as a lecturer on the prophecies, and the Second Coming of Christ*, 1853, Joshua V. Himes, Boston, MA

Boon's Lick Times, "A Modern Mohomet", Fayette, Missouri, April 4, 1846, p. 1. Article about the persecution of Bábís in Shíráz.

Edward G. Browne, Ed., *Materials for the Study of the Bábí Religion*, 1918, Cambridge University Press

Christopher Buck, *Native Messengers of God in Canada?: A test case for Bahá'í universalism*, 1993, Paper read at the 1993 Religious Studies Special Interest Group of the ABS-ESE in Newcastle, and again in 1994 at the 18th Annual Conference of the Association for Bahá 'í Studies (Cambridge, MA). Downloaded from Academia.com.

Glen Cameron and Wendy Momen, *A Basic Bahá'í Chronology*, 1996, George Ronald, Oxford

Michael V. Day, *Journey to a Mountain: The Story of the Shrine of the Báb, Volume 1: 1850-1921*, 2017, George Ronald Publisher, Oxford

Frederick M. Denny, *An Introduction to Islám, 1994, 2006, 2011, Taylor & Francis, NY, NY*

James White Elder, *Sketches of the Christian life and public labors of William, Miller, Gathered from his memoir by the late Sylvester Bliss, and from other sources*, 1875, Steam Press, Battle Creek, Michigan

Yahiya Emerick, *Critical Lives: The Life and Work of Muhammad*, 2002, Alpha Books, Indianapolis, IN

Abu'l-Qasim Faizi, *The Prince of Martyrs*, 1977, George Ronald, England, p. 38. Now available online as an eBook. Also available online. Url: https://bahai-library.com/faizi_prince_martyrs (Last accessed: 26 March 2019).

Yohanan Friedman, *Prophecy Continuous*, 1989, University of California Press

A. Guillaume, *The Life of Muhammad, A Translation of Ishaq's Sirat Rasul Alláh*, 1955, 1967, Oxford University Press, Oxford, England

Michael Hart, *The 100: A Ranking of the Most Influential Persons in History*, 1978, 1992, Kensington Publishing Corp., New York, NY

Phyllis G. Jestice, Editor, *Holy People of the World: A Cross-Cultural Encyclopedia (Volume 1)*, 2004, ABC-CLIO Inc., Santa Barbara, CA. Section on Hájí Mubarak by Anthony Lee.

Anthony Lee, *The Bahá'í Faith in Africa: Establishing a New Religious Movement, 1952-1962*, 2011, Brill, The Netherlands

Meir Litvak, *Shi'i scholars of nineteenth-century Iraq: The 'Ulama' of Najaf and Karbala*, 1998, Cambridge University Press, Cambridge, U.K.

Todd Lawson, *Tafsir as Mystical Experience: Intimacy and Ecstasy in Quran Commentary (Tafsir surat al-baqara by Sayyid 'Alí Muhammad Shirazi, The Báb (1819-1850))*, 2019, Leiden, Boston

Baharieh Rouhani Ma'ani, *Leaves of the Twin Divine Trees: An In-depth Study of the Lives of the Women Closely Related to the Báb and Bahá'u'lláh*, 2008, George Ronald, Oxford

William McCants, *The ISIS Apocalypse: The History, Strategy, and Doomsday Vision of the Islamic State*, 2015, St. Martin's Press, NY, NY

Jacqueline Mehrabi, *The Lamp: The Life Story of the Báb*, 2009, Bahá'í Publications Australia, Bundoora, Victoria

R. Mehrabkhani, *Mullá Husayn, Disciple at Dawn*, 1987, Kalimat Press, Los Angeles, CA

William Miller, *Evidence from Scripture and History of the Second Coming of Christ, about the Year 1843: Exhibited in a Course of Lectures*, 1840, B. B. Mussey, Boston

Moojan Momen, *An Introduction to Shi'i Islám*, 1985, Yale University Press, New Haven, CT

Moojan Momen, "The trial of Mullá 'Alí Bastámí: A combined Sunní-Shi'i fatwá against the Báb", 1982, *Iran: Journal of the British Institute for Persian Studies*, 20, p. 113-143

Adnan A. Musallam, *From Secularism to Jihad: Sayyid Qutb and the Foundations of Radical Islámism*, 2005, Praeger Publishers, Westport, CT

Nabíl, translated and edited by Shoghi Effendi, *The Dawn-Breakers*, 1932, Bahá'í Publishing Trust, Wilmette, IL

A.L.M. Nicolas, *Seyyed Ali Muhammad dit le Báb*, 1905, Dujarric & Cie, Paris

A.L.M. Nicolas, *Qourret-oul-Aine*, translated by Peter Terry, *Táhirih in History*, (1905) 2004, p. 97-112 (Originally from A.L.M. Nicolas, *Seyyed Ali Muhammad dit le Báb*, 1905, Dujarric & Cie, Paris, p. 273-287 and 446-452). Essay from Sabir Afaqi, editor, *Táhirih in History. Perspectives on Qurratu'l-'Ayn from East to West. Studies in the Bábí and Bahá'í Religions: Volume 16*, 2004, Kalimát Press, Los Angeles.

Ronald L. Numbers and Jonathan M Butler, eds., *The Disappointed: Millerism and Millenarianism in the Nineteenth Century*, 1993, University of Tennessee Press, Knoxville

Emily McBride Perigord, *Translation of French Foot-notes of the Dawn-Breakers*, 1939, Bahá'í Publishing Trust, Wilmette, IL

Dennis Prager, *Ethical Monotheism*, The Jewish Virtual Library: Url: https://www.jewishvirtuallibrary.org/ethical-monotheism (Last accessed: September 16, 2019). And also: https://www.jewishvirtuallibrary.org/jsource/Judaism/mono.html (Date last accessed: October 22nd, 2015)

Shaykh-ul-Islám Dr. Muhammad Tahrir-ul-Qadri, *Fatwa On Terrorism And Suicide Bombings*, 2010, Minhaj-ul-Qur'án International, London. See also: www.minhaj.org; www.minhajuk.org; and www.fatwaonterrorism.com.

Gregory J. Riley, *The River of God*, 2001, HarperCollins Publishers, NY, NY

Royal Islamic Strategic Studies Centre of Jordan, *The 500 Most Influential Muslims*, 2012, Aman, Jordan

Janet Ruhe-Schoen, *Rejoice in my gladness: The life of Táhirih*, 2011, Bahá'í Publishing, Wilmette, IL

Abdulaziz Abdulhussein Sachedina, *Islámic Messianism: The idea of the Mahdi in Twelver Shi'ism*, 1981, State University of New York Press, Albany, New York

Nader Saiedi, *Gate of the Heart: Understanding the Writings of the Báb*; 2008, Wilfrid Laurier University Press

Nader Saiedi and Omid Ghaemmaghami, The Ethiopian King, *Bahá'í Studies Review*, v 17

William Sears, *Thief in the Night*, 1961, George Ronald Publisher, Oxford, England

Sammireh Anwar Smith, translator, *Munirih Khanum: Memoirs and Letters*, 1986, Kalimat Press, Los Angeles, CA

Michael Sours, *The Prophecies of Jesus*, 1991, Oneworld Publications, Oxford, England

Robert Spivey and D. Moody Smith, Jr., *Anatomy of the New Testament: A guide to its structure and meaning*, 2nd. Edition, 1974, Augsburg Fortress, Minneapolis, MN

Adib Taherzadeh, *The Covenant of Bahá'u'lláh*, 1992, George Ronald Publisher, Oxford

Adib Taherzadeh, *The Child of the Covenant*, 2000, George Ronald Publisher, Oxford

Adib Taherzadeh, *The Revelation of Bahá'u'lláh v1*, 1975, George Ronald Publisher, Oxford

Adib Taherzadeh, *The Revelation of Bahá'u'lláh v2*, 2006, George Ronald Publisher, Oxford

Peter Terry, translator and editor, *A Prophet in Modern Times (Volume 1 of the Babi Studies Series)*, 2008, Lulu Publications. A translation of A.L.M. Nicolas, the first English translation of the first biography of Hájí Siyyid Ali-Muhammad Shírází, called the Bab. The original was published in French by A.L.M. Nicolas in 1905.

The Times of London, "MAHOMETAN SCHISM - A new sect has lately set...", November 19, 1845, p. 3. The Times Digital Archive, http://tinyurl.galegroup.com/tinyurl/93d8j8. Accessed 10 Feb. 2019. Gale Document Number: GALE | CS52590963

Sayyid Qutb, *Milestones*, 1964. Various versions downloadable from Internet.

Lawrence Wright, "The Rebellion Within: An Al Qaeda mastermind questions terrorism", *The New Yorker Magazine*, May 23, 2008 (June 2, 2008 Issue). Url: https://www.newyorker.com/magazine/2008/06/02/the-rebellion-within (Last accessed: September 16, 2019)

Shaykh Muhammad Al-Yaqoubi, *Refuting ISIS: Destroying its religious foundation an proving it has strayed from Islám and that fighting it is an obligation, Second Edition*, 2016, Sacred Knowledge (books), Herndon, Virginia

Abdullah Yúsuf 'Alí, *Commentary on the Imam Husayn and His Martyrdom*. Found at Url: https://www.al-islam.org/articles/imam-husayn-and-his-martyrdom-abdullah-yusuf-ali. (Last accessed: 24 March 2019)

John C. Zimmerman, "Sayyid Qutb's Influence On The 11 September Attacks", *Terrorism and Political Violence*, 2004, vol. 16, #2, p. 222-252, published online August 10, 2010, Url: https://doi.org/10.1080/09546550490480993

PERSIAN SOURCES

Afnan #1	Muhammad Afnan, *Collected Essays of Dr. Muhammad Afnan*, 2013, Andalib, Dundas, Ontario, Canada
Afnan #2	Muhammad Afnan, *Collected Essays of Dr. Muhammad Afnan, Vol. 2*, 2017, Andalib, Mississauga, Ontario, Canada
M. Amanat	Mousa Amanat, *Baha'iyan-e Kashan*, No date given, edited by Noura Amanat-Samimi, Fundación Nehal, Madrid, Spain
Ashraf	Faramarz Ashraf, *History of the Bahá'í Faith in Qazvin (Persian)*, 2016, Canada (Available from Bahaibookstore.com)
Baráqí	Firúz Baráqí, *Boshruyeh: Zádgáh-e Jenáb-e Mollá Hossein "Báb ul-Báb"*, No date given, Fundación Nehal, Madrid, Spain
Faizi	Muhammad-'Alí Faizi, *Hadrat-i-Nuqtay-i Ula (The Life of the Báb)*, 1976 (1987, 1994), Bahá'í-Verlag, GmbH, Hoffheim-Langenhain
Fuádi	Hasan Fuádi Bushrú'í, *The History of the Bahá'í Faith in Khorásán (Táríkh-e Díyánat-e Bahá'í dar Khorásán, 1844-1926)*, 2007, edited by Minou D. Foadi and Fereydun Vahman, 'Asr-e Jadíd Publisher, Darmstadt, Germany
Husaini #1	Nusrat'u'llah Muhammad-Husaini, *The Báb, His Life, His Writings and the Disciples of the Báb's Dispensation*, 2nd edition, 1995 (2016), Century Press Publications, Bundoora Vic, Australia
Husaini #2	Nosratollah Mohammad Hoseini, *Hadrat-i-Tahirih*, No date given, Fundación Nehal, Madrid, Spain
Khusravi	Muhammad 'Alí Malik-Khusravi, *Tarikh-i Shuhaday-i Amr, vol 1*, 130 BE (approx. 1974 AD), The National Institute of the Publication of the Faith (Bahá'í Publication, Iran), Tihran. This book is available online at the Afnan Library (www.afnanlibrary.org/malik-khusravi_tarikh-i-shuhaday-i-amr_vol1/)
Málmírí	Muhammad Táhir-i-Málmírí, *Tarikh-i-Amriy-i-Yazd (History of the Bahá'í Faith in Yazd)*, 2013, Century Press Publications, Bundoora Vic, Australia
Mázandarání #2	Asad'u'lláh Fádl Mázandarání, *Zuhúr'u'l-Haq, Vol. 2,* Unpublished. Manuscript available online. Url (Last accessed: 8 March 2019): https://www.h-net.org/~bahai/arabic/vol4/2tzh/2tzh.htm
Mázandarání #3	Asad'u'lláh Fádl Mázandarání, *Zuhúr'u'l-Haq, Vol. 3, 2nd edition*, 2008, Bahá'í-Verlag, Germany-Hofheim. Manuscript available online. Url (Last accessed: 8 March 2019): https://www.h-net.org/~bahai/areprint/vol2/mazand/tzh3/tzh3.htm
Mudarris	Fathu'lláh Mudarris, *Tarikh-i-Amr-Bahá'í dar Najafabad (A History of the Bahá'í Faith in Najafabad)*, 2004, edited by Vahíd Rafati, 'Asr-e Jadíd Publisher, Darmstadt, Germany
Rouhani	Muhammad Shafi Rouhani, *Lama'átu'l-Anvár (Depicting the Soul-stirring Episodes of Nayriz), Vol. 1 & 2*, No date given, Century Press Publications, Bundoora Vic, Australia
Shahidian	Aminullah Shahidian, *Mansuban Astan-i A'la (Khandan Afnan)*, 2009, Bahá'í Distribution Services, Bundoora Vic, Australia

ENDNOTES

1 Shoghi Effendi, *God Passes By*, p. xiv; Shoghi Effendi, *The World Order of Bahá'u'lláh*, p. 97

2 Bahá'u'lláh, *Gleanings from the Writings of Bahá'u'lláh*, p. 76

3 'Abdu'l-Bahá, *Some Answered Questions*, ch. 8, p. 30-31

4 'Abdu'l-Bahá, *The Promulgation of Universal Peace*, p. 192

5 Bahá'u'lláh, *Gleanings from the Writings of Bahá'u'lláh*, p. 65

6 Bahá'u'lláh, *The Book of Certitude*, p. 152-153

7 Bahá'u'lláh, *The Book of Certitude*, p. 153-154

8 The Báb, cited by Shoghi Effendi, *The World Order of Bahá'u'lláh*, p. 62-63

9 'Abdu'l-Bahá, *Some Answered Questions*, p. 32

10 Bahá'u'lláh, *Epistle to the Son of the Wolf*, p. 21

11 Bahá'u'lláh, cited by Baha'i International Community, 1992 May 29, *Statement on Baha'u'llah*, p. 27

12 Shoghi Effendi, *God Passes By*, p. 276

13 Nabíl, translated by Shoghi Effendi, *The Dawn-Breakers*, p. 208-209

14 Shoghi Effendi, *The World Order of Bahá'u'lláh*, p. 123

15 Shoghi Effendi, *God Passes By*, p. 276

16 Shoghi Effendi, *God Passes By*, p. 276

17 'Abdu'l-Bahá, cited by Shoghi Effendi, *God Passes By*, p. 276

18 Shoghi Effendi, in the forward to Nabíl, translated by Shoghi Effendi, *The Dawn-Breakers*, p. xxiv

19 'Abdu'l-Bahá, *Twelve table talks given by 'Abdu'l-Bahá in 'Akká*, recently translated. Url: https://https://www.bahai.org/library/authoritative-texts/abdul-baha/twelve-table-talks-abdul-baha/

20 Shoghi Effendi, in the forward to Nabíl, translated by Shoghi Effendi, *The Dawn-Breakers*, p. xxiv

21 Shoghi Effendi, in the forward to Nabíl, translated by Shoghi Effendi, *The Dawn-Breakers*, p. xxiv

22 Shoghi Effendi, in the forward to Nabíl, translated by Shoghi Effendi, *The Dawn-Breakers*, p. xxiv

23 Lord Curzon, cited by Shoghi Effendi, in the forward to Nabíl, translated by Shoghi Effendi, *The Dawn-Breakers*, p. xxxix

24 Lord Curzon, cited by Shoghi Effendi, in the forward to Nabíl, translated by Shoghi Effendi, *The Dawn-Breakers*, p. xxvii

25 Shoghi Effendi, the preface to *The Dawn-Breakers*, p. xxix-xxx

26 Shoghi Effendi, the preface to *The Dawn-Breakers*, p. xxix-xxx

27 Abdulaziz Abdulhussein Sachedina, *Islamic Messianism: The Idea of the Mahdi in Twelver Shi'ism*, p. 86, 96. See also Moojan Momen, *An Introduction to Shi'i Islám*, p. 161-165.

28 Abdulaziz Abdulhussein Sachedina, *Islamic Messianism: The Idea of the Mahdi in Twelver Shi'ism*, p. 157-166. See also Moojan Momen, *An Introduction to Shi'i Islám*, p. 166-170.

29 Abbas Amanat, *Pivot of the Universe*, p. 5. Modern-day Persia (Iran) became a full-fledged theocracy, when the clergy literally became the State. Beginning in 1979, the religious leaders stopped conferring legitimacy on the Shah when they seized the power of the State for themselves and presumptuously labeled it the Islamic State, government by God.

30 Adamantine (adjective) = unyielding, firm. Dictionary definitions include: a) rigidly firm, unyielding – example: "adamantine discipline"; b) resembling the diamond in hardness or luster. In this context, the meaning is utterly unyielding or firm in attitude or opinion; too hard to cut through, unbreakable.

31 Shoghi Effendi, in the forward to Nabíl, translated by Shoghi Effendi, *The Dawn-Breakers*, p. xxx

32 Abbas Amanat, *Pivot of the Universe*, p. 415

33 Shoghi Effendi, *The Promised Day is Come*, p. 65

34 Shoghi Effendi, *The Advent of Divine Justice*, p. 17

35 Abbas Amanat, *Resurrection and Renewal*, 1989, p. 33

36 Abbas Amanat, *Resurrection and Renewal*, 1989, p. 206

37 Abbas Amanat, *Resurrection and Renewal*, 1989, p. 36

38 Abbas Amanat, *Resurrection and Renewal*, 1989, p. 40

39 Janet Ruhe-Schoen, *Rejoice in my gladness*, 2011, p.22

40 Abbas Amanat, *Resurrection and Renewal*, 1989, p. 48

41 Shoghi Effendi, translator and editor, *The Dawn-Breakers*, p. 5-7, in a footnote, states: "A. L. M. Nicolas, in Chapter 5 of his book, *'Essai sur le Shaykhisme,'* gives a list of no less than ninety-six volumes as representing the entire literary output of this prolific writer." Shoghi Effendi lists the 10 most important works of Shaykh Ahmad in the footnote.

42 Nabíl, translated by Shoghi Effendi, *The Dawn-Breakers*, p. 1-2, 10

43 Mázandarání, footnote, p. 126

44 In general, the Shí'ih literature on the Hidden Imám emphasized that "a prolonged biological life for the Imám was not impossible" (Amanat, p. 55), that he is still alive, on earth, in one of two distant cities. The two distant cities are either Jabalqa in the East or Jabarsa in the West. Most Shí'ih religious leaders maintained that these were earthly cities. Shaykh Ahmad claimed that they were spiritual in nature, belonging to the spiritual realm of Hurqalya. He wrote: "Jabalqa is the city of the West, that is, in the direction of the beginning. Jabarsa is the city of the West, that is, in the direction of the return and ending." (Amanat, p. 53) (See Abbas Amanat, *Resurrection and Renewal*, 1989, p. 53, 55)

This theory, of course, assumed his life had miraculously continued for over a thousand years. Shaykh Ahmad would not have wondered about God's power to bring about such a miracle, but he said that God uses a more sensible and spiritual approach.

Decades later, Bahá'u'lláh was asked a question about the abode of the Imám. His answer confirmed, for all practical purposes, the approach of Shaykh Ahmad:

"All that thou hast heard regarding Muhammad the son of Hasan—may the souls of all that are immersed in the oceans of the spirit be offered up for His sake—is true beyond the shadow of a doubt, and we all verily bear allegiance unto Him. But the Imáms of the Faith have fixed His abode in the city of Jabulqa, which they have depicted in strange and marvellous signs. To interpret this city according to the literal meaning of the tradition would indeed prove impossible, nor can such a city ever be found. Wert thou to search the uttermost corners of the earth, nay probe its length and breadth for as long as God's eternity hath lasted and His sovereignty will endure, thou wouldst never find a city such as they have described, for the entirety of the earth could neither contain nor encompass it. If thou wouldst lead Me unto this city, I could assuredly lead thee unto this holy Being, Whom the people have conceived according to what they possess and not to that which pertaineth unto Him! Since this is not in thy power, thou hast no recourse but to interpret symbolically the accounts and traditions that have been reported from these luminous souls. And, as such an interpretation is needed for the traditions pertaining to the aforementioned city, so too is it required for this holy Being. When thou hast understood this interpretation, thou shalt no longer stand in need of "transformation" or aught else.

"Know then that, inasmuch as all the Prophets are but one and the same soul, spirit, name, and attribute, thou must likewise see them all as bearing the name Muhammad and as being the son of Hasan, as having appeared from the Jabulqa of God's power and from the Jabulsa of His mercy. For by Jabulqa is meant none other than the treasure-houses of eternity in the all-highest heaven and the cities of the unseen in the supernal realm. We bear witness that Muhammad the son of Hasan was indeed in Jabulqa and appeared therefrom. Likewise, He Whom God shall make manifest abideth in that city until such time as God will have established Him upon the seat of His sovereignty. We, verily, acknowledge this truth and bear allegiance unto each and every one of them. We have chosen here to be brief in our elucidation of the meanings of Jabulqa, but if thou be of them that truly believe, thou shalt indeed comprehend all the true meanings of the mysteries enshrined within these Tablets." (Bahá'u'lláh, *Gems of Divine Mysteries*, p. 34-38)

Shaykh Ahmad claimed that all of the Imáms had died a normal physical death. He said they now reside in an intermediary celestial realm of the spirit, which he called Hurqalya. Shaykh Ahmad's concept was that "a divine substance accompanies man's spirit in its descent from the realm of eternal truth to earth, and after passing through earthly life, eventually reascends to its origin." (Abbas Amanat, *Resurrection and Renewal*, 1989, p. 50-51)

Relying on a symbolic interpretation of Qur'ánic verses, and esoteric insights which he claimed to have gotten from the Imáms themselves, Shaykh Ahmad "redefined the concept of resurrection contrary to the view held by the literalists. The survival of the spiritual being in the world of Hurqalya, removes the problem of corporal resurrection from the earthly grave." (Abbas Amanat, *Resurrection and Renewal*, 1989, p. 52)

Face-to-face contact with the Imáms, in normal historical time, is entirely possible, he attested, but only through mystical contact with the intermediary realm of Hurqalya. In Shaykh Ahmad's view, the Perfect Shí'ih on earth is the one individual entitled to claim deputyship to the Hidden Imám; once he is identified, all must adhere to his guidance.

45 Abbas Amanat, *Resurrection and Renewal*, 1989, p. 53-55, 103, 283, 364

46 Janet Ruhe-Schoen, *Rejoice in my gladness, 2011,* p.25

47 Qur'án 6:103, cited by Bahá'u'lláh, translated by Shoghi Effendi, *The Book of Certitude*, p. 98, 170

48 The reader may have noticed a particular oddity concerning the wingspan of the angels. Wingspan is a concept of *distance*, but the number given is measured in years, that is, as *time*. Who measures wingspan as years? Who measures distance as time? Well, sometimes, when asked how far away a certain city may be, one can answer "It is three hours away", meaning, "at highway speeds it will take you three hours to get there".

If the wingspan statement is similarly understood, and even if we arbitrarily assume maximum speed, i.e. the speed of light, then we would be saying that, tip-to-tip, a 'wingspan of a thousand years' is actually one thousand light-years across! Obviously, this cannot be right, because nothing that big could ever exist as a viable corporeal life form.

Moreover, the concept of a light-year is a fully modern concept, which was non-existent in the time of Muhammad. According to Wikipedia:

"The light-year unit appeared a few years after the first successful measurement of the distance to a star other than the Sun, by Friedrich Bessel in 1838. The star was 61 Cygni, and he used a 6.2-inch (160 mm) heliometer designed by Joseph von Fraunhofer. The largest unit for expressing distances across space at that time was the astronomical unit, equal to the radius of the Earth's orbit (1.50×108 km or 9.30×107 mi). In those terms, trigonometric calculations based on 61 Cygni's parallax of 0.314 arcseconds, showed the distance to the star to be 660,000 astronomical units (9.9×1013 km or 6.1×1013 mi). Bessel added that light employs 10.3 years to traverse this distance… He recognized that his readers would enjoy the mental picture of the approximate transit time for light, but he refrained from using the light-year as a unit… The speed of light was not yet precisely known in 1838; its value changed in 1849 (Fizeau) and 1862 (Foucault). It was not yet considered to be a fundamental constant of nature, and the propagation of light through the aether or space was still enigmatic. The light-year unit appeared, however, in 1851 in a German popular astronomical article by Otto Ule." (See https://en.wikipedia.org/wiki/Light-year)

In other words, the traditions of Muhammad from the 7th century onwards could not possibly have intended the description of the angels' wingspan of a thousand years to refer to an actual measurement of distance, because that concept didn't even exist until the mid-1800s.

Ultimately, this entire description is an enormous "red flag" that the descriptions of the wingspans of the angels and of many of the traditions should not be taken literally. No matter how one thinks of this statement, one is forced into a non-literal interpretation.

49 Abbas Amanat, *Resurrection and Renewal*, 1989, p. 52-55

50 This word is "*zuhur*" in Arabic.

51 Moojan Momen, *An Introduction to Shí'i Islám*, p. 165

52 Abbas Amanat, *Resurrection and Renewal*, 1989, p. 52-53

53 Nabíl, translated by Shoghi Effendi, *The Dawn-Breakers*, p. 10

54 Nabíl, translated by Shoghi Effendi, *The Dawn-Breakers*, p. 15

55 The sixth Imám, Ja'far Sádiq, cited by Nabíl, translated by Shoghi Effendi, *The Dawn-Breakers*, p. 47

56 Abbas Amanat, *Resurrection and Renewal*, 1989, p. 60

57 Siyyid Kázim, cited by Dr. T.K. Cheyne, *The Reconciliation of Races and Religions*, p. 19, cited by Shoghi Effendi, translator and editor, *The Dawn-Breakers*, p. 25

58 'Abdu'l-Bahá, *Some Answered Questions*, p. 46-47

59 Michael Sours, *The Prophecies of Jesus*, p. 69-71

60 Numbers 14:34

61 'Abdu'l-Bahá, *Some Answered Questions*, p. 47-48

62 William Miller, cited by Sylvester Bliss, *Memoirs of William Miller, Generally known as a lecturer on the prophecies, and the Second Coming of Christ*, p. 49-50

63 Evidently, some versions of this quote say "1843", while others say "1844". Refer to William Miller, cited by Sylvester Bliss, *Memoirs of William Miller*, p. 79. See also: *AHP Bulletin*, "William Miller Farm, Low Hampton, New York", Summer 1990, Vol. 3, No. 2

64 William Miller, *Evidence from Scripture and History of the Second Coming of Christ*

65 *AHP Bulletin*, "William Miller Farm, Low Hampton, New York", Summer 1990, Vol. 3, No. 2

66 William Miller, cited by James White, Elder, *Sketches of the Christian life and public labors of William Miller*, p. 182

67 Ronald L. Numbers and Jonathan M Butler, eds., *The Disappointed: Millerism and Millenarianism in the Nineteenth Century*, p. 215

68 *AHP Bulletin*, "Adventism's birthplace purchased", June 1985, p. 1

69 See William Sears, *Thief in the Night*. See also Jeremiah 49:38: "And I will set my throne in Elam..." Elam is an ancient name for the region of southern Persia, the exact location where the Báb appeared.

70 Mullá Husayn, cited by Nabíl, translated by Shoghi Effendi, *The Dawn-Breakers*, p. 57. See also Nabíl, p. 24-25.

71 Siyyid Kázim, cited by Nabíl, translated by Shoghi Effendi, *The Dawn-Breakers*, p. 25

72 This is being written in 2019

73 Husaini, p. 139; Faizi, p. 71

74 Shahidian, p. 7

75 Nabíl, translated by Shoghi Effendi, *The Dawn-Breakers*, p. 72-75.

76 Husaini, p. 139. Husaini mentions (in footnote #1 on p. 150) that in a book written by the scholar 'Abdul-Hamid Eshragh-Khavari (1902-1972) that the birthplace of the Báb took place at the home of his maternal uncle, Mírzá Siyyid 'Ali, but that has no basis in fact. Perhaps the confusion is due to the fact that the paternal uncle of the mother of the Báb and the maternal uncle of the Báb (His mother's brother) have the same name – Mírzá Siyyid 'Ali. See also: Faizi, p. 71-72.

77 Faizi, p. 7-14. Interestingly, this Caliph, Umar II, was the rare Umayyad Caliph in that he was known for his righteousness and piety. He was also a reformer. The other Umayyad Caliphs have quite the opposite reputation. (For a quick overview of his life, use this link: https://en.wikipedia.org/wiki/Umar_II. Last accessed: December 13, 2018)

78 The graphic is based on information from several sources. 1) General information: Nabíl, translated by Shoghi Effendi, *The Dawn-Breakers*. 2) The paternal lineage of the Báb: A letter from the Universal House of Justice, dated 13 June 2005 published in Shahidian which cites a memorandum of the Research Department of the Universal House of Justice, dated 20 September 1993, which states that the Báb's father was Siyyid Muhammad-Rida, that His grandfather was Mir Ibrahim, that His great-grandfather was Mir Abu'l-Fath, and that His great-great-grandfather was Mir Nasru'llah. 3) The maternal lineage of the Báb: Shahidian, p. 16-17. 4) The relationship of the Báb to the chief Shí'ih religious leader (the "marja' taqlid") in the Shí'ih world at the time, Mírzá Muhammad Hasan Shírází: Shahidian, p. 11-12 and Husaini, p. 718-719.

79 Nabíl, translated by Shoghi Effendi, *The Dawn-Breakers*, p. 75. See also: Faizi, p. 64-65; Husaini, p. 717-738

80 Scholars have not been able to verify the exact date of the death of the Báb's father. Some scholars, such as Eshraq-Khavari, Habibu'llah Afnan, Balyuzi, and Faizi, agree that he passed away sometime in the period of 1243 AH (1827 to 1828 C.E.), which would have placed the Báb as about eight years old. 'Abdu'l-Bahá states, in *A Traveler's Narrative*, "The Báb was a young merchant of the Pure Lineage. He was born in the year one thousand two hundred and thirty-five [AH] on the first day of Muharram, and when after a few years His father Siyyid Muhammad-Rida died, He was brought up in Shíráz in the arms of His maternal uncle Mírzá Siyyid 'Alí the merchant." ('Abdu'l-Bahá, *A Traveller's Narrative*, p. 4). Mírzá 'Abu'l Fadl, who may have gotten his information from Siyyid Javad Karbila'i, who knew the family, in Shíráz and in Búshihr during the early years of the Báb, says He was an infant. Nabíl (p. 72) says the Báb's father passed away during His early childhood. Shoghi Effendi, at this point in his translation of Nabíl inserted a footnote (#3) which stated that Mírzá 'Abu'l Fadl claimed that the father's passing occurred during his infancy. Husaini interprets 'Abdu'l-Bahá's statement of "after a few years" to mean past the age of infancy, perhaps two or three years old, but not as far as eight years old. See Husaini, p. 141-142.

81 Shahidian, p. 9

82 Shahidian, p. 9

83 Mázindaráni, vol 2, p. 17-18

84 Nabíl, translated by Shoghi Effendi, *The Dawn-Breakers*, p. 75-76

85 The opening words of the Qur'án are: "Bismi'llahi'r-Rahmani'r-Rahím." The translation is: "In the name of God, the Compassionate, the Merciful." Alláh, the reader will recall, means "the God"; ar-Rahman means "the Compassionate"; and ar-Rahím means "the Merciful". All but one of the 114 chapters (súrih's) of the Qur'án begin with this phrase.

86 Shaykh Abid, cited by Nabíl, translated by Shoghi Effendi, *The Dawn-Breakers*, p. 75

87 Shaykh Abid, cited by Nabíl, translated by Shoghi Effendi, *The Dawn-Breakers*, p. 76

88 H.M. Balyuzi, *The Báb: The Herald of the Day of Days*, p. 36

89 Mázindaráni #2, p. 18-19

90 Husaini, p. 685-691

91 Husaini, p 138-149

92 Hafiz was a highly acclaimed Persian mystic poet and author of the 14th century. He is laid to rest in Shíráz, the home city of the Báb. Today, he is one of the most popular poets in Iran.

93 Hafiz, cited by the Báb, in H.M. Balyuzi, *The Báb: The Herald of the Day of Days*, p. 35

94 Husaini, p. 139-149

95 Husaini, p. 139-149

96 Nabíl, translated by Shoghi Effendi, *The Dawn-Breakers*, p. 75-76

97 Abbas Amanat, *Resurrection and Renewal*, 1989, p. 123

98 Abbas Amanat, *Resurrection and Renewal*, 1989, p. 127-128. See also: H.M. Balyuzi, *The Báb: The Herald of the Day of Days*, p. 39

99 Abbas Amanat, *The Early Years of the Babi Movement Background and Development*, p. 121-122. See also: Husaini, p. 155-156

100 Husaini, p. 155-156

101 Adib Taherzadeh, *The Revelation of Bahá'u'lláh, v 1*, p. 221

102 Siyyid Javad Karbilá'í, cited by Nabíl, translated by Shoghi Effendi, *The Dawn-Breakers*, p. 79. See also Husaini, page 154-155

103 Faizi, p. 93

104 Qur'án 68:51, translation by Arberry

105 Faizi, p. 87, in a footnote. The Bahá'í Faith owned this building for about ten years, but the city of Búshihr took it over and demolished it when a city plan called for putting a road through the neighborhood. The building and the seemingly prophetic door are, alas, lost to history

106 Abbas Amanat, *Resurrection and Renewal*, 1989, p. 136-137

107 Shaykh Hasan, cited by Nabíl, translated by Shoghi Effendi, *The Dawn-Breakers*, p. 30

108 'Abdu'l-Bahá, in a recently translated talk, makes this statement. The talk is entitled "*Shaykh Ahmad and Siyyid Kazim*", Number 10. 'Abdu'l-Bahá's statement is found in paragraph 10 of that talk. Url: https://www.bahai.org/library/authoritative-texts/abdul-baha/additional-tablets-extracts-talks/491087709/491087709.xhtml (Last accessed: 3 December 2018)

109 HM Balyuzi, *Eminent Bahá'ís in the Time of Bahá'u'lláh*, p. 171-176; HM Balyuzi, *Bahá'u'lláh-King of Glory*, p. 33

110 Fuádi, p. 108-110, including footnote on p. 108

111 Fuádi, p. 108-110, including footnote on p. 108

112 Faizi, p. 100-103, 112

113 Husaini, p. 161-162

114 Abbas Amanat, *Resurrection and Renewal*, 1989, p. 136

115 Abbas Amanat, *Resurrection and Renewal*, 1989, p. 138-139

116 Shaykh Hasan-i-Zunuzí, cited by Nabíl, translated by Shoghi Effendi, *The Dawn-Breakers*, p. 27-29

117 Mázindaráni, p. 82

118 Mázindaráni, p. 78-80

119 H.M. Balyuzi, *The Báb: The Herald of the Day of Days*, p. 42

120 Abbas Amanat, *Resurrection and Renewal*, 1989, p. 140-141, 146

121 The Báb, cited by Todd Lawson, *Tafsir as Mystical Experience*, p. 55.

122 Note: A disciple of Siyyid Kázim, Shaykh Hasan, tells a story which indicates that Siyyid Kázim had intimations of the greatness of the Báb's station:

One early morning, in Karbila, Shaykh Hasan was summoned to the house of Siyyid Kázim. He was "fully dressed, wearing his aba, and ready to leave his home. He asked me to accompany him. 'A highly esteemed and distinguished Person,' he said, 'has arrived. I feel it incumbent upon us both to visit Him.' The morning light had just broken when I found myself walking with him through the streets of Karbila. We soon reached a house, at the door of which stood a Youth, as if expectant to receive us. He wore a green turban, and His countenance revealed an expression of humility and kindliness which I can never describe. He quietly approached us, extended His arms towards Siyyid Kázim, and lovingly embraced him. His affability and loving-kindness singularly contrasted with the sense of profound reverence that characterised the attitude of Siyyid Kázim towards him… We were soon led by Him to the upper floor of that house, and entered a chamber bedecked with flowers and redolent of the loveliest perfume. He bade us be seated. We knew not, however, what seats we actually occupied, so overpowering was the sense of delight which seized us. We observed a silver cup which had been placed in the centre of the room, which our youthful Host, soon after we were seated, filled to overflowing, and handed to Siyyid Kázim, saying: 'A drink of a pure beverage shall their Lord give them.' [Qur'án 76:21] Siyyid Kázim held the cup with both hands and quaffed it. A feeling of reverent joy filled his being, a feeling which he could not suppress. I too was presented with a cupful of that beverage, though no words were addressed to me. All that was spoken at that memorable gathering was the above-mentioned verse of the Qur'án. Soon after, the Host arose from His seat and, accompanying us to the threshold of the house, bade us farewell. I was mute with wonder, and knew not how to express the cordiality of His welcome, the dignity of His bearing, the charm of that face, and the delicious fragrance of that beverage. How great was my amazement when I saw my teacher quaff without the least hesitation that holy draught from a silver cup… I could not explain the motive which could have induced the Siyyid to manifest such profound reverence in the presence of that Youth… Many a time I heard [Siyyid Kázim say to me]: 'O Shaykh Hasan, rejoice that your name is Hasan [praiseworthy]; Hasan your beginning, and Hasan your end. You have been privileged to attain to the day of Shaykh Ahmad, you have been closely associated with me, and in the days to come yours shall be the inestimable joy of beholding "what eye hath seen not, ear heard not, nor any heart conceived."' (Shaykh Hasan, cited by Nabíl, translated by Shoghi Effendi, *The Dawn-Breakers*, p. 25-30.)

Shaykh Hasan's surprise at the use of the silver cup is due to the fact that there is a hadith (a report) attributed to Muhammad which appears to ban their use. The hadith has been accepted in the Muslim community and jurists have interpreted the hadith as a ban. The fact that the Báb used a silver cup and that Siyyid Kázim did not balk at its use may suggest recognition of the authority of the Qá'im to abrogate the laws of Islám as well as implicit recognition of the Báb as the Qá'im. It may also indicate that neither the Báb nor Siyyid Kázim regarded the hadith itself as authentically from Muhammad. In both interpretations, the willingness of these men to depart from accepted norms is apparent.

123 Hájí Siyyid Javad-i-Karbila'i concerning the Báb, whom he knew well, cited by Nabíl, translated by Shoghi Effendi, *The Dawn-Breakers*, p. 79-80

124 Adib Taherzadeh, *The Covenant of Bahá'u'lláh*, p. 156-158

125 Abdullah Yúsuf 'Alí, *Commentary on the Imam Husayn and His Martyrdom*. He wrote: "The following pages are based on a report of an Address which I delivered in London at

an Ashura Majlis on Thursday the 28th May, 1931 (Muharram 1350 AH), at the Waldorf Hotel."

126 'Abdu'l-Bahá, *Some Answered Questions*, p. 50

127 Abu'l-Qasim Faizi, *The Prince of Martyrs*, p. 38

128 Abu'l-Qasim Faizi, *The Prince of Martyrs*, p. 38-39

129 Abu'l-Qasim Faizi, *The Prince of Martyrs*, p. 39-40

130 Meir Litvak, *Shi'i scholars of nineteenth-century Iraq*, p. 17

131 The Báb, cited by Nabíl, translated by Shoghi Effendi, *The Dawn-Breakers*, p. 253. See also Todd Lawson, *Tafsir as Mystical Experience*, p. 46

132 Nabíl, translated by Shoghi Effendi, *The Dawn-Breakers*, p. 252

133 The Báb, *Selections from the Writings of the Báb*, p. 69

134 The Báb, cited by Shoghi Effendi, *God Passes By*, p. 30

135 Abbas Amanat, *Resurrection and Renewal*, 1989, p. 146. Amanat says that the uncle, Hájí Mírzá Siyyid 'Ali, sought out the assistance of Siyyid Kázim.

See also: H.M. Balyuzi, *The Báb: The Herald of the Day of Days*, p. 45-46. Balyuzi attributes this information to the narrative of Hájí Mírzá Habibu'llah, a widely used source among scholars. Balyuzi states that the uncle, Hájí Mírzá Siyyid 'Ali, sought out the assistance of Hájí Siyyid Javad-i-Karbila'i.

136 Baharieh Rouhani Ma'ani, *Leaves of the Twin Divine Trees*, p. 27. Shahidian, p. 147, gives the date of 1820 C.E.

137 H.M. Balyuzi, *Khadijih Bagum: The Wife of the Báb*, p.1. Note: In 19th century Persia the rules were different. Marrying a cousin was not considered inappropriate.

Note: Khadijih had dreams of her future Husband more than once. One night she saw Him "in a verdant plain, with flowers in profusion, facing towards [Mecca] in an attitude of prayer." He wore a coat on which verses of the Qur'án had been embroidered in gold and He was radiant. Years later, but long before He had advanced His claim to be the Báb, Khadijih dreamed of Him again. She "dreamt that Fatimih, the daughter of the Prophet Muhammad, had come to ask for her hand in marriage to the Imám Husayn. Her mother, when she heard of the dream, rejoiced. That very day, the Báb's mother and grandmother came to her house to speak with her mother. "The mother of Siyyid 'Ali-Muhammad kissed her on the forehead before leaving. Seeing her puzzled look, her mother hastened to explain: 'That kiss implied that she has asked your hand in marriage to her Son. You see, the dream you had last night has come true.' Khadijih Bagum … was greatly elated… She recalled: 'From that day I felt a great stirring within my heart. It seemed that the gate of God's mercy and abundant bounty had been flung open before my face. I felt immeasurably proud of my coming union."" (Khadijih Bagum cited by H.M. Balyuzi, *Khadijih Bagum: The Wife of the Báb*, p.3-4)

138 Husaini, p. 171. Husaini says the marriage took place in the house inherited from the Báb's father. Balyuzi states that the home was the one in which the Báb grew up in. (H.M. Balyuzi, *Khadijih Bagum: The Wife of the Báb*, p. 5.) See also Faizi, p. 105; Shahidian, p. 147, says the home of the uncle and the home of Khadíjih were next door to each other.

139 Khadijih Bagum, cited by H.M. Balyuzi, *Khadijih Bagum: The Wife of the Báb*, p.5

140 Fatimih, the reader will recall, is the daughter of the Muhammad, who along with Khadijih, Muhammad's first wife, are regarded as the preeminent women of the Islámic Dispensation.

141 The Báb, cited by Nader Saiedi, *Gate of the Heart*; p. 153

142 Nabíl, translated by Shoghi Effendi, *The Dawn-Breakers*, p. 77. Recall that Abraham was ordered to offer up His son as a burnt offering, but in the end "offering up" meant that He was not required to sacrifice His son. The Báb, who named His son Ahmed, after Muhammad, was not ordered to sacrifice His son, but in the end lost him anyway. Spiritually, the Báb saw it as a sacrifice and He wished to also offer up His own life to God.

143 H.M. Balyuzi, *Khadijih Bagum: The Wife of the Báb*, p. 9

144 The Báb, cited by Nabíl, translated by Shoghi Effendi, *The Dawn-Breakers*, p. 252-253

145 H.M. Balyuzi, *Khadijih Bagum: The Wife of the Báb*, p. 10-12

146 H.M. Balyuzi, *Khadijih Bagum: The Wife of the Báb*, p. 12-14

147 Abbas Amanat, *Resurrection and Renewal*, 1989, p. 154-156

148 Abbas Amanat, *Resurrection and Renewal*, 1989, p. 156

149 Abbas Amanat, *Resurrection and Renewal*, 1989, p. 156-158. And also Nabíl, translated by Shoghi Effendi, *The Dawn-Breakers*, p. 333-334.

150 Abbas Amanat, *Resurrection and Renewal*, 1989, p. 156-158. And also Nabíl, translated by Shoghi Effendi, *The Dawn-Breakers*, p. 333-334; R. Mehrabkhani, *Mullá Husayn, Disciple at Dawn*, p. 193-197.

151 Siyyid Kázim, cited by Nabíl, translated by Shoghi Effendi, *The Dawn-Breakers*, p. 47

152 Mullá Husayn, cited by Nabíl, translated by Shoghi Effendi, *The Dawn-Breakers*, p. 46

153 Mullá Husayn, cited by Nabíl, translated by Shoghi Effendi, *The Dawn-Breakers*, p. 46

154 Nabíl, p. 50 and elsewhere, says Mirza Muhammad Baqir was a nephew of Mullá Husayn. Shoghi Effendi quoted Nabíl in his writings, referring to Baqir as a nephew of Mullá Husayn. Numerous scholars, however, have researched this and are united in their opinion that Baqir was a maternal cousin, not a nephew. See the following: Faizi, p. 109; Husaini #1, p.180 and footnote p. 195; Baraqi, p. 239 and footnote p. 169, and Mázindarání #3, p. 153. The scholars derived their conclusions by looking at early manuscripts. Also, logic suggests that if Baqir had been a nephew, he would have been too young to undertake the journey. Baqir was 22 years old in in 1844. Logically, in this instance, it is best to conclude he was a cousin.

When a statement of fact found in the Writings is found through later investigation to be in error, and when the error is stated by the Head of the Faith, what is a sincere Bahá'í or scholar supposed to do? To answer this question, one should refer to the following quotes from the Universal House of Justice, dated 1974 and 1977.

"Now, in the matter of the accuracy of historical fact, Shoghi Effendi had to rely on available information... The Guardian was meticulous about the authenticity of historical fact. One of the friends in Yazd wrote to him stating that the account given by 'Abdu'l-Bahá in one of His Tablets about events related to the martyrdom of some of the believers in that place was in conflict with known facts about these events. Shoghi Effendi replied saying that the friends should investigate the facts carefully and unhesitatingly register them in their historical records, since 'Abdu'l-Bahá Himself had prefaced His recording of the events in His Tablet with a statement that it was based on news received from Yazd." (The Universal House of Justice, July 25, 1974, Infallibility of the Guardian, retrieved from Ocean database.)

"Shoghi Effendi was asked several times during his ministry to define the sphere of his operation and his infallibility. The replies he gave and which were written on his behalf are most illuminating. He explains that he is not an infallible authority on subjects such as economics and science, nor does he go into technical matters since his infallibility is confined to 'matters which are related strictly to the Cause'. He further points out that 'he is not, like the Prophet, omniscient at will', that his 'infallibility covers interpretation of the Revealed Word and its application', and that he is also 'infallible in the protection of the Faith'..." (From a letter written on behalf of the Universal House of Justice to an individual believer, August 22, 1977, *Lights of Guidance*, p. 310, retrieved from Ocean database.)

155 Nabíl, translated by Shoghi Effendi, *The Dawn-Breakers*, p. 50. See also: Faizi, p. 109

156 Faizi, p. 110 footnote. Faizi mentions that the Islámic prophecy is from Ja'far ibn Muhammad, and is found in the famous book, *Bahar-ul-Anvar* (vol 13, p. 197)

157 Faizi, p. 109

158 Abbas Amanat, *Resurrection and Renewal*, 1989, p. 165

159 Baraqi, p. 57-59

160 H.M. Balyuzi, *The Báb - The Herald of the Day of Days*, p. 15

161 Baraqi, p. 57-59

162 Nabíl, translated by Shoghi Effendi, *The Dawn-Breakers*, p. 52

163 Baraqi, p. 57-59

164 Faizi, p. 111

165 Nabíl, translated by Shoghi Effendi, *The Dawn-Breakers*, p. 52-65

166 Nabíl, translated by Shoghi Effendi, *The Dawn-Breakers*, p. 52-65

167 Faizi, p. 119

168 Mázindarání #2, p. 30-32

169 Nabíl, translated by Shoghi Effendi, *The Dawn-Breakers*, p. 52-65

170 The Báb, *Selections from the Writings of the Báb*, p. 41-43. And also Shoghi Effendi, *God Passes By*, p. 6-8

171 The Báb, *Selections from the Writings of the Báb*, p. 41-43. And also Shoghi Effendi, *God Passes By*, p. 6-8

172 The Báb, *Selections from the Writings of the Báb*, p. 41-43. And also Shoghi Effendi, *God Passes By*, p. 6-8

173 The Báb, *Selections from the Writings of the Báb*, p. 41-43. And also Shoghi Effendi, *God Passes By*, p. 6-8

174 R. Mehrabkhani, *Mullá Husayn: Disciple at Dawn*, p. 70-71

175 Shoghi Effendi, *God Passes By*, p. 5

176 Khadijih Bagum, as reported by Munirih Khanum, cited by Baharieh Rouhani Ma'ani, *Leaves of the Twin Divine Trees*, p. 36. See also: *Munirih Khanum: Memoirs and Letters*, translated by Sammireh Anwar Smith, p. 34

177 We calculate Fiddih's age at this point as follows: She dies at the age of 47 in 1882. Therefore, the year of her birth must have been 1835. She is 7 when she becomes part of the Báb's household, so that means she arrives in the year 1842. Two years later, in 1844,

when the Báb declares His mission to Mullá Husayn, she would be 9 years old. This calculation is cross-referenced with the date of the Báb's marriage to Khadijih in 1842, so it is safe to conclude that she entered the household not long after they were married. See the following resources: 'Abu'l-Qasim Afnan, *Black Pearls*; H.M. Balyuzi, *Khadijih Bagum*; Baharieh Rouhani Ma'ani, *Leaves of the Twin Divine Trees*. See also Shahidian, p. 158-159; Husaini, p. 724.

178 'Abu'l-Qasim Afnan, Black Pearls, p. 21-25; H.M. Balyuzi, *Khadijih Bagum*; Baharieh Rouhani Ma'ani, *Leaves of the Twin Divine Trees*. See also Shahidian, p. 158-159; Husaini, p. 724.

179 'Abu'l-Qasim Afnan, *Black Pearls*, p. 7. See also Anthony Lee, *The Bahá'í Faith in Africa*, p. 31-33; Phyllis G. Jestice, Editor, Holy People of the World, p. 606; Kwame Anthony Appiah and Henry Louis Gates, Jr., *Encyclopedia of Africa, Volume 1*, p. 197, Section on Hájí Mubárak by Anthony Lee

180 Nader Saiedi and Omid Ghaemmaghami, "The Ethiopian King", p. 181

181 Nader Saiedi and Omid Ghaemmaghami, "The Ethiopian King", p. 181-186. See also The Báb, *Selections from the Writings of the Báb*, p. 83, 92, 213; Bahá'u'lláh, *The Book of Certitude*, p. 146. And also Matthew 5:10; 20:16; Mark 9:35; 10:31; Luke 13:30 and Qur'án 28:5

182 Mullá Husayn, cited by Nabíl, translated by Shoghi Effendi, *The Dawn-Breakers*, p. 62

183 The Báb, *Selections from the Writings of the Báb*, p. 107-108

184 The Báb, *Selections from the Writings of the Báb*, p. 106-107

185 The Báb, *Selections from the Writings of the Báb*, p. 107-108

186 Shoghi Effendi explains the dates as follows: "...The believers must hold gatherings for the Bahá'ís at exactly 2 hours and 11 minutes after sunset on May 22nd ... as this is the exact time when the Báb declared His Mission to Mullá Husayn." (From a letter written on behalf of the Guardian to the National Spiritual Assembly of India, December 27, 1941: Dawn of a New Day, June 22, 1943, p. 105, also Lights of Guidance, p. 469) And also: "... regarding the declaration of the Báb and the birthday of the Master; the Báb declared His Mission on the fourth day of the month of Jamadi I, two hours and eleven minutes after sunset, corresponding with the evening of May 22nd. But as the Bahá'í day begins after sunset, and not after midnight as in the West, the Báb's declaration is celebrated on the fifth day of Jamadi I, corresponding to the 23rd of May. "Abdu'l-Bahá was born in the course of that same night, but the exact hour of His birth has not been ascertained." (From a letter written on behalf of Shoghi Effendi to the National Spiritual Assembly of the United States and Canada November 25, 1936. Also: Lights of Guidance, p. 469)

187 The Báb, *Selections from the Writings of the Báb*, p. 107-108

188 The Báb, *Selections from the Writings of the Báb*, p. 107-108

189 The Báb, *Selections from the Writings of the Báb*, p. 78

190 'Abdu'l-Bahá was the Son of Bahá'u'lláh, and His Successor appointed in writing. 'Abdu'l-Bahá is one of the three great Central Figures of the Bahá'í Faith.

191 See 2 Peter 3:10, 1 Thessalonians 5:2, and Matthew 24:42-44

192 Nabíl, translated by Shoghi Effendi, *The Dawn-Breakers*, p. 65-66

193 Mullá Husayn, cited by Nabíl, translated by Shoghi Effendi, *The Dawn-Breakers*, p. 66

194 Faizi, p. 122-123

195 Mullá Husayn, cited by Nabíl, translated by Shoghi Effendi, *The Dawn-Breakers*, p. 67

196 Mullá Husayn, cited by Nabíl, translated by Shoghi Effendi, *The Dawn-Breakers*, p. 67

197 Nabíl, translated by Shoghi Effendi, *The Dawn-Breakers*, p. 52-65

198 Mullá 'Alí and other Shaykhis, cited by Nabíl, translated by Shoghi Effendi, *The Dawn-Breakers*, p. 68

199 Mullá 'Alí and other Shaykhis, cited by Nabíl, translated by Shoghi Effendi, *The Dawn-Breakers*, p. 68

200 Nabíl, translated by Shoghi Effendi, *The Dawn-Breakers*, p. 68

201 Faizi, p. 124-125

202 Nabíl, translated by Shoghi Effendi, *The Dawn-Breakers*, p. 68-69

203 Faizi, p. 124-125, 126 footnote.

204 'Abdu'l-Bahá , *Memorials of the Faithful*, p. 193

205 Táhirih, cited by Nabíl, translated by Shoghi Effendi, *The Dawn-Breakers*, p. 81-82

206 Private communication (by email to this writer, dated November 28, 2017) with Dr. Nader Saiedi, Professor of Bahá'í Studies, University of California, Los Angeles. At the time of this writing, Dr. Saiedi is the only scholar who has seen the actual letter written by the Báb for Táhirih, which is preserved in the Bahá'í International Archives in Haifa, Israel. Dr. Saiedi told me: "This account you cannot find in any book. The reason is that this account is given by the Báb Himself in His Tablet addressed to Táhirih. There He says that because you said to the one who was leaving to find me "Ozkorni" (odhkorni, i.e. make mention of me), I accepted you and made you a Letter of the Living. He adds that this single word uttered by her is more important than anything she has ever done in her life. No one knows about this Tablet."

207 'Abdu'l-Bahá, *Memorials of the Faithful*, p. 193-194

208 Nabíl, translated by Shoghi Effendi, *The Dawn-Breakers*, p. 69-70

209 Faizi, p. 126-128

210 Letters of the Living as listed by Nabíl, translated by Shoghi Effendi, *The Dawn-Breakers*, p. 80

211 See, for example, 'Abdu'l-Bahá, *Some Answered Questions*, 2014 edition, p. 291-293, 343-345; 'Abdu'l-Bahá, *Foundations of World Unity*, p. 45-47

212 The Báb, cited by Nabíl, translated by Shoghi Effendi, *The Dawn-Breakers*, p. 87-92

213 Nabíl, translated by Shoghi Effendi, *The Dawn-Breakers*, p. 90-92. Bahá'u'lláh singles out Shaykh Muhammad-Hasan Najafi for criticism in His most important book, *The Most Holy Book (Kitáb-i-Aqdás)*. "Call ye to mind the shaykh whose name was Muhammad-Hasan, who ranked among the most learned divines of his day. When the True One was made manifest, this shaykh, along with others of his calling, rejected Him, while a sifter of wheat and barley accepted Him and turned unto the Lord. Though he was occupied both night and day in setting down what he conceived to be the laws and ordinances of God, yet when He Who is the Unconstrained appeared, not one letter thereof availed him, or he would not have turned away from a Countenance that hath illumined the faces of the well-favoured of the Lord. Had ye believed in God when He revealed Himself, the people would not have turned aside from Him, nor would the things ye witness today have befallen Us. Fear God,

and be not of the heedless." (Bahá'u'lláh, *The Most Holy Book (Kitáb-i-Aqdás)*, p. 79-80)

214 Husaini, p. 2013-206. Husaini cites Mázindarání #3, p. 105, as his source. See also Nabíl, translated by Shoghi Effendi, *The Dawn-Breakers*, p. 87-92

215 Abbas Amanat, *Resurrection and Renewal*, 1989, p. 220

216 H.M. Balyuzi, *The Báb: The Herald of the Day of Days*, 1973, George Ronald Publisher, Oxford, p. 61

217 Abbas Amanat, *Resurrection and Renewal*, 1989, p. 205

218 Husaini, p. 203-206. See also Abbas Amanat, *Resurrection and Renewal*, 1989, p. 220-238.

219 Abbas Amanat, *Resurrection and Renewal*, 1989, p. 237

220 There are diverse accounts about the demise of Mullá 'Alí Bastámí. It is known that the Ottoman Sultan summoned him to Constantinople, the capital city of the Ottoman Empire, that he had left Baghdad and was on his way to Constantinople. In all probability, he did not arrive, but rather died on the way. See Mázindarání #3, p. 87-89 and also Moojan Momen, "The trial of Mullá 'Alí Bastámí: A combined Sunní-Shi'i fatwa against the Báb", 1982, *Iran: Journal of the British Institute for Persian Studies*, 20, p. 113-143.

221 Shoghi Effendi, *God Passes By*, p. 10

222 Husaini, p. 203-206

223 See also Abbas Amanat, *Resurrection and Renewal*, 1989, p. 214, footnote #15, in which details about this spoken chronicle are explained. The spoken chronicle was recorded from Hájí Siyyid Javad Karbilá'í himself when Mírzá Abu'l Fadl visited him between 1876 and 1881 in Tihran.

224 Hájí Siyyid Javad Karbilá'í, as told to Mírzá Abu'l-Fadl, and cited by Adib Taherzadeh, *The Revelation of Bahá'u'lláh, v 1*, p. 221-223. See also Husaini, p. 685-691

225 Husaini, p. 685-691

226 Hájí Siyyid Javad Karbilá'í, as told to Mírzá Abu'l-Fadl, and cited by Adib Taherzadeh, *The Revelation of Bahá'u'lláh, v 1*, p. 221-223. See also Husaini, p. 685-691

227 The Primal Point = A reference of the Báb to Himself, one of His diverse titles which are found in His Writings.

228 The Báb, cited by Nabíl, translated by Shoghi Effendi, *The Dawn-Breakers*, p. 92-94

229 Shoghi Effendi, *The World Order of Bahá'u'lláh*, p. 61

230 Shoghi Effendi, *The World Order of Bahá'u'lláh*, p. 123

231 About half were Shaykhis. These are the nine names of Letters who were associated with the Shaykhis that I have been able to identify so far:

Mullá Husayn-i-Bushru'i

Muhammad-Hasan, his brother

Muhammad-Baqir, his cousin

Mullá Aliy-i-Bastámí

Mírzá Muhammad Rawdih-Khán-i-Yazdi

Sa'id-i-Hindi

Mírzá Muhammad-'Aliy-i-Qazvíni

Táhirih

Quddús

232 This method of gradual disclosure has led some scholars, such as Juan Cole and Dennis MacEoin, to claim that the Báb's own self-awareness gradually developed over time, that initially He only thought of Himself as the Gate to the Hidden Imám and that only later did He conceive of Himself as a new Manifestation of God. Such a theory, without proximity to the Báb Himself, without any indication from the Báb, and without any testimony from any of the Báb's various confidants, presumes to perform a deep psychoanalysis of the Báb's internal mental state (at a distance of more than a century!), while it ignores numerous explicit indications found in the Báb's own written testimony and in His actions that He understood fully and from the beginning Who He was. Readers interested in exploring this topic further should consult Nader Saeidi's excellent rebuttal of these claims (*Gate of the Heart*, p. 19, 83-85).

Readers may also find these statements from 'Abdu'l-Bahá and Shoghi Effendi helpful:

"In the year one thousand two hundred and sixty [A.H.], when He was in His twenty-fifth year, certain signs became apparent in His conduct, behavior, manners, and demeanor whereby it became evident in Shiraz that He had some conflict in His mind and some other flight beneath His wing. He began to speak and to declare the rank of Bab-hood. Now what He intended by the term Bab [Gate] was this, that He was the channel of grace from some great Person still behind the veil of glory, Who was the possessor of countless and boundless perfections, by Whose will He moved, and to the bond of Whose love He clung. And in the first book which He wrote in explanation of the Surih of Joseph, He addressed Himself in all passages to that Person unseen from Whom He received help and grace, sought for aid in the arrangement of His preliminaries, and craved the sacrifice of life in the way of His love." ('Abdu'l-Bahá, *A Traveller's Narrative*, p. 4)

"When, at the beginning of his Mission, the Báb, continuing the tradition of the Shi'ahs, proclaimed His function under the double title of, first, the Qá'im and, second, the Gate, or Báb, some of the Muhammadans misunderstood the latter reference. They imagined His meaning to be that He was a fifth Gate in succession to Abu'l-Hasan-'Ali. His true meaning, however, as He himself clearly announced, was very different. He was the Qá'im; but the Qá'im, though a High Prophet, stood in relation to a succeeding and greater Manifestation as did John the Baptist to the Christ. He was the Forerunner of One yet more mighty than Himself. He was to decrease; that Mighty One was to increase. And as John the Baptist had been the Herald or Gate of the Christ, so was the Báb the Herald or Gate of Bahá'u'lláh." (Shoghi Effendi, *The Dawn-Breakers*, p. xxx-xxxi)

"It will help you to connect the origin of the Movement with the tenets and beliefs held by the Shí'ahs of Persia. The Báb declared Himself at the beginning of His mission to be the "Báb" by which He meant to be the gate or forerunner of "Him Whom God will make manifest", that is to say Bahá'u'lláh, Whose advent the Shí'ahs also expected in the person of "the return of Imám Husayn". The Sunnís also believe in a similar twofold manifestation, the first they call "the Mihdi", the second "the Return of Christ". By the term Báb, the Báb meant to be the forerunner of the second manifestation rather than, as some have maintained, the gate of the Qá'im. When He declared Himself to be the Báb, the people understood by the term that He was an intermediary between the absent Qá'im and His followers, though He Himself never meant to be such a person. All He claimed to be was that He was the Qá'im Himself and in addition to this station, that of the Báb, namely the gate or forerunner of

'Him Whom God will make Manifest." (Shoghi Effendi, *The Unfolding Destiny of the British Bahá'í Community*, p. 426)

233 Nabíl, translated by Shoghi Effendi, *The Dawn-Breakers*, p. 85-87

234 The Báb, cited by Nabíl, translated by Shoghi Effendi, *The Dawn-Breakers*, p. 85-87

235 The Báb, cited by Nabíl, translated by Shoghi Effendi, *The Dawn-Breakers*, p. 96

236 Isfahán religious school students, cited by Nabíl, translated by Shoghi Effendi, *The Dawn-Breakers*, p. 97-98

237 Hájí Siyyid Asadu'llah, the son of the distinguished teacher, head of the school, cited by Nabíl, translated by Shoghi Effendi, *The Dawn-Breakers*, p. 97-98

238 Hájí Muhammad-Ibrahim-i-Kalbasi, a second distinguished teacher in Isfahán, cited by Nabíl, translated by Shoghi Effendi, *The Dawn-Breakers*, p. 97-98

239 Husaini, p. 207-230

240 Nabíl, citing the Báb, translated by Shoghi Effendi, *The Dawn-Breakers*, p. 99

241 The Báb, cited and translated by Shoghi Effendi, *The Dawn-Breakers*, p. 99-100, regarding the *Persian Bayan*, vol 4, p. 113. See *Persian Bayan* 8:14.

242 Husaini, p. 207-230

243 Nabíl, translated by Shoghi Effendi, *The Dawn-Breakers*, p. 101

244 Fuádi, p. 108-110, including footnote on p. 108

245 Mázindarání, vol 2, p. 47, in a footnote

246 Husaini, p. 207-230

247 Mázindarání, Vol. 2, page 46-47 footnote

248 The father of Bahá'u'lláh

249 Mullá Muhammad, cited by Nabíl, translated by Shoghi Effendi, *The Dawn-Breakers*, p. 103-107. The question about the script in which Bahá'u'lláh excels is a reference to Arabic calligraphy. Both the Báb and Bahá'u'lláh were renowned for their highly excellent calligraphy, an important art form in Persia at the time. The question and the answer serve to indicate a high degree of refinement and virtue.

250 Mullá Muhammad, cited by Nabíl, translated by Shoghi Effendi, *The Dawn-Breakers*, p. 103-107

251 Mullá Muhammad, cited by Nabíl, translated by Shoghi Effendi, *The Dawn-Breakers*, p. 103-107

252 Mullá Husayn, quoted by Mullá Muhammad, reported by Nabíl, translated by Shoghi Effendi, *The Dawn-Breakers*, p. 107-108

253 Nabíl, translated by Shoghi Effendi, *The Dawn-Breakers*, p. 117-118

254 Mírzá Muhammad Taqiy-i-Núrí, cited by Nabíl, translated by Shoghi Effendi, *The Dawn-Breakers*, p. 111-112

255 Mírzá Muhammad Taqiy-i-Núrí, cited by Nabíl, translated by Shoghi Effendi, *The Dawn-Breakers*, p. 111-112

256 Nabíl, translated by Shoghi Effendi, *The Dawn-Breakers*, p. 116

257 Due to the family into which He had been born, Bahá'u'lláh's social class was considered nobility.

258 Núr was Bahá'u'lláh's home province, north of Tihran.

259 Nabíl, translated by Shoghi Effendi, *The Dawn-Breakers*, p. 113

260 Nabíl, translated by Shoghi Effendi, *The Dawn-Breakers*, p. 114

261 Nabíl, translated by Shoghi Effendi, *The Dawn-Breakers*, p. 118-119

262 Mázindarání, vol 2, p. 49-50

263 The Báb, *Selections from the Writings of the Báb*, p. 37

264 The Báb, *Selections from the Writings of the Báb*, p. 42-43

265 Muhammad Khán-i-Turkaman

266 Mázindarání, vol 3, p. 169

267 Mázindarání, vol 2, p. 49-50; Faizi, p. 131

268 Comte de Gobineau, cited in a footnote in French by Shoghi Effendi, translator of Nabíl, *The Dawn-Breakers*, p. 125. See the following: Emily McBride Perigord, *Translation of the French Foot-Notes of the Dawn-Breakers*, p. 16-17

269 Mázindarání #3, footnote p. 139, p. 140

270 Nabíl, translated by Shoghi Effendi, *The Dawn-Breakers*, p. 126

271 The Báb, cited by Nabíl, translated by Shoghi Effendi, *The Dawn-Breakers*, p. 123

272 Nabíl, translated by Shoghi Effendi, *The Dawn-Breakers*, p. 126

273 Nabíl, translated by Shoghi Effendi, *The Dawn-Breakers*, p. 126-128

274 The computations discussed in the following are in part based on information obtained from R. Mehrabkhani, *Mullá Husayn: Disciple at Dawn*, p. 121-122. Other specific sources are cited below.

275 Faizi, p. 132; Husaini, p. 232, Baraqi, p. 75. Nabíl and other Persian sources usually give the dates in terms of the Islámic calendar. To get the exact Gregorian calendar date, an online Hijri/Gregorian calendar converter was used. (Url:http://www.muslimphilosophy.com/ip/hijri.htm). This online resource enables easy and reliable conversion from the Gregorian calendar to the Hijri calendar, and from the Hijri calendar to the Gregorian.

276 This is calculated using Google Maps, a modern-day computer application using the modern-day road system for its calculations. We cannot identify the exact roads which Mullá Husayn, in the 19th century, would have taken or what obstacles on the way he would have encountered.

277 This is calculated using Google Maps. See the previous endnote.

278 Baraqi, p. 75

279 Nabíl, translated by Shoghi Effendi, *The Dawn-Breakers*, p. 126

280 R. Mehrabkhani, *Mullá Husayn: Disciple at Dawn*, p. 121-122

281 Shoghi Effendi, *God Passes By*, p. 8-9. See also H.M. Balyuzi, *The Báb*, p. 57

The exact date of the Báb's departure from Shíráz for His pilgrimage was listed as 26 Sha'bán 1260 AH on the Islámic calendar, which was September 10th, 1844 on the Gregorian calendar. To get the exact Gregorian calendar date, an online Hijri/Gregorian calendar was consulted. See previous endnote.

282 Nabíl, translated by Shoghi Effendi, *The Dawn-Breakers*, p. 128

283 The exact date of the Báb's departure from Shíráz for His pilgrimage was listed as 26 Sha'bán 1260 AH on the Islámic calendar, which was September 10th, 1844 on the Gregorian calendar. To get the exact Gregorian calendar date, an online Hijri/Gregorian calendar was consulted. See previous endnote.

284 Shoghi Effendi, *God Passes By*, p. 8-9. Shoghi Effendi gives the exact date in terms of the Islámic calendar: 19th of Ramadán,1260 AH. which was October 2nd, 1844 AD. To get the exact Gregorian calendar date, an online Hijri/Gregorian calendar was consulted. See previous endnote.

285 Jaddih = A port city on the western coast of Arabia, at the Red Sea. Jaddih is close to Mecca which is somewhat inland. Pilgrims arrived by boat at Jaddih and then traveled a short distance over land to reach Mecca.

286 Shoghi Effendi, *God Passes By*, p. 8-9. Shoghi Effendi listed the exact date as "the first of Dhi'l-Hajjih", which is in the Islámic calendar. This date corresponds to December 12th, 1844 on the Gregorian calendar. To get the exact Gregorian calendar date, an online Hijri/Gregorian calendar was consulted. See previous endnote.

287 Faizi, p. 141-142

288 Faizi ,p. 133

289 Meir Litvak, *Shi'i scholars of nineteenth-century Iraq*, p. 143

290 Interestingly, in addition to the mole, two other signs were "white teeth" and "laughing out loud". Javad found all three of these signs in the Báb. (Mázindarání #3, p. 80-81)

291 Husaini, p. 233; Mázindarání #3, p. 80-81

292 Mázindarání, p. 82

293 Mázindarání, vol 2, p. 55

294 Mázindarání, vol 3, p. 312 footnote

295 Abdul-Baha uses the term "gabr", which means a member of the Zoroastrian Faith, when translated. For further information see: https://en.wikipedia.org/wiki/Gabr. And also: http://www.iranicaonline.org/articles/gabr- (the hyphen is included). (Last accessed: 8 March 2019.)

296 'Abdu'l-Bahá, *A Traveller's Narrative*, p. 20-21

297 Rouhani, p. 21

298 A.L.M. Nicolas, cited in a footnote in Nabíl, translated by Shoghi Effendi, *The Dawn-Breakers*, p. 171

299 Faizi, p. 141-142

300 Mázindarání, vol 3, p. 21

301 Nabíl, translated by Shoghi Effendi, *The Dawn-Breakers*, p. 613-615

302 Husaini, p. 233; Mázindarání, vol 3, p. 80-81

303 A. L. M. Nicolas, *"Siyyid Ali-Muhammad dit le Bab,"* pp. 207-208, cited as a footnote by Nabíl, translated by Shoghi Effendi, *The Dawn-Breakers*, p. 130

304 The Báb, *Selections from the Writings of the Báb*, p. 35-38

305 H.M. Balyuzi, *The Báb*, p. 69-70

306 The Báb, cited by Nabíl, translated by Shoghi Effendi, *The Dawn-Breakers*, p. 130

307 The Báb, cited by Nabíl, translated by Shoghi Effendi, *The Dawn-Breakers*, p. 131

308 Faizi, p. 141-142

309 H.M. Balyuzi, *The Báb*, p. 69-70. See also Faizi, p. 141-142

310 Faizi, p. 141-142

311 H.M. Balyuzi, *The Báb*, p. 69-70

312 Nabíl, translated by Shoghi Effendi, *The Dawn-Breakers*, p. 141. The date given in the text is 1st of Muharram, 1261 AH. The footnote for this date on the bottom of the page says the date was January 30th, 1845. The online date converter (http://www.islamicity.org/hijri-gregorian-converter/#), however, reports the date as Friday, January 10th, 1845. In this instance, priority will be given to the online date converter.

313 Nabíl, translated by Shoghi Effendi, *The Dawn-Breakers*, p. 140-141

314 Baráqí, p. 79

315 Nader Saiedi, *Gate of the Heart*, p. 21

316 Nader Saiedi, *Gate of the Heart*, p. 21-22

317 Baráqí, p. 79

318 The Báb, cited by Nabíl, translated by Shoghi Effendi, *The Dawn-Breakers*, p. 140-143

319 The Persian name of this treatise is *Khasa'il-i-Sab'ih.*

320 Nabíl, translated by Shoghi Effendi, *The Dawn-Breakers*, p. 143

321 Faizi, p. 82-88. The first three lines are sourced from Faizi. The fourth line is sourced from Nabíl, p. 144, which was translated by Shoghi Effendi.

322 Nabíl, translated by Shoghi Effendi, *The Dawn-Breakers*, p. 144

323 Nabíl, translated by Shoghi Effendi, *The Dawn-Breakers*, p. 143-144

324 'Abdu'l-Bahá, *A Traveller's Narrative*, p. 5

325 Shoghi Effendi states in a footnote on p. 145: "According to A. L. M. Nicolas' "Siyyid Ali-Muhammad dit le Bab" (footnote 175, p. 225), this meeting took place on August 6, 1845 AD" Nabíl, translated by Shoghi Effendi, *The Dawn-Breakers*, p. 145

326 Husayn Khán attempting to quote the Báb, cited by Nabíl, translated by Shoghi Effendi, *The Dawn-Breakers*, p. 146. He did not get the quote just right. This passage is as follows in *Selections from the Writings of the Báb*, p. 41: "O concourse of kings and of the sons of kings! Lay aside, one and all, your dominion which belongeth unto God..."

327 The Báb, cited by Nabíl, translated by Shoghi Effendi, *The Dawn-Breakers*, p. 145

328 Nabíl doesn't mention Ardistani, but 'Abdu'l-Bahá does. See 'Abdu'l-Bahá, *A Traveller's Narrative*, p. 5

329 Nabíl, translated by Shoghi Effendi, *The Dawn-Breakers*, p. 145-148

330 Mullá Sádiq, cited by Nabíl, translated by Shoghi Effendi, *The Dawn-Breakers*, p. 145-148

331 An eyewitness, cited by Nabíl, translated by Shoghi Effendi, *The Dawn-Breakers*, p. 145-148

332 Nabíl, translated by Shoghi Effendi, The Dawn-Breakers, p. 147

333 Faizi, p. 82-88

334 The Times of London. "MAHOMETAN SCHISM.-A new sect has lately set..." Times, 19 Nov. 1845, p. 3. *The Times Digital Archive*, http://tinyurl.galegroup.com/tinyurl/93d8j8. Accessed 10 Feb. 2019. Gale Document Number: GALE | CS52590963

335 Boon's Lick Times, Fayette, Missouri, 4 April 1846, p. 1. Article about the persecutions in Shíráz.

336 The Basic Bahá'í chronology (available online) says the arrival date was July 7, 1845. That same source also states that Nicolas says he arrived in Shíráz August 6, 1845.

337 Shoghi Effendi, *God Passes By*, p. 11

338 Siyyid = descendent of the Prophet Muhammad

339 Nabíl, translated by Shoghi Effendi, *The Dawn-Breakers*, p. 148-150

340 H.M. Balyuzi, *The Báb*, p. 88

341 Nabíl, translated by Shoghi Effendi, *The Dawn-Breakers*, p. 150

342 Husayn Khán, cited by Nabíl, translated by Shoghi Effendi, *The Dawn-Breakers*, p. 150

343 The Qur'án, cited by the Báb, cited by Nabíl, translated by Shoghi Effendi, *The Dawn-Breakers*, p. 150

344 Nabíl, translated by Shoghi Effendi, *The Dawn-Breakers*, p. 148-150

345 Faizi, p. 165-167, identifies the Shaykh as Shaykh Husayn, with no further comment. Nabíl identifies this man as "a certain siyyid known as Siyyidi-Shish-Pari, whose function was to carry the mace before the Imám-Jum'ih". (Nabíl, translated by Shoghi Effendi, *The Dawn-Breakers*, p. 153) Interestingly and somewhat humorously, the term "Shish-Pari" means "six wings". The term, "Imám-Jum'ih" refers to the chief religious leader in the city.

346 The Báb was quoting a Muslim Tradition. The translation of this tradition is cited from H.M. Balyuzi, *The Báb*, p. 97

347 This young man's full name was: Mírzá Abu'l-Hasan Khán Mushír'ul-Mulk. The term Mushír'ul-Mulk indicates that he later became a very high ranking official in the Persian government. He was probably a consultant to the King, the Prime Minister, or one of the princes.

348 An account from an eyewitness, Hájí Mírzá Muhammad Sádiq-i-Mu'allim. See also Faizi, p. 165-167; H.M. Balyuzi, *The Báb*, p. 98

349 Husaini, p. 262-262. Husaini discusses the differences between the accounts of that day.

350 Nabíl, translated by Shoghi Effendi, *The Dawn-Breakers*, p. 153-154

351 Nabíl, translated by Shoghi Effendi, *The Dawn-Breakers*, p. 154

352 'Abdu'l-Bahá, *A Traveller's Narrative*, p. 6-7

353 Nabíl, translated by Shoghi Effendi, *The Dawn-Breakers*, p. 155

354 Faizi, p. 167-169; Husaini, p. 262-263; Nabíl, p. 155. re Vakil episode. The nephew was steadfast all his life, and eventually recognized Bahá'u'lláh as well.

355 Nabíl, translated by Shoghi Effendi, *The Dawn-Breakers*, p. 170

356 Nabíl gives the names of the three men. They were Mullá Javad-i-Baraghani, Mullá Abdu'l-'Aliy-i-Harati, and Mírzá Ibrahim-i-Shírází. (Nabíl, translated by Shoghi Effendi, *The Dawn-Breakers*, p. 159, 161

357 Nabíl, translated by Shoghi Effendi, *The Dawn-Breakers*, p. 159-160

358 Nabíl, translated by Shoghi Effendi, *The Dawn-Breakers*, p. 161

359 Nabíl, translated by Shoghi Effendi, *The Dawn-Breakers*, p. 161

360 Nabíl, translated by Shoghi Effendi, *The Dawn-Breakers*, p. 161-162

361 Faizi, p. 170-173

362 Hájí Siyyid Javád Karbilá'i, reported by Husaini, p. 143-144. See also Faizi, p. 176-177

363 Husaini, p. 143-144

364 Nabíl, translated by Shoghi Effendi, *The Dawn-Breakers*, p. 170-171

365 Baraqi, p. 84-85, gives Mullá Husayn's route as follows: Shíráz, Yazd, Kirmán, Tabas, Bushrueih, and Mashhad. Fuádi, p. 68, gives a different route: Shíráz, Yazd, Anjirak, Bushrueih, and Mashhad. Niether Faizi nor Mazindarani discuss the route. The reader will note that Fuádi omits Kirmán and Tabas, and that Baraqi omits Anjirak. When the writer attempted to test the possibility of Anjirak being on the route, it was found that there are numerous towns by that name and that the "right" Anjirak could not be located. Fuádi was written in the 1930s, and Barqi was written in the 1990s. All in all, it is felt that Baraqi's account is the more reliable one.

366 Faizi, p. 170-173

367 H.M. Balyuzi, *The Báb - The Herald of the Day of Days*, p. 98. See also Nicolas, *Seyyed Ali Muhammad dit le Báb*, p. 233

368 Shoghi Effendi, *God Passes By*, p. 11

369 Nabíl, translated by Shoghi Effendi, *The Dawn-Breakers*, p. 171-172

370 Adib Taherzadeh, *The Revelation of Baha'u'llah v 1*, p. 326. See also 'Abdu'l-Baha, *A Traveller's Narrative*, p. 7

371 Málmírí, p. 19-20

372 Vahíd, cited by Adib Taherzadeh, *The Revelation of Baha'u'llah v1*, p. 326-327. See also Málmírí, p. 19-20

373 Nabíl, translated by Shoghi Effendi, *The Dawn-Breakers*, p. 173

374 Vahíd, cited by Nabíl, translated by Shoghi Effendi, *The Dawn-Breakers*, p. 173

375 Vahíd, cited by Nabíl, translated by Shoghi Effendi, *The Dawn-Breakers*, p. 172-174

376 The Qur'án is about 6,600 verses and Muhammad revealed it over a span of twenty-three years. This is a rate of just 287 verses *per year*. According to Afnan, the Báb's revelation on this occasion was about 3,600 lines in about 5 hours (estimated). (Afnan #1, p. 491) Afnan also says the entire work is about 226 pages and each page has 19 lines, and each line has an average of nine to twelve words. (Afnan #2, p. 73) Shoghi Effendi states that it was no less than 2,000 verses (Shoghi Effendi, *God Passes By*, p. 12). Using the lesser of the two numbers for verses from Shoghi Effendi, we get the following computation. This is a rate of at least 400 verses *per hour*! According to Vahíd, the Báb's revelatory act was smooth and uninterrupted for the entire time that revelation was underway. Hence, the Báb was able to reveal a complex text, on a literary par with the quality of the Qur'án, about a third of the size of the Qur'án, with content as edifying as the Qur'án, with quotes and citations from other sources, without recourse to other reference books or time for research, without pause, without modern writing tools, in the span of about five hours.

377 Vahíd, cited by Nabíl, translated by Shoghi Effendi, *The Dawn-Breakers*, p. 176

378 Málmírí, p. 19-20

379 Rouhani, p. 25

380 Rouhani, p. 25-26

381 Siyyid Javad Karbila'i's account, written by Mírzá Abu'l-Fadl, reported in Mázindarání, p. 362-363, footnote

382 'Abdu'l-Baha, *A Traveller's Narrative*, p. 7-8

383 Mázindarání #3, p. 55

384 Málmírí, p. 19-20

385 Rouhani, p. 21-22

386 Rouhani, p. 21-26, including footnotes

387 Rouhani, p. 23-24

388 Vahíd, cited by Nabíl, translated by Shoghi Effendi, *The Dawn-Breakers*, p. 177

389 Rouhani, p. 23-24

390 Rouhani, p. 21-29 (entire chapter), 30-31. Also footnotes on p. 564.

391 'Abdu'l-Bahá, *A Traveller's Narrative*, p. 7-8

392 Nabíl, translated by Shoghi Effendi, *The Dawn-Breakers*, p. 176

393 Agent reporting to Husayn Khán, Nabíl, translated by Shoghi Effendi, *The Dawn-Breakers*, p. 194-196

394 Husayn Khán, cited by Nabíl, translated by Shoghi Effendi, *The Dawn-Breakers*, p. 194-196

395 Husaini, p. 279

396 Faizi, p. 184; Husaini, p. 283

397 Nabíl, translated by Shoghi Effendi, *The Dawn-Breakers*, p. 195

398 A citizen cited by Nabíl, translated by Shoghi Effendi, *The Dawn-Breakers*, p. 195

399 Nabíl, translated by Shoghi Effendi, *The Dawn-Breakers*, p. 194-196

400 Nabíl, translated by Shoghi Effendi, *The Dawn-Breakers*, p. 196-197

401 'Abdu'l-Bahá, *A Traveller's Narrative*, p. 9. And also Shoghi Effendi, *God Passes By*, p. 13

402 Husaini, p. 285-286

403 H.M. Balyuzi, *The Báb*, p. 106-107

404 Nabíl, translated by Shoghi Effendi, *The Dawn-Breakers*, p. 197

405 Husaini, p. 287. Paraphrased from the Persian by Husaini.

406 Nabíl, translated by Shoghi Effendi, *The Dawn-Breakers*, p. 197

407 Husaini, p. 287. Paraphrased from the Persian by Husaini.

408 Faizi, p. 184, footnote

409 Faizi, p. 185, footnote

410 M.H. Azizi and F. Azizi, *History of Cholera Outbreaks in Iran during the 19th and 20th*

Centuries, p. 51–55. (PMCID: PMC4154910). (Url: https://www.ncbi.nlm.nih.gov/pmc/articles/PMC4154910/; Last accessed: 22 February 2019). Here is some information excerpted from the article: "Between 1820 and 1903, seven major cholera epidemics with high mortality rates, particularly among children, occurred in Iran as part of the worldwide cholera pandemics.... Unsanitary public conditions, serious shortage of safe water supply, ignorance and poverty all had major roles on the emergence and spread of the infectious epidemics in Iran during the 19th and the first decades of the 20th century.... Pilgrimage to Mecca and Iraq's holy cities had a significant role in dissemination of the illness among the Iranian pilgrims during epidemics... The third epidemic occurred in 1846. The original focus was India and it spread by way of Afghanistan into Mashhad (Khorasan Province, northeastern Iran), subsequently reached Isfahán and finally extended further to Constantinople (Turkey), Russia and other parts of Europe.... Because of the high fatality rate attributed to cholera, the term 'margamargi' (death and dying) ... [was] also used in Iran. The public health status in Iran during the Qájár period (1796-1925) was poor. For instance, in the 19th century, the infant mortality rate in Iran was greater than 50% 13 while at the same time it was around 20% in France and Germany...."

411 The Báb, cited by Shoghi Effendi, *God Passes By*, p. 84

412 Nabíl, translated by Shoghi Effendi, *The Dawn-Breakers*, p. 192, 198

413 The Báb, cited by Nabíl, translated by Shoghi Effendi, *The Dawn-Breakers*, p. 197-198. In this statement the Báb indicates His foreknowledge of both His future exile to Mákú and Chihríq, in the region of Ádhírbáyján, and that when He is martyred, He will be accompanied by one of His disciples.

414 Nader Saiedi, *Gate of the Heart*, p. 239-240

415 Shoghi Effendi, *The World Order of Bahá'u'lláh*, p. 123

416 Shoghi Effendi, *The World Order of Bahá'u'lláh*, p. 123

417 Bahá'u'lláh, cited by Shoghi Effendi, *The World Order of Bahá'u'lláh*, p. 123

418 Shoghi Effendi, *The World Order of Bahá'u'lláh*, p. 123-124

419 Shoghi Effendi, *The World Order of Bahá'u'lláh*, p. 123

420 Bahá'u'lláh, cited by Shoghi Effendi, *The World Order of Bahá'u'lláh*, p. 124

421 The Báb, *Selections from the Writings of the Báb*, p. 96

422 For the reader interested in an average daily rate, the numbers are as follows: The Báb revealed, on average, 228.31 verses per day; Muhammad revealed, on average, 0.74 verses per day.

The calculation 228.31/0.74 = 308.52 reveals the comparison of the average daily rates of production. Thus, the Báb's average daily rate of production was 308.52 times faster than Muhammad's average daily rate. The purpose of this calculation is NOT to say One was better than another because, surely, each One was doing what God asked Them to do and, indeed, if They had reversed positions, They each would have done what the Other had done. The comparison therefore is an indication of what it might mean to "wield the septre of independent Prophethood to a degree unrivaled by any of the Messengers of the past. This, in turn, is an indication of the immense receptivity of the more recent era.

It must be remembered that in both cases, due to illness, travelling, or other physical constraints, there must have been some days when neither the Báb nor Muhammad would have been occupied in revealing verses. Hence, it is important to emphasize that these calculations are for average rates of production.

423 The Báb, provisional translation, cited by Nader Saiedi, *Gate of the Heart*, p. 98

424 Nader Saiedi, *Gate of the Heart,* p. 98

425 The Báb, provisional translation, cited by Nader Saiedi, *Gate of the Heart,* p. 276-277

426 The Báb, *Selections from the Writings of the Báb*, p. 100

427 The Báb, *Selections from the Writings of the Báb*, p. 144

428 The Báb, cited by Shoghi Effendi, *The World Order of Bahá'u'lláh*, p. 62-63

429 The Báb, cited by Shoghi Effendi, *God Passes By*, p. 29

430 Shoghi Effendi, *The World Order of Bahá'u'lláh*, p. 100-101

431 The Báb, *Selections from the Writings of the Báb*, p. 109

432 The Báb, *Selections from the Writings of the Báb*, p. 155

433 The Báb, *Selections from the Writings of the Báb*, p. 154

434 The Báb, *Selections from the Writings of the Báb*, p. 125

435 The Báb, *Selections from the Writings of the Báb*, p. 129-130

436 The Báb, *Selections from the Writings of the Báb*, p. 6

437 The Báb, *Selections from the Writings of the Báb*, p. 111-112

438 The Báb, *Selections from the Writings of the Báb*, p. 113

439 The Báb, *Selections from the Writings of the Báb*, p. 111, 130

440 The Báb, *Selections from the Writings of the Báb*, p. 86

441 The Báb, *Panj Sha'n*, pp. 391-392, provisional translation, cited by Nader Saiedi, *Gate of the Heart*, pp. 175-177

442 Online article, no author. *The Anathemas of the 2nd Council of Constantinople.* https://www.biblestudytools.com/history/creeds-confessions/creeds/the-anathemas-of-the-2nd-council-of-constantinople.html

443 The Báb, *Selections from the Writings of the Báb*, p. 117

444 The Báb, *Selections from the Writings of the Báb*, p. 174-175

445 Bahá'u'lláh, *Gleanings from the Writings of Bahá'u'lláh*, p. 165-166

446 The Báb, *Selections from the Writings of the Báb*, p. 75

447 The definition of "emanate" was taken from the online dictionary, Dictionary.com. (Url: https://www.dictionary.com/browse/emanate) An online thesuarus is also available at Thesaurus.com. (Url: https://www.thesaurus.com/browse/emanate)

448 The Báb, *Panj Sha'n*, p. 388-390, provisional translation, cited by Nader Saiedi, *Gate of the Heart,* p. 174

449 Nader Saiedi, *Gate of the Heart,* p. 174

450 The Báb, *Selections from the Writings of the Báb*, p. 125

451 The Báb, *Selections from the Writings of the Báb*, p. 113

452 Thanks to Nader Saiedi for this terminology. Nader Saiedi, *Gate of the Heart,* p. 264

453 Based on the following quotes, it is fitting to describe the Bayán in the following terms: "the Bayán" = the Mother-Book of His Dispensation, His most weighty book and the repository of His laws. Here are quotes that that support this designation: "...the Persian Bayan, the

chief and best-preserved repository of His laws..." (Shoghi Effendi, *The World Order of Bahá'u'lláh*, p. 62) "...the Bayan, His most weighty Book..." (Shoghi Effendi, *The Unfolding Destiny of the British Bahá'í Community*, p. 261) "...the Bayan (Exposition)—that monumental repository of the laws and precepts of the new Dispensation and the treasury enshrining most of the Báb's references and tributes to, as well as His warning regarding, "Him Whom God will make manifest"..." (Shoghi Effendi, *God Passes By*, p. 24-25) "... His Book of Laws, the Persian Bayan..." (Shoghi Effendi, *God Passes By*, p. 27) "...both the Qayyúmu'l-Asmá' and the Bayan, designed to be respectively the first and last written testimonials to the glory with which God was soon to invest Him..." (Shoghi Effendi, *God Passes By*, p. 67) "...His best-known work, the Persian Bayan..." (Shoghi Effendi, God Passes By, p. 97) "...His Persian Bayan, the Mother-Book of the Bábí Dispensation..." (Shoghi Effendi, *God Passes By*, p. 324)

454 The Báb, *Selections from the Writings of the Báb*, p. 125-126

455 For example, see Christopher Buck, *Native Messengers of God in Canada?: A test case for Bahá'í universalism*, 1993, Paper read at the 1993 Religious Studies Special Interest Group of the ABS-ESE in Newcastle, and again in 1994 at the 18th Annual Conference of the Association for Bahá 'í Studies (Cambridge, MA).

456 The Báb, *Selections from the Writings of the Báb*, p. 12

457 The Báb, *Selections from the Writings of the Báb*, p. 130

458 Adib Taherzadeh, *The Covenant of Bahá'u'lláh*, p. 39

459 Bahá'u'lláh, *The Book of Certitude*, p. 98

460 See Bahá'u'lláh, *Má'idih-Ásmání*, vol. 8 page 191-192. Url: http://reference.bahai.org/fa/t/b/MAS8/mas8-191.html (Last accessed: 24 June 2019)

461 My thanks to Behrad Majidi for suggesting this interpretation in the first place.

462 Nader Saiedi, *Gate of the Heart*. See chapter 8 and throughout the book. See the index as well.

463 The Báb, *Selections from the Writings of the Báb*, p. 38

464 The Báb, *Selections from the Writings of the Báb*, p. 174-175

465 The Báb, *Selections from the Writings of the Báb*, p. 177

466 The Báb, *Selections from the Writings of the Báb*, p. 177

467 The Báb, *Selections from the Writings of the Báb*, p. 216

468 The Báb, *Selections from the Writings of the Báb*, p. 185-186

469 The Báb, *Selections from the Writings of the Báb*, p. 125

470 The Báb, *Selections from the Writings of the Báb*, p. 125

471 The Báb, *Selections from the Writings of the Báb*, p. 125

472 The Báb, *Selections from the Writings of the Báb*, p. 86

473 "Point of the Bayán" = This is a reference to the Báb Himself. His main book was called the Bayán. As its Revealer, He called Himself the Point of the Bayán.

474 "Him Whom God shall make manifest" = Bahá'u'lláh. The Báb declared that He was the Forerunner of a Prophet greater than Himself, whom He referred to as "Him Whom God shall make manifest." This particular passage was written years before Bahá'u'lláh made it known publicly that He was the One Whose coming the Báb had prophesied. Later, He an-

nounced Himself publicly as the Promised One of the Báb and of all the prior Revelations.

475 One of Muhammad's main titles was "Apostle of God." This was discussed in the chapter on Islám. In one of the traditions (hadiths) of Islám, Muhammad is reported to have made the statement, "I am all the Prophets." Here the Báb gives the spiritual meaning of that statement.

476 The Báb, *Selections from the Writings of the Báb*, p. 125-126

477 The Báb, *Selections from the Writings of the Báb*, p. 104, 125

478 Bahá'u'lláh, *The Book of Certitude*, p. 152-153

479 Bahá'u'lláh, *The Book of Certitude*, p. 175

480 'Abdu'l-Bahá, *'Abdu'l-Bahá in London*, p. 22-24

481 Him Who is the Tree of divine Reality = This is a reference to the Manifestation of God generally.

482 The Báb, *Selections from the Writings of the Báb*, p. 106. Note: The Primal Tree = This is a reference to the Manifestation of God.

483 The Báb, *Selections from the Writings of the Báb*, p. 77

484 The Báb, *Selections from the Writings of the Báb*, p. 88

485 Nader Saiedi, *Gate of the Heart,* p. 34, 242

486 The Báb, *Selections from the Writings of the Báb*, p. 31

487 Nader Saiedi, *Gate of the Heart,* p. 11

488 Nader Saiedi, *Gate of the Heart,* p. 243

489 The Báb, *Selections from the Writings of the Báb*, p. 125

490 The Báb, *Selections from the Writings of the Báb*, p. 86

491 Qur'án 33:40, Arberry translation.

492 Yohanan Friedmann, *Prophecy Continuous, 1989*

493 The Báb, *Selections from the Writings of the Báb*, p. 86

494 The Báb, provisional translation, cited by Nader Saiedi, *Gate of the Heart,* p. 274

495 Nader Saiedi, *Gate of the Heart,* p. 274

496 The Báb, provisional translation, cited by Nader Saiedi, *Gate of the Heart,* p. 274

497 Nader Saiedi, *Gate of the Heart,* p. 274

498 Nader Saiedi, *Gate of the Heart,* p. 276-277

499 Matthew 5:31-32, NIV

500 Matthew 5:38-39, NIV

501 Qur'án 2:144, Arberry translation

502 Nader Saiedi, *Gate of the Heart,* p. 276-277

503 'Abdu'l-Bahá, *The Promulgation of Universal Peace*, p. 407

504 The Báb, *Selections from the Writings of the Báb*, p. 107

505 The Báb, *Selections from the Writings of the Báb*, p. 108

506 The Báb, *Selections from the Writings of the Báb*, p. 89

507 Bahá'u'lláh, *Gleanings from the Writings of Bahá'u'lláh*, p. 290

508 The Báb, *Selections from the Writings of the Báb*, p. 89-91

509 The Báb, *Selections from the Writings of the Báb*, p. 92

510 The Báb, *Selections from the Writings of the Báb*, p. 125

511 The Báb, provisional translation, Nader Saiedi, *Gate of the Heart*, p. 370-371

512 Nader Saiedi, *Gate of the Heart*, p. 228-229

513 The Báb, provisional translation, Nader Saiedi, *Gate of the Heart,* p. 283. From the Báb, *Fi's-Suluk II, Collection*, p.459

514 Nabíl, translated by Shoghi Effendi, *The Dawn-Breakers*, p. 309-312

515 Nabíl, translated by Shoghi Effendi, *The Dawn-Breakers*, p. 309-312

516 The Báb, cited by Nabíl, translated by Shoghi Effendi, *The Dawn-Breakers*, p. 316

517 The Báb, *Selections from the Writings of the Báb*, p. 109, Persian Bayan 2:1

518 The Báb, *Selections from the Writings of the Báb*, p. 109, Persian Bayan 2:1

519 The Báb, *Selections from the Writings of the Báb*, p. 109, Persian Bayan 2:1

520 Nader Saiedi, *Gate of the Heart*, p. 47. Note: Italics added.

521 Nader Saiedi, *Gate of the Heart*, p. 53-54

522 The Báb, provisional translation, cited by Nader Saiedi, *Gate of the Heart*, p. 74-75. From the Báb, *Tafsir-i-Suriy-i-Kawthar*, INBA 53:181

523 Nader Saiedi, *Gate of the Heart*, p. 227-229

524 The Báb, *Selections from the Writings of the Báb*, p. 123-124

525 The Báb, *Selections from the Writings of the Báb*, p. 12-13

526 The Báb, *Selections from the Writings of the Báb*, p. 88-89

527 The Báb, *Selections from the Writings of the Báb*, p. 165-166

528 The Báb, *Selections from the Writings of the Báb*, p. 89-91

529 The Báb, *Selections from the Writings of the Báb*, p. 95-96

530 The Báb, *Selections from the Writings of the Báb*, p. 124

531 The Báb, *Selections from the Writings of the Báb*, p. 98-99

532 In Arabic, the numerology system is called the Abjad. In Greek, it is the Gematria. In Hebrew, it is the Kabbalah.

533 Nader Saiedi, *Gate of the Heart*, p. 282-283

534 Nader Saiedi, *Gate of the Heart,* p. 283

535 Nader Saiedi, *Gate of the Heart*, p. 282. And also: Abbas Amanat, *Resurrection and Renewal*, 1989, p. 192

536 The Báb, *Selections from the Writings of the Báb*, p. 6

537 Nader Saiedi, *Gate of the Heart*, p. 35

538 Nader Saiedi, *Gate of the Heart*, p. 260

539 Shoghi Effendi, *God Passes By*, p. 138

540 Nader Saiedi, *Gate of the Heart*, p. 282

541 Nader Saiedi, *Gate of the Heart*, p. 282

542 Nabíl, translated by Shoghi Effendi, *The Dawn-Breakers*, p. 123

543 The Báb, cited by Nabíl, translated by Shoghi Effendi, *The Dawn-Breakers*, p. 123

544 The Báb, provisional translation, cited by Nader Saiedi, *Gate of the Heart*, p. 327

545 Notes to *The Most Holy Book*, published by the Universal House of Justice, Note #28, to Bahá'u'lláh, *The Most Holy Book*, p. 178

546 Nader Saiedi, *Gate of the Heart*, p. 327

547 The Báb, *Selections from the Writings of the Báb*, p. 77

548 The Báb, *Selections from the Writings of the Báb*, p. 106-108. Note: Paragraphs added to assist the reader.

549 Nader Saiedi, *Gate of the Heart*, p. 253. Note: Emphasis added.

550 The Báb, *Selections from the Writings of the Báb*, p. 92

551 The Báb, *Selections from the Writings of the Báb*, p. 105-106

552 The Báb, *Selections from the Writings of the Báb*, p. 203

553 The Báb, *Selections from the Writings of the Báb*, p. 6

554 The Báb, provisional translation, cited by Nader Saiedi, *Gate of the Heart*, p. 251. From the Báb, *Tafsir-i-Hadith-i-Haqiqat*, INBA 53:33

555 The Báb, provisional translation, cited by Nader Saiedi, *Gate of the Heart*, p. 46. From the Báb, *Persian Bayan 4:1*

556 The Báb, *Selections from the Writings of the Báb*, p. 111-112

557 The Báb, *Selections from the Writings of the Báb*, p. 125

558 Nader Saiedi, *Gate of the Heart*, p. 163

559 Nader Saiedi, *Gate of the Heart*, p. 339

560 Nader Saiedi, *Gate of the Heart*, p. 267

561 Bahá'u'lláh, *Gleanings from the Writings of Bahá'u'lláh*, p. 78

562 The Báb, *Selections from the Writings of the Báb*, p. 56

563 The Báb, *Selections from the Writings of the Báb*, p. 125

564 The Báb, *Selections from the Writings of the Báb*, p. 129

565 The Báb, *Selections from the Writings of the Báb*, p. 111

566 Bahá'u'lláh, *Tablets of Bahá'u'lláh*, p. 222

567 The Báb, *Selections from the Writings of the Báb*, p. 75

568 The Báb, *Selections from the Writings of the Báb*, p. 133

569 Qur'án 2:256, translation by Yusuf 'Ali

570 The next eight paragraphs are based upon Nader Saiedi, *Gate of the Heart*, p. 210-216

571 The Báb, provisional translation, cited by Nader Saiedi, *Gate of the Heart*, p. 211. From the Báb, *Tafsir-i-Sirr-i-Ha'*, INBA 86:115

572 The Báb, provisional translation, cited by Nader Saiedi, *Gate of the Heart*, p. 212. From

the Báb, *Tafsir-i-Ha'*, INBA 86:115

573 Nader Saiedi, *Gate of the Heart*, p. 212

574 The Báb, provisional translation, cited by Nader Saiedi, *Gate of the Heart*, p. 213. From the Báb, *Tafsir-i-Ha'*, INBA 86:116

575 The Báb, provisional translation, cited by Nader Saiedi, *Gate of the Heart*, p. 214. From the Báb, *Tafsir-i-Ha'*, INBA 86:116-17

576 The Báb, *Selections from the Writings of the Báb*, p. 89

577 The Báb, *Selections from the Writings of the Báb*, p. 77

578 Nader Saiedi, *Gate of the Heart*, p. 215-216

579 The Báb, *Selections from the Writings of the Báb*, p. 67

580 The Báb, *Selections from the Writings of the Báb*, p. 77

581 The Báb, *Selections from the Writings of the Báb*, p. 77-78

582 The Báb, *Selections from the Writings of the Báb*, p. 77-78

583 The Báb, *Selections from the Writings of the Báb*, p. 158

584 The Báb, provisional translation, cited by Nader Saiedi, *Gate of the Heart*, p. 248-249

585 The Báb, provisional translation, cited by Nader Saiedi, *Gate of the Heart*, p. 249

586 The Báb, provisional translation, cited by Nader Saiedi, *Gate of the Heart*, p. 175-176. From the Báb, *Panj Sha'n*, p. 391-392

587 The Báb, *Panj Sha'n*, pp. 391-392, provisional translation, cited by Nader Saiedi, *Gate of the Heart*, p. 175-176

588 The Báb, cited by Nabíl, translated by Shoghi Effendi, *The Dawn-Breakers*, p. 63

589 The Báb, *Selections from the Writings of the Báb*, p. 88. Note: emphasis added.

590 The Báb, *Selections from the Writings of the Báb*, p. 105-106

591 The Báb, *Selections from the Writings of the Báb*, p. 43

592 The Báb, *Selections from the Writings of the Báb*, p. 77

593 The Báb, provisional translation, cited by Nader Saiedi, *Gate of the Heart*, p. 177. From the Báb, *Tablet to Mírzá Hasan*, INBA 53:199

594 The Báb, provisional translation, cited by Nader Saiedi, *Gate of the Heart*, p. 177. From the Báb, *Tablet to Mírzá Sa'id*, INBA 14:439

595 Nader Saiedi, *Gate of the Heart*, p. 180

596 The Báb, provisional translation, cited by Nader Saiedi, *Gate of the Heart*, p. 311-312. Note: Formatting added.

597 The Báb, provisional translation, cited by Nader Saiedi, *Gate of the Heart*, p. 315-316

598 The Báb cited by Nader Saiedi, *Gate of the Heart*, p. 315-316

599 The Báb, *Persian Bayán* 9:4, provisional translation, cited by Nader Saiedi, *Gate of the Heart*, p. 314-315

600 The Báb, *Persian Bayán* 6:19, provisional translation, cited by Nader Saiedi, *Gate of the Heart*, p. 321-322

601 The Báb, *Persian Bayán* 6:19, provisional translation, cited by Nader Saiedi, *Gate of the*

Heart, p. 321

602 The Báb, *Persian Bayán* 6:19, provisional translation, cited by Nader Saiedi, *Gate of the Heart*, p. 321-322

603 The Báb, *Kitabu'l-Asma'*, INBA 29:152, provisional translation, cited by Nader Saiedi, *Gate of the Heart*, p. 322

604 The Báb, Persian Bayan 7:18, provisional translation, cited by Nader Saiedi, *Gate of the Heart*, p. 321-322

605 Nader Saiedi, *Gate of the Heart*, p. 322

606 The Báb, *Persian Bayan* 7:18, provisional translation, cited by Nader Saiedi, *Gate of the Heart,* p. 322

607 The Báb, *Kitabu'l-Asma'*, INBA 29:423-24, provisional translation, cited by Nader Saiedi, *Gate of the Heart,* p. 323

608 Nader Saiedi, *Gate of the Heart*, p. 339

609 'Abdu'l-Bahá, *Paris Talks*, p. 65

610 'Abdu'l-Bahá, *Paris Talks*, p. 109-112

611 The Báb, *Selections from the Writings of the Báb*, p. 178

612 The Báb, *Selections from the Writings of the Báb*, p. 191

613 The Báb, *Selections from the Writings of the Báb*, p. 75

614 The Báb, *Persian Bayan* 4:11, provisional translation, cited by Nader Saiedi, *Gate of the Heart,* p. 255. Note: Italics added.

615 The Báb, *Selections from the Writings of the Báb*, p. 88-89

616 The Báb, *Persian Bayan* 4:1, provisional translation, cited by Nader Saiedi, *Gate of the Heart,* p. 46, 181

617 The Báb, *Selections from the Writings of the Báb*, p. 88-89

618 The Báb, *Selections from the Writings of the Báb*, p. 77

619 The Báb, *Selections from the Writings of the Báb*, p. 102

620 The Báb, *Selections from the Writings of the Báb*, p. 157-158

621 The Báb, *Selections from the Writings of the Báb*, p. 78

622 The Báb, *Selections from the Writings of the Báb*, p. 191

623 The Báb, *Selections from the Writings of the Báb*, p. 161

624 The Báb, *Selections from the Writings of the Báb*, p. 77

625 The Báb, *Persian Bayán* 9:4, provisional translation, cited by Nader Saiedi, *Gate of the Heart*, p. 314-315

626 The Báb, *Persian Bayan* 7:18, provisional translation, cited by Nader Saiedi, *Gate of the Heart,* p. 322

627 Abdulaziz Abdulhussein Sachedina, *Islámic Messianism*, p. 64. And also Moojan Momen, *An Introduction to Shi'i Islám*, p. 166-170.

628 Nader Saiedi, *Gate of the Heart*, p. 1

629 Nader Saiedi, *Gate of the Heart,* p. 21

630 Nader Saiedi, *Gate of the Heart*, p. 21

631 Nader Saiedi, *Gate of the Heart,* p. 368

632 Adib Taherzadeh, *The Revelation of Bahá'u'lláh, vol 1*, p. 278-279

633 The Báb, cited by Shoghi Effendi, *The Promised Day is Come*, p. 28. And also The Báb, *Selections from the Writings of the Báb*, p. 41

634 The Báb, cited by Shoghi Effendi, *The Promised Day is Come*, p. 28. And also The Báb, *Selections from the Writings of the Báb*, p. 42

635 The Báb, cited by Shoghi Effendi, *The Promised Day is Come*, p. 28. And also The Báb, *Selections from the Writings of the Báb*, p. 43

636 The Báb, cited by Shoghi Effendi, *The Promised Day is Come*, p. 28. And also The Báb, *Selections from the Writings of the Báb*, p. 63

637 The Báb, *Selections from the Writings of the Báb*, p. 43

638 The Báb, *Selections from the Writings of the Báb*, p. 31

639 Bahá'u'lláh, mentioned by Shoghi Effendi, *The Promised Day is Come*, p. 85

640 Arabic Bayán 8:9, 10:2. Persian Bayán 8:10

641 Arabic Bayán 6:16

642 Arabic and Persian Bayán 8:15. Persian Bayán 6:7

643 Persian Bayán 6:7

644 Persian Bayán 4:18

645 Arabic and Persian Bayán 11:6

646 Arabic Bayán 8:17

647 Persian and Arabic Bayán 7:14

648 Arabic Bayán 6:16, 7:18, 9:16, 10:6, 10:17, 11:3 and 11-17. Persian Bayán 6:16

649 Arabic 11-5, Persian 5-16

650 Arabic Bayán 11:16 and Persian Bayán 4:5

651 Arabic Bayán 5:13, 8:12 to 10:3 and Persian Bayán 8:2

652 Arabic Bayán 8:17

653 Arabic and Persian Bayán 7:6

654 Arabic Bayán 9:8, 11:18 and Persian Bayán 9:7, 9:8

655 Arabic and Persian Bayán 7:11, 9:9

656 Arabic Bayán 9:17

657 Arabic Bayán 10:1, 10:5

658 Persian Bayán 6:19

659 The Báb, with provisional translation, cited by Nader Saiedi, *Gate of the Heart*, p. 315-316. See also Persian Bayán 6:2, 9:10 and Arabic Bayán 9:11

660 Husaini, p. 841-842

661 Shoghi Effendi, *Citadel of Faith*, p. 82-83, letter dated 4 July 1850

662 The Báb, *Selections from the Writings of the Báb*, p. 160

663 Bahá'u'lláh, cited by Shoghi Effendi, *The World Order of Bahá'u'lláh*, p. 167

664 Shoghi Effendi, *The World Order of Bahá'u'lláh*, p. 102

665 See Shoghi Effendi, *The World Order of Bahá'u'lláh*, p. 102, 103, 114, 167; Shoghi Effendi, *Messages to the Bahá'í World – 1950-1957*, p. 8, 40, 59, 75, 153, 156, 168; Shoghi Effendi, *Letters from the Guardian to Australia and New Zealand*, p. 41; Shoghi Effendi, *God Passes By*, p. xi, 3, 54, 57, 100, 400; Shoghi Effendi, *Directives from the Guardian*, p. 7, 61; Shoghi Effendi, *Dawn of a New Day*, p. 170; Shoghi Effendi, *Citadel of Faith*, p. 69, 80. The following is also a succinct summary: "For it should be borne in mind that in the year 1944 we celebrate not only the termination of the first century of the Bahá'í Era, but also the centenary of the birth of the Bahá'í Dispensation, of the inception of the Bahá'í cycle, and the birth of 'Abdu'l-Bahá, and commemorate as well the fiftieth anniversary of the establishment of the Bahá'í Faith in the Western world." (Shoghi Effendi, *Messages to America*, p. 62) And also: "The Báb … Whose advent at once signalized the termination of the "Prophetic Cycle" and the inception of the "Cycle of Fulfillment,"…" (Shoghi Effendi, *God Passes By*, p. 57)

666 The Báb, *Selections from the Writings of the Báb*, p. 91

667 The Báb, *Selections from the Writings of the Báb*, p. 126

668 Shoghi Effendi, *The Promised Day is Come*, p. 123-124

669 The Báb, *Selections from the Writings of the Báb*, p. 125

670 'Abdu'l-Bahá, *The Promulgation of Universal Peace*, p. 361-370

671 For info on ethical monotheism refer to these links: 1) Dennis Prager, *Ethical Monotheism*, The Jewish Virtual Library: https://www.jewishvirtuallibrary.org/jsource/Judaism/mono.html (Date last accessed: October 22nd, 2015); 2) *Ethical Monotheism*, Wikipedia article: https://en.wikipedia.org/wiki/Ethical_monotheism (Date last accessed: October 22nd, 2015)

672 Genesis 22:1-3, The Bible, New International Version

673 'Abdu'l-Bahá, *The Promulgation of Universal Peace*, p. 340

674 Exodus 34:27-29, The Bible, New Revised Standard Version

675 The first five books of the Bible are known as the Torah.

676 Deuteronomy 29, The Bible, Revised Standard Version

677 Most likely, this reference to 1,000 generations is not meant to be taken literally, but rather as a euphemism for "forever". Nevertheless, as a mental exercise, even if it is literal, and if we take a generation to be about 20 years in length, we would be talking about a promise of faithfulness from God that could endure no less than 20,000 years! If we assume (arbitrarily) that the passage was written 4,000 years ago, that would mean, if taken literally, there are still 16,000 years to go before this promise expires! However one looks at this passage, a very, very long time is indicated!

678 'Abdu'l-Bahá, *The Secret of Divine Civilization*, p. 76-77

679 Bahá'u'lláh, *Gleanings from the Writings of Bahá'u'lláh*, p. 18-19

680 'Abdu'l-Bahá, *The Promulgation of Universal Peace*, p. 85

681 Matthew 3:16-17, The Bible, New International Version

682 Luke 4:17-20, The Bible, New International Version

683 Gregory J. Riley, *The River of God*, p. 160

684 Robert Spivey and D. Moody Smith, Jr., *Anatomy of the New Testament: A guide to its structure and meaning*, p. 194

685 Interestingly, in the Old and New Testaments, the term "son of man" is used much more frequently than the term "son of God". "Son of God" occurs 58 times, whereas "son of man" occurs 210 times, a ratio of almost four to one. Some instances of "son of God" do not even refer to Jesus. Some are derisive, such as in Matthew 4:3 or 27:40 when other parties use the term to mock Jesus. Others are appreciative, such as Matthew 14:33, and are intended to affirm that Jesus was the son of God. Moreover, Jesus most of the time refers to Himself as "Son of man". Further analysis would enable precise categorization, but suffice to say, even if all "son of God" occurrences were positive, the word count shows that the term "son of man" occurs 360% more frequently than does the term "son of God". This data suggest that, theologically, Jesus' own more frequent self-description as Son of Man deserves to be taken just as seriously as those passages which label Him as the Son of God. Indeed, reflecting on both titles, in relation to one another, is likely to lead to a more enhanced comprehension of the station and claims of Jesus.

686 Bahá'u'lláh, *The Book of Certitude*, p. 19

687 Qur'án 61:6, translated by Pickthall

688 Romans 3:29-30, The Bible, New International Version

689 'Abdu'l-Bahá, *The Promulgation of Universal Peace*, p. 128

690 Nader Saiedi, *Gate of the Heart*, p. 3-4

691 Bahá'u'lláh, *The Book of Certitude*, p. 31

692 'Abdu'l-Bahá, *Some Answered Questions*, p. 22-29

693 The first written constitution in world history. See A. Guillaume, *The Life of Muhammad, A Translation of Ishaq's Sirat Rasul Alláh*, p. 231-232. See also these articles: Url: https://en.wikipedia.org/wiki/Constitution_of_Medina (Last accessed: October 14th, 2015); Url: https://en.wikisource.org/wiki/Medina_Charter (Last accessed: October 14th, 2015)

694 For general information on Sayyid Qutb see https://en.wikipedia.org/wiki/Sayyid_Qutb (Last accessed: July 28, 2015)

695 An English translation of Sayyid Qutb, *Milestones*, is available as a pdf document from http://majalla.org/books/2005/qutb-nilestone.pdf

696 Ayman al-Zawahiri cited by Adnan A. Musallam, *From Secularism to Jihad: Sayyid Qutb and the Foundations of Radical Islámism*, p. 190

697 John C. Zimmerman, Sayyid Qutb's Influence On The 11 September Attacks, *Terrorism and Political Violence*, 2004, vol. 16, #2, p. 222-252, published online August 10, 2010, Url: https://doi.org/10.1080/09546550490480993

698 Lawrence Wright, "The Rebellion Within: An Al Qaeda mastermind questions terrorism", *The New Yorker Magazine*. See also https://en.wikipedia.org/wiki/Sayyed_Imam_Al-Sharif (Last accessed: October 11th, 2015)

699 For general information on Dr. Muhammad Tahir-ul-Qadri see https://en.wikipedia.org/wiki/Muhammad_Tahir-ul-Qadri

700 Shaykh-ul-Islám Dr. Muhammad Tahrir-ul-Qadri, *Fatwa On Terrorism And Suicide Bombings*

701 Shaykh Muhammad Al-Yaqoubi, *Refuting ISIS: Destroying its religious foundation an proving it has strayed from Islám and that fighting it is an obligation, Second Edition*, 2016, Sacred Knowledge (books), Herndon, Virginia. The quotes in the next few paragraphs are found, in order, on these pages: p. 73, 73, 74, xiii, 13, 84, 109-110.

702 Royal Islamic Strategic Studies Centre of Jordan, *The 500 Most Influential Muslims*, 2012, Aman, Jordan

703 William McCants, *The ISIS Apocalypse: The History, Strategy, and Doomsday Vision of the Islamic State*, 2015, St. Martin's Press, NY, NY, p. 8ff

704 Ibn Taymiyyih of the 13th century. See article in Wikipedia. Url: https://en.wikipedia.org/wiki/Ibn_Taymiyyah#Jihad. See also these references: Natana J. DeLong-Bas, *Wahhabi Islam: From Revival and Reform to Global Jihad (First ed.)*, 2004, Oxford University Press, New York, p. 252–3. And also: Rudolph Peters, *Jihad in Classical and Modern Islam: A Reader*, 1996, Marcus Wiener, Princeton, p. 48

705 Abdul-Aziz ibn Abdullah Al ash-Sheikh's comments on Reuters are found at Url: http://blogs.reuters.com/faithworld/2014/08/25/saudi-arabias-grand-mufti-denounces-islamic-state-group-as-un-islamic/ (Last accessed: September 15, 2019). See also: https://en.wikipedia.org/wiki/Abdul-Aziz_ibn_Abdullah_Al_ash-Sheikh (Last accessed: September 15, 2019).

706 'Abdu'l-Bahá, *The Promulgation of Universal Peace*, p. 401

707 Yahiya Emerick, *The life and work of Muhammad*, p.12

708 The first written constitution in world history. See A. Guillaume, *The Life of Muhammad, A Translation of Ishaq's Sirat Rasul Alláh*, p. 231-232. See also these articles: Url: https://en.wikipedia.org/wiki/Constitution_of_Medina (Last accessed: October 14th, 2015); Url: https://en.wikisource.org/wiki/Medina_Charter (Last accessed: October 14th, 2015)

709 A hadith collected by Bukhari records this incident: "When the time of the death of the Prophet approached while there were some men in the house, and among them was 'Umar bin Al-Khatttab, the Prophet said, 'Come near let me write for you a writing after which you will never go astray.' 'Umar said, 'The Prophet is seriously ill, and you have the Qur'án, so God's Book is sufficient for us.' The people in the house differed and disputed. Some of them said, 'Come near so that God's Apostle may write for you a writing after which you will not go astray,' while some of them said what 'Umar said. When they made much noise and differed greatly before the Prophet, he said to them, 'Go away and leave me.' Ibn 'Abbas used to say, 'It was a great disaster that their difference and noise prevented God's Apostle from writing that writing for them.'" (Bukhari, Volume 9, Book 92, Number 468) Refer to: http://www.sahih-bukhari.com/Pages/Bukhari_9_92.php (Last accessed: October 3rd, 2015)

710 Michael Hart, *The 100: A Ranking of the Most Influential Persons in History*, p. 3

711 Essad Bey, *Mohammed, A Biography*, p. 90

712 Karen Armstrong, *Muhammad, A Biography of the Prophet*, p. 48-51

713 Karen Armstrong, *Muhammad, A Biography of the Prophet*, p. 49

714 Qur'án 3:84, transl. by Pickthall

715 Frederick M. Denny, *An Introduction to Islám, 2nd ed.*, p. 131

716 Nader Saiedi, *Gate of the Heart*, p. 358

717 H.M. Balyuzi, *Muhammad and the Course of Islám*, p. 157-159

718 'Abdu'l-Bahá, *Some Answered Questions*, p. 22-29

719 Hadith in the Bukhari collection, reported saying attributed to Muhammad, narrated by 'Abdullah bin 'Amr, listed in Bukhari, Volume 4, Book 52, Number 248. See this Url: https://muflihun.com/bukhari/52/248 (Last accessed: September 15, 2019). Website states: "Muflihun.com is a web platform for Qur'an and Hadith, focused on only authentic contents that people can fully rely upon." See also Url: https://www.sahih-bukhari.com/Pages/Bukhari_4_52.php. (Last accessed: September 15, 2019) Scroll down the page to #248.

720 Yohanan Friedman, *Prophecy Continuous*, 1989, University of California Press

721 Michael Hart, *The 100: A Ranking of the Most Influential Persons in History*, p. 3

722 'Abdu'l-Bahá, *The Promulgation of Universal Peace*, p. 346-347

723 'Abdu'l-Bahá, *Some Answered Questions*, p. 25-26

724 Shaykh Abid, cited by Nabíl, translated by Shoghi Effendi, *The Dawn-Breakers*, p. 75

725 The following contains a brief reference to the Báb's revelation experience and places it on a par with those of the other Divine Educators:

"It was in such dramatic circumstances, recalling the experience of Moses when face to face with the Burning Bush in the wilderness of Sinai, the successive visions of Zoroaster, the opening of the heavens and the descent of the Dove upon Christ in the Jordan, the cry of Gabriel heard by Muhammad in the Cave of Hira, and the dream of the Báb, in which the blood of the Imám Husayn touched and sanctified His lips, that Bahá'u'lláh, He 'around Whom the Point of the Bayán hath revolved,' and the Vehicle of the greatest Revelation the world has yet seen, received the first intimation of His sublime Mission, and that a ministry which, alike in its duration and fecundity, is unsurpassed in the religious history of mankind, was inaugurated. It was on that occasion that the 'Most Great Spirit,' as designated by Bahá'u'lláh Himself, revealed itself to Him, in the form of a 'Maiden,' and bade Him 'lift up' His 'voice between earth and heaven'—that same Spirit which, in the Zoroastrian, the Mosaic, the Christian, and Muhammadan Dispensations, had been respectively symbolized by the 'Sacred Fire,' the 'Burning Bush,' the 'Dove,' and the 'Angel Gabriel.'" (Shoghi Effendi, *Messages to America*, p. 100. Note: Italics added.)

See also Nabíl, translated by Shoghi Effendi, *The Dawn-Breakers*, p. 252)

726 Mullá Husayn, cited by Nabíl, translated by Shoghi Effendi, *The Dawn-Breakers*, p. 52-55

727 Mullá Husayn, cited by Nabíl, translated by Shoghi Effendi, *The Dawn-Breakers*, p. 55

728 Mullá Husayn, cited by Nabíl, translated by Shoghi Effendi, *The Dawn-Breakers*, p. 57. See also Nabíl, p. 25.

729 The Báb, quoted by Mullá Husayn, cited by Nabíl, translated by Shoghi Effendi, *The Dawn-Breakers*, p. 57

730 Mullá Husayn had been told of this key sign by his former teacher and leader of the Shaykhi movement, Siyyid Kázim. For details, see Nabíl, translated by Shoghi Effendi, *The Dawn-Breakers*, p. 57

731 Mullá Husayn, cited by Nabíl, translated by Shoghi Effendi, *The Dawn-Breakers*, p. 62-63

732 The Báb, cited by Nabíl, translated by Shoghi Effendi, *The Dawn-Breakers*, p. 85-87

733 Nabíl, translated by Shoghi Effendi, *The Dawn-Breakers*, p. 128, 129

734 The Báb, *Selections from the Writings of the Báb*, p. 77

735 The Báb, cited by Shoghi Effendi, *God Passes By*, p. 21

736 Táhirih, cited by Shoghi Effendi, *God Passes By*, p. 75

737 Nabíl, translated by Shoghi Effendi, *The Dawn-Breakers*, p. 513

738 Nabíl, translated by Shoghi Effendi, *The Dawn-Breakers*, p. 514

739 The Báb, cited by Nabíl, translated by Shoghi Effendi, *The Dawn-Breakers*, p. 85-87

740 The Báb Himself provided this number in a passage of the Persian Bayán during His imprisonment in Mákú, two years before the completion of His ministry: "Likewise behold the Point of the Bayan. His behaviour prior to the declaration of His mission is clearly evident unto those who knew Him. Now, following His manifestation, although He hath, up to the present, revealed no less than *five hundred thousand verses* on different subjects, behold what calumnies are uttered, so unseemly that the pen is stricken with shame at the mention of them. But if all men were to observe the ordinances of God no sadness would befall that heavenly Tree." (The Báb, *Selections from the Writings of the Báb*, p. 96-97, cited from the *Persian Bayán* VI, 11. Note: Emphasis added.)

741 The Báb, *Selections from the Writings of the Báb*, p. 111

742 The Báb's concept of God counteracts the human tendency to imagine that God walks, talks, thinks, feels and acts like a physical human person. As we will see later, this "humanizing thinking" goes by another name – anthropomorphism. Anthropomorphism, applying human qualities to a non-human subject, is a fine literary technique in art, fantasy storytelling, and cartoons, but it is necessarily limited when it is applied to the Highest Being in all of existence – God – and taken as a description of theological truth about God. There are some classic examples: In the Sistine Chapel in Rome, Michelangelo painted an image of God as a grey-bearded old Man. While undoubtedly one of the greatest artworks of all time, such a depiction utterly fails as a true concept of God. The Scriptures sometimes apply anthropomorphic images of God, depicting Him as walking in a garden, getting angry, or having ordinary conversation with humans, in order to tell a story or illustrate a deeper spiritual principle, but when such images are taken literally rather than figuratively, it leads to concepts of God which fall far short of His ultimately unknowable Reality and Essence. More detailed discussion of anthropomorphism is found in Volume One.

743 The Báb, *Selections from the Writings of the Báb*, p. 126

744 The Báb, *Selections from the Writings of the Báb*, p. 125

745 The Báb, *Selections from the Writings of the Báb*, p. 105

746 The Báb, *Selections from the Writings of the Báb*, p. 126

747 Bahá'u'lláh also says the same thing: "...by a word of His command all that are in heaven and on earth have come to exist, and by His wish, which is the Primal Will itself, all have stepped out of utter nothingness into the realm of being, the world of the visible." (Bahá'u'lláh, *The Book of Certitude*, p. 98)

748 The Báb, *Selections from the Writings of the Báb*, p. 125

749 The Báb, *Selections from the Writings of the Báb*, p. 12

750 The Báb, *Selections from the Writings of the Báb*, p. 130

751 Adib Taherzadeh, *The Covenant of Bahá'u'lláh*, p. 39

752 The Báb, *Selections from the Writings of the Báb*, p. 125

753 The Báb, *Selections from the Writings of the Báb*, p. 106-108

754 The Báb, *Selections from the Writings of the Báb*, p. 78

755 Nader Saiedi, *The Gate of the Heart*

756 The Báb cited by Nader Saiedi, *The Gate of the Heart*, p. 46

757 The Báb, *Selections from the Writings of the Báb*, p. 125

758 The Báb, cited by Shoghi Effendi, *God Passes By*, p. 29

759 Adib Taherzadeh, *The Child of the Covenant*, p. 103

760 The Báb, cited by Shoghi Effendi, *God Passes By*, p. 30-31

761 A. L. M. Nicolas, cited in a footnote to Nabíl, translated by Shoghi Effendi, *The Dawn-Breakers*, p. 514-515. Refer to: Emily McBride Perigord, *Translation of French Footnotes of the Dawn-Breakers*, p. 60-61

762 This statistical remark is sourced from Adib Taherzadeh, *The Revelation of Bahá'u'lláh v2*, p. 75. Taherzadeh states: "…when Bahá'u'lláh manifested His Cause, about ninety-nine per cent of the Bábí community recognized Him and embraced His Cause." See also Adib Taherzadeh, *The Covenant of Baha'u'llah*, p. 87-88. Taherzadeh states: "The great majority of the followers of the Báb, estimated by Hájí Mírzá Haydar-'Ali in his immortal Bihjatu's-Sudur to be about ninety-nine percent, embraced the Cause of Bahá'u'lláh." Hájí Mírzá Haydar-'Ali was a close associate of Bahá'u'lláh, served as His personal secretary, and was a direct eyewitness to history.

763 'Abdu'l-Bahá, *The Promulgation of Universal Peace*, p. 401-402

764 Shoghi Effendi, *God Passes By*, p. 90

765 Bahá'u'lláh, *Epistle to the Son of the Wolf*, p. 21-22

766 Shoghi Effendi, *God Passes By*, p. 113-114

767 Bahá'u'lláh, *The Summons of the Lord of Hosts*, p. 144-145

768 Bahá'u'lláh, *Gleanings from the Writings of Bahá'u'lláh*, p. 12-13

769 Bahá'u'lláh, *Gleanings from the Writings of Bahá'u'lláh*, p. 149

770 Baha'u'llah, *Gleanings from the Writings of Bahá'u'lláh*, p. 286

771 Bahá'u'lláh, *Gleanings from the Writings of Bahá'u'lláh*, p. 217

772 Bahá'u'lláh, *Gleanings from the Writings of Bahá'u'lláh*, p. 166

773 Bahá'u'lláh, *Gleanings from the Writings of Bahá'u'lláh*, p. 322

774 Bahá'u'lláh, *The Hidden Words*, Arabic #4

775 Bahá'u'lláh, *Gleanings from the Writings of Bahá'u'lláh*, p. 50

776 Shoghi Effendi, *God Passes By*, p. 139

777 Shoghi Effendi, *The World Order of Baha'u'llah*, p. 42

778 Bahá'u'lláh, *Gleanings from the Writings of Bahá'u'lláh*, p. 94

779 Baha'u'llah, *Tablets of Bahá'u'lláh*, p. 57

780 Bahá'u'lláh, cited by Shoghi Effendi, *The Advent of Divine Justice*, p. 23

781 Bahá'u'lláh, cited by Shoghi Effendi, *The Advent of Divine Justice*, p. 23

782 'Abdu'l-Bahá, cited by Shoghi Effendi, *The Advent of Divine Justice*, p. 26

783 The Universal House of Justice, *Ridván 2010 Message*

784 Baha'u'llah, *The Most Holy Book*, p. 195, note 65

785 Some ideas and phrases taken from Shoghi Effendi, *God Passes By*, p. 219

786 The Universal House of Justice, *Ridván 2010 Message*

787 Bahá'u'lláh stated that His Dispensation would endure for a minimum of one thousand years, possibly longer. Thus the next Manifestation of God will not appear "ere the expiration of a full thousand years" (Bahá'u'lláh, *The Most Holy Book*, p. 195, re. para 37) The Bahá'í Writings state that the "The intimation of His Revelation to Bahá'u'lláh in the Siyah-Chal of Tihran, in October 1852, marks the birth of His Prophetic Mission and hence the commencement of the one thousand years or more that must elapse before the appearance of the next Manifestation of God." (Bahá'u'lláh, *The Most Holy Book*, p. 195) Therefore, the earliest humanity might expect the next Divine Educator will be in the year 2852. This paragraph is being written in the year 2019, therefore, there are 833 years to go—minimum—before the conclusion of the Dispensation of Bahá'u'lláh can be expected.

788 Shoghi Effendi, *God Passes By*, p. 411-412

CPSIA information can be obtained
at www.ICGtesting.com
Printed in the USA
LVHW021211071019
633402LV00001B/41/P